ESME HOWARD

A DIPLOMATIC BIOGRAPHY

Esme Howard, First Baron Howard of Penrith (1863–1939)

ESME HOWARD

A DIPLOMATIC BIOGRAPHY

B. J. C. McKERCHER
DEPARTMENT OF HISTORY
ROYAL MILITARY COLLEGE OF CANADA

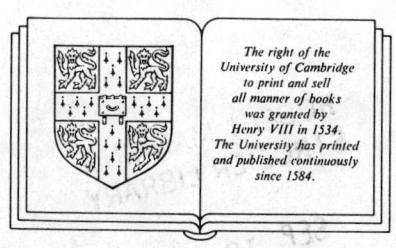

CAMBRIDGE UNIVERSITY PRESS

CAMBRIDGE
NEW YORK PORT CHESTER
MELBOURNE SYDNEY

Published by the Press Syndicate of the University of Cambridge
The Pitt Building, Trumpington Street, Cambridge CB2 1RP
32 East 57th Street, New York, NY 10022, USA
10 Stamford Road, Oakleigh, Melbourne 3166, Australia

© Cambridge University Press 1989

First published 1989

Printed in Great Britain by the University Press, Cambridge

British Library cataloguing in publication data
McKercher, B. J. C.
Esme Howard: a diplomatic biography
1. British diplomatic service, Howard,
Esme, 1863–1939
I. Title
327.2'092'4

Library of Congress cataloguing in publication data
McKercher, B. J. C., 1950–
Esme Howard: a diplomatic biography / B. J. C. McKercher.
p. cm.
Bibliography.
Includes index.
ISBN 0-521-32257-X
1. Howard, Esme. 2. Diplomats – Great Britain – Biography.
3. Great Britain – Foreign relations – 1901–1936. I. Title.
DA565.H75M35 1989
327.2'0924 – dc19
[B]   88-27440 CIP

ISBN 0 521 32257 X

For James Barrington

Contents

Acknowledgements		*page* ix
List of abbreviations		xiii
1	The making of a diplomat, 1863–1903	1
2	Crete: consulship and civil war, 1903–1906	38
3	Washington: Imperial affairs and arbitration, 1906–1908	71
4	Budapest and Berne: prelude to the Great War, 1908–1913	101
5	Stockholm: war and diplomacy in neutral northern Europe, 1913–1916	132
6	Stockholm: diplomacy and war in neutral northern Europe, 1916–1918	164
7	Paris: Poland, the Baltic States, and the Treaty of Versailles, 1918–1919	197
8	Madrid: Anglo-Spanish relations, 1919–1924	234
9	Washington *redux*: rebuilding good relations, 1924–1927	269
10	Washington *redux*: meeting the American challenge, 1927–1930	300
	Epilogue and conclusion 'A great ambassador'	352
	Notes	376
	Bibliography	438
	Index	453

Acknowledgements

I first 'met' Esme Howard when, in the summer of 1974, I did research for my MA thesis at the old Public Record Office in Portugal Street. Some of Howard's letters about the proposed League of Nations were in the Cecil of Chelwood papers, and Howard's ideas about how this new organisation should function impressed me then as striking the necessary balance between realism and idealism in making British foreign policy. When I subsequently began my Ph.D. work on official British views of the United States during the period of the second Baldwin government, and derived from this my first book, Howard had a prominent place because of his position as the British ambassador at Washington after 1924. His analyses of United States foreign and domestic policies were both dispassionate and balanced, and they played a major part in the development of Britain's American policies in the latter half of the 1920s. Thus, with the work I have done in writing this diplomatic biography, Esme Howard has been an important element in most of my scholarly life.

Howard's papers were 'lost' until 1977 when, after their discovery by his family, they were deposited at the Cumbria County Record Office at Carlisle. This is an enormously important manuscript collection in terms of the study of British foreign policy for the half century after 1885, this given the length of Howard's active life and the large number of his correspondents (he kept a diary only sporadically). Its importance was enhanced in 1984 when a further batch of his papers, his private office papers for the time he was ambassador in Madrid and Washington, was also found and deposited at Carlisle. With this, the complete private papers of one of Britain's pre-eminent diplomats of this century were available for scholarly research.

I actually began to write about Howard and his career in 1982 and, soon after, became aware of the hoary comment that historians should write a biography to find out how different from history it is. This was driven home to me by my friend, Keith Neilson, who read an early chapter and found that I had discussed a problem for more than three pages without mentioning Howard. As Neilson wrote in the margin: 'Esme, Esme, *toujours* Esme!' I have written this study with this dictum in mind, and I have called it a 'diplomatic biography' because it deals primarily with Howard's career. So many recent biographies of British politicians and diplomats are based almost solely on the particular individual's private papers, supplemented by reference to secondary sources and a smattering of references to other private manuscript collections and private archives. But, for a serving diplomat, much of what he thought and advised is not in private papers because of the need to consult London quickly by telegram or, at other times, because of the desire of the men in London for official embassy views on particular subjects. These materials are in the Foreign Office records and, if the matter is important enough, in Cabinet minutes and memoranda. Thus, just as much as on Howard's papers, there has been a heavy reliance in this study on Foreign Office and Cabinet papers where Howard's assessments and advice were analysed and discussed, and policy made. Whilst some of the private manuscript collections have, of course, been of marginal value, several have been invaluable and have been referred to often; chief amongst these are the papers of Lord Hardinge of Penshurst, all of the foreign secretaries except one under whom Howard served (Lansdowne, Grey, Balfour, Curzon, and Chamberlain), and Ramsay MacDonald, who was both prime minister and foreign secretary in 1924 and, after 1929, though relinquishing the Foreign Office to Arthur Henderson, controlled Britain's American policy. In this way, this book is not a study of the life and times of Esme Howard, nor does it purport to offer comprehensive analyses of each of the problems confronting British foreign policy during Howard's tenure at each of his posts: for instance, the 'Eastern question' whilst he served in Crete in 1903–6. Rather, this is a study of what Howard thought and did in these matters – *toujours* Esme – and, as important, how his views, ideas, and policy proposals had an impact on those who made foreign policy in London. I admit that at times in this analysis, the professional side of Howard's life dominates the personal one; but this is a 'diplomatic biography'. Still, I have tried to show Howard the man as much as Howard the diplomat.

I would like to acknowledge the help of a number of people who made my task easier in writing this book. The staff of the Cumbria County Record Office, Carlisle (Mr B. C. Jones, David Bowcock, Jeremy Godwin, and Frederick Brown) were indispensable. I would also like to thank the staffs of: the Public Record Office, the British Library, the House of Lords Record Office, and the British Library of Economic and Political Science, London; the University Library and the Churchill College Archives Centre, Churchill

Acknowledgements

College, Cambridge; the Bodleian Library, Oxford; the National Maritime Museum, Greenwich; the Liddell Hart Archives Centre, King's College, London; the Public Archives of Canada, Ottawa; the Minnesota Historical Society, Minneapolis; the Government Publications Library, the University of Alberta, Edmonton; and the Massey Library, the Royal Military College of Canada, Kingston. I would like to add to this list a special thanks to John Martin Robinson, the archivist to the Duke of Norfolk. Cathie Krull compiled the bibliography from the notes, and several typists laboured for me, chiefly Pat MacDonald. If I had listened earlier to the sage words of Tom Harkness, a number of delays in the early period of writing would have been overcome. Lastly, in this respect, William Davies, my editor at Cambridge University Press, and Mary Baffoni, who sub-edited the final manuscript, have been both patient and understanding.

Several scholars also gave me advice or commented on portions of the manuscript: Alan Cassels, Michael Dockrill, Nandor Dreisziger, Kristin Lundby, David Mills, Douglas Owram, Antony Polansky, Zara Steiner, and Wesley Wark. Professor D. Cameron Watt knows how much I owe him. David Moss and Paul Voisey, my former colleagues at the University of Alberta, were especially supportive of my work whilst I was there. Three of the department chairmen for whom I have worked also went out of their way to help: Rod Macleod and David Hall, at the University of Alberta, and Barry Hunt, at the Royal Military College of Canada. Professor Ian Nish, the chairman of the Centre for International Studies at the London School of Economics when I had a research fellowship there in 1982, removed several impediments from my path. I would like to single out for special thanks my friend, and now my colleague at RMC, Keith Neilson. His comments and support have been much appreciated.

References to and quotations from archives and manuscript collections are made by kind permission of the following: for the records of the Admiralty, Cabinet, Foreign Office, and War Office, as well as the private office papers of Lord Bryce, Lord Balfour, Lord Robert Cecil, Sir Austen Chamberlain, Lord Curzon, Lord Grey, Lord Lansdowne, Lord Carnock, and Sir Cecil Spring Rice (all Crown-copyright material in the Public Record Office), the Controller of Her Majesty's Stationery Office; for the Bryce papers at the Bodleian Library, Oxford, the Bodleian Library; for the Cecil of Chelwood papers at the British Library, Professor H. K. S. Lambton; for the Hankey papers at Churchill College, Cambridge, the Master, Fellows, and Scholars of Churchill College in the University of Cambridge; for the Hardinge papers at the University Library, Cambridge, the Syndics of Cambridge University Library; for the Howard papers at the Cumbria County Record Office, Carlisle, Lord Howard of Penrith; for the Frank B. Kellogg papers, the Minnesota Historical Society; for the William Lyon

Mackenzie King papers in the Public Archives of Canada, the Historical Resources Branch of the Public Archives of Canada; for the Lloyd George papers, which are in the custody of the House of Lords Record Office, the Clerk of Records and the Trustees of the Beaverbrook Foundation; for the copyright material from the James Ramsay MacDonald papers in the Public Record Office, London, the executrix of the late Malcolm MacDonald; for the papers of the 15th Duke of Norfolk at Arundel Castle, Sussex, His Grace the Duke of Norfolk; for the Richmond papers, the Trustees of the National Maritime Museum, Greenwich; for the Robertson papers, the Trustees of the Liddell Hart Centre for Military Archives, King's College, London; for the Spring Rice papers at Churchill College, Cambridge, Lady Arthur; and for the Wester-Wemyss papers at Churchill College, Cambridge, Mrs Alice Cunnack.

Finally, I must mention some special contributions. There is the kindness of the Lord and Lady Howard of Penrith and the Hon. Edmund and Mrs C. Howard, who on several occasions discussed aspects of Esme Howard's life with me fully and frankly. Moreover, Lord Howard made every effort to ensure that all of the Howard papers were available to me, and he and his brother, whilst answering my questions and giving me all of the assistance they could, never once sought to change any of my interpretations of their father's life and work. I owe them an immense debt of gratitude. My friends, Paul and Lynn Hurst, and their children, Kati, Sally, and Danny, understand how much I am in their debt for allowing me to stay with them whenever and for however long I was in London doing research. Malmesbury Road is my home away from home. As a last word, my wife, Cheryl, and my son, Asa, have perhaps suffered more than is usual because of the time I have spent away from home and in other ways; I am grateful that they have each come through this with me.

Abbreviations

ADM	Admiralty
AHR	American Historical Review
APSR	American Political Science Review
BD	British Documents on the Origins of the War, 1898–1914
BJIS	British Journal of International Studies
BL	British Library
BLINY	British Library of Information, New York
BR	Belligerent Rights Sub-Committee
CAB	Cabinet
CHR	Canadian Historical Review
CID	Committee of Imperial Defence
CJH	Canadian Journal of History
CP	Cabinet Paper
DBFP	Documents on British Foreign Policy
DH	Diplomatic History
EHR	English Historical Review
FA	Foreign Affairs
FO	Foreign Office
FRUS	Papers Relating to the Foreign Relations of the United States
HJ	Historical Journal
IHR	International History Review
INS	Intelligence and National Security
JAH	Journal of American History
JBS	Journal of British Studies
JCH	Journal of Contemporary History
JCPS	Journal of Commonwealth Political Studies
JEH	Journal of Economic History
JICH	Journal of Imperial and Commonwealth History
JMH	Journal of Modern History
n.a.	no author

n.d.	no date
PAC	Public Archives of Canada
PRO	Public Record Office
PSQ	*Political Science Quarterly*
RP	*Review of Politics*
ToL	*Theatre of Life*
VH	*Vermont History*
WO	War Office

For MSS abbreviations see sections I and II of bibliography.

1

The making of a diplomat, 1863–1903

Life, when I was a boy in the eighteen-seventies, was in England at least a quiet and placid stream, rather muddy in places, but still often blue and white with reflections of the sky. Now it is still muddy and turgid but broken with cataracts and whirlpools leading us – whither?

Esme Howard, July 1936

I

Esme Howard was one of the most gifted and important British diplomats in the first third of the twentieth century. He was born in September 1863. His first memory of great-Power politics was when he was 7 years old; the Franco-Prussian War had broken out and, since France was seen to be the embodiment of evil, his family were 'all passionately united in favour of Germany'. He died in August 1939, just one month before the outbreak of the Second World War. The end of his life was a counterpoint to its beginning. Like many other thoughtful and knowledgeable British observers in the late 1930s, he had worried about the worsening international situation, its effect on Britain and the Empire, and how diplomacy could be used to safeguard both international peace and security and British interests. A way had to be found around the 'cataracts and whirlpools'.

Howard's life and diplomatic career, the latter stretching from 1903 to 1930, coincided with the decline in Britain's position from the only truly global Power to just one of a number of great Powers with varying international commitments. This decline encompassed a number of issues, each of which touched Howard's career. In economic terms the emergence of the United States of America as the principal financial Power in the world, the result of the exigencies of fighting and financing the Allied war effort against the Central Powers between 1914 and 1918, eroded seriously Britain's dominance in this crucial aspect of international politics. British decline also had an Imperial dimension, centring on the perennial Irish question as well as the determination of the 'White' dominions, especially Canada because of its geographical connexion with the United States, to have greater independence in conducting their foreign relations.

Throughout the nineteenth century, pre-eminent British global power was concomitant with the potency of the Royal Navy. After 1900 Britain's decline was also pushed along by the efforts of a number of industrial countries – at first, Germany unsuccessfully and, later, the United States and Japan successfully – to build powerful navies to protect both their seaborne commerce and the maritime lines of communication to their own burgeoning empires. Finally, in the aftermath of the First World War, the relative economic and naval decline of Britain forced its leaders to restrict their diplomacy to fit new conditions. This meant a different focus in foreign policy, a focus in which the balance of power in western Europe was maintained at all costs – this had been traditional since the seventeenth century – whilst commitments in the rest of the world were limited to just a few places judged vital to British interests, chiefly in the Middle East and East Asia.

Esme Howard was an integral member of the small group of men who made and implemented British foreign policy at this critical juncture in Britain's history as a world Power. This was especially so in the period from 1913, when he went to Stockholm as the head of Legation, to 1930, when he retired as the doyen of the British diplomatic service after six very successful years as ambassador at Washington. To be honest, Howard's importance was primarily the result of the posts he held after 1913, each crucial in some way to the readjustment in Britain's international position. But crucial also were his character and unique abilities, the result of his life before 1903 as well as his diplomatic apprenticeship. Thus, Esme Howard's diplomatic career offers insight into the way in which the relative decline of Britain occurred in the first third of the twentieth century and into the problems with which British diplomats of that generation had to contend.

II

Howard once wrote: 'There was nothing remarkable about my childhood except its complete happiness.'[1] There is no doubt that the secure family life in which he was raised was, not unnaturally, one of the greatest influences on the development of his character. But there were also a number of less obvious influences on him that, in connexion with his happy childhood, were just as influential. Howard was part of the privileged class that dominated English society, politics, and economy in the late Victorian period. His immediate family, his parents and five older brothers and sisters, were northern gentry, and they were the recipients of a rich heritage dating from medieval times. His father was Henry Howard of Greystoke in Cumberland. His grandfather was Lord Henry Thomas Molyneaux-Howard, the younger brother of the twelfth Duke of Norfolk. With this there existed an important family tie with one of England's greatest aristocratic landed families who were both socially and politically prominent. In addition, Henry Howard's sister had married the third Earl of Carnarvon whose family, the Herberts, was by the middle of the nineteenth century one of England's principal social and political clans.

Howard's mother, Charlotte, was the eldest daughter of Henry Lawes Long of Farnham in Hampshire. One of her ancestors, Samuel Long, had gone out with Cromwell's forces to the West Indies in a punitive expedition against the Spanish colonies in 1655 and then settled in Jamaica. The Longs became prominent in Jamaican society and politics – Samuel Long was the first speaker of the Jamaican Parliament – and, with branches in both the West Indies and England, the family had prospered until earlier in the nineteenth century when the end of slavery and the advent of free trade savaged the West Indian sugar industry. None the less the Howards of Greystoke had a lengthy connexion with the Empire. Just as important, Charlotte Howard's mother, Catherine, was a Walpole, the daughter of the second Earl of Orford. These Walpoles, the descendants of the Whig prime minister, Robert Walpole, constituted one of the most important political families in the eighteenth century. Charlotte Howard's family, however, were not political, though they sympathised with Whiggish notions and came to count amongst their circle of friends a number of Italians exiled prior to the Risorgimento. The life of the Long family revolved around scholarship and letters. Henry Lawes Long was a classicist who dabbled in natural science and natural history, and his wife wrote 'pious and evangelical novels' to help supplement the family income.[2] The Long family were also somewhat itinerant, living variously in England, Switzerland, Belgium, and Germany. They were not at all insular, appreciating the beauty and heritage of continental countries, especially Italy, and making friends with a range of foreigners including those Italian exiles. In this way Esme Howard was the heir to an important cultural, Imperial, political, and social legacy, a legacy that suffused his childhood experiences.

Howard was the youngest in his family, a late child born when his father was sixty and his mother forty. In his own estimation he had been 'much spoilt',[3] but this is not surprising given the nature of children separated from older brothers and sisters by a large gap in years. His father, who died in January 1875, typified the entrepreneurial gentry of nineteenth-century England. Although dedicated to the traditions of his class, especially horses and the hunt, he was a hard-nosed businessman unafraid to invest his money in the new projects of the burgeoning industrial age. Charlotte Howard's financial records for the period after her husband's death show Henry Howard to have been astute in business; according to his son's recollection, he seems to have been most satisfied investing in railroads, notably the Lancashire and Carlisle Railway of which he was a co-director.[4] Howard admitted that his father did not influence him to any great extent. This is explained in part by the difference in age – contact between them seems largely to have been talking together in the evening before the boy went to bed – as well as by the father's infirmity. Memories of his father revolved around endless stories and anecdotes about his father's life and of the more colourful people he had known. Howard did admit that he had 'unfortunately forgotten' much of what his father had told him.[5] Still, he retained warm feelings for this man he had hardly known, acknowledging that 'he was always most kind and affectionate to me'.

In contrast to his relationship with his father, that with his mother was close and constant until her death in July 1896.[6] Charlotte Howard doted on her youngest child, so that for the first thirty-three years of his life she was not only his mother but his closest confidante and friend. She was not a 'society woman'. She was an unpretentious, clear-thinking, and considerate woman, tolerant of those whose opinions and ways of life differed from her own. This is not to say that she lacked resolve. She remained firm until the end in her convictions about religion – in her case, Anglicanism – politics, and the propriety of what was the 'right thing' in conducting one's affairs.[7] The Long family's peripatetic existence and their devotion to letters probably had much to do with this trait.

Charlotte Howard's life was consumed by her family, caring for her children and her progressively invalided husband at the family homes at Greystoke and at Thornbury in Gloucestershire. In this way she inculcated many of her beliefs and ideals in her children. Esme was especially influenced. As the youngest child, he spent a great deal of time with his mother; at the age of five he still slept with her. Moreover, he would accompany her on twice-yearly shopping trips to London, excursions which permitted his mother to maintain contact with an established circle of friends, including Alfred Lord Tennyson. It is not difficult to see why Howard later wrote: 'Of the *dramatis personae* in my early youth, my mother stands out head and shoulders above all.' It is also not difficult to see why to a great extent Esme Howard came to share not only his mother's cultural instincts, but the personal qualities of unpretentiousness, clear thinking, consideration, and tolerance, the qualities indispensable to a diplomat.

Although the most important influence in moulding character, family life is just one element. A second crucial one is physical environment. Howard was a northern Englishman. This translated into a decided love for the Cumberland countryside, especially that which fell within the confines of the family estate at Greystoke. His father's holding encompassed 6,000 acres: 'a series of pastures and moorland, with woods and tarns and marshes, and some limestone cliffs at the highest part which reached an elevation of twelve hundred feet'.[8] It teemed with all sorts of wildlife, and Howard called it 'our kingdom'. His childhood ties with Greystoke were translated to Cumberland as a whole. Acknowledging that its terrain might appear to first-time visitors as 'gloomy, harsh, and grey', he felt at home only there. In later life he experienced emptiness during periods of absence and unbridled joy when he returned.[9] Although he had experience of London as a child when he accompanied his mother on those shopping trips, he never really liked the city – he bought a house there only after he retired. Nor did he feel completely comfortable in any of the other cities which he either served in or visited. They provided only 'the sense of depression, exile and exasperation that the country man feels when brought to live in a great city', as well as a feeling 'of imprisonment and loss of liberty'.[10] Understanding Howard's spiritual connexion to the rugged northwest of England where he spent most of his happiest times as a child is necessary in appreciating his character.

A final factor from his childhood important in moulding his character was an awareness of England's history, with which his family had been connected intimately since medieval times. The two family homes, as well as those of his relations – Pixton Park, the estate of the Earl of Carnarvon whom one of his father's sisters had married, and Charlton Park, the residence of the Earl of Suffolk, whom his father's other sister had married – were tangible connexions with the past surrounding Howard at every turn.[11] Of Pixton Park, he remembered: 'The atmosphere surrounding the Carnarvon Herberts was literary, scholarly, political, interwoven with a spirit of travel and adventure.' Charlton House, then 'in a somewhat dilapidated condition', had a central hall 'hung with old full-length portraits of Elizabethan Howards'.

Of the two family homes, Thornbury was steeped in the Tudors. It had been built originally by Edward de Bohun, the Duke of Buckingham, to vie with Cardinal Wolsey's palace at Hampton Court; both Henry VIII and Mary Tudor had resided there. It had later fallen into disrepair and then it came into Howard hands. As a boy, Howard played in the remaining ruins, something that gave him 'endless delight and adventure'.[12] But, as in everything else in his life, Greystoke was most important. Its history was related to him in stories passed on by his parents and others. For instance, the eleventh Duke of Norfolk, who opposed George III's policies during the American revolution, had named farms and woods on the estate after rebel victories and leaders – such as Bunker Hill and Jefferson. Greystoke was much older and had a more varied history than Thornbury. Its origins supposedly pre-dated the Norman Conquest, when it was a site for a stockaded fortress, though nothing of this remained by 1860, if it ever had. Bits of Greystoke Castle did date from the twelfth century, so that by the middle of the nineteenth century it represented an amalgam of many periods. Part had been fortified during Edward III's reign; part had been destroyed by Puritan armies during the Commonwealth and later rebuilt. The original Howard owners had been Roman Catholics, and portraits of all the Stuarts from Mary Queen of Scots to Bonnie Prince Charlie hung there, as well as a needlework depiction of the Crucifixion supposedly from Mary Stuart's hands. There also hung an imposing portrait of the eleventh Duke of Norfolk, who had supported the influential Whig, Charles James Fox, in the late eighteenth century. Howard's sense of the history of the place shows in a passage from his memoirs:

Greystoke, when I was a child, was a strange mixture of Whig and Stuart traditions, of Protestant and Catholic atmosphere. The Whig and Protestant traditions and atmosphere came from [the eleventh Duke of Norfolk] who still, many years after his death, dominated the scene for us children, and whose portrait by Romney hung in the dining-room. The Stuart and Catholic atmosphere came from the place itself.

Howard's carefree childhood lasted until he was ten years old when, like so many boys of his class, he was sent away to school. He later related that this occurred to his 'immense sorrow' because, first, he was removed from the cocoon of his family and familiar surroundings and, secondly, it 'took me a long time to get accustomed to the ways of boys my own age which, at first, I thought most disagreeable'.[13] The school was Farnborough, one of the most exclusive in the hierarchy of these institutions at that time. A letter written to his mother shortly after his arrival shows his unhappiness:

I don't know what to do[,] I am so very very unhappy[.] I never was so unhappy in all my life and I hope I never shall be again...I am so perfectly miserable that I almost wish I could get very ill [so] that you should come and see me or else that I should come to Greystoke; I hardly like sending this letter but you never often asked how I like school and I now tell you plainly how I like it!!![14]

This reaction was normal for a child who, suddenly, had been taken from the warmth and security of his home and placed in what in his view was a relatively hostile and unknown world, a world in which he had to fend for himself. Nevertheless he learned to cope. Happier letters soon reached his parents,[15] the result of his settling into a routine and making friends.

The most enduring friendship he made at Farnborough was with Rosslyn Wemyss, who later entered the Royal Navy and rose to become first sea lord in the First World War. Because one of Howard's older brothers, Mowbray, knew the Wemyss family, Rosslyn Wemyss took Esme 'under his wing'. This had a positive effect on Howard in that Wemyss hated snobbery – there was an abundance at Farnborough – and Howard came to share the sentiment.[16] These personal issues aside, Howard benefited from his time at this school. He excelled at sports, becoming captain of the cricket team, and, showing qualities of leadership, he became head boy. In terms of academics, he received a good grounding in Greek and Latin amongst other mandatory subjects. Languages were Howard's strong point; he had a gift for them. His time at Farnborough helped him in later life master French, German, Italian, Spanish, Dutch, as well as passable Swedish and Hungarian.

From Farnborough, Howard went on to Harrow. Harrow was in the top rank of Victorian public schools, but Farnborough's chief connexion was with Eton. Therefore, on arriving at Harrow, Howard found himself alone once again; none of his Farnborough friends had gone on there. But this time he did not have the same despondency at being suddenly alone, and he fitted into public school life rather easily. His time at Harrow seems to have been typical of that of most schoolboys of whatever period: indulging in sports, spending time with friends, finishing assignments the night before they were due, cramming for examinations, asking his mother for extra money, and imploring his family to send on desperately needed articles – cricket boots, for instance – somehow left at home during the holidays.[17] From both his memoirs and extant correspondence of this period, Harrow appears to have been a stable and happy time in his life. The only lasting effect on his character arose from the realisation that he was not the most brilliant scholar the school had ever produced. He had never once believed that he was, but his reaction on being told so by his Latin master – 'a sarcastic gentleman' – is interesting. On being informed that he was a 'respectable mediocrity', Howard observed: 'He was quite right, and not only in regard to Latin verses. Having recognised that fact in time has stood me in good stead, for surely it is a far happier thing to be a "respectable mediocrity" than a genius of any kind.'[18] Given that he probably felt an immediate blow to his schoolboy pride, Howard was by this juncture mentally tough enough to accept harsh criticism and realise his own limitations. But he also possessed self-confidence in the abilities he did have, the result of his secure childhood and education, and was prepared to face life with the knowledge that these were not limitless. It made him at times more determined to succeed. By the time he left school, Esme Howard's character was tinged with a realism lacking in those of most men.

After leaving Harrow in 1881, he was given for the first time a choice in deciding what path his life should take. Willing to support him financially in preparing for whatever endeavour he chose, his mother presented him with two possibilities: either to continue his education by going up to Cambridge, as his older brothers had done, or to begin preparations for a diplomatic career. Anxious to have 'the advantage of getting young into Diplomacy',[19] he chose the latter. Knowledge of languages was a *sine qua non* for a diplomat, so for three years, accompanied by his mother and his unmarried sister, Maud, he lived on the continent in Florence, Paris, and Dusseldorf, paying tutors and learning Italian, French and German. In many ways mirroring what his mother's family had done when she was young, this time on the continent exposed Howard to the cosmopolitan world of the European upper classes and their attitudes, tastes and foibles.[20] During this time he began to acquire a decided admiration for Italy, a measured equanimity towards France, and an uneasiness about Germany. In addition, he found 'a real distaste for what might be called Society life', whether in Italy, France, or Germany; this was an echo of his upbringing in the rugged countryside of Cumberland.

Prior to setting off on his 'grand tour', Howard had approached the head of Scoones, one of the best cramming schools in London. Such establishments prepared young men for the rigours of writing civil service entry examinations, of which those for the Foreign Office and the Diplomatic Service were the most difficult. Scoones had given Howard a reading list to work through whilst he learned languages abroad. This in tandem with his knowledge of languages would then serve as the basis for a year of intense study at Scoones once he returned to England. By early 1884 Howard was in London, living at the home of one of his father's former butlers, preparing for entry examinations by 'hard work and little relaxation'. He wrote the examinations for the Foreign Office and Diplomatic Service late in the winter of 1884–5 and was one of only four who passed.[21]

The period from 1885 to 1903 was integral to Howard's development. He was twenty-one when he embarked on a diplomatic career but by 1890 he was unhappy with his choice in that it did not seem to meet with his expectations. He resigned in 1890 and did not decide to make diplomacy his profession until 1903 when, with a pregnant wife, he needed full-time employment and a career. His experience of a wide range of activities and his exposure to an equally wide range of people during this time helps to explain his success in the Diplomatic Service after 1903. Just as his first twenty-one years formed an important basis in the making of this diplomat, the following eighteen refined and shaped him.

Immediately after passing the civil service examinations, Howard entered the Foreign Office to begin his apprenticeship. He was fortunate that Sir Julian Pauncefote, the permanent under-secretary and civil service head of the Office, was a friend of his cousin and brother-in-law, the Earl of Carnarvon – Howard's elder sister, Elizabeth, had become Carnarvon's second wife in 1878 – making smoother the transition from student to professional man. He was put in the Western Department, but found the work tedious: 'ciphering and deciphering telegrams and copying [by hand] endless dispatches and memoranda'.[22] At this time he began to make friendships with younger colleagues who would later prove invaluable to his diplomatic career. Cecil Spring Rice was the most important of these. He was then the précis writer to Lord Granville, the foreign secretary, and 'a general favourite' in the Foreign Office.[23] This initial experience in the business of diplomacy lasted until June 1885 when the Liberal ministry of which Granville was a member resigned over failure to get Commons' concurrence to a minor budget provision.[24]

A Conservative government then formed under the third Marquess of Salisbury, and Carnarvon, who had twice served as colonial secretary under Benjamin Disraeli, accepted the vexatious post of viceroy of Ireland. At the prompting of Howard's sister, Carnarvon arranged for Howard to be seconded to his staff at Dublin as an assistant private secretary. Howard worried about this, questioning 'whether it is a good thing to identify oneself with the Conservatives'; he wrote to his mother that 'I am sorry now we did not press more for an Assistant Secretaryship for me here [the Foreign Office] as I believe I might have got it'.[25] None the less, Howard went to Dublin and worked conscientiously to fulfil the Conservative government's mandate: to keep order by reducing tensions between 'Unionists' and 'Home Rulers'. This posting lasted just seven months, but it is important for the lessons it offered Howard in Imperial policy.

Prior to his posting at Dublin, at least judging from his private papers, Howard does not seem to have had any views of consequence on the Empire. But his association with Carnarvon's viceroyalty exposed him to the difficulties of governing and preserving the Empire. For Carnarvon and many other Victorian Imperialists, the Empire was the reason for Britain's position as a great Power; it had to be preserved at all costs.[26] For Carnarvon, unlike some of his colleagues in Salisbury's Cabinet,[27] this did not mean that the Empire was a static entity. Carnarvon was not opposed to internal changes in the Empire if this meant it could be preserved. If colonials were ready for independence, whatever the degree, they should be given it. Carnarvon generally supported a gradualist approach to change, a view which implied that London should control events in the interests of both the home and colonial governments whilst preserving

Imperial unity. Carnarvon's tenure as colonial secretary in Disraeli's first ministry saw concrete evidence of this when he helped shape the legislation that gave Canada dominion status in 1867. Canadians received their autonomy, and the Empire, though altered, stood as firm as ever.

In the middle of the 1880s the Irish majority, chiefly the Roman Catholic lower classes, sought 'Home Rule'. This did not mean complete independence. Rather it meant Irish control over purely Irish matters like education. For financial and other reasons, higher policy like foreign affairs and defence would be left to the government in London. The Conservatives generally opposed 'home rule', a function of their traditionalist bent and the economic and political clout of the Anglo-Irish gentry who, as Conservative supporters, had influence at Westminster. Despite these pressures Carnarvon was amenable to change in Ireland, but change of the slower, more evolutionary type. He was beginning to move in this direction but ran out of time when Salisbury's government fell in January 1886. From the central position of Dublin Castle, Howard observed these events which portended so much for the strength of the Empire. He wrote later: 'I left Ireland...a convinced believer in the necessity, if we were ever to have peace, of giving local autonomy to Ireland, which then went under the rather elastic name of Home Rule'.[28]

After his time in Ireland, Howard began his apprenticeship in the intricacies of great Power politics with an immediate transfer to the Embassy in Rome as a third secretary. This was not the best British diplomatic establishment. The ambassador was Sir John Savile Lumley, whom Howard thought the 'typical regular diplomat of the day...doing, on the whole, what was expected of him with considerable success, as long as too much was not expected'.[29] Compounding the problem was a Chancery riven by personal dispute: the three senior members could not stand each other. Luckily, in the two and a half years that Howard spent at Rome, no major Anglo-Italian or general European dispute of any proportion arose to tax the Embassy's collective ability. In this diplomatic somnolence Howard served as 'the scrub of the Embassy', his time devoted to the same work he had done earlier in the Foreign Office Western Department: ciphering and deciphering telegrams and copying in longhand a seemingly endless series of despatches and memoranda. However, as his command of Italian was the best amongst the Embassy staff, he was given additional responsibilities; Lumley loaded him with translation work, especially of the key newspapers which the ambassador thought important, like the *Popolo Romano* and the *Corriere della Sera*.

The social connexions Howard established were as important as his exposure to the drudgery of routine Embassy work. It seems that no one at the Embassy liked to hunt, so, in exchange for two free days a week during 'the season', Howard agreed to represent the Embassy at the Roman hunt. This hunt was a high point for Roman society; it provided him with an entrée to that society and reinforced his italophile feelings, feelings that were helped by his mother's periodic visits. At this time Howard became friendly with Cardinal Edward Howard, a first cousin of Howard's father. This gave Howard a link with the Vatican. Most important in terms of his subsequent career, Howard's movements in Roman society led him into friendship with Wilfrid Blunt, a strongly arabophile English adventurer – he liked dressing like a Bedouin sheikh – who spent part of his year at Rome.[30] This friendship led to Howard joining the Crabbet Club, one of those late Victorian aristocratic societies devoted to nothing in particular. Club members met each June at Crabbet Park, Blunt's Sussex estate, for a weekend of games, speeches, and conversation.[31] Prizes were given to the best lawn tennis player and the member producing the best poem. Amongst the members was George Curzon, later the Indian viceroy and, when he served as foreign secretary from 1919 to 1923, Howard's political master. Howard and Curzon became friends.[32] So, too, did Howard and Moncton Milne who, after his elevation as the Marquess of Crewe, served as a senior minister in the various Liberal and coalition governments from 1905 to 1916 and, as ambassador in Paris from 1922 to 1928, was one of Howard's main colleagues in the Diplomatic Service.

This leisured existence ended in June 1888 when, unexpectedly, Howard was transferred to Berlin to serve as private secretary to the ambassador, Sir Edward Malet. The atmosphere of Berlin differed from that of Rome. In the first place Bismarck was chancellor and at the height of his power – no one seemed to suspect that the great man was in the twilight of his public life. Germany, centred on Berlin, was the axis on which continental affairs revolved. Added to this was the death by throat cancer of the Emperor Frederick, whose reign had lasted only a few months. He died just days before Howard arrived. Frederick's demise precipitated a minor Anglo-German crisis in that the German empress, who was Queen Victoria's daughter, was virtually imprisoned in the Imperial Palace at Potsdam. Both Frederick and his wife had supported liberal ideals, a stance that led them privately to criticise domestic and foreign policies pursued by Bismarck and the late emperor's father. Both Bismarck and the new emperor, William II, kept the empress secluded; they worried that her husband's diary which was thought to contain these criticisms might be published if it slipped out of the Palace. The empress was to remain incommunicado until Bismarck and William could lay their hands on the diary.

The difficulty was that even letters and parcels between Queen Victoria and her daughter were held up. The Embassy's intervention did nothing to help. A version of the diary was published some months later by a Professor Geffcken, a liberal friend of Frederick – it had been given to him in the later stages of the emperor's illness – and nothing of consequence emerged. The poor treatment of the empress had a lasting and unfavourable impact on Howard. As a boy, he had been raised with 'an immense admiration and affection for everything German'[33] – his favourite childhood nurse was from the Rhineland – but as he observed after this incident:

I must confess that my experience in Berlin, and everything that I have since read of transactions at the German Foreign Office, or at the Court of the Emperor William, have only confirmed the very unfortunate impression that I received during the first week of my stay at the Embassy.

During his posting at Berlin, because of his more senior position, Howard received more demanding tasks to perform. The nature of Bismarck's government in the 1880s was to entrench the monarch's position and protect the privileges of the upper classes. Bismarck's opponents in this were the German socialists, who wanted to reduce monarchical power and curtail privilege. The practical expression of Bismarck's policies was to undercut the domestic appeal of the socialists by introducing legislation to protect the working classes. In the middle of 1889 Bismarck's government secured a law to protect workers against the economic ravages of illness and old age by contributory national insurance. Howard was assigned to evaluate this and prepare a report for the Foreign Office.[34] Despite his growing antipathy to the conduct of high policy in Germany,[35] Howard found this piece of social legislation to be a landmark. It appealed to his own whiggish-liberal notions about helping those less fortunate than himself, something that was driven home to Malet with the observation that 'by the provisions [of this act] every labourer, workman, or servant in the Empire may look forward to receiving some material assistance when rendered unable to earn his living'. Lauded by Malet, Howard's analysis was circulated to the Cabinet as a confidential print, a signal achievement for so junior a man.

The most important work Howard did in Berlin occurred with his secondment in May 1890 to assist Sir Percy Anderson, the head of the Foreign Office African Department, who was sent to Berlin to negotiate an Anglo-German colonial settlement for East Africa. Salisbury, again prime minister and foreign secretary, found the Germans willing to resolve differences in Africa; given the nature of international politics at the time, these had the potential of upsetting the balance of power in Europe – a vociferous press campaign on both sides of the Channel was creating a crisis-like atmosphere. Anderson's mission removed the possibility of Anglo-German conflict in East Africa, this mainly because Salisbury suddenly offered to give Germany Heligoland in exchange for concessions in Africa.[36] An island off the North Sea coast of Germany, Heligoland had been British since 1815. The Germans wanted it and, as its waters were too shallow to anchor warships, the British lost nothing in relinquishing their control. The Germans responded by granting Britain a free hand in the East African island of Zanzibar, now a key staging point on the route to India because of French activity in Madagascar. Both at the time and later when he wrote his memoirs, Howard argued that this agreement was the best one possible.[37] He remained cognisant of its arbitrariness – 'It was easy, perhaps, to call in question the rights of two Great Powers thus to indulge in map-making at the expense of "ignorant savages".' But the world was imperfect. Diplomats and statesmen had to guard the interests of their people and states. As he observed pragmatically: 'The practical issue was both for [the natives] and for us, that a settlement of the question, which was inevitable at the time, should be carried out peacefully and by agreement.' After five years learning the craft of diplomacy, Esme Howard understood completely the hard edge of great-Power politics.

Whilst he involved himself with the Anderson mission, Howard realised that a diplomatic career was not meeting his expectations. This had been building up since his short time at Dublin. Then, only six months after passing his civil service examinations, he had worried whether he would end up 'a specimen of dry, withered officialism by the time I am 65'.[38] These feelings grew to such an extent that by the middle of 1890 he was preparing to leave the service for a few years to find himself. South Africa appealed to him, and he began secretly to learn Dutch. The situation in Germany, and especially Berlin, forced his hand. In a candid letter to his mother, he confessed that 'I dislike this place & the life here.'[39] He felt constrained. He chafed at the conventions of 'society'. He wished to get away, to explore those places which, outlined on the maps that he, Anderson, and Germans poured over, were names and nothing more. Inspired by the success of his brother, Stafford, who had been elected a Liberal MP, he also entertained political ambitions. 'It will be like getting a cool, antiseptic mouth wash into one's mouth after a heavy German dinner', he wrote, 'to rough it away in an altogether new world.' He was a young man in a hurry – he admitted that 'I have no Time to lose' – and he had much to accomplish.

He therefore arranged with London to take two years' leave *en disponibilité*, that is, he could return in two years without losing his seniority, from the Diplomatic Service beginning on 1 January 1891.[40] This decision of his led in June to a strained correspondence with his mother who, in addition to being confronted with her son's seeming impetuousness, also had to contend with Carnarvon's sudden death and Elizabeth's early widowhood.[41] Charlotte Howard asked Esme to consider three issues: his personal finances, the effect his leave would have on subsequent promotion, and his 'capability' to pursue a life outside the Diplomatic Service. She had provided £9,000 in 1889 for him to invest and live off the proceeds;[42] assuming that he would have to take some of the interest and re-invest it, this would leave him with an annual income of £400. Could he live on this? He said he could. Unlike in diplomatic life, in private life he would not have to spend vast sums on keeping up 'appearances'. About his career, Howard argued that by leaving at the end of 1890, he would have served two and a half years at Berlin, the normal tenure at a post for someone of his rank. Thus, there would be no stain on his record. Indeed, he pointed out that Malet found nothing improper in him leaving at the appointed time. Finally, he was typically realistic about his 'capability': 'I don't think you or anyone else[,] myself included[,] know much about it as it has never been tried.'

His ambition dominated. He pointed out that, even by the time he turned 50, the odds were against him getting an embassy of his own. What would this do to help England? It was necessary to strive for greatness whilst he was still young. Perhaps he might have erred by entering the Diplomatic Service at an early age. 'I believe that, if one desires to become a great man, one can only do so by applying oneself to a great idea.' This was the crux of his desire to strike out on his own. Howard felt that there were 'two great ideas at present in embryo in England. 1. the so-called "Federation of Empire"[.] 2nd. State Socialism.' With poignancy, he added:

If I can help in anyway – in the smallest way – to assist in the development of either or both of these two, I think I shall die a more or less contented man, tho' as you say, and I confess I am glad of it, I shall never be satisfied all my life.

Realising that she could not dissuade her son, Charlotte Howard abandoned her opposition. In March 1891 Howard set out for South Africa to explore for gold; his mother accompanied him, as she 'could never bear to be very long, or very far, away from [him]'.[43] Prior to leaving, Howard consulted Percy Anderson. This led to introductions to a few men in London 'with African experience' who advised him on how to plan his expedition. More important, through his brother, Stafford, he received a letter of introduction to Cecil Rhodes written by Albert Grey, a friend of both Stafford and Rhodes who later, as Earl Grey, became governor-general of Canada. Rhodes was premier of the Cape Colony, the driving force behind the rich and influential British South Africa Company, and one of the most vocal proponents of British Imperial expansion in Africa and of Imperial federation. As luck would have it, on the ship carrying the Howards to South Africa were friends of the Carnarvons: Sir Henry Loch, the governor of Cape Colony, his wife, and Seymour Fort, Loch's private secretary. This chance meeting not only provided Charlotte Howard with friends to see during her stay in Cape Town when Esme left on his expedition, but it gave Howard another entrée into the Cape's social and political elite.[44]

Once at Cape Town, Howard prepared immediately for his first great adventure. On the sea passage from Britain he had become friendly with Algernon Caulfield, the stepson of a British diplomat, Sir Horace Rumbold. Although Caulfield went to South Africa to join the South Africa Company's police force, Howard persuaded him to join the expedition. Howard and Caulfield then befriended four Australians also in South Africa to make their fortunes. The six men formed a partnership – with Howard, because he funded the expedition, the senior partner.[45] In the month or so before he was ready to set off, Howard tried to meet as many people as possible to learn about local conditions. Because of his letter of introduction and his shipboard friendship, this meant exposure chiefly to prominent Cape politicians and businessmen: Rhodes, Jan Hofmeyr, a prominent Dutch leader, Leander Jameson, one of Rhodes' principal disciples, and others.[46]

Howard found his views about Imperial unity which he had gained in Ireland were shared by most of these men. For them, there were two ways to keep South Africa within the Empire – by autocratic fiat issued from London or through constitutional changes akin to Home Rule. There was opposition to the former way as it might promote a reaction and probable separation. The latter was more feasible, especially if the Cape Colony could expand and consolidate its position: '...if therefore we are to retain this Colony within the Empire we must rely entirely on the Constitutional approach, giving the Colony the freest hand possible in the administration of internal affairs, & allowing, even to urging on – the annexation of the Colony of Bechuanaland & the other native Protectorates'. Despite the fact that these views, prevalent amongst prominent men in the Cape, corresponded generally with Howard's beliefs, they reflected to a great extent the prejudices of Cape interests, especially those of the South Africa Company. After his venture into the interior, Howard retained his beliefs about more colonial local autonomy, but he became extremely critical of Rhodes' Company.

Howard's trek into the South African heartland began in June 1891 and over the next five months he and his partners searched in vain for gold.

They travelled as far north as Fort Salisbury in Rhodesia and then, realising their quest was fruitless, pushed east to the Portuguese colony of Lourenço Marques in Mozambique. From there, by steamer, Howard made his way back to Cape Town.[47] His experiences with the South Africa Company's administration in areas where it had been given a monopoly made him question its policies. As the whole region was rich, with potential for all sorts of development, Howard contended that 'people with capital' should be encouraged to develop dams, irrigation, and other projects to provide a basis for such development. The 'ignorant, land-greedy & backward Boer farmers' would only retard development.[48] But the South Africa Company was as rapacious as the Boers. Howard believed that he, his companions, and other adventurers had been grossly misled by the Company. People thought 'they were coming to a land of milk & honey & gold – & they found that instead they had run their heads into fever, privation, & want'.[49] Almost everyone Howard met, including junior officials of the Company, criticised Rhodes, Jameson, and others: 'The universal complaint against the Administration is that they are a clique of financiers from Kimberley, knowing nothing of Government or organization, while they are all bent on developing their own special interests in the country even to the detriment of those of the country at large.'[50] Howard felt the criticism levelled at Jameson might be misplaced as he seemed 'a thoroughly sterling man'. But in spite of this, Jameson did not have 'sufficient experience in his work to justify his position as ruler of the country virtually as absolute or more so than the Czar of Russia'. A political administration responsible in some way to the people would be preferable to that of the Company responsible to itself.

Before he returned to Britain, Howard had one more conversation with Rhodes. This is important because Howard expressed views about the Empire, refined by his Irish and South African experiences, that altered little during the rest of his life.[51] There were two dimensions to this, one political and the other economic. Rhodes complained about how the expansion of his Company – which, he argued, would strengthen the British position in southern Africa – was constrained by its being bound tightly to Britain. Howard thought this unrealistic. Any Company expansion affected immediately European great-Power politics. Without Britain's support, the Company and the British colony dominated by it would have been prevented by the Powers from achieving and holding their present position. Howard asked how Rhodes would respond to German expansion into the Company's sphere if there existed no firm British connexion. Rhodes was forced to admit that 'in spite of the difficulties which sometimes occurred owing to [the British] connection, he was strongly in favour of it'. Howard's perception of a strong Empire was, in part, that the colonies, as they achieved good government and sought independence, need not be bound tightly to Britain. But the *sine qua non* for Imperial security remained British power to defend the colonies and dominions in their endeavours.

Rhodes and Howard also discussed the economic aspect of Imperial unity. Rhodes believed that international economics were changing, that free trade was a thing of the past. He pointed to the new tariff system established in the United States by American protectionists adding that it was designed 'not for revenue or protection, it was simply for prohibition of foreign goods'. The British Empire had to respond with what he called a 'Customs Federation', in essence a system of Imperial Preference. Unless Britain gave the colonies and dominions a favourable advantage in trade by raising tariffs against competitors like the United States, the colonies and dominions would seek preferential agreements with those competitors. Rhodes alluded to American economic pressures on Canada, adding that the British West Indies were seeking a special tariff arrangement with the United States if an Imperial 'Customs Federation' proved illusory. Howard supported wholeheartedly Rhodes' ideas on Imperial Preference; if realised, they could strengthen the Empire against economic competitors and, in the bargain, weaken those competitors. Thus Howard left South Africa as dedicated as ever to the political and economic preservation of the Empire – especially as it seemed to entail the 'great idea' of Imperial federation – but he was aware of the limitations of Imperial agents like Rhodes and his Company, and he realised that Britain's power was indispensable in protecting the colonies and dominions from political and economic encroachments by others.

On returning to England in early 1892, Howard wanted to run for parliament. His support for Irish Home Rule meant that his fortunes lay with the Liberal Party, since the Conservatives, united to a group of former Liberals who had bolted from the party in 1886 because they opposed concessions to the Irish, would never endorse a candidate with such views.[52] Howard turned to his brother, Stafford, a Liberal MP, to help him find a seat. The selection committee at Dursley, Gloucestershire, near Thornbury, agreed to interview him. But in this interview, Howard was too frank.[53] He acknowledged his support for Home Rule and then outlined his strong commitment to social reform – he mentioned non-contributory old-age pensions like those which he had analysed in Germany and were now being proposed in Britain by the social reformer, Charles Booth – and Imperial Preference. Advocating Home Rule did not cause any flutters since the Liberal leader, Gladstone, was committed to it. But on social reform and Preference, Howard's views were too advanced: 'when I let myself go on Tariff Reform, I felt that the tea froze'. He learnt his lesson, though he thought the whole incident amusing. He would have to be more circumspect about social and tariff issues.

Rejection at Dursley did not end Howard's political future. With Stafford's intervention, Arnold Morley, the Liberal chief whip, agreed to help Howard find a seat. By May 1892, Morley informed Howard that he could contest Worcester in the general election scheduled for July. Liberal success there was not certain; in fact, the chances of a Gladstonian candidate winning were remote.[54] More qualified men, established in the area, had declined to run since the possibility of success was slim. *The Birmingham Daily Gazette* observed dryly that 'Mr. Howard's name has been submitted for the consideration of the local Liberal Council. That is one way of saying that the constituency has been submitted to the consideration of Mr. Howard.' Howard's ambition to succeed led him to accept the challenge. He seems to have thought that he had a good chance of winning – that he never again ran for political office after this indicates that he never considered seriously that, if he did well carrying the party's banner, the party might at the next election find him an easier constituency to contest. He lost, judged that politics were not for him, and pushed on in pursuit of the great idea.

In retrospect Howard remarked that at Worcester: 'Besides Home Rule I accepted the whole Liberal programme to that date, lock, stock, and barrel, and only attempted one serious addition on my own initiative, which was the Charles Booth proposal for non-contributory old-age pensions, besides a general pensions system for workmen incapacitated by accidents or sickness.'[55] Although later expressing fond memories for this part of his life, he could not have had such feelings at the time. The local Conservative newspaper, *The Daily Times*, subjected him to withering editorial criticism.[56] Because Charles Booth's father founded the Salvation Army, Howard's views about pensions brought rebukes like the 'sprightliness of the juvenile politician has brought him into line with the Socialist-Salvationist exponent'. After discussing foreign policy, he was chastised for rushing in 'where older men fear to tread'; his youth and diplomatic experience were deprecated equally with remarks such as 'he should be well advised not to attempt to enlighten the electors of Worcester respecting events which happened when he was boy at school, and the history of which, probably, he has not carefully studied during the time of his performance of very light duty abroad'. The most sustained criticism from local Conservatives came over Irish Home Rule: 'A measure of Home Rule which cannot be explained, a sop to Liberationists, and a little tinkering with the franchise – that is all the Gladstonian candidate here [Howard], can talk about with any definiteness.' Whilst the local Liberal newspaper, *The Worcestershire Echo*, sought to extol Howard's virtues –

'Mr. Howard's...sympathies are with the working classes, and with the reforms, political as well as social, which they ardently desire' – and emphasised the warm reception accorded by Liberals and other electors – 'Mr. Esme Howard, who was received with enthusiastic applause...' – it was not enough to overcome the entrenched position of the sitting Conservative MP;[57] nor was it enough to surmount the obvious dislike of the majority of Worcester voters for Liberal policies like Home Rule. Howard received 2,540 votes; his Conservative opponent 3,353. The Conservative majority was 813, a marked improvement on the majorities of 143 in 1886 and only 84 in 1885.[58] It was a bitter result for Howard, but it did not cool his desire to achieve some great purpose.

The problem was that nothing seemed to present itself immediately after Worcester. He did nothing of consequence for almost a year. After spending the rest of the summer and autumn of 1892 in Cumberland and Scotland, he wintered with his mother in Italy, at Portofino, Elizabeth's estate. There he met one of Carnarvon's cousins, Arthur Herbert, and his wife. They were planning a camping trip in Morocco – with private sleeping tents, a common tent for dining and sitting, servants, a chef, and all the other paraphernalia of a major expedition. With the Herberts was Walter Harris, a *Times* correspondent who knew much about North Africa. Howard joined them. This trip's importance lay not so much in the experience Howard gained by viewing at first hand a different society and culture, though that had value. For instance, whilst at Fez, he, Harris, and Herbert risked death if caught when they observed secretly a number of harems taking the air at dusk, on supposedly secure rooftops of the city out of the sight of men – Howard and his friends managed to get to a higher roof.[59] The importance of this trip came from Howard's assessment of Morocco's diplomatic and strategic importance to Britain. Although Morocco in 1893 appeared 'rather beautiful, quiet, peaceful, and dignified', change was imminent. It was a kingdom honeycombed with financial corruption: 'The Sultan squeezed the Treasury, the Treasurer the tax-gatherers, and the tax-gatherers the people, and the userers squeezed them all.'[60] Local British businessmen looked to Britain to establish a protectorate over Morocco to safeguard their investments, but the French also wanted to annex the kingdom.

Howard looked at the problem from the point of view of Britain's strategic interests. According to his memoirs, he was then keeping a correspondence with Percy Anderson and Sir Thomas Sanderson, the permanent under-secretary at the Foreign Office. Howard wrote to them that it would be in Britain's interest to forgo a protectorate and allow the French to create one, the trade-off being French approval of a British free hand in Egypt. Interestingly, this arrangement formed a key part of the

Anglo-French entente in 1904, something which Sanderson then acknowledged that Howard had seen clearly a dozen or so years before.[61] Howard reckoned that the principal British interest in the western Mediterranean was the security of Gibraltar and its command of the Straits. Morocco touched none of these crucial interests, thus it would be an expensive diversion, expensive financially as well as in terms of Anglo-French relations. Although his views were not appreciated at the time, Howard's realistic appraisal of what was and what was not a British interest showed a quality indispensable for success in diplomacy.

On returning to Britain in the spring of 1893, an opportunity presented itself for Howard to pursue the great idea of 'State Socialism'. He had long admired Charles Booth's ideas on social reform and, at that point, Booth and a number of his disciples were enquiring into the living and working conditions of London's poor and labouring classes.[62] Booth's assistant, George Duckworth, a friend of Howard who knew of Howard's admiration for Booth, asked him to join the enquiry as an unpaid researcher – Howard's private income permitted such an arrangement. Here was the sort of opportunity that Howard wanted, a chance to observe at first hand the problems of the lower classes and, perhaps, contribute to the introduction of needed reform. Accepting Duckworth's offer, Howard worked for Booth for most of the rest of 1893 investigating conditions in a number of industries: china, glass, brush-making, musical instruments, leather, matches, rubber, paints, and varnishes. The nature of the work involved sending letters to factory managers in these industries in London, arranging meetings, and interviewing them about their employees. A parallel enquiry would then be arranged with trade-union leaders, heads of workingmen's clubs, churchmen, and any others who might offer opinions about lower-class living and working conditions. Once Howard and the other investigators compiled statistics from those willing to co-operate – and many did not – other enquiry members would collate and co-ordinate these findings, put them in the relevant chapters of the report, and thereby give Booth's enquiry its final shape.

Howard's work confirmed his beliefs about the need for reform to help the lower classes.[63] The economic distress of the lower classes was, he felt, exacerbated by overpopulation. Together these two factors constituted 'the secret of the "iron law" of the tendency of wages to [stay at] a minimum so that eventually manufacturers & employers generally would if they could employ Chinamen who would live on 6d a day'. Each industry he investigated had its own unique problems for which Howard tended to blame the 'free-trade', *laissez-faire* economy. Artisans who blew glass were being put out of business – and their craft lost – by unrestricted entry into Britain of cheap, mass-produced Belgian and German glass. The

Belgians and Germans each had tariffs to protect their glass industries. London workers in trades where chemicals and volatile liquids were essential for production were exposed to needless danger and their health suffered accordingly. In the match industry, for instance, because of a lack of basic precautions, numbers of workers each year contracted 'phossy jaw' from handling and unavoidably ingesting phosphorus. This disease was marked by the slow disintegration of the bones. More lethal than this was white-lead poisoning, the danger faced by workers in the paint- and varnish-making industries.

The insensitivity of the majority of the employers angered Howard; he saw employers' claims that workers' carelessness and uncleanliness caused these industrial diseases were less than true. Indeed, for Howard these were only excuses to shift blame and prevent the expenditure of capital on workers' safety, expenditures that would reduce profits. None of this is to suggest that Howard was arguing for a turn-about in industrial ownership; this would be anathema to his upbringing, though as he observed, one need not accept 'all Karl Marx's theories and conclusions' to see the problems in Britain's industrial society. But it is to say that he saw a dangerous imbalance between capital and labour. He came to advocate that establishing balance be the goal of government, owners, and workers. This would prevent 'the unavoidable conflict between capital and labour' that might lead to the collapse of British society from within. To this end, Howard formulated an 'economic credo' which he believed would bring about, if not domestic tranquillity, at least greater domestic cohesion.[64] Howard never had the opportunity to implement his credo, though he never abandoned it. However, as a consequence of his work with Booth, Howard became a convinced 'protectionist' – this accorded with his views about Imperial federation – and supported more state intervention in the economy to bring about the needed balance between capital and labour.

In early 1894 Howard convinced his sister, Elizabeth, to accompany him and Walter Harris on a second trip to Morocco. She agreed, bringing along her two young sons, Aubrey and Mervyn.[65] When the party reached Tangier in March, Howard received a letter from a friend in London, a fellow Liberal named Armine Wodehouse, the son of the first Earl of Kimberley. Wodehouse offered Howard the position of assistant private secretary to the foreign secretary, an unpaid post but one offering Howard another chance to pursue the great idea. Gladstone had resigned in March 1894 to be replaced as Liberal leader and prime minister by his foreign secretary, the Earl of Rosebery. In forming his Cabinet, Rosebery found Kimberley to replace him at the Foreign Office. With the offer to serve under Kimberley, admittedly from a position outside the civil service,

Howard was given access to the mechanisms that made high policy. He jumped at the offer. He became the most junior private secretary in Kimberley's inner office. Wodehouse served as his father's private secretary and Henry Foley, a career man, was Kimberley's précis writer. By his own admission, Howard's work was not that onerous:

> We made an excellent *ménage a trois*: Armine dealt with the bulk and the most important part of his father's correspondence, Henry Foley with all matters of ceremonial and personal affairs relating to the office, while I dealt with minor personal matters and also docketed and put by a great part of the Cabinet and other letters for which Armine prepared replies or wrote replies at his father's dictation.[66]

As so often in his life to this point, Howard's actual work was secondary to the experience gained and the contacts made. Most important at this time, he became friends with Edward Grey, Kimberley's parliamentary under-secretary. It was to be under Grey, who served as foreign secretary from 1905 to 1916, that Howard's diplomatic career advanced rapidly. Howard saw Grey in a variety of roles. Since Kimberley was a peer, Grey had not only to perform the usual tasks of a parliamentary under-secretary, for instance, answering questions in the Commons; he in effect served as the official government spokesman in the lower house for the Rosebery government's foreign policy. Moreover, on a personal level, Howard and Grey were both northerners – Grey was from Northumbria – and they shared an interest in bird-watching. About Grey, Howard commented later: 'Though he was a granite column there was hidden within it a vein of gold and, though it may seem incompatible with granite, he had a keen sense of humour.'[67]

This time in the Kimberley Foreign Office, which lasted until Rosebery's government lost the general election of June 1895, also provided Howard with two indispensable lessons about politics and diplomacy. It gave him insight into the way in which political affairs at the highest level were conducted. Coupled with his experience of constituency politics at Worcester in 1892, any illusions he might have had about political parties of like-minded men working together for some common good were sheared away completely. Rosebery represented the conservative wing of the Liberal Party; William Harcourt, the chancellor of the exchequer in both the Gladstone and Rosebery ministries, was the focal point of the more radical element. They divided on a range of domestic, foreign, and Imperial policies, and it fell to Kimberley to act as a buffer between the two men in the Cabinet.[68] Howard became fully aware of the cut and thrust of politics and, crucially, of how one's most powerful enemies can often arise within one's own party. Finally, at least in conducting foreign policy, Howard became convinced that diplomacy should be less the province of politicians and their appointments and more that of the professionals. Howard became a 'service' man, supporting strongly the notion that only those trained in diplomacy fill positions in the Foreign Office at home and the embassies abroad.[69]

Howard's experiences with the Booth enquiry and in the Kimberley Foreign Office affected him profoundly. Prior to this he had been consumed by the ambition of making a name for himself and pursuing the great ideas. A Commons seat had been integral to this and, as late as July 1893, he was thinking about trying to find another constituency.[70] But two years later he had mellowed. He admitted that 'my ambitions were much watered down'. He still wanted to pursue the great ideas, especially Imperial federation, but the key now was to put all that he had learned in South Africa, Worcester, and London into practice. His more modest ambition was to make enough money to 'enable me to buy a small property in a fruit-growing district in England and there start a fruit farm on co-partnership lines such as I have sketched in my Economic Credo'.[71]

The best way to begin was to make his fortune in the Empire. In working for Booth, he had met Christian Gray, the manager of one of Britain's largest rubber works, who showed him the 'tremendous potentialities of rubber'. In the middle of the 1890s this commodity had limited uses, but Gray held that in the future it would be a crucial commodity in any industrial economy.[72] Existing rubber-tree cultivation would be inadequate to meet anticipated demand. Howard saw the challenge and hit upon the idea of beginning a rubber plantation in the West Indies. The West Indies appealed to him for two reasons. First, its connexions with the Long family attracted him. Secondly, he knew that the sugar industry had collapsed there with little chance of revival, and that the West Indian lower and working classes were suffering as a result. As Howard observed realistically: 'What could be a more delightful plan for a young man at a loose end than to start a new industry in an impoverished part of the British Empire, while at the same time making a little money for himself and his friends.'[73]

The best rubber cultivation was then in the Amazon basin of Brazil. Howard approached Booth about his idea and Booth, agreeing the project had potential, offered help. As part-owner of a Liverpool shipping line whose vessels plied the Atlantic between Britain and the Americas, Booth arranged for Howard and any friend to travel free to Brazil. This was so that Howard could study at first hand the methods of rubber cultivation and latex production. Booth also wired ahead to the agent of his company in Brazil to help Howard by making arrangements for him to visit local plantations and meet men in the industry. For a companion, Howard convinced an old Harrow friend, George Crawley, to accompany him, and the two set off in August 1895. The result of this journey, which included a 900 mile expedition up the Amazon River to visit plantations in the deep interior, proved to be inconclusive in gauging the potential of transposing the techniques of Brazilian rubber cultivation to the West Indies – Howard did add immensely, however, to his experiences by hunting alligators, going bird-watching, and participating in all manner of social events in Brazil.[74] Howard and Crawley travelled to three rubber-growing districts, but none of the rubber trees under cultivation nor the methods used would work well in the West Indies. One tree with good latex flow – the *hevea brasiliensis* – could achieve this flow only if it was flooded with a metre or so of water during the rainy season. This natural irrigation would never happen in the West Indies. But the main problem with this investigation centred on Howard not preparing well enough beforehand by reading and interviewing experts. After returning to Britain empty-handed in late 1895, he determined to go back better prepared so that he could realise his ambitions.

His mother's health delayed that return. In December 1895 Charlotte Howard decided that she should convalesce in a warmer climate. She chose to travel to Italy where Elizabeth was wintering and where a number of her friends had also decided to pursue the sun. Howard went along, not only to be with his mother but to see a young Italian noblewoman, Donna Isabella Giustiniani-Bandini, whom he had met on earlier visits and to whom he was attracted. This Italian trip would also allow him time to assess his Brazilian visit and plan better his next expedition there. In the end, he had little time to think about rubber cultivation. The steady deterioration of his mother's health preoccupied most of his time. By Easter, Charlotte Howard knew she had not long to live and wished to return to Cumberland to die in her own house surrounded by all that was dear to her. The trip was cut short as Howard took his mother back to England.

Whilst at Rome, Howard had made no headway in forging a relationship with Isabella Bandini, who, for her part, seemed attracted to him. The Bandini occupied a prominent place in the upper reaches of Roman society, a society governed by exceedingly strict rules of conduct, especially concerning young, unmarried women. It proved impossible for Howard to be alone with Isabella, either indoors at parties or outdoors at promenades. As Howard related: 'So strict was the supervision in my father-in-law's house that his elder daughters have told me that they were never allowed to cross the "*anti-camera*" or entrance hall of their house in Rome without a maid or a governess, because a footman was always stationed there to open the door for guests.'[75] Not confessing his feelings to anyone lest word get back to Isabella's parents, Howard did what any other infatuated young man might do: he attended functions where he suspected she might be and he sought out those from whom he could gather information about her, especially the English Catholic colony at Rome, most of whom he knew well – the Bandini were linked to this colony as one of their ancestors, the Earl of Newburgh, had fled to Rome during Cromwell's Commonwealth and remained there after the Stuart restoration. By later admission, his infatuation transformed itself into love.[76] But the strictures of Roman society prevented him being alone with her for a 'heart to heart talk'. When his mother's frailty and the subsequent need to return to Cumberland forced him to leave Rome in the spring of 1896, he did so without ever having had a chance to let Isabella know how he felt.

Four months after returning to England, Charlotte Howard died. This had a devastating affect on Howard. For the first time he was completely alone – his brothers and sisters each had their own lives and families, so that he had finally to face life on his own. He went into seclusion with the family of his eldest brother, Henry, at their home on Ullswater in Cumberland. After several weeks of soul-searching – a 'spell of rest in surroundings both of people and places that I loved helped me to recover my balance'[77] – he struck on a two-part plan. He would resolve his relationship with Isabella and, at the same time, work to achieve the financial security he believed was possible by rubber cultivation in the West Indies. The need for such security was now doubled: it would provide for both the pursuit of economic 'co-partnership', as well as give the means to support a wife and family.

Howard embarked on his plan with gusto. His first trip to Brazil failed because of inadequate preparation. Accordingly, he travelled to London to make enquiries in Kew Botanical Gardens as to who possessed expertise in the field of rubber cultivation. Howard was lucky. The curator at Kew, Sir Thisselton Dyer, supported enthusiastically more extensive rubber cultivation in the Empire; he directed Howard to a young Cambridge botanist, Rowland Biffen, who had been conducting experiments to increase latex flow and production. Biffen had discovered that latex from a Mexican rubber tree, the *castilloa elastica*, produced superior rubber to that of the *hevea brasiliensis*. Although the West Indian climate was more like that of Mexico than Brazil, the problem remained: could profitable amounts of latex be produced in the West Indies? After consulting with Dyer and Christian Gray, both of whom saw great potential in Biffen's work, Howard made arrangements for himself and Biffen to travel extensively in the Americas to investigate the practicability of Biffen's ideas.[78] Whilst he had been making enquiries about the practical aspects of rubber cultivation, Howard had begun to consider the establishment of a syndicate of 'a small circle of friends' to invest in West Indian rubber growing. This syndicate was still in the planning stages when Howard and Biffen left Britain in July 1897.

For six months the two travelled in the Americas: from Brazil to the West Indies; from the West Indies to Mexico; and, after a side trip to the United States because it was so close, back to Mexico.[79] The result of this investigation was the decision that *castilloa* cultivation in Trinidad held the most potential for profitable enterprise. Based on their finding, Howard succeeded in putting together a syndicate with an initial capitalisation of £5,000.[80] Using his social connexions, Howard attracted support 'in influential quarters'. Charles Booth was a willing investor and agreed to sit on the board of directors. So, too, was Sir Edward Jenkinson, later the chief of the British Secret Service and chairman of the Daimler Company. A distant cousin of Howard, Charles Morpeth, later Lord Carlisle, also agreed to join. In a signal coup, Howard persuaded Lord Stanmore, the ex-governor of Trinidad, both to invest and to serve as chairman of the board. Stanmore could use his influence to smooth over any difficulties the syndicate might encounter. The board agreed that nothing on a large scale should be attempted at first. An experimentation phase funded by the initial £5,000 would have to be completed and assessed; only then could a decision for further development – and investment – be made. To manage the plantation, Morpeth recommended a friend from Oxford, an Anglo-Dane named Thorleif Orde. Orde's principal qualification centred on his having 'spent some years in South Africa and was thoroughly accustomed to roughing it and to managing coloured people, besides being in character and physique one of the finest and best men'. Orde managed the plantation until his death in 1934, and he remained firm friends with Howard throughout.

With these plans for his goal of financial security moving ahead, Howard approached the delicate matter of Isabella Bandini. In the spring of 1897, after his first meeting with Biffen showed there to be a chance of success in the West Indies, he went to Italy on a brief trip to make certain that his feelings were reciprocated. His one ally in this was his sister, Elizabeth, who was friendly with Isabella and her family. Howard confided everything to Elizabeth.[81] He did essentially what he had done a year earlier: arranging to meet with Isabella briefly at tea parties and other functions. This time, however, he let her know of his devotion to her – 'I don't fancy she has any doubts now about my feelings' – and he was convinced that Isabella realised his intentions were honourable. The only difficulties that he foresaw concerned his own economic future and the problem of religion. Although Howard did not reject Christianity, he had long since ceased to be a practising Anglican and was somewhat of an agnostic. The Bandini were devout Roman Catholics, so-called 'Black

Romans', putting the pope on a plane above the Italian king and, in fact, blaming the Italian monarchy for stripping the papacy of its temporal power during the Risorgimento. Howard believed both problems could be overcome. He was even reconciled to the possibility of going back into government service if the West Indian project failed.

In April 1898, following the dictates of Roman custom by writing to the Princess Bandini, Isabella's mother, he indicated his wish to marry her daughter and sought an audience with mother and daughter to discuss the matter directly.[82] After receiving 'a most friendly reply', he went to the Palazzo Bandini to press his case. He left the meeting in despair.[83] Isabella would accept his proposal of marriage, but she could not because he was not Roman Catholic. When Howard suggested that a 'mixed marriage' was not unusual, Isabella replied 'that she could not think of a married life in which she did not see eye to eye with her husband in what was to her the first question of life'. He could not accept what he called 'the Faith of Christianity'; if he could, he would have no hesitation about converting to Catholicism. 'So it is an impasse', he confided to Elizabeth, 'she loves me, & I her, but there is a barrier that for the present seems stronger than steel.'

It was not hopeless. Isabella Bandini loved Howard as much as he loved her. She wanted to marry him and, as a result, she worked to convince him both of her deep feelings and the genuineness of Catholic Christianity.[84] At her suggestion, Howard went to discuss both Christianity and Catholicism with a close friend of the Bandini family, Monsignor Raphael Merry del Val, a member of the Accademia Ecclesiastica and a favourite of the then pope, Leo XIII. Howard met twice with Merry del Val in the latter's rooms at the Vatican and, before leaving Rome in late April, Howard received a number of books to read on Catholicism and theological subjects. Isabella's efforts – she and Howard met secretly at the home of a mutual friend without the knowledge of her parents – coupled with his discussions with Merry del Val began to suggest to Howard that he might be wrong in his disbelief. He noted after his second meeting with Merry del Val that 'it seemed to me suddenly as if I was surrounded by the Divine'. But he could not stay at Rome any longer. The rubber syndicate wanted him to travel to Trinidad to purchase land and begin the experimental phase of the project. So, armed with Merry del Val's books, Isabella's support, and a few unresolved questions about the 'Faith of Christianity', Howard left Rome at the end of April. His trip to the West Indies would lead him to complete the two-part plan he had struck upon in the weeks after his mother's death.

After a short stay at London, Howard left for Trinidad with Orde. The information they received from property sellers and others, including Sir

Hubert Jerningham, the governor, proved Trinidad to be a loss. Most land was either unsuitable or not for sale. That on the market was too expensive. Jerningham and a few others suggested they investigate Tobago, an island just thirty miles to the northeast, where property was cheaper. On Tobago's Windward Coast, Howard and Orde found exactly what they required at a fair price.[85] It had been a sugar estate, and its buildings were in disrepair. Although unworked for some time, the land was unspoilt. From the highland in the interior, a river ran through the middle of the property, providing the necessary water supply, and the river valley itself was broad and flat enough to allow for experimentation. Just as important, a large village existed within the estate; this could provide the necessary labourers. Until October 1898, when Howard returned to London to report to the syndicate, he and Orde worked feverishly to get the estate ready for the 1899 growing season. They repaired the main house and a number of buildings, contacted local notables, bought and stored supplies, and assured themselves of enough labourers. They also built a nursery and began immediately to cultivate rubber-tree seedlings. By the time Howard left, the plantation was moving ahead quickly and seemed to offer the prospect of success.

Just as important, whilst in Tobago, Howard converted to Catholicism. He had been meditating on his talks with Merry del Val, and the religious reading he had done had a decided impact on his beliefs.[86] Two letters written to Elizabeth just prior to and after his conversion show the end of his religious odyssey.[87] A few days before converting, although he could observe that 'the more I see of Catholicism the more I begin to understand what a living everyday power it becomes in one's life', his thoughts were suffused by residual guilt that he was rejecting the religious faith of his family, especially of his mother. But a few days after converting, this guilt evaporated and he was a new man:

I have gone on with my everyday work just the same...but the sense of religion now pervades even the everyday work, & gives a lightness & freedom from worry that I never felt before. Indeed, it is a great and glorious thing, and makes the struggle for a good life so much easier, in spite of raising the standard infinitely both as to thoughts, words, & acts.

The question naturally arises as to whether Howard converted out of conviction or because it was the only way he could marry Isabella. He converted out of conviction. If he was disingenuous, he would have taken the plunge at Rome in April. But he was not, and he did not. He began to question his scepticism in April; however there was a diffidence that precluded conversion. Only when he got away to the West Indies, immersed himself in work, and had time to meditate and consider the arguments proffered by Isabella and Merry del Val, and study those books, could he convert in good conscience. In the end there was no reluctance; he became in every sense of the term a 'born-again Christian'.

As soon as Howard reached London, he had to depart for Rome. Howard had been in constant contact with Isabella – Elizabeth acted as an intermediary[88] – and with Merry del Val. Prince and Princess Bandini now welcomed Howard as a son-in-law. But Isabella's mother was gravely ill and, sensing that she would soon die, wished the marriage to occur as soon as possible.[89] On 17 November 1898 in the private chapel at Palazzo Bandini, Esme and Isabella were married by Merry del Val. By Roman custom, the next day they were also married in a civil ceremony. Moreover, as Howard had married into 'the Black Society' of Rome, he, Isabella, and Prince Bandini followed the dictates of that society by paying their respects to Leo XIII in a papal audience; this first meeting with the pontiff had a profound effect on Howard.[90] The newly-weds had no opportunity for a honeymoon. Isabella wished to stay with her mother during her illness and, with the death of Princess Bandini on 15 December, the couple went into seclusion at Elizabeth's villa at Portofino. Howard and his new wife travelled to England in the New Year and, after a short stay at London which gave Howard's family a chance to meet Isabella, they went north to Cumberland. They remained there until the autumn. The rubber plantation was now in its first phase – Howard was not needed just then – and he wanted to enjoy married life by spending as much time as possible with 'Isa'.

Whilst Howard had been setting about realising his two-part plan, Anglo-Boer relations in South Africa were worsening. Rhodes' British South Africa Company and the colonial policy of Salisbury's third government, directed by Joseph Chamberlain, the colonial secretary, were leading to a crisis with the independent Boer republics of the Transvaal and the Orange Free State.[91] In October 1899 the armies of these republics, guided by the Transvaal president, Paulus Kruger, invaded the British colonies of Natal and the Cape. A number of issues intertwined to make the struggle of importance to British foreign and Imperial policy. First, the diamond and gold wealth of the region could not be ignored. Secondly, South Africa was important strategically in protecting the sea routes to India and the eastern portions of the Empire. Finally, there loomed the spectre of possible European involvement in the war on the Boer side – British relations with both France and Germany had been under increasing strain in the late 1890s.[92] The Boer republics had begun this struggle believing that there would be diplomatic and other support for them from Britain's European adversaries, especially the Germans.[93] This support was an illusion.

Howard had gone to the plantation – now called Louis d'Or – in the autumn of 1899. All was progressing well; the seedlings were planted, so that all the syndicate could do was to wait to see how good the latex flow was. When Howard left Louis d'Or in October 1899, he assumed that the South African war would be over in a few months because of obvious British military superiority. This did not happen. The Boers were successful initially, besieging British garrisons at Kimberley, Ladysmith, and Mafeking. By the time Howard reached Britain, he and most of his countrymen realised that the war was going to drag on. Some, the critics of the Empire, were willing to let the Boers dominate South Africa, since they had as much right there as the British South Africa Company. But for those like Howard who were deeply attached to the Imperial idea – Howard because he supported the notion of Federation, and others, like Rhodes, for baser reasons – the problem centred on retaining South Africa as an integral part of the Empire. This could not be achieved simply by giving the region the equivalent of 'Home Rule'. If the Boers came to dominate, they would drive the British out and South Africa would be removed from the British orbit. Britain's position in the world would be diminished because its control over the Empire would be seen to be weakened.[94]

Howard felt he had to help in some way. He wanted to join the army but, at thirty-six, he was too old to enlist. However, as he had had experience of South Africa and could ride, shoot, and speak Afrikaans, he made enquiries. He found that he might serve as a trooper in one of the 'yeomanry' companies, squads which did not participate in combat but performed ancillary work, like guarding railways and bridges, that freed younger men to fight. 'Yeomen' soldiers were 'gentlemen' soldiers, paying their own expenses in kit and forgoing wages; they were there to serve their country or to seek adventure, or both. After discussing the matter with Isabella, Howard enlisted in a company called 'The Duke of Cambridge's Own' – the DCO. With other gentlemen soldiers, Howard left for South Africa in February 1900 in the second-class cabins of a steamer called *Dunvegan Castle*.

Howard served in South Africa for less than a year. Although he went out to keep that vital region firmly within the Empire, his tour of duty became a full-scale adventure. After rudimentary training at Matjesfontein, a camp near Cape Town, the DCO were sent inland to support the main British army which was striking north into the Transvaal and the Orange Free State in an attempt to crush Boer military power.[95] By the end of May, the DCO was with regular troops near Lindley, in the north central region of the Free State. On 30 May a Boer army counterattacked and captured the British force at Lindley. With two hundred prisoners, the Boers feared a British advance to free their men; they therefore marched their captives to the town of Vrede, a safer place in the extreme northeast of the Free State. The trek was difficult for Howard, who had become ill from drinking tainted water. He had also lost his kitbag, which contained a number of crucial bits of equipment, especially his blanket. With his already poor health, the cold nights on the veldt saw Howard become deathly ill. On 14 June the bulk of the British soldiers were transferred further inland, but Howard and another sick soldier, Herbert Mappin, were too ill to travel. As a consequence, Howard and Mappin were left at Vrede – it was still firmly in Boer control – and the Boer commander found them an English doctor in the town to treat and care for them. Howard's health remained poor for almost two months.[96] For the first two weeks, he was bedridden with a low fever. When this began to clear up, he got a chill that developed into a mild case of typhoid.

Howard and Mappin were well treated by their Boer captors.[97] They were nursed by that British doctor. They lived in an English family's boarding house. They had a certain amount of freedom within Vrede. In fact, the Boers even returned to Howard some gold jewellery which was of sentimental value: a locket containing a portrait of his mother, a crucifix, and a holy medal. This affected Howard profoundly:

This naturally made a great impression on me, as did our treatment by the Boers all through, and since that date I have never been willing to hear any abuse of Boers, from whom I had from the first a genuine respect, but for whom from that time I have always felt a real affection as a people.

Howard's opinion of the Boers in 1900 differed markedly from his view ten years before – 'ignorant, land-greedy & backward'. Now, thanks to his good treatment during his captivity, they were obviously men like any others.

He now recognised the animosity that separated Englishmen from Boers, but he believed his experiences indicated that a basis existed for reconciliation, something that could only foster Imperial unity.[98] But Britain and the Boers were still at war in August 1900. Vrede was endangered by a British offensive and the Boers were going to withdraw taking Howard and Mappin with them. The two had learnt much about the strengths and weaknesses of Boer forces in the area, so it would be folly for the Boers to leave them behind to provide invaluable intelligence for the British army. Knowing this, and fearing they might be shot to prevent their passing on knowledge, Howard and Mappin decided to escape. With the help of pro-British sympathisers at Vrede, Howard and Mappin eluded their captors on 12 August and four days later, after a perilous journey through Boer-held territory, they reached a British position.[99] By August 1900 the conventional military phase of the Boer war was winding down. British forces had occupied Pretoria, the Transvaal capital, on 5 June, Kruger had fled to Europe, and the British had begun consolidating their hold on South Africa. No one knew that it would take Britain two difficult years fighting Boer guerrillas before South Africa would be subdued.[100] Howard rejoined the DCO and served guarding railway lines in the interior until the DCO disbanded in October 1900. On 7 November Howard was reunited with Isabella and his family when he arrived in London.

In 1901 and 1902 Howard and Isabella lived in London whilst he attended to the business of the rubber syndicate. Under Orde's management, Louis d'Or was doing well; the difficulty was that it was not yet returning, nor would it for some time it seemed, the sort of profits that would allow Howard to pursue his newer goal of economic co-partnership. He had told Elizabeth in 1897 that, if the rubber plantation did not work out, he was willing to go back into government service. At that time he wrote that 'that will be the last string in my bow'.[101] It was clear that, by the end of 1902, he had reached that last string. He was entering his fortieth year; he had not really accomplished much in pursuit of the great ideas, even in their modified version; and he now had a wife not only to provide for, but to offer some security. He too needed something secure. Government service seemed to offer the only avenue for his talents.

III

In late 1902 Esme Howard had no way of knowing – no one did – that those first forty years were the preparation for a diplomatic career in the service of Britain during three crucial decades of its existence as a great Power. It was his personal misfortune that he did not achieve the ambitions he had set grandly for himself in 1890. But it was his country's good fortune that he was prepared to go back into government service – though there was uncertainty in late 1902 that this meant diplomacy. It was also his country's good fortune that his first forty years transformed him into a gifted diplomat. At twenty-seven he had the raw materials. He had social grace, a sense of his family's place in Britain's history, and an unaffected manner. He also possessed a number of important attributes necessary in diplomacy: a facility for languages, the capacity for hard work, and, most crucially, an icy realism that permitted him to see to the heart of a problem and propose policy in Britain's best interest. But those raw materials could never have been developed fully by the Esme Howard of 1890, and for one simple reason: by his own admission, he was a young man in a hurry. He had written to his mother in 1890 that his 'capacity' had not been proved. He left diplomacy to realise that 'capacity'. For more than a decade his ambition had dominated. This was crucial to his development. If he had never had the opportunity to pursue his ambitions, his mind would always have been preoccupied with 'what might have happened'. For someone with his intelligence, never to have tried would have made him miserable. It was not a recipe for success.

The Esme Howard of 1902, on the other hand, was ready to be a great diplomat. By 1902 he was older, reconciled to his own limitations, confident in his abilities, and possessed compassion and consideration. It was the experiences of the 1890s in pursuit of the great ideas which brought about this metamorphosis in his character, and it is ironic that the unquenched ambition of 1890 was responsible for the reasoned character of 1902. Howard's explorations of the alien societies of Africa and the Americas, markedly different from that shared by Britain and the European continent, broadened him to such an extent that he was not an insular Englishman. He was tolerant of other views and opinions and tried to understand the points of view of others, although he might not agree with them. The rough and tumble – and uncertainty – of local and national politics and of business gave him exposure to life which can only go to one who does more than observe. His taste of the harshness of modern industrial society that came during his work for the Booth enquiry demonstrated the necessity of compromise. Recognising that capitalism was essential to the economic well-being of England, he sought to soften its hardness by working towards co-partnership with labour. More dogmatic men would either have ignored the abuses of industrial capitalism or sought to abolish it. Most important, the Esme Howard of 1902 possessed an inner peace and a strength of character that might always have been there, but that were brought to the surface by the love of a good woman and his complete and genuine acceptance of Roman Catholicism. This inner peace and strength suffused both his private and public lives, so that never once in critical moments representing his country did he have a crisis of conscience in carrying out difficult policies. Esme Howard had matured during the 1890s. He was the most reasonable of men, and he was ready to serve his country in any way it saw fit.

IV

After living in London for most of 1902 attending to business and taking part in the 'season' – Edward VII's coronation took place in June – Howard and Isa travelled to Rome to spend the winter with the widowed Prince Bandini. In making the customary social rounds soon after he arrived, Howard visited the British Embassy at Rome. The ambassador at Rome, Sir Francis Bertie, a career diplomat, had known Howard since the days when Kimberley was foreign secretary. When Bertie discovered that Howard was unemployed, he enquired if Howard would consider serving as honorary secretary at the Rome Embassy.[102] This was an unpaid post involving routine administrative work rarely of a sensitive nature. How this matter was raised – and which of the two men raised it – can only be guessed.[103] At this time Howard was looking for some sort of employment – his memoirs make this clear. However, it is doubtful whether he planned in advance to find work with the Diplomatic Service in Rome. It is more probable that Bertie, who liked Howard and recognised his abilities, decided to do what he could to help his friend. In any event, Bertie made it clear that 'there was no sort of possibility of [this appointment] leading any further'.[104] Bertie lobbied the Foreign Office, overcame the opposition of some key officials who felt that Howard should be denied even an honorary position because he had left the Service in 1890 – Sanderson was one of these[105] – and by Christmas 1902 Howard had employment. As Howard observed dryly in his reflections on this: 'I was again installed in the Embassy in Rome with the hitherto unknown rank of Honorary Second Secretary.'[106]

Presented with an unexpected opportunity, Howard seems to have decided to use this appointment as a means of impressing Bertie and others with his abilities, thereby to gain readmittance to the Diplomatic Service in a regular capacity. His chance came in early 1903 when Edward VII decided to travel to Rome on an unofficial visit. The king had planned a Mediterranean cruise, along with a visit to France, for April and May 1903. He wanted to undertake some unofficial diplomacy to improve Britain's relations with a few countries, especially France, which had suffered as a result of the Boer War.[107] In visiting Italy, tied to Germany and Austria-Hungary by the Triple Alliance, audiences had to be arranged with both the king and the pope, who were still at odds over the loss of the Papal States by the pope during the Risorgimento, whilst at the same time seeking not to antagonise Protestant opinion within Britain.

There proved to be little difficulty in arranging one meeting with the Italian king and a second with the pope. A precedent had been established by William II, the German emperor, who had first met with the king at the Quirinal, the royal palace at Rome. However, since the pope did not acknowledge the existence of Italian royal authority, it was impossible to travel immediately after to the Vatican. William II had returned to the German Embassy and, suitably cleansed by being temporarily on 'neutral' soil, then proceeded to the Vatican for an audience with Leo. Edward adopted this procedure. He would meet the Italian king at the Quirinal, return to the British Embassy, and then make his way to the Vatican. Italian royal and papal susceptibilities would be safeguarded.

Edward's visit created two difficulties none the less. The first was convincing the Conservative Cabinet, led by Arthur Balfour, the prime minister, that a domestic crisis would not ensue in Britain. As late as 12 April, two weeks before Edward was to set foot in Italy, Balfour had written to the king about the danger 'that ordinary Protestant prejudice might fasten on [the] visit, and declare it part of [a] settled scheme to buy off Roman Catholic opposition, and secure passage of [the] Irish Land Bill and [the] success of your Majesty's visit to Ireland'.[108] This did not dissuade the king. Whilst Prince of Wales, Edward had met Leo on three occasions. In 1902, on the fiftieth anniversary of Leo's election as cardinal, Edward had sent a member of his household to represent him at the jubilee celebrations at Rome. Moreover, the English Roman Catholic community, led by Howard's kinsman, the fifteenth Duke of Norfolk, was lobbying both Edward and Balfour to find a way to allow the meeting to take place.[109] Edward needed little prompting. Balfour relented when both the king and Norfolk assured him that Edward's visit to the Vatican would be 'private and unofficial'. Balfour's only condition in all of this was that Bertie and the Embassy should 'arrange [the] unofficial visit, if possible on [the] initiative of [the] Pope'.[110] In the event of a reaction to the meeting developing within Britain, Balfour could use Bertie and his staff as scapegoats on which to heap any blame.

Balfour's condition led to the second problem: ensuring that the initiative for the meeting did not come from the royal party then *en route* to Italy on the king's yacht. For domestic political and religious reasons, Edward could not ask for an audience with the pope, not even a private and unofficial audience. This would place the head of the Church of England in the role of supplicant to the head of the Church of Rome. For the same reason, however, Leo could not be seen to invite Edward to meet with him. This created a major diplomatic impasse which Howard was able to remove.

Howard had several problems to overcome. The British government and the Vatican did not have formal diplomatic relations. As a result, any time discussions or negotiations occurred, they required an intermediary who had the confidence of both the Embassy and the Vatican Secretariat of State, the arm of the papal government which handled such matters. In this matter, the role of intermediary was entrusted to Monsignor Edmund Stonor, an English ecclesiastic living at Rome who was close to Cardinal Rampolla, the Vatican secretary of state. By 18 April, Stonor's efforts to co-ordinate the king's meeting with the pope were going nowhere. Three days earlier Stonor and Rampolla had conferred.[111] Rampolla made it clear that his master could not invite Edward to meet with him. The invitation would have to be sought by the English king. As Rampolla noted: '...should the

King of England wish to do him the courteous attention of making him a visit, I can assure your Lordship that the courtesy of His Majesty would be acceptable and duly appreciated by His Holiness'. Bertie and Sir Charles Hardinge, an assistant under-secretary at the Foreign Office accompanying the king, believed that Stonor's efforts were coming to nothing. In addition, they felt that Rampolla was not consulting the pope in this matter.[112] Bertie and Hardinge therefore tried a different tactic. Hardinge wired Norfolk in England to put pressure on Rampolla to secure a meeting between Edward and Leo.[113] Bertie, knowing of Howard's connexions with the Vatican, asked him to approach someone else in the Vatican hierarchy who had the ear of the pope and could put the matter directly to him.[114]

Howard's subsequent efforts proved to be decisive in this twisted process.[115] He sought out Merry del Val, apprised him of the situation, and showed him some of the correspondence that had passed between the royal party, the Embassy, and the Vatican. Merry del Val's immediate reaction was that Rampolla's letter to Stonor summarising their meeting of 15 April 'had quite met the King's wishes'. Howard disagreed. The king would have to seek an audience with the pope and 'it could not be allowed to appear that the king was going to throw himself at the feet of the Pope'. Merry del Val countered that the same held for the pope. After desultory conversation, Merry del Val mentioned that Norfolk had written a letter which had just been received at the Vatican – this meeting between Howard and Merry del Val occurred on 21 April, so Hardinge's telegram to Norfolk had obviously elicited a quick response. Howard and Merry del Val saw that Norfolk's efforts offered a way around the impasse. After consulting their superiors, Howard and Merry del Val agreed that an audience was possible if 'all burden of initiative would be thrown onto the shoulders of the Duke'. Thus Norfolk simply indicated to both the king and the pope that it would be beneficial for them to meet. Naturally both accepted. On 29 April 1903, the head of the Church of Rome met with the head of the Church of England in the papal apartments at the Vatican. They did so as equals. A large part of the credit for this went to Esme Howard.

Howard was lucky in being at Rome at this time, and also for impressing not only Bertie, but Hardinge as well. Hardinge and Bertie were in the midst of a private campaign to modernise what they saw to be 'the red tape' and 'the red tapism' of the old regime in the Foreign Office.[116] This regime had worked well in the days of Granville, Rosebery, and Salisbury, but times had changed: Britain was entering a new period in its foreign relations when the Foreign Office and the Diplomatic Service had to work with efficiency and speed to respond to the challenge proffered by a united Germany, a more powerful Russia, and other states with a desire to achieve the global status enjoyed by Britain. Sanderson and others of the old school were the focus of the disapproval of Bertie and Hardinge. Men like Howard, if they showed ability, were the type of diplomat needed to modernise the conduct of British foreign policy. Hardinge was back at London by the middle of May 1903; within weeks, Lord Lansdowne, the foreign secretary, had selected Howard to serve as the new British consul-general for the island of Crete.[117] Hardinge's part in Howard's appointment is undeniable. The consul-generalship in Crete was usually the private preserve of the so-called 'Levant Service', a division of the Diplomatic Service controlled by Sanderson. As Hardinge wrote to Howard soon after he arrived in Crete: 'I hear that the Levant Service would like to tear me in pieces for your appointment to Crete but I am quite content to trust you to justify the appointment...'[118] The point was clear. Howard was being given the chance to remake a career in the Diplomatic Service, the new one being fashioned by a new school of diplomats. Such chances were rare,[119] and Crete was to be his proving ground.

2

Crete: consulship and civil war, 1903–1906

> Personally, looking at the question simply as regards Crete and Crete only, I feel sure that the sooner England can get rid of the Cretan incubus by inducing the other Powers to allow annexation to Greece the better for us, the better for P[rin]ce George, and probably, taking all considerations together, the better for Crete[,] tho that is open to doubt and is not a question that need much concern us.
>
> *Howard, October* 1904

I

Arriving in Crete on 11 July 1903, Howard faced a daunting task as consul-general. In a personal sense, he saw that success at this post would give him the career he needed to provide for his wife, and, with Isa now pregnant – the baby expected in the autumn – the pressure to succeed had increased. In a professional sense, he realised that he had been sent to the island to ensure that British influence and interests were not diminished. Crete was one of two provinces of the crumbling Ottoman Empire seeking independence from the Porte; Macedonia was the other. As such, Crete and Macedonia were the flashpoints of the on-going 'Eastern Question', which Powers like Britain with an interest in the Near Eastern balance of power sought to control for their own ends. Britain's chief rival in the region was Russia, whose policy focussed on the Balkans where Russian dominance might lead to the demise of Turkey-in-Europe and Russian control of the Straits. The British could not allow this for strategic reasons tied to the vital sea lanes that ran across the Mediterranean and through the Suez Canal. The principal British goal in handling the 'Eastern Question' centred on propping up the Ottomans as a bulwark against Russian expansion. In Crete, Howard would be integral to this general policy, reporting on the situation and carrying out policy directives sent from London. On this hinged his chances for regular employment in the Diplomatic Service.

Crete had been an increasingly important post in the British Diplomatic

Service since 1896.[1] In that year fighting broke out when Christian Greek-Cretans, supported by patriotic clubs in Greece, attempted to break Moslem Ottoman control over the island. Crete's population was overwhelmingly Greek, the majority of whom sought union – in Greek, *enosis* – with Greece. The Cretan rebellion led to a Greco-Turkish war in 1897, which forced the Powers to intervene in order to maintain the Near Eastern balance of power. In this the British and Russians were at one, as they attempted diplomatically to keep the Germans from gaining a foothold in the region – Turco-German relations were warming. A settlement in 1898 saw Crete remain an autonomous province of the Ottoman Empire, with a high commissioner appointed by the Powers to run the Cretan government. Ostensibly subservient to the Porte, in reality the high commissioner answered to the consuls-general of the Powers posted to the island, who jointly oversaw the general administration, thereby protecting the sultan's interests and preserving the balance of power in the eastern Mediterranean. To assuage Greek feelings, including those of Greek-Cretans, Prince George, a younger son of George I of the Hellenes, was chosen as high commissioner. In the end only four Powers – Britain, France, Italy, and Russia – agreed to supervise the prince's administration; Germany and Austria-Hungary refrained as they wished to ingratiate themselves with the sultan, who was unhappy about this great-Power interference within his Empire.

Howard's work involved collaborating with the other three consuls and, through this body, working with Prince George. In the first few years of his rule, the prince fashioned a constitution as well as a code of law and a local gendarmerie to enforce this code and keep order. A Cretan Assembly had been elected to help in governing. The four Protecting Powers stationed troops on Crete – the island was divided into four occupation zones – and these troops ensured that the 1898 settlement was not overthrown from outside. The difficulty in this was that Prince George supported *enosis*. He had begun his initial three-year term in December 1898 and, before it expired, had recommended *enosis* to the Powers. They refused this course, and a second proposal that the Greek king be given control of the island's administration. In order to maintain the status quo, the Powers persuaded the prince to serve a second three-year term and, accordingly, this began in December 1901.

This situation greeted Howard in July 1903. On the surface all seemed well. Crete remained within the Ottoman Empire. A balance existed amongst the Powers with an interest in the Near East, especially between Britain and Russia. But, underneath, tension had not diminished. Cretans – and Macedonians – still wanted to break away from the Porte. Britain and Russia, and the lesser Powers, competed for advantage. The sultan was not happy. Athens wanted union with the island, a goal supported by Prince George and the majority of Cretans and Greeks. It was obvious that Howard's time on the island would not be easy.

Controversy exists over the instructions Howard received before he took up this post. Apparently Sanderson and Hardinge briefed the new consul-general about the situation in Crete, its connexion with Macedonia, and the absolute necessity of ensuring that Cretan union with Greece did not occur.[2] The problem centred on Prince George. British diplomatic circles recognised that he was working, within the strictures imposed by the Powers, to effect *enosis*.[3] This the British could not allow. But Prince George had some residual diplomatic leverage thanks to dynastic links between the Greek royal family and the British and Russian Imperial families: King George of Greece, the dowager Tsarina Marie, and Queen Alexandra of England were siblings. According to Howard, he was 'given to understand at the Foreign Office before taking up [his] new post that the Prince was a favourite nephew of King Edward and Queen Alexandra, and it must be [his] particular job to let him down gently'.[4]

Howard's phrase 'let him down gently' is the focus of the controversy. When Prince George wrote his Cretan reminiscences twenty-five years after Howard's appeared, he latched upon this phrase to characterise Howard and the Foreign Office as his arch-enemies in Crete: 'Ostensibly [Howard] was just the new British Consul-General, but in fact (and we have this from his own memoirs) he was the chosen envoy of the Foreign Office in London who, according to pre-arranged policy, was to stab me in the back.'[5] Apart from misreading Howard's memoirs, the prince failed to appreciate Crete's importance in the Near Eastern balance of power. The British were not opposed to *enosis*. Hardinge and others not only saw this as a reasonable solution, they believed it would happen eventually given the close cultural ties between the island and the mainland.[6] But at this juncture *enosis* would benefit the Russians. The Russians were willing to sanction Crete's union with Greece. In return, however, they argued that the other Balkan Powers would have to be compensated for Greek gains, and the only place where equitable compensation could be given was in Macedonia, which Bulgaria and Serbia, Russian clients, desired.[7] St Petersburg sought to tie the Cretan and Macedonian questions together. London worked to keep them apart.

Howard saw that if Crete could be absorbed by Greece without giving the minor Slav Powers an advantage in the Balkans, so much the better. This could not be arranged in 1903. Given Russian influence at Sofia and Belgrade, the Near Eastern balance of power would shift to Russia's advantage. Since Britain opposed this, as did Germany and Austria-Hungary, then working to bolster their positions at Constantinople, the chance of great-Power conflict existed over this question. At a lower level, Athens would never allow its exclusion from any division of Macedonian territory. Hence, the possibility of a Balkan war if the 'Eastern Question' was mishandled. Working hard for union, Prince George ignored the diplomatic interests of Britain and the other Powers in the equation. Therefore, Howard had to 'let him down gently', to delay *enosis* until some more fortuitous moment. Rather than 'a stab in the back', it was part of a diplomatic strategy to prevent a conflict amongst those Powers concerned about the demise of Turkey-in-Europe.

Howard's predecessor as British consul-general, Robert Graves, remained in Crete for a week after Howard's arrival; he provided valuable information about the problems on the island, as well as the difficulties encountered in dealing with Prince George.[8] Although Greek-Cretans generally supported *enosis*, Howard learnt that this support did not extend necessarily to the prince's administration. With his royal mien, Prince George tended to govern without consulting members of his government. Tied to a tendency to see issues in black and white, this saw him view anyone disagreeing with him as an enemy. But Graves did not see the prince as the chief villain. This role belonged to the prince's private secretary, Andrew Papadiamondopoulos, a royalist and pro-*enosis* Greek who had come with the prince's entourage in 1898. In Grave's estimation, Papadiamondopoulos 'had a really sinister effect on the Prince's character in certain ways making him suspicious and ready to take offence'. Captain Clarke, a Royal Marine seconded as the prince's medical adviser, reinforced this view. Clarke informed Howard that Papadiamondopoulos ran a 'system of espionage' to monitor Cretan opposition to the prince. As Clarke put it: '...if one's cook or butler is a supporter of the opposition, H.R.H. is at once informed of it, & a black mark put against the master of such suspicious services'. These views coloured Howard's assessment of the situation, causing him to vow 'to keep out of all suspicion of taking the slightest personal interest in Cretan internal politics'.

When Howard arrived, princely suspicion and ire were directed against the Italian consul-general, Count Negri.[9] This touched Howard because of Isa, and the subject arose in almost his first meeting with Prince George. When questioned about his wife, Howard 'laid great stress on her Scotch descent [through the earls of Newburgh] & patriotic adoption of England as her country, which, it is hoped, calmed his suspicions'. The prince's suspicions were calmed and, learning the lesson, Howard distanced himself from the petty squabbling that tended to mark Prince George's relations with the other consuls-general. In addition, Howard strove for a good working relationship with the high commissioner, something seen when over two years later the prince confided his feelings about Howard to Hardinge, whom he had discovered had engineered Howard's appointment:

> [Prince George] sent the Greek minister to see me to thank me [for getting Howard appointed] & to say that he thoroughly appreciated and liked Howard, that he is the only Consular official with whom he can talk openly and treat as a friend, and that his wife is charming. He added that though Howard did not always agree with him he always acted loyally towards him.[10]

This explains Howard's success at Crete. He distanced himself from the real or imagined conspiracies that the prince and Papadiamondopoulos saw emanating from the other consulates, and he avoided taking sides between the high commissioner and his Cretan opponents – something Papadiamondopoulos' spies would have unearthed if there was even a hint of Howard's collusion with the domestic opponents.

When Howard succeeded Graves, Prince George was in the midst of a campaign to secure *enosis* before his second term as high commissioner ended in December 1904. This entailed several issues touching Crete's internal affairs as well as its external relations with the four Powers and the Porte. In domestic affairs, Prince George moved to increase his control over the island's political life by isolating his opponents. Concerning the four Powers and the Porte, the prince did everything he could to weaken the few bonds remaining between the sultan and Crete and to lessen four-Power control over Cretan affairs. In most instances, the line separating internal from external Cretan policy remained blurred.

The first difficulty Howard encountered involved the prince's attempt to achieve full authority over the gendarmerie and the occupation troops of the four Powers. Gaining control over the forces which carried out the will of the high commissioner's government would be a signal accomplishment. By four-Power agreement, Italian soldiers officered the gendarmerie, a move to ensure the Powers had some control over this important arm of the Cretan government. In September 1903 the gendarmerie commander, Count Caprini, completed his tour of duty and, in discussing the situation with Howard, outlined the difficulties confronting the gendarmerie.[11] These stemmed from Prince George asserting that its officer corps was under the direction of the Cretan government, a situation which found the gendarmerie torn between the Powers and the prince. Howard commented:

> Unfortunately, [the Italian officers'] status in Crete is ill-defined and readily leads to misinterpretation, for while the High Commissioner apparently looks upon them entirely in the light of Cretan officers dependent upon him alone, they are still on the active list of the Italian army, in receipt of full pay, and figure as under the Officer Commanding the Naples district.

Howard found prescient Caprini's prediction that pressure from Canae, the prince's capital, would continue and create difficulties for Captain Monaco, the new commander.[12] But the Foreign Office could do nothing just then to deflect the prince. Hardinge wrote privately to tell Howard that Cretan affairs had a low priority.[13] Macedonia and troubles brewing in the Far East between Japan and Russia were far more important. Hardinge noted candidly that London 'would be ready to stretch a point or two merely to keep things quiet in Crete'. Therefore, Howard spent the next eighteen months observing Prince George encroach on the authority of the gendarmerie – and watching the High Commission's relations with Italy worsen – not agreeing formally with what was occurring but conceding privately to the situation.

There were other matters to which Howard could not remain so indifferent. In the event of a major crisis like an insurrection against the 1898 settlement, the international troops and not the gendarmerie would maintain the status quo imposed by the Powers. In the middle of March 1904 Howard met with the prince who 'spoke, while referring casually to the foreign troops in Crete, as if they were under his command'.[14] Howard had earlier been assured by a French officer, Captain Destelle, that such responsibility did not reside with the prince, although he was nominal commander of the international troops on Crete. Howard sought clarification from London. If left unsettled this issue could have led to difficulty if a crisis arose, difficulty which might impair quick and decisive action. Howard found that, unlike the way it responded to the question of the gendarmerie, the Foreign Office would brook no interference here by Prince George.[15] Richard Maxwell, the head of the Foreign Office Eastern Department, informed Lansdowne that the Protecting Powers agreed in April 1903 that each contingent of foreign troops was under the sole jurisdiction of their commanding officers, who were to work with their respective consul-general. Military and diplomatic expediency could be combined on the spot. Neither Maxwell nor Lansdowne saw any need for Howard to explain the matter to the prince until 'the contingency which he apprehended' arose. The chance came a month later when a minor dispute developed between Prince George and Destelle over having international troops guard prisons, a job normally accorded to the gendarmerie. Showing talent for seizing the initiative, Howard sought out the prince and explained in an anodyne way that British troops were under the direction of their commander. This did not mean that British troops would never be used to help maintain order; however, British authorities had to make that decision. Howard's success in this can be judged by the prince noting that he had no complaint with the British troops or the officers commanding them.

Cretan finance was another problem with which Howard had to deal. To make his administration independent, the prince sought financial autonomy for Crete. In 1898 the four Protecting Powers had each loaned the new government one million francs.[16] This helped provide effective government and served as the basis for increased trade with the outside world. Cretan revenues depended on customs, and thus on foreign trade, but, once the loan monies ran out, Crete suffered a recession, imports declined, and government revenues fell. The prince now had in place an expensive governing apparatus, especially the gendarmerie, which consumed one quarter of the budget. It proved impossible to reduce in a meaningful way this 'extravagant expenditure'. Paying back the four-Power loan was difficult and for the fiscal year 1903–4, Howard's first year at Crete, the prince's government faced a deficit of nearly 500,000 francs.

Howard found that the other consuls-general believed little chance existed for repayment. The French consul-general, Drouin, confided in Howard that 'the High Commissioner had almost ridiculed the idea that the Powers would insist on the payment of the interest of the Loan'.[17] This presented the four Powers with the possibility of a monetary crisis in Crete. It meant that either the Powers could let the island suffer such a crisis or they could lend Crete more money. The first course might lead to an anti-foreign reaction, promoting calls amongst the island population for *enosis* with Greece. The second amounted to throwing good money after bad and thereby postponing the day of reckoning. For the British neither possibility was palatable. The Treasury balked at increasing the level of British loans[18] whilst the Foreign Office, because of the 'Eastern Question', could not countenance an immediate change in the Near Eastern status quo.[19] Added to this, the Cretan government owed money to foreigners and foreign-protected nationals whose property had either been damaged or destroyed by Greek-Cretans during the troubles of 1896–8. By the middle of 1903 the indemnities had yet to be paid out of a fund established especially for this purpose. The fund's capital came from a 3 per cent surtax imposed on a range of imported goods and, in July 1903, it totalled nearly one million francs. Given that the indemnities fund was under Cretan control and not that of the Powers, Howard and his consular colleagues were uneasy about the security of this money.[20]

Therefore Howard, within weeks of arriving at the British consulate-general in Candia, divined that not only was the economic situation desperate, but that Prince George and Papadiamondopoulos were striving to circumvent the Powers' economic authority over the High Commission. Their efforts had two parts: raising money by legislative action in Crete and securing a new loan without reference to the Powers. To raise additional monies, Prince George engineered passage of legislation to permit the construction of utilities on the island. Just before Howard arrived, for instance, a law was passed granting a concession for the construction of a telephone system on the island.[21] This occurred without consulting the consuls-general, so it seemed as if Prince George's government would exclude the nationals of the Powers from bidding on a contract. This was a direct challenge. In the 1898 agreement establishing the High Commission, the four Powers had been given capitulary rights in Crete. One of these was that British, French, Italian, and Russian business concerns would have special rights in bidding for contracts like that dealing with telephone construction. Howard reported on the situation to the Foreign Office and, at the direction of Sanderson and Lansdowne, joined with Sir Nicholas O'Conor, the ambassador at Constantinople, and the other consuls-general to protest this action by the Cretan government.[22]

Howard also learnt of the prince's attempts to raise money independently of the Powers. In September this entailed Cretan negotiations with the Bank of Greece for a loan of five million francs,[23] a move to tie Crete and Greece closer together; however, by December, these negotiations faltered. Howard then suggested privately to London that some effort be made by the Powers to aid the Cretan government.[24] Though financial, the issue was fraught with political considerations, something Howard emphasised with cogent analysis of the Cretan situation:

The state of things financially is thoroughly unsound & no one is more ready to admit this than [Prince George] himself, in fact he often insists upon it as a reason for annexation to Greece. What I really particularly fear is that, when the pinch comes, and that it will come either in the shape of a financial or a currency crisis or both is almost certain, the discontent of the Cretans at the prolonged uncertainty of their fate, and their natural and innate distrust of the foreigner will be roused to the boiling point; the Greeks who surround the Prince may then make use of this state of things to push the hill people to an extreme course, such as raising the Greek flag, probably telling them that it is [Prince George's] wish to do so.

To avoid another Cretan crisis with the potential of inflaming the 'Eastern Question', Howard suggested that Crete be encouraged to seek a loan on the European money market. This would obviate closer financial links between Crete and Greece whilst keeping Prince George's government solvent. Although Sanderson initially seemed reluctant to sanction such a move – his tendency to dally already irritated Howard[25] – by March 1904 the permanent under-secretary was investigating the possibility of a loan guaranteed by the Powers. It was for 200 thousand pounds, or five million francs.

Handling Cretan financial issues gave Howard an object lesson in the need for patience in diplomacy. He found the Foreign Office willing to allow the financial problems of Crete to slide throughout 1904. No other option existed. Macedonia continued to divert the Powers' attention within Europe whilst, in the Far East, worsening Russo-Japanese relations, which led to war in Manchuria in February, pushed this and every other issue in international politics into suspended animation. London avoided taking the initiative to correct the deficiencies in Cretan public finance. This had been constant in British policy from at least the time Howard arrived at Candia.[26] If the other Powers were to suggest some way around the impasse, then the British government would listen attentively. Until that seemingly distant moment, however, London had no intention of re-opening the matter on its own. Sanderson explained this to Howard in May 1904:

I am not sure that much can be done at present. If we get through to the winter without having a row in Macedonia, and the situation there really mends, there might be some chance of making progress in regard to Cretan affairs. But it is a misfortune that the Russians who have always been jealous of any other Power taking the initiative, should at present be so much occupied elsewhere.[27]

In terms of Cretan finance, Howard's task remained ensuring that the 1898 settlement was not disrupted, reporting on possible infringements by the Cretan government, and keeping the prince and Papadiamondopoulos in line by concerting with the other consuls-general. Frustrated from time to time, Howard pointed out to his superiors simple and effective means to resolve a few of the minor but nagging problems – for instance, establishing a mixed commission to help Turkish-Cretans seeking indemnities[28] – but his counsel fell on deaf ears.

The final problem with which Howard had to deal involving Prince George's efforts to secure *enosis* before his second term ended revolved around achieving absolute control of domestic Cretan politics. Of all the things the prince did to distance Crete from the Powers and bring it closer to Greece, this caused Howard the most difficulty. Prince George's problem was that his view of *enosis* clashed with that held by some influential native-born Greek-Cretans led by Eleutherios Venizelos. As a Greek, the prince wanted Crete's complete absorption by the Greek state, in effect making it another province of the kingdom. Venizelos and his supporters envisaged a different arrangement whereby the island would be an autonomous principality within the Greek polity – an arrangement which not coincidentally would enhance the power of Cretan leaders like Venizelos.[29] A philosophical division also existed between the prince and Venizelos. The prince tended to govern autocratically, looking askance at constitutional limitations on his power. For Venizelos, constitutional limitations on the exercise of power remained fundamentally important.

By the time Howard arrived, the prince had used his position as high commissioner to remove Venizelos and his supporters from public life on the island.[30] Venizelos, who had been counsellor for justice during Prince George's first term, had been forced out in 1900. Thereafter his followers were squeezed out of executive office and, with Papadiamondopoulos' manipulation of elections, the Cretan Assembly. By March 1903, in control of the Assembly, the prince engineered passage of legislation permitting him to appoint officials at every level of government, including mayors. By the middle of 1903, the prince and Papadiamondopoulos controlled every facet of Cretan domestic politics. Not content with this, the high commissioner moved to discredit Venizelos. Using his control of the Cretan courts, the prince had Venizelos convicted on trumped up charges of libel and gaoled for a week. Although nominal, the punishment served the purpose of stifling the Venizelist opposition and simultaneously strengthening the political hand of those advocating Crete's complete absorption by Greece. Upon his release from gaol, just after Howard's arrival, Venizelos 'kept very quiet and studiously avoided all demonstrations which might offend His Royal Highness'.[31]

Howard saw that dominance over Cretan politics was crucial to Prince George's position *vis-à-vis* the Powers. With the apparent support of the Cretan people through the Assembly, trotted out periodically in resolutions favouring *enosis* on his terms, the prince seemed to have strength in arguing his case.[32] But this was sham, having no influence on Howard or the other consuls-general,[33] and even less on their home governments. None the less, early in 1904, secure in the belief that the opposition in Crete stood helpless, the prince mounted a diplomatic campaign to end Ottoman suzerainty over the island. A calculating man, he realised that the Powers required a solution that would maintain the façade of the 1898 settlement. In 1901 he had struck upon an ingenious ploy: Crete should be treated exactly like other Ottoman territories tied to the Porte but administered by another Power. For instance, in 1878 two Balkan provinces, Bosnia and Herzegovina, were turned over to Austria-Hungary. In 1901 the prince had pursued this 'Bosnian' solution, suggesting that Greece should assume Crete's administration in the name of the sultan. Not surprisingly, because of their differing interests, the Powers rejected this proposal. But in 1904, unworried by the Venizelist opposition and working hard to achieve control over the island's security forces and autonomy in fiscal affairs, the prince again advocated the 'Bosnian' solution.

Howard became actively involved in all these problems when, on 14 May 1904, Prince George broached the matter in a private conversation.[34] His argument centred on the obvious dislike of Greek-Cretans for the

1898 settlement: 'Everyone in Crete was tired of waiting for a definite solution of the question, & the fact that the present situation was obviously only provisional led [to] a state of general unrest.' Suffusing this conversation were two issues: Prince George's complaint, an old one, about his difficulty in balancing amongst the Powers, the Porte, and Athens, coupled with a new one about his reluctance to serve a third term. This second point was crucial in his renewed campaign to achieve four-Power support for the 'Bosnian' solution, since he repeated this same refrain to the other consuls, and even their wives,[35] whenever he had the opportunity over the summer. The implication in this was that if he retired in December 1904, the Cretan question would re-emerge as a major foreign policy problem for the Powers. Hence, it would be in the Powers' interests to arrange a 'Bosnian' solution for Crete, ending the matter once and for all. It amounted to diplomatic blackmail of a high order.

In reporting this to Sanderson, Howard noted that he shared the prince's view of the situation – though he apportioned blame for dissatisfaction in Crete to Papadiamondopoulos who had the 'impulse towards administrating by wirepulling'.[36] As well, he pointed out that the Russian consul-general, Baron de Etter, was equally convinced about the difficulty of the prince's position and, like Howard, felt that an adjustment to the regime in Crete had to be made. Howard told Sanderson that Etter, in the midst of being transferred from Crete, had written his final despatch to the Russian Foreign Office in these terms. Aware that his immersion in Cretan affairs might influence unduly his views about a readjustment, Howard hammered home the implications of policy as seen by the man on the spot: 'It may be much better to let things shape their own course here, in view of the other possibilities elsewhere, but it is useless to deny that there are rocks ahead, and I take it to be my business to point them out.' Whilst carrying out his instructions to the letter, Howard cautioned the Foreign Office about the weaknesses of policy. Unless there emerged a reasonable response to the prince's entreaties, there would soon be a political price to pay by Britain and the other Powers interested in the 'Eastern Question'.

By late April 1904 Howard discerned that two separate opposition movements to the efforts of the prince and Papadiamondopoulos seemed to be emerging.[37] One was amongst hill people in the western part of the island, led by Hadji Mihalis, an old chieftain who had 'taken a leading part in every Cretan revolution since 1866'. As Howard observed perceptively:

The important feature of this movement, if true, is that it comes not from the town in which there is always likely to be political opposition to any administration among disappointed place-hunters and others, but from the country districts on the absolute support of which the High Commissioner has hitherto entirely relied. It seems to be principally directed against Mr Papadiamontopoulo [sic] His Royal Highness' Private Secretary of whose unpopularity there is little doubt.

The other opposition group developed in the towns, clustering around Constantine Foumis, a Venizelist and former counsellor also driven from office by the prince and Papadiamondopoulos. Foumis appeared to be an interim leader who would step down once Venizelos gave up his self-imposed political isolation. Foumis' group criticised Cretan public finance, the officering of the gendarmerie, and the matter of the indemnities, but, like Mihalis and his supporters, focussed on Papadiamondopoulos: 'the person really responsible for what is done and left undone, but that having constitutionally no locum standi [sic] for such a position...is beyond the reach of effective criticism.'

Howard found himself by July 1904 faced with a potential crisis stemming from Prince George's treatment of the opposition on Crete. All vocal opponents were harshly treated with gaol sentences. This increased the resentment of the opposition, making their resistance more deep-seated;[38] it created a round of press comment in Britain and the other major Powers;[39] and it fostered an unfavourable reaction amongst diplomatists like Lansdowne, who began to doubt the prince's ability to govern.[40] In the short term, however, it provided the prince and Papadiamondopoulos with the chance to make the crucial approach to the Powers about the 'Bosnian' solution without a crisis in Crete erupting to scuttle their diplomacy. At the end of July, Prince George announced unexpectedly that he would travel to Rome, Paris, London, and St Petersburg 'to obtain some modification of the Status Quo in Crete'.[41] He then held private conversations with each consul-general.

Of his meeting with the prince, Howard reported that 'His Royal Highness spoke as if it was practically his last effort, as High Commissioner, to obtain a settlement'.[42] First, he emphasised that if he did not achieve some modification to the 1898 settlement, his prestige with the Cretan people would evaporate since they would question his sincerity in securing *enosis*. Dissatisfaction amongst the Cretans, after six years of the High Commission and four-Power occupation, would probably result in open rebellion against his administration coupled with declarations for union with the mainland. The second issue devolved from the first: if his tour failed, he would not seek a third term. He had no wish to lead the Cretan government in suppressing Cretans who shared generally his views about union. He ended his talk with Howard by condemning the Venizelists. The prince indicated that he had taken a major part in 'combatting the aims of Mr Venizelos' to ensure order. His purpose, he said, had been 'to prevent the country being divided into two hostile camps, which would have certainly led to internal disorders, which it might have been exceedingly difficult to suppress'. The implication was that something had to be done to prevent an outbreak of armed violence, and the tour of the capitals was the last chance to do this.

In commenting on this conversation, Howard decided to put on the official record his most candid assessment of the situation. He had done so privately a number of times since his arrival a year before but, whilst Hardinge and others sympathised with these private entreaties, his views and suggested policies were fobbed off by those in whom he confided. However, in July 1904, with the prince's tour in the offing and the very real chance of the Cretan question re-emerging as a major foreign policy problem, Howard decided that he had to enclose his views in a despatch. 'I must reluctantly admit', he told Lansdowne, 'that there is, to the best of my belief, much truth in Prince George's arguments.'[43] After six years of being on 'trial' before the Powers and 'of waiting and hoping for something better', Greek-Cretans wanted closer ties with Greece. Little doubt existed, observed Howard, that if the Powers refused to sanction some modification, opposition to the prince would grow and seek to modify unilaterally the status quo. This would force Britain and the Powers to make a difficult decision: 'whether or not they were prepared to maintain [the 1898 settlement] by force'. Howard refused to blame solely the prince for the situation – interesting given the prince's subsequent charge about a stab in the back:

I venture to take this opportunity of saying, with reference to the severe criticisms on the High Commissioner[']s Administration that have lately appeared in the Press, that, while no doubt mistakes have been made, the want of material progress is more attributable to the apathy of the country people and the intrigues of the different party leaders than any fault of the Government...

The Foreign Office appreciated Howard's candour. Maxwell, characterising Howard's effort as 'an important despatch', informed Lansdowne that the Italians had recently approached the Foreign Office about 'an exchange of views', an unexpected development suggesting that Rome suspected a change in Crete and wanted its senior partners cognisant of Italian feelings. It was decided to survey the views of the French, Italian, and Russian governments.[44]

Throughout August, as the prince prepared for his tour, Howard continued to apprise London about the island's situation.[45] Prince George was making every effort to reduce tensions between his government and the Powers. He even dined with the Italian consul-general, 'whom he always denounced with the vigour of a nautical vocabulary, & in whose house he loudly protested he would never set foot'. But his problems with the Cretan opposition, now spilling over into Greece,[46] could not be contained indefinitely. Attacks on Papadiamondopoulos were now 'aimed, if not openly at least secretly, at the Prince himself'. Howard now surmised that the prince and Papadiamondopoulos, on one side, and Venizelos and his followers, on the other, each wished to take the glory for achieving *enosis* whilst denying any to the other. The reaction of the statesmen with whom Prince George would meet on his tour would determine the resolution of the Cretan question.

The prince's efforts kept him away for six months: he left in late August 1904, returning only at the end of January 1905. In each capital he made the same argument about the difficulties of rule that he had put before the consuls prior to his departure. His remarks to the Russian foreign minister, Count Lamsdorff, were typical:

> In consequence of these difficulties he felt that unless annexation to Greece or the military occupation of the island by Greek troops in the place of the international troops was granted by the Protecting Powers in accordance with the aspirations of the Cretan population, he would lose so much prestige with the people that he would not be able to return to Crete, nor to accept an extension of his present mandate on its expiry in December next.[47]

By the autumn of 1904 the chanceries of the Protecting Powers, and not just Howard and his consular colleagues, had to cope with the prince's endeavours.

Whilst Howard was involved centrally in Crete, neither he nor Crete was central to decisions reached at London and St Petersburg. It was Prince George's misfortune that Britain and Russia, the key Powers, could offer nothing more than cosmetic changes to the island's administration. For Lansdowne, the time was inopportune: not only had the Russo-Japanese war yet to be decided, but the Germans were provoking a crisis in Morocco to split the recently concluded Anglo-French entente.[48] A balance of power in southeastern Europe based upon an Anglo-Russian condominium of interests to counter German penetration of the Porte suited Lansdowne.[49] It mirrored that emerging in western Europe, based on the Anglo-French entente, to restrain German adventurism. Lamsdorff proved even more anxious to avoid any change in Crete. With the war against Japan diverting Russian attention to the Far East, every chance existed that a change in Crete's status, with implications for the 'Eastern Question', might occur to Russian disadvantage. Despite antipathy towards Britain developing out of a belief that the Anglo-Japanese alliance had encouraged Japanese aggression in the Far East, the Russian government sought to avoid antagonising Britain unduly. For instance, in a rare display of public contrition, the Russians admitted their responsibility for the 'Dogger Bank incident', when the Russian Baltic fleet, steaming towards the Far East in October 1904, fired on British fishing vessels in the nervous belief that they were Japanese torpedo boats.[50] Until the war in Manchuria ended and Russian military power could again be brought to bear to support tsarist foreign policy in the Balkans, Lamsdorff was compelled to maintain the status quo in Crete and Macedonia.

Howard's role in the Cretan affair remained central through Lansdowne's realisation that steps had to be taken to break the obvious diplomatic stalemate. Lansdowne recognised that the other Protecting Powers, as well as Germany and Austria-Hungary, were unwilling to make any suggestions; thus, after the prince's tour ended, Lansdowne suggested a compromise which, conceding nothing of substance, sought to salvage both the prince's esteem amongst the Cretan people and the eastern Mediterranean status quo. On 30 November he circulated a note to the other three Protecting Powers to this end.[51] Whilst the Powers had to reject the 'Bosnian' solution because of promises made to the sultan, they could guarantee that neither they nor any other Power would annex the island unless the Cretans desired such a course. Always a realist, Lansdowne added that Germany and Austria-Hungary should consent to the guarantee. Efforts could also be made to reduce Cretan agitation by making some troop withdrawals and arranging a new loan for public works construction. Finally, increasingly critical of the high commissioner,[52] Lansdowne argued the time had come to end the prince's continual carping about *enosis*. The Powers had to state unequivocally 'that the terms offered represented the utmost that the Protecting Powers could sanction and that if they were rejected the responsibility for the consequences must rest with the Cretan government'. The three occupying Powers accepted Lansdowne's note 'with alacrity and some trifling alterations'.[53]

Lansdowne's note provided Howard with an opportunity to demonstrate his skill at carrying out an unpalatable British policy for, as he wrote afterwards, 'I still remember how my heart sank when I read this document, the futility of which must have been as apparent to those who drafted it as it was to us in Crete.'[54] The central issue, he believed – Lansdowne's note ignored it – concerned meeting the national aspirations of people who had suffered Turkish domination for centuries: 'It was a case of panem et circenses only the circenses in Crete were insurrections.' This pessimism about Lansdowne's note derived from Howard's monitoring of the activities of the prince's opponents over the autumn of 1904. For instance, in September he had reported that Venizelos and some of his lieutenants had returned from Athens after a two-week visit 'for the purpose of enlisting the sympathies and cooperation of the Greek public with their aims in Crete'.[55] Howard observed that it was 'impossible not to see in this an attempt to discredit Prince George'. Venizelos and his cronies were mounting a political counter-offensive to the prince's tour, seeking to undercut the prince's support in Greece.

Howard's despatches found an appreciative audience at the Foreign Office and were considered in the drafting of Lansdowne's note. Lansdowne saw that the Cretan opposition would never agree to a 'Bosnian' solution and, more important, 'that Prince George himself perceives this and has no intention of proposing that the precedent should be <u>strictly</u> followed'.[56] However, the difficulty in this derived from the prince's threats of resignation. If he remained unplacated, a renewed Cretan crisis might inflame the 'Eastern Question'. On the other hand, going too far in appeasing the prince might lead to a Venizelist insurrection, which had threatened since before Howard's arrival. Consequently Bertie, at London filling in for an infirm Sanderson, sought Howard's advice on how to prevent the Prince's resignation.[57]

Bertie's enquiry gave Howard an opportunity to pen his most candid assessment yet of Cretan affairs.[58] Given the situation after 1898, Prince George by 'his method of personal intervention has done much to keep the peace'. Howard surmised that such tactics, understandable and effective in the short term, were adopted because the prince believed in 1898 that *enosis* would be possible by December 1901. But it was still not possible in 1904 and this, coupled with the dissatisfaction of the Cretan opposition and the machinations of Papadiamondopoulos, placed the high commissioner in difficulty. Within Crete, though muzzled, the Venizelists were agitating for change on their terms. Thanks to princely efforts to control island finance and the international troops, the Powers were unhappy. Ideally, contended Howard, 'the Cretan incubus' could most easily be removed by the four Powers abandoning the island to Greece. The international situation prevented this. Changing high commissioners offered the only solution: the Powers should induce Prince George to renounce his position in favour of one of his brothers. His disappearance would probably soften opposition criticism: 'People would be disposed to give the new High Commissioner a fair chance, and with good luck we might tide over another three years without a crisis.'

Of course Lansdowne's note side-stepped the matter of replacing Prince George and, in almost his last despatch of 1904, Howard reported that the 'most complete tranquility reigns for the present in the Island', a function of all parties waiting to learn the Powers' response to the prince's overtures[59] – as Berlin and Vienna had to be consulted about the proposed guarantee, public disclosure of Lansdowne's note, even to Prince George and the Greek government, had to be delayed. By December, as well, the prince backtracked by declaring his intention to remain as high commissioner in order to achieve *enosis*.[60] By the prince's return to Canae in late January 1905, the Cretan question was entering a new phase. Howard was to find new challenges.

II

The prince's decision to remain in Crete set the stage for the final phase of 'the Cretan drama' during Howard's tenure as British consul-general. Although ignorant of the contents of Lansdowne's note, Prince George and the Greek government had indications by the middle of January 1905 of four-Power reluctance to make substantive changes to the 1898 settlement.[61] In a calculated gamble, the prince and Papadiamondopoulos decided to force the Powers' hand by calling new elections. Through precluding Venizelos and his allies from the new government, the High Commission could use a renewed mandate to push for its brand of *enosis*. Within a week of returning to Canae, the prince called elections for 2 April. The elections were not an end in themselves. Coupled with continued efforts to control the island's economic and military affairs, they were integral to the prince's overall effort to give the High Commission greater independence.[62] The prince and Papadiamondopoulos also manoeuvred to create division between the Protecting Powers, on the one hand, and Germany and Austria-Hungary, on the other, this by deliberately misinterpreting a statement by Count Goluchowski, the Austro-Hungarian foreign minister, about having Greek troops replace those of the four Powers.[63] Whilst not endearing himself to the four Powers, the prince did not care. The Powers' determination to delay political changes meant he had nothing to lose and everything to gain by playing off the Powers against each other.

The pressing question for the Powers did not concern plots emanating from Canae; these had been repelled successfully before, so every reason existed to assume they would be handled similarly again. Real difficulty revolved around the actions of the Cretan opposition. Rumours of insurrection had circulated since before Howard's arrival. Now, with the advent of new elections and the certainty that the High Commission could keep the Venizelists out of the new legislature, the Cretan opposition confronted the spectre of a massive political victory by the prince at a critical juncture. If they did nothing, they faced political oblivion since the prince's formula for *enosis* might be accepted by the Powers. Even before Prince George arrived back, Howard warned Sanderson that 'everything is quiet, rather too quiet, I think...Generally [the opposition] are loud in their declaration of what they are going to do under certain circumstances and I do not much like this conspiracy of silence.'[64] By the first week of March, Monaco's agents discovered the opposition leaders were 'determined to attempt some demonstration against the Government, with the object at any rate of disturbing and, if possible, invalidating the elections'.[65] Although a Venizelist lieutenant appeared to be organising this demonstration, Venizelos told Howard that he was 'averse' to this course. Howard disbelieved Venizelos; his suspicions were well-founded. Just two weeks before the elections, Howard learnt that an armed Venizelist insurrection, led by Venizelos himself, would break out shortly; he also informed the Foreign Office that the Venizelists were doing this to undercut any support for the high commissioner which the elections might engender in Greece.[66]

On 24 March 1905 Howard found himself in the middle of the long predicted insurrection.[67] Venizelos, with other opposition leaders and 'several hundred persons, many of whom were armed', met at Therisso, a village south of Canae, and raised the Greek flag. A squad of gendarmerie despatched to investigate were ambushed and suffered two casualties: one wounded, one dead. The high commissioner reacted decisively, issuing a proclamation which implored Cretans to 'adhere to the laws', whilst asking the insurgents to give up their arms and return home. To contain the insurrection, the gendarmerie prepared to move inland. Most important, the consuls of the four Powers were asked to allow the international troops to support the gendarmerie. Although Monaco had made such a request only two days before so that he could prepare contingency plans in the event violence broke out,[68] the immediacy of the crisis led to a meeting of the consuls on 24 March to consider what role the international troops should have. Each consul decided to consult his home government. But Howard and his Italian and Russian colleagues agreed that, until precise instructions arrived, their garrisons should take over any gendarmerie duties in their respective sectors which would free the prince's forces for operations against the insurgents. However, these troops would not engage in hostilities against the insurgents.

London reacted swiftly to Howard's joint action. The government, in the person of Balfour, decided that British forces should 'as far as possible...confine operations to protecting life[,] property and order in centres of population'. Howard was informed without delay.[69] Given the international situation, the determination of his government to ensure the Cretan status quo provided Howard with the acid test of his diplomatic skills. The civil war in Crete – Greek-Cretans were fighting Greek-Cretans – lasted only eight months, until November 1905, and in this short span Howard demonstrated decided diplomatic ability and so ensured receiving full employment in the revamped Diplomatic Service being structured by Hardinge and Bertie. Moreover, Howard also won the admiration of Edward VII who, given his interest in his nephew, received from Lansdowne most papers dealing with the crisis. Howard's task was not easy. Lansdowne and the Cabinet wanted the status quo maintained with a minimum British commitment of money and men. Although the foreign offices in the four capitals did much to preserve the 1898 settlement, decided responsibility for doing this devolved upon the consuls. This meant Howard's constant involvement in the thorny matter of deploying international troops, as well as guaranteeing orderly elections, preserving as much domestic tranquillity as practicable, and discovering a compromise which could end the civil war. Naturally, regular consular work, like getting the High Commission to resolve its financial woes, was not suspended during the crisis.

Howard dealt first with the elections. Since their call had precipitated the rash act of the opposition, they were essential to upholding the 1898 settlement. Accordingly, with international troops substituting for the gendarmerie in routine security work like guarding prisons, the scheduled 2 April elections went ahead under the protection of Monaco's forces. Still the insurgents disrupted polling in a few locations by carrying off or breaking ballot urns, and by exchanging rifle fire with the gendarmerie. This helped the Venizelists. 'It must, however, be noted', Howard reported, 'that the number of abstentions from the polls has been very large and the insurgents will doubtless declare that the Chamber does not represent the country.'[70] Howard did not hide his belief that: 'It is the action of Messrs Venizelo [sic] and Foumis in resorting to arms in order to force their views on the country which must be characterized as unjustifiable.' The consuls thus acted. On 9 April new elections were held replacing those 'invalidated' by the 'insurgents'; this time international troops guarded the polls.[71] In analysing these results, Howard reckoned that 'the figure of abstentions attributable to the Venizelist [two words obscured] must still be further reduced, and the adherents of his party may be properly set down at not more than ten per cent of the total number of voters'. Decisive action by Howard in concert with the other consuls gave the High Commission a needed appearance of legitimacy.

Guaranteeing orderly elections amounted to short-term policy for Howard and the consuls. The insurgents were not about to lay down their guns since their desperate gamble to disrupt the selection of a new Cretan Chamber had failed; long-term goals involved preserving domestic peace on the island despite the presence of an armed opposition. With the differing interests of the Powers, the prickly personality of Prince George, and the growing concern of both Athens and the Porte in internal Cretan affairs, this proved difficult. On the British side and increasingly in terms of the general consular reaction to the civil war, Howard played a pivotal role. As the British diplomat on the spot, his judgement was paramount whether making proposals to London or tendering advice to the British military and naval commanders in Crete. Political expedience had to be melded with military and naval action on the island; speedy decisions were the order of the day.

To conduct effective diplomacy, Howard needed latitude in working with both the prince and the other consuls. The Foreign Office acknowledged this by the end of April as a result of the prince's unrelenting pressure throughout that month to have the Powers assist in crushing the Venizelists. After the 9 April elections, the resolve of the Venizelists still intact, Monaco, on the prince's instructions, asked for additional foreign troops. Such troops could either occupy the coastal towns, depriving the insurgents of control of customs houses but allowing chaos to reign in the interior, or they could join in squashing the insurgency quickly. In relating this request to the Foreign Office,[72] Howard emphasised the soundness of the former course. Costing little in 'lives or money', it would put 'the odium of the financial wreck that would follow' on the insurgents, who were responsible for the immediate crisis. The latter course, conversely, would assuredly result in both a lengthy occupation and the rise of discontent amongst Cretans certain to undermine the political settlement built around the High Commission. Lansdowne gave Howard's assessment unqualified support: 'The case could not be more clearly stated.'[73] Consequently, neither the British nor their occupation partners retreated from the position established within two days of the Therisso incident: Prince George's administration had to quell the disturbances in the interior. The British and their partners did despatch additional troops to assist in protecting the population centres on the coast.[74] Despite problems in co-ordination and agreement of zones of occupation, their warships also patrolled the coast to intercept clandestine arms shipments to the Venizelists.[75] But sharing this misgiving voiced by Howard, they would not join actively in defeating Venizelos.

This decision about reinforcements had taken time, a valuable commodity in the heat of a civil war. Thus Howard received instructions on 27 April 'to meet with your colleagues periodically to consider in consultation with the High Commissioner, the measures necessary for the re-establishment of order & to discuss proposals to be submitted'.[76] All major questions, of course, had to be cleared by London. However, as the civil war developed, he received more and more leeway in handling the situation from Candia. In mid July, for instance, he enquired if London was 'absolutely opposed to any military operations being taken against insurgent villages, who may in future attack our troops'.[77] The Foreign Office replied that he and the British commanding officers had to make that decision, ensuring only that 'such measures will be effective and will not lead to prolonged operations for which the force at their disposal could not be adequate'.[78] In this instance and a number of others, Howard made crucial decisions about where, how, and in what way British military and naval power was brought to bear to help the gendarmerie.[79] His success can be gauged by the prince's criticism that British troops did not do enough[80] and by senior British officials, like Hardinge, who saw Howard's efforts to be prudent, effective and in Britain's best interests.[81]

The turning point in Howard's diplomacy came during the summer. By the end of June the insurgents seemed as strong as ever. Despatching additional troops, coupled with the naval quarantine of the coast, had not forced the Venizelists to surrender. In fact Prince George's government seemed near collapse.[82] Insurgent control of some coastal customs houses meant the chance of the High Commission being unable to pay the gendarmerie; this would lead assuredly to desertions 'in large numbers'. Added to this were defections by some prominent members of the Cretan government to the insurgents, the determination of others to protect their positions with arms should the Venizelists succeed, and a growing laxity by judicial authorities who, uncertain about who would triumph ultimately, were backing both sides. This apparent weakening of the prince's regime and the corresponding growth in insurgent power pushed Maurouard and Fasciotti, the French and Italian consuls, and, through them, their governments into open criticism of the High Commission. Howard now faced a decided problem in maintaining his government's policy about underwriting the status quo, since the 1898 settlement confronted extreme political pressure inside and out.

Howard surmised that Maurouard and Fasciotti now believed that the Venizelists did not actually seek the overthrow of the High Commission, rather they were 'actuated mainly by liberal principles and only desiring reforms'. The French and Italian consuls now suggested that 'before taking steps for the re-establishment of order by force, an effort should be made to come to an agreement with the insurgents on the basis of internal reforms, if they will accept them'. Problems faced by the tsarist government in containing the outbreak of a revolution that followed Russian defeat by Japan in the Far East led the Russian consul, de Bronewsky, to support maintaining the status quo. Howard's diplomacy therefore entailed working on one side with the prince, increasingly irritated with four-Power reluctance to shore up his eroding power with more troops, and on the other with Maurouard and Fasciotti, turning in favour of insurgent demands for reform. Howard sought to reconcile these divergent views and at the same time to protect the status quo.

In the normal course, Howard would not have much influenced this reconciliation process. He was just one of four consuls and had been on Crete only two years. But in those two years, the Russian and French consuls who had been there when he arrived had been transferred. Moreover, on 2 June 1905, Negri, the Italian consul so antagonistic towards Prince George and Papadiamondopoulos, died suddenly. This meant that, at a crucial moment, Howard became doyen of the diplomatic corps on the island. He now chaired the four-Power consular meetings, which gave him control over matters like the agenda, and he met with Prince George as spokesman for the consuls. This latter point was decisive. Whereas the prince entertained deep suspicions about Negri, little doubt existed that Howard was *persona grata* in the eyes of the high commissioner.[83] Howard's superiors at London greeted his sudden elevation as doyen with sanguine approval.[84] He could have a decisive influence on events if he chose to exercise it, especially since the Foreign Office trusted him to make certain political and military decisions. Coming on the eve of the most important phase of the civil war, his rise to doyen proved fortuitous to both British policy and his subsequent employment.

Howard had ideas about how to restore order in Crete from the moment he heard of the Therisso incident and, in a series of letters and despatches sent in April, May and June, he outlined them.[85] He never jettisoned his long-held belief that the best solution would be to permit *enosis*. As he told Sanderson privately in late April, he advocated this:

not because I am a Philhellene, please don't be afraid of that, but because I think it is the only way for England to get out of an infernal mess. What happens after Union, & whether Cretans & Greeks cut their throats as is most probable, w[ou]ld not concern us. They will have made their own bed & lie in it.

But with the determination of London and St Petersburg to maintain the 1898 settlement, this radical course was impossible. The question then was what was a practicable solution? Howard saw the basis of the crisis to be 'personal hatred' between Venizelos and Foumis, on one hand, and Prince George and Papadiamondopoulos, on the other. Moreover, despite the elections, the prince's popularity was faltering. Howard's cold assessment was '[Prince George] is accused of caring more to satisfy his personal hatred of Venizelo [sic] than the Greek national cause.' This did not cause him to doubt that having the prince continue as high commissioner would be preferable to Venizelos emerging by means of the insurrection as the *de facto* Cretan ruler. But the sticking point was Papadiamondopoulos. Whether he was at fault was not the issue; the Venizelists and many other Cretans unsupportive of the insurrection perceived him as being at fault. To improve the image of the High Commission and ensure the prince's political survival, Papadiamondopoulos had to go. The other consuls shared Howard's view, though all agreed that Papadiamondopoulos should go only after order was restored – a tactic that would avoid weakening further the prince's reputation during the crisis.

Howard saw two ways to restore order. The first involved direct negotiations with the insurgents, though the Powers should stay out of this given the pool of venom separating the prince from Venizelos. The second involved offering an amnesty. Even Prince George, reported Howard, did not oppose this, though he attached three conditions to be met before he would endorse the offer: additional four-Power troops to enforce it; a deadline by which the insurgents had to comply; and its issue by the Powers rather than the High Commission. Lansdowne found nothing wrong with these conditions and urged Howard to press the notion of an amnesty on his consular colleagues.[86] Howard did so but, until Negri's death, he lacked the authority to force his will on the consuls. In addition, just at the moment he became doyen, the civil war favoured the insurgents. In early June the idea of direct negotiations between the Cretan government and the insurgents proved hollow.[87] Cretan politicians who had fought and won the April elections felt that entering into talks with Venizelos might weaken the legitimacy of those elections. Thus the consuls had to act.

This gave Howard his opportunity. He moved quickly to bring together the disparate elements involved in the crisis. He cleared the ground with Prince George in order to get a face-to-face meeting between the consuls and the insurgents; he wished to avoid being seen as going behind the high commissioner's back.[88] Such a meeting fitted into the calculations of all the interested parties: Prince George, because it might re-establish his regime's power; the insurgents, because it might reinforce their apparent dominance; and the Powers, because each might better protect its particular interests. A meeting occurred on 15 July at a monastery in a neutral village. Prior to this, under Howard's direction, the consuls drafted a proclamation outlining the position of the Powers: there could be no alteration to the status quo at present; the Powers would consider internal reforms; an amnesty would be granted for all insurgents who surrendered within fifteen days, except those guilty of common law violations and desertion from the gendarmerie; and, if the insurgents did not surrender, the Powers would act in the best way they saw fit to restore order.[89] The proclamation appeared on the day of the meeting. At that gathering, Howard spoke on behalf of the consuls, elaborating on the proclamation, reaffirming the impossibility of *enosis*, and emphasising that internal Cretan reforms were possible but only after insurgent surrender.[90] Venizelos refused to budge – Howard surmised because of his several hundred armed followers who were in revolt because they wanted union with Greece.[91] The meeting ended without result.

The meeting showed Howard that the insurgents were not as formidable as had been earlier assumed. Given the Powers' military support, especially that of the British and Russians,[92] Prince George's regime had stabilised. The High Commission had the military and economic resources to survive, resources which the Venizelists could not diminish to their advantage.

Insurgent inability to bring the prince's government to its knees lay with the Powers' success in controlling the waters surrounding the island, as well as crucial stretches of its littoral. Howard's words to Lieutenant-Colonel Panton, the British commanding officer in Crete, written a week after the meeting with Venizelos, show this: 'the status quo in Crete, the maintenance of which is the principal reason of the presence of our troops on the Island, cannot be really changed by the insurgents so long as we hold the Coast towns...'.[93] Whilst a few coastal customs houses were insurgent-controlled, creating some problems for the High Commission and traders with established markets in Crete, the success of the naval blockade in intercepting arms and other supplies destined for the Venizelists weakened the insurgency. The 15 July meeting had also weakened Venizelos politically. His failure to accept the proclamation had bankrupted his credit with Maurouard and Fasciotti, since it was they who had pushed for a public consular statement that internal reforms would be considered if the insurgents accepted the amnesty. It mattered little whether Venizelos would not or could not compromise; his hardline led to greater four-Power unity within Crete than had existed since early April 1905.

Following Venizelist rejection of the compromise, the Powers remained firm. Under Howard's instructions, British forces were 'to hit back, as hard as we can, when attacked, and to do all in our power to protect life and property where they are threatened, and to punish those guilty of firing on our troops whenever and wherever this can be done without too great subsequent danger to our troops'.[94] However, since the control of the coast and coastal waters gave the Powers certain tactical advantages, Howard pointed out to Panton that 'it is therefore not worth while risking serious loss of life in order to maintain detachments in the interior if there is real danger in doing so'. Howard's mixture of firmness and caution paid immediate dividends. On 12 August an insurgent attack on a small British detachment was foiled by that detachment taking the offensive and being supported immediately by reinforcements.[95] The insurgents retreated. This demonstrated clearly that Venizelos lacked the will or the resources – or both – to risk provoking the Powers who, despite the political problems it might engender for them on Crete, might feel compelled to despatch a large number of troops to the island to end the civil war as soon as possible. All this would do was keep the prince in place and further delay *enosis*.

Lansdowne approved Howard's efforts when the report of the 12 August attack reached his desk.[96] The hardline adopted by Howard in the British sector of the island, and mirrored in the Russian one, weakened the insurgent position. By late August Howard reported that the insurrection was beginning to collapse in the regions controlled by the British, the Russians, and the prince's forces.[97] A significant shift in fortunes had occurred. On 21 August, the consuls met to discuss the rise in anti-insurrectionist sentiment; Howard wrote to Lansdowne:

In the Rethymo [Russian] and Canae districts the anti-insurrectionist movement is also gaining ground and requests are coming in from different villages, especially in the former secteur[,] for permission to form armed tower guards in order to defend themselves against the insurgents.

These requests have been granted by the Russian Authorities in the Rethymo district and at their desire the Consuls have today given their consent, with the approval of the High Commissioner, to three hundred rifles being supplied from the Gendarmerie arsenal for the purpose in question.[98]

Coupled with this news were Russian intercepts of letters from and to Venizelos, which de Bronewsky forwarded to Howard.[99] One of Venizelos' commanders wrote tellingly on 25 August that 'I have no hopes whatever. If an amnesty is granted, I fear I shall be left alone...I am asking for help and I can get none.' More important, this and other letters indicated that wrangling amongst insurrectionist commanders existed; such division sapped the fighting ability of insurrectionist forces. The result, Howard contended, was that Venizelos was now 'making the most desperate efforts to rally his supporters'. In addition, Venizelos' letters showed Howard that 'the insurgent leaders are now openly allied to the anti-dynastic party in Greece'. Howard suggested that this might explain further the mutual hostility between the prince and Venizelos which precluded a settlement. Whilst Venizelos saw 'encouragement' for his armed uprising 'from the inaction of France and Italy', British, Russian, and gendarmerie success in the rest of the island was taking its toll. Howard observed:

Summing up the general situation, the actual power of the insurrection seems to be so reduced in the island... that some energetic combined action taken by the four Powers together in these districts, such as the occupation of one or two important places, might possibly deal a blow to the movement, which, if not ending it at once, would certainly hasten its end considerably.

By September Howard's reports showed that the civil war would soon end with the failure of the insurgency and the preservation of the 1898 settlement. With this turn of events, Howard's part in 'the Cretan drama' came gradually to assume less importance. The return of peace meant that once again the crucial decisions about Crete would be made almost exclusively outside the island. This resulted, at least in Howard's case, in a return to the role he had had prior to 24 March 1905: tendering advice to London, carrying out instructions, but having little to do in initiating policy on the island. This shift on the British side showed on 11 September when Lansdowne, on holiday at his Irish estate, wrote at length to Sanderson on Crete.[100] Any settlement would have two parts: ending the fighting and, then, initiating internal reform. Suffusing both of these elements had to be an 'equality of effort as between the four Powers'. The dilatory attitude of the French and Italians had antagonised the Russians, thereby threatening unity of action. A break had to be prevented. Lansdowne noted realistically: 'We shall however not bring the laggards up to the mark unless we can produce a practical policy holding out some hopes of good results.' Practical policy involved post-civil-war reform. The notion was circulating that an international commission comprised of the four Protecting Powers might serve the purpose and, luckily, the wording of the consuls' 15 July proclamation which mentioned reforms allowed for such a body. A reform commission would certainly bring the French and Italians back into the fold. But reforms would not be enough. Lansdowne concluded that Prince George had to go. The foreign secretary had just seen an article in *The Fortnightly Review*[101] which outlined the litany of princely misdeeds. Although recognising it to be 'a one-sided account of the case', Lansdowne reckoned: '...unless [the author] wholly disregards the truth, H.R.H. has surrounded himself by a gang of Greek intriguers, and does not allow the representatives of the Cretan population any voice, even in their municipal affairs'. An indication of the improving situation occurred in early September when Howard received permission to travel to Rome to be with Isa for the birth of their second child, expected in early October – she had left in the summer to be with her family during her confinement just as she had done in 1903 when their first child, a boy named Esme, was born.[102] Howard had been denied a scheduled leave in May because 'Lansdowne [would] not hear of entrusting the Consul General to anyone but [Howard] during these troubles'.[103] With the promise of a month's holiday suddenly before him after the difficult summer, Howard greeted the reduction of tension in the autumn with relief. He departed from Crete on 22 September, was at Rome for the birth of his second son, Francis, on 5 October, and set foot on the island again on 21 October.[104] By the time Howard resumed his duties, the civil war was sputtering to a halt.

The main task confronting him on his return concerned negotiating the insurgents' surrender, a process in which by virtue of his position as doyen he had a key role. Venizelos and Manos sent a letter to the consuls on 18 October outlining their conditions for surrender and, knowing that Howard would be back in a few days, a consular meeting to discuss the conditions was delayed until 22 October.[105] There were two insurgent demands: first, that the rebels be allowed to keep their weapons after the surrender and, secondly, that the amnesty outlined in the 15 July proclamation be extended to include deserters from the gendarmerie. In an important adjunct to the second condition, Venizelos, Manos, and Foumis indicated their willingness to shoulder personally the guilt of all of their followers, including any deserters; they would 'accept punishment and go into exile'. Under Howard's chairmanship, the consuls discussed these demands. Although the first condition could not be met – and the consuls decided that between 800 and 1,000 rifles and 'a sufficient quantity of cartridges' had to be turned over to the international troops – a compromise was possible over the second. Fasciotti proposed that all insurgents, whether or not they were deserters, could be amnestied, with the exception of those who were guilty of non-political offences against common law or who had been sentenced by international or Cretan military tribunals. Thus, those deserters who had not broken the common law would have nothing to fear. Howard supported this proposal, indicating to London that Fasciotti and de Bronewsky could agree to it without consulting their home governments.

By the first week of November there existed some insurgent diplomacy to secure great-Power support for specific reforms to be instituted once peace was achieved, but this proved fruitless because of Howard's opposition. He still had some latitude in conducting British policy and took this firm line, as he told the Foreign Office, because 'it appeared to me that this would be tying the hands of the Commission of Enquiry, which is to come for that very purpose, and further because we are by no means certain whether the reforms, which the insurgents would like, would be agreeable to the Cretan people at large...'.[106] Final negotiations ensued between the consuls, led by Howard, and Venizelos on 15 November at a neutral site.[107] Insurgent weapons were to be deposited at various locations on the island to be picked up by the international troops. As a number of gendarmerie deserters and 'intransigent deserters' did not wish to surrender, arrangements were made for them to leave the island before the publication of the Proclamation of Amnesty, the formal end of the civil war, scheduled for 24 November. With the surrender of the insurgents, units of the gendarmerie and the international forces would move into the interior.

The final surrender was almost wrecked by Prince George. To assert his faltering authority, he claimed on 23 November that any Proclamation of Amnesty had to be issued by him.[108] Summoning Howard to his palace, he argued that under the Cretan constitution only he could amnesty wrongdoers. Howard responded that, as the consuls had declared martial law and negotiated with Venizelos under the authority of the Powers, they were empowered to issue the final amnesty. But he agreed to raise the matter with his colleagues, doing so at a hurriedly convened meeting the next day. The consuls struck upon a compromise: two proclamations should be issued simultaneously, one by the consuls covering cases within their purview and another by Prince George for cases falling within the competence of the Cretan courts. At an audience with the prince held immediately afterwards, this compromise was accepted.

However, when the two proclamations were sent to the government printing office at Canae, the printer informed the consuls' messenger that the consular proclamation would have to be vetted by Papadiamondopoulos. The prince compounded the situation by arriving at Howard's home to claim that the consuls had gone too far; he had understood that the consuls were publishing only an 'explanatory declaration' and not an amnesty. Unflappable, Howard calmly indicated that he would take the matter up with his colleagues the next day, but at that meeting, marked by annoyance at the prince's tactics, the consuls refused to be badgered. Their proclamation would be posted on all buildings controlled by them and their troops. It was clear to the insurgent leaders that the prince and Papadiamondopoulos were attempting to spike a settlement not to their liking. Venizelos wanted an explanation. Howard invited him to meet with the consuls on the afternoon of 25 November. Venizelos' concern was that the prince's proclamation differed slightly in its wording from that of the consuls, a crucial point as it restricted those who could be amnestied. Under Howard's guidance, the consuls explained that there was nothing to fear. All contested amnesties were to be heard by a five-man board, the four consuls and the president of the Cretan court of appeals. Prince George could safely be ignored as 'the Consuls-General would certainly interpret according to the spirit of the instructions they received [from their governments]'. To reassure Venizelos, the consuls reaffirmed the primacy of the amnesty commission in a notarised procès-verbal. That day, the insurgents surrendered and the civil war ended. Even to effect peace on Crete, Howard and his colleagues had to out-manoeuvre the prince and Papadiamondopoulos.

III

Howard remained on Crete for almost a year after the end of the civil war, a time marked by determined political efforts of the Powers to ensure domestic tranquillity on the island. The insurgents' surrender marked the passing of the high point of Howard's tenure as British consul-general. For eight months, the need for quick decisions in response to the crisis had given him a taste of 'high' policy-making. He had been at the centre of a major diplomatic maelstrom, especially after his unexpected rise as doyen; he now faced a period in which his work would be routine. Thus, with the restoration of order, he resumed his pre-civil-war role as a conduit for British policy on the island, attending to regular consular duties and tendering advice to London whenever it was sought or when he felt the need to do so. Given his character, he did not chafe at this diminution of responsibility. Instead, as he did before March 1905, he fulfilled his assigned tasks willingly and to the best of his abilities.

This was important to his subsequent promotion. In the autumn of 1905 Balfour's government, tired and riven by internal discord, was losing the will to rule. In a twisted political process, Balfour decided to resign and allow the supposedly divided Liberals under Henry Campbell-Bannerman to take office.[109] On 5 December 1905, though a minority in the Commons, the Liberals took office, buried their differences, called elections, and, early in the new year, formed a majority government. This meant the advent of a new foreign secretary, Sir Edward Grey, who had served as the Foreign Office parliamentary under-secretary when Howard worked in Kimberley's private office. One of Howard's friends was now his political master.[110] Just as significant, Hardinge had been chosen to replace Sanderson. The one man determined to revolutionise the conduct of British foreign policy, and who had been instrumental in finding Howard a post when he wanted to return to the Diplomatic Service, now controlled the Foreign Office administration. If and when a post fell vacant in which Howard's talents could be brought to bear, he would find favour with the two men who decided ultimately on appointments. Howard's work during the final ten months he served on Crete underscored the confidence Hardinge had in him and showed Grey his diplomatic abilities.

Two factors militated against Howard's inclusion in 'high' policy-making. The first came with his exclusion from the International Commission on Cretan Affairs, the body promised by the Protecting Powers to the insurgents which was to visit Crete, investigate, and make recommendations for internal reforms. This exclusion occurred through pressure exerted by Prince George and his father, the natural result of the antipathy shown by the high commissioner to the efforts of the consuls, especially the Italian, during the insurrection.[111] Four fresh representatives of the Powers were sent to Crete in February and March 1906, so Howard's contribution to the International Commission amounted to arranging meetings for the British commissioner, Sir Edward Law, and, when the need arose, giving his observations on pressing matters.[112] He also ensured that others with experience of the island, like Panton,[113] had their assessments of the situation put before the proper authorities. The second factor was the interest of King Edward in his nephew's welfare. The king had been kept fully apprised of all the developments on the island, especially during the civil war, and he had acknowledged during the troubles 'how difficult the task is to satisfy Prince George and [that] some of his ideas are vy wild'.[114] The International Commission tendered its report at the end of March and the next month, on another of his 'unofficial' Mediterranean cruises accompanied by Hardinge, King Edward took the opportunity to call on King George at Athens to impress on him the need to have Prince George work honestly in instituting the reforms advocated by Law and his associates.[115] In this way Howard was bypassed completely in the diplomacy surrounding Cretan reforms.

None the less, Howard's final months on Crete were marked by important accomplishments. New elections for all town councils and the Cretan Assembly were to be held once the civil war ended. During the civil war, Athens had convinced the prince to surrender his right to appoint municipal officials, a major criticism of the insurgents.[116] Following from this, just as they had done in April 1905, the consuls used the military power afforded by the presence of international troops to ensure orderly municipal elections in January 1906. But these elections saw no decisive result: the prince's supporters captured forty-two councils, the Venizelists twenty-six, and independents six.[117] Far more important were the Assembly elections scheduled for late May; in these, Howard and the consuls played a major part. On 20 March they met with an opposition delegation, led by Venizelos, anxious to ensure electoral probity.[118] The opposition leaders sought a number of guarantees, including a method of adjudicating disputed returns and the presence of international troops at polling stations. Howard and his colleagues met most of the opposition concerns, for instance, arranging to have a mixed committee of three Cretans and the four consuls – so that the consuls had a majority – to decide on contested elections. In broaching their proposed concessions to the opposition with Prince George, the consuls were surprised at the high commissioner's reasonableness. His only condition involved having the elections held on two different days in order to ensure maximum protection of polling stations by the gendarmerie and international troops. This was agreed; the elections were to be held on 20 May in the western portion of the island and seven days later in the eastern portion.

Howard led the way in co-ordinating four-Power supervision of the Assembly elections: removing additional concerns of the opposition leaders, keeping the consuls united, and making certain that the responsibilities of the international troops were defined clearly within assigned zones.[119] Both the prince's supporters and those of the opposition worked within the limits established through consultation with Howard and the consuls. The political advantages that capture of the Assembly entailed were too great for either party to risk endangering by subverting the electoral process; consequently the elections passed off smoothly. Though the prince's supporters were the clear victors, the opposition demonstrated that it, too, had firm and substantial support.[120] As Howard confided to the Foreign Office:

It is therefore obvious that, while the Government must be considered as still retaining the confidence of the majority of electors, the Venizelists constitute a growing force in the country, and are far from being the small and contemptible body which the Government believed them to be at the beginning of last year.

Thanks to their deft handling of a potentially explosive situation – the recrudescence of civil strife remained near the surface – Howard and the consuls made a major contribution to sustaining order in southeastern Europe just at the moment that Macedonia and the outbreak of revolution in Russia complicated international politics.[121]

More important than this were Howard's efforts in the post-civil-war reconstruction of the island. In his memoirs, Howard referred to a despatch he sent Lansdowne during the last phase of the civil war, one in which he attributed four causes of the troubles: the personal quarrel between Prince George and Venizelos; the interminable squabbling amongst the various Cretan political factions; the economic plight of the island; and the matter of *enosis*.[122] 'I concluded by saying', Howard added, 'that the best way temporarily to tranquilise the people would be, while introducing such financial and administrative reforms as might immediately improve the economic condition of the country, to give at the same time some pledge that union with Greece would not be indefinitely postponed.' His prescience showed here, as these were precisely the points addressed by Law and the commissioners. Without addressing explicitly the matter of the feuds existing between the prince and Venizelos and amongst the various factions, the commissioners recommended numerous financial and administrative reforms, coupled with a proposal that only the prompt union of the island with Greece would resolve the Cretan problem. Although unstated, *enosis* would permit the factional bickering to disrupt domestic Greek politics and not the balance of power in the eastern Mediterranean. More crucially, all of the recommendations and proposals amounted to an implicit but stinging rebuke of Prince George as high commissioner.

Grey was determined that the International Commission's report be accepted; he had more pressing problems to settle. Consequently, Howard's work until he left Crete in August 1906 amounted to carrying out Foreign Office directives concerning the report, chiefly in the matters of the economic reconstruction of the island, protecting the interests of Moslem Cretans, and indemnifying claimants from the war of 1896–8. On each of these main issues, Howard and the consuls were at odds with the International Commission. Since the consuls agreed generally with the thrust of the report in easing the island into the Greek orbit, the problem remained one of means rather than ends. Resolving the indemnities question is a case in point. In April 1906 the consuls of the four Powers, plus those of Germany and Austria-Hungary, decided that monies raised by the surtax on imports should be paid to claimants in September 1906 when the surtax was to lapse.[123] Calculations indicated that Greek and Cretan claimants would recover $5\frac{1}{2}$ per cent of their claims whilst citizens of the six Powers would receive 51 per cent. However, if a loan could be arranged with the Powers' help, Greek and Cretan claimants could realise an additional $5\frac{1}{2}$ per cent. Difficulty arose when the Foreign Office consulted Law, since the consular recommendations ran counter to the report.

Where Howard and the consuls were willing to allow the Cretan Chamber to debate whether an additional loan should be raised to double Greek and Cretan indemnities, Law and his colleagues disagreed.[124] They wanted the Chamber to be forced to vote for a loan as 'an essential condition' for the Powers helping the prince's administration set Cretan finances in order. Since the vast majority of Cretans seeking indemnities were 'Mohammedans and other classes of the population who are partizans [sic] of M. Venizelos', the High Commission opposed raising such a loan. A trade-off existed. The prince's administration wanted to extend the surtax past September, using the new monies generated to build public works. Under the 1898 settlement, the Powers had to be consulted about issues like an extension. If the Cretan government wanted a public works programme, it would have to approve the indemnity loan. The issue amounted to who controlled Cretan public finance: the Powers or the prince. Howard's support of the consular decision forced Grey and his advisers to choose between the consuls and the International Commission. They supported Law.[125] Thus Howard was compelled to follow Foreign Office directives about the indemnity, a situation which created deeper antipathy between Prince George and the British government.[126] From this it is clear that the prince's subsequent anti-Howard sentiments were more the result of London overriding Howard's views about how to maintain order on the island and less a result of Howard 'stabbing' him in the back. More importantly, in terms of Howard's diplomatic apprenticeship, he learnt the valuable lesson that the man on the spot's advice, though sound in every way, does not necessarily fit into the 'big picture' which the Foreign Office had always to consider.

IV

Howard's work on Crete was recognised by a range of people within the British diplomatic establishment to have been of a high order. He had the ability to deal with difficult personalities in a way that did not cause offence but which, firm and resolute, ensured British interests would not suffer. He possessed impressive analytical skills, which showed in his faculty dispassionately to assess confused and complicated events and, then, translate these into accurate perceptions for his superiors in London. Finally, whilst showing that he could carry out orders with which he disagreed, Howard also showed his willingness to take responsibility and make important decisions in the most rational way possible, even during the crisis atmosphere of a civil war. On his return to the Foreign Office after serving as ambassador at St Petersburg, Hardinge had been warm in his praise.[127] With the necessity for an Anglo-Russian accommodation in terms of the 'Eastern Question', the British Embassy at St Petersburg had kept close tabs on the difficult time Howard had had and on his diplomacy. 'Your despatches are most interesting and amusing', his friend Spring Rice wrote from Russia, 'You have made quite an impression here and [the Embassy] are much pleased with the way you are acting with your Russian colleague.'[128] But the appraisal that really counted came from Grey, who wrote glowingly in early April 1906:

You have got an impossible job in Crete which might well depress anybody. All I can say to encourage you is that I recognise how impossible the job is, and that everyone here thinks you are making the very best that can be made of it. No one could have done better, and it is not likely we should have found any one else who could have got on so well.[129]

The Foreign Office's private appreciation had twice been translated into public recognition during his time on the island: in November 1904, membership in the Royal Victorian Order, and in April 1906, just after Grey wrote, elevation to a commander of that order.

As important as they were, such distinctions did not necessarily mean a renewed diplomatic career. But Howard did not wait long to realise his goal of permanent employment in the Diplomatic Service. By June Hardinge was moving to improve the Service and the Foreign Office, and Howard fitted into his plans. Problems existed in British relations with the United States and Hardinge believed that the qualities Howard had shown in Crete, and the lessons he had learnt in dealing with the difficult Prince George, could be brought to bear with success at Washington. Howard's time on Crete was over.

3
Washington: Imperial affairs and arbitration, 1906–1908

I have travelled over great stretches of the United States and come into contact with men of all kinds, except unfortunately the real backwoodsmen and cowboys whom I should have liked to meet, but I have not been able to formulate in my mind any of those easy generalisations about America and Americans with which travellers from Europe who have spent a month or two there so often return home; generalisations they can easily pack into a small 'grip-sack' and offload on audiences at home eager for news of that land full of unexpected contradictions.

Howard, 1936

I

Howard reached England with his small family in August 1906 for a vacation and, avoiding London, went immediately to Greystoke, from which he had been away for more than three years. Two months were devoted to his wife and two young sons, to fishing, grouse shooting, and generally restoring spent energies within a circle of relations and close friends in the place he loved most in the world. On 18 October he called at the Foreign Office to receive instructions for his return to work. There, Grey and Hardinge disclosed the surprising news that the ambassador to the United States, Sir Mortimer Durand, was being recalled. More surprisingly, Grey and Hardinge wanted Howard to go to Washington as the counsellor, the senior diplomat under the ambassador, at the Embassy to take charge until a new ambassador could be found and sent out. Once Durand's replacement arrived, Howard would continue serving in the normal capacity as counsellor.

Howard accepted the offer – he could do little else given his determination to get regular employment in the Diplomatic Service. The offer constituted an appointment of decided importance, given the high rank Howard would receive and the fact that Washington, although not as prestigious as Paris, St Petersburg, or Vienna, was in the first rank of diplomatic postings. In his memoirs Howard remarked: 'This was, naturally, a most gratifying appointment for me. It meant a definite return to the Diplomatic Service and to have to act as Chargé d'Affaires at one of the principal Embassies showed, I suppose, that my chiefs had a confidence in me which I myself was far from feeling.'[1] In his diary at the time, however, his misgivings were more pronounced as he commented that he possessed 'rather mixed feelings on this score'.[2] Given the cost of living in the United States and the expense of transatlantic travel for holidays in England or on the continent, a posting in the American capital would stretch Howard's financial resources. His counsellor's salary would not cover his living and entertainment expenses; in addition, by this time the rubber syndicate he had put together had decided that the project at Louis d'Or was not feasible. Unwilling to give up on the scheme, Howard had taken control of the plantation, with the result that much of his money was tied up in Tobago in the hope that some sort of breakthrough would occur.

Since the American president, Theodore Roosevelt, demanded Durand's recall, Grey and Hardinge wanted Howard in the United States as soon as possible. As Howard's household was still intact in Crete, however, he was given permission to go there first, settle his affairs, and then get to Washington to take over the Embassy.[3] It was not until 14 December 1906 that Howard disembarked at New York City to begin his service in the United States.

His initial problem centred on ensuring that Durand's departure would not further damage Anglo-American relations – they had suffered from a succession of irritants over the past few years. Durand had no idea why he was being recalled; this angered him. In discussing the matter with Howard several times, Durand went 'over the past few years wondering what could have gone wrong, of complaining with justice that he had been over to England in the summer and had been given no hint whatever that his recall was contemplated'.[4] But, unknown to him, Roosevelt had long wanted his removal.[5] In late 1904, just a year after arriving in the United States, Durand had annoyed the president by knowing little about big-game hunting and by tiring too quickly during a presidential rock-climbing expedition. The ambassador was not a robust outdoorsman, the kind of man much admired by Roosevelt.[6] More crucially, in diplomatic exchanges between London and Washington over the ending of the Russo-Japanese war in the summer of 1905 and the progress of the Algeciras conference in January–April 1906,[7] issues in which both Britain and the United States had played important roles, Roosevelt saw Durand as singularly unhelpful. Although much of this was not Durand's fault, since he followed Foreign Office directives, Grey had to recall him given White House pressure and a British desire to keep Anglo-American relations running smoothly. As Durand had not been long at Washington, his removal might have caused a stir; Grey sought first to set up an alternative line of communication between the Foreign Office and the White House through the military attaché at the Embassy, Lord Edward Gleichen, a Boer War veteran and man of action. This did not placate Roosevelt, who caustically described Durand as 'a worthy creature of mutton suet consistency' with 'a brain of about eight-guinea-pig-power'.[8] Durand could not be saved, thus there had to be changes at the Washington Embassy.

Hardinge and Grey apprised Howard of the situation prior to his departure for Washington.[9] Howard had to work to keep on Roosevelt's good side in order to improve the relationship between the Embassy and the White House. In addition, he had to make certain that Durand knew nothing of the reason for his recall nor of the antipathy felt towards him by Roosevelt and by the United States secretary of state, Elihu Root, since this might create strain in Anglo-American relations just at the moment when Grey was seeking to improve them. Howard proved successful in both endeavours. In his first meeting with Roosevelt a few days after arriving, Howard and the president had a pleasant conversation about Cretan archaeology and Cumberland. Roosevelt impressed Howard and, it seems, he the president. Howard wrote later that the president 'had a just and generous soul, he genuinely cared for the under dog and was a good friend. But he was also a good hater who did not hide his feelings and was hated in return, especially by the "Old Guard", or as we should call them the "Die-hards", among the Senators.'[10] That Roosevelt never hated Howard speaks highly of Howard's diplomatic abilities. Indeed, Howard's efforts to ensure a good relationship with the president were helped when, subsequently, he and Isa became friends with Roosevelt's sister, Anna Cowles, 'who occasionally asked us to dine alone with the President and Mrs Roosevelt so that we could enjoy his wonderfully racy conversation.'[11]

However, Howard's immediate problem involved getting Durand out of the United States without discovering the reason for his recall. This, too, passed off easily. In those private conversations when the ambassador speculated about his recall, Howard said nothing which gave away the game. When he accompanied Durand to the White House when the latter submitted his letters of recall, and both Roosevelt and Root were effusive in praising Durand – the president even uttering the words 'For my own part I wish to say officially that I have never had to do with any foreign representative whose proceedings inspired more entire confidence'[12] – Howard dutifully kept silent in Durand's presence about the hypocrisy of the two American leaders. Telling Durand the disagreeable details of his recall later fell to Hardinge. The permanent under-secretary first vented his spleen about American duplicity to Howard: 'I cannot get over the falseness of the President & Root to Durand at the time of his departure after the way they had worked to obtain his removal.'[13] This became more poignant when Durand reached London certain he stood high in Roosevelt's estimation. 'Whether the President's and Mr. Root's volte face was necessitated or not by political considerations', Hardinge confided to Howard, 'it was very hard on Durand who arrived here with the absolute conviction that they both deeply regretted his withdrawal, an illusion which we had fortunately some documentary evidence at hand to dispel.'[14] But Durand's sacrifice had been necessary to appease Roosevelt – though it caused Howard to reflect when he became an ambassador about 'whether suddenly and unexpectedly the axe might fall and decapitate me as swiftly'[15] – and the ground had been cleared to improve Anglo-American relations. Howard had done much in this regard, impressing Roosevelt and making certain that Durand remained ignorant about why he was being dumped.

That Howard had been sent out to handle the volatile Roosevelt is clear. After three fruitful years on Crete contending with Prince George, Howard's strong character and anodyne personality were useful at Washington in the transition from Durand to his successor, Sir James Bryce. Howard was not sent as an expert on America. This is evident from some preliminary observations of the American question sent by Hardinge to Bryce just after the latter's selection to succeed Durand. Bryce was commended to direct any queries he had to Ronald Lindsay, the second secretary at Washington, since 'Howard, the Councillor of Embassy, has only just gone there & has no previous experience with America'.[16] The Foreign Office did not want Howard wasting his time initially with matters about which he knew little and whose study would take up his valuable time. Howard was there to set in train a new approach, to help inaugurate a new tone in British representation in the United States. His superiors had given him the chance to pursue 'high' policy for a short time at one of the more important British diplomatic missions, to lay the ground for Bryce to exploit; this came above all else.

In his first weeks in the United States, Howard met socially with a number of influential people:[17] Maurice Low, *The Times* correspondent; Mrs Leiter, a *grande dame* of Washington society and the mother of Curzon's wife; J. P. Morgan, senior, the anglophile doyen of New York's banking fraternity; the Boardmans, a Washington family with important State Department and United States Diplomatic Service connexions; and Mrs Henry Cabot Lodge, the wife of the chairman of the Senate Foreign Relations Committee. Within a short time, Howard's circle of acquaintances expanded to include other prominent members of the select

'Eastern Establishment', that charmed circle who dominated pre-Great War America through their entrenched positions in the economic, political, and social life of the Boston–New York–Philadelphia–Washington axis.[18] Among these people were Oliver Wendel Holmes, the renowned justice of the United States Supreme Court; Henry Adams, the scion of the Massachusetts family that had given the United States two of its early presidents and, in his own right, a literary figure of importance in turn-of-the-century America; Mrs Cameron, whose father was General William Sherman, the civil war hero, and whose daughter, Martha, was engaged to Lindsay; and James Garfield, Roosevelt's secretary of the interior and the son of the assassinated president. At the same time, Howard made contact with the members of the Roosevelt Administration with whom he would have to deal, especially Robert Bacon, an assistant secretary in the State Department and Root's righthand man.

Although Howard did nothing extraordinary in this respect – it was incumbent on any diplomat to do this sort of thing, and even Durand had attempted to do so – he seems to have been decidedly successful at it. For instance, Garfield became the 'closest and most intimate friend' Howard made at the time, and he continued to be so after Howard left Washington at the end of 1908.[19] Just as crucial, Howard's entrance into the patrician circles of the 'Eastern Establishment' saw him make connexions largely with supporters or partisans of the Republican Party. Roosevelt was a Republican, as were Lodge, Garfield, Bacon, Mrs Cameron, and Mrs Leiter. This meant that Howard's political duties were made easier through his social contacts. Because of them, including his later friendship with Anna Cowles, Howard could use social occasions as appropriate to speak about issues of concern to his government to people from the president on down. These friendships simply added to his effectiveness as a diplomat, complementing the skills he had refined at Rome, Berlin, and in Crete, and the strength of character he had developed in the 1890s.

II

As important as Howard's appointment to Washington was in a personal and professional sense, it amounted to just one part of a strategy by Grey and his Foreign Office advisers to improve Anglo-American relations. For almost a decade, from the Venezuela border dispute of 1895–6 through the Alaska boundary question in 1903 to the recall of Durand,[20] these relations lacked cordiality. In 1905, as a result of the growing German menace in Europe and the need to concentrate more ships and men closer to the home islands, the British withdrew strategically from the western hemisphere.[21] From this flowed the need to protect British interests in the

Americas with diplomacy since, despite notions of transatlantic pan-Anglo-Saxonism, there existed in Britain some concern about United States ambitions following victory in the Spanish–American war.[22] Thus, the quality of diplomatic representation at Washington became crucial. The Campbell-Bannerman government made concerted efforts to ensure that Durand's successor would have Roosevelt's confidence, as well as a general appeal to the American people through their representatives in Congress. In addition the new ambassador had to possess special skills to deal with the peculiar nature of the American political process, dominated as it was by a heterogeneous populace not necessarily sympathetic to Britain. A number of men were considered: Spring Rice, judged too junior to win a major embassy; Lord Rosebery, felt never a serious candidate; and even Hardinge, who turned it down despite pressure from the king.[23] In fact Hardinge claimed that, after he turned down the post, he wracked his brain and came up suddenly with Bryce's name.[24]

Although it is difficult to accept Hardinge's assertion about Bryce unexpectedly coming to mind given his other machinations, it constituted a brilliant suggestion. Bryce had travelled extensively in the United States; he had a wide circle of acquaintances there, including Roosevelt, with whom he was not only an equal in outdoor pursuits but had discussed all manner of political and philosophical subjects; he was an academic with strong americophilia, having written one of the standard texts on the American political system;[25] and, finally, at the time of his consideration for the Washington post, he had served for a year as chief secretary for Ireland in Campbell-Bannerman's government and was in the midst of bringing reforms to Ireland to ease the difficult situation there.[26] This made Bryce ideal for Washington. He knew the United States and its political processes intimately; he got on well with Roosevelt; his reputation as a scholar and statesman added an aura of prestige; and, because of the importance of Irish-American voters in most of the northeastern big cities, he might not come under automatic attack from that vociferous and irrational quarter. With so much at stake the Campbell-Bannerman government persuaded Bryce to take the post, which he accepted because of the importance of the task;[27] he left for Washington in the middle of February. According to one source Bryce's selection came about 'after more careful consideration than any cabinet ever gave a diplomatic appointment'.[28]

The announcement of the appointment came just as Durand departed and, Howard reported, it was 'received in the American Press with a chorus of approval'.[29] He added that Bryce's selection was 'generally accepted as the expression by His Majesty's Government of their desire to follow the example set by the United States in regard to their Embassy in

London, by sending here an Ambassador distinguished both in the world of politics and letters'; since his posting in 1905, the American ambassador at London, Whitelaw Reid, the owner and editor of the New York *Tribune* and a staunch anglophile, had made a decidedly favourable impression at all levels of British political and social life.[30] Grey's effort to improve Anglo-American relations had begun auspiciously. For personal reasons, however, Howard's initial reaction to Bryce's appointment was not one of unbridled optimism. Howard's own lack of a university education seems to have been at the bottom of his concern.[31] Having met Bryce a few times before in only a cursory way, Howard knew him by his reputation as a major academic and senior Liberal statesman: 'I knew him as Professor of Civil Law at Oxford, as a great Latin scholar and as a ready debater in the House of Commons. Altogether I looked forward to his regime with some trepidation as I feared it would be too highbrow for me.' This worry evaporated immediately upon Bryce's arrival. Howard found 'nothing the least superior in his manner'. Ironically, Bryce confided to Howard that he, too, had some personal apprehensions about his new post, deriving from his being outside the Diplomatic Service. Bryce feared the Embassy staff would criticise him 'for all sorts of shortcomings in conventional etiquette and ambassadorial dignity' – given Howard's established belief in the need for professionals to conduct diplomacy, it is surprising that he possessed no concern about the obvious political nature of Bryce's appointment.

Within days of Bryce arriving at Washington, both he and Howard were relieved that their worries were unfounded. They quickly formed a firm friendship that lasted until Bryce died in 1922[32] and, in terms of Anglo-American relations in 1907–8, this was crucial. Bryce had been sent to improve those relations and, to do so, needed a good working relationship with his staff, especially his number two. Because Howard and Bryce found each other to be kindred spirits, sharing interests in art, history, politics, and a range of other subjects, strong personal bonds strengthened their professional relationship. Bryce, accordingly, possessed confidence in Howard's diplomatic abilities and in his innate skill in handling difficult situations and people with grace, tact, and in Britain's interests. On the other hand, Howard never fretted about Bryce lacking confidence in him; hence in his time as the second British diplomat in the United States, Howard pursued his duties knowing that his superior supported him unequivocally. 'Personally I may say', Howard confessed later, 'that I found him the most agreeable of Chiefs.'[33]

All of this says much about Bryce's subsequent success in the United States, especially in his first two years when Howard served as counsellor at the Embassy. To be honest, the nettled problems in Anglo-American relations had yet to be resolved when Howard left for his next posting in late 1908. But they were all settled before Bryce departed in 1912, and the groundwork had been laid in the first two years when the team of Bryce and Howard moved with diplomatic prudence and consummate social grace to raise the tone of transatlantic relations. Howard was always the junior in his dealings with Bryce, whether at Washington in 1907–8 or subsequently, but their relationship constituted one based on mutual respect and shared interests. This is crucial in understanding the course of Anglo-American relations from early 1907 to late 1908 and, in addition, in assessing Esme Howard's pivotal role in the whole process.

III

In this period, the normal diplomatic work of the Washington Embassy was compounded by its responsibility for handling American relations with both Canada and Newfoundland. Though an autonomous dominion, Canada possessed neither a foreign ministry nor diplomatic representation abroad; the conduct of both its foreign and Imperial policy resided with its governor-general, who, although he worked with the Canadian government in these matters, took instruction from London.[34] As a Crown Colony, Newfoundland's position within the Empire differed from that of Canada but, like Canada, its governor had responsibility for its foreign and Imperial relations; he also received direction from London.[35] This meant that when the Canadian and Newfoundland governments conducted their relations with the United States – even though a colony, Newfoundland had a limited form of self-government – they did so through the Imperial government in London, which in turn dealt with American authorities through the Washington Embassy.

Responsibility for the Embassy's work in handling Canadian and Newfoundland affairs with the United States was delegated to Howard, because Bryce's principal concern focussed on improving Anglo-American relations and took most of his time. Therefore, from the moment Bryce arrived in Washington in February 1907, Howard's duties concentrated on co-ordinating Canadian and Newfoundland relations with the United States. He became involved heavily in foreign and Imperial policy, a complicated diplomacy that entailed not simply ensuring a smooth relationship between Ottawa and St John's, on the one hand, and Washington, on the other, but in working with a byzantine bureaucratic system at London. The Colonial Office held responsibility for Canadian and Newfoundland external affairs; the Foreign Office for Britain's relations with the United States. In all questions touching the United States and the two bits of the Empire in North America, the Colonial and Foreign Offices had first to agree on policy. All of this meant that Howard's work at

Washington was complicated by a need to consider the susceptibilities of American politicians, Canadian and Newfoundland leaders, and the interested departments of state in London.

Howard's responsibility for co-ordinating American relations with Canada and Newfoundland does not suggest that Bryce abdicated his interest in this sphere. He did not. In addition to his American duties, Bryce saw his appointment as a means of strengthening Britain's relationship with the senior dominion, a goal shared by his friend Albert Grey, the Earl Grey of Howick, who had been appointed governor-general of Canada in December 1904.[36] Despite this, Bryce could not spend vast amounts of time on the Canadian question. Ameliorating Anglo-American relations was far more important to British diplomacy, which meant making contacts and establishing firm friendships with powerful Americans: the president, key members of the Administration, senators, congressmen, the economic and social leaders of the 'Eastern Establishment', and leading journalists. As Bryce believed strongly in the efficacy of public speaking in the United States – and knowing that his words would reach the vast American audience through newspapers – he also undertook lengthy tours to speak before large groups outside of the northeast.[37] He thus involved himself in Canadian issues only when the ambassador's power could ensure some initiative fostered by Howard would succeed or, less often, to arbitrate between the Embassy and the Canadian government. Howard, therefore, had a relatively free hand in his diplomacy, assured by Bryce's confidence in him and the support this engendered.

Actually, Howard's baptism in handling Imperial affairs at Washington preceded Bryce's arrival. It involved a minor diplomatic crisis over action by the United States Navy in Jamaica in the wake of a major earthquake at Kingston on 14 January 1907.[38] Roosevelt's Administration decided to help, immediately despatching a three-ship squadron with medical supplies and tents, doctors and nurses, food, and other much-needed goods. The initial reaction in Jamaica, especially from the governor, Sir Alexander Swettenham, was one of decided appreciation. But within days a dispute broke out between Swettenham and the American naval commander, Admiral Davis. A mutiny had broken out amongst black prisoners at the local penitentiary. Fearing for their safety, the American community in Kingston appealed to Davis for protection when British troops were distracted by the need to restore order in other areas. Davis despatched Marines to help quell the mutiny, but he did so without first getting Swettenham's permission. The governor asked for the withdrawal of the American troops and Davis complied. However, two days later, the American community again appealed to Davis for protection and, after unsuccessfully trying to get a message to Swettenham, the admiral sent another band of Marines into Kingston. When Swettenham heard of this, he immediately wrote a strongly worded letter to Davis castigating him for his actions. Davis responded by loading up his medical staff, tents, and supplies and returning to the United States. The publication of Swettenham's letter in the American press on 20 January precipitated the crisis.

For Howard, and, hence, for the British and American governments, the 'Swettenham incident' did not become a matter of who in Jamaica had been correct – Swettenham, because the rule of international law was on his side, or Davis, because an extraordinary situation called for unusual measures. Both governments could argue that their representatives were correct, a situation that would see Anglo-American relations suffer further. Both Grey and Roosevelt wanted to avoid a transatlantic shouting match. Bryce's appointment was recognised in both capitals to be the beginning of a new chapter in Anglo-American relations; both governments accordingly sought to bury the matter. Roosevelt made the first move by telephoning Howard.[39] Emphasising that the American press had to be silenced over this issue, the president suggested that the best way to do this would be if the British government sent him 'a friendly message of some kind expressing their regret at the language used by Governor Swettenham in his letter to Admiral Davis'. Roosevelt would then have the British message published, a move he believed would staunch the vitriol pouring forth from American newspapers. Given that the president had telephoned him – 'an unusual step' – and seeing immediately that this tactic had a chance of succeeding, Howard agreed. The same idea had occurred independently to Grey, who had already sent a note to Reid along the lines sketched by Roosevelt. When the president had Grey's message published, 'all agitation in the newspapers stopped as if by magic'.

Summoned to the White House a few days later, Howard talked the situation over with Roosevelt in a relaxed and casual atmosphere, one punctuated by presidential jokes and hearty laughter on both sides. Howard observed that 'the President's mirth was really infectious and his informal way of treating diplomatic incidents was to me novel and pleasing. But I began to understand why a grave and reverend Signor like Sir Mortimer Durand, who had learnt his diplomacy in Eastern countries, could not appreciate him nor he Sir Mortimer.' When Bryce began his Washington duties in late February, nothing immediate existed to impede his task of improving Anglo-American relations. That Howard worked well with Roosevelt in helping bury the 'Swettenham incident' had much to do with this.

When Howard began his work in co-ordinating Canada's dealings with the United States, however, impediments existed which made smooth relations difficult not only between Ottawa and Washington, but also between Ottawa and London. This devolved from Canadian pique at the way in which Britain had handled Canadian interests in 1903 during a diplomatic squabble with the United States, the so-called 'Alaska boundary dispute'.[40] The frontier between Alaska, which the United States purchased from Russia in 1867, and Canada remained unclear, the result of rather hazy clauses in an Anglo-Russian treaty of 1825 which delimited the two empires in North America. Although Canada and the United States inherited the undelimited boundary, there existed no problem until 1896 when the discovery of gold in the Yukon gave the region decided economic importance. The gold fields were inland in Canadian territory, whilst the Americans controlled the Alaska panhandle with the ports through which supplies entered and the precious bullion was exported. Controlling the ports meant reaping substantial economic benefits and, since the precise boundary remained uncertain, Canadian and American locals quarrelled, sometimes violently. Although the Canadians had a better legal claim to the headlands of two deep inlets extending far into the interior, the Americans had occupied them for years. As legal claims in international law are tenuous at best and since the Canadians involved in the gold rush were as unscrupulous and rapacious as the Americans, in 1903 Britain wisely sacrificed Canadian claims to improve Anglo-American relations. Its global strategic requirements dictated this. However, there was a price to pay in that the Canadian government and a large segment of the Canadian people were angered at what they saw as American greed and British duplicity. The echoes of Canadian displeasure – despite the Canadians being as grasping as the Americans in the matter – were the impediments Howard faced at Washington in 1907.

In first looking at the task confronting him, Howard discovered something in the order of sixteen outstanding issues in Canadian–American relations waiting to be resolved. Dealing with matters like reciprocal mining rights and alien labour laws, the majority of these issues lacked importance. Four of them, however, possessed in varying degree decided economic and emotional significance to both Canada and the United States. These concerned Canadian demands for compensation over pelagic seal hunting in the Bering Sea, the rights of both countries in using boundary waters, the delimitation of North Atlantic fishing zones, and tariff reciprocity. As early as 1898 a diplomatic mechanism, the Joint High Commission, had been established by Canada and the United States to resolve all their outstanding questions.[41] After three years of fruitless discussion, the Commission went into abeyance because the commissioners failed to reach agreement on the crucial problems, especially at that juncture the vexing matter of the Alaska boundary.

Howard learnt that when this boundary was settled in American favour,

Canadian resentment surfaced in the Canadian House of Commons with a scathing attack by Sir Wilfrid Laurier, the Canadian prime minister, on both Britain and the United States.[42] Official Canadian displeasure transformed into an inflexible diplomatic position over the next few months, a position from which Canada refused to take any initiative in the settlement of Canadian–American differences. Laurier made this clear in answer to an opposition question in March 1904 about whether the Joint High Commission still existed.[43] The prime minister said that it did, but he also indicated unequivocally that, if the Americans wished to resolve the network of outstanding issues, they would have to put forward proposals for Canadian consideration. Just before Howard's arrival in Washington, the Roosevelt Administration had begun the process of renewing discussion of the outstanding issues. In May 1906, after months of exploratory talks, Root wrote to Laurier via Durand suggesting the settlement of all Canadian–American differences.[44] Thanks to Lord Grey pushing Laurier hard over the need to settle these differences, Root travelled to Ottawa in the middle of January 1907 to impress on Canadians the Roosevelt Administration's desire to put Canadian–American relations on an even footing – by doing this, the Americans seemed to defer to Laurier's hardline, though Root's task remained doubly difficult as he had been one of the three American commissioners during the Alaska boundary settlement.

Root's Ottawa visit came during Howard's service as chargé d'affaires at the Washington Embassy, which meant Howard and Lord Grey co-ordinated the British end of things. Howard and Lord Grey were old friends – when Howard went to South Africa in 1891 exploring for gold, he did so armed with Grey's letter of introduction to Cecil Rhodes. Thus, before Root arrived in the Canadian capital, Howard had received Grey's personal congratulations on the Washington appointment – 'I have always looked upon you as one of the men in the diplomatic service who has it in his power to be of use to the Empire in high ambassadorial positions' – as well as vice-regal observations on Canada's positions in the matter of the outstanding questions.[45] For the Canadian government, tariff reciprocity remained most crucial. The Canadians had long sought to break through American tariff walls so that their industries could prosper through access to the rich American market. Once a single Canadian product received special consideration by the Americans, a chink in that tariff wall would exist, a chink Ottawa could then exploit to push through other commodities.

Howard was told by Lord Grey that the fishing industry was the key and, here, Newfoundland impinged on Canadian–American relations. Twice, in 1891 and 1902, Newfoundland's premier, Sir Robert Bond, had negotiated treaties with the United States permitting the free access of Newfoundland fish into the American market. The first, the Bond–Blaine treaty, had been scotched by Canadian pressure on London to secure similar treatment for Canadian fish. The ratification of the second treaty, the Bond–Hay treaty, had been forced into limbo, partly because of Canadian pressure and partly because of domestic American opposition – the American North Atlantic fishing industry was based in Gloucester, Massachusetts, and the senior senator from Massachusetts was Henry Cabot Lodge. Lord Grey told Howard point blank that the fish tariff was essential:

I cannot think that [the Americans] will show less readiness to receive Canadian fish, particularly when they can represent, that, in return for giving Canada the same favour that they are prepared to give to Newfoundland, they can establish an Entente Cordiale between Canada and the United States.

Howard shared the governor-general's hope that Root's visit would inaugurate a new era in Canada's relationship with the United States, thereby making the Embassy's more important task of improving Anglo–American relations easier.[46] But Root took nothing to Ottawa except pious words about the need to wipe clean the Canadian–American slate.[47] In informing Howard of Root's few days in Canada, Lord Grey tried to put the best light on the American overtures by stating that a key speech by Root produced a 'favourable impression'.[48] Howard was also told that discussions with Laurier permitted the secretary of state 'to learn and to appreciate the Canadian point of view'. This remained a thin sugar coating over a bitter political reality. Root bluntly informed the governor-general 'that the Atlantic Fisheries question was a small matter in American politics compared to the position which it occupied in Canadian'. More critically, Root observed 'that the American Nation is profoundly indifferent to all outside matters, including their relations with Canada, and that consequently the influence of an affected interest like the Gloucester Fleet was powerful in Congress'. The Senate would never permit duty-free Canadian or Newfoundland fish into the United States. Howard found that Root believed the big issues in Canadian–American relations could not be resolved at this time. The Americans might have come to Ottawa to help salve Canadian irritation over the Alaska boundary, but they brought nothing substantial. All Root would say was there were 'several minor matters which do not involve national rights, which may be wiped off the slate'.

Root's Ottawa visit crystallised the diplomatic problem with which Howard would have to contend. It was imperative to improve Canadian–American relations given their intimate connexion with the overall Anglo–American relationship. But improving Canadian–American relations meant settling the outstanding issues, and in this a fundamental divergence of opinion existed between Ottawa and Washington over how this should be done. Laurier's government wanted to settle the major issue of reciprocity first, believing that, once this was done, tackling the rest of the problems whether major or minor would pose little difficulty. On the other side, the Roosevelt Administration showed interest only in resolving the minor issues, happy to wait for a more propitious moment to confront the major ones. Represented by the Washington Embassy and the governor-general, Britain would have to pursue policy with probity to make certain that Anglo-Canadian relations improved and did not, as they had done after the Alaska boundary settlement, threaten to disrupt the North American balance of power to Britain's disadvantage. Suffusing the whole situation was a diplomatic spoiler: Newfoundland's single-minded determination via Bond's duty-free fish treaty with the United States to break through the American tariff wall come what may.

The lack of substance in Root's overtures to the Laurier government convinced Howard and Lord Grey that it would be necessary to use Bryce's appointment as a means, first, of bringing fresh air into Anglo-Canadian relations and, secondly, of beginning to bridge the gap between Ottawa and Washington. Bryce could do this soon after his arrival by discussing Canadian–American relations with Root and then, as soon as possible, travelling to Ottawa to be instructed by Laurier in the Canadian case.[49] Bryce's mind was already moving in this direction before he left England,[50] thus he needed little persuasion to undertake a mission to the Canadian capital in late March 1907, a month after he took up his post at Washington.

Howard waited for the ambassador to undertake an Ottawa visit. Accordingly, after meeting with Root to sound out the official American position, Bryce went to Canada.[51] Coupled with what he learnt from Root, Bryce's discussions there confirmed for him and Howard that neither Ottawa nor Washington was prepared to budge over the major issues, though a suggestion by Root that the Americans might permit duty-free Canadian coal into the northeastern and northwestern United States in return for Canada allowing duty-free American coal into Central Canada was rebuffed by Laurier after he consulted with his political advisers. None the less, seeing an opening, Laurier indicated that American tariffs should be taken off 'all natural products, including fresh lamb, eggs, vegetables, fruit and hay'. But the Canadian prime minister did not press this, something which relieved Bryce, knowing 'the [American] Protectionist forces would rally against it. They are wonderfully well organized'. In terms of Canadian–American relations this haggling over reciprocity meant nothing more than a cheap American ploy to show good faith; both Ottawa and Washington could not yet move on this issue as there were domestic impediments in each country to overcome. Although Bryce faced pointed public criticism by some Canadians during his visit because of the record of British diplomacy in North America since 1903,[52] the ambassador discovered a glimmer of promise for putting the Canadian problem to rest. Laurier seemed agreeable to entering into discussions with the Roosevelt Administration on some of the minor issues, most especially the matter of international waters. This suggested to Howard and Bryce that the Canadian problem could begin to be resolved by removing the minor issues in Canadian–American relations, so that, once these were out of the way, the bigger ones would be more amenable to settlement.

Once Bryce made his journey to Ottawa, he turned to his more important job of improving Anglo-American relations. For most of 1907 this involved establishing and cementing social ties with prominent Americans, undertaking speaking tours to Illinois, Maine, Missouri, and Oklahoma, and handling sensitive political issues for which the Embassy was responsible, chiefly explaining Britain's position at the second Hague conference. All of this meant Howard's independence in co-ordinating Canadian–American relations. The immediacy of ameliorating Canadian–American discord receded for a time after March 1907: Laurier left for London in April to attend a Colonial conference that had as its focal point greater Imperial unity and this, and the policy considerations it spawned, preoccupied his government for months.[53] On the other side, the Roosevelt Administration had arrogated to the United States a leading role in the discussion of maritime rights at the Hague conference, which began in June, and this absorbed American diplomatists for the rest of 1907 and into 1908.[54] This respite afforded Howard time to build on the promise that Bryce had brought back from the Canadian capital.

Howard's immediate consideration involved coming to terms with the Newfoundland government's determination to break into the American market with duty-free fish and the impact of this on Canada. Once the matter of Newfoundland fish was removed, a main impediment blocking good Canadian–American relations would be gone. Thus the focal point of Howard's diplomacy for the rest of 1907 concerned dealing with the government at St John's. His problem hinged on Bond's willingness to use the most belligerent and abrasive tactics to force the Roosevelt Administration to secure Senate support for a duty-free fish treaty. This led Bond's government to create legal difficulties for Americans who fished off the Newfoundland coast: making it illegal for Newfoundlanders to work on American boats, restricting the sale of bait to American fishermen, and so on.[55] The idea was that the Roosevelt Administration would then do all it could to end these hindrances – and so improve the Gloucester fleet's profits – by getting a treaty favourable to Newfoundland. Bond did seek to make it understood that these actions were directed not against the

Roosevelt Administration, but against those narrow-minded New England fishermen whose success depended upon Newfoundland sailors and bait. Bond seems to have calculated both that the American fishermen would buckle, thus asking Washington to settle the issue by giving Newfoundland fish unrestricted access to the American market, and that Britain would support him. He miscalculated badly. Root's words to Lord Grey about the 'affected interest' of the Gloucester Fleet in Washington proved true; in an Alaska boundary dispute writ small, Roosevelt supported rapacious Americans against equally rapacious foreigners.[56] Moreover, just as in 1903, the British did not see it in their interests in 1905 and 1906 to imperil their relations with the United States by pushing Imperial unity to the limit. Indeed, in October 1906 the Campbell-Bannerman government concluded a *modus vivendi* with the American government which permitted New England fishermen to pursue their livelihood off Newfoundland.[57] The basis of this was an Order-in-Council which overrode the legal impediments thrown up by the Bond government. The predictable result was a shrill cry of 'sell out' by Bond and other powerful interests in the colony who supported his government.[58]

For a convinced Imperialist like Howard, London's treatment of the Bond government demonstrated a callousness which had the potential of opening a fissure between the home government and that at St John's. However, whilst Howard sympathised with Bond's plight, there were wider political issues to consider. Britain's relationship with the United States was far more important to the Empire's security in the wider world, given the increasing naval rivalry with Germany. In terms of the Imperial position in North America, ensuring that Canada's *amour propre* did not suffer any further abatement had a greater regional significance than did keeping Newfoundland content over exports of its fish harvest. Of course, this did not mean that Britain should concede to every American demand respecting its two protégés in North America. With its international position to consider, Britain's continual appeasement of acquisitive Americans could not be countenanced.[59] In the cold, hard world of international politics, however, states in a weakened position have to make some sacrifices in their diplomacy. Britain was in an exposed position in North America, the result of its strategic withdrawal and strong desire to keep the Americans sweet. The easiest way to avoid a squabble with the United States, the path of least resistance, lay in overriding Newfoundland's desire to break into the American market. Howard recognised this from the moment he arrived at Washington in late 1906.[60] Whilst he would do everything to settle Newfoundland's problems, it remained more important to improve Anglo-American and Anglo-Canadian relations. Throughout 1907, this stood at the centre of his handling of Canadian and Newfoundland relations with the United States.

The chance that the Bond–Hay treaty would be ratified existed until 4 March 1907, the day the American Congress rose for its break. The Foreign Office and the Colonial Office agreed that the British government should not put any pressure on the Roosevelt Administration to push the thing through the Senate. Supported by Grey, Hardinge saw the American failure to ratify as a means by which Britain could then inform Washington that the whole matter would have to be reconsidered; Howard was informed of this in early February and ordered to say nothing about the matter until after Congress adjourned.[61] By 4 March, the Bond–Hay treaty was dead and, with Bryce's discussions with Root and Laurier in late March and early April, the stage had been set to find some new diplomatic arrangement to resolve the Newfoundland fisheries problem. Whilst Bond's government continued to work for ratification – for instance, it prosecuted two Newfoundland sailors who, though working for an American master under rights granted by the *modus vivendi*, had supposedly broken the Newfoundland laws prohibiting them from doing so[62] – Howard and Root sought a way around the impasse.

Since the annual fishing season began in October, Howard found time constraints hampering a permanent solution. By the middle of May with the talks still in an exploratory stage, and with only a few months till the Gloucester fleet set sail, Root proposed that the *modus vivendi* be extended to cover the new fishing season.[63] Because of the Colonial Conference, Bond was then in London lobbying Lord Elgin, the colonial secretary, to use his powers to prevent the extension of the *modus vivendi*.[64] Seeing his position weakening, Bond appeared to make an atypical attempt at constructive diplomacy by suggesting that Newfoundland and the United States conclude a set of joint regulations to govern American fishing off the colony's coast – the basis of these regulations would be an Anglo-American treaty of 1818 which allowed American fishermen certain rights, like where precisely off the coast to fish, and which had served as the basis of Bond's two treaties with the Americans and the *modus vivendi*. Howard saw merit in this idea;[65] it accorded with established diplomatic practice in American relations with the British dominions in North America – a joint Canadian–American commission to establish regulations governing the use of fresh waters had been revived by the improved relations between Ottawa and Washington. Acknowledging that fishing regulations could easily be drawn up by a small Joint Commission of arbitration, Howard cautioned that there might be difficulty given the emotive nature of the question; 'Unless a strong and impartial person is chosen as Umpire in any such Commission', he added, 'I fear there will be trouble in securing any agreement.' Unwilling to gamble at this stage, the Foreign Office took Howard's admonition to heart – Bond would probably do all he could to delay a settlement which avoided giving Newfoundland reciprocity;[66] accordingly, Grey squelched all notion of negotiating joint regulations, plumping instead for the extension of the *modus vivendi* for 1907. This would allow for a diplomatic solution unblemished by the need to conclude it rapidly, and so eliminate the Newfoundland problem in order to pursue more pressing problems. Over the summer, as a result, London and Washington negotiated, extending the 1906 agreement to cover the 1907 fishing season and making minor modifications to overcome the legal impediments thrown up by St John's.[67] Given the diplomacy that took place over the next year, the Newfoundland question ceased to have importance any more in Anglo-American relations.

For Howard, the central consideration in submitting this question to arbitration was Canada's position. Clearly, Bond could be ignored, given London's refusal to support Newfoundland's objection to the extension of the *modus vivendi*. Whatever the decision, St John's would have to accept it. But Canada was a different proposition. That country's constitutional autonomy within the Empire meant London could not pass an Order-in-Council forcing Laurier's ministry to bend to Britain's will. Moreover, even if legally sound, such a course would be impolitic. Echoes of the Alaska settlement had not died away; London needed to avoid arbitrary policies. Canada had to be consulted; its wishes had to be incorporated into the British diplomatic strategy devised to safeguard Imperial interests at The Hague.

In June 1907, Howard saw the need for a general Canadian–American settlement underscored when Ottawa and Washington argued about American fishing rights off the Magdalen Islands, Canadian possessions in the Gulf of St Lawrence. In late May Canadian authorities refused to allow an American schooner, *The Alert*, to drop its nets off the Magdalens. Despite Canadian laws enacted to control the times and methods of fishing for all vessels whether Canadian or not – notably conservation laws prohibiting purse-seines as they depleted too rapidly fish stocks – the Americans claimed that the 1818 treaty gave them unrestricted rights in the region.[68] Laurier's government refused to bend, taking the sensible line that Canadian laws applied to all those fishing in Canadian waters and overrode the treaty. Although a minor nuisance, *The Alert* incident pointed to the necessity of a final settlement of Canadian–American differences. A number of such trifling problems might, if left unresolved, combine in the future and undermine all the good that had begun to be done in the Anglo-American relationship.

Root decided to act first and, on 12 July 1907, Whitelaw Reid handed a letter to the Foreign Office which proposed that all questions between the United States, on one hand, and Canada and Newfoundland, on the other, arising out of interpretations of the 1818 treaty be submitted to the Hague

Tribunal for arbitration.[69] Although some concern existed in the Foreign Office about the soundness of the Newfoundland case, general agreement existed that 'arbitration should be accepted'.[70] By August, supposing that their interests would be better protected by arbitration rather than by direct negotiation with the Americans, both the Newfoundland and Canadian governments agreed that the Hague Tribunal should decide on the matter;[71] it fell to Howard to co-ordinate the Imperial response.

He went on an official trip to Ottawa, Montreal, and Quebec City in September 1907.[72] Consulting with a range of 'notables' confirmed that 'a certain feeling existed rightly or wrongly against the Embaassy [sic] for having "neglected Canada"'. In fact, Canadian feeling was in a 'rather suspicious state' about British policies. This did not mean that Canadians harboured ill-feelings toward Britain. Sir Charles Fitzpatrick, the chief justice of the Supreme Court, believed that Canadians had 'always come out of disputes with the U.S. more advantageously than they could have expected considering their case'. Still, Fitzpatrick voiced the worry of his countrymen about arbitration when he emphasised the need to have Newfoundland and Canadian judges on the arbitral panel; they would have knowledge about local matters of which a British judge would be ignorant. With the Alaska boundary arbitration in mind, Howard warned Hardinge: 'Besides there was always the fear that English judges might be again, however unjustly, accused of having sacrificed Canadian interests. This ought to be avoided at all costs.' If London truly wanted to shore up the British position in North America, every effort had to be made to avoid antagonising Canada. Wounded Canadian pride would prevent an amicable settlement of outstanding Canadian–American differences, which in turn would do Anglo-American relations no good.

Over the next few months, Howard wrestled with the problem of how best to approach the Hague Tribunal. Before states put their disputes before that body, a joint treaty outlining the points of contention had to be drafted; with this, and the cases and counter-cases argued before it, the Tribunal would then arrive at a decision and the issue would be settled by ratification of the treaty encasing the Tribunal's interpretation. By suggesting arbitration, the Americans believed they would derive some advantage out of the procedure; hence, they could not complain if the decision went against them. With this in mind, Howard drew upon the knowledge gained from his Canadian trip, and an exhaustive study of the fishing question and the history of arbitration decisions, to produce a proposed strategy to safeguard Newfoundland and Canadian interests against American encroachments. He outlined this in two insightful memoranda.[73]

Howard surmised that Britain had only two options. The first involved an active role in preparing the Imperial terms of reference to be submitted in treaty form to the arbitral panel. This meant negotiating with the Bond and Laurier governments, on one hand, and with the Roosevelt Administration, on the other; in essence serving as a conduit between the two sides. The second was passive. Britain could let Canada, Newfoundland, and the United States each formulate its case independently. All that London should insist upon in the preparation of the draft treaty was the absence of any reference to specific issues. As all the major points of contention derived from interpreting Article I of the 1818 treaty – for instance, where precisely Americans could fish and where they could seek shelter, repair damages, and purchase wood and water – having the Tribunal decide simply on 'the true construction of Article I' held a better chance of success for the Imperial case.

Supported by Bryce, Howard argued that the second option be followed. Three advantages could accrue to Britain by doing so. First, the negotiation of the treaty to be submitted to the Tribunal would be easier and quicker because useless wrangling over details, especially with the 'fractious' Bond, would be eliminated. Next, given the Senate's penchant for blocking treaties entered into by the Administration – Bond's two fish treaties were a case in point – a general statement of the problem at hand would add to the speed with which the settlement would occur. Finally, Britain would avoid the danger of antagonising either side; about this, Howard noted perceptively:

If the terms are not specified, but the points to be decided are to be stated later in the cases and countercases submitted by the Newfoundland, Canadian, and United States' Governments respectively, and argued before the Tribunal by Newfoundland, Canadian, and United States' advocates, His Majesty's Government will incur no responsibility for the presentation of the cases, for the elimination or retention of such and such terms of reference, or for the success or failure of the suit.

Implicit in this proposed strategy was the assumption that every effort had to be made to ensure Imperial solidarity as the best means of preserving the British position in the North American balance of power. This conformed to those deeply held Imperial sentiments which helped shape Howard's view of Britain's place in the World; in this instance, Canada remained fundamentally important. Given the need to be as objective as possible in advising the Foreign Office about policy options, his personal view had no place in official memoranda. But, where he could in his proposed strategy, he stressed the Canadian viewpoint and London's need to keep it at the fore in constructing Britain's American policy. For instance, he pointed out that the real reason why Ottawa wanted Newfoundland not to receive preferential tariff treatment in terms of a fishing treaty stemmed from Canadian beliefs that Newfoundland would eventually be absorbed into Canada. 'Divided jurisdiction over a province lying at the mouth of the St Lawrence would, in Canadian opinion', he observed, 'give to the United States a hold over Canada which Canadians desire to avoid.'[74]

Privately, Howard held an impassioned view about the need to placate Canada, something that showed in a letter to his brother, Stafford, written two days before the Canadian trip ended.[75] As a rapidly growing country, Canada would soon demand a larger voice in international politics. Britain had to recognise this fact. Howard found that 'the English-speaking Canadians [the vast majority of the population] seem to want a larger national development. I don't believe that as population & wealth increases they will be content to occupy for much longer the rather subordinate part of the world's theatre which they fill at present.' Canadian susceptibilities had to be weighed in creating Britain's American policy. Britain could not continue bartering away Canadian interests with impunity for, once Canada stood on its own internationally, it would be an indispensable ally. The Empire's future diplomatic strength would suffer if London did nothing to help the dominion in its present disagreements with the United States. For Howard, avoiding this meant eliminating the network of outstanding Canadian–American differences so that Canada did not suffer unduly and, to do this, the fisheries question had to be resolved quickly in Ottawa's favour. Howard's proposed strategy represented a realistic and rational method of doing this.

The Foreign Office saw the wisdom in Howard's memoranda,[76] so that they became the leitmotif of London's diplomacy pursued until January 1909 when Britain, representing Canada and Newfoundland, exchanged notes with the United States outlining the specific case for submission to the Hague Tribunal. Though coming after Howard had moved on to his next post, in large part the draft put before the arbitral panel conformed to his submission that 'the true construction' of Article I of the 1818 treaty should be all that was sought.[77] Moreover, in his memoranda, Howard had emphasised that, by looking at the whole article instead of 'specific points picked out by this side or that', 'American fishermen stand to lose rather than to gain by any decisions of an Arbitration Court'.[78] His judgement was flawless, since the Tribunal's decision rendered in September 1910 resulted in an overwhelming victory for Canada.[79] Anglo-Canadian relations were not undermined but were strengthened by these developments.

Of course, the Washington Embassy's task was not smooth in the time between Howard tendering his views and the exchange of notes. The Americans and the Canadians each tried to squeeze the maximum advantage out of the process of getting agreed terms of reference – so, too, did Newfoundland, though the Foreign Office ceased to have anything to do with Bond once his government accepted the proposal to arbitrate; the Colonial Office became saddled with handling Newfoundland given its status as a colony subject to London's foreign policy dictates.[80] The continuing dialogue between Ottawa and Washington preoccupied Howard because, until departing in November 1908, he remained responsible for co-ordinating Canada's relations with the United States. The major obstacle had been to agree on a method of settling the fisheries dispute and, then, hit upon the best strategy safeguarding British interests. This had been overcome with Laurier and Bond approving Root's suggestion of approaching the Hague and Howard's superiors accepting the kernel of his two memoranda. His diplomacy from January to November 1908 lacked, therefore, the urgency of that pursued throughout 1907 over fisheries, but it contributed to his diplomatic apprenticeship and added to his knowledge of the American scene.

Howard's problem in 1908 was to balance between American desires to get an agreed draft without delay and Canadian opposition to being rushed. Root sought a result well before the combined presidential-congressional elections took place in November 1908, this to provide the Republicans with another political success to brandish before American electors. The Roosevelt Administration recognised the weakness of their case in the summer of 1907; hence their willingness to arbitrate. Roosevelt himself made this plain to Reid two weeks after the ambassador suggested arbitration to Grey: 'I have never felt that the matter was of such vital importance to us, or that our rights were so clear, that we could afford to take an extreme position in reference to it – such a position as we took on the Alaska boundary business, for instance.'[81]

Throughout the winter and early spring of 1907–8, Root pressured the British Embassy to submit the Imperial terms of reference and, in turn, Howard appealed to the Foreign Office to have the Colonial Office cajole Ottawa and St John's into action. In the middle of January, Howard reported that Congress would probably rise in May and not sit again until after the elections. Given Senate tendencies to demand 'ample time to consider draft Treaties', no time should be wasted in getting this question out of the way.[82] Bond's government sent its terms of reference to the Colonial Office at the end of March, and these were duly forwarded to the Washington Embassy.[83] But the Canadians delayed. This caused Howard to complain to Mallet, Grey's private secretary, about the snail's pace at which the Foreign Office seemed to be moving.[84] Though appreciating Howard's concern, Mallet replied: 'We are doing all that is possible here to hurry up the C.O. but I believe they can get nothing out of Canada.' All hinged on the Colonial Office's ability to get Laurier to put the Canadian position on paper, but he would not. Matters were not helped when Campbell-Bannerman, diagnosed as having cancer, resigned on 5 April 1908. In the subsequent shuffling of the Cabinet by the new prime minister, Herbert Asquith, Lord Crewe, Howard's old Crabbet Club friend, replaced Elgin as colonial secretary. Crewe had to gain knowledge of his new post, something that delayed further the effort to get Canada to move.

Canadian reluctance to submit terms of reference is explained in two ways. First, with the Alaska boundary dispute still fresh, Laurier's government was not about to move until certain of Canada's case being as strong as possible. There might also have been an element of revenge in this, causing both Britain and the United States some irritation after the unfavourable arbitral decision of 1903. Secondly, the breakthrough in the fisheries question had led to progress in settling some of the minor Canadian–American questions – Howard's prediction in 1907. For instance in February, seeing improved relations with Ottawa, Root proposed a draft treaty to regularise procedures for conveying prisoners and for wrecking and salvaging privileges.[85] Since the American proposals treated Canada fairly, and as Root wanted to settle these issues prior to the elections, Laurier exploited the situation by making minor amendments to show Canadian firmness and then concluded a treaty covering these matters on 18 May.[86] Canadian–American negotiations were under way concurrently on the more substantive problems of pecuniary claims and the use of boundary waters, and Laurier worked these to milk every possible concession out of Root whilst conditions allowed.[87]

Howard's balancing between the Americans and the Canadians over the fisheries arbitration ended on 9 May when the Embassy received a Foreign Office telegram reporting that the Canadian terms of reference had been sent to the Colonial Office the day before.[88] An exasperating time for Howard had ended. The Americans were obviously annoyed with Canada's failure to formulate quickly its terms of reference once agreement to go to the Hague had been achieved. Howard's complaints to Mallet showed this, though, because of the decision to adhere to Howard's strategy, there should have been little complaint. If the British were to distance themselves from the detailed negotiation of the joint submission to the arbitration tribunal, they had to be patient when delays ensued. But neither Howard nor Bryce wanted to risk damaging needlessly the improving Anglo-American relationship and, whilst valid in Canada's interest, Laurier's torpor served only to create unfavourable impressions of the northern dominion within the Roosevelt Administration. Howard and Bryce saw this emerge with 'Root's disappointment & impatience';[89] they had additional concerns since Roosevelt would not be seeking another term as president. Bryce put this forcefully to Lord Grey: 'If things don't move much faster, nothing will be done before Roosevelt & Root vanish a year hence. After them who knows what will come.' On the other hand, Laurier did not see a change of Administration as worrying, since it was no coincidence that the draft Canadian terms were given to London just before Congress rose for the last time prior to the elections.

None the less, with the Canadian submission of their terms in early May and the American release of theirs three weeks later[90] – Root had decided to hold off until Ottawa finally moved – the hardest part of the diplomatic process over the fisheries arbitration ended. Subsequent negotiations involving technical details over the precise document to be submitted to the tribunal, the choice of a neutral presiding judge, and the number of national judges were relatively easy.[91] Although Howard did not play a leading role in this – the Foreign Office, working closely with Reid, did so – he remained the crucial link in Washington between the authorities in London and the Roosevelt Administration. This was especially so from July to September when Bryce spent his annual leave in Britain and Howard ran the Embassy.[92] Howard made his task easier by taking a second trip to Canada, in the latter part of June before Bryce's departure, seeing Laurier, Fitzpatrick, and others important in formulating and executing Canadian policy over the arbitration. This trip also provided him with the opportunity to learn from Canadian officials their government's position on the other outstanding issues in Canadian–American relations, most especially the anticipated Canadian tack in the pelagic-sealing issue.[93]

By the summer of 1908, thanks to Bryce and Howard's concerted efforts to break the circle of outstanding Canadian–American questions by first tackling the North Atlantic fisheries dispute, the strain between Ottawa and Washington which threatened good Anglo-American relations seemed to be ebbing away. For the ultimate amelioration of Anglo-American differences in this period, the recognised legacy of Bryce's embassy,[94] the groundwork had been laid by the team of Bryce and Howard. Of course, other problems cropped up between Britain and the United States during Bryce's tenure which had the potential of disrupting the smooth relationship sought by Grey, his Foreign Office advisers, and the Embassy; American determination to build a United States controlled Panama Canal and involvement in Mexico which might damage British interests there were two important ones.[95] Britain had to concede somewhat to American demands given the more pressing problems in Europe, but accommodation was possible as a result of the new tone in Anglo-American relations established in 1907 and 1908. Much of the credit for this derives from the conscious British effort to improve Anglo-

American relations that began with Durand's recall in December 1906 and to which Esme Howard contributed in an important way.

Howard's American experiences were not limited to those gained by his concentration on Imperial affairs and the achievement of an arbitration proposal for the Hague. He served for almost two years at the centre of the American political process, during which time he learnt a great deal about how that process worked. The American constitution might possess all the theoretical perfections of political democracy, with defined separation of powers between the executive and the legislature, but in reality it created a complex method of arriving at foreign policy. The president and his secretary of state could chart the course of American diplomacy, for instance, the Roosevelt Administration's efforts to use Durand's removal as a starting-point in repairing Anglo-American relations. Root's visit to Ottawa in early 1907, a recognition that improved Canadian–American relations were essential to this new course, showed the direction this policy began to take. To this point, the policy-making process differed little in Britain and the United States. Here, however, all similarity ended. In Britain, a government in power could undertake new directions in foreign policy without undue worry about that policy being deflected by Parliament; in fact in 1907, over the frenzied shrieks of radical Liberals with their pathological hatred of tsarist absolutism, Grey concluded an entente with Russia without endangering the government.[96] In the United States, on the other hand, Administration officials had always to be cognisant of Congressional opinion, notably that in the Senate which, with committees like that on foreign relations integral to treaty-making, could and did deflect policy. Since the average American cared little about international matters – Root's candour about the power of the Gloucester fleet in garnering public and political sympathy showed this – Congressional members became embedded in parochial politics. These considerations were more pronounced during presidential election years. Thus, Howard found that American diplomatists had not only to consider the interests of foreign states in their calculations, they had also to weigh carefully to a greater extent than in Britain the interests of domestic pressure groups and their Congressional mouthpieces.

The intimate connexion between American domestic politics and foreign policy impressed itself on Howard. This showed in April 1908 when the Embassy prepared the annual report on the United States for the calendar year of 1907.[97] Bryce delegated Howard to prepare the sections on national and state politics; this resulted in a cogent analysis of a range of subjects from economic and commercial legislation to abject corruption in the Pennsylvania state government. With this information and additional advice and observations from Howard, Bryce then wrote the portion of the report dealing with 'Public Opinion and the Subjects that interest it'. In regard to public opinion and foreign policy in the United States, Bryce wrote: 'I...need only here observe that public opinion occupies itself very little with [foreign affairs]. Not one man in ten thousand, hardly even one politician or journalist in a hundred, knows or cares what happens in the Old World or realizes the silent influence which the Old World exerts on America.' These comments related to historical tendencies in the United States, not simply to the course of American opinion in 1907. Of course some extremist blocs of the American public, especially the implacably anglophobic Irish-Americans,[98] possessed decided opinions on what course American foreign policy ought to take, and worked to pressure Washington to adopt policies to conform to their beliefs. Because of their extremism, these views could usually be discounted. However, an indelible impression had been left on Howard during his service as counsellor on Bryce's staff: British diplomatists at their peril could ignore American domestic politics in pursuing their policies towards the United States.

Howard was influenced by Bryce's iconoclastic approach to ambassadorial service. This is interesting, as it represented the influence of a man with 'shortcomings in conventional etiquette and ambassadorial dignity' on Howard, a 'Service' man. Yet, many of Bryce's unconventionalities became standard procedure when Howard returned to Washington as the British ambassador in 1924. Until Bryce, no other British ambassador had bothered to travel to the distant parts of the country to be seen and heard, let alone visit Canada so vital to Britain in the North American balance of power. The value of such trips came from the senior British representative at Washington putting the British case to local interests in Oklahoma, Maine, or Illinois. There is no doubt that these tours helped improve the British image in the United States after Bryce's arrival.[99]

Just as important, Bryce believed that his principal subordinates should also travel within the United States. With such a large territory, heterogeneous population, and obvious regional interests and diversity, the complexity of 'the American scene' could be appreciated only at first hand. Consequently Howard made a number of trips to the South, as well as one memorable one to Chicago in June 1908 to attend the Republican Party's presidential nominating convention.[100] Added to these excursions were his two trips to Canada. Howard intended to take a major tour of the West with his friend, James Garfield, Roosevelt's secretary of the interior, in the summer of 1908, but Hardinge had him cancel because Bryce's absence on leave at this time meant that someone with authority had to be in charge of the Embassy.[101] None the less, the utility of junior members of the Embassy seeing various parts of the United States had been ingrained on Howard, and it became an essential part of his approach to his duties when he returned as ambassador in 1924.

Howard's time in Washington throws new light on Bryce's ambassadorship. It has been suggested that Bryce, despite his knowledge of the United States, failed to appreciate the power of the press as an arbiter of American public opinion.[102] The implication is that, whilst Bryce did use the American press to get the British point of view across in the United States, he did not do so as effectively as he might have. This is wide of the mark. Bryce and his staff did recognise this basic fact of political life in the United States.[103] Bryce had Herbert Grant Watson, a third secretary at the Embassy, prepare a major report on the American press and its methods in early 1908. Grant Watson, in his analysis of the American concept of the freedom of the press, emphasised that 'this freedom is so misused that the censorship with all its injustice is keenly regretted by the many who suffer from its daily budget of lies and horrors'. In despatching this report to the Foreign Office, Bryce made the telling comment: 'Mr Watson has couched his comments in language whose moderation I appreciate all the more because I should have felt inclined to paint in darker colours the reckless irresponsibility of a large section of the American press.' Hence, it was not a matter of Bryce failing to exploit the American press to the full; it was instead one of ensuring that the British case did not become too distorted by this unpredictable institution in American life.

Howard had discovered this at almost the moment he arrived in Washington in December 1906.[104] At that time American newspapers speculated wildly about the reasons for Durand's recall. Some eastern newspapers, led by the *New York Evening Post*, were suggesting that the recall derived from a Court intrigue in London where Lady Susan Townley, apparently jealous of the king's mistress, Alice Keppel, had engineered Durand's fall. Durand supposedly enjoyed Mrs Keppel's confidence. Durand worked feverishly to prevent wide circulation of this story by discussing the matter personally with a *Post* representative, impressing on him 'that publication must do great harm especially if the King's name was prominently dragged in'. As a result, whilst the stories appeared, Durand's 'representations [had] considerable effect and the stories have been a good deal watered down in comparison with what was originally intended to be published'. By digging around to learn the truth about this sordid business, Howard discovered that the rumours were probably started by Roosevelt's friends, chiefly Senator Lodge. These men, 'feeling that the P[resident] had sometimes spoken in not too friendly a spirit about Sir Mortimer[,] probably wanted to draw a red herring across the track by making Lady Susan responsible for what has occurred'. This lesson about the American press, its power, and its manipulation was not lost on

Howard during his tour of duty, nor when he returned nearly twenty years later as ambassador.

Canada's importance in the Anglo-American relationship amounted to one of the most important impressions made on Howard during his two years as Bryce's counsellor. The Canadian situation confirmed Howard's ideas about Imperial evolution that had formed in Ireland and South Africa. When parts of the Empire were ready and wanted full independence, this should be granted without delay; to avoid doing so would create difficulties and, perhaps, ill-feelings towards Britain which could sap Imperial strength. In the Canadian case, Ottawa possessed full sovereign rights except over foreign policy – British strategic withdrawal from the western hemisphere saw Canada inaugurate policies to ensure its terrene defence.[105] Both Bryce and Howard believed that Canada should handle its own foreign affairs through its own foreign office at Ottawa. This would improve the speed with which decisions were made,[106] whilst giving the country the international presence desired by its English-speaking majority. Though left unspoken, in terms of Britain's narrow national interests this could only augment Imperial unity since the British could not be blamed for any resulting Canadian shortcomings. Although entrenched opposition existed within the British government about allowing a Canadian foreign ministry – Elgin personified this view[107] – Bryce and Howard agreed completely on this much-needed department; percipient men like Hardinge were of the same opinion.[108] Hence, within eight months of Howard departing Washington, Canada established a Department of External Affairs, and in this the Bryce Embassy with its decided view on the need for Canadian political autonomy played a decisive role.[109]

Howard believed that, although Canada should have loose foreign-policy ties with Britain, Britain should tighten its economic relationship with the dominion. In other words the sort of Imperial tariff federation which Howard had discussed with Rhodes almost twenty years before – and which had become a hot political issue in Britain with Joseph Chamberlain's Imperial Preference campaign[110] – had to be created as soon as possible. He had put this case to his brother Stafford, still a Liberal free-trade MP, in September 1907: 'As to a preferential tarif [sic], that is essential if the Empire is to be maintained & you free-importers will have to make up your minds some day whether you prefer the gospel of Cobden to the Empire or not.'[111] These feelings intensified over the next year. A few months before being transferred, Howard again poured out his heart to Stafford.[112] In the narrow context Britain would benefit from Imperial Preference since government revenues would increase in step with national wealth. The American experience offered a telling endorsement of protection, since United States tariffs made 'the [American] working man...infinitely better off than he is in England or Europe as a whole'. However, the broader context counted more. Britain and the Empire could both prosper by Imperial Preference, with a concomitant increase in international strength. The obvious implication was that, being less dependent on American markets, Canada would be tied more closely to Britain, so that the international position of Britain, Canada, and the Empire would each be decidedly improved.

Finally, Howard left the United States as an admirer of that country. First and foremost, he felt that Americans were a friendly and unpretentious people. His first months at Washington showed this when he set about making social calls: 'Friendly hospitality is indeed an outstanding feature of the United States, and if sometimes the visitor is in danger of being killed with kindness, he is yet always ready to run the risk a second time.'[113] His relationship with Roosevelt, especially during the Swettenham incident, demonstrated that informality extended to the highest political office in the land. But more than just these personal contacts, the United States showed Howard the vibrancy of the 'New World' in its economic life, its lack of social sanctimony relative to that in England, and its democratic politics enshrined in the Constitution. His assessment of the expansiveness of the American economy and how and why Britain should imitate it had a profound impact on him; he still extolled its virtues twenty years later.[114] He lauded the relaxed attitude of Americans towards life in general, even towards that pursued by dignitaries. Howard often spent Sunday morning with his eldest son, Esme, carrying him pick-a-back on explorations of Rock Creek Park at Washington. 'That was a thing which, I suppose,' he wrote, 'a First Secretary of Embassy could hardly do in a major European capital without loss of – what shall I say? – of face, but Washington was still kindly enough – and small enough in size but big enough in heart – not to take offence.'[115] The democratic ideals of Jefferson, Adams, and Franklin, which had had the support of the old twelfth Duke of Norfolk and had surrounded Howard as a boy at Greystoke, found practical expression in such purely American institutions as the presidential nomination conventions of the major political parties. Whilst he knew that all of the major decisions at these conventions were made by power-brokers behind the scene, it gave the average American, more so than the average Briton, the necessary illusion that his voice counted at the national level.[116]

None of this suggests that Howard surveyed the American scene uncritically. A number of aspects of American life did not appeal to him. Given his own firm beliefs about the need to find a compromise between capital and labour, he found distasteful the efforts of the two major parties to stymie the growth of trade unionism in the United States.[117] There also existed a certain hypocrisy between the constant American refrain about protecting individual rights and the abject lack of rights given to black Americans, especially in the southern states. Howard was not immune from racist tendencies of his own; his correspondence had many references to 'darkies', for instance. Moreover, many Englishmen discriminated against blacks in the Empire. But Howard was far more tolerant of non-white peoples than most people of his class and background at that time on both sides of the Atlantic, this the result of his African and South American adventures. Hence, he reported with a certain disgust the maltreatment of blacks in the United States, the land where those lofty Jeffersonian ideals were supposed to reign supreme.[118]

The United States existed in Howard's view, therefore, as a land of contradictions. Because he could not, he did not generalise about this country, refusing to offload any 'grip-sack' of opinions on his family, friends, and superiors containing trite little characteristics of America and Americans which could be contradicted almost as soon as they fell from his lips. His work at the Embassy led him to approach every facet of the American scene with which he came into contact on its own merits. The value of this not only to his expertise about the United States but to his growing skill as a diplomat is undeniable. The refusal to see the United States in simple terms of black and white, and to categorise American policies accordingly, underscored his talent to assess coldly and realistically complex issues. It helped make a success of his apprenticeship in Bryce's Embassy,[119] convincing the Foreign Office of his talents, and ensuring his rise up the ladder of the diplomatic establishment in the service of Britain and the Empire.

4

Budapest and Berne: prelude to the Great War, 1908–1913

It is a most curious thing that in foreign politics the English radical has always[,] ever since I can remember, been absurdly & ignorantly in the wrong. I suppose it is because they never try to learn the grammar of foreign affairs.   *Howard, March* 1913

I

After a year at Washington, Howard found his financial resources stretched thinly. A third son, Hubert, had been born in December 1907 and this, in combination with the social responsibilities of a counsellor, began to erode his inheritance. Moreover, in the autumn of 1907, he had made a trip to Louis d'Or and learnt the disheartening news that the experimental rubber-growing would not succeed. Latex flow remained well below that needed for profitable enterprise and, worse, could not be expected to improve. He and Thorlief Orde therefore made the decision to begin anew with cocoa cultivation. All of the rubber groves would have to be cut down and replaced with cocoa trees.[1] It would be a while before he could rely on any substantial income from this venture, let alone have enough annual profits to consider retiring once again from the Diplomatic Service. These financial strictures convinced him of what had been evident since he rejoined the Embassy at Rome: his future and the security of his family lay in a diplomatic career.

On returning from Louis d'Or he enquired discreetly of his friends at the Foreign Office about the possibility of an early transfer from Washington to some less costly post. When news of this reached the permanent under-secretary's office, Hardinge wrote to Howard with a mild rebuke for seeking to leave Washington after such a short time there. 'It is a pity', admonished Hardinge, 'that you should want to move as we consider that constant changes in the upper levels of the Service are disadvantageous in every way.'[2] Hardinge did indicate that changes in a number of posts would occur in the following autumn, but he could make no guarantees. The message was clear. Not only had Howard been favoured by appointment to a senior post at a major Embassy after proving himself on Crete, but more important considerations existed in conducting British foreign policy than his immediate financial problems. No doubt Hardinge believed that the delicacy of British–Canadian–American relations at that moment – the draft terms of reference for the fisheries arbitration had yet to be exchanged – demanded that Howard remain at Washington. After all, he was the key Embassy official in the co-ordination of this question. Hardinge did say that he would keep Howard's request in mind. Howard continued in his duties with decided vigour, and it is no coincidence that, once the initial exchange of the draft terms of reference occurred, he received encouraging news about a transfer from Hardinge.[3] At the end of August, William Tyrrell, Grey's private secretary, telegraphed Howard that he would soon be transferred to the Vienna Embassy as counsellor; Vienna, one of the four postings in the charmed circle of the European great Powers. Bryce confirmed this news after meeting with Grey and Hardinge at the Foreign Office prior to returning to the United States from his leave.[4] Howard therefore began preparations to move his family to Vienna in the latter part of 1908.

Before Howard had finalised his plans, a major crisis erupted in the Balkans when Austria-Hungary suddenly annexed the Turkish provinces of Bosnia and Herzegovina in October.[5] By great-Power agreement at the Congress of Berlin in 1878, Austria-Hungary had occupied these provinces, governing them in the sultan's name but, in reality, developing them as integral parts of the Dual Monarchy – this was the 'Bosnian solution' so favoured by Prince George for Greek control of Crete. In July 1908 the Balkan equilibrium had wobbled when a group of progressively minded and liberal army officers seized power at Constantinople and, whilst keeping the sultan on the throne, announced a programme to modernise and strengthen the Ottoman Empire. The 'Young Turk' rebellion threatened not only Austro-Hungarian control of Bosnia and Herzegovina, but also tsarist Russian ambitions to break through to the Straits. Thus Alexander Isvolsky, the Russian foreign minister, broached to his Austro-Hungarian counterpart, Baron Alois von Aehrenthal, a joint approach. At a friend's estate at Buchlau in September, the two men agreed that the Concert Powers should be canvassed to allow Austria-Hungary to annex Bosnia-Herzegovina whilst Russia secured a favourable change in the status of the Straits. The two states would provide mutual support in this endeavour. But whilst Isvolsky then toured the other Congress capitals to garner their support for an alteration in the Straits' regime in Russia's favour, Austria-Hungary unexpectedly annexed the two provinces, claiming Russian support. Aehrenthal had out-foxed Isvolsky, and the net result was chaos in the Balkans. Bulgaria announced immediately its full independence from the Porte. Crete proclaimed *enosis* with Greece. With its own designs on the two provinces, Slavic Serbia felt betrayed by its chief protector, Russia, whilst Italy, worried always about Austro-Hungarian power, looked askance at this obvious increase of territory by the Dual Monarchy.

Howard was affected immediately by the Bosnian crisis, a crisis that put Hungary at or near the centre of the Foreign Office's concerns in the winter of 1908–9.[6] As Bosnia and Herzegovina were contiguous with Hungary, Budapest might govern them as domains of the Magyar realm. The Foreign Office needed someone with proven diplomatic talents, as well as experience of the 'Eastern Question', to represent Britain at Budapest. Since he had yet to take up his post at the Vienna Embassy, Howard emerged as the obvious choice. In changing their plans for Howard, Grey and Hardinge seem to have had three considerations in mind.[7] First, the Hungarians were pursuing vigorous policies to enforce the 'magyarisation' of their subject peoples: Romanians, Ruthenians, Slovaks, and others. Such policies might now be pursued in Bosnia-Herzegovina, peopled mainly by ethnic Serbians. This led to the second consideration: the reaction of Serbia and its protector, Russia, to the fate of the Serbians in the two provinces. With Russian interest in Bosnia-Herzegovina, as well as Aehrenthal's brilliant diplomatic success scored at Isvolsky's expense, this area of the Balkans would be a focus of great-Power rivalry for the foreseeable future. Finally, a political struggle was under way within the Dual Monarchy between the Magyars and the Austrian 'Germans' over how much independence should be accorded the Hungarian army – lesser ones also existed over problems of joint finance and Austrian opposition to Magyar treatment of the subject Slavs. Coupled with the divisions it spawned between Budapest and Vienna, this would tell on how well the Dual Monarchy could function as a great Power. In aggregate, these considerations had a decided impact on British foreign policy.

On 1 January 1909, ensconced in a Budapest hotel until he could find accommodation for his family, Howard began a new period of his diplomatic career, one which thrust him full tilt into great-Power politics in Europe. For the next four and a half years, whilst serving at Budapest and then Berne, Howard confronted one aspect of the central problem which British diplomats faced prior to 1914: responding to the machinations of the 'German' Powers of the Triple Alliance. These were the final years of peace before the outbreak of the Great War, a war begun by Austro-Hungarian and Serbian quarrelling over events in Bosnia. Howard's image of an aggressive Wilhelmine Germany, formed when he served Malet at Berlin in the late 1880s, was confirmed by his experiences at Budapest and Berne. Howard worked hard to ensure that British influence and that of its two Entente partners, France and Russia, were not lessened in terms of the European balance of power by the policies of Germany or its client, Austria-Hungary.

II

In both Crete and the United States, Howard had had to conduct involved negotiations which cut into his routine diplomatic work. His two years at Budapest proved to be different. There, his principal task was to report on events in Hungary and on any external issues which, though treated prominently in Hungary, might not come to the attention of either the Vienna Embassy or the Foreign Office. Of course Howard also fulfilled regular diplomatic duties, for instance, making it easier for visiting British subjects who came to Budapest for business, personal, or other reasons.[8] But these were really secondary. Given the impact of the Bosnian crisis on the general situation in the Balkans, it was imperative that those who made British foreign policy had reasoned and realistic assessments of events in that vital region – which Howard had proved he could provide – in constructing their diplomatic initiatives.

For the first time in his service since 1903, however, Howard came up against superiors who, unlike Bryce, did not accept uncritically what he had to say about people and events within his bailiwick. Both Sir Fairfax Cartwright, the ambassador at Vienna, and Sir Eyre Crowe, the head of the Foreign Office Western Department, tended to disagree with his views. This developed because Howard came gradually to see the Hungarians in a favourable light. Such had not been his first impression. Setting foot in Budapest in January proved disheartening: 'The weather was grey, foggy, and cold. There was a slush of melting snow under foot. Big blocks of ice covered with dirty snow were floating down the river.'[9] He had come without his family, knew no one, and his predecessor at the consulate had already departed. Even the arrival of Isa and the children failed to lift his spirits, since almost at once the two oldest boys, Esme and Francis, contracted scarlet fever. 'It was an inauspicious beginning', he wrote, 'but all in the day's work of a diplomat's family. Still, perhaps it unconsciously prejudiced me against Budapest, and that prejudice took some months to wear off.'[10] The wearing off began with the coming of spring and his establishing social contacts with a range of Hungarians. Budapest now seemed 'far more cheerful and attractive', whilst the Hungarians were 'delightful', '[h]ospitable, full of life, if somewhat irresponsible, eager sportsmen and good riders, keen musicians, travellers, [and] excellent linguists, often well versed in the literature of other countries'.[11] Here were a people who shared a number of his cultural and intellectual ideals.

More than this, Howard came to sympathise with Hungarian sentiment on two crucial issues. On a trip to the Banat and Transylvania, he saw at first hand why Budapest enforced, 'somewhat drastically perhaps', the Magyar language on Hungarian subject peoples.[12] In this one region over half-a-dozen languages were spoken; if the Hungarians were to create a unified state, enforcing language laws was essential: 'where, one asked oneself, was the use of perpetuating for all time the babel of languages which obtained for instance in and around Temesvar, the capital of the Banat?' In Howard's view, it would be hypocrisy for a British diplomat to chide Hungarians about their language policies given the forced primacy of English throughout the British Empire, from polyglot India to Boer South Africa to French Canada. Secondly, he found Hungarians to have little love for Austrian 'Germans', something which mirrored his own increasing dislike.[13] The roots of Magyar anti-Germanism lay with the brutal suppression of Louis Kossuth's rebellion against the Habsburgs in 1849 and, despite the *ausgleich* of 1867 – or maybe because of it – this germanophobia had not abated. Sitting in Budapest, Howard came to see little difference between Austrian 'Germans' and their Wilhelmine cousins in the apparent desire of both to dominate. Although in retrospect he probably erred by lumping all Germans together, and he certainly downplayed the more rebarbative aspects of the Budapest government's 'magyarisation' policies which touched more than language, he saw a division between 'German' Vienna and 'Magyar' Budapest which could be exploited to British advantage.

Howard's sympathies were not shared by Cartwright and Crowe. Taking up his appointment only on 1 November 1908, Cartwright's previous service in Bavaria and Württemberg had suggested to him a lack of unity within the German world. In August 1908 he had outlined these ideas for Grey in the context of Austria-Hungary's position within the European balance.[14] The nub of his argument was that the Austrian 'Germans' could be persuaded by careful British diplomacy to rely less on Germany by devices like reducing Austro-Russian tensions in the Balkans or educating 'Austrian public men' that 'neither Liberal nor Conservative Governments in England have now any intention of opposing legitimate Austrian aspirations in the Near East'. The purpose of this diplomacy would be to erode Austria-Hungary's reliance on the Triple Alliance. Coming only days before Cartwright began his service as ambassador, the Bosnian crisis only accentuated the need for London to make every effort to improve Anglo-Austrian relations. Hence Cartwright tended to view 'German' Austria in a favourable light and those, like Howard, who saw things differently had to be chastised. As time progressed, Howard's relationship with Cartwright became subjected to decided strain because of this divergence of opinion.

By the time of Howard's transfer to Budapest, Crowe was the Foreign

Office expert on German affairs.[15] From his vantage point, Crowe reckoned that Germany was working to dominate both in Europe and the world by building up its military strength and alliances, constructing a potent fleet, and acquiring an overseas empire. He had adumbrated these views in an important memorandum dated 1 January 1907.[16] German goals to dominate in Europe and the world struck at the heart of British security and, particularly, the balance of power in Europe, and had to be resisted at all costs. Crowe's basic premise was that British ententes with France and Russia – when he wrote this memorandum, the Anglo-Russian entente seemed imminent – were crucial to maintaining the balance. Hence, Crowe did not want Germany reduced to 'the rank of a weak Power', since the 'German' threat would assuredly be replaced by 'a Franco-Russian predominance equally, if not more, formidable to the British Empire'. In this equation Austria-Hungary played a fundamental role. The Franco-Russian alliance balanced the Austro-German one and, as a result, Crowe found it impossible to differentiate diplomatically between Austrian 'Germans' and Magyars. They were locked in a symbiotic political and economic relationship which could not be altered without the *ausgleich* collapsing.[17] More than this, the Dual Monarchy's existence relied upon close diplomatic ties with Wilhelmine Germany. Just as it was impossible to split the Hungarians from the Austrian 'Germans', it was impossible to split the Dual Monarchy from Germany. In addition, Crowe possessed anti-Magyar sentiments because of Budapest's inflexible policies towards its subject nationalities, sentiments which intensified in the final decade of peace.[18] Thus Crowe's view of Austria-Hungary, internally and in the context of the European balance, differed from those held by Cartwright at Vienna and Howard at Budapest. But, while Howard's views on Hungary led to strained relations with Cartwright, Esme did not suffer an estrangement from Crowe. This derived from Howard and Crowe each being more cerebral in their conduct of British diplomacy than was the over-emotional ambassador.[19]

Prior to arriving at Budapest, Howard spent a few days at Vienna to meet with Cartwright and Theo Russell, the new counsellor of the Embassy. This was essential since Howard had never met the ambassador and, as the Consulate-General at Budapest was technically an adjunct of the Vienna Embassy, he reported to Cartwright. Given the ambassador's self-appointed mission to mitigate Anglo-Austrian differences, Howard discovered that he would have little supervision in performing his duties: 'I gathered from Cartwright that he was not deeply interested in Hungarian affairs, and that I was not expected to make reports on matters outside the borders of the Magyar Kingdom, unless something unusually important came to my knowledge.'[20] Howard would be 'semi-independent', a factor which seems to have reconciled him to his transfer to Budapest.[21]

However, with the charged atmosphere created by the Bosnian crisis, Howard's semi-independence proved impossible to achieve, at least for his first few months at Budapest. The Hungarian reaction to the great Powers' efforts to resolve the crisis peacefully had to be weighed carefully in carrying out British policy; this necessitated close co-operation between the Consulate-General and the Embassy. The British predicament stemmed from the Anglo-Russian entente. To save face, Isvolsky now supported Serbian claims, because of the obvious change in the Balkan status quo, for territorial compensation. This put Grey in a difficult position but, to maintain good relations with Russia, he was willing to voice support for Isvolsky.[22] Here was the rub. Flushed by his success and certain of German support, Aehrenthal refused to compensate Serbia with Austro-Hungarian land; on the other hand, no one would countenance any further territorial sacrifices by the Ottomans. By January 1909 the two alliance coalitions were at loggerheads over whether Serbia should gain by Aehrenthal's coup. War seemed a possibility.

On arriving at Budapest, Howard stepped into the middle of a violent anti-British press campaign mounted by three prominent 'German Hungarian' newspapers, *Pesther Lloyd*, *Neues Pesther Journal*, and *Budapesther Tageblatt*. This campaign had at its base Britain's apparent support for Serbian territorial ambitions. According to these important press organs, Britain, with 'the Teutophobe spirit now rampant' and 'no very material interests' in the region, sought to make the Dual Monarchy pay for being Germany's ally.[23] Although a distinction was made between the British government and traditionally anti-Magyar newspapers like *The Times*, 'the British Govt. is accused of hypocrisy because while it continued to speak fair & moderately it did not gag "its" press'. For Howard, the lesson in this could not be missed: if Britain desired good Anglo-Hungarian relations, circumspection in its Balkan policy was necessary. 'The long & short of all this', he observed, 'seems to be that openly expressed sympathy with Servia or southern Slav aspirations is not compatible with Hungarian friendship, for Hungary is as bitterly hostile as Austria to the erection of any powerful Slav state on its southern borders, believing that such a State would menace her very existence.'

Despite being at Budapest a short time, Howard showed shrewd analytical judgement in these views. Supporting Isvolsky might entail paying the highest price possible in the event of an Austro-Serbian war. Howard drove this home to Cartwright in the middle of February, when such a war seemed imminent: the Dual Monarchy had 110,000 troops on its border with Serbia – twice the normal number – something costing the

Hungarian exchequer an extra ten million kronen a month.[24] Although Howard's reports were not the only factor influencing Grey and the Foreign Office in this crisis,[25] they added to sentiment within the British government that nothing stood to be gained by underwriting Serbian ambitions. Consequently, although mouthing sympathy for Serbia's plight, Grey distanced himself from Isvolsky throughout February and March – the French did the same. The British position was saved when, on 22 March, Germany showed its unequivocal support for the Dual Monarchy by issuing an ultimatum to Russia and Serbia to recognise the annexation of the two provinces or face the consequences, presumably war.[26] Isvolsky capitulated; his country lacked the military strength and the diplomatic support of its allies to back its Serbian client. Thus, whilst the Triple Entente had been forced to bow to Austro-German pressure, it had not been broken, and Britain had avoided going to war over a squabble in the Balkans.

Howard took the opportunity presented by the end of the crisis to inform the Foreign Office privately of Hungarian feelings towards Britain and British policy and what this portended for the balance of power in southern and central Europe.[27] It made unhappy reading. Hungarians had traditionally been pro-British because Britain had granted sanctuary to Louis Kossuth after the failure of his revolution in 1849, but this credit was now exhausted. This only benefited Germany because:

> it is only too clear that the intense hatred of everything Slav which is the dominant note at present of the Hungarian mind in matters of foreign politics, has roused an extraordinary feeling against England on account of her supposed support of the Slav races and of her entente with Russia. On the other hand Germany is looked on by all classes as their one salvation from the Slav peril...

The 'German Hungarian' press attacks on Britain, apparently funded clandestinely by the foreign offices at Vienna and Berlin, had been unrelenting. This could only be expected. But unexpected, flowing from the obvious germanophobia of Hungarians, was public praise by Hungarian politicians for the Dual Monarchy's diplomatic connexion with Germany. 'I was told, and I well believe it', Howard informed Hardinge, 'that the demonstration in the House of Deputies when Wekerle [the Hungarian premier] spoke of the German Alliance as having struck roots in the heart of the Hungarian Nation, was something astonishing in warmth and enthusiasm.' The Foreign Office had to recognise that Hungary, 'as a factor in Balkan politics', now stood as a staunch German ally. British policy had to be developed and pursued accordingly.

Howard penned this pessimistic assessment after just three months at his new post, a time of extreme diplomatic tension suffused by the threat of war. It also coincided with that difficult time in his family life when he, Isa, and the children had to adjust to living at 'grey, foggy, and cold' Budapest. But the advent of warmer weather, a healthier family, and a better understanding of Hungarian domestic affairs led him to modify the view that Hungary would support its 'German' allies, both in Austria and Germany, come what may. This change came about through his assigned task of reporting on Hungarian politics and making contacts at Budapest; this showed Howard the weakness of Austria-Hungary caused by the volatility of Magyar nationalism.

Howard found much of his time throughout 1909 and early 1910 devoted to assessing a seemingly insoluble ministerial crisis within the Hungarian government. This crisis requires closer examination, for its twists and turns illustrate the insightful way in which Howard interpreted domestic Hungarian politics and their impact upon the strength of the Austro-Hungarian state and its foreign policy. A three-party coalition constituted the Hungarian government: the Independence Party, the Constitutional Party, and the Catholic People's Party.[28] Although this coalition possessed an overwhelming majority in the House of Deputies – 363 to 46 – Howard realised almost as soon as he arrived that its size presented 'a source of weakness'.[29] This stemmed from a division between the Independents and their partners over Hungary's position within the Dual Monarchy. Led by Francis Kossuth, the son of the revolutionary leader of 1848, and Julius de Justh, an ardent nationalist, the Independence Party sought complete autonomy for their state, the only connexion with Austria being the emperor-king, Francis Joseph. The Constitutionals, headed by Wekerle, and the People's Party supported the *ausgleich* because of the additional strength this gave Hungary internally and externally, a stance which meant accepting joint Austro-Hungarian control of foreign, financial, and military policy. In the coalition, however, the strengths of the two major parties had not been translated into Cabinet seats: with just 70 deputies, the Constitutionals had four posts including the premiership; the Independents, with 270 deputies, had just three appointments. This was the work of Francis Joseph, who, under the *ausgleich*, could appoint his ministers. He had appointed this ministry in 1906 following a bitter dispute over electoral reform; the coalition was to govern provisionally until it could arrange a new election law extending the suffrage, a law that it was anticipated would permit more non-Magyars to participate in the political process, thereby lessening internal tensions. The coalition still chugged along in early 1909, and issues which had simmered for nearly three years were boiling to the surface: electoral reform; the establishment of a state bank for Hungary, and the use of the Magyar language, as well as Hungarian flags and coats of arms, by Hungarian regiments in the army.

When he sent his assessment of Hungary's position within the German alliance to Hardinge in late March, Howard had been pessimistic about the closeness of Hungary to its 'German' neighbours. The ministerial crisis led him to be more optimistic. In April, the coalition collapsed through the failure of Hungarian attempts to alter the joint banking system of the monarchy, a failure prompted by Austrian refusal to concede to Hungarian demands. Howard immediately informed Cartwright that Magyar newspapers, notably those sympathetic to the Independence Party, had erupted into a blind rage, blaming official and banking circles at Vienna, because of their apparent worry about Russian support for pan-Slavism within the Dual Monarchy, for the failure.[30] To mitigate Slavic unrest, Magyar interests were being sacrificed. Suggestions surfaced about the necessity for Hungarians to consider seeking friends elsewhere to protect 'their national aspirations and language and historical mission'. Though sensing that this bluster was designed to pressure the Austrians into making concessions to Budapest, Howard implied that perhaps Hungary was not as close to 'German' Austria as he had earlier surmised. A public statement by Kossuth – 'The influence of those circles in Austria which have never been sympathetic to Hungary, appears to be stronger to-day than ever...We have now been entirely disillusioned' – suggested this.

Howard found over the next year, as the political crisis dragged on, that the inherent distaste of Magyar nationalists for the strictures placed on Hungary by the *ausgleich* overshadowed any desire for a much-needed external perception that the Dual Monarchy functioned as a strong, unified state in European affairs. Clearly, Francis Joseph and pro-*ausgleich* elements in Hungary were working hard throughout 1909 and into 1910 to ensure that when new elections were held the electoral support of the Independence Party would be markedly reduced.[31] This created angry reactions from the Independence Party, especially when the House of Deputies was dissolved in March 1910 over the opposition of the majority of deputies.[32] The subsequent electoral success in June of Francis Joseph's hand-picked candidate, Count Khuen-Hedevary, a result of political manoeuvring by the Court in Vienna in league with pro-Austrian politicians in Hungary which saw a decided reduction in Independent deputies, only made divisions worse. Even moderate Magyar opinion, Howard found, could not be relied upon to give unconditional support to the pro-*ausgleich* government now in place. Howard dutifully recorded the reaction of a prominent Magyar newspaper:

Times have changed and it is useless to disguise the fact that Hungary cannot any longer work hand in glove with Austria. Hungary cannot altogether give up the fight against Austria for the emancipation of her commercial interests and the establishment of her constitutional rights.[33]

By the end of his first year at Budapest, Howard had come round to the idea that a British advantage might accrue from treating Hungary with some deference. This constituted a more sophisticated view of the Dual Monarchy than that held by Cartwright – a result of Howard's analysis of the 1910 crisis – and the policy line it suggested was that exploiting the German–Magyar split in Austria-Hungary might make the Dual Monarchy a less valuable alliance partner to Germany. The Entente could benefit from playing on the racial balance in Austria-Hungary, a relationship that remained volatile and, hence, more easily exploited than that of kindred Austrian 'Germans' with their cousins in the Wilhelmine Empire. A chance to build a small bridge between Britain and Hungary arose in late 1909 when the Hungarians complained about reference in official British documents to the 'Austro-Hungarian Empire'.[34] Howard supported conceding to Budapest on this minor point, since 'Hungarians believe that it is misleading and causes people to think that they are the subjects of the Austrian Emperor instead of being subjects only of the King of Hungary... they have been struggling for almost four centuries against the idea of "Gross Oesterreich"'. After some grumbling by Crowe – 'I am all in favour of humouring absurd people, so far as we can, and I have asked Law [the head of the Foreign Office Commercial Department] to get the objectionable words altered' – efforts were made to respect Hungarian sensitivities on this issue. It did not cost the Foreign Office anything to do so.

But on larger issues, Howard found his superiors at London intractable. During 1910 the Hungarian government sought a substantial loan in, first, Paris and, then, London for railway construction and redeeming Treasury Bills about to come due. Howard accepted the reasons given for the loan, but the suspicious Crowe did not, arguing there was 'more behind these loan negotiations than appears in [Howard's] despatch'.[35] However, when the Hungarian negotiations with French financiers failed because of pressure from the French government, a syndicate of London banks was prepared to underwrite the loan provided the Foreign Office had 'no objection'.[36] Crowe immediately lobbied Hardinge and Grey to 'prevent the transaction', pointing out that the French government blocked the floating of the loan at Paris because 'the money is practically certain to be used for improving the armament of the triple alliance (building dreadnoughts, etc.)'.[37] In this, French industry would not profit. Hence, protecting unity amongst the Entente Powers stood as a more important diplomatic consideration than any Hungarian goodwill that might emerge from underwriting the loan on the London money market.[38] Under pressure from Grey, the London syndicate abandoned the project,[39] forcing the Hungarian government to seek monies from the Rothschild banking interests in Vienna and Berlin at higher interest than it would have had in either Paris or London. Whilst accepting this as the harsh reality of power politics, Howard put on record his view that 'an impartial observer may be pardoned for considering it one more link in the chain which binds the Dual Monarchy *nolens volens* ever tighter to Germany, a link, moreover, for which Hungary has to pay somewhat dear'.[40] The Foreign Office's decision grated on him as the man on the spot; an opportunity to weaken the Triple Alliance had been lost. However, nothing would be accomplished by pursuing the matter, so Howard let it drop; he was learning the valuable lesson that those at London, aware of the whole diplomatic picture in Europe, knew best.

To learn as much as he could about domestic Hungarian affairs, Howard used similar methods to those he had employed so efficaciously at Washington to gain entry into the upper levels of Budapest life. 'I am trying', he wrote a few months after arriving, 'rather to get into the world of journalists, politicians, & professors than into that of sport & society but cannot tell yet all what sort of advantage one will get from them.'[41] The advantage he got was a realisation that those who influenced, made, and executed Hungarian foreign policies were not a homogeneous group of men with a common outlook. By May 1909 Howard had met most of the important politicians, including Wekerle, his principal lieutenant, Count Julius Andrassy, Count Albert Apponyi, the architect of the Magyar language laws, and Kossuth.[42] Individually, they were genteel and able. Collectively, however, their differing points of view and the passion with which they practised politics suggested that the Habsburg Empire lacked the cohesion a great Power needed to pursue effective foreign policy. As a result of the ministerial crisis, Howard discerned three 'currents of opinion' within Hungary.[43] The first he characterised as the 'imaginative', that which revolved around ideals, 'the independence of the country and...the maintenance of its individuality at all costs, even at the risk of losing a certain quantum of material prosperity'. The second he labelled the 'economic'; this current deprecated 'the catchwords of the imaginative', pursuing instead 'the material advantages of the Austrian connection so highly that it sometimes loses sight of non-material objects altogether'. Between these two extremes ranged a third current which he could not label though it 'highly prizes national independence, but is inclined to think that the compromise of 1867 safeguards that independence from all Austrian encroachments'. In general the 'imaginative' men represented agrarian interests, whilst the 'economic' ones were urban and drawn from 'the industrial, commercial, and professional classes'.

This view of Hungary, established through Howard's political contacts and by observing their twists and turns in policy, did not alter much throughout his stay in Budapest.[44] These assessments found a receptive audience at the Foreign Office. Crowe lauded Howard's analysis as 'a clear account of a very complicated situation, and will repay careful reading'; Grey not only praised Howard's assessment in a minute, but sent thanks for his 'most useful' reporting.[45] But where Howard tended to the idea that this inherent division might be exploited by Britain, the Foreign Office saw little to be gained by such a tack. For instance, in December 1909 Howard was approached by Leo Lanczy, a financier, the president of the Hungarian Chamber of Commerce, and a member of the House of Magnates. Anxious to encourage foreign investment, Lanczy informed Howard that any British textile manufacturers prepared either to run such concerns themselves or, at the least, employ Hungarian managers trained in Britain would meet 'with every encouragement'. Lanczy also indicated that it would not be difficult to get Hungarian partners and capital involved in such ventures. His only proviso involved a demand that the British government avoid encouraging 'faiseurs – people who wanted to float companies & then get out of the business as soon as they had made something of it'. Anxious to diversify and improve the Hungarian economy, the 'economic' men were willing to encourage British investment to do so. Howard informed the Foreign Office immediately.[46] His report was shunted off to the Board of Trade, and there, because the Foreign Office does not seem to have pushed,[47] the matter died. Unlike the Hungarian government loan sought in Paris and London, this venture did not touch Entente unity. But the result was the same. Howard's idea of using British economic strength to loosen the ties between Hungary and the Triple Alliance 'Germans' had been lost because of official unwillingness at London.

Other contacts Howard made indicated that the Dual Monarchy's ties to the German alliance were not favoured by a range of important Hungarians, including those who were members of the 'Hungarian-German' community. For instance, in his early days at Budapest, Howard met Dr Ferdinand Leipnik, an academic and the foreign editor of the *Pesther Lloyd*. Friendship with this man provided Howard with decided insight, as Leipnik not only wrote for the most prominent 'Hungarian-German' newspaper but had firm links with official circles in Vienna and Berlin. Howard did not fall in with Leipnik simply to pump him for information; such calculating callousness was alien to Howard's character. Rather, the two men found that they shared a range of cultural and artistic interests and, from this, formed a close friendship that lasted till Leipnik's death thirty years later.[48] But whilst at Budapest, Howard found Leipnik's knowledge of central-European and Balkan affairs to be so insightful that he drew often upon it and with some success commended the Foreign Office to do the same.[49]

A good example of how valuable Howard found Leipnik's views occurred in May 1910. At that time, Howard met with Leipnik, who had just returned from Berlin.[50] As a member of the Albert Association, a group promoting cordiality between Britain and Germany, Leipnik had been canvassed by the Association to publish a paper on Anglo-German relations. Accordingly, he travelled to Berlin to learn at first hand from prominent Germans their ideas on this subject. Leipnik returned disheartened. He had interviewed amongst others Otto Hammann, the head of the Wilhelmstrasse Press Bureau, and Walter Rathenau, a leading industrialist and friend of Emperor William, Hammann disclosed that Germany was about to launch a major diplomatic offensive in Persia to acquire railway concessions. This meant that the Germans were prepared to sacrifice good Anglo-German relations, as well as take the serious risks involved in running up against both the British and the Russians who, by the entente of 1907, had buried their differences in Persia. Leipnik also learnt of a Wilhelmstrasse plot to have the French consul-general at Budapest, de Fontenay, recalled because he appeared 'somewhat aggressively anti-German in his talk'. This would affect German relations with the Entente; so, despairing, Leipnik decided not to write his piece. His conversation with Rathenau proved to be equally disquieting. In enquiring if Rathenau and other industrialists found burdensome the heavy taxation necessary for producing armaments, Leipnik received an emphatic 'no'. In the first place these massive expenditures occurred within Germany, thereby helping the economy. But more important, Rathenau observed:

Germany must have not only the strongest army for defence, but also one of the strongest navies to be able to dictate her terms to the world at large & obtain the concessions and advantages her expanding commerce required. Therefore industrial and commercial circles recognized the advantage of spending money on a big fleet, while the agrarian vote was always to be had for a little extra protection to some agricultural product.

Such implicitly anti-British views only confirmed to Leipnik the wisdom of refusing to write the proposed article. The whole affair suggested to Howard that some prominent Hungarians, even those with close links to Germany, did not support the goals of German foreign policy.

Howard realised that men like Leipnik, despite their positions of influence, did not constitute any sort of majority within the Hungarian ruling elite. In addition, their opposition to the Germans did not necessarily mean that they would seek to undermine the Triple Alliance if it went to war. However, the contacts Howard made suggested that there were divisions within the Dual Monarchy that sapped its ability to influence European affairs. In assessing Hungary after the Bosnian crisis had lost its immediacy, Howard had written that 'the Austrian Empire in a few years at the rate we are going will be little more than a polite fiction, one of the conventional lies of our civilization, which will stand just as long as Prussian bayonets will that it should'.[51] More than a year later, his pessimistic view remained unchanged. In commenting on Leipnik's Berlin conversations, Howard observed: 'This little incident makes me realize to what extent Hungary is but the province of a province. For it is in reality but a province of Austria & Austria – for all Aehrenthal's talk about independent policy etc – is since last year more than ever – at least so it appears to me – a province of Germany.'[52]

Howard's despondent view of Austria-Hungary accorded with the prevailing view in the Foreign Office, as espoused by Crowe and those like him. But it ran counter to the strong pro-Austrian views of Cartwright, who, by the middle of 1910, became extremely critical of Howard's interpretations of affairs within the Dual Monarchy. In the first months of their professional relationship, Howard and the ambassador got on rather well. This can be seen in the ready co-ordination between the Consulate-General at Budapest and the Vienna Embassy during the final tense months of the Bosnian crisis. When Howard arrived at Budapest, he discovered that his staff comprised two German-Hungarian clerks. This meant the security of his despatches could not be guaranteed; as he told Hardinge: 'I dare not lay stress on these little things in my Despatches because with my German type-writer everything I write is as good as reported at once.'[53] Accordingly, until he received permission to hire a more reliable secretary, F. Chambers, an Englishman living at the Hungarian capital who had worked for a commercial firm there, as well as have a regular diplomatic bag for all correspondence,[54] he arranged to send Cartwright confidential private letters in a numbered series. The arrangement worked well in that the Embassy received full and regular assessments of Hungarian affairs, especially about the anti-British press campaign, which helped Cartwright in his political dealings with the emperor and his advisers at Vienna. Initially, therefore, little discord existed between Howard and Cartwright.[55]

But Howard's growing sympathy for the Hungarian predicament, notably the recognition that the language laws were indispensable if the Magyars were to create a strong and cohesive state, seems to have created distance between the consul-general and the ambassador. Whilst

Cartwright could see that Austrian policies were not without fault, a function of the Austrian government having 'its hands tied by constitutional forms', he apportioned most of the blame for difficulties within the Dual Monarchy on the 'extremely troublesome' Hungarians.[56] By 1910, at least from the lack of any sort of private correspondence in the available archives, Howard and Cartwright ceased to have much to do with each other. In fact, by this time, Howard's principal correspondent at the Vienna Embassy seems to have been Theo Russell.

Howard's differences with Cartwright boiled to the surface in the summer of 1910 over the consul-general's assessments of newspaper articles on Hungarian affairs written by two British subjects: Robert Seton-Watson, a slavophile author, and Henry Wickham-Steed, *The Times* correspondent at Vienna. Seton-Watson had travelled to the Slovakian provinces of Hungary during the final days of the 1910 election campaign and, on returning to Vienna, published articles in a couple of newspapers in that city which charged Hungarian authorities with electoral corruption.[57] His vivid description of local police preventing Slovakian voters from casting their ballots, thereby ensuring the election of the Magyar candidate, led to blistering attacks on his veracity by the Budapest press. At the same time Wickham-Steed sent equally damning reports to *The Times*, which when published[58] roused anti-Magyar feelings in Britain, especially in the Foreign Office, and created an anglophobic reaction in the Hungarian press. When Howard wrote to Grey to suggest that the anti-Habsburg, anti-Magyar sentiments of Seton-Watson and Wickham-Steed should be discounted within the Foreign Office, Crowe rose to the defence of the two British writers. He suggested that Howard 'has been unconsciously influenced by the feelings entertained for Mr Steed at the Vienna Embassy'.[59] With his pronounced animus for the Dual Monarchy, Crowe also minuted: 'Mr Howard cannot make us forget that the Austrian and Hungarian records in the matters of corrupt administration and police brutalities are of the very darkest.'

As far as the Foreign Office was concerned, the matter ended at this point. Howard had given his views, and his superiors were unwilling to accept them. Conditioned by an anti-Germanism, which touched even this multi-racial German ally, these men had a perception of the Dual Monarchy perhaps expressed best by Walter Langley, an assistant under-secretary, who noted, when Howard's despatch crossed his desk: 'It is of no great importance to us whether Mr Seton-Watson's accounts are accurate or not. No one appears to have any doubt that the election was most corrupt.'[60] However Cartwright, anxious always to improve Vienna's image in London, involved himself in the matter by sending the Foreign Office a stinging criticism of Howard, who, in other despatches, had sided with Wickham-Steed in stressing that the anglophobic press reaction within Austria-Hungary on this matter originated with Aehrenthal's ministry. Cartwright argued that the blame really lay with Magyar nationalists in Budapest and, since Leipnik was now known as Howard's chief contact there, singled out the *Pesther Lloyd* for special condemnation. 'It should be remembered', prattled Cartwright, 'that the "Pesther Lloyd" is run by German Jews, but in internal Hungarian affairs it defends Magyar supremacy.'[61] But Cartwright went further than this, and, with comments like 'Howard unfortunately does not give us the full text of the article', 'Howard is entirely in error', and Howard writes 'interlarding his summary with what seem to me to be rather superfluous remarks', undertook to discredit his consul-general at Budapest.

With his own stock declining in the Foreign Office because of inaccurate information sent to London and the apparent social failure of the Embassy,[62] Cartwright's views found little support in London. 'The comments of Sir F. Cartwright on Mr Howard's despatches do not seem to be just', minuted Crowe, and in this Crowe was supported by Langley, Hardinge, and Grey.[63] But this mattered little for good relations between Howard and his superior at Vienna. Whilst the Foreign Office might continue to have every confidence in Howard and his analytical abilities, even though it did not always agree with him, Cartwright did not. By the end of the summer of 1910 Howard saw his position to be untenable; thus, in the autumn, he enquired discreetly of his friend, Tyrrell, about a transfer.[64] The chance for a move came early in 1911 with a sudden vacancy at the Legation in Berne. The Foreign Office probably saw this as a chance to separate Howard and Cartwright, thus preventing any weakening of Britain's representation in Austria-Hungary. Being the junior diplomat, Howard was obviously easier to transfer than an ambassador who had been at his post less than three years. In addition, as his family had grown again, with the birth of his fourth son, Edmund, the increase in salary that came with heading the Berne Legation would be helpful. Howard seized this opportunity and, on 1 February 1911, began his duties as British minister to the Swiss Confederacy.

In this way Howard left Budapest after two years of demanding work. He had represented his country's interests successfully, especially during the final stages of the Bosnian crisis. His time in Hungary had made him, if not supportive of Hungarian domestic policies toward subject nationalities, at least appreciative of why they had to be imposed. He also left with a deeper understanding of the inherent weakness of the Dual Monarchy, the result of the antipathy between Austrian 'Germans' and Hungarian 'Magyars'. This suggested to Howard a diplomatic advantage for Britain if exploited properly. That such division, if it existed, remained unexploited was not

Howard's fault. Neither the Hungarian search for a loan on the London money market nor the desire by commercial circles in Hungary to attract British investment had found support in the Foreign Office. Hardinge, Crowe, and others were more concerned with the general diplomatic balance in Europe, one which for them by 1909–10 divided sharply into two competing spheres, the Entente and the Central Powers. There existed no Entente advantage in helping a part of the Central Powers, especially a weak part, strengthen itself. It was Howard's job as a diplomat to report on what he saw and, when necessary, make recommendations for policy. If his superiors chose not to act on his suggestions, he could only continue in his assigned duties. As an experienced member of the Diplomatic Service, this is what he did. He had also gained a valuable, if perhaps unpleasant, lesson about the problems resulting from having a superior, in this case, Cartwright, who did not agree with or even respect his views. Later in his career, in dealing with junior members of his staff, Howard worked to avoid the needless disputes within his embassies which served only to weaken Britain's diplomatic representation.

Beyond this, as a result of his own observations and through contact with men like Leipnik, Howard's long-held suspicions of Germany were confirmed. German policy during the Bosnian crisis showed this with clarity, the ultimatum to Russia and Serbia a blunt indication of the limits to which Berlin would go to ensure the humbling of its continental rivals and the corresponding increase in the strength of its alliance coalition. Leipnik's report of those discussions with Hammann, Rathenau, and the rest, a good cross-section of the German foreign-policy-making elite, served only to underscore further Howard's belief about German desires to dominate in Europe. But Leipnik's words had a more ominous twist; little doubt now existed that in the wider world, Britain and its Empire faced danger from an aggressive Germany intent on building a high-seas fleet to force British acquiescence to German overseas expansion. It was this impression of a dangerous Germany which Howard carried away from Budapest above all else, and it was this that coloured heavily his diplomatic work in the few years of peace left before the conflagration of the Great War.

III

During the little more than two years Howard spent at Berne, nothing arose to create discord in Anglo-Swiss relations. As Howard observed in his annual report for 1912: 'The relations between Great Britain and Switzerland have continued as heretofore to be excellent.'[65] But what remained true of Switzerland's relations with Britain did not hold for those with its four contiguous neighbours: Austria-Hungary, France, Germany, and Italy. The Swiss found themselves in the unenviable position of being geographically at the centre of great-Power politics in western Europe. Switzerland's neutrality had been a constant in European diplomacy for more than three centuries and, in the period after 1894 when the continent began to divide into two mutually hostile alliance coalitions, Swiss leaders worked to ensure that their country remained outside the swirl of power politics which increasingly threatened the sub-continent with war. Two additional factors compounded this situation. First, Switzerland was a multi-cultural, multi-lingual state whose population comprised three main ethnic groups: French, German, and Italian. Especially in the case of the former two, the press organs of each group tended to support the foreign policies of their respective mother countries, a situation that put pressure on political leaders at Berne. Secondly, Italo-Swiss relations were chilly at the best of times, something which from the perspective of the Swiss derived from Italian irredentist ambitions in southern Switzerland. From this it follows that Howard's tenure at the Berne Legation involved reporting on affairs in Switzerland, which, because of the country's geographic position, could affect the balance of power in Europe. The Foreign Office had to be kept fully apprised of Switzerland's relations with its neighbours because, should some change occur in Swiss political or military orientation, British policy would have to be modified accordingly.

At the moment of Howard's transfer, some officials in the British government entertained the belief that German military planning for the next war involved a co-ordinated assault on France across the Franco-German border with two concurrent pincer attacks, one through Belgium in the north and the other through Switzerland in the south. This view had been advanced by the British military attaché at Rome, Colonel Charles Delmé-Radcliffe, whose responsibilities included Switzerland.[66] Delmé-Radcliffe based this supposition on the recent construction of German rail lines to northern Switzerland that, taken with existing Swiss track which carried on to the French border, suggested the possibility of a rapid deployment of German troops through Switzerland into south-central France. Apparently a gifted student of military strategy, Crowe supported this view because he saw no other reason for the construction of these new rail lines.[67] He also contended that this German military strategy meshed with a diplomatic one designed to isolate France politically – the 1911 Moroccan crisis was in the offing;[68] once isolated, France would suffer 'a gigantic concentric attack' and be knocked out within ten days. The balance of power would be overthrown in Germany's favour. 'The matter seems to be one of very serious importance', Crowe wrote alarmingly. 'It concerns in some way the position of Great Britain.'

Howard's first task at Berne involved determining if Delmé-Radcliffe's notions had substance. The key to any German use of Switzerland as a staging base for a major operation against France had to be official Swiss sanction. Swiss neutrality could not be compromised unless the Berne government consented, this because the passes and tunnels through the Alps from Germany to Switzerland and from Switzerland to France remained firmly under the Swiss Army's control. For Delmé-Radcliffe's thesis to be true, a Swiss–German agreement would have to exist to permit the passage of German troops through Switzerland. By the middle of April 1911, after an exhaustive enquiry, Howard concluded that the Swiss were determined to protect their neutrality against any violation by any of their neighbours. He worked with the French minister, Count d'Aunay, on this. On 13 April Howard reported a conversation which d'Aunay, as the senior Entente diplomat at Berne, had had with the Swiss president, Ruchet.[69] Ruchet emphasised in the strongest terms that no secret Swiss–German agreement existed, that his country would defend its neutrality at all costs, and that the Swiss people would support its government without equivocation. Over the next several months, information from a variety of sources confirmed Howard's enquiry. Alwyn Parker, a member of the Foreign Office Western Department, had met with 'a very rising officer' attached to the War Office who believed that the main German attack on France would come through Belgium, a view supported by Grey and Arthur Nicolson, Hardinge's recent successor as permanent under-secretary.[70] Later reports from the Embassy in Paris suggested that if Franco-German war broke out, Switzerland if anything would adopt a pro-French position.[71] By this time Parker had consulted with the director of military operations at the War Office, a conversation that disclosed the surmise of British military circles that the new German rail lines were 'merely a feint' designed to divert French troops to the south and away from the anticipated German attack in the north.[72]

Throughout 1911, despite the hollowness of Delmé-Radcliffe's assertions, Howard found himself assessing the implications of a round of press comment in Switzerland, Germany and Italy about whether Swiss interests demanded closer ties with Germany. The matter began with the publication of an article by a German-Swiss scholar, Professor Scollenberger of Zurich University, asserting that Germany was Switzerland's natural ally should the country be threatened by either France or Italy; implicit in this was the suggestion that France and Italy threatened Swiss security.[73] The press debate created by this article provided Howard and, through him, the Foreign Office with a decided appreciation of the intractability of Swiss leaders about the policy of neutrality and, more important, Italy's unreliability as a member of the Triple Alliance. Not surprisingly, French-Swiss newspapers embarked on a derisive condemnation of talk about close Swiss–German relations. But despite one of the more important German-Swiss-language newspapers, the *Züricher Post*, ridiculing any idea of formal Swiss ties with Germany, Howard found it significant that the original article had appeared simultaneously in both German-Swiss and German newspapers. Although unstated in his despatch, Howard saw in the articles a campaign orchestrated by the Press Bureau of the German Foreign Office designed to divert French attention and tie up needlessly French military resources in a region that would be untouched by a German attack.

More important, Howard reported the reaction of military and nationalist elements in Italy to Scollenberger's article. Scollenberger had noted that Italy had never recognised the validity of the Treaty of Vienna of 1815 by which, amongst other things, the great Powers recognised Swiss borders. He then made the telling remark that 'Switzerland would therefore be free to attack Italy if she thought good'. A senior Italian officer, General Perrucchetti, reacted to this in the authoritative Milan newspaper, the *Corriere della Sera*, with an article that had at its heart the argument that 'neither the government nor any section of the public in Italy have ever entertained designs of any kind against Switzerland'.[74] Perrucchetti then suggested that a secret Swiss military agreement existed with Germany and Austria-Hungary permitting troops of those two Powers to pass through Switzerland for operations against Italy. Clearly the Italians feared for their security in the northern Alpine region, one contiguous with both Switzerland and the Dual Monarchy, a perception encouraged by the Swiss construction of fortifications in the mountain regions separating the two countries. The Swiss could use these positions as bases for a co-ordinated assault on northern Italy.

Howard watched as this domestic and external press speculation forced Ruchet to assert publicly what he had told d'Aunay privately: no secret convention existed between Switzerland and either Germany or Austria-Hungary. In meeting with Ruchet after he issued this statement, Howard learnt that the president had seen the Italian minister at Berne and that the latter had left 'convinced of the complete lack of foundation of these rumours and treated them with ridicule'. Although concern within northern Italy continued over the possibility of a Swiss threat – another major article appeared in the *Corriere della Sera* in September suggesting the existence of an 'aggressive attitude of Switzerland towards Italy'[75] – Howard and the Foreign Office recognised that the Swiss were completely neutral, that they could and would defend that neutrality themselves, and that the Italians entertained deep suspicions about their two Germanic partners in the Triple Alliance.

Howard found himself concerned increasingly with assessing Switzerland's strained relationship with Italy, despite the fact that the idea of a Swiss alliance with the two German Powers became daily more chimerical. This was largely due to the political situation in Europe. Part of the reason for Italian worries in 1911 and, later, 1912 about Swiss intentions came from Italy's involvement in a war with Turkey. The Italians fretted that whilst they fought this war – it focussed in North Africa and led in 1912 to the Italian annexation of Libya – the Swiss might exploit the situation by launching at attack on northern Italy. Of course the Swiss had no intention of attacking Italy; Italian suspicions about other Powers stabbing Italy in the back was a result of judging others by Italian standards. However, Italian success against the Turks altered dramatically the German-Swiss perception of their southern neighbour. 'The economic, industrial and, be it said, military awakening of Italy', Howard suggested to Grey, 'has come like a sudden shock to the slow-thinking German people who still dreamt of nothing but oranges and palms and moonlight and mandolines.'[76] Along with Delmé-Radcliffe's assertions about Swiss desires to absorb Italian territories on Switzerland's southern frontiers,[77] these developments at the nexus of the two great-Power alliance coalitions portended much for the balance of power in western Europe and, therefore, for British foreign policy.

In watching these events unfold, Howard observed the correctness of formal Italo-Swiss relations. But whilst the two governments never criticised officially each other's policies, the recriminations and counter-recriminations continued to surface in the nationalist press on both sides of the border. The ventilation of such remarks by these newspapers created an atmosphere of unease in Italo-Swiss relations. In noting in his annual report for 1912 that 'certain organs of the press on both sides of the frontier have done their best to create an atmosphere of suspicion and even hostility between the two peoples', Howard concluded that 'these efforts seem to have met with considerable success' in Switzerland.[78] Interestingly, however, in the first months of the Italo-Turkish war, when German-Swiss nationalist newspapers were joined by German and Austrian ones in attacking Italian policies in the war, the result was equally vituperative attacks by the Italian nationalist press on the 'Germans' to the north. Howard saw that this had an impact on Switzerland in that the Swiss public began to be convinced that Italy now posed 'a possible menace' to their country.[79] Acknowledging that this Swiss perception found basis with 'the foolish clap-trap and post-cards of certain extreme Italian Irrendentists and Nationalists, exaggerated by the German-speaking press here', Howard was convinced that this had the potential of 'creating a lasting atmosphere of suspicion between the two countries'. The Foreign Office divided in assessing Howard's reports. In November 1911, Lord Drogheda, a member of the Western Department, supported the consul-general's views about the legitimacy of Swiss fears of Italian irredentism, whilst Walter Langley, an assistant under-secretary, tended to endorse Delmé-Radcliffe's judgement that Switzerland had designs on northern Italy.[80]

Chance and family connexions enabled Howard to get another perspective on Italo-Swiss relations when he spent Christmas 1911 at Rome with Isa's sister and brother-in-law, the Count and Countess Colleoni. The Colleonis were close friends of Antonio Di San Giuliano, the Italian foreign minister, so that Howard had the opportunity of meeting with Di San Giuliano several times during the holidays. After returning to Berne, Howard sent Nicolson a private letter outlining the 'small talk' he had heard whilst at Rome which shed light on Italy's difficult position within the Triple Alliance.[81] The strain of the war had affected Di San Giuliano's health: gout paralysed him. Moreover, the usually loquacious foreign minister was unusually quiet. But with Italian victories by the New Year leading suddenly to an end of his gout attack, Di San Giuliano 'perked up wonderfully and became as cheerful and entertaining as ever'. Britain had adopted a policy of strict neutrality in this war, hoping not to antagonise either belligerent. Howard discovered that Di San Giuliano believed that the government in London, James Rennell Rodd, the ambassador in Rome, and Lord Kitchener, the viceroy of Egypt, had all acted properly. In fact, in front of Howard, Di San Giuliano 'defended [the British] from charges of slackness as regards neutrality & all allowances for the difficulties Lord K. had in maintaining strict neutrality in face of a population which sympathized altogether with the [Moslem] Turks'. Perceptive enough to suspect that 'I thought that this might be due to my presence', Howard learnt 'afterwards that in speaking to an Italian in private [Di San Giuliano] had expressed himself as highly pleased with recent British actions in this respect'.

Howard's conversations and intelligence-gathering had shown that Anglo-Italian relations escaped damage during the Italo-Turkish war, but this could not be said for Italy's relations with its two German partners in the Triple Alliance. Vienna's lukewarm attitude towards Italy's venture in North Africa had 'brought out to an astonishing extent...the almost universal dislike of Austria' in Italy. Newsreels of a recent Habsburg marriage ceremony had been 'hooted and hissed' in Roman cinemas. Young Italians, who a few years before had been apolitical, now decried Austria as 'the enemy'. In Howard's estimation, anti-Austrian sentiments seemed to inhabit all classes of Italian society. This had a diplomatic dimension. At one of his luncheons with Howard, Di San Giuliano was accompanied by the war minister, Paolo Springardi. Springardi suggested to Howard that Italy's renewal of the Triple Alliance, coming up in 1912, might now be doubtful. Italian germanophobia, in evidence in the press war with German-Swiss nationalist newspapers, indicated a major division within the Triple Alliance.

Although Howard's reporting suggested that Britain and its allies might with effort pry Italy loose from the Triple Alliance – and Nicolson, for one, viewed Howard's remarks as 'very interesting' and sent them to the king[82] – Grey had no inclination to do so. On personal grounds, the foreign secretary found distasteful this Italian adventure and, more important, in terms of Britain's wider interest, reckoned that a break-up of the Triple Alliance would disrupt the European balance of power.[83] Even if Grey had warmed to the idea of bringing Italy into the Entente's orbit, his French partners were not keen to do so. Franco-Italian relations were cooling over the disposition of spheres of influence in North Africa – Di San Giuliano had counselled the seizure of Libya because French success in Morocco in the wake of the Agadir crisis in July 1911 suggested that France might be encouraged to move eastwards from Algeria.[84] Accordingly, Grey and his allies left Italy to its own devices, and Italy, needing allies to bolster its claim to membership in the circle of great Powers, renewed the Triple Alliance in the autumn of 1912. Whilst the North African crisis had subsided by late in that year – inaugurating war in the Balkans as the little states there, smelling Turkish blood, also moved to profit by Ottoman weakness – Italo-Swiss relations continued to suffer through the mutual suspicion of nationalist newspapers on both sides of the border. Although Howard reported, just before his transfer from Berne, that the Swiss president had calmed the situation somewhat through public statements, it remained that Italy entertained suspicions about its Germanic neighbours to the north. From Howard's vantage point at Berne little doubt existed that the Triple Alliance was a sham. This to a degree also reflected his own italophilia. Howard felt that its two Germanic members comprised a bipartite alliance, and it was of this combination only, not Italy, that he and his colleagues within the British diplomatic establishment had to be wary.

Howard spent most of 1912 monitoring 'German' diplomatic pressures on Switzerland, this as the Italians dithered about renewing the Triple Alliance. At the end of January, a Vienna newspaper with ties to the Ballhausplatz published an article which suggested that if Italy abandoned the Triple Alliance, Germany and Austria-Hungary should 'knit up relations' with Holland, Belgium, and Switzerland.[85] Inspired by 'an eminent Austrian diplomatist', no doubt in league with the Foreign

Ministry at Berlin, the article argued that those states which followed foreign policies of neutrality were actually embracing 'a kind of conventional defencelessness'. The state of European affairs directed that a neutralist foreign policy was a thing of the past, thus these three small Powers should combine with Austria-Hungary and Germany. Not only were these three Powers closer culturally to the two German Powers, but their commercial and financial positions would be enhanced; they could remove themselves from the oppression of French bankers – an ironic comment in light of the Hungarian government's efforts in 1910 to arrange a railway loan at Paris given the less usurious interest rates there than prevailed at either Berlin or Vienna. Better economic well-being would add to the crucial connexion with 'a great military Power', Germany. By these words, the 'German' Powers were telling the Italians that if they abandoned the Triple Alliance, every effort would be made to nullify that defection with a series of treaties with the small Powers on France's eastern flank.

Like every other sensible observer, Howard knew that this proposal could work only if it was taken up by all three small Powers. Howard reported immediately that the Swiss government, through the *Bund*, a Berne newspaper used to issue semi-official communiqués, poured cold water on the Austrian article.[86] Not only would abandoning the policy of strict neutrality violate the Swiss constitution but, the *Bund* added, Switzerland's historical experience with alliances – an oblique reference to the Franco-Swiss alliance of 1798[87] – suggested that the country's interests could be better defended if it kept out of great-Power politics. Howard saw this speedy and categorical denunciation of the Austrian proposal as an 'attempt to cut short any Teutonic aspirations of this kind'. Relieved, the Foreign Office acknowledged that the Swiss reply constituted an 'excellent' riposte to 'German' probing about Switzerland acceding to a modified Triple Alliance.[88] Swiss success in this regard emerged within a month. The Vienna correspondent of the *Journal de Genève* wrote that Ballhausplatz officials deprecated any idea of an 'alliance of rapprochement' amongst Austria-Hungary, Germany, and Switzerland, citing the 'German Powers' satisfaction with a neutral Switzerland and Swiss determination to enforce that neutrality. Disingenuously, Austrian diplomats added that they could not understand why an obscure article in an even obscurer Viennese newspaper could have caused such a stir – French and Italian press comment had been equally critical. 'This question', Howard now believed, 'has been so fully and publicly discussed in one way or another during the past year, and it has been so evident that there is no intention on the part of Switzerland to alter her present status and join one or other group of the Great powers, that only the deaf and blind could continue to entertain a hope that she would voluntarily do so.'[89] The Foreign Office Western Department put it more succinctly: 'The "ballon d'essai" collapsed.'[90]

Whilst Howard and his colleagues in London were satisfied that Swiss neutrality could be relied upon should a crisis erupt involving the Triple Entente and the Triple Alliance, they were still wary when the Germans moved to improve Swiss–German relations. This came in September 1912 when William II undertook an official visit to Switzerland to attend army manoeuvres. Long-planned, it was in part an effort by the Berne government to show the evenhandedness of its diplomacy – the French president had been received on a state visit a few years before. On the German side, the visit seemed designed to improve Germany's image in Switzerland, an image recently tarnished by difficult negotiations over railway concessions, as well as border incidents involving the pursuit of criminals from one country to another.[91] Just before the visit began, Howard speculated that the emperor's movements would attract 'a more vivid interest than generally attends such Royal visits in other countries' since for the first time a reigning monarch would be received officially at the capital.[92] However, given all that had happened in the past year, little probability existed of Switzerland being drawn closer to its 'German' neighbours.

Howard's reports during the visit confirmed his earlier surmise. William's chief purpose concerned observing army manoeuvres, a result of recognised increases in Swiss military strength thanks to a series of reforms begun by the central government in 1907;[93] and, whilst the emperor attended the military exercises and a limited number of public gatherings, Swiss leaders took every opportunity to state their determination to keep their country neutral – the unspoken lesson being that the reformed Swiss Army could do this handily.[94] Thanks to Howard's reports, the Foreign Office did not see the dark hand of German diplomacy at work.[95] This did not dissuade Howard from cautioning London about the long-term effects of Germany trying to push Switzerland into support for the 'German' Powers. A political alliance between Switzerland and Germany did not pose the real danger to the balance of power. The problem for the future, Howard reckoned, involved instead 'the economic and intellectual penetration of Germany into Switzerland which causes uneasiness amongst many Swiss in the German cantons, as well as in the French, and may eventually become a serious factor in the situation'.[96] For the foreseeable future, however, Howard's reports showed that Britain and its allies had little to worry about Switzerland aligning with the 'German' Powers.

From September 1912 until his transfer to Stockholm in the spring of 1913, Howard was not confronted with any new crisis. This derived from Italian renewal of the Triple Alliance and the Powers being forced yet again to consider the interminable 'Eastern Question', this time because of the outbreak of the first Balkan war. With their attention diverted to southeastern Europe, the great Powers had little time to jockey for diplomatic and strategic advantage in the west. Although Howard still witnessed the Swiss and Italian nationalist newspapers railing at one another, Di San Giuliano took the initiative of making a public statement about his country's lack of 'hostile intentions' towards Switzerland.[97] But this was now small beer. Once Italian relations with its two 'German' allies were on the mend – and neither Howard nor his colleagues at the Foreign Office seemed to have suspected that ploys like the Vienna article about Switzerland joining a modified Triple Alliance were designed to put pressure on the Italians to renew – Switzerland ceased to be drawn into the vortex of great-Power politics. Besides, as Howard's despatches had shown, the Swiss had no desire to abandon their neutrality and they would use their reformed army to defend this and their territory. The only incident of any note during Howard's last months at Berne concerned German efforts to strengthen a fortress at Hüningen, just north of Basle. After some initial worry, it transpired that the Germans were doing this for defensive rather than offensive purposes.[98] The Germans were taking no chances that, should the Reich become involved in a struggle elsewhere, the Swiss would be able to exploit German weakness in this area.

Howard's period of diplomatic inactivity at Berne over the winter of 1912–13 allowed him time to contemplate the problems facing British foreign policy. His thoughts surfaced in a series of letters to Stafford, his brother, now the chief whip for the Liberal government in London. These musings are important because they show how a decade's experience in the Diplomatic Service, especially during the preceding four years of uninterrupted contact with the 'German' question, had fixed Howard's view of Britain's place in the world and how to maintain it. The fact that Grey and the senior members of Britain's foreign-policy-making elite were then struggling to maintain a balance of power in southeastern Europe in the wake of the first Balkan war added piquancy to Howard's ideas.

Howard's essential view was that the country's foreign policy was not as effective as it might be because of the strictures the Liberal Party itself placed on Grey. His belief that the Liberal Party circumscribed Grey's foreign policy perhaps owed something to Howard's growing disenchantment with Liberal domestic politics. This seemed to reach a peak in 1910 when Asquith and his chancellor of the exchequer, David Lloyd George, emasculated the House of Lords by removing its veto power over

Commons' legislation. At that time Howard, seeing the upper house as a necessary check on the Commons, characterised the Liberal government's move as akin to running 'a coach and four through the constitution'.[99] His disapproval continued during the Asquith government's subsequent handling of the Irish question.[100] By the winter of 1912–13, his criticism of Liberal policies shifted to the foreign-policy sphere. This derived from two issues: radical attacks on Grey's policies and the Liberal failure to deliver on promises to strengthen the Territorial Army. It amounted to a rebuke of those who sought to make foreign policy an issue of partisan politics, as well as of those who would deny British diplomatists the force necessary to support policy.

In assessing the reason for the success of the Balkan League in throwing off 'that rotten & putrid corpse of Turkish domination', Howard felt that the small states' superior military strength had proved to be the deciding factor.[101] Observing that the Swiss military reforms allowed the Berne government to stand aside from European power politics, he told Stafford: 'It is another great object lesson for us of the absolute necessity of military preparedness and efficiency.' In the autumn of 1912, it was significant that the South African government had sent a mission to Switzerland to learn at first hand about the reforms there; the South Africans were going to structure their territorial forces on the Swiss model. That Pretoria had not gone to Britain, Germany, or any other major Power spoke forcefully, Howard opined, about the effectiveness of a small Power like Switzerland – and by implication, the four small Powers of the Balkan League – using its maximum military potential to support foreign policy. The lesson was obvious. If a major Power like Britain harnessed its potential military strength *à la mode Suisse*, its foreign policy would be that much stronger. With the obvious military threat to the European balance of power posed by Germany and its allies, it was incumbent, Howard felt, on Britain's Liberal government to do something constructive in terms of British military preparedness. This would make Grey's work, and that of his advisers and diplomats, more effective, whilst at the same time allowing for the better protection of British interests in Europe. Howard despaired at the retrenching policies of the government. 'I fear however', Howard admonished Stafford, 'that we shall have to be taught the necessity of self-defence by some disaster before we begin to understand something of it.'

The central criticism levelled by Howard against the government's military policies concerned Liberal timidity in introducing peacetime conscription. Conscription stood as a cardinal element of the Swiss system. 'It is an axiom with me', Howard wrote, 'that there can be no real Democracy without a people in arms to back it. If a man will not defend his country neither should he vote... You [Liberals] will continue to fight against this idea tooth and nail. But someday perhaps the people will get to understand it & then you will think it splendid!' Whilst this constituted a most unBritish sentiment and a certain detachment from the political reality which Stafford and his party daily had to consider if they wished to remain in office – though Howard's words showed that he knew his countrymen as a whole did not support the concept of 'national service' – Howard reckoned the government was doing nothing to educate the people about the need to support British diplomacy with the threat of force. The Royal Navy was not enough; without terrene strength, British foreign policy would not be as effective. None of this is to suggest that Howard wanted war against the Triple Alliance. He did not. He wanted to ensure the maintenance of the balance of power in Europe against the possibility of the 'German' Powers upsetting it. Never once during the second Balkan war did he believe that 'a European war' was on the cards. Nevertheless, as far as the military course of the Balkan struggle and its diplomatic implications were concerned, the lessons for Britain in maintaining its position as a world Power were obvious. The Liberal government refused to learn.

Howard's criticisms of radical Liberal attacks on Grey had been simmering for some time, but were brought to the surface by the war in the Balkans. A year earlier Grey had been the object of a bitter attack by critics within his own party over his Persian policy. The radical bugbear was the Anglo-Russian entente of 1907, part of which delineated spheres of interest in Persia. That 'Liberal' Britain had by Grey's policies found a condominium of interests with 'absolutist' Russia raised the ire of the radicals.[102] At the time, Howard deprecated in the strongest possible terms to Stafford the lack of realism in the rantings of the foreign secretary's critics.[103] The central point about Grey's Anglo-Russian entente was that it gave Britain another ally which could help off-set any growth in the power of the Triple Alliance. The radicals, for partisan reasons which ran counter to the national interest, threatened the balance of power:

I have never seen anything quite so imbecile as the attacks made against Edward Grey by the Radicals. But as that party have only one idea of Foreign Policy which is to quarrel with our friends of the time being in order to get on good terms with one's enemies for the time being, to whom in order to induce them to smile, one must make every conceivable sacrifice...

Blinded by their hatred of tsardom, the radicals also did not consider that secondarily the Anglo-Russian entente had been 'the one hope for the maintenance of Persia as an independent country'.

During the first Balkan war, Howard watched as Grey did all he could to localise the conflict by ensuring that the great Powers, especially the

Dual Monarchy and Russia, did not come to blows over the collapse of Turkey-in-Europe. Using his influence with the Russians via the 1907 entente, Grey succeeded in bringing them into a conference of the Powers in London, under his chairmanship, to settle the dispute. This successful diplomacy brought Grey accolades from home and abroad, at the same time raising his international prestige and that of Britain. Still, grumbling from the radical wing of the Liberal Party continued, something which caused Howard to vent his anger about these amateurs to Stafford:

The agreement between Austria and Russia has been a triumph for Edward Grey, and the principal credit for the preservation of European peace must be ascribed to him. I don't suppose this will put an end to the attacks on him by [the radicals]. It is a most curious thing that in foreign politics the English radical has always[,] since I can remember, been absurdly & ignorantly in the wrong. I suppose it is because they never try to learn the grammar of foreign affairs.[104]

Here were the words of a 'Service' man who saw the injection of partisan politics into the direction of British foreign policy as holding the potential for deflecting that policy away from the national interest.

In his aggregate of a decade and a half as a diplomat, Howard had served under both Conservative and Liberal foreign secretaries. He had seen that changes in government, whilst they might mean wholesale changes in domestic policy, did not alter much the course of British foreign policy. For instance, once the Liberals took office in December 1905, Lansdowne's policy of developing close ties with the French against the expansion of German power had been accepted and further developed by Grey. Later, despite obligatory criticism of the Anglo-Russian entente because they formed the Official Opposition, the Conservatives generally were willing to accept Grey's Anglo-Russian entente. That was the way consistent policy to protect the national interest had to be conducted. The radicals threatened to disrupt this by ill-conceived criticisms of the domestic policies of an ally. They were justified in despising the rebarbative nature of the tsarist government, but personal feelings had to be sublimated for the protection of Britain's national interests; this is the crucial lesson Howard had learnt when he helped Sir Percy Anderson in his negotiations with the Germans over East Africa in 1890, and which had been confirmed at Crete, Washington, Budapest, and Berne. As a professional, Howard was not wedded to the notion that Britain's allies in 1912–13 would be Britain's allies in five, ten, or fifteen years. His words about 'friends of the time being' and 'enemies for the time being' indicate his support for the old maxim that 'Britain has no permanent friends or enemies, just permanent interests'. The radicals in Britain had lost sight of this. Howard was telling his brother during the winter of 1912–13 that, if Britain was going to survive as a Power of the first rank, its foreign policy must not be subject to the whims and caprices of partisan politics.

By Howard's own precepts about separating private from professional life in diplomacy, none of these ideas that he conveyed to his brother found expression in his despatches, telegrams, and letters sent to the Foreign Office. But these ideas about the problems facing the conduct of British foreign policy, along with his decade of experience since Hardinge and Bertie had brought him back into the Service, gave him the desire and the capacity to handle any challenge to Britain's international position which he, as a diplomat, would have to face. In the spring of 1913 he was selected to take charge of the Legation at Stockholm. Howard did not know, indeed no one knew, that a year after his transfer to Sweden, general European war would break out between the Triple Entente and the Triple Alliance. The greatest challenge to Britain's position as a world Power was at hand, and Esme Howard was ready and able to use his considerable talents as a diplomatist to the benefit of Britain's national interests.

5

Stockholm: war and diplomacy in neutral northern Europe, 1913–1916

> I hope you won't think that I am weak in dealing with the Swedish Government. What I have had constantly before my mind in dealing with them is the necessity of sparing His Majesty's Government and the Russian Government any unnecessary trouble and anxiety on their account.
>
> *Howard, April* 1916

I

For personal reasons, Howard did not relish the thought of a transfer to head the Legation at Stockholm. Berne lay at the centre of western Europe, making it easy for Howard and Isa to visit both Italy and Britain. By the same token, friends and family had to make only a slight detour when travelling to pass through Switzerland. Stockholm, on the other hand, seemed 'practically at the end of the civilised world and not on the road to anywhere, so that it was unlikely that many acquaintances would come along that way'.[1] Added to this, the Swedish climate, with its long, dark winter days, did not seem appealing. However, in terms of his career, this transfer amounted to a major step. When writing to congratulate Howard on the Berne post in 1911, Bryce had suggested: 'You will be at Brussels or Stockholm in a year or two & then go to an Embassy...'[2] Bryce spoke wisdom. Stockholm served as a final proving ground for those junior British diplomats judged by the Foreign Office to be of ambassadorial material. A number of the men who had served in Stockholm since 1851 had gone on from there to embassies, including Howard's two immediate predecessors: Rennell Rodd to Rome and Spring Rice to Washington. In fact, Rennell Rodd wrote to Howard after learning of his transfer to say that, whilst Stockholm was 'so far from Italy', 'it is at any rate more often than not in the prelude to an Embassy'.[3]

The professional gains to be made by such a transfer were undoubtedly in Howard's mind after his friend, Tyrrell, wrote privately in February 1913 to inform him that Stockholm might become available in April and asking if he would like to be considered for it. That Howard had the option of refusing until something else came along is clear from Tyrrell's remark: 'Should you for personal reasons wish to remain where you are, it would not earn you a "black mark" if you told me, as my enquiry is just personal.'[4] Deciding that his chances for subsequent promotion would be enhanced by taking Stockholm, Howard accepted the offer.[5] There was also the added inducement of more money for this post – Nicolson moved to prevent the Treasury from reducing the pay for this post as part of a long-planned economy measure[6] – a prime consideration for a man with a growing family; a fifth son, Henry, had been born in Berne in March. Accordingly, Howard arrived in Stockholm on 10 June 1913.

The reason for Howard's transfer derived from the Foreign Office's determination to have a seasoned diplomat in what was becoming an increasingly sensitive post. This sensitivity stemmed from two intertwined issues that were to be the stuff of Howard's time in Sweden: first, Sweden's growing animosity towards Russia which was matched by a corresponding closeness in Swedish–German relations; and, secondly, the publicly avowed intention of Sweden to enforce its neutrality should general war in Europe erupt. Howard appeared as the obvious choice for Stockholm, given that Spring Rice, the incumbent minister there, had been deemed essential for Washington. Howard had had over four years' experience in dealing with the 'German' question and, more important, for the preceding two years had served in a country whose government had also vowed to enforce its neutrality should general European war break out. Howard, of course, was not unfamiliar in coping with Russian policies; his time on Crete, though it had ended seven years before, had provided him with this indispensable knowledge. Howard was a worthy choice to take the Stockholm Legation at a crucial point in Anglo-Swedish relations.

On his way to Stockholm, Howard spent time at London seeing Crowe and being briefed on the problems facing him at his new post.[7] He learnt that neutral Sweden presented a very different problem for Britain than did neutral Switzerland. Where the Swiss made every effort to treat equally each great Power, the Swedes on the whole were unabashedly germanophile. In the event of some major crisis precipitated by the conflicting interests of the Triple Entente and Triple Alliance, the Foreign Office felt that the pro-German sentiments of the vast majority of Swedes would probably mean the benevolent neutrality of their country towards Germany. Even if such a crisis did not lead to war, Swedish favouritism towards Germany would have a tremendous impact on the British strategic position in northern Europe, especially in the Baltic Sea; and what affected Britain's position, in turn, affected that of its Entente partner and traditional Swedish adversary, Russia. The pro-Germanism of the Swedish population, particularly those who made or influenced foreign policy at Court and in the government, army, and bureaucracy, had been hammered home by Spring Rice for five years in a steady stream of despatches and private letters to London.[8] Howard pored over these official papers in his short time between assignments.

But he also received Spring Rice's private assessments of the Swedish situation. When rumours circulated in November 1912 that Howard might move to Stockholm, Spring Rice wrote to his friend: 'Sympathies here are entirely against the Slavs mainly because Russia, the black beast, is Slav and Germany, the white angel, is anti-Slav...'[9] Once Howard accepted the post, Spring Rice continued to send perceptive appraisals. Howard would daily have to conduct business with the highest political circles in Sweden; as the king, Gustav V, and the majority of those surrounding him were unrestrained in their admiration of Germany, Spring Rice opined that 'I think the Court officials are the very devil: Berlin and putty. You will loathe them.'[10] He cautioned Howard that the matter of Swedish russophobia had implications for Anglo-Swedish relations and the balance of power in Europe. Although Britain had concluded the entente with Russia in 1907 to obviate British and Russian imperial differences in south-central Asia, by this act Britain had allied with a Slav Power, *the* Slav Power. This touched Europe. Germany and Austria-Hungary opposed Russian ambitions in eastern Europe and the Balkans; this opposition had a racial dimension for the Swedes – the 'black beast' versus the 'white angel' – since Sweden had been for more than two centuries the chief Russian adversary in northern Europe. It followed that the existence of the Anglo-Russian entente made Britain and British policy suspicious in Swedish eyes. In representing British interests at Stockholm, Howard would have to tread warily in carrying out directives from the Foreign Office.

As had been his custom at each post since 1903, Howard set about soon after his arrival to meet as wide a range of people as possible. He had been provided with a list of contacts who had been useful to Spring Rice; it included a smattering of courtiers, some politicians, a few men with Swedish Foreign Ministry connexions, and a small number of anglophiles outside of official circles.[11] Significantly, Spring Rice's list failed to include any army officers who, because of the threat Russia seemed to pose to the kingdom's eastern frontiers, were the focal point of germanophilia in Sweden. One of the most important contacts established by Howard on his own was the Crown Princess Margaret, an English princess, the cousin of George V, whom Howard had first met when she and her family stopped at Crete briefly on a yachting holiday.[12] Howard and Isa established a close friendship with Princess Margaret, a course aided by the fact that there was a certain solace in 'English' companionship in the increasingly 'German' atmosphere of the Swedish capital. Very quickly, Howard's network of contacts expanded.[13] An honorary attaché at the Legation, Charles Madeley, 'a general favourite in Swedish society', provided Howard with an entry into the upper reaches of that society. Within weeks, for example, Howard was invited to take a yacht cruise of the eastern Baltic with a prominent member of Stockholm's monied classes – he had to decline because of the pressures of Legation work. Howard also became friendly with Axel Munthe, the doctor of the Swedish queen; Alwyne Maude, an Englishman who married into the Swedish aristocracy; and Axel de Bildt, a prominent financier with strong anglophile tendencies. Within the diplomatic community at Stockholm, Howard formed a good working relationship with his French and Russian opposites – essential if the Entente was to have some solidarity in this crucial European capital.

Howard's contacts with members of the Swedish government proved to be difficult to make, a result of political instability within the country for the first eight months of his tenure as minister. This instability centred on the fact that the government in power, a Liberal/Social Democrat coalition, had a weak position within the Swedish parliament, the Riksdag, and did not really enjoy the confidence of Gustav V.[14] Spring Rice's list had indicated that the premier, Karl Staaff, and his foreign minister, Count Ehrensvärd, would be difficult men with whom to work; Staaff became animated only when one spoke German, whilst Ehrensvärd 'has caught the big head and is pomposissimus'. Despite these words of caution, Howard managed to forge a good business relationship with these two men.[15] It mattered little, for the government soon collapsed over the issue of funding for the army.[16] This brought into office a conservative coalition and new leaders, the most important of whom for Howard were the premier, Hjalmar Hammarskjöld, and his foreign minister, Knut Wallenberg. Thus, Howard had to begin establishing a working relationship with new Swedish diplomatists only months before the outbreak of general European war.

Howard's network of contacts remained relatively small for the duration of his five years at Stockholm, the result of a conspiracy of circumstances and increasing Swedish germanophilia. He had begun making his initial contacts after arriving in June 1913 and, since he, Isa, and the boys had not been in England for two years, took leave in November and December to stay with Stafford at Thornbury. He and his family returned to Stockholm on 29 December and, the next day, the dowager Queen Sophie died. The Court immediately went into six months' official mourning, abruptly curtailing all social events which had the potential of bringing Howard together with Swedish courtiers, politicians, civil servants, diplomats, and army officers. After February 1914, he had the added burden of creating professional friendships with Hammarskjöld and Wallenberg and, once the mourning period ended, the July crisis was gathering momentum. When this led to war between the Triple Entente and the 'Dual' Alliance of Germany and Austria-Hungary – the Italians would not fight – the pro-German sympathies of Swedes limited Howard's opportunities to round up much support for British policy. Constrained social intercourse – and social contacts are a key element in the work of a diplomat – lay at the bottom of Howard's difficulties. As he later observed, 'it seriously restricted our [his and Isa's] contacts with Stockholm society and to that extent perhaps our general usefulness'.[17] None the less, once the war broke out, Howard used his small circle of acquaintances as best he could. Whilst Swedish germanophilia became more pronounced as the war dragged on, late in the war the Swedes in general, sensing German defeat, turned unblushingly toward Britain and its allies. Such naked self-interest did not deflect Howard. Since returning to the Diplomatic Service in 1903, he had learnt the necessity of ignoring those who opposed or sought to undermine British policy. Following the directives of the Foreign Office whilst at the same time remaining *persona grata* within the country he served had been a distinguishing feature of Howard's diplomatic work; his time in both Crete and Hungary had shown this. This skill, in part, explains much about Howard's success at Stockholm between 1913 and 1918.

II

In the year between arriving at Stockholm and the outbreak of the war, Howard found himself preoccupied with the problems that the 'Russian' question injected into Anglo-Swedish relations. This confirmed all that Spring Rice had written about the pro-German and anti-Russian tendencies of the Swedes; it also fixed in his mind, once the war began, the need to consider carefully Swedish reactions to British policies which involved Anglo-Russian collaboration. In the early autumn of 1913 the conservative campaign to force greater military spending by the Staaff government entered a new phase when some prominent Swedes openly suggested that Russia posed the greatest threat to Sweden and its Norwegian neighbour because of St Petersburg's desire for year-round warm water ports.[18] These men argued that Sweden could survive only if it abandoned its outmoded policy of neutrality, concluded 'an alliance or understanding with Germany', and increased the fighting capacity of the army and navy. It could not draw closer to Britain and France because those countries were tied to Russia, thus Sweden's only salvation lay in membership with the German alliance system. Whilst the case for abandoning neutrality might have been overstated, Howard reckoned that '[t]here seems to be little doubt that public opinion in this country is being gradually roused over the defence question'.

Howard warned the Foreign Office that this Swedish debate, now being heatedly discussed not only in the Riksdag but also on the public platform, at university forums, and in the press, could lead to a shift in the direction of that country's foreign and defence policy. Staaff, Howard argued, was committed to neutrality. However, his parliamentary majority depended on his minority Liberal Party being supported by the Social Democrats. To garner Social Democratic support, Staaff had agreed to endorse a number of domestic programmes that diverted money from the armed forces. Howard saw that a growing number of the premier's fellow Liberals, caught up in the emotion of the debate and obviously worried about their political lives, were demanding that a compromise over defence spending be made to blunt conservative attacks. But the Social Democrats would not budge. Hence, Howard felt, a political crisis which might alter radically the direction of Swedish foreign policy and the balance of power in northern Europe could not be discounted.

Whilst this foreign- and defence-policy debate with its strong russophobic undertones raged in Sweden, Howard and the Foreign Office found themselves confronted with the disquieting news that the Swedes had unearthed a Russian spy ring operating out of Stockholm. In October 1913 the Russian military attaché in Stockholm, Colonel Assanovitch, had been implicated in 'purchasing secret information from two Swedish non-commissioned officers'.[19] Noting that Assanovitch was the second Russian military attaché in two years in Sweden compromised by espionage activities, Howard told the Foreign Office 'that this story when it becomes known will add fuel to the fire of anti-Russian propaganda which is being carried on by the military party'. Worried about the conservative attacks on the Staaff government, Ehrensvärd appealed to Howard on 30 October to have Grey intervene at St Petersburg to keep Assanovitch out of Sweden – arrogantly, the Russians were indicating that Assanovitch might remain as the proof against him remained inconclusive.[20] On the same day, Howard also reported that the Swedes had proof that Assanovitch was the paymaster for a Russian spy ring operating in Austria-Hungary.[21] Assanovitch had paid Colonel Alfred Redl, an Austro-Hungarian staff officer recently exposed for selling secrets to the Russians. If the Russians persisted in keeping Assanovitch in Stockholm, Ehrensvärd would be forced to make public the hard evidence he had about the Redl case. The political and diplomatic repercussions would be difficult to predict if this sordid business saw the light of day. Similar information reached Grey through the Swedish ambassador in London, Count

Wrangel.²² Although it is difficult to determine how much pressure Grey was able to exert on the Russians to remove Assanovitch permanently from Stockholm, the military attaché was gone by the New Year.

Once this particular issue had died down, Howard assessed its impact in a letter to Grey.²³ The Assanovitch case not only enhanced Swedish suspicions about Russia, which were legitimate given that the Russians did have spies in Sweden, but it also showed how easily Russo-Swedish relations could be subjected to strain. In addition, Howard placed on record his scepticism of the arguments proffered by some Swedish politicians that if the conservative opposition came to power, cooler heads would prevail and there would be no attempt to forge an anti-Russian alliance with Germany. Howard observed:

The officers of the Army and Navy, especially the younger ones, seem all to hope for a war with Russia, and therefore all their influence which is very considerable with the King at any rate would be used to bring about an alliance with Germany. It seems to me doubtful whether the Conservative leaders could resist this pressure in a time of crisis.

At least whilst Staaff held power, Howard advanced, the chance of a Swedish–German alliance seemed remote.

A good indication of this came just before Christmas 1913. Wrangel sought out Crowe at the Foreign Office to suggest that Britain 'reaffirm her policy concerning the maintenance of the status quo in northern waters'.²⁴ Crowe spoke generally about the northern-European balance to Wrangel, later informing Grey that Britain was no party to any agreements about the Baltic; Britain's only commitment was to maintain the status quo in the regions bordering on the North Sea. But to keep Anglo-Swedish relations sweet, Crowe suggested that 'perhaps we may treat his suggestion, at least for the present, as of the nature of an "obiter dictum" rather than a serious proposal'. In this way, Howard's worry about a shift in the north to German advantage seemed remote.

Within two months, however, Howard's concerns came back to the fore when King Gustav moved to topple the Staaff government by his appeal to the Swedish people to support increased arms spending and an extended military service. Howard had been reporting on increasing pressures on the Liberal/Social Democratic government from both inside and outside of Sweden for several weeks before the king moved. The most alarming of these reports suggested that the Germans were working with conservative elements to persuade Swedes generally of the Russian menace and, therefore, to reject neutrality and 'look to German friendship not only on account of military considerations but also on account of the blood relationship between them'.²⁵ This effort by the Germans and their sympathisers in Sweden followed the by now familiar German practice of a co-ordinated press campaign orchestrated in the same way as those which Howard had observed at Budapest and Berne. The original suggestion for closer Swedish–German ties appeared in an authoritative German newspaper, in this case the *Militär Wochenblatt*, characterised by Howard as 'the well-known German Military paper'; significantly, it then reappeared untouched and without comment in one of Sweden's most important conservative, pan-German newspapers, the *Svenska Dagblad*. In reporting on this press campaign, Howard thought that any additional comments by him would be 'superfluous': 'it fits in with the present agitation for increased armaments in Sweden of which that paper [the *Svenska Dagblad*] is one of the principal supporters'. Howard's reports found ready acceptance in a Foreign Office becoming dominated by germanophobes. The publication of the article in Sweden and Germany seemed a 'well-organised campaign' to secure Swedish adherence to the German alliance system.[26]

Three weeks after Howard reported on the *Militär Wochenblatt* article, Gustav made his appeal to the people and brought down the Staaff government. In analysing the king's efforts, Howard believed that the 'German party' at Court – Queen Victoria, Gustav's consort; Sven Hedin, a russophobe academic; Verner von Heidenstam, 'an *exalté* patriotic poet'; and Count Douglas, the earl marshal – had engineered the whole thing.[27] Howard remained convinced that conservative leaders in the Riksdag had no forewarning of the king's speech and reported that, whilst publicly proclaiming that the king's words did not exceed his constitutional rights, in private they confessed that this action was 'decidedly unwise'. Howard drew an important conclusion from the change of government. Enquiring into the circumstances surrounding Gustav's unorthodox assault on his own ministers, he came to doubt the king's political savvy. 'The King is not either a strong man or an able man', Howard wrote to Grey, '& he is besides far from well. He positively hated Mr Staaff if all accounts are true and so did the Queen, & the speech seems to be the impatient gesture of the weak & nervous man to get rid of a dominating personality whom he could not bear.'

But whilst Howard and his Foreign Office colleagues could ruminate endlessly on why Gustav had acted as he did, more important issues beckoned. Conservative disquiet over the king's actions did not prevent conservative politicians from seeking to benefit by the fall of Staaff's government to form one of their own. It remained that change might now occur in Swedish foreign and defence policy, probably to the detriment of Entente interests. Howard did not hide his concern: 'Should…the Conservative and military element come into power as a result of an outburst of patriotic enthusiasm, I should be much afraid that Sweden may abandon her policy of neutrality and cast in her lot for better or worse with that of the German Empire.'[28] Just as concerned about the possibility of a change in the northern-European balance of power, Grey circulated Howard's warnings to King George and the Cabinet.[29] There was no doubt that at the bottom of the political crisis in Sweden resided Swedish fear of Russia. Whether this fear was legitimate or not was beside the point, though issues like the Assanovitch case suggested, perhaps, that it might have been. In cold diplomatic terms, however, a powerful sector of Sweden's court, political, and military elite believed in a Russian menace. To Howard and the Foreign Office it appeared that, as Sweden searched for an ally to help allay such fears, Germany was the obvious choice.

Howard watched as Gustav began to sound out politicians to form a new government. Fortunately for the British and their allies, the heavy political bargaining and compromises necessary in the Cabinet-making process that led to the rise of Hammarskjöld resulted in a ministry not as conservative as the king and his coterie wanted. As Howard informed London, Wallenberg's inclusion augured well for a continuation of a foreign policy based on neutrality: 'The Minister of Foreign Affairs is Mr Wallenberg, the leading financier in Sweden. He has considerable business connection with England.'[30] By the same token, the new premier and his Cabinet were men like any other men in power. They had a particular vision about the way Sweden should evolve and, despite the constitutional crisis brought on by the king and general conservative support for the royal prerogative, they were not about to permit a palace clique to dominate policy. Once the Hammarskjöld government took office, the view prevailing within Sweden was that it was 'strong'. Howard accepted this view, as did the Foreign Office.[31] The rise of Hammarskjöld suggested to Howard that, whilst defence spending might rise and Sweden might draw closer to Germany, there was no worry at that juncture of a full-scale Swedish–German alliance directed against the Russians. 'The present ministry', Howard confided privately to Grey, 'is fortunately composed of strong sensible practical men who will not, I believe, allow His Majesty to be ruled by a monstrous regime of women and poets. If the latter had continued they might together with the military jingoes have brought about a change in Swedish foreign policy, abandoned neutrality, and thrown themselves into the arms of Germany.'[32]

By the end of March 1914, as the dust settled on the political crisis in Sweden, Howard had spent almost six months considering the impact of the 'Russian' question on Sweden. For the moment, however, it seemed as if Russo-Swedish relations were entering a quiescent phase. In late April, an interview given by Wallenberg to a Russian newspaper appeared in the Stockholm press.[33] When asked point blank about the 'so-called Russian danger' and the likelihood of a Swedish–German alliance, the Swedish foreign minister moved to dispel publicly the belief that his government would reverse the traditional policy of neutrality. Pouring cold water on the idea that the Hammarskjöld government's commitment to increased arms spending and the extension of military service was directed against Russia, he argued that this was designed to meet 'the necessity for being prepared for all sorts of eventualities'. Wallenberg cunningly brought these issues together by attacking the palace clique surrounding the king. He did so with a stinging criticism of Hedin, who continued to utter anti-Russian diatribes on the public platform: 'He is, it seems, an inconsequent and unbalanced man, and the present leaders of foreign policy cannot be in any way held responsible for the exaggerations of such people.' Despite some disingenuousness surrounding Wallenberg's assertions, for instance, that Sweden's arms build-up had little to do with Russia, Howard understood this to be a calculated endeavour 'to re-establish confidence in Russia as regards Sweden's future foreign policy under the guidance of [Hammarskjöld's] "Defence Party"'.

None the less, whilst the 'Russian' question was being played down by the new Swedish regime, Howard remained fully aware that it had not disappeared as a major consideration in Swedish foreign policy. Another minor crisis like the Assanovitch affair might see renewed truculence towards Russia. A major crisis, on the other hand, like a war between the Triple Entente and Triple Alliance, where German and Russian armies would certainly clash, would be far more disruptive. The situation in diplomatic terms remained fluid. Thus, British policy towards Sweden had always to be made with an eye on the possibility that some crisis might arise which could inflame Swedish passions against the Entente Powers. This would have a decided impact on the balance of power in northern Europe which Britain could ignore only to the detriment of its interests.

The wisdom of Howard's view surfaced in the final months of peace when the *amour propre* of Sweden suddenly imposed itself on the functioning of the Anglo-Russian entente in Persia. By the 1907 agreement, Persia had been divided into three zones: a northern one dominated by the Russians; a southern one dominated by the British; and a central one remaining neutral. Because of mutual suspicions and the fact that the shah retained nominal control over his kingdom, the British and Russians agreed that some disinterested Power be asked to have its soldiers lead the gendarmerie established under the entente. Swedish officers were then invited to perform this duty. By the time Howard came to Stockholm, the Anglo-Russian entente in Persia seemed on the edge of collapse. In violation of the original agreement, the Russians were attempting to annex the north by a series of actions including seizing public revenues, interfering with local government, and so on.[34] The

Swedish gendarmerie proved incapable of enforcing the shah's will. Suddenly, in May 1914, Wallenberg asked Howard if the British government 'appreciated the efforts made by the Swedish Gendarmerie to restore order in Persia'.[35]

Howard had been reading circular despatches sent to every British mission about the problems in Persia. It seemed to him that the Swedish gendarmerie was failing to keep order there, not only in the Russian zone, but in others as well. When Howard went on a short leave to Britain in late May, he met with Crowe at the Foreign Office to discuss the matter of whether the Swedish officers should be retained and, if not, how to handle informing Hammarskjöld's government of this fact. The need for caution came from the problems that might ensue if the matter was handled intemperately. Howard put the issue before Crowe: '[The Swedish officer corps] are so sensitive and so proud of their military qualities that the slightest hint that we were dissatisfied...would not only cause great irritation in the country against us, but would quite probably result in a demand for the immediate recall of the Swedish Officers in Persia which might be very inconvenient.'[36]

Howard and Crowe agreed that the matter should slide for the time being – the Foreign Office was then in the midst of a high-level debate about how to handle the Russian violation of the 1907 agreement. Howard returned to Stockholm, saw Wallenberg, and, with consummate skill, explained the British position.[37] As a result, Wallenberg seemed amenable to the gradual withdrawal of the Swedish officers and their replacement by others, British or otherwise. In fact, Wallenberg even went so far as to suggest that if the British government wished to use the matter of the Swedish gendarmerie to open fresh negotiations with the Russians over Persia, the Hammarskjöld ministry would say nothing. Crowe's reaction, penned the day before the assassination of the Austrian heir apparent at Sarajevo, showed that the Foreign Office was moving towards a division of Persia into two contiguous zones: a Russian in the north and a British in the south.[38] Hence, the gradual phasing out of the Swedish officers would probably occur as their contracts for service in Persia expired. In the areas under British control, British officers would replace them. But until that time, it would be incumbent on Howard to refrain from saying anything about the fact that 'the Swedish officers are a complete failure, and that there is no reason to expect that they will be any better in the future'. However, the onset of the July crisis and Britain's declaration of war on Germany on 4 August made the whole matter academic. The significance of this final Anglo-Swedish diplomatic exchange before the war, however, showed the premium that London attached to keeping Sweden as friendly to Britain as possible. Along with the other questions which had touched the balance of power in northern

Europe since his transfer to Stockholm, this made Howard conscious once the war broke out of the monumental task confronting him to make certain Sweden, with its anti-Russian and pro-German tendencies, did not turn against Britain and the Entente.

III

Since at least his time at Budapest, Howard had joined the ranks of the so-called anti-Germans in the British foreign-policy-making elite.[39] Like Hardinge, Nicolson, Crowe, Spring Rice, and others, he saw in German foreign, military, and naval policy the most lethal threat to Britain's position as the pre-eminent world Power. His perception since the Bosnian crisis had been that much of the blame for the problems in the Balkans stemmed from clumsy Austro-Hungarian efforts to eliminate Serbia, Russia's client, and the Slav threat in southeastern Europe.[40] As he observed the unfolding of the July crisis from the vantage point of Stockholm, he concluded that Germany had set in train the events that led to the final breakdown of peace in Europe.[41] Behind German policy lay a determination to destroy the British Empire. It followed that responsibility for the failure to find a peaceful solution to 'the third Balkan war', chiefly Berlin's rejection of a Grey proposal for a conference of the Powers to do what they had done successfully in 1912, resided with the 'German' Powers. Howard's anxiety was that Britain might not come into the war, that it might not live up to its obligations to its two Entente partners because of the determination of radicals in the Asquith government to have Britain stand aside whilst the continental Powers fought.[42] When the Germans sent their armies through Belgium in an effort to knock France out of the war, he knew the turning point had been reached. Thus, after learning on the morning of 5 August that Britain had finally declared war on Germany because of its violation of Belgian neutrality, his worries vanished. 'It came almost as a relief', he recorded in his memoirs, 'after all the uncertainties of the last days and the overpowering fear that perhaps my country might not live up to her plighted word.'

All of this demonstrates that, once the war began, Howard entertained no doubts that the 'German' Powers were to blame for it. He perceived that the essential struggle was an Anglo-German one. If Germany came to dominate the continent, Britain would not long survive as a Power of the first rank, let alone a world Power. Aggressive Germany had to be defeated if there was to be real peace and security for Britain and the Empire in the future. This attitude coloured Howard's work at Stockholm during the war years – he left only at the end of August 1918, a little more than two months before the armistice on the Western Front. It gave him the will to do all in his power to ensure that British policy carried out from

Stockholm was successful. Howard had to pursue a two-front war of his own in Stockholm. The first front was against the Swedes, with their pro-German interests and attitudes. The second front was more sporadic, with Howard often engaging in disputes with his superiors in London and with his colleagues in the Diplomatic Service to influence the shape of British policies in neutral northern Europe in the way he judged would be most effective for achieving victory. This constituted the essence of his wartime activities, and he brought to it all the skills, talents, knowledge, and experience that he had gained since he first entered the Diplomatic Service in 1885. As Howard had shown since at least 1903, effective diplomacy was marked by a realistic appraisal of the situation and a hard-nosed application of policy. But, as he had also known since at least 1903, success as a diplomat came from presenting unpalatable issues to host governments in an anodyne way. His accomplishments in his preceding four posts showed this. Howard's war service in Stockholm was distinguished by an appreciation of the big picture of British foreign policy, an attempt to understand and adapt to the point of view of and pressures put on the Swedish government, and a decided skill in pursuing policies that, whilst not offending the Swedes, helped Britain win the war.

Immediately upon Britain's declaration of war on Germany, Howard received instructions from the Foreign Office that his work at Stockholm now had 'two main objectives': first, ensuring that Sweden kept out of the war; and, secondly, preventing Sweden 'from assisting Germany to obtain a mass of overseas supplies which the Germans needed for the prosecution of the war, and therefore, for the slaughter of our sailors and soldiers at the front and those of our Allies'.[43] The more important of the two involved keeping Sweden neutral; the Entente did not need another enemy, this time in northern Europe, to drain men, money, resources, and energy from the crucial fronts in eastern and western Europe. Sweden's germanophilic proclivities meant, however, that working to prevent Germany being supplied with needed war materials would entail a cautious diplomacy. Pushing Sweden too hard over selling raw materials and industrialised goods to Germany might push Sweden into declaring war on Britain and its allies.

Howard's principal diplomatic concern in pursuing his two objectives lay with the Russian question. Of the three Entente Powers, Britain had the dominant voice in the determination of Entente policy towards Scandinavia. This derived from the use of the Royal Navy to enforce a very stringent maritime blockade of Germany.[44] The blockade was also imposed against those neutral states which, like Sweden, were in a position to supply war materials to Germany and its allies. Such war materials, labelled contraband, were subject to seizure by the Royal Navy. If a neutral state could show that the goods in question were for its exclusive use and not for re-export to Germany or its allies, the British would let the goods through – this particular aspect of the British blockade, so-called 'rationing', emerged later in the war and touched commodities as diverse as coal, raw cotton, and machine parts – the amount of such commodities permitted ingress by the British was based on pre-war levels of consumption by the blockaded neutral.

The fact that the British were responsible for the blockade of the neutral Powers tied Howard's 'two main objectives' and the Russian question together. Generally speaking, the significance of a possible Swedish entry into the war against the Entente Powers had two aspects. The first was the effect which it would have had on Russia's trade, both with the Entente and with Sweden and other neutrals. The other was the consequence which Swedish military intervention could have had on the Eastern Front. Germany's declaration of war and, subsequently, in November 1914, that of Turkey meant that Russia's overseas trade shrank virtually to nil by the end of 1914. With Germany and its allies blocking the land-trading routes in Europe, and the Dardanelles and Scandinavian straits closed to Russian shipping, Russia became reliant on the port of Vladivostok and those in the White Sea for external trade. An exception to this stranglehold was trade with Sweden via the Gulf of Bothnia and overland from the Swedish railhead at Haparanda to the Finnish rail line at Tornea. This 'Swedish connexion' was now important to Russia for two reasons: Russia was dependent on Sweden for some vital aspects of its war industry, especially imports of precision engineering equipment; and, by trans-shipment from Norwegian ports, Sweden provided a year-round ingress for essential war supplies from Britain and France.

In all of this lay a complex diplomatic situation that taxed Howard's abilities until at least early 1917, when revolution in Russia followed by American entry into the war on the Entente side changed the complexion of the struggle. If Britain alone had been fighting Germany, Howard could easily have advocated a far more stringent application of British economic, military, and naval power to cow Sweden into neutrality and prevent it from helping Germany. However, Britain was not alone; it was a member of a three-Power coalition fighting Germany and, as the war progressed, this Allied coalition grew to include other Powers. Consequently, Allied interests, especially Russian ones, had to be considered every time Howard advocated a policy line or, in following orders from London, undertook some action in Stockholm. Such was driven home to him in his relations with Anatole Nekludoff, the Russian minister at Stockholm. Within weeks of the British declaration of war, Howard, Nekludoff, and their French colleague, Thiébaut, were meeting almost daily to discuss all manner of issues touching Sweden and inter-Allied trade.[45] Given Russia's need for a neutral Sweden, Nekludoff consistently stressed flexibility in dealing with Sweden. Russia's exposed position was also impressed on Howard by a telegram sent by the Russian chief of staff to London, and repeated to Stockholm, that Sweden entering the war on Germany's side would be 'incalculable and disastrous' for Russia. 'This telegram', Howard later wrote, 'burned itself into my memory in letters of fire.'[46]

For Howard, then, his work in neutral Sweden involved balancing diplomatic expediency with military necessity. Russian needs provided Sweden with the diplomatic lever to pry off British attempts to control Swedish trade with Germany. That Vladivostok was too remote from both potential suppliers and Russian industry to service the needs of Russia in the war and that the White Sea ports were ice-bound six months of the year meant that Sweden had a strong position from which to negotiate modifications to the British blockade. This position, however, was not unassailable. Once the Russians completed the construction of a rail line to Nikolaev – now Murmansk – an ice-free port, much of the leverage enjoyed by Sweden would disappear. Thus the progress of the building of this line became a matter of importance for Howard and his colleagues, not only for the impact it would have on Russia's war effort, but also for the impact which it would have on Sweden's ability to circumvent the British blockade. The military situation on the Eastern Front also affected the Swedish lever. Prior to the war, despite the disproportionately large amount of money spent on the Russian Baltic Fleet, the Russian Admiralty had conceded control of the Baltic to the German navy. The role of the Russian navy was to be largely defensive, designed to protect the approaches to the three vital gulfs of Bothnia, Finland, and Riga.[47] Should Sweden combine with Germany and its allies, such an aim would be difficult, if not impossible. Swedish ports in the Gulf of Bothnia would be closed and the vital Aland Islands would be unavailable to the Russians. There was the additional possibility that the Swedish army might join with the Germans in an attack on St Petersburg, either through Finland or by an amphibious descent. Here, the Russian key was the military position in Courland and Livonia. If Riga fell, the way to St Petersburg would be open; therefore, concern about Swedish intervention could not be overlooked. Thus, the military situation on Russia's Northern Front, that is, the area of the Baltic States, became an issue influencing Anglo-Swedish relations: the better the Russian military position, the less influence Sweden could exert on Britain and vice versa.

In this way, when the war broke out in August 1914, Howard's twofold task of keeping Sweden neutral and preventing it from helping the Germans was immediately reckoned to be of the highest importance for the

British. Sharing the general expectation that the war would be a short one, Howard recommended to the Foreign Office throughout the autumn of 1914 that Sweden not be pressed too sharply to conform rigidly to the provisions of the British blockade. As he saw it, the principal goal of British policy should be 'to prevent the Scandinavian neutral states becoming a regular channel of supply for Germany and Austria, and, at the same time, not to create a feeling of serious hostility or irritation to ourselves'.[48] Howard's concern over this second point was profound. As early as 7 August he had advised Grey that it was unlikely that Sweden would enter the war on the side of the Central Powers.[49] Over the succeeding four months his views on the Swedish situation remained unchanged, and they proved to be decisive at the Foreign Office despite some opinion there to the contrary.[50]

The Anglo-Swedish negotiations in 1914 showed the dominance of Howard's views. On 3 November Sweden was sent a memorandum offering to allow it to import contraband providing it was willing to agree not to re-export these goods, or an equivalent amount of its own material, with the ultimate destination being the Central Powers.[51] But Howard felt this was not enough given the conservative climate of opinion in Sweden. Throughout November he kept track of bellicose statements by important Swedes, so that on 22 November he was able to report to Grey that not only were Swedish soldiers and sailors anxious to join the war on Germany's side, but that Gustav had been reported as saying to a number of people 'that if Germany was hard pressed by Russia, Sweden would have to come to her aid & would probably be at war in a few months'.[52] One way to reduce Swedish antipathy towards the Entente resided in a less stringent application of the British blockade; by 8 December, Howard succeeded in getting the Foreign Office to go further than the 3 November memorandum and grant even more generous exemptions.

Whilst Howard had been able to persuade his own government to go easy on the Swedes during the first five months of the war, by the beginning of 1915 the situation had changed and the Swedes were unwilling to accept the British terms. Much of this derived from the military situation. The short war of pre-war expectation seemed less certain: the Russian 'steamroller' had failed to win a decisive victory in the east; the stalemate of trench warfare had emerged in the west; and the Dardanelles had been closed to Russian shipping by the Turks.[53] In these circumstances, Russian control of northern sea lanes to Sweden became of great importance, so much that Vice-Admiral Ivan Grigorovich, the Russian minister of marine, wrote to his foreign minister, Sergei Sazanov, that the Aland Islands had to be fortified if Russia was to remain secure in the Gulf of Bothnia.[54] When Nekludoff informed Wallenberg of this Russian action, Wallenberg indicated that his government would not object, though he stressed that the matter be kept secret. But, having made such a concession, the Swedish government was not willing to bow further to Allied pressure. Just five days after accepting the Russian demand, on 13 January, the Hammarskjöld government announced that the transit of arms across its territory would be banned.[55]

Stockholm's ban on arms shipments across Sweden, coupled with the fact the war did not 'end by Christmas', put Howard in a difficult position. For the first five months of the war, he had advocated a tolerant attitude towards the Swedes and had been successful in getting it accepted by the Foreign Office. Although London seemed willing during that time to follow Howard's lead at Stockholm given other more pressing diplomatic problems – notably seeking to keep Turkey and the Balkan states out of the German alliance – the failure of Grey's diplomacy at Constantinople and Sofia by the New Year brought calls by British advocates of a tough blockade for increased pressure on Sweden. As Howard continued to urge some restraint in applying the blockade to Sweden, he found himself at odds with the British minister at Christiania, Mansfeldt Findlay, and the naval attaché for all of Scandinavia, who worked out of the Legation at the Norwegian capital, Captain Montagu Consett.

Howard had his hands full with Findlay and Consett throughout most of the war. Both of these men had little use for the Swedes because of the pro-German attitudes dominant in the court, government, officer corps, and so on at Stockholm,[56] Speaking for both himself and Consett early in the war, Findlay put his views on record. A major consideration in their thinking was the belief that Sweden, through its minister at Christiania, was seeking to push Norway into the German camp.[57] Findlay's essential criticism was that, despite everything Howard was doing to get Sweden a better deal with British blockade authorities in London, the Hammarskjöld government could not be trusted. Findlay went so far as to put this to Grey in a private letter in November, a copy of which he sent to Howard and in which he emphasised that this was not a 'personal dispute' but rather one of 'different points of view'.[58] When in December 1914 Howard suggested that Britain support an entente of the neutral Scandinavian states – and Grey had been explicit in August 1914 that Britain and its allies expected them to maintain their neutrality and that, in return, the anti-German Powers would help them to defend that neutrality – Findlay torpedoed such an idea. 'I foresee that, although a Scandinavian Entente may have great advantages in so far as it strengthens Wallenberg & the party in favour of Swedish neutrality,' Findlay wrote to Howard, 'it will have the great disadvantage of dragging Norway more or less into the orbit of Sweden and Baltic politics where Germany can exercise a great deal of pressure.'[59]

Howard's task now became doubly difficult. With the changing military situation by early 1915, he had not only to worry about Swedish reactions to British policy, but also to contend with increasingly powerful voices in his own government which criticised his assessment of the Swedish problem and how to respond to it. Little doubt existed that the Swedes were doing all in their power to circumvent the somewhat loose blockade, based on the November and December 1914 memoranda, that Howard had been able to get London to adopt. That London would go no further than the 8 December memorandum was made abundantly clear to Howard and the Swedish government when the Foreign Office refused to help a Swedish delegation, led by Marcus Wallenberg, the foreign minister's brother, secure a British loan. Despite Howard's strong support for such a loan, Grey himself intervened with the Treasury to prevent it. The foreign secretary did this after the Foreign Office had received information from Spring Rice at Washington that the purpose of the loan, ostensibly to stabilise the kronor, was really 'intended for German purchases abroad'.[60]

Howard watched as, by March 1915, the positions on both sides hardened because authorities in London believed that the blockade had to be tightened to put as much pressure as possible on the Germans. The British government passed an Order-in-Council on 11 March stating that all ships bound for German ports would be detained. In response, the Swedes put forward a policy of 'compensation', that is, that they would allow only as much material to be exported to Russia – either from domestic Swedish production or of foreign manufacture – as the British would permit the Swedes to export to Germany.[61] Howard remained unsure that this Order-in-Council was necessary. Just a week before it came into effect, he had written to Bryce that blockade work at Stockholm was increasingly less rancorous:

> We are on the whole getting on better here for the moment. Our arrangements with the S[wedish] G[overnment] as to the restriction of contraband are working with greater smoothness & I have not heard half so many complaints as I did in January when the atmosphere was thick with theirs & I was told daily that we were ruining Sweden & throwing Swedish work men [sic] out of work.[62]

Howard's difficulty lay with the Foreign Office's inability to see the 'greater smoothness' of the situation. Hence, when the increased restrictions came into force, Howard complained to the Foreign Office that this demonstrated a lack of confidence in his appraisal of the situation. This led to Crowe, now the head of the Contraband Department in a restructured wartime Foreign Office, putting the matter into perspective.[63] Although the Contraband Department had agreed to the softer blockade policies advocated by Howard in late 1914 – and Crowe allowed that this had been done with 'misgiving' – the Swedish attitude in the first months of 1915 had made hard policies necessary. The Foreign Office saw the Swedes, both the government in Stockholm and the diplomats in London, as the culprits in this affair. 'It is no use pretending', Crowe observed icily, 'that our confidence has not been rudely shaken. Things have gone through, en masse, openly under our noses and those of the Swedish authorities.' In addition, the Foreign Office believed that the Swedes were advancing German interests by stirring up anglophobic sentiments in Denmark and Norway, as well as conspiring with Italy which, though a neutral, still remained a member of the Triple Alliance. Crowe argued that Allied interests could be advanced only by letting the Swedes know frankly that British blockade policies would be enforced to the letter.

For the remainder of 1915, Howard's work at Stockholm entailed balancing between hardening positions on both sides of the Anglo-Swedish relationship. In this period, as well as for the duration of the war, it must be emphasised that Howard had little personal regard for the Swedish policy of neutrality. He referred to Sweden, as well as other neutral Powers, as *tertii gaudentes*, 'laughing third parties'; he did so, as he wrote in his memoirs, because 'I became convinced that one object of neutral Powers is to make all the money they can out of war by trading with belligerents and thus, intentionally or not, helping to prolong war to the latest hour possible'.[64] His condemnation of the mercenary aspects of neutrality was not limited to 1914–18. As he also wrote in his memoirs: 'I do not accuse the neutrals of the Great War only of this rather unsavoury rôle, but neutrals in all wars at all times, including my own country.'[65] But as a serving diplomat during a war in which Britain was fighting for its survival as a world Power, Howard could not let his personal beliefs colour his diplomatic work. His twofold task, first outlined in August 1914, had not altered. The changing military situation, the failure to keep Turkey out of the German alliance, and the need to tighten the economic screws on the Central Powers meant his task was both more important and more difficult than ever. Thus, for the remainder of 1915, he swallowed the hard words of Crowe and the criticisms of Findlay and Consett and worked to follow through successfully on his assignment.

Howard saw the 11 March Order-in-Council as a decision which reflected on more than purely British strategic and diplomatic considerations. Russian needs had to be weighed in any blockade calculations. The tsarist government supported the tightening of the blockade as long as supplies which had to cross Sweden were not endangered in any way. Howard reported on 13 April that Nekludoff and the Russian commercial attaché at Stockholm 'regard it as essential' that Russia should continue to get certain material from Sweden and did not feel that 'there was any particular harm' in accepting the compensatory principle.⁶⁶ Two months later, Sir George Buchanan, the British ambassador at Petrograd – St Petersburg's name had been changed because it sounded too German – wrote to support Howard's view that danger lay in 'allowing the contraband question to outweigh political considerations of still greater importance'.⁶⁷ This derived from the worsening Russian military situation.⁶⁸ Beginning in May 1915, the Germans launched a major eastern offensive which led to massive Russian retreats that ended only in September. A major concern was a shortage of supplies, therefore foreign orders and shipments were viewed as essential. For Buchanan, and through him Howard, this meant Russian concerns took on a new urgency as there were fears of a separate Russian peace or, perhaps, political upheaval in Russia to the detriment of the war effort. Rumours were also circulating that Sweden was contemplating joining the Central Powers, which were compounded by the certain knowledge that Finnish nationalists in Germany were working to bring Sweden into the war against Russia.⁶⁹ The Finns were prepared to buy Swedish help in liberating Finland from tsarist rule by ceding the Aland Islands to Sweden. The Russians had no desire to be seen suppressing a nationalist revolt in Finland during the war, and furthermore did not welcome the military threat involved in defending against the Germans on the whole of the Eastern Front. In the event, whilst the Swedes rejected these Finnish overtures, Russian concern remained.

Howard's letter from Crowe suggested that the blockade authorities at London were concerned about the policy of leniency adopted towards Sweden. Although Howard remained unaware of it, some at London believed Hammarskjöld and Wallenberg had duped him.⁷⁰ This stemmed from a series of reports which showed that the Swedes were evading the spirit of the blockade and passing on strategic goods to Germany. In late March, for instance, when the Stockholm Legation reported that a major Swedish firm was exporting an increasing number of horseshoes to Germany, little doubt existed that these horseshoes, once in Germany, were melted down and remanufactured to produce shellcasings.⁷¹ The British problem derived from horseshoes not being covered in the contraband lists outlined in the two memoranda sent to the Swedish government in late 1914. Thus, Howard's efforts to minimise Swedish irritation with the blockade by getting a range of exemptions for Sweden created difficulties for Crowe and the Contraband Department.

But Howard's concerns about the wider political and strategic context of Swedish problems were also recognised by the Foreign Office. When Findlay had been remonstrating against Howard in late 1914, Grey had minuted: 'There is not really much difference between the two controversialists: on the whole I think Mr Howard has the best of it.'[72] There were also those rumours of possible Swedish entry into the war on the German side, rumours which assumed decided importance when the German offensive in May 1915 threatened the Baltic States. This roused the Russians over blockade policy towards Sweden, as both Sazanov and General Nikolai Ianushkevich, the army chief of staff, pointed out the disastrous consequences of a possible Swedish intervention.[73] At the same time, Buchanan impressed on London the unfavourable reaction of Russian opinion on recent Anglo-French efforts to aid Russia's war effort.[74] The Hammarskjöld government, recognising it now had a strong hand, moved to exploit the situation by setting up the State Commerce Commission on 8 June, a body to deal with balancing licences for exports to Russia against those for Germany.[75] All of this led to a Foreign Office decision to send a four-man mission headed by Robert Vansittart, of the Western Department, to Stockholm in late June. Although sent ostensibly to negotiate a new blockade agreement, the mission's real purpose was to ensure Swedish neutrality.[76]

Although at first glance Howard's ability to represent Britain might seem to have come under question because of the despatch of this mission, the decision really amounted to Foreign Office recognition that Sweden remained of vital importance to both the application of the blockade and the wider political interests of Allied unity. Once the British mission arrived in Stockholm, an impasse in the discussions quickly emerged. The British sought to reduce Swedish imports to their pre-war level as a means of ensuring that no goods were passed on to Germany; the Swedes wanted British recognition of the compensatory principle. In all of this, the Russians advocated moderation.[77] But the Foreign Office was not too concerned about getting an agreement, since the mission's purpose seems to have been to stretch out negotiations, thereby reducing the chance of Sweden entering the war against the Allies at this crucial time – the rail line to Nikolaiev would likely be completed in 1916. This goal was achieved, thus few tears were shed when Vansittart left Stockholm empty-handed in October. The British were not about to put their trust in an agreement with the Swedes anyway. The real thrust of British policy was spelled out by Grey to Buchanan in August: whilst the British were willing to sacrifice with respect to the blockade for Russia's sake, 'we have it in our power to refuse Sweden supplies which she cannot do without, and we fully intend, with or without agreement, to use this lever for insisting, among other things, on equivalent or larger supplies needed by Russia going through'.[78] Clearly, Vansittart's mission was to complement Howard's diplomacy, not to supplant it.

Howard played a crucial part in the negotiations undertaken by

Vansittart and his three colleagues, providing them with information about the situation in Stockholm and smoothing over as many difficulties put in the way of the negotiations as possible.[79] A consequence of this was that Howard and Vansittart became firm friends – just before Vansittart left London, his brother, Arnold, had died on the Western Front, and Howard and his family played a major part in helping Vansittart overcome his grief.[80] Just as important, the problems Howard faced at Stockholm, permeated as it was with pro-German and anti-Russian sentiments, were driven home to the members of the mission. This came about through the ongoing debate between the Legations in Stockholm and Christiania about the rigour of the blockade in neutral northern Europe. Throughout 1915 the divergence of opinion between Howard, on one hand, and Findlay and Consett, on the other, widened. Both Howard and the Foreign Office were subjected to a barrage of letters from Findlay which suggested that Britain could apply the blockade against Sweden as tightly as possible with impunity, this because of Consett's belief that the Swedes would never dare go to war against the Allied Powers.[81] In fact, in the summer of 1915, Howard quarrelled so heatedly with Consett about the application of blockade policy that the normally patient minister sought clarification from Crowe over who precisely advised the Foreign Office on this matter. Crowe responded with a categoric statement that the responsibility resided with Howard.[82]

No question existed in the minds of Vansittart and his colleagues when they left Stockholm about the enormity of the task confronting Howard. They duly informed the Foreign Office. One mission member, H. H. Cleminson, had travelled to Christiania to consult with Findlay. The stark contrast between the attitude to the war in Norway – the court and political circles there were pro-British – and that in Sweden impressed Cleminson markedly. As he wrote immediately to a colleague in the Contraband Department at London:

Of course Howard's job is one of much more difficulty. By comparison Findlay's is child's play. Howard is just the man for it and it's mighty lucky we've got him here. He has a real diplomatic problem to handle which does not exist in Christiania and all the commercial work of Norway is or should be half of Sweden.[83]

The upper echelons of the Foreign Office appreciated the disparity between war work at Stockholm and Christiania, something made abundantly clear by both Vansittart's verbal report to Crowe and Howard's summary of the four months of fruitless negotiation.[84] After assessing the situation, Grey wrote to express his approval of Howard's war work.[85]

Throughout 1915, apart from the blockade activities, Howard's routine diplomatic work remained much as it had before August 1914. This was a function of Britain and Sweden being at peace. Howard, therefore, conducted business on a routine basis with the Hammarskjöld government. However, as the war raged on the periphery of neutral northern Europe, that routine work assumed much more importance. Stockholm was the most important neutral capital in the region, a function of both Sweden's economic importance to the German war effort and its contiguity with Russia. Moreover, given that the Central Powers maintained Legations in Stockholm, Howard had to keep conversant with all that transpired between the pro-German Swedish government and Berlin – a burdensome duty given that, once the war broke out, Howard and the Allied ministers had no formal contact with those of the Central Powers.[86] At this point, peacetime diplomacy melded with that necessary for Allied success in the war.

Howard's contact with the Swedes did not disabuse him of the notion of *tertii gaudentes*. Hammarskjöld, who had risen to prominence as an international lawyer, took every opportunity when seeing Howard after the war broke out to castigate British blockade politics. The premier argued that the declarations of Paris (1856) and London (1909), both of which advocated complete neutral rights in wartime including freedom of the seas, were violated by the British blockade.[87] Hammarskjöld's words had a bitter twist. Since Britain supported both declarations before the war, he implied that Howard's government stood guilty of the basest hypocrisy by its rigorous application of maritime belligerent rights. Three times during the first eighteen months of the war, Hammarskjöld summoned Howard to protest personally against the blockade.[88] These were unusual diplomatic practices, as heads of government rarely delivered such disapprobations to envoys. Twice Howard said nothing except that he would report the premier's views to London. But the third time, with the war stalemated and tremendous losses inflicted on Britain on land and sea, he refused to bite his tongue. Hammarskjöld's hiding behind the advocacy of neutral rights whilst his country made no secret of its support for Germany comprised, Howard argued, the real hypocrisy. Alluding to the pro-German sympathies in Sweden, Howard enquired how the Swedish premier viewed the German violation of Belgian neutrality and, more to the point, whether he supported the German submarine offensive against unarmed merchantmen. Britain had not invaded any neutral state whilst its blockade, which involved the capture of merchantmen not their sinking, indicated that British policy towards neutral states remained starkly different from that of Germany. Combining both the official British position and his personal views, Howard put the case bluntly:

The ordinary rules of war came to an end when Germany entered Belgium. That act of hers killed the Declaration of Paris and the Declaration of London at one blow as well as other provisions guaranteeing seaborne trade with belligerents...The old rules of maritime warfare no longer obtain: it is therefore no use protesting about these matters any longer or quoting these rules to me.

Reluctantly, Hammarskjöld admitted the merit of Howard's argument.

Howard never again met with the premier. His contacts thereafter with the Hammarskjöld government – it survived in office until March 1917 – were limited to meetings with Wallenberg. For whatever reason, the Swedish foreign minister tried to ensure his country's neutrality. His efforts, especially over the opposition of the Court clique, led in June 1915 to the Germans and their Swedish sympathisers seeking to have him removed. Howard reported a press campaign in Sweden that suggested that Wallenberg was 'too favourably inclined towards the Allies, on account of his large financial interests and connections in Great Britain and France'.[89] But Howard saw that Wallenberg's personal disposition to keep Sweden formally neutral did not prevent Swedish interests from seeking to supply the Germans with as many goods as possible. Thus, whilst Howard maintained normal diplomatic contacts with the Swedish government – and through Wallenberg getting a fair hearing at the Foreign Ministry[90] – he was aware of the chief goal of Swedish foreign and economic policies: circumventing the British blockade to trade with Germany.

Howard's regular diplomatic work also involved gathering information and, when he judged necessary, tendering advice to the Foreign Office. The information he was able to gather often amounted to bits of political gossip that came his way, an indispensable part of diplomatic life. In 1915, he reported on the pro-German machinations of the Court clique led by Queen Victoria, as well as the efforts of the German minister, Baron von Lucius, a 'dangerous diplomat', to erode Wallenberg's resolve to support strict neutrality.[91] He passed this sort of information on to his superiors in order to let them know about the delicacy with which the Swedes had to be approached and, more crucially, to counteract the ideas of Findlay and Consett that the possibility of Sweden entering the war on the German side constituted a bogey.

He also sent along information about other matters outside of the Anglo-Swedish relationship. In July he learnt that a director of the Deutsches Bank, then at Stockholm, had approached Nekludoff through a prominent Russian businessman to broach the idea of a separate peace between Germany and Russia.[92] German gains in Poland at Russian expense would be compensated by giving Russia 'possession of Constantinople', as well as areas of eastern Europe including Galicia. Von Lucius had apparently endorsed this approach. Howard told Nicolson that Nekludoff had immediately wired Sazanov, and Nekludoff expected that the Russian foreign minister would inform Grey. Other reports sent by Howard related to internal conditions in Germany – that is, that the blockade was creating economic hardships – as gleaned from Swedes and others who had travelled there.[93] Howard knew that this sort of 'intelligence' only supplemented that sent in by British diplomats in every other post, but that it was necessary if the Foreign Office was to come to grips with the big diplomatic picture for which it was responsible.

Howard's tendering advice was a different proposition. If his twofold political task had any chance of success, those who directed the war effort in London had to be made fully aware of the diplomatic impact of their blockade, and economic and military policies on Sweden. In such circumstances, Howard strained every resource to influence the shape of British policies in neutral northern Europe in the way he judged to be most effective. A case in point arose just as the Vansittart mission arrived in Stockholm. Howard complained to Crowe that it appeared as if the Legation in Stockholm was being ignored by the blockade experts in London when they devised policy that touched his political work of keeping Sweden neutral and ensuring that Russia's war effort would not be imperilled by any closeness in Swedish–German relations.[94] The crux of Howard's remarks was that Consett's views and advice about how best to balance a stringent blockade with keeping Sweden neutral were taking precedence over those of Howard and his staff. Because the Legation was being bypassed in this decision-making process, the political consequences were difficult to assess and effective responses made harder to formulate. The issue at hand involved the consigning of hardening metals to consumer industries in neutral nations. London had suddenly, and without telling Howard, begun restricting all traffic in those metals that, by an earlier agreement, were to go to Sweden. Surmising that Consett had had a hand in the decision, Howard also noted that it seemed as if a range of corollary issues touching the blockade, for instance the matter of licences to export commodities like metals, were being discussed and decided in London without reference to the Stockholm Legation or the efforts it was making to keep Anglo-Swedish relations steady.

Howard's words caused Crowe to respond with a lenitive letter to impress on the minister that the particular matter of metal exports was one beyond the control of both the Foreign Office and the Contraband Department.[95] Instead it was a special arrangement governed in this instance by the Admiralty. American metal merchants had been restricted to trade limitations with neutral consumers because of the British blockade; British ones were not. The Americans complained, justly thought Crowe, that this constituted unequal competition. To be as fair as possible, the Admiralty had decided that restrictions must be universal. This affected Sweden adversely, but Sweden was just one of a number of neutrals so bothered. Consett may have advised the Admiralty in this; however, about his counselling the Foreign Office, Crowe observed: 'I cannot imagine what put it in your head that we were consulting or being advised by Consett. I have so far as I can remember not seen a line of his since the war began, and had, in fact[,] become entirely oblivious to his existence.'

Crowe's response to Howard is interesting in two ways. First, it shows clearly that the Foreign Office Contraband Department was pursuing its politics quite independently of the Admiralty. This meant the pursuit of blockade policy with more emphasis on the wider political and economic issues and less on the technical ones that preoccupied the Royal Navy. Although the Admiralty might dominate in this particular matter, the Foreign Office still held responsibility for the vast majority of blockade decisions which the British government had to make.[96] Secondly, and more important, it demonstrates visibly that, although Consett divided his time amongst the Legations in Stockholm, Copenhagen, and Christiania, almost a year after the war began one of the pivotal officials in Britain's blockade establishment had not seen any of his reports. Thus the Foreign Office remained concerned primarily with the political ramifications of policy – the domain of Howard and the other diplomatic agents – more so than with the purely naval and technical ones. From July 1915 on, Howard knew that his advice had decided weight with his superiors at London.

That Howard's advice had an impact on the shape of British blockade policies in Sweden emerged most clearly in the immediate aftermath of the Vansittart mission; this led to Howard's greatest diplomatic success in the first half of the war, the establishment of the Transito company. Although Vansittart failed to arrange a new Anglo-Swedish blockade agreement, the need remained for the British to have some device to ensure that goods destined for Russia were not diverted to Germany. As mentioned earlier, Howard's understanding line towards the Swedes did not equate with a personal support for the policy of neutrality, far from it. He knew and remained concerned that goods, especially those supposedly ticketed for transit across Sweden to Russia, were ending up in Germany. One of the things he had done during the first months of the war was to create an intelligence-gathering network to determine the extent of the movement of goods in and out of Sweden; he accomplished this by using the existing British consuls in key ports like Gothenburg and, then, lobbying London to get additional help for these men.[97] His information, when compared with that available in the Contraband Department and at the British Embassy in Petrograd, by early 1915 indicated that large quantities of goods imported by the Swedes were ending up in Germany. In March, Howard had advised that the British create a trade organisation in Sweden to control 'transit traffic' of goods assigned to Russia.[98] An equivalent body, the Netherlands Overseas Trust, had been set up, with the blessing of the Dutch government, by Dutch businessmen and traders to guarantee that goods imported into Holland would not be exported to Germany.[99] With Nekludoff failing to persuade the Hammarskjöld government to do the same thing in Sweden[100] – and with the tsar's government, through Buchanan, pressing London to improve supply[101] – Howard suggested that the British government unilaterally establish an Overseas Trust in Sweden.

Howard's advice in March 1915 came to nought after a decision that Vansittart should settle the matter. When Vansittart failed, Howard returned to the charge. Intelligence showed that goods, notably armaments and the materials necessary for producing munitions, were being diverted to Germany even as Vansittart wrangled throughout the summer with Hammarskjöld and Wallenberg.[102] Howard now realised that the Hammarskjöld government would never allow a British subject to establish an equivalent of the Netherlands operation in Sweden. But a Swedish citizen could, and if this Swede could be persuaded to be a nominal head and allow the British to run the organisation, then both the British blockade and Russian supply would be that much easier. Such a Trust would have no control over imports from neutral Powers but, since Russian supply occurred through the British, a pro-Allied, Swedish-owned trading organisation would not only prevent the diversion of Russian goods to Germany, it would also permit improved application of the British blockade since the precise amount of goods imported for transit to Russia would be known.

With Vansittart leaving empty-handed, and Russian pressure to do something continuing, Howard was given freedom to act. He induced his anglophile friend, the businessman, Axel de Bildt, to form a company to handle the transit of goods across Sweden to Russia.[103] He then, with great caution, approached Wallenberg to ensure that the Swedish authorities would not put legal impediments in the way of the British puppet company; in a signal diplomatic achievement, he obtained Wallenberg's formal agreement that no problems would ensue as long as 'legitimate Swedish interests do not suffer'.[104] By the end of December 1915 a private Swedish company, Transito Aktiebilag, ostensibly owned by de Bildt, began operations to handle transit traffic to Russia. Though owned by de Bildt, Transito was run by Howard and the British Legation in conjunction with the Russians.[105] Its operations, legally speaking, were unlawful as the Swedish prohibition on arms shipments of January 1915 was still in effect. But British pressure over imports and the turning of a blind eye towards some Swedish exports to Germany led to a sort of uneasy *modus vivendi*. As Howard subsequently put it, this arrangement was 'a very clumsy makeshift for a more general agreement...[but] we were glad to get anything we could that would to some extent satisfy the perpetual clamour of our Russian friends'.[106]

By early 1916 Howard had fulfilled the double task set out for him by the Foreign Office within twenty-four hours of the declaration of war on Germany. It had not been easy. General Swedish sympathy for Germany, tied to Hammarskjöld's pontificating, had forced him to tread warily. British policy had had to reckon with the pro-German clique surrounding Gustav, the anti-Russian sentiments of political and military men, and the constant rumours about Sweden joining the Central Powers. The unceasing nagging by Nekludoff in Stockholm and the diplomats and soldiers in Petrograd about keeping Russian supply lines across Scandinavia open had justified Howard's temperate approach to the Swedes in the name of intra-Allied solidarity. He had paid a price for this with criticism from some quarters in London and from Findlay and Consett in Norway. Still, his diplomacy was held to be sound by the senior members of the Foreign Office, especially after Vansittart's mission. To show his appreciation of Howard's work in a substantive way, Grey arranged for Howard to be included in the king's New Year's Honours List – he was made a Knight Commander of the Order of St Michael and St George on 1 January 1916. 'Sir' Esme Howard had received recognition for his valuable service to the state at a dire point in its history. However, as the war had yet to be won, this reward amounted to encouragement from his political chief to continue along the path Sir Esme had been padding since August 1914.[107]

IV

By the early months of 1916, Howard found that the emphasis of his work had changed because of Transito's existence. The control of goods bound for Germany had become easier for the Legation to monitor and, through liaison with the Contraband Department and the Royal Navy, the blockade made more effective. It followed that the second part of Howard's twofold task – preventing Sweden from assisting Germany in obtaining supplies – had fewer difficulties. It meant, however, that the first part – keeping Sweden from joining the Central Powers – consumed more time and effort. A tighter blockade led inevitably to increased Swedish discomfort amongst politicians like Hammarskjöld who spouted 'neutral rights' at every opportunity, those at court who worried about German defeat, and traders and businessmen who were concerned about the reduction of their profits. Howard found that he spent more of his energies in soothing frayed

Swedish nerves. He could do little to assuage the bitterness of outright opponents of the Allied Powers who, seeing the blockade as the most visible evidence of the Allied war effort, lashed out at Britain. For instance, Howard informed Grey privately in January that Queen Victoria was engaged in a discreet lobbying campaign to convince prominent Swedes of the necessity for Sweden to join Germany as soon as possible in its war against Britain and Russia.[108] When he could, however, he did all in his power to have blockade authorities at London stretch a point to reduce their harassment of Swedish firms that he judged could be excused for minor transgressions against the Allied cause. In the early months of 1916, for example, he approached Eric Hambro, an Anglo-Swedish banker and a member of the War Trade Committee in London, to help remove two Swedish banks from a British 'black list' that precluded them from raising money on the London money market.[109]

Howard still believed that the Swedes had to be handled with care because of the chance they might, if pushed too hard, join with Germany against the Allies. Wider diplomatic considerations had to have precedence over the most stringent application of the blockade. By the beginning of 1916, however, the circumstances which had dominated British policy towards Sweden were changing. In 1914 and 1915, Howard had been able to make his advice accepted largely because of the situation on the Eastern Front. With Russia supporting a softer line towards Sweden, the advocates of a rigorous blockade, chiefly Findlay and Consett, found little support in London: Russia was too valuable an ally to risk either losing or offending. But as 1916 dawned, the differing views of the military men and the diplomats over the situation on the Russian front and in Scandinavia, especially in terms of the Swedes using the threat of entry into the war against Russia as blackmail to get trading concessions, emerged sharply. In late January General Sir William Robertson, the new chief of the Imperial General Staff, argued that the Swedish threat was largely negligible. He informed the Cabinet that the 'only hostile action which Sweden can take against Great Britain will be to place restrictions on trade...it does not appear at present that the intervention of Sweden in any other form than aiding a German attack on Petrograd would seriously affect the course of war'.[110] In private, Robertson showed contempt for Russian fears about Sweden.[111] Therefore, whilst Howard continued to press for restraint in the application of the blockade, British military opinion was becoming less concerned about Sweden's entry into the war. Such notions were reinforced by views and events in Russia. A British military mission to Russia reported that 'the Russians seem to be reassured as to the Swedes'.[112] Buchanan, in an interview with Tsar Nicholas, discovered that Petrograd was not too concerned with the situation on the

Northern Front since the Russians were planning a major offensive further south under General Brusilov for the summer.[113] In addition, spring meant the end of the dependence on the Swedish overland route, whilst there was optimism about the Nikolaev line being open by the end of 1916.[114] With the Northern Front more secure and another season of complete dependence on Swedish forbearance respecting trans-shipment unlikely, good reason existed to be firmer at Stockholm.

Howard continued in his work whilst the political in-fighting over policy towards Sweden broke out at London. Whilst Robertson's concerns had force, there were other issues at stake when the Foreign Office considered Sweden and blockade. Grey and his advisers were not convinced that Robertson had considered everything in a wide enough context. The Foreign Office position was circulated to the Cabinet in a memorandum prepared by Cecil Hurst, the legal adviser.[115] In commenting on the possibility of blockading the Baltic, something implicit in Robertson's musings, Hurst noted frankly that Russia would be reluctant to sanction such a move 'lest it should drive Sweden to join the enemy'. The political lesson of the blockade as it affected neutrals was obvious: the application of belligerent rights had to be done prudently. At this time, the Foreign Office argument found support from the fact that Anglo-American relations were being pushed to breaking point because of the blockade.[116] The Foreign Office memorandum implied that the military men ought to be more concerned with the diplomatic repercussions that might result if the blockade screws were tightened too firmly on Sweden.

Howard's work in 1915, the culmination being the creation of Transito, had done much to improve the economic struggle against Germany. But, with Robertson's attack on Britain's Swedish policy, the Foreign Office moved in February 1916 to improve the general blockade apparatus by restructuring the blockade administration. Since May 1915 the centre of blockade policy had resided with the Foreign Office under Lord Robert Cecil, a political under-secretary, and Crowe. Despite this, other ministries, like the Admiralty and Board of Trade, were able to follow their own blockade policies in particular instances. This tended to cause inter-departmental friction – the Admiralty decision about metal consignments being a case in point. Attempts at resolving this by a co-ordinating body failed, so in February 1916 Grey approached Asquith about creating a Ministry of Blockade.[117] Asquith agreed; Cecil became minister of blockade, though he remained at the Foreign Office. Although this meant a diminution to some extent of Grey's power over foreign policy, in purely administrative terms it meant that the Admiralty and those other ministries, military or otherwise, were virtually excluded from blockade policy making. The Foreign Office again moved to the fore.

Once the dust settled on these changes, Howard wrote to Cecil to impress on the new minister the need for caution in applying the blockade against Sweden.[118] Writing just as Marcus Wallenberg left London after fruitless negotiations with the Ministry of Blockade for a new Anglo-Swedish agreement, Howard reaffirmed the need to put political considerations above all others. Cecil had written a week before that Wallenberg had been 'entirely vague as to any prospect of a commercial agreement' and, more, suggested that 'Germany was invincible'.[119] Of this Howard conjectured:

I feel certain that the ambition of the Wallenbergs is to act as intermediaries between the belligerents, for which they no doubt think that their financial relations in both camps render them particularly suitable. The idea of playing a great rôle at the end of the war seems to have taken hold of the Swedes of all Parties, and I think it is quite useful not to nip it in the bud, as it certainly acts as a weight in the scale in favour of their maintaining their neutrality.

But, as he told Cecil, an agreement was a mirage at this stage of the war. Hammarskjöld in his inflexibility over neutral rights would never agree to one. Embargoing commodities like coal – Sweden received most of its coal from Britain – would only increase Swedish unemployment and make 'the Swedish public like a flogged donkey, back us into a ditch, instead of going along the road we want it to go'. Over all of this remained the question of Russian supply. Howard went on record to state that, if a tougher blockade increased anti-British sentiments in Sweden and the Germans had success in the Baltic provinces, 'I will not answer for the consequences'. Howard did not oppose a more stringent blockade, but its application had to conform to the political reality. The Foreign Office, the Ministry of Blockade, and the military and naval authorities in London had to be cognisant of this. 'I would further like to repeat what I have so often said in despatches,' he told Cecil, 'that <u>this Spring and Summer are the critical months as far as Sweden is concerned</u>...So I feel strongly that pressure should be applied <u>gradually</u> during these critical months' (emphasis in original).

Although Cecil supported Howard's words of caution and moved to follow through on them in applying the blockade against Sweden in the months that followed,[120] Howard's credibility came under attack from Consett. This threatened Howard's diplomacy at Stockholm, as Consett was obviously moving to emasculate those diplomats in neutral northern Europe with whom he disagreed – evidence exists suggesting that he engineered the recall of Edward Lowther, the British minister at Copenhagen, at this time.[121] Consett saw the changed circumstances of 1916 as an opportune moment to press his views on blockading Sweden and thereby discrediting Howard. By 1916, Howard was better placed than he had been in 1914 – when some felt he had been duped by the

Swedes – to withstand Consett's broadsides. His KCMG, implying Foreign Office recognition that his analysis and handling of the Swedish question were correct, coupled with the new-found hegemony of the Foreign Office in setting blockade policy, strengthened Howard's position. Consett did not recognise this and, in fact, Howard's new pre-eminence seems only to have antagonised the truculent sailor.[122]

In the middle of 1916, Howard found himself defending his diplomacy against attack from Consett. Whilst reflecting the strained relations between the two men, these quarrels touched in a major way the twin matters of how to treat the Russians and the Swedes. In late April, for instance, Howard wrote to Consett complaining about the treatment which two Russian emissaries – a naval attaché and his military counterpart – had received on a visit to Christiania.[123] The two Russians had apparently been snubbed by the Legation, which was under Consett's direction because Findlay was bedridden with phlebitis. The Russians had sent a report to their government, a report which was then circulated to the other Allies. The report misinterpreted Norwegian events and the blame for this was laid at the feet of the British Legation. Howard received an immediate rebuke from Consett in which the latter made plain his 'many misgivings' about Howard's assessment. Consett indicated that the Russians were untrustworthy in that they had not consulted the British Legation – nor, for that matter, the French one – and their misinformation came from other, unofficial sources. Consett wanted Howard to agree that 'this Legation at any rate is in no way responsible for any opinions expressed by the Russian Naval or Military Attachés'. Though no doubt justified in complaining, Consett did so with a vehemence suggesting he was not balanced in his appreciation of the problem and, moreover, exhibited a tendency to over-react at the slightest criticism. Howard had made an enemy of a man determined to force as quickly as possible an airtight blockade against the Swedes. Such a policy, if adopted, would have incalculable political repercussions within Sweden and, more ominously, on the strategic position of Russia at a dangerous time in the war. By the middle of 1916, Consett's pressing for the most stringent blockade possible was threatening Howard's thus far successful diplomacy of keeping Sweden out of the war and ensuring Russian supply. Howard had to remove the Consett threat or see all he had done for two years turn to ashes.

6

Stockholm: diplomacy and war in neutral northern Europe, 1916–1918

> The position as far as Sweden is concerned is now very much altered. We have not got to bother about Russia, for the present at any rate, & although Swedish iron & steel & some chemicals are still of great importance to the Allies, yet I presume that we could if necessary do without them.
>
> Howard, December 1917

I

As Howard moved to protect his diplomacy from being deflected by Consett in the latter half of 1916, a series of military and political events conspired to change the focus of Howard's work at Stockholm for the rest of the war. On 1 July 1916, to relieve pressure on their French allies who faced a massive German attack at Verdun, the British launched an offensive on the Somme. Lasting until October, this battle cost the British over 400,000 dead and many more wounded for little apparent military or strategic gain.[1] The Somme had a political impact on Britain that altered the country's policy-making apparatus at the highest level for the rest of the war and into the post-war period. First, a range of British politicians and generals felt that the British war effort was flagging through Asquith's inability to lead his coalition government effectively – this Liberal–Unionist coalition had been formed in May 1915 following the failure of the Dardanelles campaign. Accordingly, Asquith fell from power in early December thanks to a coup engineered by Lloyd George and a group of Liberal and Unionist politicians anxious for wartime decision-making to be carried out in the most expeditious way.[2] Asquith's replacement by Lloyd George gave Grey, tired after ten years in office and a critic of the new prime minister, an excuse to resign. Arthur Balfour succeeded to the foreign secretaryship, but this portfolio was not considered important enough to merit inclusion in the new five-man War Cabinet created by Lloyd George to manage Britain's war effort. Regular diplomacy was held to be less vital than more pressing issues like strategy and supply, a view that Grey had shared since August 1914.³ None the less, by the end of 1916, as a result of the Somme offensive, fundamental changes had occurred in both Britain's political leadership and the mechanism that made national policy. For the Foreign Office and diplomats like Howard, the advent of Balfour meant a foreign secretary lacking the political muscle to get his ministry's views consistently before the new War Cabinet.

Howard's work in Sweden was affected by other developments in the war. Their failure to break the French at Verdun led to a fateful decision by the German war lords to embark on a campaign of unrestricted submarine warfare, this to starve Britain and France of foodstuff and raw-material imports and deny them exports of industrialised goods.⁴ This decision accentuated the economic side of the struggle on both sides and, since unrestricted submarine activity involved sinking neutral merchant-men, especially American ones, brought the United States closer to the Allies. By April 1917, the United States declared war on the Central Powers. American entry into the war made Howard's work of limiting Swedish exports to Germany much easier; until that moment, the Americans had been the source of most of Germany's overseas purchasing and the neutral most likely to complain if Sweden were squeezed. Contrasted with the growing adherence of the United States to the Allied cause by late 1916 were severe internal problems in Russia which began to sap its effectiveness as an ally. The failure of the Brusilov offensive in the autumn of 1916, tied to difficulties with food distribution to Russia's urban population, demonstrated the seeming inability of the tsarist regime to cope with the war and domestic distress. These internal Russian problems, which led in March 1917 to the overthrow of the Romanov dynasty and the proclamation of a republic, began to alter the war on both the Eastern and Northern Fronts by the end of 1916.⁵ For Howard, it meant that the Swedes had less effect in blackmailing the British over the matter of Russian supply.

For Howard, the change at the top of the British foreign-policy-making establishment caused by Grey's retirement did not create any problems. Despite being tied together by bonds of friendship going back to the Kimberley Foreign Office, Howard and Grey had worked within a professional relationship since the former's last year on Crete. Howard's subsequent rewards and promotions had resulted from his record of success, not from political nepotism. Little changed with the advent of Balfour to the Foreign Office. Howard and his new political chief forged a good working relationship, albeit not one marked by any sort of personal amity. Besides, a number of senior Foreign Office colleagues – Crowe, Theo

Russell, Cecil, Tyrrell, and Vansittart – held Howard in high regard. In this way Balfour, in his own estimation and that of his principal advisers, saw little about which to complain concerning Howard's diplomacy.

Howard's position also received a fillip from two other personnel changes in the foreign-policy-making establishment. In June 1916, before any hint existed that Grey was in the twilight of his tenure as foreign secretary, Nicolson retired. In an unprecedented move, Hardinge, who had completed his service as viceroy of India, returned to replace him. Whilst in India, Hardinge had kept abreast of Howard's career, was impressed with his protégé's work, and could be relied upon to give Howard a fair hearing in London.[6] Equally important for the application of British policy in Scandinavia, the British minister in Copenhagen after August 1916 was Ralph Paget. Prior to his transfer, Paget held the assistant under-secretaryship at the Foreign Office responsible for treaty affairs, a post concerned largely with the legal application of belligerent rights. Hence, Paget understood completely the wider political issues which preoccupied the Foreign Office.[7] By the end of 1916, despite Consett's apparent hand in Lowther's recall, Paget came to share and support Howard's views about the situation in neutral northern Europe and he did so with more vigour than his predecessor.

Howard's effort to remove the Consett threat, which turned out to be the final phase of the diplomatic–military conflict that had been raging since late 1914, occurred whilst that series of military and political events described above took place. In August, despite Brusilov's initial success and the improvement in the Swedish question, Howard still cautioned the pursuit of prudent diplomacy towards Sweden. He outlined his views to Hardinge.[8] Howard concurred with the general view that 'all people here are now convinced that any chance of Sweden's coming into the war is practically at an end'. This did not mean, however, that the Swedes would never countenance entering the war, especially against the Allies. Swedish belligerency seemed possible in two ways. The first was obvious: a direct attack on Sweden. The second concerned the blockade for, if applied too tightly, every chance existed that Sweden could enter the war on Germany's side. As Howard noted: 'unless we really reduce working people here to the verge of starvation by stopping raw materials altogether and so causing factories to close I believe the war may close without a really bitter feeling against us having been created in this country generally'. Obviously the blockade, tied to 'black lists', 'navicerts', and other reforms instituted since February by the Ministry of Blockade, was sufficient to put economic pressure on Germany through neutral suppliers like Sweden;[9] this, whilst simultaneously keeping anti-British feeling in key states like Sweden at manageable levels.

Howard learnt that the Foreign Office felt inclined to sanction a more rigorous application of belligerent rights. Hardinge wrote that Robertson still believed strongly that Swedish entry into the war against the Allies would be meaningless.[10] Earlier, Cecil had suggested to Howard the necessity of having a uniform policy towards all of the Scandinavian states because the diplomatic problems would be less: 'if we sometimes seem to you rather stiff here, you will not, I am sure forget the great importance of not treating the repentant Sweden better than the relatively virtuous Norway and Denmark'.[11] But Howard stuck to his assessment. He warned the Foreign Office and the Ministry of Blockade that the Germans were still intent on getting Sweden into the war on the Central Power side; this had to be a major consideration in any belligerent rights policy that touched Sweden in any way.[12] Whether the Germans could have succeeded in this endeavour is another matter,[13] but this possibility had to be weighed when applying the blockade against Sweden. Hardinge admitted in October 1916 that Howard's admonitions about Russia 'being practically cut off from all direct communication with the West in the event of Sweden going to war' were legitimate.[14] Clearly London, or at least the diplomats who controlled the blockade administration, were willing to follow Howard's lead in keeping the delicate balance in the application of their policies.

Howard's ability to swing the architects of British blockade to his side induced Consett to bring the matter of military necessity and blockade diplomacy to a head. Ultimately, it concerned more than just Howard and Consett, bringing into play all three British legations in the Scandinavian capitals, as well as the Foreign Office and the Admiralty. In November 1916, in the aftermath of the Somme, Consett pressed hard for a more effective blockade in Scandinavia. His reason was perfectly sound in military terms, reflecting a concern for the tremendous British losses being suffered on the Western Front: it was 'the only fair thing to our men in the trenches & would end the war in a comparatively short time'.[15] Suffusing this was his perception of Swedish policy as bluff, since Sweden 'would not fight no matter what happened & if [it] made [itself] disagreeable could be starved out in a matter of two months'. He suggested that the threat of Swedish intervention against the Allies was hollow and that there was no way in which Sweden either would or could move against a more rigorous blockade. Hence Russian fears, which he deprecated at every opportunity, were groundless.

Howard found himself at odds with Findlay over the probable repercussions of Consett's proposals. Just as he had done since late 1914, Findlay continued to parrot Consett. In early October 1916, he wrote to Hardinge that 'I sincerely hope we may be able to come to an agreement with the Swedes if we can do so without giving them more than other

Scandinavians...no Scandinavian can bear seeing his neighbours getting any advantage.'[16] Where Howard advocated the need to consider each northern neutral separately in devising blockade policy and diplomatic strategy, Findlay argued for a single Scandinavian policy that did not treat Sweden better than the others. Whilst it is apparent in retrospect that the Hammarskjöld government had no desire to go to war,[17] it was not then obvious. In addition, the Russians were still nervous about the pro-German and anti-Russian tendencies of Sweden's political and Court elites.[18] This put pressure on Howard and the Foreign Office. As Howard observed in a memorandum on the subject two weeks before the fall of Tsar Nicholas:

The question of the blockade and the question of Russian transit are...most intimately connected, as far as Sweden is concerned, and it must always be remembered, in judging the case of every commodity which for some reason or other is being stopped from coming to Sweden, that this may, sooner or later, injure the transit to Russia, and cause irritation and vexation in Russia, which it is most important to avoid...if I have appeared less zealous as regards pushing the blockade, in so far as Sweden is concerned, than my colleagues in other neutral countries, it is because I have been, since the beginning of 1915, face to face with this transit problem...[19]

Howard's memorandum sought to answer the scathing criticism of his policies that emanated from the Legation at Christiania. In November 1916 when he began to press hard for a more stringent blockade, Consett made his point about the mirage of Sweden's ability to fight, and of the mistaken perceptions of the Russians, in such forceful and blunt terms that the normally patient Howard was offended. Howard saw Consett as a military man with no sensitivity to the very real political problems on the diplomatic side of the blockade. This led to Howard penning a rebuke, putting his wounded pride before Findlay, and expounding his views to the Foreign Office.[20] Findlay sought to soothe Howard's hurt feelings with a few carefully chosen words, but he still supported Consett unflinchingly. As Findlay told Howard, 'the whole question is whether we can or cannot afford to hurt neutral feelings & what they will do when hurt'.[21] For Consett and Findlay, the answer remained that neutral feelings could be hurt with impunity.

Howard's endeavour to remove Consett's threat to sensible diplomacy in northern Europe, ironically, received help from an unexpected quarter – Consett himself. This developed when the naval attaché overreached himself in his campaign to get a firmer blockade policy. In doing so, he not only antagonised Howard; he also made an enemy of Paget and brought the wrath of the Foreign Office hierarchy down on his head. This occurred when Consett tried to get the blockade authorities in London to tighten the noose more firmly around the Danes. Consett reckoned that, despite

Germany and Denmark sharing a common border, there would be no danger of a German occupation of Denmark if key Danish commodities were withheld completely from the Germans. Paget disagreed. Initially Paget had seen little to quarrel with in what Consett was doing; however, within months of his appointment, friction developed between the two men.²² The reason was the same as that lying at the bottom of Consett's differences with Howard: Consett's failure to square military expediency with diplomatic necessity. Hence, when Consett began pressing for a more stringent blockade, he became as uncompromising with Paget as he had been with Howard.²³

Howard's words of caution, now supported by Paget, led both Cecil and Grey privately to discount Consett's appraisal of the situation.²⁴ Cecil minuted laconically that 'Captain Consett is a very dangerous adviser with an *idée fixe* that we ought to coerce Denmark in every possible way.' More detailed in his criticism, the foreign secretary surmised that the Germans would make every effort to occupy Denmark if forced into the position to do so; he doubted also Consett's certainty that Sweden would remain neutral. More crucial than diplomatic concern about northern Europe was the situation in Russia and Eastern Europe, especially Romania. Consett ignored this. Grey opined that these factors militated against a stronger blockade and, in a wider sense, there existed the matter of the United States. At that juncture, just before the German decision to embark on unrestricted submarine warfare, Anglo-American relations had reached a half-century nadir because of the incompatibility of the British doctrine of maritime belligerent rights with the American theory of the freedom of the seas. As Grey observed realistically: 'It is improbable that the Americans would stand a wholesale blockade of neutral ports.' With British reliance on American money and supplies, the risk of unduly antagonising the Americans could not be countenanced.²⁵

Howard, joined by Paget, had exhausted his arguments to dissuade Consett. The naval attaché continued pressing hard his arguments about squeezing the northern neutrals. In this, he had Findlay's complete support.²⁶ This forced Howard and Paget to combine to scupper Consett, who by late November was making his case for a total blockade to the Admiralty. Paget did this in an artful way, damning Consett's efforts with faint praise in remarks like '[h]e is not aware in what way he has transgressed in respect of intemperance of language'.²⁷ Howard offered a more straightforward critique, informing Cecil that Consett's tendency to spend most of his time at the Legation in Christiania distorted his image of Scandinavia as a whole:

Living, however, entirely in Norway and having before he left here a strong prejudice against [Sweden], and which I may say in parentheses, I quite sympathize, he has overlooked in his burning zeal for the blockade the question with regard to Sweden which is in my opinion of the most really vital importance, i.e. what effects our policy towards Sweden may have on Russia.[28]

This prompted Cecil to seek Consett's removal as naval attaché in Scandinavia. Unfortunately the 'Consett question', as Hardinge now called it, threatened to escalate into 'a serious row' between the Admiralty and the Foreign Office.[29] The Admiralty had no intention of pulling a man they judged to be doing a good job out of an area like Scandinavia – and, to be fair to Howard and Paget, neither of them quibbled about Consett's purely naval abilities.[30] The Foreign Office wanted to avoid a major interdepartmental crisis – Asquith's government had just been replaced by that of Lloyd George and the political situation in London remained one of extreme delicacy – and let the matter drop. All Cecil succeeded in doing amounted to getting an Admiralty promise to pressure Consett about being more appreciative of the problems in enforcing blockade policy in northern Europe.[31]

Howard had earlier learnt that promises mean nothing unless backed by some sort of sanction – Prince George of Greece had shown this. Despite knowing that two of the three ministers in Scandinavia were so critical of his activities that there was a move afoot to replace him, Consett persisted in pushing a hardline at all costs. This led to continual complaints about Consett, as well as emphasis being put on the delicacy of the diplomatic situation in Sweden and Denmark, being sent to London by Howard and Paget.[32] It led Hardinge to apprise both Sir Edward Carson, the first lord of the Admiralty, and Sir John Jellicoe, the first sea lord, of Consett's actions.[33] None the less, by early spring 1917, Consett was again at full steam in his campaign to force London to impose an impenetrable blockade. This exasperated Howard and Paget and, adding to their discomfiture, was 'the fact that Consett boasts that the F.O. cannot remove him as the Admiralty will not allow it'.[34]

At this stage, Howard and Paget found their diplomacy threatened by Consett's actions. They were lucky in that Consett, assuming he could do what he wished without risking his recall, overreached himself. Consett remained deeply suspicious of the political leaders of each of the three Scandinavian countries, no matter what their political stripe or previously announced commitment to good relations with Britain. Hammarskjöld was perhaps the most prominent but, as time passed, H. N. Andersen, the Danish premier, also gave him concern. In an effort designed to discredit Andersen in both Denmark and Britain, Consett started a rumour that the Danish premier had once been a brothel-keeper in Siam. When this rumour reached King George V, a friend of Andersen, the Foreign Office found its opportunity to ask for Consett's recall. By April 1917 Consett was gone.³⁵ Although he returned as the British naval attaché in Stockholm and Christiania later that year with no diminution in his beliefs about the need for the most stringent blockade possible, his effectiveness as a lobbyist within the British government had vanished completely. He fulfilled his naval duties till the end of the war, though afterwards, to vent his spleen, he published a devastating critique of Howard, the Foreign Office and the Ministry of Blockade, to which Howard responded as forcefully.³⁶ None the less, Consett's recall in early 1917 removed a major irritant in Howard's performance of his duties, not to say that of Paget. The diplomatic side of blockade policy took precedence over its purely naval and military side.

II

Although Howard, Paget, and the officials in London did not realise it, the 'Consett question' as it affected British policy towards Sweden and relations with Russia had become anti-climactic by late 1916. The glittering success of Brusilov's summer offensive, pushing two hundred miles to the west, renewed the Russians' traditional disinclination to discuss the Aland Islands. Sazanov's dismissal as foreign minister in July provided a pretext for abandoning Russo-Swedish talks on whether the islands' fortifications, built in 1915, should be dismantled at the end of hostilities. There was no agreement to renew them until December 1916, by which time Brusilov's offensive had turned to dust. But, even then, Petrograd showed little interest in the matter; the Nikolaev railway would soon be completed.³⁷ In addition, since the Northern Front had remained a backwater throughout 1916, with the bulk of the fighting on the Eastern Front occurring in the southwest,³⁸ Swedish military threats in the north and questions of transport through Swedish territory seemed remote.

Howard pursued his twofold task into the early months of 1917; by April, he knew that the situation confronting him had altered fundamentally. This derived from two factors: first, the change in the general military and political situation of the war created by the overthrow of the tsarist regime on 15 March 1917 and, secondly, in a narrower sense, the fall of Hammarskjöld's government. These two events, occurring within weeks of each other, changed both the objectives of Howard's diplomacy in the Swedish capital and, more important, the style of that diplomacy.

Howard was not surprised that Nicholas' government collapsed under the strains of war in early 1917. For months he had received information from a variety of sources which showed that, with the failure of Brusilov's offensive and concurrent domestic difficulties involving food distribution to the cities, the bankruptcy of the tsar's regime was obvious to most Russians. For instance, in October 1916, as Central Power counteroffensives forced Brusilov's forces into a retreat that quickly became a rout, Howard informed Hardinge and Buchanan of rumours circulating at Stockholm that a separate Russo-German peace might soon be concluded.[39] Both men dismissed this possibility because of the tsar's firm commitment to the Allied cause.[40] However, here lay the problem. If Nicholas changed his mind or was replaced, Russian adherence to the anti-German alliance would be uncertain. Buchanan's reply to Howard indicated that anti-Allied feeling permeated important circles within Russia. Howard learnt from Buchanan that a powerful group of pro-Germans existed at Petrograd; this group seemed apprehensive about British economic aid to Russia – 'Russia, they declare, will never be able to repay the hundreds of millions advanced her by England' – and worried that Britain, with its naval and military strength, might move after the war to collect its debts by seizing Russian railways and customs as a guarantee of payment. A separate peace with Germany might obviate this. Although such Russian fears were groundless, their existence demonstrated that Russia's allegiance to Britain and France remained a tenuous commodity.

Howard's residence in neutral Stockholm permitted him to meet a large number of travellers of various nationalities who passed through the city. By late 1916 and early 1917, those arriving from Russia painted a dark picture of political conditions there. Distressed at what he heard, Howard related these 'accounts [which] all tally in principal particulars' to the Foreign Office.[41] Talk of revolution seemed everywhere, a consequence of the inability of the Court to handle both the war and the domestic problems deriving from it – Nicholas had commanded his armies at the front since September 1915, leaving Alexandra to run the government; she had surrounded herself with a coterie of arch-reactionaries and placemen. Howard wrote that 'the Council of the Empire [the Cabinet], the Duma and the officers and rank and file of the Army are heartily sick of the present régime with its constant shifting of Ministers and consequent disorganization and general incompetence'.

Howard's sources suggested that the Court reactionaries looked to Germany 'as their only support against a revolution'. The problem was that, as far as Howard could judge, a revolution of some sort seemed imminent. Not only Alexandra, but now Nicholas was being blamed for Russia's malaise, so that 'the possibility of his removal if he will not appoint men to the Government that have the confidence of the Nation is openly and widely discussed'. Howard also reported that even the Guards regiment at Petrograd shared this increasingly critical view of the tsar; thus, instead of helping Nicholas enforce his will, they would probably join in his ouster. 'The general opinion therefore', Howard impressed on Hardinge, 'seems to be that Russia is on the verge of a very serious crisis.'

Although he did not have to do so, Howard spelled out the military and diplomatic problem facing pro-Allied Russians:

> The great desire of all parties who wish to carry the war through successfully is that anything in the shape of a popular revolution which would result in street fighting and severe repression may be avoided, as they naturally fear that this might be disastrous for the prosecution of the war.

For Howard the seriousness of the Russian situation was driven home in a private conversation he had with Nekludoff at this time.[42] Not only did the Russian minister condemn the ineptitude of those who controlled his government, but he was prepared to leave the Russian Diplomatic Service because of it. Moreover, long a devoted supporter of Nicholas, Nekludoff now joined the ranks of Russians who believed that, unless changes were made by the tsar's government, the tsar should go.

Howard observed equally momentous events occurring within Sweden over the fate of the Hammarskjöld government. Just before the creation of Lloyd George's ministry, a new round of Anglo-Swedish negotiations had began at London over Sweden's trade policy toward the Allied Powers.[43] These negotiations dragged on until the first week of February 1917 and, in that time, two events occurred which prompted Cecil, who led the British delegation, to take the hardest line possible. First, the advent of Lloyd George brought much-needed vigour to the prosecution of the British war effort, especially to diplomacy towards the neutral Powers. This translated into increased British intransigence to any watering down of their blockade. Secondly, because of Berlin's announcement of unconditional submarine warfare, made on 31 January 1917, the United States broke off its diplomatic relations with Germany. Until that moment, the United States had been the chief spokesman for the neutral Powers in their opposition to the British blockade, a function of its decided economic power and of British reliance on American capital and commodities to fight the war. Suddenly Sweden and the other neutral Powers stood alone in their opposition to Britain, facing the daunting prospect of American entry into the war on the Allied side. These events helped bring about Hammarskjöld's downfall.

Howard remained divorced from the Anglo-Swedish negotiations, which began on 7 November 1916. In fact, only after complaining to Cecil that the Stockholm Legation knew nothing about what was transpiring in London did Howard receive assurances that he would be kept abreast of developments.[44] He thereafter received periodic reports about the course of the talks,[45] but his chief responsibility in this matter revolved around assessing domestic Swedish reaction to the events in London. All hinged on Hammarskjöld, who had been forced to sanction renewed negotiations because of domestic pressures from concerned Cabinet ministers like Wallenberg, business interests worried about trade, and the opposition parties angered by his tendency to ignore the Riksdag.[46] Believing that the negotiations would prove feckless, Hammarskjöld out-manoeuvred Wallenberg to win the right to appoint the Swedish delegation. Although three of the four principal members were supportive of an Anglo-Swedish agreement – Johannes Hellner, a jurist and director of the Wallenberg bank; Erik Frisell, a businessman; and Marcus Wallenberg – the fourth was not. Hammarskjöld chose this man, Claës Westman, a Swedish Foreign Ministry official, to ensure that agreement remained difficult to attain. The premier also won the right to draft the delegation's instructions; these were designed to preclude a workable solution to the blockade issue. Cecil recognised Hammarskjöld's hand in this from the beginning,[47] and Howard, after assessing the political atmosphere in Stockholm, confirmed that, should an agreement be reached, Hammarskjöld would do all possible to prevent its implementation. 'It is an open question whether if any agreement is reached with His Majesty's Government', Howard confided to Hardinge, 'he will ratify it, or make up his mind to go rather than do so...It would seem almost more likely that he will stick on and, even if he cannot wreck the agreement, saboter whenever he can in the German interests.'[48]

Howard observed the course of political events in Sweden, whilst the negotiations continued into December and January. Hammarskjöld began to be singled out for criticism by his opponents, now unwilling to remain silent during the war emergency – food rationing had been introduced in December 1916, a result of the British blockade. None the less the Swedish premier managed to withstand a blistering attack on both his government's domestic and foreign policies in the Riksdag in late January. Sensing that Hammarskjöld would be able to hang on to power, Howard suggested to the Foreign Office that the negotiations be abandoned in favour of the existing system of *ad hoc* trade agreements;[49] Transito's success had much to do with this. But decisions were being made in London concerning the overall strategy of the war, the most important occurring within the new War Cabinet. By late January, the War Cabinet had concluded that the war would extend into 1918, thus Britain and its allies had to do all possible to squeeze Germany economically, militarily, and politically.[50] Because of these and other decisions – for instance, to resist German calls for an immediate peace based on the post-1914 territorial status quo[51] – Howard's counsel about abandoning the negotiations was disregarded.

Howard's tendency to argue for some leniency in dealing with the Swedes began to run counter to beliefs at London that Sweden had to be treated firmly in order to weaken Germany. In fact, anti-Swedish feeling had been mounting for some time. Such notions were accentuated in June 1916 when the Hammarskjöld government closed the Kogrund Passage, linking the Baltic and North Seas, to British shipping, thereby trapping several British vessels in the Baltic. Accordingly, on 2 February, the day the United States severed diplomatic links with Germany, Cecil unexpectedly delivered an ultimatum to the Swedish delegation in London.[52] He demanded that the Swedes accept all tentative arrangements discussed to that point in the negotiations, chiefly those dealing with blockade rationing and trans-shipment to Russia, as well as that Sweden honour assurances given over the course of the discussions to deliver to Britain commodities like ball-bearings. Showing his government's firmness, Cecil said nothing about Britain relenting over blockading foodstuffs destined for Sweden. Neither did he mention Britain allowing neutral merchantmen, impounded in British ports on the day that the Germans announced their unrestricted submarine campaign to prevent them from scurrying to their home harbours for the war's duration, to be released.

Howard watched as Swedes divided over the ultimatum. Hammarskjöld became the focus of criticism from within both his own and the opposition parties for all the difficulties confronting Sweden. Howard's private view was that Hammarskjöld should remain in office:

His Anti-British Agreement Policy has on the whole served our purpose very well, since, owing to it, Sweden has been kept on the shortest possible commons & the export to Germany of all kinds of foodstuffs with the one exception of fish has been tremendously reduced, while the odium of it all has fallen upon the P.M. and his pedantic obstruction to any kind of Agreement.[53]

But this constituted wishful thinking. Howard's surmise from the information he could gather was that the Cabinet was split and, more important, that a fundamental division existed between the government and the Riksdag.[54] This split centred on Hammarskjöld and, although the real issues underlying the crisis concerned his high-handed attitude toward a section of the Cabinet and his failure to consult the Riksdag, the ostensible point of departure became the proposed Anglo-Swedish agreement: his opponents tended to support it; his sympathisers did not. Since Sweden lacked responsible government, Hammarskjöld needed to retain only the king's confidence to stay in office. But on 3 March the government suffered a major defeat in the Social Democratic-dominated Riksdag over a defence bill. Hammarskjöld saw his political capital running out and, contrary to Howard's belief, decided to resign. Throughout March, whilst a façade of political normalcy ensued, intense negotiations occurred behind the scenes as conservative factions sought to hold on to the government, a course aided by Gustav who had no desire to work with a Social Democratic ministry.[55] So secret were these political manoeuvres that, a week before Hammarskjöld resigned, Howard remained unaware of the impending changes.[56] On 29 March a new conservative government took office. Two men dominated it: Carl Swartz, the premier, and Admiral Arvid Lindman, the foreign minister. With Hammarskjöld gone, a new chapter in Anglo-Swedish wartime relations had begun. Coupled with the emergence of a liberal republican regime in Russia at the same moment, suggesting, perhaps, an improvement in Russo-Swedish relations, the diplomatic situation confronting Howard by April 1917 was transforming.

III

Howard and his superiors entertained little doubt that the advent of the Swartz government would change the substance of Swedish foreign policy. Both Swartz and Lindman were perceived to be as pro-German as Hammarskjöld and, importantly, as protective of neutral rights as the former premier. But the circumstances which had permitted Hammarskjöld to assume an intransigent guise had changed. The Russian revolution and, within days of the Swartz government taking office, American entry into the war on the Allied side had altered radically the international situation. Within Sweden, commodity shortages created by the British blockade along with the abject failure of Hammarskjöld's government to build up stocks of foodstuffs produced severe domestic problems. These problems were linked – the United States remained the principal source for an array of Swedish imports; together they gave the British the upper hand in dealing with the new Swedish government. For instance, amongst the neutral merchantmen detained in British ports since February were Swedish ships loaded with American grain. To ensure that needed imports found their way into Sweden, the Swartz government had to conform more closely to the British blockade.

Seeing this shift occurring even before the change of government, Howard was astute enough to realise that it devolved from the impact of Swedish domestic politics on foreign policy. The new government's chief concern centred on preventing the parties of the left, the Liberals and Social Democrats, from achieving significant political gains at conservative expense. Time constraints aided the British cause since regularly scheduled elections were to occur in September. Less than two weeks before Swartz came to power, Howard told Hardinge that the real struggle within Sweden revolved around whether 'there shall be Representative Parliamentary Government in this country or not'.[57] The conservatives sought to uphold the king's constitutional right to select a government regardless of Riksdag opposition, a situation which not coincidentally protected the political and economic advantages enjoyed by the generally upper-class conservatives. The parties of the left made no bones that their ultimate goal was constitutional change – to have a government responsible to the Riksdag. This issue dominated the political jousting between the conservatives and their opponents throughout the summer of 1917, having a decided impact on Swedish foreign policy towards Britain and the blockade. If Lindman could achieve some sort of agreement with Britain to safeguard neutral rights whilst securing foodstuff and raw material imports, the conservatives would be in a better position in the election campaign. Failure in this regard would only help their political opponents, who were making political capital out of scarcities resulting from the blockade.

Howard realised that the pro-German sentiments of conservative Swedes did not diminish because of the change in government. Gustav remained 'very pro-German', 'evidently hoping in the success of the submarine campaign'.[58] In addition Lindman, who had been premier for five years after 1907, was widely known to be sympathetic to the Germans, having played a prominent part in helping raise a German war loan in Sweden.[59] None the less, given the compelling problems the new ministry faced, Howard reckoned that it would be 'more reasonable than the late Government'.[60] As he confided to Hardinge, the Swartz-Lindman regime 'continues to be friendly in a practical sense'. Here lay material with which the British could twist the economic noose around Germany more snugly. The need for the Swedes to find a practical solution to the problems engendered by the blockade meant that they would have to deal with Britain on British terms. Underscoring Howard's assessment during April and May 1917, there occurred a series of 'hunger demonstrations' throughout Sweden by workers and regular soldiers and sailors which were exploited by the Social Democrats.[61] On May Day, Howard reported that socialist leaders addressed 75,000 people in the open air at Stockholm, many of whom wore red rosettes and small Belgian flags. In the early part of the war, Howard had advised the Foreign Office that a tight blockade might push Swedish workers into support for joining the war on Germany's side; now, with changed conditions and the obvious failure of Hammarskjöld's government to arrange a blockade agreement with Britain, the general anger of ordinary Swedes fell on their government. Given recent Russian events, conservative politicians could ignore this anger at their peril.

Howard's diplomacy now altered because little danger existed that Sweden would enter the war against Britain, given food and raw material shortages and the political divisions created thereby. Indeed, Howard found himself in the period between the formation of the Swartz government and the September elections involved, first, in overcoming Lindman's scruples about settling with the British and, secondly, in ensuring that trans-shipment to Russia remained unimpeded. Howard's diplomatic goals had altered subtly: he still had to keep supply lines to Russia open, but he could use the changed circumstances of the war and in domestic Swedish affairs to force some agreement out of the Swedes. That times were different was confirmed when Lindman, on the day he took office, approached Howard about getting Swedish grain ships out of British harbours.[62] Sensing that Lindman's motivation stemmed from a desire to weaken opposition attacks, Howard none the less believed this offered a chance of getting the trapped British ships through the Kogrund Passage. By the first week of April, he had worked out an agreement with Lindman whereby Allied ships trapped in the Baltic, on a ton for ton basis, would be allowed through the Kogrund in return for grain ships leaving Britain. As 90,000 tons of Swedish shipping remained in British ports, 90,000 tons of Allied shipping in the Baltic would be allowed out.[63] A start at reducing the Swedish commitment to neutral rights had begun.

Neither Howard nor his colleagues in London held any illusions about this minor agreement signalling an about-face in Swedish foreign policy. Based on Howard's reports, Cecil and Balfour took pains to instruct the War Cabinet about the 'dangerous and reactionary tendencies of recent Swedish political changes', with the result that Lloyd George and his colleagues concluded that Sweden needed careful watching.[64] When Lindman indicated a desire to negotiate an Anglo-Swedish agreement spelled out in Cecil's ultimatum of 2 February, Howard learnt from Crowe the impossibility of this course: Sweden could only accept the ultimatum or reject it.[65] Whilst Britain would settle willingly minor problems like that over the Kogrund Passage, on the major issue, Cecil's ultimatum indicated the irreducible British position.

During the six-month life of the Swartz government – one composed of parties of the left replaced it after the September elections – Howard did all he could to get the Swedes to come to terms. Despite some success on lesser issues, he failed to persuade Swartz and Lindman to settle based on Cecil's ultimatum. But achievement in this regard increasingly ceased to be important. This stemmed from the changing military situation throughout the summer and autumn of 1917 caused by accelerated domestic turmoil in Russia. Howard learnt this from Buchanan and his staff.[66] As Russian military power crumbled during the middle months of 1917, and as the British and French were becoming more reliant on American economic, military, and naval aid to defeat Germany in the west, the War Cabinet and Foreign Office saw less and less need to placate the Swedes. As early as May 1917, the decision had been made by blockade authorities in London that no urgency existed in getting Swedish concurrence to Cecil's ultimatum.[67] British naval power, combined with American determination to enforce a rigorous blockade, meant that Sweden would have to conform to the Allied blockade come what may.

None of this suggests that Howard's work became easier. His mind now turning to the post-war period, he became concerned about the need to keep Anglo-Swedish relations on a firm footing. For instance, he and Isa continued to cement close personal ties with Crown Princess Margaret who, aside from any political advantages that might accrue to Britain once her husband succeeded to the throne, had been suffering social snubs and material deprivation at the hands of the pro-German court clique. Isa solicited Margaret's help to arrange for Red Cross collections in Sweden, whilst Esme used his influence with London to ensure that the Crown Princess received simple commodities, like coffee, being denied her.[68] More important, at the official level, as the Swedes moved to bring the Kogrund Passage into operation in June – they had to ensure that the Germans would not sink British merchantmen – Howard gave private assurances to Lindman that the embargoed grain ships would be freed first. This vexed the Foreign Office in that Howard seemed willing to give way to the Swedes without seeing whether they would abide by their promises.

Tired and overworked – he had had no vacation since before the July crisis – Howard became angry. He wrote to Hardinge to defend his action.[69] He indicated brusquely that three reasons existed why little harm would result from his assurances: first, no hard evidence obtained to suggest that the Swedes would break their promise should they receive grain before the Passage opened; next, if the grain arrived unfit for human consumption through unnecessary British delays, anglophobia in Sweden might impair future Anglo-Swedish relations; and, finally, the combined power of Britain and the United States in blockade and ancillary economic and diplomatic matters was so dominant that the Swedes had no choice but to honour their commitment. For the first and last time since rejoining the Diplomatic Service in 1903, Howard threatened to resign. If forced to withdraw his assurances to Lindman, he would ask to be recalled. He did not hide his conviction that, in this case, he remained the best judge of how to implement the Kogrund Passage deal. This agreement had nothing to do with the wider and more important February ultimatum; instead, it was a local arrangement designed to free needed Allied merchantmen for the war effort. The Swedes had neither the inclination nor the power to resist the combined strength of the Anglo-Americans, hence, it would only help future Anglo-Swedish relations to release the grain ships. Realising Howard's worth and the force of his argument, the Foreign Office buried its opposition, and the Kogrund Passage agreement went into operation with the release of the embargoed grain ships.

Howard took his first vacation in three years during the first two weeks of August 1917, returning to work in time to assess the Swedish elections which were to begin on 1 September and continue for twenty days. He had reported on political conditions periodically over the summer,[70] and the electoral campaign saw no new issues raised. The country's economic plight and the matter of acquiring 'real parliamentary and constitutional government' remained at the fore, resulting in the campaign 'becoming increasingly bitter as the polling day approaches'.[71] The focus of the polemics on each side centred on foreign policy. The parties of the left argued that the conservatives since August 1914 had not been neutral, that is treating both the Entente and the Central Powers equally, but had followed 'the old activist movement' favouring Germany. For their part, the conservatives railed against the 'alleged Ententephilism' of Hjalmar Branting, the Social Democratic leader and the individual who would dominate any left-party government. The conservatives made a great deal out of their resistance to the February ultimatum, a tack which aroused general support for continuing the existing policy of neutrality. Howard stood convinced that not even a Branting government would be more pro-Allied. But in terms of who might capture votes, little doubt existed that the Social Democrats would gain. The question was which of the conservatives or the liberals, the allies of the Social Democrats, would lose seats? In late August, the answer proved elusive.

Two days before the voting period ended, however, Howard reported that the conservatives had lost, a result of a diplomatic crisis which robbed the Swartz ministry of its claim to be the guardian of strict neutrality.[72] On 9 September the Swedish Foreign Office, a bastion of conservative sentiment, was exposed as a conduit for secret German despatches which, passing as Swedish messages from neutral countries to Stockholm and then shunted to Berlin, had military and other non-neutral contents. These messages were sent in the German cipher which, unknown to either the Germans or the Swedes, British Naval Intelligence had cracked late in 1916. The messages sent by Count Luxburg, the German minister at Buenos Aires, were particularly damaging as they recommended the sinking of Argentine ships. In a convoluted plot by Naval Intelligence, which saw leaks of Luxburg's messages to the American newspapers, Hammarskjöld, Wallenberg, Swartz, and Lindman were all implicated in the affair.[73] For a variety of reasons, especially a determination by anti-Swedes within Britain's naval community to influence the course of the elections, the 'Luxburg affair' exploded like a bomb-shell in Sweden. It did the same at the Foreign Office which, because of inter-departmental rivalry, knew nothing of the matter until Spring Rice telegraphed from Washington after the story broke there.

Howard watched intently as the conservatives relinquished power to a Liberal-Social Democrat coalition on 19 October. Nils Eden, a Liberal, assumed the premiership; Branting became minister of finance; and Johannes Hellner, an independent and member of the Swedish delegation to London in late 1916 to early 1917, took the foreign ministership. A fundamental change had occurred within Sweden's body politic. As Howard observed perceptively whilst this shift in domestic Swedish politics was unfolding: 'When this blessed change does come and Sweden is no longer governed by Junkers and Courtiers, it should be a very good country to deal with and to live in.'[74]

Howard and his Foreign Office colleagues had realised that the diplomatic and military situation in neutral northern Europe had begun a period of transition in March and April 1917 with the fall of Hammarskjöld and the overthrow of the tsar. At that moment, no one knew whether the transition would be reversed. By October and November, thanks to the rise of the Liberal-Social Democrat coalition in Sweden and, three weeks later, the Bolshevik *coup d'état* in Russia, there had been a complete metamorphosis in the diplomatic and military milieu in which Howard functioned. This derived from the Russian situation impinging on Anglo-Swedish relations. The Lloyd George government's growing belief over the summer that the new Russian republican government would not have much success against the Central Powers had led to reduced exports of arms and other commodities eastwards.[75] This is why Crowe informed Howard in May that it mattered not a whit whether the Swedes accepted Cecil's ultimatum. With the end of conservative rule in Sweden and the advent of the Bolsheviks in Russia, the focus of Anglo-Swedish relations transformed dramatically. As soon as Vladimir Lenin, the Bolshevik leader, achieved power, he moved to take his country out of the war by signing a separate peace with the Germans.[76] Suddenly, the Swedes lost their only diplomatic lever to keep the British blockade as loose as possible: threatening to cut trans-shipment to Russia. With Russian withdrawal from the war, the Allies were forced to concentrate all of their effort to defeat Germany on the Western Front, the more so as the Germans would assuredly transfer troops from east to west once the Bolsheviks agreed to peace terms. This alteration in the diplomatic and military situation in northern Europe, which had been gestating for months, *ipso facto* affected Howard's diplomacy. He could now be as tough as possible on the Swedes to put the maximum economic pressure on Germany. That the new

Swedish government was much less pro-German than its two conservative predecessors, as well as less inclined to follow the advice of the Court, made Howard's new diplomacy much easier.

Howard saw this two weeks before the Bolshevik coup. On orders from the Foreign Office, he had met with Hellner on 23 October to inform the new foreign minister that, whilst Britain wanted to settle its differences with Sweden, the record since 1914, especially the Luxburg affair, led London not to trust Stockholm to live up to promises of strict neutrality.[77] When Hellner emphasised that the Liberal-Social Democrat coalition would observe strict neutrality to avoid the diplomatic pratfalls which had discredited its conservative predecessors, Howard became convinced of the genuineness of these words. He held this as an unprecedented opportunity to get Sweden to conform formally to the Allied blockade of Germany. With the food situation remaining precarious, and tied to the conservatives' determination to regain office, there existed weakness within Sweden which could be exploited to British and Allied advantage. The Allies did not possess enough shipping to get American troops from North America to Europe to shore up the Allied position on the Western Front. Swedish ships could be used for this purpose. This had the double advantage of denying maritime transport for the export of Swedish commodities to Germany. The quid pro quo in this was that the Allies had to agree to help the Swedish economy by purchasing those commodities which otherwise would go to Germany, especially iron ore. There would also have to be some Allied concession over food exports.

Howard knew by late October that the nature of the Anglo-Swedish relationship had undergone fundamental change. Thus, when Lenin and the Bolsheviks seized power in early November, the situation had altered to such an extent that the British hardline over the 2 February ultimatum became archaic. New times called for new policy. Howard convinced the Foreign Office and Ministry of Blockade of this, so that by December renewed Anglo-Swedish talks began in London. The Swedish delegation was led by Marcus Wallenberg who, working with Hellner to ensure that there would be no repeat of the Hammarskjöld-Westman obstructionism of a year earlier, won the right to choose the delegation members. This delegation, loyal to its leader and the government in Stockholm and, in turn, supported by the Eden Cabinet, arrived in London in the first week of December to break the blockade and shipping stalemate.

Though Howard played the pivotal role in getting renewed talks started by convincing his superiors in London, notably the anti-Swedish Cecil, that the basis for an agreement existed, he had little to do with the negotiations once they started. Everything happened in London. Howard's essential purpose during the six months of negotiation entailed keeping pressure for settlement on the Swedish ministers when they complained of inflexible British demands, like that over restricted re-export to Germany.[78] He also combined with Thiebaut and Ira Morris, the American minister, in establishing an inter-Allied Trade Committee in Sweden to control import applications once the new agreement was finally arranged.[79] The signing of that agreement on 28 May 1918 represented a stunning diplomatic triumph for the British and their allies.[80] They received shipping required to transport the much-needed American troops to Europe, something made more urgent when, in March 1918, the anticipated German offensive taxed seriously the military capacity of the Allies in France. In addition, the Swedes caved in further by agreeing to prevent the export of a range of goods and commodities to Germany: foodstuffs, textiles, ores, and metals. As a trade-off, the British permitted the Swedes to fulfil an extant contract for the export of molybdenum and a new one for ferro silicon demanded by the Germans; in this nettled process, the Swedes had to apprise Berlin about the course of the Anglo-Swedish talks to prevent German reprisals against Sweden. If the Germans wanted these needed commodities, they had to make concessions. As Howard noted later: 'Strange to say the Germans gave these assurances and thus our negotiations with Sweden, which had begun in May, 1915 [with the Vansittart mission], only resulted in an agreement in May, 1918, and that agreement was in force for about four months up to the end of the War.'[81]

For Howard, this agreement represented the signal achievement of his wartime diplomacy. Whilst it is true that his superiors at London took the direct negotiations out of his hands after May 1915 – the result of that suspicion that he had been duped by Hammarskjöld – it is clear that his assessments of the Swedish situation before and after this had been correct. His reports showed that as long as the conservatives, whether the intransigent Hammarskjöld or the slippery Lindman, controlled Swedish foreign policy, an abrupt change favouring Britain and the Allies remained impossible. Whilst minor agreements like that over the Kogrund Passage were feasible, the political and economic climate in Stockholm until late 1917 precluded a major agreement regulating the blockade. Moreover, until the middle of 1917, the Swedes had the Russian lever with which they could loosen the strictures placed on their trade with Germany. Only with the rise of the Liberal-Social Democrat coalition, a result of food shortages brought on by the British blockade, and occurring at the same time as the failure of the liberal republican regime in Russia and its overthrow by the Bolsheviks, did the situation with which Howard had to contend at Stockholm change. By late 1917, the Swedes were vulnerable to the British lever of restricted ingress and egress of goods and commodities indispensable to Sweden's economic welfare.

Howard showed his mastery at this juncture. He knew that all talk about upholding strict neutrality and following the dictates of international law was so much diplomatic camouflage. The issues at stake since August 1914 were the national interests of Britain and its allies and those of Sweden. Until the political shifts in Sweden and Russia in 1917, the Swedes had had the diplomatic strength to ensure that their national interests, tied to trade with Germany, were not jeopardised. He never quarrelled with this. Such attitudes had suffused the international politics with which he had contended since Crete. What angered Howard was the hypocrisy of Hammarskjöld and other conservatives who decried the British blockade, yet said nothing about the violation of Belgian neutrality by Germany. But, by late 1917, once conditions had altered so much that following the hoary policy of the conservatives endangered Swedish national interests, a change had to occur. Hellner's words to him just days after the Eden government took office showed this. The Liberal-Social Democrat coalition had come to office, in part, because it offered a different approach to protecting the country's interests. It was not just Swedish workers who suffered. Swedish businessmen and financiers had grown richer from the war, everyone from the Wallenbergs, with their vast interests in both belligerent camps, to Lindman, whose bank had loaned money to Germany. Howard's derisive term, *tertii gaudentes*, spoke the truth. But the unregulated blockade now also hurt Sweden's economic well-being. Trade with Germany could not be balanced by trans-shipment to Russia. It was with decided accuracy that Howard noted in his diary: 'There is no doubt the agreement would be very popular here among businessmen particularly.'[82] In addition, the ongoing domestic crisis in Sweden over food supplies had not abated. The Germans had earlier promised to offset any Swedish shortfalls in grain supplies from the West with Russian deliveries. But the chaos in Russia and the exigencies of the war prevented this. Again, Howard's diary makes clear the changed situation within Sweden: 'Since all hope of getting food from the Ukraine has vanished all parties here realize that they are dependent on [the] agreement if there is not to be a very serious shortage of foodstuffs [?next] year.' Any Swedish post-war diplomatic pretensions, say leadership of the Scandinavian Powers, would evaporate if a domestic crisis arose within the country serious enough to destroy the economic, political, and social balance.

Howard's advice in October and November 1917 led to the abandonment of Cecil's ultimatum and the inauguration of new negotiations. This, tied to accurate reports about Sweden's internal conditions and their impact on Swedish foreign policy, impressed Cecil and others and helped them handle the Wallenberg mission.[83] Howard helped in a major way to pave the way which led to the agreement of May 1918. No one knew then that the war would end within six months. The Germans were in the midst of a major offensive that seemed to hold the possibility of either ending the struggle on the Western Front or, at the least, prolonging the struggle into 1919.[84] Either way, any diplomatic mechanism to tighten the economic screws on Germany was welcome. Howard's role in the three years of difficult diplomacy preceding that agreement, especially in initiating the final six-month phase, remained pivotal from the perspective of the Foreign Office. Along with his KCMG and the recognition of his abilities that showed when, for instance, Hardinge backed down over Howard's threatened resignation in June 1917, this decreed that he would continue in his country's service once his time at Stockholm ended.

IV

Howard's final year at Stockholm found him occupied with a number of other questions less critical than the diplomacy surrounding the Anglo-Swedish agreement. One of the most important of these concerned the dissemination of Allied news despatches to Swedish newspapers. Because of economic constraints imposed by the relatively small Swedish population, only one organisation existed in Sweden to distribute news despatches sent from abroad. This organisation, the Swedish Telegram Bureau, was controlled by pro-German Swedes. By early 1918, in the wake of the Luxburg affair, Howard and his Allied colleagues, mainly Morris, became concerned that the distribution of Allied news was being hampered severely by the Swedish Telegram Bureau. Cables from Germany relating to any issue would be distributed first, whilst those from Allied countries, sent to Stockholm by the Reuters, Havas, and Associated Press agencies, tended to be delayed until their contents could have little impact or be overshadowed by new German wires. Coupled with this was the fact that the majority of Swedish newspapers, led by the *Svenska Dagblad*, were unabashedly pro-German. As the Anglo-Swedish negotiations were then under way, and as the massive German offensive in the West began in March, it became obvious to Howard and the other Allied ministers that Allied news had to be disseminated as quickly and as widely as possible if there was to be any hope of the Allied case being understood by ordinary Swedes. But the fact that this news had first to get out of the Swedish Telegram Bureau militated against this.

Accordingly, Howard and Morris took the initiative in early 1918 of creating a rival telegram bureau.[85] This new organisation received the exclusive right to receive and distribute Allied news despatches. Since the new bureau had to appear to be Swedish-controlled, Howard used his friendship with the faithful de Bildt to entice a number of pro-Allied Swedes on to the board of directors; these included de Bildt himself, as well as a number of politicians and businessmen. Moreover, Howard persuaded de Bildt to put up the capital for the nascent organisation, something approaching 800,000 kronor. De Bildt also purchased two newspapers, the *Aftontidningen* and the *Svensk Handelstidning*, to aid in distributing Allied news; these two investments cost him an additional 1.5 million kronor. Realising that 'a Telegraph Agency in a small country like Sweden cannot live on the distribution of telegrams alone', Howard and his colleagues 'agreed to the new Bureau having an affiliated Trading Co[.] which should supply printing and other requisites to the newspapers in order to make profits thereby, so as to cover their loss on the Telegraph Agency and also to obtain a hold on the papers'. Using their control over the inter-Allied Trade Committee in Sweden, Howard and Morris guaranteed the import of these goods, as well as others, like 200 tons of copper, which the trading company could also sell to keep the entire news organisation afloat.

Apart from the financial issue, Howard knew that any success this pro-Allied bureau would enjoy depended on two political factors: co-ordinating Allied information from abroad, and the removal of bureaucratic impediments in Sweden. Howard and Morris worked with a representative of the Ministry of Information, the wartime propaganda arm of the British government, during the planning stages of the bureau. To ensure that the Eden government would not block the establishment of an Allied propaganda organ in neutral Sweden, Howard sought out and won the support of powerful pro-Allied Swedes like the Wallenbergs and Hellner. On 27 May 1918, the *Nordiska Presscentralen* came into existence. When news of its impending creation leaked to the pro-German Swedish press two weeks before, an attack on its credibility was launched by pro-Germans within Sweden, an attack which included the public displeasure of the German minister. 'If the Germans are annoyed', Howard recorded with satisfaction at the time, 'it must be a good thing.' It was. During the final stages of the war, the litany of Allied successes in the West after July 1918, which led to German military defeat in November, had an outlet in Sweden undistorted by the Swedish Telegram Bureau. Working with his Allied colleagues and using his contacts, Howard had scored another diplomatic victory over Britain's enemies.

Another question which occupied Howard during his final months in Stockholm involved the impact of the chaos in Russia on northern Europe. This had several strands, all of which were tied in some way to the efforts of the Finns to establish an independent state contiguous with both Sweden and Russia. Until July 1917, Finnish nationalists had moved to weaken tsarist Russian control over their homeland by seeking support from Russia's enemies – the Grand Duchy of Finland had been an integral part of the Russian empire since the Napoleonic wars, thus the British and French, in the best interests of inter-Allied unity, could not support Finnish nationalist efforts to dismember Russia. As a consequence, Finnish nationalists worked to cement ties with Germany during the war, and twice, in 1914 and 1915, even offered Sweden the Aland Islands if it would join in a campaign to throw the Russian yoke off Finland.[86] Sweden had refused these overtures, but the onset of the Russian revolution and the collapse of Russian military power changed the situation. On 29 July 1917, the Finns declared their independence from Russia, establishing in Helsinki a moderate government supported by Finnish military power, the Civil Guards.[87] This put the Allies in a quandary; they still entertained hope that republican Russia would be able to fight the Germans, thus they could not recognise the Finnish declaration of independence. This gave the Germans an advantage, since they could with impunity move to regularise Finno-German relations.

Howard could do little at Stockholm about these events until the New Year. Then, with the Bolshevik coup in Russia and the beginning of Russo-German peace negotiations at Brest-Litovsk, he took it upon himself to advise Balfour that it remained essential for Britain to recognise the new Finnish regime.[88] But, he warned, recognition had to be just a first step, one followed immediately by military and economic assistance; the new Finnish regime, moderately rightwing, faced the very real possibility of being overthrown by radical socialist Finns supported by Bolshevik Russian troops still in the country. If Britain failed to act soon and decisively, the Germans would certainly achieve decided diplomatic and strategic gains because they were likely to give succour to the Finnish government. By recognising and supporting the fledgling regime, Britain could look to future friendly relations with a strategically important small Power in the eastern Baltic.

Howard's advice was apposite but, before his despatch could reach Balfour, events in Finland got away from the British government. On 27 January, civil war in Finland broke out between 'Red' Finns and Bolshevik Russians, on one hand, and the 'White' forces of the legitimate government, on the other. The 'Reds' seized Helsinki and the southeastern portion of the country, whilst the 'Whites', based at the port of Vaasa in the northwest, controlled the rest. The civil war lasted until May, but the problems it spawned for the British remained until just before Howard left Stockholm in August. These derived from the course of the war, chiefly from a German decision to do all possible diplomatically and militarily to help the 'Whites'. In the Treaty of Brest-Litovsk, the Germans included a provision that all Bolshevik troops were to leave Finland and, in April, 12,000 German troops, joined by a Finnish battalion which had been fighting in the German Army since 1916, arrived in Finland.

Howard advocated a pro-'White' policy from January to August 1918, the reasoning for which lay with his belief that the 'Whites' would win, thus it would serve British interests in the post-war period to have helped the Finns achieve their independence from Russia and Bolshevism. This belief developed out of his contacts at Stockholm with agents of the 'White' Finn military commander, General Carl Mannerheim, and, after May 1918 when he relinquished his command because of his animosity towards the Germans and went into exile in the Swedish capital, Mannerheim himself.[89] Howard's policy throughout remained that which he advanced the day before the 'Reds' took Helsinki and the south: formal recognition followed by material support. The problem resided with Foreign Office reluctance to recognise Finnish independence. Balfour and his advisers did not wish to offend either the Americans, who at this stage of the war thought only of an indivisible Russia, or anti-Bolshevik elements in Russia, who would view British recognition as an affront to Russian dignity.

Howard found his pro-'White' stance difficult to maintain in the first half of the civil war. 'White' reliance on German support to achieve victory meant that following Howard's line held the risk of helping a German ally strengthen itself. Howard conceded as much in March when he concurred with a Foreign Office decision to deny foodstuff exports to the Vaasa government, though he implied in a private letter to Hardinge that British inaction since January had much to do with the 'White' Finns turning to the Germans.[90] Still, the force of events by April – Brest-Litovsk, the beginning of the German offensive in the West, and the realisation that the 'Red' Finns would lose – led to Foreign Office willingness to compromise with the 'Whites'. In the middle of April, the Vaasa government was informed that Britain would give it official recognition if two ultimata were met: first, all British subjects arrested by the Germans in supposedly neutral Finland had to be released; and, secondly, the security of Allied goods and subjects passing through Finland had to be guaranteed.[91] As an inducement, London allowed that it would not oppose the resolution of Finland's independence, based on the principle of self-determination, at the anticipated post-war peace conference.

Howard took no part in the formulation or delivery of this ultimatum – the Foreign Office did everything. He could do nothing until after the 'White' government, flushed by victory over the 'Reds' and in no mood to bargain, replied in the middle of May. The 'White' Finns then indicated that their country's independence was a fact and would not be subject to some peace conference debate.[92] Moreover, whilst noting that all efforts had been made to effect both the release of British nationals gaoled by the Germans and the passage of Allied subjects and goods crossing Finland, it would be difficult to do more for Britain which had failed to offer the new state *de jure* recognition. A stalemate had emerged. The 'White' Finns were not about to compromise, a result of their military success and the pressure of their German benefactors; the British, discounting any Finnish claim to neutrality, were reluctant to negotiate with a German client. Moreover, the state of Anglo-Finnish relations worsened as the British and their allies had landed troops at Nikolaev on the Murman coast, an area coveted by the Finns, to prevent the Germans seizing it and basing submarines there. By late June, the threat of war between the Allies and Finland seemed imminent as Allied troops appeared to block 'White' Finnish efforts to occupy the Murman coast and the Pechenga Peninsula, both parts of Russia. On 27 June, a 'White' Finnish agent at Stockholm handed Howard a note demanding that British troops be pulled out of 'Finnish territory' and any support the British were giving 'Red' Finns be halted.[93] Worried about a war with Finland, Howard decided to act.

Since the middle of May, Howard had kept abreast of Finnish developments. Meeting several times with Mannerheim, he had reached the conclusion that pro-Allied Finns, the majority, could be strengthened within Finland by British recognition of legitimate Finnish demands. He also concluded that Britain's failure to recognise the Finnish regime and react favourably to its territorial demands at Russian expense constituted a major mistake. After receiving the 27 June note, he despatched his views to Balfour, emphasising that if Britain and its allies wanted to avoid poisoning their future relations with this emerging Power, it would be in their interests to break the stalemate by offering recognition.[94] That such a move involved paying a heavier price than might have been the case two months earlier, because of Finnish territorial demands, had to be accepted. He argued that Britain should agree to the cession of those Russian territories even though, because of the strategic importance of the Murman coast, this area had to remain under Allied control until the war's end.

Howard's advice found decided opposition in the upper levels of the Foreign Office. George Clerk, the head of the War Department, and John Gregory, its Russian Section head, both argued against territorial concessions at Russia's expense.[95] Gregory objected on political grounds, asserting that other Russian subject peoples would use the Finnish case as a precedent to seek British support for their nascent regimes. The result would be chaos in eastern Europe, since such regimes might not accord with British diplomatic, economic, or strategic interests and, in addition, would antagonise anti-Bolshevik Russians who, should they take power, might otherwise align with Britain and its allies. Clerk's resistance was founded on legal arguments. Only a Russian government could cede Russian territory or, if that proved impossible, the eventual peace conference had to do so. Either way, Britain lacked the right to accord unilaterally the *de jure* recognition envisaged in Howard's despatch. At the highest level Balfour, reluctant to move on this issue until the uncertainty of events in Russia dissipated, looked for an excuse that would allow him to refuse support for Finnish territorial demands. He thus took the logical line that, as Britain had not yet recognised the new Finnish government, it must refrain from recognising Finnish territorial claims at Russia's expense.[96] He underscored this with the argument that, as long as Finland remained a German client, Britain had to do everything to prevent the Germans from basing submarines on the littorals of the Arctic Ocean and White Sea. The Foreign Office ignored Howard's advice.

With so much at stake for Britain in northern Europe, Howard refused to relent. An Anglo-Finnish war would do British interests no good because, win or lose, Finland would harbour anglophobic sentiments for a long while thereafter. Howard's continued contacts with Mannerheim and anti-German 'White' Finns at Stockholm reaffirmed that a large and powerful section of Finnish opinion was pro-Allied. London could scupper German ambitions by recognising Finland and its territorial demands; this would enhance pro-Allied sentiments and strengthen the hand of anti-German Finns. Howard sent Balfour a strongly worded despatch outlining these points, arguing that such a course should be followed after the Germans withdrew from Finland.[97] Once the Germans left, Howard implored, Britain and its allies had immediately to recognise the 'White' government, ensure the export of foodstuffs, and encourage 'neutral' Finland to align with Norway, Denmark, and Sweden in an 'informal association' of Scandinavian Powers. Additional benefits might accrue if Britain could guarantee Finland a northern port. Pressure could then be put on the Finns to cede the Aland Islands to Sweden, a ploy that would tie both Finland and Sweden to Britain in the post-war period, assuring Britain influence in the northern European balance of power.

Howard's despatch reached the Foreign Office amid a series of events that put his views in a more favourable light. By the middle of July the German offensive in France sputtered to a halt as the Allied armies counterattacked. This necessitated the transfer of all possible German troops to the Western Front from less critical theatres of war like Finland. At London, both the War Office and Admiralty now endorsed the need for a softer line towards Finland. Based on reports from the commanders of the British forces on the Murman coast, the War Office argued that the majority of Finns were pro-Allied, thus British forces could have support from 'White' Finnish troops against the Bolsheviks who, seeing Russian territory invaded by the Allies, were preparing to counterattack.[98] The first lord of the Admiralty, Sir Eric Geddes, fresh from a tour of northern Russia, now supported granting Finland a port in the north, as long as the Finns were made to understand that this would not be ceded until the German departure and Finland ceased to be under German control.[99] The changed situation led the Foreign Office to adopt a more reasonable line towards the 'White' Finns.

Howard's pro-'White' Finnish views, adumbrated after he had received the Finnish note of 27 June, formed the official British reply to that note. On 9 August the Finns were informed that Britain acknowledged Finnish sovereignty as long as Finland was not a German ally, that Britain's sole purpose in having troops in northern Finland stemmed from a desire to keep lines open to Russia and prevent the Germans building submarine bases, and that Britain had no territorial ambitions in this region.[100] The British note purposely said nothing about submitting Finnish territorial aspirations in the north to either a Russian government of any political stripe or the eventual peace conference. This constituted a signal achievement for the legitimate Finnish government and the pro-Allied Finnish elements, the objectives of which were shared by and promoted by Howard. This British note allayed 'White' Finnish worries about British support of Bolshevik or 'Red' Finn goals in the north and led to a sudden amelioration of Anglo-Finnish relations. Moreover, Mannerheim's return to Finland and his rise to power as regent in December 1918 saw a further warming of Britain's relations with this new state. Howard played a crucial role in settling this problem, in putting Anglo-Finnish relations on a firm base, and in assuring that British interests in this part of northern Europe were not imperilled but, rather, strengthened.

Howard also ensured that British interests in the Baltic were buttressed when the fate of the Aland Islands agitated Swedish opinion. Although these islands as part of the Grand Duchy of Finland formed part of the tsarist Empire, the disintegration of authority in Russia after the Bolshevik coup gave the Alanders an opportunity to break away from Russian authority.[101] They wanted union with Sweden, and the majority of them signed a petition to this end in December 1917. Although the Swedish government would not receive this petition until February 1918, the knowledge that the islanders wanted to break away from Russia added to the complexity of British diplomacy in northern Europe. To get the Eden government to support German ambitions in the Baltic, the German government was prepared to allow the Swedes to take the islands. Although Howard and his Allied colleagues did not know about secret German overtures made to Hellner in November and December 1917, which the Swedish foreign minister rejected because he sensed the offer was designed to trap Sweden into breaking its announced neutrality,[102] they learnt in early January that the Eden government was considering sending a delegation to Brest-Litovsk to participate in discussion of the Alands when they appeared on the conference agenda. Because of pressure from the Allies and the refusal of the other Scandinavian Powers to send delegations to Brest-Litovsk, the Eden government decided to stay away from the conference.[103] In watching these events unfold, Howard concluded that it would be in Britain's best interests to encourage Swedish acquisition of the islands.

Howard found himself at odds with his Allied colleagues in Stockholm, chiefly Thiebaut, in advocating such a course. But, as he advised the Foreign Office, Swedish control of the Alands would prevent both the Germans and the Finns from possessing them[104] – at this stage, though Howard stuck to his pro-'White' policy, Finland's ability to break free of German domination for the foreseeable future remained uncertain. Since control of the Alands portended much for control of the Baltic, Swedish possession, especially if encouraged by the British, would augur well for Britain. On the other hand, should the British fail to support Aland union with Sweden, they would risk not only giving ammunition to anglophobic Swedes, they would also provide the Germans with a chance to resolve the matter in their interests. By taking this tack, Howard looked to the long-range impact of this question on Anglo-Swedish relations. Sweden's possession of the Islands would probably force it to align more closely with Britain, since the Swedes would then have to consider German ambitions in the Baltic – the Eden government's prevarication over whether to attend Brest-Litovsk, and its final decision not to do so, made Berlin wary of the orientation of Swedish foreign policy under the direction of Eden and Hellner. For Howard, here lay a golden opportunity to push Sweden away from Germany and into the Allied orbit. This notion coloured all of Howard's efforts with respect to the fate of the Aland Islands for the remainder of his time at Stockholm.

Howard's words found support at the highest levels of the Foreign Office. Cecil reckoned it to be an 'admirable despatch', whilst Hardinge concurred with the long-term gains to be made by Britain 'by adopting a sympathetic attitude towards Sweden's claims'.[105] Encouraged to cultivate the Eden government in this regard – though unstated, such a ploy might ease along the Anglo-Swedish negotiations then in progress at London – Howard's diplomacy seemed to pay dividends by late February. Though he had taken a firm line with Hellner over the despatch of a Swedish delegation to Brest-Litovsk,[106] each time the two men discussed the Aland Islands, Howard showed sympathy for the idea of union. When Swedish troops were sent to the islands early in the New Year, Howard said nothing, accepting the Swedish justification for doing so that these troops were there for a 'humanitarian mission' and to ensure 'the security of Russian property'.[107] After meeting with Hellner on 20 February 1918, Howard was sure that the British had scored a major diplomatic coup by supporting the Swedes. He took solace in Hellner's words 'that [the] temporary Swedish occupation of the Islands would be respected by Germany during the war'. As Howard told Balfour: 'at least [the Swedish occupation] would guarantee [the] Aland Islands from falling into the hands of Germany'.[108] He erred in this assumption. Four days after meeting with Howard, Hellner announced a Swedish delegation would not travel to Brest-Litovsk. Worried about their position in the Baltic, and desirous of defeating the 'Reds' in the Finnish civil war, German troops landed on the Alands on 2 March.[109]

Suddenly Howard was confronted with a situation which, though it spelled difficulty for Britain in the immediate future because of German control of the islands, offered the chance to tie Sweden closer to Britain. In early February he saw that even 'the Conservative Press' in Sweden began to entertain fears about 'German supremacy in the Baltic'.[110] Immediately after the German occupation, the Swedish press became agitated about the action and there was much comment about the strain in Finno-Swedish relations caused by the Aland question.[111] Now it seemed as if the very real possibility of a pro-German client on Sweden's eastern frontier, in tandem with German domination of the Baltic, was altering the way in which important elements of Swedish opinion saw the protection of their country's interests. In many Swedish minds, Germany seemed to be replacing Russia as the chief threat to Sweden. But, as a seasoned diplomat, Howard realised that the pendulum had not yet swung completely to the other side. Pro-German Swedish newspapers, crowing loudly about the inevitability of German victory after the March offensive began, along with the appointment of a few pro-Germans to key positions in the Swedish Foreign Ministry, disabused him of this.[112] None the less, with the Swedish reaction to the Aland question lay material with which to enhance Britain's position in neutral northern Europe.

Howard therefore continued to sympathise openly with the Swedish desire to annex the Alands. Twelve days after the German troops landed on the islands, Howard informed Hellner that Britain would stand by Sweden 'whenever the final settlement of the Aland islands question comes up for discussion',[113] an obvious reference to the anticipated post-war peace conference. The Foreign Office had asked Howard to give this assurance, one Britain had a legal right to give as a signatory of the Treaty of Paris of 1856, an article of which concerned the islands.[114] Even after the Germans began to withdraw their troops from the Alands as the Finnish civil war wound down and fresh soldiers were needed for the fighting in France, Howard worked to assure the Eden government of British willingness to support Sweden over this matter.[115] He also continued to press the Foreign Office on the need to appease the Swedes in this regard – his suggestion to Balfour about the benefits that would accrue to Britain if the Finns were pressured to surrender their claim to the islands to Sweden in exchange for a firm promise of a Murman port is indicative of this train of thought.

For Howard, following such a policy seemed more promising than ever by July as the German offensive in the West lost steam. He saw several clear indications that Sweden could be turned into supporting the Allies. Pro-German Swedes were beginning to acknowledge that Germany might now lose the war and be forced to sue for peace; Sven Hedin emerged as the most prominent of these.[116] More important, formal diplomatic relations between the German government, now controlled by two senior general officers, Paul von Hindenburg and Erich Ludendorff, and the Eden-Hellner-Branting coalition boded well for Britain. Howard discovered that Ludendorff and his advisers were concerned 'about the anti-German attitude of the present Swedish Gov.t'.[117] More telling than this, in the middle of July, he learnt from private sources that the 'new dispositions of the Swedish General Staff are now being framed against Germany as the presumptive enemy'.[118] Without equivocation, Howard knew that political and military circles within Sweden were increasingly wary of the old connexion with Germany. The Aland question existed as a diplomatic litmus indicating this fundamental change.

Howard realised that the Swedes were opportunists, as his term *tertii gaudentes* implied. German setbacks and the attendant increase in Allied strength by the middle of July 1918 suggested that Swedish interests might better be protected by distancing Sweden from Germany. But the chance of a negotiated peace to end the war still seemed possible in the summer of 1918. Thus, Howard saw British support for Sweden's claim to the Alands, tied to other diplomatic measures, beginning to pay dividends – Howard advocated using the prospective League of Peace, an organisation being bandied about as an Allied war aim, as a mechanism to tie Sweden and other neutral states to Britain in the post-war period.[119] Whilst some questions had the potential of creating disharmony between London and Stockholm – the Eden ministry mirrored its conservative predecessors by seeking ways to circumvent the blockade, despite the May 1918 agreement, something Howard felt came 'not so much from dishonesty as from weakness of character'[120] – Anglo-Swedish relations stood in a vastly improved condition by August 1918. Howard played a major part in this turn-about: through his efforts to get the British view across to Swedish leaders in private conversation and to the Swedish people at large through the new telegram bureau. In addition, by cultivating friendships with pro-Allied Finns like Mannerheim and imploring successfully Foreign Office officials to support a pro-'White' Finn policy, he had accomplished much in tying the new Finnish state to Britain. By August 1918 the British strategic position in terms of the northern European balance of power was decidedly enhanced over what it had been in August 1914, April 1917, or even May 1918. Although the course of Swedish domestic politics, the impact of the Russian revolution, and the deterioration of Central Power military strength also contributed to this enhancement, as much credit has to go to the patient and dogged diplomacy of Esme Howard. Without him, representing Britain's interests with force at Stockholm whilst simultaneously advising the Foreign Office about how best to cut and trim policy, the British position in neutral northern Europe would have been much weaker than it was as the Great War ground to a close.

V

By the summer of 1918, Howard was a tired man. Except for his two-week vacation in August 1917, he had had no rest since before the July crisis of 1914. Although he never complained directly to the Foreign Office about this – he knew that everybody else was just as overburdened, something driven home to him as early as March 1915 when he learnt that Tyrrell had broken down[121] – his superiors knew this indirectly.[122] But he was too valuable to transfer. They did all they could to make his work easier, especially in the autumn of 1917 when Hardinge got the director of Public Prosecution to begin action against *The Tatler* magazine which had libelled Howard about supposed leaks of secret documents from the Stockholm Legation to the German secret service.[123] In early 1918, Drummond, Balfour's private secretary, received instructions to tell Howard that he would be considered for an embassy at the end of the war 'if there is any diplomatic service existing'.[124] These were words which gave Howard the will to continue.

But Howard still had a difficult row to hoe whilst the war continued. As the chief British diplomatic agent in Sweden, it was incumbent on him to make certain that his staff continued to work at peak efficiency. The main problem in this regard stemmed from tremendous price inflation over basic commodities that his people needed to survive – food, coal for heating, and clothing. The diplomats at Stockholm were as inconvenienced by the blockade as were the Swedes, and their pay packets were slow to be topped up. To give his staff the necessities of everyday life, he informed the Foreign Office that he would willingly sacrifice his salary if it was used to supplement that of his subordinates.[125] This action, which was not accepted by the Foreign Office which moved to do what it could, constituted a major oblation by Howard since, shortly afterwards, he was forced to sell some of his and Isa's family heirlooms to survive financially at Stockholm.[126] More importantly, his two eldest sons, Esme and Francis, were at school at Downside, and their letters to him created within him a need to have his family together at Greystoke.[127]

In May 1918, as the Anglo-Swedish negotiations neared completion, he wrote privately to Hardinge to request leave as soon as practicable.[128] Realising that Howard had performed a succession of difficult tasks with efficiency and despatch, Hardinge agreed to receive 'most sympathetically' any application Howard made for leave. He could not yet make such an application, given the dangers presented by Finland and the Aland issue. However, by the middle of July, with the only problem on the horizon being the Eden government's efforts to circumvent the May agreement, Howard requested leave; permission to travel to England reached him on 29 July.[129] Isa and the three younger boys had left a week earlier to join Esme and Francis, now on summer vacation. The pressures of work kept Howard at Stockholm another month but, on 1 September 1918, he set foot in Aberdeen. He wrote in his diary: 'It is splendid to feel oneself back again in the U.K. after nearly $4\frac{1}{2}$ years of absence. I had a feeling I should <u>never</u> get back again – seems too good to be true.'[130] He raced to his family's estate near Carlisle, apprehensive that his rejoicing might not be shared by his sons, especially the two older ones who had been at school. He approached the door of the house with trepidation. 'It was glorious', he recorded the same day. 'Arrd at Lyulph's Tower about 11 and was greeted by Isa and the youngs with joy. No British coldness about them thank goodness and school has not made them ashamed of giving me a good hug.'[131] His much-needed rejuvenation in the place he loved most with those he loved most had begun. He assumed he would be back in Sweden in two months, refreshed and ready to go again. It was not to be.

7

Paris: Poland, the Baltic States, and the Treaty of Versailles, 1918–1919

> Lloyd George evidently does not want to see me. So I am writing him a long letter on Poland. It is all I can do & when I have done that I shall shut up.
>
> *Howard, April* 1919

I

After two weeks in the Cumberland countryside, hiking with his sons, seeing the families of his brothers and sisters, and taking part in several grouse and snipe shoots, Howard travelled with Isa and the children to spend a few days at London before the four oldest boys began their term at Downside. At the capital, the family went to the theatre, visited the zoo, and took tea with a number of relatives and friends. On 23 September, as Howard had never been to Downside, he and Isa accompanied Esme, Francis, Edmund, and Hubert there, spending two days seeing the school, meeting the head master, and finding out at first hand about the curriculum and religious instruction. Howard and his wife planned to travel to Italy – they could not embark until 18 October – and in the three weeks before leaving, he met with the king, and discussed Swedish and northern European affairs at the Foreign Office with Curzon, Tyrrell, Cecil, and others. He also travelled to Penshurst to talk matters over with Hardinge, then laid up with a broken leg. He conferred with British trade officials and Swedish commercial representatives about encouraging postwar Anglo-Swedish trade. He even had time to see both Bryce and Grey, and with each talked about the ability of the proposed League of Nations to ensure international peace and security in the post-war period. In this, Howard agreed with Grey that 'the idea had now gripped the mass of the people in England, and that it was certain to go through in some shape. The difficulty would be to find the best [shape]. Cooperation with America was essential.'[1] Over a lunch with Drummond, the subject of Howard's next posting surfaced. When Drummond enquired about Howard's preferences, the response had been 'Madrid or if Vienna still existed Vienna'.[2] In this way, except for a few days devoted totally to his family, Howard's first six weeks of leave amounted to a working holiday. It was with some relief that he and Isa set out for Rome in the middle of October.

Howard's short time in Britain occurred during a period of increasing optimism that the war would end soon with an Allied victory. His diary is full of references to daily newspaper reports recording Allied breakthroughs on the Western Front, the capture of thousands of German prisoners and guns, the softening of Berlin's war aims, and the crumbling of Austria-Hungary, Bulgaria, and the Ottoman Empire. Howard's optimism increased on his journey across the continent to Italy. In Paris for a few days *en route*, he discussed the situation with colleagues at the British Embassy; and in Rome, Rennell Rodd, still the ambassador, showed him up-to-date telegrams and despatches about the improving military situation and German efforts to sue for peace on the basis of President Wilson's fourteen points, which had been announced the previous January but which failed to strike a response at Berlin as long as the Germans thought they could win. In Rome, the enormous price of fighting the war was driven home to him when he met with friends and members of Isa's family whose sons had been killed in the fighting. With pathos he recorded how his sister-in-law was 'inconsolable' at the loss of her only boy.[3] The same sentiment emerged after he and Isa had called at the home of an acquaintance and had 'talked much of poor Joey and saw his portrait and military medal'. Some of his friends in Britain had also suffered losses, such as Tyrrell and Vansittart, but he had been removed to a degree from their grief. In Italy, amidst the news of constant Allied triumphs and the mounting evidence of Central Power collapse, the war's deadly impact on individual families surrounded him.

All of this affected Howard profoundly, steeling him inwardly to work hard once the fighting stopped to prevent the outbreak of another Great War and adding to his already pronounced anti-German sentiments. William II, especially, became an object of Howard's anger. When reports reached Rome that radical socialists were being cheered in the streets of Berlin, Howard observed caustically:

Rumours of German Emperor's abdication continue but not confirmed. In a recent speech in the Reichstag his abdication was openly advocated. Leibnicht [a radical socialist leader] has at last been set free in Germany and addresses the crowd in Berlin in a carriage filled with flowers. A different picture indeed to that, which the Kaiser must often have dreamt of, of his own triumphant entry into Berlin in shining armour.[4]

When additional news filtered through that Ludendorff and Hindenburg were to relinquish their power, uncharacteristic acid flowed from Howard's pen: 'Ludendorff's departure is generally interpreted as marking the end of the military caste in Germany. He was their high priest...If Ludendorff was the high priest, Hindenburg was the idol and a rather discredited one at that.'[5] All of Howard's emotions, which had had to be bottled up inside him in pro-German Stockholm during the war, now had a release. For Howard, the responsibility for the war lay with Germany and, to a lesser degree, its allies. This underpinned his beliefs about German brutishness and aggression that had begun to form in Bismarck's Berlin and were confirmed at Budapest, Berne, and Stockholm. Naturally, Howard refused to see that Britain bore any responsibility for the war; no man blames his own country easily in such matters, especially a diplomat.

But Howard had also never shied away from the use of diplomacy supported by armed strength to restrain the Germans from upsetting the European balance and, thereby, imperilling British security. His defence of Grey's foreign policy and of the proposals to arm Britain more heavily, made to Stafford before the war, attests to this. In addition, once the war began, which Howard saw as a struggle into which Britain found itself unwillingly dragged in order to protect its national and Imperial existence, he advocated tightening the blockade of Germany by the Royal Navy as a necessary evil. He knew that German women and children suffered deprivation because of the blockade, but that constituted the price that the German people had to pay for the folly of their leaders. Moreover, in Allied countries like Britain, women and children suffered deprivations as well with lost husbands and fathers. Thus, as the war drew to its victorious end for Britain and its allies, the opportunity existed to rid Europe and the world of militaristic, aggressive Germany. A peaceful Germany, or at least one whose expansionist tendencies could be contained, had to be the order of the day. With sanguinity, Howard received an urgent telegram from Hardinge on 8 November to return to London in haste to help prepare for the anticipated Peace Conference. 'If this means that I shall take part, however humble, in the Conference', he recorded that day, 'my highest ambition will be realised.'[6]

II

Howard reported to the Foreign Office on the morning of 13 November. There Hardinge was in the midst of creating what he assumed would be the British Delegation for the Peace Conference. Howard learnt that he had been selected as one of six senior officials, which Hardinge called 'diplomatic advisers', responsible for policy in six areas of Europe and the world where post-war adjustments had to be made. As the head of that section responsible for northeastern and eastern Europe, Howard would direct British policies concerning the region to the east of Germany or, to be precise according to Hardinge's directive, the 'Baltic Provinces, Russia,

Poland, Ukraine, Caucasia &c'.[7] About this Howard entertained private reservations: 'A large order. While I know something of [the] Baltic question and Poland and a little about Russia, I am quite ignorant of Ukraine and Caucassus [sic].'[8] But Hardinge's purpose at this moment, as the Central Powers crumbled more rapidly than almost everybody expected, involved getting the ablest men in the Foreign Office and the Diplomatic Service to serve in senior positions for the arduous task of peacemaking. Howard and the other five 'diplomatic advisers' had all shown that they could handle difficult assignments and, as important, understood the need to sublimate their personal beliefs in favour of Britain's foreign policy interests as defined by senior officials and ministers in London. Howard's colleagues in the proposed Delegation also responsible for European questions were to be Crowe, charged with co-ordinating policy for northwestern Europe – France, Alsace-Lorraine, Luxemburg, Belgium, and Holland – and Paget, responsible for southern and southwestern Europe – Austria-Hungary, Italy, Trentino, Trieste, the Balkans, and Turkey-in-Europe. Men like Findlay, who had continually quarrelled throughout the war with the Foreign Office view, were bypassed.

The selection of Howard, Crowe, Paget, and the others had a deeper significance in Hardinge's long-range plans. The permanent undersecretary's efforts in late October and early November 1918 concerning the British Delegation, supported by Balfour and Cecil, also had as their goal the re-establishment of Foreign Office primacy in the making and execution of foreign policy. Hardinge's scheme, outlined in his instructions to Howard, envisaged that the Foreign Office would dominate the British Delegation.[9] For several reasons, Foreign Office ability to determine the shape and direction of British diplomacy had been eroded seriously during the war. In the first place, the Foreign Office had become the target of general criticism in Britain, fostered by radical organisations like the Union for Democratic Control, through its pursuit of 'old diplomacy' before 1914.[10] Seen in things like secret conversations and secret agreements, such diplomacy had supposedly sucked Britain into the struggle on the continent. Secondly, during the war itself, the Foreign Office had to a large degree been superseded in the formal processes that made foreign policy.[11] Winning the war meant co-ordinating strategy and supply with the other allies; thus, during the four years of fighting, the service ministries, the Treasury, the Board of Trade, and other departments concerned with these overriding questions slowly replaced the diplomats with their own officials when negotiating or holding conversations with their opposites in other governments. Finally, the rise of Lloyd George to the premiership had emasculated the Foreign Office politically within the government.[12] Because diplomacy contributed little to strategy and supply and Balfour had been denied a seat in the five-man War Cabinet, Lloyd George and his principal private secretary, Philip Kerr, decided foreign policy, such as it was, by themselves without reference to the professionals. With an open contempt for the Foreign Office as the bastion of aristocratic privilege, and deprecating the work done by its officials and the diplomats, Lloyd George by the end of the war sought to revolutionise the conduct of British foreign policy by directing the country's external relations from Downing Street and appointing his political cronies as ambassadors abroad. Hardinge's attempt to get a Foreign Office-dominated Delegation in place as the war suddenly ended has to be seen in this context.

To what extent Howard understood the deeper significance of Hardinge's endeavours in early November 1918 is a moot point. None the less, immediately after seeing Hardinge on the morning of 13 November, he began to prepare for his part in the anticipated Peace Conference.[13] In Hardinge's scheme, the full resources of the Foreign Office were to be at the disposal of the 'diplomatic advisers': the Political Intelligence Department – PID – directed by Tyrrell; the Library, under the stewardship of Alwyn Parker, the head librarian; and the Historical Section, led by G. W. Prothero. Howard acquainted himself with these divisions on his first day back; he also met with the young expert on eastern Europe assigned to him as a private secretary, Edward Hallett Carr.[14] Within hours of arriving back at London to begin preparations for the Peace Conference, Howard immersed himself in his work.

In the two months between the time he took up this assignment and his departure for Paris, the site of the Conference, on 8 January, Howard found his position in the British Delegation modified. This derived from the Foreign Office being unable to convince the prime minister that it should dominate in the Delegation. This does not seem surprising given Lloyd George's determination to shape policy himself, and his poor estimation of the Foreign Office and the diplomats. What does surprise is that Hardinge and the other professionals should have believed that they could easily push aside those who had replaced them at the centre of Britain's foreign-policy-making elite during the war. For a variety of reasons, Lloyd George decided to bring a large delegation with him; not only did the Foreign Office have representation but so, too, did the service ministries, the Treasury, the Ministry of Shipping, the law officers of the crown, and several other departments of state.[15] Added to this diverse group of experts were full delegations from the dominions and India, a special adviser on Anglo-American relations, Kerr and several private secretaries, and Sir Maurice Hankey, the secretary to both the Cabinet and the Committee of Imperial Defence, to whom the prime minister gave complete administrative authority over the Delegation. Hardinge's plans were scuppered, though he received the distinguished sounding rank of 'Superintending Ambassador' to assuage his sensitivities; as Hardinge quickly realised, this amounted to a largely empty position. Hankey had received real influence over the day-to-day functioning of the British Delegation, along with constant access to the prime minister. The leading lights of the Foreign Office and Diplomatic Service, represented by Howard, Crowe, Paget, and the others, became known as the 'Political Section' of the Delegation. Through Lloyd George's conscious efforts, the professional diplomats received a secondary role in peace-making, a role that ultimately rankled Howard and his colleagues and made them increasingly critical of the prime minister and his revolutionary methods of foreign-policy-making as the Conference progressed. But Howard's dissatisfaction with Lloyd George, like the dissatisfaction of the other senior diplomats, really developed after the conference commenced in January; at that time, the prime minister, meeting with the other principal Allied leaders, Wilson and George Clemenceau, the French premier, decided issues on his own with minimal reference to his ostensible advisers.

Although Howard had been chosen by Hardinge to handle British policy concerning northeastern and eastern Europe, he soon concentrated on issues relating to Poland and the Baltic States. Howard's role and general ideas in the making of the Treaty of Versailles as it affected Germany's eastern frontiers are well-established thanks to a number of studies.[16] He worked as a 'diplomatic adviser' from the middle of November 1918 to early February 1919. He then served as the senior British delegate on an inter-allied mission sent to Poland to examine and report on conditions there and, after returning to Paris in the first week of April, offered some advice on Polish and Baltic affairs until the signature of Versailles. On 15 May, he began service as chairman of the Baltic Commission of the Peace Conference, a body whose work had yet to be completed when he left Paris to prepare for his next posting. These same studies have also outlined to some extent Howard's ideas about how the peace settlement in eastern Europe should be achieved and, based on this, have sought to explain his contributions to British policies of peace-making. Howard's general view held that, with the collapse of Germany, the disintegration of Austria-Hungary, and the advent of Bolshevism in Russia, stability in eastern Europe required strong successor states. Concerning the area of his specific responsibility, Howard's ideas when translated into an expression of practical politics meant a viable Poland and the independence from the Russian yoke of the small and isolated Baltic Provinces which, supported by Britain, should align diplomatically with Finland and Sweden in a pro-Allied Baltic League. Wedded to the principle of the balance of power in Europe, Howard's experience gained over two decades led him to argue that German aggressive tendencies had to be limited in the east, that Bolshevik Russia had to be hemmed in on its western frontiers, and that, for the sake of general European security, Germany and Bolshevik Russia had to be kept apart. This meant giving Poland and the Baltic States defensible borders and sound demographic, economic, and territorial bases to sustain their independence. 'Apart...from my personal sentiment in favour of the freedom of all the subject nations', he later observed, 'I was strongly convinced that their national spirit formed the best bulwark against Bolshevik fanaticism which, had it then gained Germany, might have swept away our civilization, Mr Lloyd George included.'[17]

All studies that touch on Howard's role in the creation of Poland in 1919 observe that he held strong 'pro-Polish' views. Except for Lloyd George, who was quite explicit at the time,[18] subsequent analyses of Howard's efforts imply that his Catholicism led him to champion Catholic Poland as the best buffer in the east and blinded him to some of the more extreme actions of the new Polish government in eastern Europe.[19] In addition, the charge has been levelled, without any substantiation, that in Paris Howard 'had great charm, a romantic adventurous spirit and some thought a certain instability of judgement'.[20] Howard did advance pro-Polish views during his service on the British Delegation. Moreover, on some issues, his opinion did change during the course of the Conference. However, his efforts in peace-making were neither unstable nor conditioned by his Catholicism. Howard's approach to the problems involved in creating Poland and the three Baltic States squared with the advice he had tendered from Stockholm throughout 1918 – before he knew he would serve in a senior capacity at a Peace Conference – about the need for British support of independent Finland in northern Europe. And, whilst no doubt exists that Howard can be characterised as pro-Polish, he never allowed personal sentiment to soften the hard-edged policies which he and the other members of the British Delegation advanced to ensure the protection of Britain's continental interests. Hence, although he supported more often than not Polish aspirations, at crucial times he also disagreed strongly with those Polish policies which threatened to undermine the balance of power, and he would then advise using such power as Britain could muster to force Warsaw's compliance with the decisions reached by the major Powers in Paris.[21] In this way, a continuity existed in Howard's diplomacy during the making of the Treaty of Versailles that stretched back to his time on Crete: working within the constraints of what can best be described as *realpolitik* to produce policies to protect British interests.

Howard's selection by Hardinge to handle British policy concerning northern and northeastern Europe came about because during the war Stockholm had been a centre of contact between eastern European nationalists, seeking independence for their respective homelands, and the British government. Howard's main contact with such people, apart from the Finns described earlier, came through the endeavours of Polish nationalists to resurrect Poland as a sovereign state. The question was complex.[22] The kingdom of Poland had ceased to exist in the 1790s, when Austria, Prussia, and Russia joined together to finish conquering and partitioning it. Although subsequent adjustments occurred to the three empires' frontiers within what had been the Polish kingdom, the Poles were divided amongst these three Powers until the great War. Polish nationalism remained a strong force by 1914, this because the Catholic Church had served as a focus for that nationalism throughout the partition and by the fact that the Polish language and culture had not been subsumed by those of the dominant Germans and Russians. This does not mean that Poles possessed uniform views about their position and those of their conquerors when the war began in 1914. Conservative elements in each empire remained generally loyal to their central government. More moderate elements, tending to be represented by socialist and peasant parties, inclined to support Germany and Austria-Hungary. Within Russian Poland, another group, the National Democrats, threw in their lot with the tsarist government. Finally, a fourth segment, mainly radical socialists, opposed the war altogether. During the war, the belligerents sought to exploit this division to their advantage. Vienna courted Polish nationalism to its cause by organising a Supreme National Council in August 1914, which had as its avowed goal the ultimate unification of Austrian and Russian Poland, a union which would owe loyalty to the House of Habsburg. In Russia, the tsarist government permitted the National Democrats to form the Polish National Committee, the mandate of which involved the unification of all Polish lands under the suzerainty of the tsar.

By 1916 and 1917, events continued apace. As Central Power armies occupied Russian Poland, Germany and Austria-Hungary moved to exploit Polish manpower and resources in their war effort. The trade-off for this came with a decision by Berlin and Vienna to establish a Polish kingdom in the east, but one subservient to them. When the Russian revolution began in March 1917, the new regime there, desperate to shore up the nation's war effort, declared its intention to accord Poland independence after the war. However, the increasing radicalisation of Russia led the Polish National Committee, dominated by conservatives, to despair of achieving full independence from the Bolsheviks, so it moved its headquarters to Paris and immediately had its agents lobby the British, French, and Americans for a promise of full independence once the war ended. In September, Berlin set up a Regency Council in occupied Poland, along with a government and a legislature, all dependent on Germany. Four months later, in outlining American war aims by publicly adumbrating his 'Fourteen Points', President Wilson bent to the pressures of National Committee lobbying and the demands of Polish-Americans by advocating 'an independent Polish state' with 'a free and secure access to the sea'. In June 1918, the British, French, and Italians followed suit with a declaration favouring 'an independent and united Poland'.

Although it is somewhat of an over-simplification, two influential competing groups had emerged amongst Polish nationalists by the closing stages of the war: the National Committee, under the leadership of Roman Dmowski, which was conservative, pro-Allied, and strong in the West; and the Regency Council, situated in Warsaw and nominally pro-German. As the armistice neared, some contact occurred between the National Committee and the Regency Council about joining to form an independent government once the Germans surrendered. At this juncture, however, a new factor developed when a respected Polish soldier, General Joseph Pilsudski, returned to Warsaw from German imprisonment. He had fought with the Austrian army early in the war, won respect amongst Poles for his gallantry against the Russians, and won even more by not supporting what he saw as the toadying of the Regency Council to the Germans in 1917. On returning to Warsaw in early November 1918, his popularity led to his becoming commander-in-chief of the army and head of state. A self-described socialist, a proven anti-Russian, and a man of principle who had not prostituted himself with the Germans in 1917, Pilsudski was in a strong political position in Warsaw by the end of 1918. By this time, therefore, two groups of Polish nationalists existed ready to create a sovereign Polish state: Dmowski in the West, who had the ear of the Allied governments; and Pilsudski in Warsaw, gaining strength within Poland day by day. The problem confronting Howard and the other Allied experts assigned to handle Polish affairs centred on coming to terms with the disunited Poles and, as both groups of Poles and other subject nationalities like the Balts, Czechs, and Ukrainians held competing irredentist designs on Austro-Hungarian, German, and Russian territories, achieving a stable settlement in this troubled region of Europe.

Howard's first exposure to the labyrinthine world of Polish politics came in May 1916 when one of Dmowski's emissaries approached him seeking British assistance in lobbying Petrograd to accord the anticipated Russian-sponsored Polish state more autonomy than it was willing to give. Howard promised nothing, though he dutifully reported this meeting to the Foreign Office.[23] When London approved his non-committal reply, noting this existed as a domestic Russian question, Howard responded by warning Grey that 'it seems to me to be of the highest importance that we should take some action to make the Poles of the conquered Provinces understand that they can rely on us for the reestablishment of their ancient liberties'. This reflected Howard's sympathy for subject peoples being allowed to run their own affairs. The Poles clearly deserved a degree of independence; perhaps, the British granting of Home Rule to Ireland on the eve of the war was in his mind at this time.[24] However, neither the British nor the French would do anything at this stage to push the Russians on this matter. Allied unity was more essential than seeking to win the support of subject nationalities which might or might not benefit Britain in the future. The French were then enmeshed in Verdun, and the British were soon to launch the Somme offensive. Only after the tsarist regime collapsed the next year and the Russian Empire began to crumble, and with it its military strength, did Paris and London begin to warm to the idea of an independent Poland.[25]

Howard's contacts with Polish nationalists, from both Dmowski's National Committee and the German-controlled areas, continued and with increasing frequency until he left Stockholm in August 1918. His reports show his sympathies in this period more and more with the National Committee,[26] not unnatural given its ties to the Entente cause since 1914 and its work in the West after the Russian revolution to win the support of western leaders for their vision of a revived Poland. Also, in the course of his periodic meetings with Dmowski's supporters, Howard formed a friendship with Count Wladyslaw Sobanski, the National Committee agent responsible for securing British support. This friendship, reinforced by social meetings and the fact that the Howard and Sobanski children were friends at Downside, continued into the Peace-Conference period. Just as important, Howard did not avoid seeing Poles from the German-controlled areas when they wished to press their case at the British Legation. In late 1917, for instance, when it was evident that Germany's creation of a Polish kingdom under Berlin's control was designed to permit the conscription of Poles to fight alongside the German army and allow for the easier exploitation of Polish economic resources for the German war effort, a representative of the Regency Council, Prince Lubecki, appeared in Stockholm. He approached Howard about the Regency Council serving as a channel for a peace settlement between Germany and the Allies.[27] Although it remains unclear whether Lubecki had German support for such a proposal, his motivation was to ensure that the political faction he represented controlled Poland once hostilities ceased. Though lacking specific instructions, Howard replied in the strongest terms that there could be no question of a peace settlement at this point. Because of the blockade, Germany would be forced 'sooner or later to come to us hat in hand, in order to obtain the raw materials she will require after the war, which are necessary for her existence'. Whilst Howard's germanophobia shone through here, in an unequivocal way he also let Lubecki know that this was a war to the finish and that the Allies were not going to smile on any regime at the eventual Peace Conference that had supported the Central Power war effort in any way.

Howard's generally favourable view of Dmowski and his followers helped contribute to the formal British recognition of the National Committee as an official voice of Polish nationalism – though, significantly, because the situation in Poland remained unclear, not as any sort of government-in-exile.[28] This recognition did not find favour in a number of quarters in Britain. An anti-semite, a conservative, and a man who embodied his organisation's unhidden desire to acquire large tracts of eastern Europe for reborn Poland, Dmowski provoked critics ranging from Cecil, who put his concerns privately within the Foreign Office, to Jewish groups and the leading articles of the liberal *Manchester Guardian*, which offered public admonitions.[29] Howard did not blindly endorse Dmowski and the National Committee. He knew there were questions about their actions and policies.[30] It would have been out of character for Howard, given his life since 1885, especially considering his experiences since returning to the Diplomatic Service in 1903, to assume that the leaders of the National Committee were motivated by altruism or lacked flaws of character and politics. But Howard was a realist. Dmowski, Sobanski, and the others were seeking to recreate an independent Poland against the real and bitter opposition of the Germans and the Bolshevik Russians. The National Committee supported the Allies against the Central Powers or, at least, did so most of the time; they did so because they judged that this would lead to the independence of their homeland and the establishment of a regime according to their economic, political, and social proclivities. Howard knew this, as he knew that such new regimes would be beholden to Britain for helping them achieve power. Thus, Howard's reasons for supporting pro-Allied Poles remained consistent with the endorsement he gave Mannerheim and his Finnish nationalists at this same moment. In this, he shared Hardinge's view of the situation in northern and northeastern Europe penned at the end of 1917, that '[o]ur object has been to encourage as much as possible those elements which we knew to be in favour of the defeat of the Central Powers'.[31] With such sentiments, Howard undertook his peace-making tasks a year later.

In London until early January 1919, Howard worked to make sense of the swirl of events that developed with the defeat of the German army, the successful revolutions in Berlin and Vienna, and the emergence of new states in eastern Europe. It remained his task to assess this ferment and arrive at policies that would best protect British interests on the continent.

This meant conferring with Balfour, Hardinge, Crowe, and other senior officials from the Foreign Office, holding discussions with his assistants, and working his way through seemingly endless papers on the various questions relating to his assignment that had been prepared by the PID, the Library, and the Historical Section.[32] It also entailed coming to grips with information, much of it contradictory, reaching him about the state of affairs within defeated Germany, revolutionary Russia, and the emerging states in between. Such information came from regular diplomatic channels, and even more from people like Mannerheim, Sobanski, and others representing the new regimes who descended on the Allied capitals to sway the great Powers in their favour.[33] Howard's work in this period came to centre almost exclusively on the issues relating to the Baltic States and Poland; almost from the beginning, the pressures of events saw him have little to do with the Caucasus and the Ukraine. In fact, his only consideration of these latter two regions arose over frontier disputes between Poland and the new Ukrainian state, both of which desired the former Austrian province of Eastern Galicia.

With the collapse of the Central Powers, Howard and his colleagues understood that Allied efforts to achieve stability in eastern Europe through the Peace Conference would entail adjudicating amongst the competing territorial claims of Germany, Bolshevik Russia, and their new neighbours: Poland, Czechoslovakia, the Ukraine, and the Baltic Powers of Finland, Estonia, Latvia, and Lithuania. Frontiers in the east remained undefined. As had occurred in Poland when Central Power defeat seemed imminent, groups of nationalists in the former Russian Baltic provinces, in the Ukraine, and in the former Habsburg lands of Bohemia, Moravia, and Slovakia, each declared the independence of new states. They each had territorial claims that, first, impinged on old Germany and Russia and, secondly, conflicted with the demands of the other new states. In Germany and Russia, despite each being governed by republican forces which promised radical approaches to domestic problems, the new leaderships in Berlin and Moscow shared their imperialist predecessors' desires to resist any territorial surrender to the irredentism of the successor states. In Bolshevik Russia's case, Lenin began to use the guns of the Red Army to reclaim lands lost during the war and revolution. On the other hand the Baltic States, the Ukraine, and Poland, whose territories had been largely within the confines of the former tsarist Empire, wanted space and defensible borders in the east at Russian expense. Lithuania, Czechoslovakia, and Poland desired portions of what had been Wilhelmine Germany in their western reaches. But matters did not end there. The Poles and Lithuanians quarrelled over control of the city of Vilna and its hinterland. The Poles and Czechs each coveted Silesia, a German province, and Teschen, a Habsburg duchy; these regions were rich in mineral resources that Warsaw and Prague each judged essential to their new state's economic development. The Poles and Ukrainians coveted Eastern Galicia, an area of agricultural abundance, and by November 1918 fighting had broken out between the two for ownership. Finally the Poles, fearful of being landlocked through German control of the southern Baltic coast and, thus, being susceptible to German control of Polish trade and economic development, sought access to the sea in line with Wilson's promise made in January 1918. This demand lay pregnant with danger as it threatened to separate East Prussia from the rest of Germany. In this way, there existed several strands of the peace settlement in eastern Europe, and Polish ambitions touched them all. It is not surprising that within a week of taking up his new job, Howard noted in his diary that Poland constituted 'my most difficult problem'.[34]

Before departing for Paris, Howard made a number of suggestions for diplomatic means by which Britain could profit by helping to bring stability to northern and northeastern Europe. He met with Mannerheim on 18 November and succeeded to a large degree in squelching some proposals made by the Finnish leader which had the potential of inflaming Allied opinion against the 'White' Finns.[35] Mannerheim asked if German advisers might remain in Finland to help the 'Whites' resist a potential Bolshevik attack. Howard indicated that the Allied governments would not look kindly on this. When Mannerheim then enquired about Allied reaction to a Finnish occupation of Petrograd and the establishment of a 'government of law and order there' should the Finns be attacked by the Bolsheviks and defeat them, Howard did not answer. His silence was taken as a polite rebuff to this Finnish suggestion. But Mannerheim also sought official British recognition of his country, and the immediate despatch of food and warships to help it resist any Bolshevik attack. Howard endorsed this and, though Balfour proved reluctant at that moment to extend formal recognition – there had to be Allied agreement for such action, and the French wanted certain guarantees like a Finnish government devoid of Germans, the evacuation of all German troops from Finland, and early elections – the British did send foodstuffs to Finland and a naval squadron into the Baltic in early December.[36] In seeing Howard after this, Mannerheim outlined his satisfaction 'that foodstuffs were at last allowed to go to Finland'.[37] Although one of many British officials supporting Mannerheim – Kerr was another; he and Howard attended a private dinner at Elizabeth Carnarvon's on 13 December to celebrate with Mannerheim on his appointment as Finnish Regent[38] – Howard helped contribute to the emergence of a pro-British Finland in the post-war period.

At the end of November, Howard sought to build on his pro-Finnish advice by lending his support to the proposal for a Baltic League comprised of Finland, Estonia, Latvia, and Lithuania; its purpose would be to keep open the Baltic in war and peace. As one observer has noted, it would also be 'directed against both Russian and German sovereignty' in that region.[39] But Howard went further. As he had done in Stockholm during 1918, he argued that Sweden should be encouraged to join and take a leading part in this League. Swedish economic interests in the region would be enhanced, allowing Stockholm to play a major role in Baltic affairs, something that would 'flatter Sweden's vanity' and, because Britain supported the endeavour, weaken Swedish–German bonds. Howard deprecated bringing Poland into this proposed arrangement, first, because of Polish–Lithuanian differences and, secondly, because Sweden might see the membership of a Power of equivalent strength as a threat to any dominance it might hope to enjoy. He admitted that the military potential of this League would be minimal; however, it could have a positive political and economic impact in this important region. In this Howard had the guarded support of his superiors, mainly Balfour and Hardinge, both uncertain that the League could resist revived Germany and Russia in the future and, with their experience, believing that it would take several years for such a League to develop. But they did not dismiss Howard's notion, being willing to watch benevolently whilst events unfolded. The Admiralty saw strategic advantages in Howard's ideas, whilst the War Office doubted whether the Bolshevik Russians would long tolerate being denied crucial ports on the Baltic. Although this met with less success than Howard's support of Finland – and ultimately the Baltic League proved a mirage – it shows Howard continuing to work towards the establishment of a regional balance of power in the Baltic that would owe much to Britain, and through which Britain could lessen the influence of its traditional German and Russian adversaries and increase its own.

Howard's principal preoccupation in these first months lay with the Polish question. He saw Poland as the key to the regional balance of power in northeastern Europe, and he remained a strong supporter of the National Committee, becoming even more so after 13 December when, at a dinner arranged by Sobanski, he met Ignace Jan Paderewski, the world famous pianist and the National Committee's agent in the United States.[40] Paderewski had done well in the United States by winning the ear of Colonel Edward House, Wilson's chief foreign-policy adviser, and in getting the president to include an independent Poland with access to the sea in the 'Fourteen Points'. Moreover, on a more subtle plane, this man's artistic talents and cultural achievements found sympathy with the private side of Howard.[41] When Paderewski became the Polish premier in the middle of January 1919, a result of Pilsudski's men and the National Committee ostensibly burying their differences to achieve a better hearing at Paris and provide a unified front to handle internal problems, Howard reckoned reborn Poland had a chance for survival. With Pilsudski as head of state and Paderewski leading the government, a new phase of Polish history had begun. 'So it seems [the] breach between [the] Polish Parties is healed & we may hope for a really united Govt. at last', Howard noted at the time. 'It is the only thing to save Poland.'[42]

Howard's contribution to Britain's Polish policy in the run-up to the Peace Conference is well known. On 9 December the Foreign Office experts produced a major memorandum which argued that Britain's Polish policy as it affected Germany should have several goals. Though a compromise document reflecting a month's discussion amongst the experts, Howard's ideas dominated its contents.[43] First, there should be a viable state whose population should be ethnically Polish and did not contain large numbers of minority Germans and others. The underlying assumption here held that Germany and Russia would revive to some extent; thus, to keep to a minimum future disputes between these two giants and Poland, the new Polish state should be as homogeneous as possible. Secondly, whilst Poland should have access to the sea, it should be denied the port of Danzig, an ethnically German city, then being demanded by the National Committee. Instead, Poland should be given the adjacent port of Neufahrwasser and its hinterland, with appropriate transportation links to the south across German territory. On the same lines, Poland should receive that part of German Silesia populated mainly by Poles, which meant, except for a few German-speaking mining districts, the area as far north as the town of Oppeln. The experts' idea involved tying East Prussia to the rest of Germany and keeping the loss of territory to Poland to a minimum so as to reduce German irredentism. Finally, in the event that problems arose over the transfer of German lands to Poland, say in East Prussian areas like Mazuria, which contained several Protestant communities, plebiscites should be arranged to allow local populations to choose in which country they should live.

Howard's ideas about Poland's eastern borders took another month to gel. By early January 1919 he supported Polish claims that justified expansion into areas of western Russia that would provide the new state with economic resources and defensible frontiers.[44] The alternative would be the spread of Bolshevism closer to western Europe; thus, Howard 'preferred the dangerous results of Polish imperialism to the collapse of Poland under Bolshevik conquest, which would be to the advantage of Germany'. Although not squaring with the ideal outlined in the 9 December memorandum about subject peoples, it was not a perfect world. A price had to be paid to have Poland succeed in maintaining the balance of power in northeastern Europe. Seeking to put some restraint on Polish pretensions, Howard argued that the Peace Conference could mitigate the 'possible unfortunate effects of such Polish imperialism'. But it remained that for Howard, reborn Poland, despite the difficulties that it might create for the Allies, had to be large enough and of sufficient strength to offset Germany and Russia.

Finally, Howard took pains in the two months before the Peace Conference convened to restrain the Poles. When Paderewski returned to Warsaw in late December 1918 to hold discussions with Pilsudski about creating a common political front, Howard appointed a British Delegation to accompany him: Colonel Harry Wade, the military attaché at Copenhagen whose analytical skills had impressed Howard during the war; Richard Kimens, a former British consul at Warsaw, fluent in Polish, who had contacts amongst rightwing politicians there; and Rowland Kenney, a member of the PID with socialist leanings who knew many leftwing Polish nationalists.[45] Whilst some debate exists about the purpose of this mission, Howard's papers indicate that it was 'political', designed to assess the situation in Poland and send accurate reports of conditions back to the British Delegation in Paris.[46] Mixed in personnel and political persuasion, such a mission on the ground in Poland would prevent the policy-makers in Paris from being flim-flammed by the National Committee and Pilsudski's followers. Indeed, just before he left for Warsaw, Howard delivered a gentle warning to Sobanski that London opposed any Polish intention to fight the Germans for territory, this though the French seemed not averse to such a course.[47] An army of Polish volunteers stood ready in France under the command of General Joseph Haller, an army that to a large extent had been the fruit of Paderewski's efforts in the United States before the armistice to get Polish-Americans and Polish *émigrés* to return to Europe to fight the Germans. Howard's verbal warning, followed by a formal message to Pilsudski at Warsaw, was that Britain would not countenance sending Haller's army to Poland at this stage because of the fragile state of relations along the as yet undefined German–Polish frontier. The point in this was that Howard shared with his colleagues a desire for a strong, united Poland, but one that would not overreach itself and, by its actions, foster continued instability in northeastern Europe.

Whilst Howard's record of actions and general views concerning the Baltic region and Poland are well known, his precise reasons for advocating the policies he did were until recently less certain.[48] However, the availability of his papers now removes this uncertainty for, with respect to his efforts at peace-making, they contain two major documents which outline precisely why he took the lines he did: a lengthy memorandum, drafted in June 1919 which, submitted to Balfour, seems not to have gone any further; and a letter written to Curzon six months later, at the latter's request after he succeeded Balfour at the Foreign Office, in order to help him come to grips with the Russian problem.[49] Howard's reasoning behind his policies, stemming from his diplomatic experience, remained purely strategic:

> Whatever the future [sic] political future of Russia may be, whether it is again united in one great State, whether it becomes a Federation of States or whether it is split up into several independent States, the great danger of the future for Europe and Great Britain will lie in a rapprochement or alliance between Germany and Russia and in the economic domination of the latter by the former.

Howard looked to the past and, although not necessarily with complete accuracy, argued that 'from the time of Peter the Great up to the war in 1914, Russia was organised and administered almost entirely commercially, financially, militarily, and politically in the main by men of German birth or of German extraction'. Germans did this because Russia and Prussia/Germany were close geographically, there existed colonies of Germans within Russia, especially in the Baltic Provinces, and Germans proved to be better administrators and organisers than Russians in the service of the tsar. For a century, from the final partition of Poland to William II's dismissal of Bismarck, the Prussian/Germans and the Russians shared a common interest in northeastern Europe: keeping the Polish people subdued. Howard quoted Frederick the Great who

> cynically put it [that] Russia and Prussia had by partitioning Poland taken the Sacrament together and divided the Host and thus laid the foundations of a common policy which must bind them together for better or worse, as a war between them would probably result in the resurrection of Poland which it would in future be in the interests of both co-partageants to avoid.

However, William II's *Drang nach Osten* 'brought Russia and Germany into conflict over Constantinople and the Turkish Empire and for the time the Polish Sacrament was forgotten'.

Howard opined that the war had resolved the matter of Constantinople as far as Germany and Russia were concerned, as well as ended 'the German dream of domination in the [Near] East'. But this meant that Germany and Russia 'will once more be in a position to unite in a common policy in the East of Europe'. Here lay the nub of the problem. A renewed Russo-German condominium in northeastern Europe appeared possible given the changes in the southeast wrought by the war. Howard stated candidly:

> ...it has always seemed to me that our principal aim should be to cut off Russia as far as possible from Germany by supporting the Baltic Provinces and Poland in every way in their struggle against both Russian Bolshevism and Germany and

> thus create a chain of States, some independent and some possibly with a wide autonomy, within an ultimate Russian Federation which would prevent Germany becoming a State contiguous to Russia. Unfortunately, we have never given sufficient support to the Baltic States whatever it may be considered we have done for Poland.
>
> A very small fraction of the money which we have spent on Denikin and Kolchak ['White' Russian commanders fighting the Bolsheviks in Russia] would have sufficed long ago to set the Baltic States on their legs and organise an adequate army for their home defences.

Howard held that British foreign policy had to be applied boldly in northeastern and eastern Europe. For him, three intertwined ways existed, a judicious blend of force and economic and political diplomacy, to keep Russia and Germany divided. The first, the most difficult, entailed fostering a 'truly democratic' Russian government; this would increase the chance of a regime 'less likely to be imperialistic and more likely to support the League of Nations'. Hence, aid to men like Denikin and Kolchak should continue but be conditional on assurances that they would encourage a representative political system once the Bolsheviks collapsed. To be avoided was 'a return to re-actionary Government in Russia which is what many of the Russian emigrés openly aim at'. The second way involved the 'erection and maintenance of a series of buffer States from the Baltic to the Black Sea'; such a course would 'prevent Germany the great geographical advantages she has hitherto enjoyed of conterminous frontiers with Russia'. He stressed the importance of the Baltic States, to which should be despatched without delay goods, credits, military equipment, arms, and ammunition, followed when possible by technical advisers for 'all branches of their administration' and recognition of their *de facto* existence. 'It is essential', he cautioned, 'that, unless the whole policy of the "cordon sanitaire" against Bolshevism, which should develop into the line of buffer States, is to collapse, the Baltic States must be given the support necessary to enable them to defend themselves against Bolshevism on the one side and German influence on the other'. The third way concerned 'the effective competition of the Western Powers and America with Germany in Russia on the economic terrain'; diplomacy of this sort would reduce Russian dependence on Germans in commercial, trade, and related endeavours. Britain could take the lead in this via the Department of Overseas Trade, the encouragement of Russian studies in British universities and secondary schools, and the subsidisation of a 'British Commercial School at Moscow' to prepare British businessmen for their work in Russia. Just as with the Baltic States, British technical advice should be given to 'every branch of the administration' in Russia and, fundamentally, that Britain encourage American, French, and other 'commercial enterprise' in the country: 'There is room in Russia for all and we [alone] cannot attempt to compete with Germany whose natural advantages are so great.'

These records show that Howard approached peace-making from the viewpoint of ensuring that the balance of power in northern and northeastern Europe would not be upset by the revival of Germany and Russia and, based on his historical analysis, of Germany's probable dominance in the Russo-German relationship. If the peace settlement had any hope of lasting, close Russo-German relations had to be prevented. To accomplish this, Howard argued that Britain should help to create and sustain a line of smaller, viable countervailing Powers in the region between the two giants. More than this, he made the point that the chief problem that Britain would face in Europe after the Conference ended would be Germany. Despite its socialist, republican garb, Germany would not abandon the expansionist tendencies which had marked its development after 1870–1. The only potential German ally of note would be Russia, so British leaders had to do all possible to make Russia a responsible Power, or, perhaps, more responsible, something that could come only by the Allies fostering a liberal government there and by reducing German influence to a minimum using the same tactics by which the Germans had previously been successful. It might seem that Howard's ideas about Russia and the potential for Britain and its allies to achieve political and economic influence in its internal affairs represented uninformed wishful thinking. Perhaps to a degree it did, but his proposals were largely based on information and policy proposals he had received in Stockholm and London from British experts on Russia during the fourteen months following the Bolshevik *coup d'état*. Before they left Petrograd, Buchanan and Lindley kept him abreast of the political morass into which Lenin and his cohorts had plunged their country.[50] A young British scholar, Bernard Pares, a russophile anti-Bolshevik working to establish Russian studies at the University of London and who advocated the 'British Commercial School at Moscow', had passed through Stockholm on visits to Russia and left Howard with a series of memoranda on internal Russian affairs.[51] Once the Bolsheviks achieved power and moved their capital to Moscow, Howard received reports from Robert Bruce Lockhart, the British secret agent at Moscow.[52] And, of course, once it became known about Howard's responsibility for policy towards Russia within the British Delegation, 'White' Russian *émigrés* like Sazanov and others sought to prime him with their ideas about British aid to counter-revolutionary operations within Russia.[53] Added to this were entreaties from former colleagues like Bryce, who did not want to see Russia weakened to any great extent by the loss of territory.[54]

But Howard was a realist. Every chance existed that the Bolsheviks might survive, or that the anti-Bolsheviks might triumph and seek to establish 'a greater Russia on the old basis, such as is the avowed object of the Denikins, Kolchaks, Sazonoffs and others'.[55] Either way, strong centralised Russia would emerge, creating difficulties for Britain not just in Europe but in the wider world where British and Russian imperial interests confronted one another. In Europe the rise of a powerful Russia, 'Red' or 'White', would assuredly lead to some sort of Russo-German rapprochement and a political and military imbalance. Howard felt that Britain had two diplomatic options to prevent this. The first, presupposing that the Bolsheviks would have nothing to do with the Allied Powers since the latter had sent forces into Russia in 1918 to tie down German troops and had given support to the 'Whites', allowed that Britain encourage 'White' leaders to look towards the creation of a federated state in which former subject peoples could have a large degree of autonomy. Such encouragement would take the form of continued and increased support against the 'Reds'; however, to ignore Allied wishes would be to face the Bolsheviks alone – the successor States would have no interest in helping the 'Whites' defeat the Red Army if a greater united Russia was to be the result. As Howard told Curzon: 'For these reasons, the support of the Border States should, I think, be a cardinal point of our Russian policy, though we should make it clear to the ['White'] Russians that we should in no way support [the Border States'] complete independence provided a satisfactory scheme of Federation can be evolved.' The second option, predicated on the possibility of either the 'Reds' or the 'Whites' winning the civil war and then establishing a strong centralised state, involved ensuring that the Baltic States and Poland possessed the strength to meet the challenge posed by such a state and, just as important, survive should their traditional enemies in the east and west again sit down together to take the Sacrament and divide the Host.

These were Howard's views as they affected the advice he gave his superiors during his service as a member of the British Delegation to the Peace Conference. They indicate several things about his role. First and foremost, he saw the creation of stability in northern and northeastern Europe to be the *sine qua non* of British policy. In this he remained a dedicated anti-Bolshevik, something easily understood given the barbarity of Lenin and his followers, their atheism, and their determination to export revolution to the rest of Europe.[56] Secondly, he did not perceive Russia to be the greatest threat to the balance of power and, thus, to British interests. Germany stood as the chief culprit in this respect, as the course of German history since 1870–1 attested, so that every effort had to be made to keep Russia and Germany apart and to make Russia more amenable to western influence through Allied aid, technical advice, and economic penetration.

Finally, flowing from the need to keep Russia and Germany separated, and in order to respect the legitimate desires of subject nationalities to determine their own lives, came the need to support the Finns, Balts, and Poles in nation-making. Even at the end of 1919, when he had finished with peace-making and had taken up his next post, he did not hold that these 'Border States' should necessarily have complete independence. It would be preferable to have them integrated into a federated Russian state – this would make German penetration of such a state more difficult – though this was not an indispensable condition. In all of this, there was no question of sympathy for Poland purely because its people were Catholic. He saw Finland and the Baltic States, peopled predominantly by Protestants, in the same light as he saw Catholic Poland. A *cordon sanitaire* from the Baltic southwards had to be created should a greater united Russia emerge from the ferment of the Russian civil war. About Howard's alleged 'instability of judgement', his support for the balance of power in northern and northeastern Europe as the best defence of British interests accorded with the dominant thinking within the Foreign Office – the prime minister's office was a different matter. He reckoned that this balance could not be achieved without support for Britain amongst the emerging states in that region; therefore, he argued that Poland and the Baltic Powers be built up to provide this support. If these states had to trim some of their national aspirations by being included in a new Russian federation, here stood the sacrifice to be made for peace and stability. If a federation proved impractical, then the small Powers had to be able to stand on their own. Such realism marked Howard's approach to peace-making before and after he reached Paris on 8 January.

III

For his first ten days at Paris, Howard had little to do. The conference's formal opening was scheduled for 18 January, the anniversary of the proclamation of the German Empire in 1871, so that Lloyd George, Wilson, and Clemenceau found themselves preoccupied with matters concerning the formal structure of this congress. Howard busied himself settling in at his room at the Hotel Majestic, setting up his office at the British headquarters, the Hotel Astoria, and using luncheons, suppers, teas, and a few preliminary meetings with other delegations to see old friends and become acquainted with other men with whom he expected to work over the next several months. In this short time, he met Wilson and Colonel House for the first time, held a short discussion on Poland with Baron Degrand, a French Foreign Ministry expert, and was introduced to Dmowski over a dinner arranged by Sobanski. Howard was impressed with the Polish leader – 'whom I thought interesting & v. clever. Everyone is agreed about this' – and he learnt at this stage that negotiations were then progressing between Dmowski and an emissary from Pilsudski about arranging a coalition government in Warsaw.[57] Howard also met with British experts from the Board of Trade about problems concerning the freedom of transit, problems which would have to be addressed if Poland was to secure unrestricted access to the sea. Still, within a week of arriving at Paris, Howard found himself at a loose end: 'Again nothing special to do. This inaction is becoming rather tiresome. It is of course v. flattering to feel that one has a share in this greatest conference in the world's history but one would like to do something.'[58]

None the less, Howard did see representatives of the new states in the East who continued to press their needs on him. On 16 January, Lithuanian and Estonian agents canvassed him about British loans, coupled with formal recognition as belligerent Powers. Their fledgling governments needed money to survive, and recognition as belligerents would give them places at the Conference.[59] Whilst Howard acknowledged their importance in the general scheme of things as he saw it, and the Estonians were having some success at repelling Bolshevik aggression,[60] he could do nothing. The loudest demands, of course, came from the Poles. Even before the Paderewski-Pilsudski government emerged on 16 January, Howard heard complaints from Sobanski 'that England was doing nothing to help the Poles & that even the request he had made some weeks ago for some aviators & aeroplanes had met with no reply'.[61] Howard sympathised: 'If we could only get arms & ammunition to Poland, I believe that [the] Poles would smash the Bolshies.' But no decisions emanated from above, as other matters preoccupied Lloyd George and the other leaders. Howard's feelings about the aimlessness of British policy reached their peak on 14 January. He had been asked by Balfour 'to prepare a paper for the Prime Minister showing the proof of Bolshevik attack on Esthonia and to go at 2.30 to Hotel Crillon where P.M. is to meet [Wilson]'.[62] Howard complied, but the meeting had been moved unannounced to another site. Howard rushed there only to sit for two and a half hours in an ante-room with Kerr, Drummond, Carr, and another diplomat. Then Lloyd George, Wilson, Balfour, and the other notables sauntered out of their meeting and past the little group of experts. Balfour apologised to Howard for his not being called in. He added that he wished Howard had as he might have helped in the final stages of the conversation, comparing the characters of Napoleon and Frederick the Great!

Howard believed that the course of events in northeastern Europe was being allowed to develop without any effort by the Allied Powers to shape them. If the Powers wanted to achieve lasting peace in those regions, and have a hand in the settlement, they would have to do something. As well, by this time reports from Wade indicated that the situation in Poland required actions in Paris; if the Allied Powers were serious about helping the new government at Warsaw, decisions needed to be made about sending arms and other aid to the Paderewski-Pilsudski regime.[63] Howard decided to act. On the day the Conference formally opened, he recommended to Balfour that a sub-committee, an Inter-Allied Committee on Poland, be established 'for collating Polish information, reporting thereon, and making suggestions to respective Govs. There seems to be special need for some such body at the present time in order to secure rapid decisions avoiding delays which may be disastrous.'[64] Balfour accepted this recommendation but chose not to send it on to the prime minister. He knew that Lloyd George and Wilson wanted to settle the Russian question before attempting anything else in eastern Europe. Moreover, several members of the British Delegation did not see the revival of Poland in the same terms as Howard. It seems that one such expert, Lewis Namier, a member of the PID who had been born in Eastern Galicia to Jewish parents and, hence, entertained a pathological hatred of Dmowski that was returned equally, had the ear of Lloyd George through Kerr.[65] In fact, in the months before the Conference convened, whilst Howard pushed his pro-Polish line, Namier fought an effective rear-guard action that sought with a degree of success to denigrate Polish ethnographical, legal, and other claims to territories also claimed by the Lithuanians, Ukrainians, and others.[66] In this way, Howard's efforts to get movement on a settlement in the east foundered on the rocks of disinterest of his superiors and criticism from well-placed colleagues within the Foreign Office.

As Howard waited for his superiors to move on Poland and the Baltic Powers, the Peace Conference began considering the Russian question by inviting Allied diplomats who had served in Petrograd to speak to senior delegates. This occurred on 20–21 January though, as Howard saw, those who spoke against the Bolsheviks seemed 'not to have made a great impression'.[67] Howard suspected that 'President Wilson & Mr. Lloyd George have made up their minds somehow or other to establish relations with [the] Bolsheviks & whatever one says to the contrary will have no effect'. His suspicions were well founded. On 23 January, the Allied Powers invited representatives from all of the competing factions in Russia to meet with an Allied delegation at a neutral site, the island of Prinkipo near Constantinople, to arrange a Russian peace settlement. With a return to normalcy in Russia, Allied leaders hoped that eastern reconstruction could begin. This conflicted sharply with Howard's view about how to achieve a balance of power in the western borderlands of Russia, a view based on a range of expert opinion from Pares through to Lockhart. Distressed after he learnt that the invitation would be made sometime after 21 January, he wrote: 'I fear this will only result in our being caught in some Bolshevik trap. It is disheartening to get the constant appeals from all quarters against these Bolshevik criminals & see nothing done against them.'[68] His discomfiture increased. On the day the Prinkipo invitations were announced publicly, Lloyd George summoned him to lunch and asked that he serve as the British delegate to the conference. For the first and last time since returning to the Diplomatic Service, Howard refused an assignment. This was important because, first, the offer came from the prime minister and, secondly, Lloyd George rarely accepted opposition from Cabinet ministers, let alone civil servants.

Howard put his views before the prime minister:

I told him frankly that if his object was to come to terms with [the] Bolshies he had better take another man & said that I thought that anything done to confirm in power Lenin, who was a great danger to Britain especially in India where he was carrying on a tremendous propaganda, was too dangerous a policy for me to wish to see carried into effect. I said that if we could make peace with Bolshevism by eliminating Lenin and Trotsky etc, that was another question.[69]

Howard received thanks for his candour; Lloyd George agreed that another British delegate should be selected. The next day Drummond informed Howard that, as he had refused Prinkipo, Lloyd George wanted him to join 'a special mission' which the main Powers at the Conference were assembling to travel to Poland.[70] This body, the Inter-Allied Commission to Poland, was to have two delegates from each of these Powers and, although at the moment of Howard's appointment its precise instructions had yet to be decided, a consensus existed that it would aid the Powers in Paris by making swifter, surer policy concerning Poland. 'I confess', Howard commented about this turn of events, 'the prospect of going to Warsaw at this time of year does not quite smile on me but there it is.'[71]

Howard's time before leaving for Warsaw on 9 February suddenly became filled with work.[72] Although he disagreed with the idea of the Prinkipo conference to the extent he would not attend, when approached by 'White' Russian emissaries at Paris about whether they should make the journey, he dutifully advised them to do so. As he told Sazanov, the 'anti-Bolshevik parties might impose conditions such as proper food distribution, free press, free speech etc. which wd. be difficult for [the] Bolshies to refuse'.[73] He also conferred with Degrand and the chief American delegate, Dr Robert Lord, an American historian, a friend of House, and a staunch polonophile,[74] to settle on travel arrangements for the Commission and its specific instructions. As a French diplomat, Joseph Noulens, a former ambassador at St Petersburg, had been chosen to chair the Commission, the French Foreign Ministry drafted the instructions. When given to Howard for observations on 27 January, he thought them 'too vague', so there ensued additional consultations to make them specific.[75] On top of this, the Polish–Ukrainian armed struggle for control of Eastern Galicia continued threatening eastern European stability, and on 23 January additional problems developed when the Czechs suddenly invaded the Polish zones of Teschen, claiming the Duchy to be historically Czech and fundamental to Czechoslovakia's economic survival. Howard was drawn into this dispute when he suggested to Balfour that the Inter-Allied Commissioners work with Czech and Polish diplomats at Paris to agree to a ceasefire. This border dispute would touch the Commission's ultimate report; after a few tiring days, a ceasefire for Teschen was achieved on 3 February.[76]

Howard's most important and time-consuming task occurred with a series of private discussions he held with Lord to arrive at a joint Anglo-American position on the Polish question. On 1 February, the Council of Ten, the senior decision-making organ of the Peace Conference, accepted the instructions for the Inter-Allied Commission which had been negotiated by Howard, Degrand, and the others at lower levels.[77] In line with a Council of Ten decision of 24 January about bringing peace to the regions between Russia and Germany, Howard and his colleagues were to end any fighting then occurring by establishing armistices. They could pressure those resisting peace by threatening to prevent the importation of needed war materials and food supplies, and do so by invoking the fiat of the Peace Conference. In this the British and American delegations agreed; the difficulty lay with the French, anxious to keep Germany weak in the east and angry with the Bolshevik regime for refusing to honour tsarist debts, a policy that adversely affected French banks and bondholders. The French endorsed any Polish actions that would have at their end the enfeebling of Germany and the punishment of Russia. The Anglo-Americans, on the other hand, wanted stability as quickly as possible; this meant ending armed struggle in eastern Europe without delay.

Two days after the Inter-Allied Commission's instructions were fixed, Howard began his conversations with Lord to determine where the frontiers in the east should be set when those armistices came into force. Between 3 and 8 February, they held five meetings, the result of which was the Howard–Lord agreement.[78] This deal has been minutely examined in other studies, so its main points need only be summarised here.[79] Poland's western frontier would remain much as it was, though with a slight adjustment in Upper Silesia in Poland's favour. Concerning the Polish border with East Prussia, there would be an equitable settlement along linguistic lines though, because of the need to have defensible frontiers and unimpeded railways, there were to be slight variations in this. Owing to the dispute over Teschen, to which another Inter-Allied Commission was being despatched, Howard and Lord made no mention of a settlement there. In the same vein, Poland's eastern frontier was to be settled by an international commission sent specifically for that purpose; but until that time a provisional border could be set. Howard and Lord looked to divide Eastern Galicia to the west of the city of Lvov, giving the Poles that western portion and the Ukrainians the eastern. With respect to the Baltic States, the two could not agree. As a matter of record, therefore, the agreement indicated that Britain supported the independence of Estonia, Latvia, and Lithuania, whilst the United States withheld recognition in the hope that the three states might rejoin Russia.

The most contentious part of the Howard–Lord agreement held that Danzig should be turned over to Poland and that this port should be connected with Poland proper by a corridor to the south. This meant severing East Prussia from the rest of Germany, but Howard and Lord saw no other way of giving Poland economic security. As one observer points out about this proposal: 'The Polish corridor to the sea was justified on the grounds that it would be a lesser evil to cut off 1,600,000 Germans in East Prussia from the rest of Germany than to leave 600,000 Poles in West Prussia and to expose 20,000,000 Poles to "an awkward and precarious commercial outlet subject to the will of an alien and presumably hostile power".'[80] This represented an about face for Howard in that he had recommended earlier the Neufahrwasser solution. But this solution proved to be unworkable, which Howard discovered in his discussions with Board of Trade officials over freedom of access questions and by looking at the logistic difficulties posed by giving Poland this port.[81] What Howard and Lord were seeking to do was to provide Poland with a tenable national position once the fighting on its frontiers stopped. For Howard, it went further by his inclusion of independent Baltic States in the British quest for stability in northern and northeastern Europe.

By the time Howard left for Warsaw, Balfour had moved on that proposal of 18 January to create a Polish Commission in Paris to collate, report, and make suggestions.[82] The result of this was British success in convincing the Council of Ten on 12 February to establish a Commission on Polish Affairs 'to deal with reports and requests from the Inter-Allied Commission to Poland'; Tyrrell became the British representative.[83] Whilst this body did not conform precisely with the sub-committee first envisaged by Howard three weeks before, at least a mechanism existed to facilitate 'rapid decisions' and avoid potentially disastrous delays. The only limitation on this body's actions came with the Council of Ten wanting all 'questions of high policy' referred upwards. But whilst the mechanism for facilitating the Peace Conference's decision-making accorded with Howard's wishes, his contribution to the agreement with Lord found almost no support from the British Delegation. The focus of this disagreement derived from the unfavourable opinion that Germans would have of the Danzig settlement. This suggestion was proffered by James Headlam-Morley, an influential member of the PID, who usually occupied the middle ground between Howard and Namier; it was endorsed by Crowe, Hardinge, and Lord Milner, the colonial secretary, then deputising for Lloyd George who had returned to London for parliamentary business.[84] This opposition from all levels of the British Delegation boded ill for Howard's ideas about how policy should develop to maintain the balance of power in northern and northeastern Europe achieving fruition.

On the day the Inter-Allied Commission left Paris, Howard lunched with Kerr, 'who spoke to me about Mr. Lloyd George's views as regards Poland'.[85] Kerr outlined the prime minister's concern that the Pilsudski-Paderewski government 'may not represent public opinion [in Poland] & therefore that there may be a revolution towards [the] extreme left'. Howard surmised that Lloyd George did not want to be 'accused of helping the "forces of reaction"'. Thus, at Downing Street's request, Howard had 'to enquire into the strengths & views of socialists, peasants' party etc. & how they view present Govt.'. Apart from the work the Inter-Allied Commission was to do to arrange ceasefires, it seems that Howard's political masters wanted him to augment the work of the Wade mission. More to the point, it probably amounted to an effort by the prime minister to rid the British Delegation at Paris of the strongest voice supporting Polish aspirations in the debates which were soon to take place about the Polish settlement.[86] It is difficult to ignore the notion that, as Howard had crossed the prime minister over the Prinkipo conference, the diplomat was being taught a lesson about where true power in the making and execution of British foreign policy now resided, and his exile to Poland at this critical juncture in the peace-making process stood as a blunt reminder in this regard.

After travelling to Warsaw via Basle, Linz, and Prague, Howard and the other commissioners arrived in the Polish capital on 12 February and immediately set about their tasks as outlined in their formal instructions. These tasks are well known.[87] The Commission met with Pilsudski, Paderewski, and an array of Polish leaders to assess the situation. After a week, Lord and General Adrian Carton de Wiart, the junior British delegate, departed for Eastern Galicia to try to arrange a truce between the Poles and the Ukrainians fighting in the area near Lvov. Shortly afterwards, the French and Italian junior members, respectively, General Niessel and General Romei, went to Teschen and Prague to pressure both

Czech authorities and the other Inter-Allied Commission, which had arrived in the disputed duchy, to implement the ceasefire arrangement which Howard, Lord, and Noulens had arranged with Czech and Polish delegates at Paris on 3 February. On 1 March, after further discussions with various Polish interests at Warsaw and co-ordinating communications between Paris and the Eastern Galician and Teschen missions, Howard, Noulens, and the bulk of the Commission went to Poznan to negotiate a German–Polish settlement with the German authorities still clinging to that province. Howard and his colleagues sought to conclude three separate agreements: to end the fighting; to assure the protection of German and Polish populations once hostilities ceased; and to resume normal economic relations with the return to peace. The Inter-Allied commissioners met with difficulty everywhere. It proved impossible to end the armed struggle in Eastern Galicia because the Ukrainians, temporarily with the upper hand, were obstructionist; so, after travelling to Poznan to consult with Howard and Noulens, Lord and Carton de Wiart returned to Paris to report. As the Czechs had no intention of compromising their hold over Teschen, the resolution of this problem at this stage proved elusive. Finally, although Howard and Noulens were able to get the German delegation at Poznan to agree to the three conventions, they could not get them signed because of excuses that Berlin, unwilling to abandon this region to the Poles, refused to send its approval. Thus, on 19 March, the Commission broke off negotiations and returned empty-handed to Warsaw.[88]

In this way, the goals set out for Howard and his fellow commissioners in the instructions agreed in Paris proved abortive. Ceasefires could not be arranged and to a large degree matters on the Polish frontiers were essentially allowed to run their course, which meant in some areas, like Eastern Galicia, many months of armed struggle.[89] But for Howard, who arrived back at Paris on 6 April, this mission enhanced his pro-Polish tendencies whilst, at the same time, confirmed and deepened his anti-Germanism. Within hours of setting foot in Poland, he concluded its people were 'beset on four fronts, by Germans, Bolsheviks, Ukrainians & Czechs & we were expected to save them & bring them food, clothes, arms etc.'.[90] His several meetings with Paderewski etched deeper his genuine feelings of respect which had first emerged when the two met two months before and, just as important, his interviews with Pilsudski led him to hold this man in as high regard. Pilsudski made conscious efforts to charm Howard, given Howard's pro-Polish sentiments and his supposedly high position in the British Delegation, and Howard succumbed.[91] But Howard did not form political opinions because of his personal regard for other leaders – his experience with Theodore Roosevelt showed this. British policy had to be set on a firm base not on sentiment. Howard recognised that political life within this new country was fluid at best. Therefore, he made contact with as many people as possible: high society, peasant and religious delegations from places like Poznan and Mazuria, trade unionists, financial men, peasant party and socialist politicians, landowners, Jewish leaders, and Roman Catholic and Protestant churchmen; this showed him that the government had reasonable support, despite some criticism from socialist quarters concerning the government's policies concerning Lvov.[92] Certainly, the regime was not viewed as reactionary, crushing the political aspirations of various political and social groupings within the new state. Thus Howard continued pressing for as much Allied aid as possible for Pilsudski's Poland if it was to resist its adversaries and take a prominent part in post-war European affairs.[93]

Howard's anti-Germanism was increased by the poor treatment accorded the Poles by the Germans and through the way in which the German delegation conducted itself during the Poznan negotiations. Prior to the mission to Poznan, Madame Paderewska took Howard to one of several refugee camps near Warsaw, places where Poles displaced by the retreating German armies were concentrated so they could be helped. Howard recorded:

I never saw a more heart breaking sight than these poor people all in destitution & completely ragged. One one[-]legged man from Russia had lost wife, children, home all. One little boy of fourteen begged to join the army as he had lost father & mother etc. 35 children died of cold in a train recently arrived from Germany as they are sent in unheated cattle trucks. Lord! it's awful, & little food & no clothing to give them.[94]

The plight of these people, especially the children, assumed greater poignancy for Howard as his son, Edmund, was then ill with appendicitis, about which Isa was extremely concerned. None the less, Howard found little to commend turning over to the Germans territories containing Poles so that they could suffer from harsh policies at the hands of their former masters. This ill-treatment, which he saw at first hand, also led him to accept uncritically reports which reached the Commission about a German 'reign of terror' against Poles in West Prussia,[95] and which saw him take a firm hand in the negotiations at Poznan.

At Poznan, Howard found the German delegation to be extremely difficult.[96] At the first meeting set for 7 March, the Germans refused to attend because they were to be escorted by Polish officers. A few times after this, the Germans also begged off because of claims that they lacked specific instructions from Berlin. At one meeting the translator on the German delegation, who translated from French into German for his superiors, announced suddenly that he refused to continue in his task. Even after the three conventions were finally agreed, as noted earlier, the German delegation refused to sign, citing again the now familiar refrain that specific instructions had not been received from Berlin, a result of a supposed inability of the civilian and military authorities there to agree. Howard believed that this German obfuscation was designed to prevent any agreement. With no settlement, the Germans could 'keep up full [military] strength on [the] Posen front so as to attack if necessary'. This also explained why the 'reign of terror' was occurring in regions still controlled by German forces: 'There is considerable agitation amongst Poles in W. Prussia & Silesia and an armed rising may take place as [a] result of German persecutions. It is probably that the Germans will try to provoke this.' If the Poles were to take up arms against the Germans, then the Germans might be perceived as the persecuted by the statesmen in Paris, especially by Lloyd George whose lack of sympathy for Poland was now well known, thanks to press leaks at the French capital. When clarifications about the conventions were sought by Berlin almost a week after they had been agreed at Poznan, Howard and Noulens broke off the talks. With disgust, Howard noted: 'It is clear that [the] Germans are only playing with us & creating delays.' Obviously the senior delegates in Paris would have to deal with this matter in the general German settlement and, to force Berlin's compliance, threaten to use the considerable economic and military resources of the Allied Powers. The Poles simply did not possess the strength to move the Germans from this region.

By the time Howard returned to Paris, he found that the Commission on Polish Affairs and the senior delegates had made a number of decisions concerning the Polish-German borderlands.[97] The most important of these concerned Danzig. Although Poland would be given a corridor to the Baltic, which would split East Prussia from the rest of Germany, Danzig, at the head of the corridor, would become an international city under the control of the new League of Nations. The city would be tied economically to Poland, which would have unfettered access to it for the import and export of goods. So, except for internationalism, this aspect of the Polish settlement accorded with what Howard and Lord had suggested in the first week of February. In the same way, the basic demarcation between Poland and Germany in Silesia and along the frontier abutting East Prussia was to follow ethnic lines modified by certain economic and administrative factors. There were also to be appropriate plebiscites in some areas, though these and the problems surrounding them were to be handled after conclusion of the peace settlement with Germany. In early April, firm decisions about Teschen and Eastern Galicia had yet to be reached, although Lloyd George had made clear his opposition to Polish acquisition of the latter as this would serve only to embitter the Bolshevik Russians and delay any normalisation of relations with their state and western Powers.

During his mission to Poland, Howard knew that decisions were being made in Paris that did not square exactly with his conception of how policy in northeastern Europe should develop. Before he left for Warsaw, he knew that men like Namier disagreed strongly with his support of Dmowski and of the form which the new Polish state should take which accorded largely with the demands made by the Poles. In the few despatches that reached him during the two months he was away, despatches which contained minutes by experts including Namier, he saw that the proposals made in his agreement with Lord were being modified by the anti-Poles in the British Delegation.[98] He even received one important letter from Headlam-Morley that indicated there would be changes to that agreement, especially over Danzig, but that on the whole the spirit of compromise with Lord would be kept.[99] Howard accepted this as the normal course of events. He knew from his experience that foreign policies developed only after many twists and turns. But what concerned him on his return from Poland was Lloyd George's obvious antipathy towards the Poles and their place in the new European order. Stories were circulating about the prime minister's private disparaging remarks about Poland and its claims – 'one might as well "give a clock to a monkey as Upper Silesia to the Poles"'.[100] More important as far as Howard was concerned was the prime minister's determination to keep Germany as strong as possible, and his willingness to accept the *de facto* existence of and do business with the Bolshevik regime in Russia.[101] For Howard, if a return to the pre-1914 conditions in northeastern Europe had a hope of being prevented – Germany and Russia contiguous in the east with the attendant problems this meant for maintaining the balance of power – then Poland and the Baltic had to be supported by Britain and its allies.

In his first days back at Paris, Howard tried to get an appointment with Lloyd George in order to put his concerns before the chief architect of British policy. He had no success. The prime minister had made up his mind about how policy should develop, hence, he had no intention of wasting his time with a second-level expert about to press a case which he had chosen already to ignore. Not dissuaded by Lloyd George's unwillingness to meet him, Howard decided to write to the prime minister; he recorded in his diary: 'It is all I can do & when I have done that I shall shut up.'[102] Howard's main point in this letter centred on outlining why the Poles, beset with all of the problems that had led to revolution in Russia – high unemployment, a weak economy, problems in food production and distribution, and the scourge of displaced people – did not seem likely to embrace Bolshevism. There were efforts to make the political life of the country responsive to the needs of the people. About this Howard outlined how a 'meeting of representatives of landlords' was prepared to introduce policies of land reform so as to free up to about 20 per cent of their holdings for purchase by peasants. He alluded to the Sejm, the Polish parliament, which, despite some difficulties given the inexperience of its members, seemed to be meeting the political needs of the population: 51 per cent of the Sejm, Lloyd George learnt, was composed of worker and peasant representatives. Howard emphasised how the Poles were decidedly pro-Allied, evidence for which had emerged in a unanimous resolution in the Sjem favouring 'an alliance with the Entente Powers'. As Lloyd George wanted information about the attitudes of the socialists and peasants leaders towards the Pilsudski-Paderewski regime, Howard recorded support accorded by the labouring classes to the government. Patriotism dominated partisan political gain:

I emphasize these points at some length to show that nothing but the strongest patriotic feeling among the working classes could have prevented the outbreak of disorders, as all classes undoubtedly rightly believed that such disorders at the present time would be fatal to the future of their country. It is impossible to say, however, how long this spirit can be maintained unless help in kind is forthcoming.

Howard believed that if Britain and its Allies really wanted to cement firm ties with the new Polish state, they could offer that help. Two ways existed to do so. First, arrangements could be made to despatch 'experts to give advice in almost all branches of government, which I do not doubt the Polish Government would accept'. He recorded that the French had already sent military advisers, and that Paderewski had suggested that British experts be sent out to 'organize their police force on British models'. British expertise could be useful in other areas, too, which he stressed by indicating that the Polish Ministry of Labour had expressed interest in having 'British advisers on labour problems, insurances etc.'. The Americans might be induced to send out financial advisers. The second way involved compromising over Poland's territorial demands. Howard acknowledged that the Poles might be willing to abandon all claims to Teschen if Danzig was turned over to them and not internationalised. 'The great fear of the Poles', he observed, 'is that if Danzig is made a free city it will remain German in character, and will attract numerous German rather than Polish emigrants.' In the Protestant areas adjoining East Prussia, chiefly Mazuria, the population wanted union with Catholic Poland. If the Peace Conference decided to prevent Mazuria from fusing with Poland because of the religious question, this might create difficulty. So, too, might attempts at Paris to prevent areas in southern Lithuania from uniting with Poland; Howard's enquiries whilst on his mission showed this region to be 'though in the main White Russian, practically Polish in sentiment'. Finally, he reported Pilsudski's declaration 'against any encroachment on Ukrainian territory [so] that in the future Poland

and Ukraine ought to live in harmony in the interests of both'. Because of the bitterness created by the fighting in Eastern Galicia, Howard suggested that an international gendarmerie under the control of an administrator responsible to the Powers occupy the province for a few years to restore order and allow tempers to cool. There could then be a settlement, acceptable to both sides, achieved by the Powers. In this, Howard's Cretan experiences showed.[103]

Howard knew that opposition to the Polish government controlling areas containing peoples of different nationality and religious beliefs circulated at all levels in Paris. Pogroms against Jews in areas controlled by the Poles had received particular consideration, especially from men like Namier.[104] But Howard's mission to Poland led him to argue that the Poles would be tolerant of minorities like the Jews. In his last days at Warsaw, he spent long hours with several Jewish delegations who were prepared to accept Polish rule as long as they could have their own schools and the like.[105] Howard stressed in his letter to Lloyd George that 'leading Poles told me that they not only approved of Jews having all religious and political rights just as other Polish citizens, but that they would support their having separate Confessional Schools under State Control as in England. This would practically satisfy the Jewish Orthodox Party which is the largest Israelite Party in Poland.' Polish authorities were determined to remove 'what may be called the "pogrom" atmosphere', though Howard argued that the pogroms which had occurred 'were clearly not organised affairs but the result of civil war and the lack of any proper police consequent on the German evacuation'. Howard even believed that any Germans coming under Polish control would be treated fairly. He drew on his observations of the situation in Poznan to buttress this argument: 'I may add that in Posen nothing was more striking than the moderation of the Poles towards the Germans who had really oppressed them for 150 years.'[106] He pointed out that German schools continued to operate, that German officials continued to perform their duties, and that elections to fill the new Diet in Germany were permitted.

Howard's missive amounted to putting his advice on the official record. There had to be some give and take in the Polish settlement and, it seemed to him, that unless Britain and the other Allied Powers were more accommodating, Poland would use what resources it could muster to take by force and hold territories it felt belonged to Poland and were needed for the survival of the state. If this happened because of the bloody-mindedness of the chief peace-makers at Paris, it would constitute a recipe for continued instability in this pivotal region of Europe. Given Howard's assessment of the ultimate aims of Germany and Bolshevik Russia, especially if the Germans revived to any great extent, the British and their partners would have won the war but, at least in the east, lost the peace. Lloyd George had to understand that the Poles sought ties with the western Powers, and that their deep-seated antipathy to both of their more powerful neighbours would probably preclude any sort of long-term understanding between those neighbours and Poland.

Although Howard's letter reached Lloyd George, as is seen by the fact that it is retained in his papers, there is no indication that he read it. This is not surprising. By the time that Howard returned to Paris, his power within the British Delegation had been reduced significantly. Lloyd George seemed to be relying more and more on Kerr, Hankey, and others who worked in his private office in the formulation and pursuit of policy. The message to Howard about his being shuffled off to the side came on 22 April when the Polish Commission underwent some changes in personnel; this was the day after Howard sent Lloyd George a memorandum outlining his ideas about Russia and the balance of power in the east.[107] 'I am not to be on the Polish Commission in Paris...', he wrote that day. 'Evidently the Warsaw Commission is much discredited & anyone connected with it. This comes of not saying what people want to hear.'[108] But, in this regard, Howard suffered the fate of almost all of the professional diplomats and Foreign Office officials within the British Delegation. Hardinge, Crowe, and most of the others knew that their papers on important issues, their minutes seeking advice, and their enquiries about what policies were being determined by other sections of the British Delegation – the various sections were working almost in isolation from one another, the prime minister's office apparently keeping tabs on what was being done[109] – were not reaching Lloyd George. He did not want to be bothered by such impedimenta as he sought to make a peace he believed would work, though his low opinion of the Foreign Office and the diplomats probably also had much to do with this. Kerr acted as a screen, and he, rather than the prime minister, saw papers reaching Lloyd George's office, initialled them, and sent them back. Even Balfour was unable to penetrate this bureaucratic wall on several occasions. An indication of the low point to which the professionals had been pushed, and the frustration this engendered, can be seen with Alwyn Parker's sudden decision to resign from the Foreign Office in March. Feeling down and depressed, Howard asked for a short leave after being left off the Polish Commission.

Howard spent two weeks with his wife and sons in England from 25 April to 6 May. He returned to Paris only a few days before the final draft of the German treaty was handed to the German delegation; thus, the decisions about Poland's borders were set and he could do no more. For the next two months, he busied himself with a series of minor assignments, most of which had to do with problems in the Baltic States where Bolshevik

Russians, German troops still there, and Baltic nationalists fought each other to achieve an advantage. Although Howard was appointed head of the Baltic Commission on 15 May, this proved to be an assignment that, until he left in early July for his summer leave, achieved little because of more pressing problems concerning the German signature of the peace treaty and the civil war in Russia.[110] Howard watched as the fighting in Eastern Galicia continued, and as new fighting broke out between the Poles and the Lithuanians over control of the city of Vilna and its environs. The Poles were clearly taking matters into their own hands, something which Howard did not like, something for which he criticised the Poles,[111] but which he knew was inevitable given Lloyd George's failure to recognise their plight. By the time the Germans signed the Treaty of Versailles on 28 June, Howard was ready to take his summer leave. He knew that when it was over he would have a new post and could get on with his career.

IV

Howard's service as a member of the British Delegation at the Paris Peace Conference constituted the low point in his thirty years in the British Diplomatic Service. He had gone to Paris fully expecting to help shape a new international order so that peace and security could be assured for Britain and its Empire for some time to come. Four years of war had exacted a heavy cost on both sides: a blood-letting the likes of which had never been seen; the expenditure of an enormous treasure to prosecute the struggle; and the anguish of families whose sons had been killed or crippled in the fighting. In Howard's own case, there had been the hard slog at Stockholm. Now, Europe had changed irrevocably: great pre-war Powers had disappeared; new, smaller states appeared in their stead, clamouring for legitimacy and sound economic and territorial bases; and revolution had become commonplace as the dislocation created by the war unleashed Bolshevism and its attendant barbarity. The victory of the Allied Powers, and Britain's contribution to that victory, had to count for something. Howard had said when he received Hardinge's orders to return to London that if he could 'take part, however humble', in peace-making, his 'highest ambition' would be realised. His subsequent work in London and Paris and during his mission to Poland had been difficult, mentally and physically draining, and compounded by the in-fighting within the British Delegation and between it and other delegations. Lloyd George's penchant for personal diplomacy and his cavalier treatment of the experts created disillusionment and resentment within the Foreign Office and Diplomatic Service.

Howard did play a humble part in peace-making. However, because of

Lloyd George's revolution in policy-making, Howard and his diplomatic colleagues had also been humbled. In all of his posts from Crete to Stockholm, Howard had come to understand and appreciate that the men on the spot had to defer to the wishes of those at the centre responsible for the big diplomatic picture. In Paris, where he became briefly one of those responsible for a part of that big picture, he learnt the more telling lesson that the politicians, especially skilful and determined ones like Lloyd George, had the final say on how that big picture emerged. Howard was glad to have had this experience, but his inability to make much of a mark beyond getting Poland a corridor to the sea rankled. His assessment of his service on the British Delegation, penned just before leaving Paris in July, is telling:

My part has had little to do with [the] Peace Conference. None of the Russian problems have been settled & I have been put out of the Polish Commission on account of my supposed ultra Polish tendencies. No one sees that Poland & the Baltic Provinces are the keys to the whole situation in E. Europe. I have been vox clamantis in deserto [a voice crying in the wilderness] & a vox et praeterea nihil [a voice and nothing more]. Still it has been a wonderful thing to have been in Paris & I am v. thankful.[112]

Howard had begun his efforts at peace-making believing that a new departure in international politics was at hand. This came from having the United States, via Wilson, in the negotiations. When the president made a series of visits to the principal Allied capitals before the Conference convened in January, at each stop his reception by the masses of people increased in enthusiasm, Howard entertained guarded hope that United States' power could be tied to that of Britain to keep the balance of power in Europe stable. It was not that the 'Fourteen Points' did not offer encouragement – they did, and this was why European crowds greeted Wilson so feverishly – but that the United States seemed finally ready to assume its responsibilities as a great Power.[113] This does not mean that Howard dismissed the president's war aims. He did not. He supported Polish access to the sea, as well as other proposals like the League of Nations, as positive developments in the new international society being constructed in Paris. But Howard's hopes for American participation in that society crumbled as the conference progressed. This derived from Wilson's attitudes. In Howard's estimation, the president had assumed an arrogance in his dealings which antagonised many European leaders. Wilson did not hide his belief that the European Powers were in Paris to protect and extend their own narrow national interests with the discredited concepts of old diplomacy. The United States, conversely, was there with only the noblest intentions, supposedly doing all possible in international interests by following a new diplomacy imbued with high moral purpose.

With such attitudes, Wilson was squandering any advantages he and his country might hope to achieve. For Howard, the evidence of this came with Wilson's approach to the Italian demand for the city of Fiume, which the Yugoslavs also sought.[114] Howard sympathised with the Italians and, for him, Wilson did not help settlement by issuing a communiqué in the middle of the negotiations 'in which he declared with a lot of sentimental rubbish attached that Italian views could not square with his 14 Points'.[115] Subsequent poor diplomacy, like telling the Italian premier, Vittorio Orlando, 'that he had the people of Italy behind him (Wilson)!', only aggravated the situation and showed Wilson's complete ignorance of Italian opinion.[116] Coupled with Wilson misjudging the ability of Congress to emasculate his diplomacy – and this led to the Senate rejection of Versailles in October 1919 – Howard was unsure about the position of the United States within the new international system being hammered out in Paris.

None the less, that new order was beginning, and Howard would have to serve in the Diplomatic Service to protect British interests within it. He was to have an embassy, the question was where? He also knew that changes within the Foreign Office were imminent. Unhappy with his position and beset with some personal problems, Hardinge wanted out. He would soon leave to take the Paris Embassy and Crowe would replace him as permanent under-secretary. Moreover, during the Peace Conference, Balfour had served as foreign secretary, but whilst he remained in Paris, Curzon, the lord president in the Cabinet, ran the Foreign Office in London. By October 1919, Curzon would succeed Balfour as foreign secretary. Thus, there were fundamental changes occurring within the upper levels of the Foreign Office as Howard prepared to take up a new post.[117] With Lloyd George seeking to control British foreign policy, with shifts in senior personnel at the Foreign Office, and with an uncertain international situation caused by the ending of the war and the Peace Conference, Howard's career really was about to take a new departure.

8
Madrid: Anglo-Spanish relations, 1919–1924

> If the people of [Spain] only felt that *we* want to be friends I have little doubt they would respond. What they resent is just that the Spanish people are so often considered a 'byword for cruelty, incompetence and corruption'. They call this the 'leyenda negra'. I have often to put pressure on myself to avoid an attitude of irritation at happenings here. But I believe it pays not to give way to this natural irritation.
>
> Howard, February 1922

I

Howard remained in Paris for ten days after the signing of the Treaty of Versailles, tying up loose ends in the Baltic Commission and saying farewells to friends and colleagues he expected not to see for some time. Then, with his work finished, he and Isa returned to Britain to spend the summer vacation with their sons in Cumberland and Scotland. Until September, the family enjoyed six carefree weeks of visiting relatives, hiking, boating, and picnicking in the Lake District, relishing the company of one another. He took the two oldest boys, Esme and Francis, on their first bird-shooting parties and spent as much time as he could with the three younger ones. He even bought two bicycles on which he – at the age of 56 – and each son in turn used to go on day trips on the roads and pathways near Ullswater. Knowing that he would soon be posted abroad again, he felt the need to surround himself with his loved ones. With the experience of Stockholm still fresh in his mind, and with the four older boys at school in Britain, he did not know when and if such an opportunity would return. Although neither he nor his family knew it at the time, the summer of 1919 was the last happy one the seven of them would share together.

Whilst Howard was on vacation, his next posting was decided upon by his superiors. Even before the signing of the German treaty, newspapers published rumours that he would succeed Sir Arthur Hardinge as ambassador in Madrid; this caught Howard unawares.[1] But no formal decision could be made at that time. Although Howard knew that he was under consideration for a major embassy and that Madrid seemed likely, Balfour and Curzon could make no firm decisions about promotions and transfers. The Foreign Office, the traditional arbiter in these matters, could not make this decision alone, given what Drummond called 'the present state of affairs which really amounts to a complete dictatorship by [Lloyd George]'.[2] With the prime minister's attention diverted by more pressing foreign and domestic problems, a decision on ambassadorial appointments had to wait. As early as January 1919, Howard's name had been included on the short-list for the Washington Embassy but, because Curzon and Balfour concurred with the view that a prominent man, perhaps a former Cabinet minister rather than a Service diplomat, should represent Britain in the United States, Howard did not become a serious candidate for this post.[3] With the signature of the Treaty of Versailles, Lloyd George moved to complete needed administrative housework and, endorsing the decision of a Foreign Office committee on promotions, agreed to Howard's appointment to Madrid on 24 July.[4] As this embassy stood as one of the first rank, Howard had to travel to London for two days in the third week of August to be sworn in as a privy councillor. It was then determined that he would travel to Spain sometime in the autumn to take up his new post. Since, technically, he was still minister in Stockholm, he left for the Swedish capital on 13 September to arrange for the disposition of his goods and furniture remaining at the Legation, submit his letters of recall to Gustav, and bid goodbye to those like de Bildt who had befriended him and helped Britain during the war.[5] By 7 October he was back in London receiving briefings on the situation in Spain.

Howard learnt in detail that Britain's primary interest in the Spanish question concerned maintaining the post-war balance of power in the western Mediterranean.[6] This balance involved three Powers – Britain, Spain, and France – and derived from the various agreements concluded in the decade after 1904 that sought to resolve the Moroccan question. Morocco had been divided into two protectorates by a Franco-Spanish convention of 1904 negotiated in the wake of the Anglo-French Entente of the same year. Whilst Britain had recognised France's exclusive rights as a Protecting Power in the kingdom – the sultan ostensibly still ruled – the French, to obviate Madrid's worry about French control of the North African littoral from Casablanca to Tunis, ceded Spain a slice of northern Morocco adjacent to the Straits of Gibraltar to administer also as a Protecting Power. Because of its part in these agreements, Britain found itself balancing between competing Spanish and French Moroccan interests. This meant that Howard would have to rely fully on his considerable analytical abilities and diplomatic skill to ensure that British strategic interests in this vital region were not imperilled by France, the stronger Power, stealing a march on the much weaker Spain. Gibraltar's fate weighed heavily in this, as key sea routes for trade and Imperial defence passed by there. Rowland Sperling, the head of the Foreign Office American and African Department, emphasised for Howard: 'Briefly, we have always regarded it as a matter of paramount strategic interest that no strong power should establish itself on the Moorish coast between & including Tetuan & Tangier.'

Howard also had instruction on the problems surrounding Tangier. Lying within the Spanish zone in Morocco, this port had not been turned over to Spain before 1914; instead, it had been accorded the status of a neutral city. By 1919 both the Spanish and the French wanted to resolve Tangier's status in their own interest. Loath to give either Power the advantage over Tangier, the British feared that favouring either would make the other instantly antagonistic towards Britain; the balance of power in the western Mediterranean would be upset. Howard was told that the Foreign Office supported internationalising the city, that is, having its various municipal agencies controlled jointly by the three Powers. This would have the benefit of assuring London a say in any future discussions concerning the city, whilst allowing Britain a sustaining role in arbitrating between Spanish and French interests there. However, the Spanish worried that Britain might back the French should a tripartite conference on Tangier be held, this because Madrid surmised that 'Allied sympathy had been alienated by the toleration of German intrigues in the Spanish zone during the war.' But, it was impressed on Howard, British interests would not be served by abandoning Tangier to either Power. Sperling, again, put the matter succinctly: 'Meanwhile there appears no reason to doubt that we shall firmly maintain our attitude about Tangier whether as a permanent policy or as a pawn in some territorial arrangement with France in the future. Spain has therefore no reason to fear for the present that we shall leave them in the lurch.' To keep Anglo-Spanish relations stable, it became one of Howard's chief tasks in Madrid to reassure Spanish leaders that Britain would not abandon them over Tangier.

Howard also became aware that his diplomatic work in Spain would have to be concerned with trade matters. Britain and Spain had had no treaty regulating their trade since the 1890s. All that existed was a *modus vivendi* that had been concluded in 1894 and could be abrogated unilaterally with just six months' notice. During the war, the Department of Overseas Trade, an adjunct of the Foreign Office, had established a commercial organisation to provide business opportunities for British firms operating in Spain. This body had had decided success and, supported by the Federation of British Industries, Cecil lobbied to have the organisation remain in place.⁷ The reason was simple. If Britain had any chance of reestablishing its pre-1914 trading patterns, disrupted by the war and now facing the threat posed by the dramatic increase in American economic strength, a concerted effort had to be made to hold and expand commercial ties with countries like Spain. Howard shared this concern though, unlike Cecil, he looked beyond Britain to emphasise that the mother country and the Empire, together, should take a hand in expanding trade. He took the time to put his ideas in this regard before senior Foreign Office and Department of Overseas Trade officials when he passed through London on his way to summer in Cumberland. At this meeting, he made a strong case about creating British Chambers of Commerce in countries 'where there are practically no British firms or merchants to form them'.⁸

Although Howard's focus centred on Sweden – and a British Chamber of Commerce in Spain already existed – his general argument suggested that the stimulation of trade remained a central element in the economic survival and global strength of Britain and its Empire. Moreover, still advocating his 'economic credo' about partnership amongst government, capital, and labour, he held that the revitalisation of British trade would have a positive impact domestically. If Britain re-established its pre-war trading patterns, and strengthened them, much of the industrial demand would increase and unemployment would be lessened. Not only would continued industrial unrest threaten Britain's ability to trade – Howard saw the potential of this in a Yorkshire miners' strike in the summer of 1919 which adversely affected energy supplies for industry – it also threatened Britain's domestic political and social stability, something that might allow the Bolshevik bacillus to take hold.⁹ Consequently, Howard realised as he departed for Spain that he had to help Britain's external and internal position by improving Anglo-Spanish trade. In this way, the negotiation of a new Anglo-Spanish commercial treaty assumed as much importance for him as maintaining the strategic balance in the western Mediterranean.

II

Since Howard did not have to be in Madrid until 15 November, he and Isa took the opportunity to visit relatives in Italy for a few weeks. Giving Isa additional time to rest within the confines of her family and friends in Rome – the hectic life of an ambassador's wife would be tiring – he travelled by himself to Madrid in the middle of November to meet with Arthur Hardinge and other members of the Embassy before presenting his letters of appointment to King Alfonso XIII. For a week, he held a series of valuable conversations with Hardinge; Mervyn Herbert, the first secretary and Howard's nephew; and Frederick Deakin, the press attaché.¹⁰ The

Embassy councillor, Charles Wingfield, had taken up his post only two weeks before the new ambassador's arrival. From these conversations, Howard became aware of a series of problems fostering domestic instability within Spain: Catalonian separatism, a poor economy and concomitant rise of working-class radicalism, political uncertainty, and a debilitating war against Rif rebels in Spanish Morocco which poisoned civil–military relations.[11] Howard became aware that the problems combined to create decided instability and this, in turn, affected Spanish foreign policy.

Howard has been criticised because he did not apparently understand the subtle nuances of Spain's confused domestic situation, that he 'too frequently used the "Latin" and "Spanish temperament" as a handy explanation for the complexities of the Spanish scene [and] did not cease to see from every corner and under every bed the "imminent revolution from below"'.[12] Apart from being a sciolistic assessment both of Howard's character and achievements prior to arriving in Spain and of his four years' service in Madrid, this critique is based on a single despatch, written two months before his departure, loosely tied to some lines attributed to but not written by him.[13] In other words, this rebuke suggests without much evidence that the ambassador's personal feelings, notably a supposed antipathy towards working-class radicalism, coloured his professional observations and advice. The question to consider, therefore, is what were Howard's views of domestic Spain?

Although Howard lacked previous political experience with Spain – on his way to South Africa in 1891, he had visited Madrid and Toledo and been impressed with Spain's cultural heritage[14] – he did not take up this post ignorant of recent Spanish affairs. His Foreign Office briefings, his conversations with Hardinge and the Embassy staff, and his observations of the situation that greeted him shortly after arriving, when a crisis involving a military junta and the politicians saw the resignation of the entire civilian cabinet, allowed him to form an opinion of the domestic situation within two weeks of presenting his credentials. He recounted this in his first annual report:

> In the first survey of the situation which I wrote after my arrival in this country I drew attention to three dominant factors in the state of affairs then existing: the activities of the juntas, the labour unrest and the bankruptcy of parliamentary institutions. These elements were perhaps not so immediately threatening as they then seemed, but they are still elements of political mischief.[15]

Hence, within six weeks of taking charge of the Madrid Embassy, Howard discerned a triad of disruptive forces within the country, not simply the threat of 'imminent revolution from below'. More telling, a year later his basic assessment had not changed. The immediacy of a major upheaval within Spain had passed, yet the naked self-interest of the juntas, the paucity of effective leadership by the civilian politicians, and the dissatisfaction of large sections of the working classes remained. The potential for a major domestic crisis lingered.

For Howard, this domestic unrest affected Spanish foreign policy. In this equation, he did not see working-class disgruntlement as the main threat to order, rather he reckoned that this responsibility lay with the crippling power struggle between the other two disruptive forces then at work: the civilian politicians and the military juntas. This power struggle, at times involving King Alfonso, had a greater impact on Spanish foreign policy than did labour problems. Weakness and uncertainty in the political and military bodies that were charged with the defence of Spain and its Empire affected Spanish relations with Britain and other Powers. Howard's perception of who bore responsibility for Spain's domestic malaise conformed to the generally held view about the nature of Spanish politics in this period.[16]

About working-class discontent, Howard and his staff did not see this being fostered exclusively by leftwing agitators. Rather, Embassy reports suggested that the problem derived from a complex situation involving the competing interests of the various components of domestic Spain. As a country dependent on foreign trade, Spain did not escape the economic dislocation caused by the end of the war. Its agricultural sector and burgeoning mining, steel, and shipbuilding industries, which experienced unprecedented growth during the war, began to contract. Economic constriction led to worker lay-offs and reduced wages; labour unrest emerged. In 1920, Howard's first full year in Spain, the country suffered 1,060 strikes.[17] Howard and his staff assessed the industrial situation in weekly reports for the Foreign Office. One problem lay with the government's inability to enforce industrial peace. In most cases, for instance a strike by Madrid bakers in November 1920,[18] divisions amongst the politicians delayed settlement until only feelings of bitterness remained amongst workers, owners, and the government. Other reports showed that the hardline industrial relations policies of Spanish owners and, in instances of foreign-owned concerns like British Rio Tinto Mines, on-site managers helped engender unrest. In La Coruna, in October, a general strike verged on settlement when some workers indicated a willingness to return to work; but, lamented the Embassy, 'the Employers Association insists on a simultaneous settlement of all disputes, so the deadlock continues'.[19] Finally, Howard's Embassy saw further problems caused by some powerful Spanish capitalists anxious to weaken foreign-controlled companies operating in Spain. Enmeshed in a grim strike in the autumn of 1920, Rio Tinto found itself the object of a virulent attack in newspapers controlled by such capitalists; the danger existed that worker grievances against their foreign masters could be whipped up so as to force passage of anti-foreign legislation.[20] The Howard Embassy demonstrated that much of Spanish labour unrest stemmed from a combination of weak government, insensitive owners and managers, and greedy Spanish capitalists intent on weakening or driving out foreign-controlled competitors.

None of this suggests that Howard or his advisers believed leftwing agitators stood blameless. The weekly reports also catalogued a litany of bombings, shootings, and other 'outrages' perpetrated by radical groups intent on creating havoc for the authorities.[21] But, crucially, Howard and the British diplomats saw leftwing extremists, instead of creating labour unrest, exploiting a situation pregnant with revolutionary possibilities through government indecision and the owners' intransigence. Howard made this plain in his 'Annual Report' for 1920: 'The general lock-out by the Employers Federation in Catalonia, began in 1919, was continued into 1920, and a similar measure adopted in the Madrid building trades led to a long and bitter struggle during which all work was stopped in those trades, and the already serious shortage of dwellings was rendered more acute.'[22] Nor did the Howard Embassy discern anything homogeneous about Spanish worker unrest. There existed decided regional variations in the willingness to compromise, the resort to violence, and so on. Barcelona, the heart of the industrial north, was the most radical part of the country, but other places, like Seville in the south, were much less so.[23]

Howard had his staff educate the Foreign Office in the political intricacies of the Spanish labour movement, which divided sharply into a radical, syndicalist one, enamoured by Bolshevik success in Russia, and a moderate one, the vast majority of members, seeing ballots not bullets as the way to improve working-class life. 'The National Confederation of Labour representing the extreme syndicalists', the Foreign Office learnt during national elections in December 1920, 'were opposed to any political action and advocated violent methods beginning with a general strike throughout Spain, but the General Workers' Union, which is led by Socialists, decided to present candidates in yesterday's election, and also refused to join in a strike, pointing out the inopportuneness of the moment and the defenceless condition in which the strikers would soon find themselves.'[24] Along with the moderates' decision a month earlier to remain outside of the Bolshevik Russian-dominated Third International, the Howard Embassy surmised by late 1920 that 'more moderate counsels are beginning to prevail'.[25]

Howard's diplomacy in this sphere was limited to keeping British economic interests as untouched as possible by labour unrest. Given his social and political position, he had little chance to meet Socialist and trade-union officials. Neither could he influence Spanish-owned firms in the conduct of their industrial relations. But he did have some leeway and used it whenever he could. For instance, he went occasionally on goodwill tours to improve the British image. In November 1920 he accepted an invitation to visit the Basque region of the north. Not only were prominent industrialists there anti-British – for example, the Marquess de Arriluce who, during the war, had supported Germany – but the Basque people, given their distaste for the central government at Madrid, saw a parallel between themselves and Irish nationalists fighting British forces in Ireland. At Bilbao, Howard visited mines, foundries, and shipyards owned by de Arriluce, supplementing this with a number of dinners with local politicians, industrialists, society leaders, and British businessmen.[26] He also made contact with the de Sota family, whose head was 'one of the leading Basque nationalists, and perhaps the richest man in Spain'. This contact had added merit since de Sota had been 'very pro-English during the war, and rendered considerable services to our officials at Bilbao'.

Howard's detached approach did not extend to British-owned firms. He could influence these companies, doing so when he judged the moment appropriate. This can be seen in his intervention in the Rio Tinto strike of 1920. Rio Tinto workers struck on 9 July over a variety of issues, but the intransigence of Walter Browning, the on-site manager, and Sir Charles Fielding, the chairman in London, prevented a compromise. Howard saw the two men's personalities blocking a settlement and, moreover, to Howard's personal distaste, Browning had bribed Spanish politicians and journalists to support the company.[27] Matters reached a peak in October. Through Howard's reports, the Foreign Office realised that Britain's reputation was suffering throughout Spain; as well, Alfonso told Howard that Browning seemed to be at fault.[28] Howard decided that something had to be done, and he then won Foreign Office support to approach privately his friend, Lord Denbigh, a senior director of the Rio Tinto board.[29] Howard's intervention led the company to send an executive, Sir Rhys Williams, 'to enquire' into the situation. Williams made several suggestions to alleviate social distress amongst the workers and, in meeting with Howard, indicated that they would be implemented after the strike settlement. More important, Howard learnt that Williams found 'no traces of Bolshevik, German, or other influences seriously at work at Rio Tinto, and believes that the strike movement, such as it is, is entirely autochthonous'.[30] This confirmed Embassy assessments. When the strike ended in early 1921, Williams' suggestions were instituted, problems at Rio Tinto disappeared, and, in this context, Britain's image remained relatively untarnished over the next several years. Much of this derived from Howard's sympathetic assessment of worker grievances and his ability to resolve the matter through pressure from his Embassy and the Foreign Office.

Howard saw that the bankruptcy of Spain's parliamentary government created decided domestic instability. This, Howard and his staff believed, derived from the plethora of parties seeking power. In the December 1920 elections to fill the 408-seat Cortes, an Embassy report identified twenty-one successful parties, whose strength varied from one to 192 seats.[31] The fractiousness of Spanish party politics resulted in a series of coalition governments and, whilst coalitions do not necessarily mean weak and ineffective government, in Spain's case, the unceasing struggle between 'ins' and 'outs' precluded strong and capable governance. What this meant in practical terms, and what Howard and his staff saw clearly, was the Cortes existing as the preserve of political managers and, as an institution of government, lacking the resolve to tackle serious economic, political, and social problems.

Summing up the political situation after his first year in Madrid, Howard informed Curzon that 'it is by no means an easy task to give an accurate, intelligible and useful account of Spanish politics at the present time. A mere recapitulation of the principal events of the year would no more give an idea of the situation than reading Baedeker's Guidebook would give of the artistic treasures of this country'.[32] However, in reporting on the various problems confronting Spanish central authorities during 1920, Howard and the Embassy showed London that the seeming impotence of the parliamentary government had much to do with the unsettled state of internal politics. Nothing existed in the reportage to suggest that British diplomats, especially Howard, were guilty of racial stereotyping, of suggesting that the problems derived from a 'Latin' or 'Spanish' temperament. During his first twelve months, Howard conducted business with three different governments. All were 'conservative' and possessed continuity in that some ministers, notably the Marquess de Lema, the foreign minister, held the same portfolio. But in terms of solving national problems, these governments accomplished little; their members were concerned more with parliamentary manoeuvring to protect their interests and dish their enemies. In the Madrid bakers' strike, the central government refused to get involved, labelling the problem one for municipal jurisdiction.[33] Although this stance seemed reasonable, Howard pointed out that the matter had to be seen in the context of the impending national elections. Madrid's conservative mayor was loyal to the Cabinet; his deputies supported opposition parties. Hence the national government could not assure its followers of victory over opposition candidates. A political crisis over bread supplies might allow the Cabinet to replace the opposition deputy-mayors with loyalists of the national government. Although letting the bread crisis continue until the eve of the elections, Cabinet machinations failed to elect government candidates in Madrid.[34]

Howard perceived that jockeying for power and influence were just symptoms of the malady afflicting Spanish parliamentary government. The illness derived from the civilian politicians' determination to use every legal and extra-legal means possible to ensure their hold on the levers of power in Madrid. Such actions saw paltry effort expended to solve the problems engendered by the post-war economic and social dislocation of the country. Howard and the Embassy showed in a stream of reports sent to the Foreign Office in 1920 that the politicians failed for two reasons. First, they were corrupt, especially in electoral practices. This showed in the 1920 elections. The Cabinet engineered a crisis over whether to allow railway-rate increases and won a decree of dissolution from Alfonso. About this, Howard observed: '...it is the aim of every politician in the country to obtain a decree of dissolution while in power, which gives the Government great advantages in – as it is called here – "making the elections"'.[35] Subsequent manipulation of municipal politics, coupled with arrests of polling committees and the destruction of ballot boxes on election day, led to Embassy lamentations about 'government interference' and 'such outrageous proceedings'.[36] The second reason came from the politicians' need for extra-parliamentary support from vested interests in the country. This charge had equal weight for both the politicians on the right, supporting and being supported by the Church, the army, and landed and industrial interests, and those on the left, supporting and being supported by a large number of intellectuals, trade unions, and unorganised workers. This polarised the country.

Later in life, Howard reflected on the Cortes' weakness in 1920: 'The Extreme Right prescribed a military government, while the Extreme Left wished to adopt the Dictatorship of the Proletariat and the Soviet system. All that could be said was that Parliamentary Government as we understand it in England was becoming more and more discredited, and this naturally encouraged revolution in one sense or another.'[37] This retrospective view squared exactly with that held whilst he served at Madrid, one on the whole reasonably accurate.[38] As Spanish politicians failed increasingly to come to grips with Catalonian distress, strikes, labour unrest, the juntas, and financial and ancillary questions, extremist elements on both the right and left came to regard the Cortes as weak and ineffective. Hence the extremists took matters into their own hands. Howard and his staff witnessed the abject failure of the politicians to combat extremism from the right and left, that is 'revolution in one sense or the other'. Given the infighting in the Cortes, the civilian government rarely used parliamentary law to settle crises; rather it relied on draconian executive actions like suspending constitutional guarantees.[39] Here lay exposed the problem with the civilian politicians. They pursued short-term solutions for deep-rooted problems, tending to do so when in power by extra-parliamentary means. The bankruptcy of parliamentary government proved a disruptive force within Spain. Spaniards showed their contempt in the December 1920 elections with a low voter turn-out, something not lost on Howard and his diplomatic staff.[40]

By the time Howard arrived at Madrid, the military juntas – or to give them their proper name, *Juntas de Defensa* – formed an integral part of Spanish political life. The juntas first surfaced in May 1917 in response to a severe economic crisis which threatened the status and income of low- and middle-rank officers; coming from the ranks of colonel and below, these men were dissatisfied equally with their generals and the civilian politicians.[41] Their initial purpose entailed ensuring that their members' promotions and pay remained untouched by a government intent on retrenching during a period of tremendous inflation. They succeeded in 1917 but, once the crisis passed, did not melt away. Anxious to use the military in suppressing strikes and other forms of direct action by syndicalists and other radical elements amongst the working classes, the government granted the *Juntas de Defensa* legal status. By 1919 juntas existed amongst all branches and ranks of the Spanish armed forces: the artillery, cavalry, engineers, general staff, infantry, and so on.

Howard saw junta disruptiveness during his first months as ambassador.[42] A dispute developed when the officers' junta moved to break the exclusivity of the Army General Staff – once a staff officer entered this august body, he remained there until his retirement. No chance existed for the promotion of regular officers into the General Staff, hence the demand for reform. When a group of twenty-five young officers from the Escuela Superior de Guerra – the elite staff college whose graduates passed easily into the General Staff – published a pamphlet attacking the junta and its reformist ideas, the junta demanded and got tribunals of honour to try the young officers for breach of discipline. Eighteen of these young men were found guilty and, when the Supreme Tribunal of the Army quashed this verdict, a crisis ensued. Howard observed these events. The junta flexed its political muscle by conferring with leftwing parties in the Cortes which, if they came to power, would introduce a number of reforms including that of the General Staff. At the same time, junta leaders indicated that, unless the young officers were punished, they would take industrial action. The civilian government admitted defeat by arranging for new tribunals of honour. This time twenty-three young officers were found guilty but, before the matter could be referred to the Supreme Tribunal, where a second quashing of the verdict seemed likely, the government resigned. This was the fourth time since the *Juntas de Defensa* had emerged in May 1917 that they toppled a civilian government. Of this Howard observed piquantly: 'The intervention of the army in Spanish politics is no new thing, and the crisis...illustrates how serious such intervention may be, for the juntas threatened, if their wishes were not met, to paralyse the country by a railway and transport strike. The position of the King was, of course, rendered one of extreme delicacy.' The potency of the juntas was underscored further in Howard's mind in 1920 by some minor crises resolved in their favour.[43] Of the triad of disruptive forces which the ambassador saw in Spain, by virtue of their raw power and the deference shown them by the forces of order, the juntas posed the main threat to Spain's domestic stability.

An eventful year in Madrid had shown Howard that the problems within Spain were complex and interconnected. He had grasped the basic situation within six weeks of taking up his post; over the next twelve months, he then broadened his knowledge and imparted this to Curzon and the Foreign Office. As difficult as it might be to offer 'an accurate, intelligible and useful account of Spanish internal politics', he put the situation succinctly in his first annual report:

If I had to paint an impressionist painting of Spain in 1920, for which accurate and detailed drawing was not required, it would be an easier task. I could then take a large canvas and produce a stage in a state of chaotic welter on which various politicians would prominently figure pulling strings in different directions and to no purpose across a background of strikes, bombs and outrages, and apparent general discontent, of committees of military officers springing suddenly into the foreground and retiring as suddenly into obscurity for no apparent reason, of railway companies carrying on systematic sabotage against themselves in order to force the country and Government into raising rates, of banks and profiteers indulging in wild speculations in foreign exchanges, undermining all the advantages the country obtained by her policy of neutrality throughout the war, of regionalism in an extreme form increasing in certain provinces and extreme centralisation clinging to straws of hope in maintaining itself, of governments coming and going without serious programmes of reform, and, above this turmoil, of King Alfonso the only stable element apparent in it all, serenely trying now this expedient, now that, to carry on against great odds until some sane, wise and strong man should emerge on the stage to put all these tragi-comedians into their right places and allow the play to proceed to the benefit and content of the public in the house.[44]

Given Spain's central position in the western Mediterranean balance of power, Howard's assessment foreshadowed difficult times for Britain's position in the region.

III

For most of Howard's first two years at Madrid, no movement occurred on the matters of Morocco, Tangier, or the new commercial treaty. This developed mainly from the inherent political instability within the Spanish government, something which saw foreign policy take a back seat to domestic politics. Given a series of niggling problems involving the two countries, Howard's essential task in this period concerned keeping Anglo-Spanish relations on an even keel. For instance, despite its neutrality during the war, Spain, like Sweden, had supported Germany and its allies rather than the Entente. True, Spain had profited in Morocco by the policies of Britain and France before 1914, but subsequent Franco-Spanish rivalry in North Africa and the continued British possession of Gibraltar rankled Madrid. In the British case after 1918, a residue of this wartime antipathy existed amongst some extreme rightwing politicians and increasingly, as troubles in Ireland mounted, in some Catholic and liberal quarters which deplored the use of British military power to subdue Sinn Fein 'freedom fighters'. Consequently, Howard took decided interest in Spanish–German relations, especially when a new German ambassador, Baron Langwerth von Rimmern, the first since the end of the war, arrived in Madrid in October 1920.[45] An expert on Morocco, von Rimmern's chief purpose involved keeping Spain friendly to the new republican regime in Germany for both economic and political reasons; Spain supplied raw materials to Germany and purchased manufactured goods, and Germany needed to secure as many friends as possible in post-war Europe. Howard's efforts in this regard were passive, keeping an eye on the German Embassy and reporting on developments to the Foreign Office.[46]

On the other hand, Howard assumed an active role in the matter of Spanish sympathy for Irish rebels. Throughout 1920 and 1921, a number of Irish Roman Catholic ecclesiastics disseminated material 'containing violent accusations against His Majesty's Government'.[47] Although Howard's long-standing sympathy for the legitimate grievances of Irish nationalism had not diminished, he perceived that Britain's image in Spain and other countries would be darkened if the wild accusations of Sinn Fein extremists circulated unanswered. As Howard realised the Spanish authorities' inability to prevent the spread of this anti-British propaganda in Spain, he argued that the Foreign Office should mount a counter-campaign. Accordingly, the News Department prepared the relevant material and, whilst sending this to Deakin, also circulated copies to other Embassies where they might be useful.[48] Not content to sit idly and let matters run their course, Howard availed himself of his contacts within the Church to use his influence to neutralise anglophobic attacks from churchmen resident in Spain.⁴⁹ Although the Foreign Office looked askance at times on these actions as they appeared 'a little undignified' for an ambassador,⁵⁰ Howard helped mute these criticisms of Britain's Irish policy.

Although Howard devoted much effort to these minor issues, he could not ignore the larger ones of Morocco, Tangier, and commercial relations. There might be no movement towards settling these problems, but they still consumed valuable diplomatic time. In terms of Morocco and Tangier, he had to contend with Spanish disquiet about aggressive French policies. Because Britain had acceded to but never formally acknowledged the Spanish protectorate in Morocco, Madrid sought British recognition to help shore up its hold over this vital piece of territory. Spanish concern was underscored by French preponderance in the court of the sultan, as well as French demands that the Paris Peace Conference recognise 'that Tangier formed a part of the French zone, and that Spain occupied in the Spanish zone the position of a sub-tenant of France'.⁵¹ Seeking to maintain the North African territorial status quo, Curzon and his advisers had decided, before Howard's appointment, to resist both French and Spanish demands. As a result, in 1919 the British hesitated to take up a Spanish offer to recognise the British protectorate in Egypt in return for British recognition of the Spanish one in Morocco. To salve Madrid's irritation over this, Curzon used his influence with the fledgling League of Nations to secure Spain one of the four non-permanent seats on the new Council.⁵² None the less, the Spanish continued to press for British recognition in 1920 and early 1921.⁵³

Howard and his Foreign Office colleagues recognised that the Spanish possessed some trumps in this game. Britain had capitulary rights in Spanish Morocco dating from before the war. The Spanish wished to end these to satisfy their *amour propre* as a Protecting Power; Crowe worried that Madrid might unilaterally cancel such rights unless the British were more forthcoming in areas like the recognition issue.⁵⁴ Moreover, several British subjects with property in the Spanish zone had filed pecuniary claims against Spanish authorities because of damage caused during military operations against rebel tribesmen.⁵⁵ Unless Britain proved more amenable to Spanish colonial ambitions, little chance existed of a speedy claims settlement. Whilst the Spanish sought to tie all of these questions together, the British endeavoured to keep them apart. It fell to Howard to do so. He did this by meeting periodically with de Lema, parrying Spanish demands, and countering with arguments despatched from London.⁵⁶

Tangier presented Howard with an equally thorny problem. The solution favoured by Curzon and the Foreign Office, given that Britain possessed the deciding voice in the disposition of the port, involved convening an Anglo-Franco-Spanish conference to achieve a settlement agreeable to all three Powers. In a conference *à trois*, Britain could mediate between France and Spain.[57] Howard's problem in this stemmed from the Spanish reluctance to lessen their rights in Tangier. Conceding to the French demand that the city be considered 'a part of the French zone' would never pass the Cortes, and any Spanish government that introduced a treaty for ratification that contemplated this would be forced from office immediately. Although less objectionable, an international regime to administer the municipal government would also create domestic difficulties for Spanish leaders. Their intransigence over this issue was coupled with the worry that, because of Spain's attitude towards the Anglo-French allies during the war, Britain would sell out Spain should a conference *à trois* meet. For most of his first two years in Madrid, Howard spent much time and effort convincing Spanish leaders that Britain had no intention of selling out beforehand either Spain or France.[58] Moreover, when his own government at times seemed insensitive to Spanish self-esteem, Howard had to intervene to have London stroke the sensitive Spanish ego. 'I feel that if we are to rely on the Spaniards co-operating with us when the time comes for dealing with the Tangier question,' Howard admonished the foreign secretary, 'it is necessary to take into consideration their rather sensitive susceptibilities.'[59] That Anglo-Spanish relations did not suffer because of the intertwined Moroccan and Tangier questions in the period before the middle of 1921 had much to do with Howard.

Howard's diplomacy also prevented a disruption of relations that might have developed through the efforts of Spanish commercial and financial circles to weaken foreign economic interests in their country. Although some nationalist feeling probably coloured this anti-foreign agitation, the principal motivation lay in the efforts of those like Catalan bankers[60] to increase profits. With the obvious connexions between and the overlapping interests of Spanish capitalists and politicians, the various conservative governments in Spain bowed to these pressures; this resulted in Madrid's denunciation of a series of bilateral commercial treaties by early 1921.[61] With the concomitant increase in Spanish customs duties, this placed Howard in the midst of a dispute between bodies representing British commercial interests in Spain – mainly the Federation of British Industries and the British Chamber of Commerce in Spain – and the Spanish government.[62] In terms of his own government, Howard had not only to be wary of the political repercussions of his actions, the Foreign Office's interest, but also the economic ones which preoccupied the Treasury and Board of Trade.

Howard found his efforts blocked by Spanish unwillingness to resolve their commercial relations with Britain. Indeed, the Spaniards were in no hurry to settle, preferring instead desultory discussions for a new Anglo-Spanish commercial treaty; the longer it took to arrange a settlement, so the Spanish seemed to believe, the better the deal they might realise, especially if lengthy negotiations were coupled with the pressures put on British trade through increased customs duties. Howard's initial response to this Spanish diplomacy concentrated on cooling tempers; the British Chamber of Commerce in Spain was hot to counter with British economic pressures on Spain. As this occurred at the same time as the damage to the British image in Spain by the Rio Tinto strike, Howard sought to limit further loss to Britain's reputation. He prevailed,[63] which allowed official discussions to occur in an atmosphere of relative calm. But, as the Spaniards proved to be unyielding, Howard came round to the idea that the only way to achieve a compromise would come from threatening British reprisals.[64] This would be part of a determined effort to conclude a new commercial treaty, the best safeguard of British interests. He began preparing the diplomatic ground for this treaty in early 1921 and, by the middle of April, had set the stage for preliminary discussions between the Spanish government and a British delegation comprising the commercial counsellor at the Embassy and a mission despatched by the Federation of British Industries.[65] Through Howard's efforts, the course of Anglo-Spanish relations had not been disturbed much by anti-foreign economic policies in Spain.

IV

For most of Howard's first two years in Madrid, Spain created discomfort but not distress for British diplomatists. Then, unexpectedly, the Spanish army in Morocco suffered a devastating defeat in Annual at the hands of Riff rebels in July 1921.[66] Howard witnessed the eruption of a major domestic crisis in Spain over who bore responsibility for the Annual disaster – the civilian politicians or the army – a crisis that accentuated the power struggle between the politicians and the juntas. These worsening political circumstances profoundly affected Spanish foreign policy. Internal bickering deflected attention from foreign affairs which, with crumbling Spanish authority in Morocco, exposed the Spanish Empire in North Africa to the possibility of French poaching. Howard and the Foreign Office did not doubt that, if Spain's hold on its protectorate weakened, the French would do all they could to profit thereby. This had to be prevented for strategic reasons: prohibiting a first-class Power from controlling the North African littoral from Casablanca to Tunis. In most respects, Howard and his colleagues were helpless in the face of Spain's domestic instability. They could only watch as the politicians and soldiers fought to affix responsibility. But in the immediate aftermath of Annual, Howard and the Foreign Office recognised that they had to use what leverage they could to bolster the Spaniards. As Britain could not sacrifice its own interests in this vital region, these moves were tactical and short-term. Stability in the western Mediterranean could come only with stability in Spain, and in this context Howard, Curzon, and the other British diplomatists waited for the return to order in Spain.

Howard's first reports about Annual mentioned little about the specific circumstances of the defeat.[67] The number of casualties, the extent of Riff penetration, and the fate of outlying Spanish posts remained a mystery as the Spanish government sought to minimise the damage. Within two weeks, following exhaustive detective work, Howard found that the Spanish had experienced a decisive defeat. He warned that the political consequences of this meant the eruption of a major crisis between the 'ins' and the 'outs', not only over who should shoulder the responsibility for failure, but also over the expense of Morocco to the Spanish exchequer and the whole nature of Spanish colonial policy.[68] The liberal opposition supported announced government policies to undertake massive public works on the mainland essential for Spain's economic health. These projects, as well as opposition support for the government, would be jeopardised if it was decided to pour money into a military reconquest of the lost territories. Given the national debt, the Spanish exchequer could not afford both. About Spanish colonial policy, Howard surmised that Annual would 'react very seriously on the position of all European states with possessions and interests in North Africa, owing to the growth of a chauvinistic Pan-Islamic movement there'. About this, Gerald Villiers, of the Foreign Office Western Department, reckoned that the French, worried about their Moroccan possessions, could not allow events to progress in the Spanish zone.[69] His superiors disagreed. Crowe saw that the extension of the French protectorate would create problems for Britain but, also, that the French would do nothing until the situation became less cloudy.[70]

Howard's warning about another ministerial crisis came true as the Foreign Office speculated on the French reaction. On 14 August 1921 the conservative coalition of Manuel Allende Salazar fell, replaced by another led by a seasoned conservative, Antonio Maura. Despite this change in government, political uncertainty in Spain did not abate, so that the cloudiness of Spanish policy in Morocco remained. It remained for just over two years, as the country continued to polarise over who bore responsibility for the defeat of the Spanish army. Government and opposition leaders railed at each other to achieve political advantage; the juntas on the mainland and the army in Morocco attacked one another to protect their positions; the politicians sought to pin the blame on the military, and the military on the politicians; and the king, who had advised the discredited commander in Annual, General Manuel Fernandez-Silvestre, flitted from side to side to shore up the throne. Finally, in September 1923, a group of senior officers led by General Manuel Primo de Rivera, tired of the squabbling amongst the politicians, concerned about Spain's hold on its portion of Morocco, and opposed to civilian attempts to curtail the army's ability to influence events, overthrew the civilian government and established a military Directorate to govern Spanish affairs.[71] The extent of the dislocation in Spanish political life is seen easiest by the fact that, beginning with the fall of Allende Salazar's ministry and ending with the rise of the Directorate, the country experienced four changes of government. Only with Primo and his cohorts achieving power, given the relatively impregnable position of the Directorate supported by the army, did Spanish policy in Morocco become clear.

Howard found that the course of Spain's domestic politics after the middle of 1921 retarded British efforts to protect their interests in the western Mediterranean and on the trade issue. Because of the need for Spanish leaders to concentrate on the high stakes of domestic politics, the unresolved issues in Anglo-Spanish relations were held in abeyance. Although Howard wished to push on with at least the trade discussions, this proved impossible because of unwillingness of both the Foreign Office and Spanish authorities to make any concessions. On the contrary, London and Madrid each sought to have the other make the first move.[72] The Spanish ploy in this regard, designed to obviate domestic criticism about caving in to the British, involved doubling tariffs on a range of British goods. The Foreign Office, on the other hand, impressed on the Cabinet, which endorsed free trade, the need to consider commercial retaliation to back up the British position that the Spanish customs tariffs be lowered.[73] Howard had supported making such threats earlier in 1921 but, as the domestic problems in Spain mounted over Annual, he asserted that the British should be flexible,[74] perhaps imposing a tariff on just one key Spanish export, fruit. His reasoning stemmed from indications that Spanish leaders, worried about French designs in Morocco and concerned about strained Franco-Spanish relations caused by already imposed increases of Spanish tariffs on French goods, wished to avoid a breach with Britain.[75] Quite obviously, Howard believed, the Spanish were amenable to a settlement with Britain, a settlement he could achieve if his government softened their bargaining position.

Late in December 1921, Howard concluded that British policy towards Spain needed clarification since, as the division between his Embassy and the Foreign Office showed over the retaliation issue, British diplomats lacked a uniform position on the Spanish question. Although Howard had long understood the need for men on the spot to defer to those at the Foreign Office on major issues – the matter of the 'big picture' – he judged in this instance that his colleagues in London ought to see the Spanish question from the Embassy's perspective. Thus, he put his views to Crowe as the year ended.[76] Howard focussed on the strategic importance to Britain in ensuring Spain's control of its Moroccan protectorate by referring to the course of the Washington conference on naval limitation then in progress. He observed that the lesser Powers led by France would now succeed in overcoming efforts by Britain to place restrictions on submarine construction:

> What I wanted to emphasize was this, that if France is allowed to maintain a considerable force of submarines and if she is ever able to acquire the Spanish Zone of Morocco[,] the Mediterranean becomes a French sea. If France held the coast from Melilla to Tangier she could (I speak with the diffidence of one who has no technical knowledge) probably bar the entrance of the Mediterranean to any very superior fleet.

Howard pressed the point that France had to be prevented from absorbing the Spanish zone. Whilst acknowledging that Britain had always supported the Spanish in this regard, he suggested that this had been done 'without enthusiasm of any kind'. Understandable given the inefficiency of Spanish colonial administration, such feelings, however, had no place in determining foreign policy. Britain's interests demanded giving the Spanish encouragement to remain in Morocco, especially now that important voices in Spain were recommending the abandonment of the protectorate. How could Britain do this? Howard argued that the easiest way would be to recognise formally the Spanish protectorate. As Lloyd George's government had just granted quasi-independent status to Egypt, Spanish recognition of the British protectorate was no longer necessary.[77] A change of tactics seemed opportune. Britain could begin simultaneous discussions with the Spanish on both the commercial treaty and the recognition of Morocco 'without in any way connecting the two questions, but so that the Spaniards would understand, and they would do so quickly enough, that a satisfactory commercial Treaty would materially contribute to such recognition'.

Howard then considered whether Britain's ability to influence events in this region hinged on preserving its control of Gibraltar. He told Crowe that 'it has always seemed to me [that] Gibraltar is a source of weakness for us viz-a-viz Spain which country we cannot afford to treat, even if we so desired, as a negligible quantity'. It was not that Spain would suddenly attack the peninsula, though that could be possible if a first-class Power like France offered support. Spain could make the British position in Gibraltar difficult by denying supplies and services from the mainland fresh water, meat, and vegetables, as well as workers. Spanish pique with Britain's control of the peninsula had surfaced most recently in August–September 1921 through official complaints that Gibraltar served as a base for smugglers who, carrying North African tobacco, found a rich market in Spain.[78] It followed that Gibraltar's security was tied to both the settlement of commercial relations and Morocco. The Spanish had to be convinced that Britain would not abandon them to their fate in North Africa. Taking the Spanish for granted and refusing to offer any initiative in settling the problems in Anglo-Spanish relations might jeopardise British interests in the western Mediterranean.

Howard's letter created a stir at the Foreign Office. Villiers played down the likelihood of the French ousting the Spaniards from northern Morocco given the uncertainty of the situation there.[79] With as little 'technical knowledge' as Howard, he pontificated on the strategic problem, arguing that French submarines operating from Oran and Casablanca could as easily play havoc with British sea lanes as any using Tangier and Melilla. About Gibraltar, Villiers saw no serious Spanish threat in the offing; more to the point, there seemed little Britain could do to halt tobacco smuggling since that was a Spanish responsibility. Most important, Villiers deprecated strongly any notion of offering formal recognition of the Spanish zone in Morocco to achieve a breakthrough in commercial relations. This would not induce the Spaniards to compromise. 'On the other side', he wrote, 'is the very natural reluctance of decent Englishmen to encourage or bolster up an administration which is a by-word for cruelty, incompetence and corruption.'

Howard's letter received more cerebral treatment from Crowe and Curzon. Crowe saw 'no reason whatever for our offering special concessions to Spain in order to persuade her to remain in northern Morocco'. He doubted whether Spanish leaders of any political stripe would contemplate seriously pulling out of North Africa. About Gibraltar he said nothing except that 'smuggling can only be prevented by the importing country, and is not the business of the exporting country'. The foreign secretary agreed with Howard that Britain preferred 'an incompetent Spain to a competent France' in Morocco 'for political and strategic reasons'. However, little need existed to appease Spanish leaders over Gibraltar or the recognition issue. Britain had no intention of abandoning Gibraltar, 'whatever the Spaniards may do or threaten'. Additionally, he wished to avoid tying recognition of the Spanish protectorate with the commercial negotiations; as he minuted: 'Let us reserve the former for something much more important.'

Howard learnt of the Foreign Office assessment of his views privately from Crowe and, after a few days thought, responded with a second letter, the contents of which he described as 'a simple matter of "Realpolitik", and for the guidance of our general policy towards this country, what, as I see it, we want from Spain and what we can offer her in return'.[80] Although taking comfort that the Foreign Office sought to maintain Spain in Morocco, Howard hinted that to do so reluctantly because of the 'cruelty, incompetence and corruption' of Spanish colonial policy indicated a lack of the sang-froid necessary to conduct effective foreign policy. Personal distaste for a Power's internal policies had rarely prevented British diplomatists from overcoming their scruples 'for the sake of larger and wider purposes of Policy'; drawing on his Cretan experiences, he referred to Britain's former support of the Ottoman Empire. Spain after 1921 differed little from Turkey in 1903–6. He emphasised again that, if the situation in Morocco so deteriorated that a groundswell arose within Spain to force its abandonment, only France would gain. Britain had leverage in this regard, something it had to use effectively.

Next, Howard argued, Britain had to secure Spanish support for internationalising Tangier. This could be done by conceding to Spain on some other matter. Avoiding concessions or, worse, not encouraging Spanish policy in Morocco might force a Franco-Spanish accommodation on Tangier, a possibility brimming with danger for Britain's strategic position in North Africa. Thirdly, Gibraltar lay in an exposed position. The Spanish could take it whenever they wished – a point conceded in Crowe's letter. If the peninsula fell to Spain in a moment of national crisis, say if Britain found itself engaged in a struggle elsewhere, the impact on Britain's position in the Mediterranean would be incalculable. Hence, 'cordial relations' with Spain were essential to protect Gibraltar. One way to foster such relations could come by being more forthcoming over tobacco smuggling because 'if the Gibraltar Government can discover some way of penalising [the smugglers] – even though they do not actually smuggle tobacco from Gibraltar itself – we shall have made a big step in the right direction'. Finally, Britain had to get a better Spanish tariff – in his first letter, he emphasised that this would help alleviate the distress of 'over 2,000,000 unemployed in England'. The problem here resided with Spanish protectionism which the Embassy and the Foreign Office had to overcome in the negotiations.

Howard then posed the question: 'Now, in return, what can we offer Spain?' His answer did not disguise the fact that the British had little more in their diplomatic arsenal than acting as if they valued good relations with the Spanish; hence, supporting them in Morocco, reducing friction over Gibraltar, and seeking goodwill had to become the order of the day. As already noted, he put the matter succinctly:

What [the Spaniards] resent is just that the Spanish people are so often considered a 'byword for cruelty, incompetence and corruption'. They call this the 'leyenda negra'. I have often to put pressure on myself to avoid an attitude of irritation at happenings here. But I believe it pays not to give way to this natural irritation.

By giving this cold assessment of Britain's relatively exposed position vis-à-vis Spain, Howard simply did what any ambassador must when representing his country's interests. If London really wanted to protect the status quo in the western Mediterranean, it had to take a sensible first step. 'If my premises are all false, then the above is all foolishness', he told Crowe, 'and as we are friends of long standing, you will no doubt tell me so plainly. If they are true, let us direct our policy accordingly.' Crowe decided not to reply.[81] Howard took this studied silence as a Foreign Office admission that his premises were correct, that Curzon and Crowe were giving him a relatively free hand in his diplomacy. He moved accordingly. Howard had already sought Spanish goodwill by getting the British community in Spain to contribute to a fund established by Queen Victoria Eugenia, Alfonso's consort, to aid sick and wounded soldiers from the Moroccan campaign.[82] This led to other initiatives during the remainder of Howard's tenure in Spain to improve the British image in that country whilst, as much as possible, creating a better atmosphere in which the settlement of outstanding political questions could be made easier. The most important of these goodwill gestures began in April 1922 when Howard pressed Curzon to arrange for eminent British men of letters to undertake lecture tours of Spain. As the French and Germans had had apparent propaganda success amongst Spanish scholars on such tours, Howard reckoned the British must counter. His entreaties found a receptive audience at the Foreign Office, especially with Sir Stephen Gaselee, the Foreign Office librarian, a man of influence within the diplomatic establishment, and a leading light of the Anglo-Spanish Society in London.[83] The Foreign Office accepted Howard's views, quickly arranging for the noted writer, Hilaire Belloc, to speak at a number of engagements in Madrid.[84] This amounted to the first phase of the operation. Even before Belloc's arrival, Howard lobbied several prominent anglophile Spaniards about creating a permanent organisation for Anglo-Spanish intellectual exchanges.[85] This led to the formation of the English Committee in Spain, under the patronage of the Duke of Alba, a Spanish cousin of the Duke of Marlborough. By 1924 this committee had begun to arrange university student exchanges between the two countries and had embarked on an annual series of lectures involving distinguished British speakers travelling to Spain.[86] Thanks to Howard and his network of contacts, a new medium had emerged in Spain by which Britain could be better understood by prominent Spaniards.

With his goodwill efforts in train, Howard lost no time in getting the stalled commercial treaty negotiations moving. The preliminary discussions on settling commercial relations, concluded before Annual, led the British to produce a draft treaty by December 1921.[87] The result of consultations amongst Howard, the Foreign Office, and the Board of Trade, this draft had been despatched to the Madrid Embassy the next month. To achieve the maximum advantage, London wanted a treaty rather than a simple agreement to reduce duties; broader in its coverage, a treaty would better protect other British financial interests, like banks and insurance companies, operating in Spain. The draft treaty contained an appendix of tariff revisions, and Howard received instructions to 'negotiate the tariff proposals with priority and separately; our view being that these are the essential part and without substantial success in this respect we should not dream of concluding a treaty'. The Foreign Office realised that Howard could do little to get the Spanish, still reluctant to move on this issue because of its importance to their export trade and the unsettled political situation following Annual, to bargain seriously unless provided with a diplomatic stick with which to prod them. In writing to Crowe, Howard had indicated that he would 'bluff' the Spanish over the issue of fruit exports to Britain to get them to the bargaining table, this because the 'Spanish Government is ... genuinely frightened of the possibility of another tariff war besides the [present] one with France'.[88] The difficulty in this arose from the Cabinet not yet making a decision about whether to impose increased duties on crucial Spanish exports like fruit, though Curzon took the line that 'I should certainly threaten, as I think it can be done without risk'.

Howard reckoned that he had to present the British draft as soon as possible – the new Spanish tariff had come into force in the middle of February.[89] Seeing nothing in London's delay that prevented him from getting the negotiations under way, on 2 March he presented the Spanish foreign minister, Gonzalez Hontoria, with the draft British treaty.[90] In doing this, Howard emphasised that his government did not dispute Spain's right to raise duties to compensate for inflation, but it did oppose 'a wholly prohibitive tariff'. Hontoria replied that 'Great Britain was mainly a free trade country in her own interests, and that Spain believed it in her own interest at present to have a protectionist tariff. [The British] could not claim to be entitled to any special favours on account of a policy which [they] had adopted because it suited [them]'. Not dissuaded by Hontoria's transparent bargaining tactic, Howard indicated that, once the Spanish reply had been received, an expert would be sent from London 'to discuss the treaty'. The negotiating lines were drawn.

Howard made no progress in these talks until late April, the result of another ministerial crisis centred on the continuing struggle between the politicians and juntas over the Moroccan crisis.[91] In the month between his presentation of the British draft treaty and his first meeting with the

Spanish Treaty Commission, which responded to the British overtures, his hand had been strengthened in a number of ways. First, Lloyd George's Cabinet authorised him to threaten retaliation over fruit imports into Britain if the Spanish refused to relent over raising their duties.[92] To pressure the Spaniards as they prepared their reply, Howard spread rumours that he had been empowered 'to threaten reprisals'.[93] Secondly, the Spanish government lacked unified support from powerful interests in Spain over the tariff issue. The landed interests, whose power and livelihood depended on agricultural exports, worried about provoking the British needlessly, whilst the Madrid press, except for two government newspapers, united in condemning the new Spanish tariff.[94] Thirdly, an important Catalan industrialist, Viscount de Cuso, 'who has had much to do with the framing of the devilish Spanish Tariff', had approached the local representative of the Federation of British Industries. He wished to advise Howard's Embassy to help it achieve 'the best possible advantage' in the negotiations.[95] Although the commercial attaché, Captain Ulick Charles, looked on Cuso 'as a very dangerous person', Howard inclined to the view that, whatever Cuso's motives, he 'might be very useful'. The Foreign Office responded that no agents of the two British commercial organisations in Spain receive any hint about the draft treaty's contents – it wished to avoid even a breath of conflict-of-interest allegations that particular business groups were favoured by the British government; but it gave Howard permission to use his discretion in seeking Cuso's advice.[96]

In this way, Howard embarked on his first meeting with the Spanish Treaty Commission on 28 April 1922, possessing some advantages in the negotiations. He told the Treaty Commission, a body of four Spanish senior civil servants representing the Foreign Ministry, Customs Department, and Ministry of Public Works, that he and Charles had not come to negotiate; instead, they sought only the Spanish counter-proposals to pass them on to London.[97] The Spanish representatives apologised for being unable to give 'definite proposals' since the coal interests, an influential lobby, had not yet replied about suggested tariff reductions on British coal. But there was value in this meeting. It came from a Spanish admission that their government understood the importance of a treaty with Britain, Spain's best customer, and that 'the Spanish Commission were in agreement with the text of the treaty from the general point of view, and that no difficulty was anticipated with regard to the vast majority of articles'. This position no doubt reflected the success of Howard circulating rumours about British retaliation. But, he also reported, whilst the Spanish quibbled with some minor points, like the use of trade marks, they intended to resist at all costs the British attempt to secure most-favoured-nation treatment, explicit in the draft treaty, 'for all British imports into Spain'. Howard left this meeting convinced that the Spaniards entertained 'a real desire' to settle, and suggested that once the coal interests responded, perhaps in a week, the Board of Trade might have their expert ready to travel to Madrid.

Howard's optimism about an early Spanish reply proved unfounded. It took two further sessions with the Trade Commission in the middle of May to elicit the full Spanish reply, the contents of which led the ambassador to despair over the British getting anything like the treaty they desired.[98] Though willing to concede to a number of British tariff demands on a range of goods and commodities, the Spaniards would compromise little on coal, cotton cloth, and locomotive engines, the first two being basic British exports. More important, the Spanish refused to budge over most-favoured-nation status. This constituted the sticking point. Howard saw merit in Hontoria's argument about British policies of free trade conflicting with Spanish protectionist ones. It would be hard for him to argue that Spain should alter a policy judged essential for its economic survival. More to the point, the Trade Commission demanded that Spain's chief exports to Britain – iron ore, fruit, almonds, olive oil, and vegetables – be exempt from duty and that Spanish wine be subject to preferential tariffs. As Howard told Henry Fountain of the Board of Trade:

...if we insist on this [most-favoured-nation status] as a principle, we are likely to lose, not only the advantages that might accrue to our trade from such concessions to specified articles as we can screw out of the Spanish Government, but also to see our modus vivendi of 1894 denounced, in order to get rid of that part which refers to most-favoured-nation treatment.[99]

Unless the British were prepared to drop their quest for most-favoured-nation status, Howard saw little chance for the conclusion of a treaty. Until he could survey the situation and come up with a new approach, the Board of Trade expert had to delay his departure for Spain.

Howard's reports precipitated a heated debate involving the Foreign Office and Board of Trade over whether to conclude a treaty lacking most-favoured-nation status or to drop the matter, impose high tariffs against Spanish goods, and fight what would certainly be a mutually debilitating trade war at a time when the British economy needed renewal. The Foreign Office held the Spanish counter-proposals to be 'an insult to our intelligence' and 'perfectly monstrous'.[100] Reflecting the attitude that had surfaced when Howard corresponded with Crowe early in 1922, the Western Department chafed at any suggestion that Britain lacked the power to force its will on Spain. With a mixed metaphor indicating a lack of clear thinking in that department, Nevile Butler minuted: 'Sir Esmé [sic] rather assumes that Spain has the whip-hand in the negotiations, whereas we believe the boot to be on the other leg.'[101] The Board of Trade, represented by Fountain, agreed that the Spanish counter-proposals were

Madrid: 1919–1924

'very unsatisfactory'.[102] Fountain argued, nevertheless, that 'a rupture of commercial relations' had to be avoided and that 'for the present, at any rate, the negotiations should be continued'. Board of Trade determination to achieve an agreement, despite Foreign Office political objections, did not come as a surprise. Stanley Baldwin, the president of the Board of Trade, had prevailed on Crowe to approach the Marquess Merry del Val, the Spanish ambassador in London and not Howard's friend in the Vatican, on 16 May about the thorny matter of most-favoured-nation status.[103] Deferring to the Board of Trade because the economic issues in this case overrode the political ones, the Foreign Office swallowed its opposition to conceding to Spanish desires to deny Britain most-favoured-nation status.

Howard received instructions to continue negotiations, during which he was to impress British disappointment at the Spanish reply.[104] At the same time, he had to let the Spaniards know that London would examine the Spanish position 'carefully with a view to making some counter-proposals'. On receiving these instructions, Howard decided to speed up the process. He sensed that, unless he moved quickly and decisively, the negotiations might stretch on until the autumn with little result.[105] His plan of action involved getting the Treaty Commission to grant most-favoured-nation status to at least that group of goods and commodities about which it had not fussed, whilst approaching the influential Cuso for advice.[106] He began by meeting privately with Cuso. This proved to be a valuable conversation as Cuso outlined a strategy that would force the Treaty Commission to treat the British draft seriously and with despatch. He confirmed the impossibility of wringing general most-favoured-nation treatment out of the Spanish government given the domestic situation. However, the same result could be achieved by asking for reductions already granted to other countries, like Switzerland, which had signed commercial treaties with Spain, and by getting an article inserted that would grant Britain automatic reductions which might in future be accorded other states. Drawing on his intimate knowledge of the Spanish situation, Cuso advised that, as an inducement to get the Treaty Commission to sit up and take notice, Howard should indicate that, unless these future and unknown reductions were conferred on British goods, Britain would have the right to denounce the Anglo-Spanish treaty.

Howard reported that Cuso outlined bargaining tactics respecting a number of specific items important to British trade, including woollens, heavy machinery, and a range of chemical products including pharmaceuticals. Cuso also emphasised tactics concerning British coal and cotton exports, which Howard deduced to be his main reason for approaching the Embassy; Cuso's wealth derived from Catalonian iron foundries and textile mills, hence he had a desire to ensure large supplies of cheap British coal whilst dampening British intentions to achieve a breakthrough on cotton exports. About the latter, Howard was advised that nothing would come by demanding reductions on cotton textiles because of the importance of the industry to Spain. About coal, Cuso told him that the amount Britain exported could be increased substantially over the million ton limit envisaged by the Treaty Commission. This could come through the British demanding two million tons of coal exports annually at a minuscule 3 pesetas per ton. Cuso believed that, after the bargaining process, Britain 'should get one and a quarter million[,] but it was necessary for us to ask for more in order that [the] government might be able to prove to Spanish coal owners they had not accepted all our demands'. Cuso concluded his remarks to Howard by stressing two points. First, the Board of Trade expert should be sent to Spain as quickly as possible. The Spanish government wanted to settle both to enhance its image within Spain and because it was 'tired of negotiating after [a] long struggle with the French'. Secondly, Cuso would support a treaty along the lines he had outlined, a telling remark since he admitted to Howard that he would be the chief adviser to the Treaty Commission.

Howard judged that the moment had come to move on the treaty. He based this on his discussion with Cuso, as well as on other sources including newspaper articles in the government organ, *Epoca*.[107] He pressed Curzon to get both the Foreign Office and the Board of Trade to agree to Cuso's suggestions and, with that achieved, have the Board of Trade expert sent to Madrid without delay to assist in what Howard anticipated would be the final phase of the negotiations. Seeing that this new approach, now supported by Howard, would give Britain most of what it sought, the Foreign Office and Board of Trade endorsed a modified treaty along the lines suggested by Cuso. By 6 July, J. J. Wills, a senior member of the Board of Trade, had made preparations to leave for Madrid, having had additional consultations with the Colonial Office about the proposed treaty's coverage of exports from the Empire to Spain.[108] Three days later, Wills arrived in Madrid to advise Howard in the final phase of the negotiations.

Howard, accompanied by Charles and Wills, conferred with the Treaty Commission on 10 July, a meeting that set in train a series of discussions over the next seventeen days that resulted in the Anglo-Spanish commercial treaty being initialled on 27 July. Although some difficulties emerged in these negotiations, stemming from Howard seeking as much of a reduction as possible on British cotton and metal exports, and the Spaniards desiring to protect their exports of fruit, vegetables, and wine, nothing of consequence emerged to prevent an agreement.[109] At the first meeting, on 10 July, the main stumbling block as far as the British were concerned disappeared when Howard got the Treaty Commission to accept that Britain be granted all present and future reductions that had or would be granted to other states.[110] The only problem emerging after this concerned the duration of the treaty before it could be denounced by either side. Although the British originally wanted a treaty of ten years' duration, it became necessary to agree to one of just three years, after which either side could denounce it with six months' notice.[111] Given that the 1894 *modus vivendi* had survived for almost thirty years with the same provision, little chance seemed to exist in 1922 that this new treaty would last just forty-two months. But even if it did, an unlikely possibility, the British had put their commercial relations with Spain on a firm footing for the foreseeable future, an important consideration in British economic diplomacy as the Americans were now pressing for the settlement of the British war debt to the United States. But Howard's concern was that settlement of the tariff question with Spain had strengthened the British position in the western Mediterranean whilst, at the same time, helping in a minor way to improve employment opportunities for British workmen who laboured for firms that traded with Spain.

Howard received warm congratulations from Balfour, then filling in for the absent Curzon: 'His Majesty's Government regard the conclusion of the new treaty with no small satisfaction, and they realise that it is largely due to the judgement, tact and unwearying efforts which your Excellency has displayed throughout.'[112] At the request of the Board of Trade, Balfour empowered Howard to sign the treaty without delay and arrange for an exchange of notes bringing it into operation as soon as the ink on those signatures dried; such notes would permit the treaty to come into force prior to ratification. Recognition of Howard's integral part in this achievement came from both the British government, which made him a GCMG, and from British commercial organisations, like the Federation of British Industries, which showered him with praise.[113] As all attempts at concluding a new treaty had been stymied by intransigent Spaniards since the early 1890s, Wills put Howard's success in perspective by observing that 'the successful issue of the recent protracted negotiations (much appreciated by British traders) is therefore a matter on which the Embassy is to be very warmly congratulated'.[114]

On the heels of this achievement, Howard began gently to push the Spaniards to settle the Tangier question. Using unconfirmed reports of secret Franco-Spanish conversations about the city in December 1922 as an excuse to reaffirm the British desire for tripartite talks, he met with the new Spanish foreign minister, Santiago Alba[115] – a liberal ministry had taken power only on 5 December. This meeting suggested that both Madrid and Paris were ready to fix the status of the city. Howard had not the same independence in this question as over the commercial treaty as

Anglo-French relations were involved. Curzon was then enmeshed in negotiations for what in July 1923 became the Treaty of Lausanne, the final peace agreement with Turkey.[116] Since Curzon's success at Lausanne depended on Anglo-French collaboration – the main beneficiaries of Ottoman collapse in the Near East were to be Britain and France – the foreign secretary wished to avoid damaging his relationship with the French by falling out needlessly over less important matters in North Africa. It followed that Howard and the Foreign Office worked more closely together over this issue than over any other since Howard's arrival at Madrid.

Howard understood completely the need to follow the foreign secretary's lead in this. Curzon's strategy in the negotiations amounted to one of absolute impartiality. Any hint of favouritism would lead assuredly to one side or the other taking offence, the result of which would be either an immediate end to the settlement process or a lengthening of it. On orders from Curzon, Howard took pains to assure the Spaniards that Britain would not conclude a separate agreement with the French to exclude Spain from the Tangier settlement. For the first months of 1923, Howard's diplomacy centred on relaying such assurances to both Alfonso and the liberal ministry in Madrid.[117] In this time, the Spanish pushed for an early conference. Although Howard, supported by Arnold Robertson, the British consul at Tangier, also argued for an early conference in order to avoid charges that Britain obstructed the settlement process, neither Crowe nor Curzon were prepared to consider such a course whilst the Lausanne negotiations inched along.[118] Curzon would do nothing until the Turkish settlement had been achieved, since those negotiations had corroded any faith the foreign secretary and his advisers might have had in the good intentions of the French to reach an equitable settlement in the Near East or anywhere else. But by May, with the Lausanne talks progressing, Curzon accepted a French proposal for preliminary talks by experts on Tangier to prepare for the main conference *à trois*.[119] Anxious to settle, the Spanish endorsed this idea, paving the way for a meeting of experts in London beginning in late June to remove the diplomatic impedimenta which might complicate the business of the main conference anticipated for later in the year.

Throughout this process, Howard followed directions despatched from London, sent analyses of the Spanish situation to the Foreign Office when he judged them appropriate, and, depending on the circumstance, cajoled, coddled, or threatened the Spanish to force them along the road to settlement.[120] The experts met from 29 June to 17 July but, as a need arose for the French and Spanish delegates to consult with their home governments, at that point they adjourned temporarily. The final set of preliminary discussions was set for August, but was delayed further, until October. In the interim, Primo de Rivera seized power in Spain.

For Howard and the Curzon Foreign Office, Primo's overthrow of parliamentary government had the potential of bringing much-needed political stability to Spain. Before Annual, domestic Spanish unrest had created some diplomatic difficulties for Britain, none insurmountable. After the Riff victory, despite decided advances made in 1922 and 1923 on the tariff treaty and Tangier, Howard and the Foreign Office became distressed at what the ambassador characterised as 'the sort of whirlpool into which Spanish politics have been plunged'.[121] Before Annual, the power struggle between the politicians and the juntas had been relatively straightforward. Afterwards, not only did division exist between the politicians and the soldiers, but arguments arose over the question of responsibility. Amongst the politicians, the 'ins' and 'outs', the left and the right, the republicans and monarchists attacked each other to acquire political advantage. Within the armed forces, the juntas on the mainland and the army in Morocco fell out over promotions, the fate of the Moroccan military governor at the time of Annual, and other issues. The struggle amongst the various factions of politicians and soldiers continued until Primo moved in September 1923 to bring order to the country. Thus, for two years, Morocco served as the focal point for domestic unrest in Spain.

Howard realised that in cold diplomatic terms, Britain faced uncertain Spanish policy in Morocco. This affected the western Mediterranean balance of power. Until the political situation in Spain stabilised, which could come only with a resolution of the responsibility debate, Spanish Moroccan policy fell subject to the caprices of whatever political wind happened to be blowing from Madrid. That such a wind could blow in the direction of a substantial reduction in the Spanish presence could not be discounted. Howard stressed this when he and Crowe sought to clarify Britain's Spanish policy in early 1922: 'If Morocco proves a millstone around the neck of Spanish finance for any considerable time, there may be a reaction against keeping it, which the King, the Conservatives, and the Army may not be able to resist.'[122] Whilst Howard and his colleagues in London reckoned a complete Spanish withdrawal to be unlikely,[123] there existed the likelihood of a substantial paring of Spanish troop levels in the protectorate. But it remained difficult for the Foreign Office to respond to the situation in the western Mediterranean because of the unsettled condition of Spain's political and military circles. It would be easier determining a response if consistent policy emanated from Madrid. Even if such a policy meant a reduction of Spain's imperial presence in North Africa, at least British policy could be set within defined limits. With all of the other major problems facing the Curzon Foreign Office – besides

Lausanne, the French occupation of the Ruhr beginning in January 1923 threatened the Paris peace settlement – it was necessary for Spain to recede as a diplomatic worry. Hence, Howard observed developments in Spanish internal politics with interest throughout 1922 and 1923.

Howard watched as three governments came and went in the year and a half after Annual. In December 1922 that liberal ministry had come to office chiefly on the promise that it could settle the Moroccan question. United from a hodge-podge of liberal factions earlier in 1922, this coalition produced political pronouncements on a range of issues, pronouncements 'mainly concerned with the extremely vague generalities'.[124] An exception concerned Morocco, where the liberals suggested 'co-operation with France and an early conclusion of military operations'. When the liberals took office, they did so as a minority, refusing to form a coalition with any conservative faction. But they did begin political manoeuvring to force a crisis in the Cortes, which would allow them to call elections to provide the parliamentary majority necessary to deal with 'the burning question of responsibility for the Annual disaster'.[125]

Howard was not sanguine about a return to stability. His assessment of the domestic situation penned after his first year remained as true two years later. The emergence of 'some sane, wise and strong man' to impose stability still offered the best hope for Spain in terms of British foreign policy interests. The emergence of Mussolini's fascist government only six weeks before the crisis that brought the Spanish liberals to power might provide a paradigm for Spain. In discussing this latest crisis with prominent Spaniards, including liberals, Howard and his staff found general support for the contention that 'Spanish politics have for years consisted in competition in intrigue and corruption between bands of politicians and in whom the country has lost all faith and for whom they have no longer any respect.'[126] Alfonso's political credit stood low: to protect his position and throne, he now colluded openly with favoured politicians and army officers. According to one Embassy liberal source, the juntas stood as 'a reaction against this "Kaiserism"'. Moreover this liberal, appalled by political squabbling and royal machinations with the monarchist parties and senior officers, saw a volatile situation emerging: 'Out of such material, could leaders only be found, might be developed a movement like the "Fascismo" of Italy; the regeneration of Spain might be achieved could they only find a Mussolini.'

Howard's pessimism about Spain's domestic plight did not abate during the first eight months of 1923, a time marked by the continued bankruptcy of parliamentary government and junta activities. Labour unrest had declined markedly after the bad year of 1920[127] and, though the extreme left periodically burst on the scene with some 'outrage' to discredit the constitutional system, the moderate left, the vast majority, eschewed any connexion with the Third International and the Red Syndical International and began to involve itself in the political process.[128] Whilst some authorities argue that the advent of the liberals provided Spain with a chance for normalcy, based on honest administration and social reform,[129] the Howard Embassy witnessed the traditional wire-pulling of a government assuring its survival.[130] The Foreign Office shared Howard's despondency, agreeing with his assessment that 'the corruption of political life is such that an urgent reform is needed, though whether that reform should take the shape of a Fascista movement in Spain is naturally a very different matter'. An attempt to emasculate legally the juntas had occurred just before the liberals took office, which only forced the juntas into rare quiescence. But the juntas remained unhappy because a number of junior officers from amongst their number were being indicted for dereliction of duty during the Moroccan campaign. Although the juntas' response remained unclear, the Embassy felt the juntas had the power to disrupt the trials of their members or, should guilty verdicts be handed down, employ a range of legitimate blocking tactics within the army to delay sentencing indefinitely.[131] During the period preceding the April 1923 national elections, the politicians and the juntas jockeyed for advantage, the politicians in the glare of publicity, and the juntas in the shadows. The showdown would come after the election when the responsibility question would have to be resolved by the new government.

Howard concluded, watching this civilian–junta manoeuvring, that a revolution might occur and, if it did, that it would come from the military on the right. 'Signs are not wanting that a Fascista revolution is being considerably canvassed and discussed in this country', he discerned before the elections, 'although at present the organisation necessary for such a movement is, I believe, non-existent.'[132] The advent of a majority liberal government after the voting stimulated the growth of such an organisation. The reason was not hard to find. After appointing a civilian high commissioner in Morocco, a break in the tradition of appointing a soldier, the liberals began to back-track on the responsibility question. Whilst the Supreme Military Court began to impose 'severe sentences' on officers cited in an official army enquiry, the new ministry had no desire to bring any civilian politicians to account for Annual. A succession of conservative and liberal governments had followed much the same policies in Morocco for fifteen years. The new Cabinet seemed content to let soldiers shoulder public responsibility and include the army amongst targets for reform.[133]

Within three days of liberal victory, Howard heard rumours of a junta plot 'to declare a military dictatorship, unless the civilians alleged to have had a share in the responsibility for the disaster...are brought to trial'.¹³⁴ Although this plot proved groundless, junta discontent remained. In May, the juntas joined with socialist deputies to demand civilian leaders be tried for their part in Moroccan policy. Masking their real intent behind constitutional and other arguments, these disparate elements were inspired by base concerns, the socialists to discredit their political opponents, the juntas to assure their 'opportunities for graft' and seek 'the blood of certain of their enemies among the civilian Ministers'.¹³⁵ Howard surmised that the likely candidate to lead a military dictatorship was General Francisco Aguilera Egea, the president of the Supreme Military Tribunal. Aguilera's purpose in getting severe sentences imposed on indicted officers seemed designed to force the new government to bring former civilian ministers to trial.

Howard deprecated Aguilera's potential as a military strongman: 'He is not the stuff of which successful dictators are made.'¹³⁶ But, in May, the situation remained unclear. Three months later, it did not. In the last week of August a ministerial crisis erupted over Morocco. With the exception of the war minister, the Cabinet favoured cutting military expenditures in the protectorate to divert money to reform programmes on the mainland. This could be accomplished only by having the army in Morocco retreat from its forward positions – permitting rebel control of more territory – consolidate nearer the coast, and then repatriate large numbers of unneeded troops. However, after a fact-finding mission by a senior officer, the General Staff supported holding the forward positions and, if possible, advancing from these. When the Riffs exploited this division in Spain by launching an offensive, the liberal government was forced to despatch reinforcements to help the beleaguered forces in Morocco; another Annual had to be avoided. Within Spain, the small Communist Party also sought to capitalise on the crisis by fostering a mutiny in the ranks of reinforcements destined for Morocco, a mutiny to be accompanied by revolution in Spain. More pitiable than anything else, this Communist intrigue failed almost as soon as it began, and the agitators within the departing troops were tried quickly and sentenced by a military court. Sensing the despatch of reinforcements might be ill-conceived, the liberal Cabinet halted the troop ships and recommended clemency for the single soldier-agitator sentenced to death. A crossroads within Spain had been reached: were the civilians or the soldiers to dominate?

Unknown to Howard and almost everyone else in Spain – including Alfonso – Primo de Rivera, the captain-general of Catalonia and a junta supporter, had over the summer replaced Aguilera as the focal point of army discontent with the politicians.¹³⁷ In an unexpected move, Primo declared martial law in Catalonia on 13 September, sought support from the other captains-general, and called on the king to dismiss the government.[138] The liberal government crumpled. Seeing that his position could be saved only by throwing in with the generals, Alfonso asked Primo to form a government. Within a week a military Directorate stood in place of the constitutional government – the Cortes was dissolved by the Directorate. By December 1923, four hundred army officers were appointed as 'Government Delegates' to direct and control municipal affairs throughout the country.[139] For better or worse, a strongman had emerged in Spain with the avowed purpose of 'cleaning up' the country.[140]

Howard and the Curzon Office remained unsure that in the long run Primo and the Directorate could make things right. Howard, who had met Primo a few times socially, had been aware of only one previous political act by the general, a December 1921 speech advocating that Spanish Morocco be traded for Gibraltar.[141] Howard opined that Primo was 'a distinguished officer, but of an impulsive character'.[142] The Foreign Office doubted the ability of 'a junta of Spanish generals' to govern effectively and, echoing Howard's misgivings about Primo, cautioned that 'there is no reason to think he is another Mussolini'.[143] Yet, despite holding the new Spanish leader in less regard than Mussolini, Villiers minuted two weeks after the coup: 'On the whole I think one is justified in believing that the bloodless revolution will effect some purification of and improvement in the highly diseased Spanish body politic.'[144] Primo had indicated initially that his government would hold power for a short time. Howard disbelieved this and, by the year's end, Primo proved him prescient with a speech indicating that the Directorate had a long and hard road to travel.[145] For the British, at least, this meant stability in Spain and consistent Spanish foreign policy. This made Howard's final months in Madrid relatively easy in a diplomatic sense since Primo's rise brought significant benefits to British interests in the western Mediterranean. First, the Tangier question was settled by the middle of December; the second phase of the experts' conference met between 6 and 10 October, the main conference from 29 October to 18 December, and, although the Spanish delegates objected to some points in the final draft of the convention, Primo ordered them to sign.[146] Secondly, in Morocco, the Directorate endorsed immediately the liberal cabinet's decision to withdraw Spanish forces from the indefensible interior to strategically sound positions nearer the coast.[147] Though this decision opposed the wishes of the juntas and some senior officers, the Directorate had a politically impregnable position from which to impose its will. But a tactical military withdrawal had to be supported by Powers willing to back Spain against French expansionism. Showing decided diplomatic skill, Primo secured Mussolini's support, using a long-planned state visit by Alfonso to Rome to do this, a visit during which a number of public references to fascist solidarity figured prominently.[148] He worked hard to get the British on his side against the French by accepting a Tangier settlement that did not exactly square with Spain's interests. Primo also discussed the aims of Spanish foreign policy with Howard, stressing that the one 'orientation he wished to give Spanish foreign policy was close cooperation with Great Britain...[as the Spanish] could not go on indefinitely shouldering this burden [in North Africa] alone without at any rate diplomatic support against French pretensions and schemes in Morocco and on behalf of interests which were almost as much those of other countries as their own'.[149]

Howard reckoned that Primo's desire to keep Anglo-Spanish relations running smoothly was genuine. The Foreign Office rejoiced, believing that as 'a military dictator, General Primo de Rivera displays a rather statesmanlike grasp of the situation and needs of his country'.[150] Whilst the Foreign Office still assessed cautiously the change in the western Mediterranean balance of power, Spanish foreign policy seemed to be entering a less erratic, more predictable phase. For Howard and his colleagues, protecting British interests in that region would be less difficult, reducing the chance of another crisis which would deflect British attention away from other more important areas such as western Europe, where the continuing Franco-German strain in the wake of the Ruhr occupation was important to the balance of power for the whole sub-continent. Thus, at the end of 1923, Howard could talk about his work in Madrid being marked by 'new-found peace'.[151]

9

Washington 'redux': rebuilding good relations, 1924–1927

> If...we act on the assumption that, war between Great Britain and the United States being impossible, we are indifferent as to what action the United States Government may take with reference to their navy, and that we have no intention of competing with America in the matter of naval armaments, I am inclined to think that one of the principal arguments of the Big Navy School here will disappear and that the mass of voters, and consequently Congressmen, will be less willing to spend money on the armaments desired by that School.
>
> Howard, October 1924

I

In the months following Primo's coup, Howard enjoyed the 'new-found peace' in Anglo-Spanish relations that conducting business with a stable regime entailed. 'Life for the moment', he later recorded, 'was, therefore, moving on more comfortable lines than it had for the past three and a half years.'[1] Turning 60 in September 1923, he now seemed content to end his diplomatic career in Madrid building on the success he had achieved in the difficult two years after Annual. However, this did not happen, for unexpectedly, on 14 December 1923, Curzon wired his intention to have Howard succeed Sir Auckland Geddes as ambassador in Washington.[2] The foreign secretary's laconic offer was accompanied by a telegram from Tyrrell, now an assistant under-secretary at the Foreign Office, who as 'an old friend' urged Howard to ignore any personal misgivings about accepting this transfer in 'consideration of the best interests of the country and your service'.[3] As Howard wrote in his memoirs, 'a bombshell fell on me to disturb my new-found peace'.[4]

After two days of soul-searching, Howard felt that, for both personal and professional reasons, he might not be the best choice for this post. He put these in a private letter which he sent to the foreign secretary through the Duke of Sanlucas, a Spanish friend leaving Madrid on 17 December and expecting to reach London before the next scheduled diplomatic pouch.

Howard explained that, although he might possess some of the qualifications as ambassador in Washington, he lacked 'the principal ones which are I think legal training and ready speech'.[5] He referred to Bryce and his achievements, noting that 'I should feel hopelessly inadequate for the task remembering what he was'. Howard stressed, too, that his sons were attending school in England, hence he could either take them to the United States for schooling there or resign himself to seeing them just once a year during his annual leave. Since he and Isa 'would deplore' depriving the boys of an English education, the latter course would have to be followed. 'I have very strong feelings about the duty of parents in educating children to grow into good citizens and I may say frankly that they are the chief joy of my life and that long separation from them would be the greatest misfortune that could happen to me.' He ended by noting that Isa was 'a wretched sailor' who would find regular crossings of the Atlantic difficult. Given all of this, Howard suggested that Curzon might reconsider his offer. But putting duty to his country above all else, he indicated that he would transfer if Curzon thought it in the best interests of Britain to do so. Knowing that Sanlucas would not arrive for a day or so, Howard telegraphed both Curzon and Tyrrell to say he had written and they could soon expect his letter.[6]

By a twist of fate, Howard's letter did not reach the Foreign Office until 20 December. Sanlucas had been 'unable to resist the temptations of Paris, and had lingered there several days'.[7] In the interim, Curzon put Howard's name to the Americans as Geddes' successor. Complicated reasons existed for doing so, which the foreign secretary explained carefully to Howard.[8] The Conservative government of which Curzon was a part would soon have to relinquish power to the Labour Party led by James Ramsay MacDonald. In a minority in the Commons following a general election on 6 December, the Conservatives, now led by Stanley Baldwin, could not long survive the combined opposition of Liberals and Labour. Curzon sought to avoid a Labour Party hack taking the Washington Embassy, 'one of the two or three blue ribands of the Service' given the growing power of the United States in the post-war world. Therefore, he had to appoint a successor to the infirm Geddes as soon as possible. Curzon assured Howard that he was being transferred because he possessed unequalled qualification – '[Bryce] hoped one day you would be his successor...I thought you the best appointment & indeed the only one <u>in the service</u> that I could contemplate with sending...' (emphasis in original). Whilst understanding Howard's personal misgivings, Curzon observed realistically that 'we all of us have on occasion to subordinate our feelings in such matters of public duty'.

Howard also received information on his appointment from Crowe.

Crowe and Tyrrell had a hand in Howard's transfer to Washington,[9] and their reasons for having Howard move, apart from having the most gifted diplomat there, stemmed from wanting to re-assert Foreign Office primacy in the process that made British foreign policy. Like Curzon, Crowe emphasised that of those of ambassadorial timber, Howard had the most experience and knowledge of the United States to represent British interests in Washington.[10] That Howard would make sacrifices to do so was 'fully realized and[,] by all who understand the situation, appreciated at its full value'. But just as important as the quality of representation stood the need for the Foreign Office and the Diplomatic Service to reverse the trend begun by Lloyd George of having British foreign policy dominated by unschooled political appointees. Ambassadorial appointments had to go to seasoned professionals to reverse the Lloyd Georgian revolution in foreign policy-making. 'It is a critical moment for our much-suffering service', declared Crowe, 'and to recapture the embassies from the outsiders is a thing which I have very much at heart.' The permanent under-secretary admitted his clandestine efforts to affect appointments to other major embassies, especially Berlin, but acknowledged 'hitherto I have failed'. As Howard planned his move, he realised that he would be both representing his country and helping re-establish professionalism in the making and execution of British foreign policy.

II

Howard knew a daunting task faced him in his new post. For almost a decade, British representation in Washington had lacked the dynamism and purpose of action that marked it under Bryce. Indeed, the renewal of good Anglo-American relations accomplished by Bryce, helped in its first phase by Howard, had been allowed to decay by a series of poor ambassadorial appointments. Spring Rice, a Service man and Bryce's successor, had been a disaster. Priggish, unwilling to modify his attitudes, and possessing an acerbic wit which he used undiplomatically, he alienated Americans and their leaders. On his appointment, Spring Rice wrote Howard that 'I shall get a good many bricks hurled at my head especially when they realise that I am not a Bryce and do not intend to kiss Sunday school girls or lay foundation stones.'[11] Within two months of Spring Rice arriving at the American capital, Howard learnt: '[Bryce] had made himself extremely popular here & although many people are very kind there is no doubt that the change of ambassadors is not altogether welcome. But the worst of it is not *that* feeling but the impression which appears to prevail that the British ambassador is to represent the US in London as much as, or more than, London in the US.'[12] Tied to the fact that he had been selected for Washington because his friends there were Republicans like Roosevelt – Grey's Foreign Office assumed the Republicans would win the 1912 elections – his stock with Wilson's Democratic Administration which took office in early 1913 remained low until his removal in 1917.

Howard knew, too, that following Spring Rice, Lloyd George's political appointments had failed to represent British interests effectively in Washington.[13] One of the prime minister's oldest cronies, Lord Reading, succeeded Spring Rice. A gifted jurist, he served in Washington from January 1918 to May 1919, a difficult task as he had been appointed Lord Chief Justice in 1913 and did not relinquish this post until 1921. This and business interests meant Reading's Washington work had been interrupted by intermittent trips to Britain. Following Reading's final departure, there was no ambassador for ten months; this saw the counsellors at the Embassy managing affairs. Geddes took over in March 1920 but, in his four-year tenure, deriving from inept public relations and his advancing blindness, his achievements went from weakness to weakness. For instance, he had been impolitic enough to criticise publicly United States immigration authorities in New York whilst, for most of his last year as ambassador, he had been invisible as he sought to cure his eye problems at clinics outside of the United States. Failure by a Service man and political appointments had been compounded by a special mission sent by Lloyd George in late 1919 to discuss with Wilson the critical questions of Ireland, naval policy, and the League. Comprised of Grey and one assistant, Tyrrell, this mission had been singularly unsuccessful. Wilson had suffered a stroke, so that his wife seemed to run affairs. With the president unwilling to meet Grey because of a misunderstanding involving a junior member of the Embassy and Mrs Wilson, this personal pique precluded even tacit Anglo-American understanding on those questions. Marking in essence the transition from the Reading to the Geddes embassies, Grey's mission only compounded the ineffectiveness of British diplomatic representation at its highest level in the post-war United States.

Howard's experiences had taught him that an ambassador sets the tone for the diplomatic representation of his country. Edward Malet had been a success in Bismarck's Berlin; Fairfax Cartwright a mediocrity in Habsburg Vienna. The impact of British diplomacy had varied accordingly in these capitals. Howard surmised that Curzon and Crowe wanted him in Washington to re-establish the civility and polish, coupled with an understanding of Americans and their problems, that had distinguished the Embassy under Bryce. Howard's diffidence in accepting this post shows this, a diffidence deriving from the enormity of the task facing Geddes' replacement: reviving an effective ambassadorial presence and, on this, building a firm Anglo-American relationship. It was not that Howard doubted his particular diplomatic skills, which had brought him a knighthood, awards, and the Madrid Embassy. But he felt that the ambassador in the United States had to possess special qualities – a legal mind and an ability to make speeches. Clearly, the foreign secretary and his advisers did not see it that way. They wanted a proven diplomat with sound analytical skills and a calm approach to problems, in short supply since Bryce's departure in 1913. Moreover, the United States at that time had a Republican as president, Calvin Coolidge, with two Republican-controlled houses of congress. It was no secret that Howard's American friends were chiefly Republicans, like James Garfield. But, just as important, his circle of American acquaintances had widened, through his work in Stockholm and Paris, to include influential Democrats and others like Edward House. Should the Republicans suffer electoral defeat in scheduled elections in November 1924, Howard, unlike Spring Rice, would not suddenly find himself cut adrift from those holding power.

Also in Howard's favour lay his knowledge of and experience with the United States and its foreign policy. When Curzon and Balfour chose Reading's successor, they agreed that he should be politically prominent in Britain to add lustre and prestige to an already beleaguered Embassy;[14] at that time Geddes, a wealthy businessman, served as president of the Board of Trade. However, Geddes' ignorance of the United States, surfacing in events like his *faux pas* concerning New York immigration authorities, impaired his ability to represent Britain. This was not so with Howard. His varied American contacts since 1906 had provided valuable first-hand lessons about United States diplomacy and its domestic context. The fisheries dispute in 1907–8, with Root's comment about the 'affected interest' of the Gloucester Fleet, had shown that American politicians at times cared more about the parochial concerns of their electors than the national interest, in this case good relations with Canada. Howard's blockade diplomacy in Sweden and his work in Paris demonstrated that in other instances the men at the top of the American foreign-policy-making establishment had to balance between ensuring American national interests and appeasing powerful domestic groups like traders, manufacturers, and Irish-, German-, Polish-, and other hyphenated Americans. On top of all of this, Howard comprehended the division of responsibility between the executive and the legislature in the United States over treaty-making. In his time in Washington in 1907–8, he watched as Root manoeuvred to find a settlement with the Canadians that would pass the Senate. More recently, Wilson's inability to secure Senate ratification of the Treaty of Versailles stood as a striking example of the power of the national legislature in the United States to force the executive along a road it had no wish to travel.

Howard understood, too, that American leaders tended to assert that their foreign policy was imbued with a high moral tone lacking in that of other states, especially of Britain. Phrases like 'protecting the freedom of the seas' or 'ensuring national self-determination', tumbling easily from American lips and bandied about by the American press until they became dogma in the United States, served simply to mask the efforts of Democratic or Republican leaders to pursue or defend their country's narrow national interests. It mattered little if Americans believed such phrases, deluded themselves into thinking they were true, or cynically mouthed them. They were a fact of diplomatic life. Howard realised that Americans did not have a monopoly on moralising about diplomacy. Lloyd George was a master of this. But Howard had been able at every post since 1903 to separate the rhetoric from the substance in assessing his host government's foreign policy and formulating his responses accordingly. The Foreign Office did not doubt that Esme Howard would avoid encumbering himself with trite phrases of American leaders, that he would look beyond them to see the real intent of United States foreign policy.

Whilst Howard may have been somewhat diffident in assessing his ability to handle the Washington Embassy, he possessed no illusions about what he had to do as ambassador and how he should go about it. Howard was an 'Atlanticist', one who believed that Anglo-American diplomatic collaboration could resolve not only European threats to international peace and security but also those in the Pacific and Far East.[15] Along with other 'Atlanticists', a diverse group ranging from decided pro-Americans like Kerr and Cecil to more cautious ones such as Balfour and Lloyd George, Howard saw the United States as the best ally Britain could have in defending its position as the pre-eminent global Power. His American experiences had also shown him that the United States had emerged as a Power which, with its massive economic strength and growing interests outside of the western hemisphere, had the potential to hobble Britain in the wider world. Given American isolationism, coupled with anglophobic sentiment amongst important sections of United States public opinion, especially Irish-Americans and people of that ilk, Howard understood that American leaders would be reluctant to combine with Britain in keeping international peace in those areas where British and American interests coincided. Consequently, Howard took his chief task whilst at Washington to be ensuring an amicable Anglo-American relationship and, should anti-British feelings arise in the United States either in government or amongst public opinion, working to defuse any American threat to Britain and its Empire.

Complicating Howard's work were powerful men in Britain with little love for the United States, let alone Anglo-American collaboration. Imperialists like Hankey, who saw the United States as a threat to Britain's global Power status, and an array of politicians, like those angered at American intransigence over the settlement of Britain's war debt to the United States, were intent on not conceding to the Americans on any diplomatic issue.[16] They seemed prepared either to isolate Britain within the Empire, defending both against the United States and any other interlopers, or to ignore the United States in British diplomatic calculations. Thus, for Howard, as he prepared to move to Washington, Spring Rice's comment ten years earlier about the British ambassador representing 'the US in London as much as, or more than, London in the US' had not lost any of its relevance.

Howard outlined the method by which he would conduct Britain's diplomatic business in Washington in a speech on 1 February 1924. This occurred at a dinner organised by the Pilgrim Society, a private organisation dedicated to improving Anglo-American amity, to honour Howard and the American ambassador in London, Frank Kellogg.[17] Since Ramsay MacDonald, who had become prime minister and foreign secretary just eight days before, attended this function and said nothing afterwards about Howard's words, the new ambassador's ideas clearly had the approval of his new political master. 'I have been accused of being an old diplomatist', Howard confided to his audience, 'an accusation to which I at once plead guilty.' But, whilst allowing that many people in the post-war world reckoned that 'the mentality of the old diplomatist is one in which vanity and futility have laid down together and red tape and guile have kissed each other', Howard argued that 'old diplomacy' was not 'all wholly bad'. He outlined with examples a series of maxims that had been handed down to him by successful 'old diplomatists' under whom he had served, chiefly Malet and Sanderson. These maxims were: 'the diplomat is the servant of [his] Government...and must always obey his instructions though he may soften and tone down their asperities'; 'Never write or speak if you feel indignant, however righteous you may think your indignation, for you are likely to offend the other party and regret it'; 'Don't trouble about style so long as you make your meaning perfectly clear'; 'Never create incidents'; 'Never do anything very secret or very clever; it will land you in trouble'; and 'Always give your opponents credit for being in good faith.'

Howard's Pilgrims speech did not entail a simple defence of old diplomacy. The new international order hammered out at Paris had created new challenges which would have to be overcome if Britain, with its Empire, was to maintain its global presence. Appreciating American strength in that new order, and realising since serving under Bryce that the political culture of the United States posed some unique problems for British diplomacy, he understood the need to get the British message across to Americans in all regions of their vast country. He told his audience that he would have to make speeches whilst ambassador – this had been preying on his mind since Curzon's offer and had been a major consideration in his correspondence with the departing foreign secretary. Howard's peroration emphasised a commitment to reversing the failure of effective British representation in the United States, this by following the maxims of old diplomacy and mixing them with a visible ambassadorial presence:

> I may say this in conclusion, that by carrying on the tradition of the old diplomacy, in which I have been schooled, and by following to the best of my ability in the footsteps of another friend and chief, James Bryce, that great master of Anglo-American goodwill, I hope, with God's help, to do my duty as His Majesty's representative in Washington, and to promote that real and abiding friendship between the two countries which each Pilgrim here present wishes to see maintained and increased.

Knowing that Washington would certainly be his last post before retirement, Howard was going to make certain he capped his career with success in the United States to safeguard Britain's position as the only global Power.

III

In late February 1924, Howard arrived in a United States that had changed in many ways from that which he had left sixteen years before. 'Skyscrapers had multiplied and were continuing to multiply', he later recorded, 'and everywhere there was much noise of riveting steel bolts, a very characteristic noise in the streets of New York and other American cities.'[18] Here stood the United States at the height of 'the Roaring Twenties', and it impressed the new ambassador as a place of excitement, innovation, and change. Here lay the reason why the United States had altered since 1908, something Howard analysed in his memoirs by recalling visits to three successful American corporate enterprises, the Ford Motor Company in Detroit, the *Chicago Tribune* presses in Chicago, and the Eli Lilly drug plant in Indianapolis:

> As I see it the difference between English and American methods of industry is that while the former often regard any new thing or even the idea that there may be any new thing under the sun with the deepest suspicion, in America the mere hint that there may be a new method of producing some article at once creates a tingling desire to try to see whether it is not better than the one in use.[19]

Howard surmised that British policy had to respond wisely, not precipitously, to the Republican America of the 1920s, with its ability to absorb new concepts and transform them into practical expressions of industrial power. Here lay the substance of the American challenge to Britain in this period: a people willing to change if change meant improvement, whilst at the same time possessing the scientific, technological, and economic capacity to do so. Howard did not see the United States outstripping Britain in this regard – Britain had advantages of its own like established trade patterns – but he and other British diplomatists had to be wary of the potential international power of the United States deriving from its strong and adaptable domestic economy. Britain had other diplomatic concerns besides the Anglo-American relationship, principally maintaining the European balance of power and defending the Empire in the east. It could not divert all of its attention and resources to the American question.

Howard saw, as well, that in one fundamental way the United States had not changed since 1908: there existed a self-satisfaction within the United States that precluded appreciation for anything not American. President Calvin Coolidge, who took office in August 1923 following Warren Harding's sudden death, personified this attitude. Soon after the Howards arrived, Coolidge told Isa 'that he thought he would never visit Europe because America had everything he needed to learn, against which singular belief she, <u>Romana di Roma</u> and citizen of no mean city, in her own direct fashion and to his amusement, vigorously protested'.[20] A diplomatic corollary of this attitude emerged as a tendency to be insensitive towards, and in some cases to ignore purposely, other Powers' viewpoints because they did not square with American ones. Howard had seen this in the Roosevelt Administration's handling of the Canadian question in 1907–8 and, at the Paris Peace Conference, in many of Wilson's endeavours. Howard's American experiences had taught him about the necessity for prudent diplomacy towards the United States, but one that did not surrender British advantages for the sake of appeasing American self-esteem. He put the matter succinctly in his memoirs: 'My American friends will, I hope, understand that if I do not always in these pages attempt to prove everything in their country is – in my humble opinion – perfect, this does not mean that...I left Washington less sure that the safety of our world depends more than any other proposition on a good understanding and friendship between the United States of America and the British Commonwealth of Nations, but without capitulations on either side.'[21]

For most of his first year as ambassador, Howard did not face any major problem in Anglo-American relations. In fact, he began his tenure at Washington during a period of unusual diplomatic calm. Until the middle of 1923, those relations had suffered from a series of issues deriving from the war and the Peace Conference: settling Britain's war debt to the United States; ensuring European security without American help thanks to Senate rejection of Versailles; and grappling with the American demand for naval equality with Britain.[22] By the time that Howard arrived in Washington, all of these questions had seemingly ceased to be divisive. In January 1923, Baldwin, then the chancellor of the exchequer, negotiated a debt settlement with the Harding Administration. Although this agreement created some anti-American sentiment in Britain, the canker of the war debt had begun to heal. Whilst Anglo-American economic diplomacy continued in 1924 over German reparations, through each country's participation in the Dawes committee, this was a multilateral endeavour; however, as these reparations discussions were held in London, they bypassed Howard's Embassy completely.

Howard found, too, that the problems relating to European security and naval limitation caused his Embassy little concern. By early 1924, his political masters in London, both the Conservatives and their Labour successors, had decided to ignore the Americans in resolving the problem of European security, which had become acute after January 1923 when French paranoia about Germany led to the Ruhr occupation. The general British idea involved relying on the collective power of League members to ensure peace and security. Although the final shape of this policy had yet to emerge when Howard arrived in Washington – Baldwin's government seemed ready to endorse the Draft Treaty of Mutual Assistance, by which League members would be obliged to undertake mutual support if any of their number were attacked, and MacDonald seemed unwilling to conclude a security arrangement approved by the Conservatives – continuing discussions in Europe on this matter had little impact at that stage in the United States. The thorniest problem of the three, naval arms equality, had been partially settled at the Washington conference in late 1921–early 1922 when Britain and the United States agreed to formal parity in capital ships, those over 10,000 tons. Whilst the Washington conference failed to eliminate Anglo-American naval tensions – lesser warships had not been limited, notably cruisers, the principal weapon for attacking and defending maritime routes and imposing blockade – these tensions had for the moment ceased to be an irritant. For Howard, the diplomatic calm that marked Anglo-American relations throughout 1924 allowed him to dedicate much time and effort to the task of improving Britain's image in the United States, this without having his attention deflected by the need to consider more pressing problems.

Prior to sailing for New York, Howard received briefings from Crowe, Tyrrell, and Vansittart about relations with the United States. Significantly, after serving as Curzon's private secretary for three years, Vansittart had become head of the Foreign Office American Department on 2 February, the very day that Howard's appointment to Washington became official. Not only was the Foreign Office seeking a new departure in diplomacy towards the United States by changing both the ambassador and the chief department official responsible for monitoring American affairs, but it was doing so by having these two key positions filled by men who were close friends. Although conclusive evidence has yet to surface, this probably stemmed from the conscious efforts of Crowe and Tyrrell to improve British handling of the American question.[23] Howard supplemented these London briefings with consultations with his senior advisers at the Washington Embassy: Henry Chilton, the counsellor, and Hugh Tennant, the ambassador's private secretary. These discussions aided Howard in understanding the political intricacies of the American capital, since knowing about the general lines of issues whilst outside a country does not make up for the intimate knowledge of local affairs held by men on the spot.

Within a month of arriving, Howard became acquainted with Coolidge, the senior members of the Administration, and the heads of the other diplomatic missions in Washington.[24] In submitting his letters of appointment to the president, Howard met the antithesis of Theodore Roosevelt. Where Roosevelt had been 'rather careless about clothes, affecting a little the bluff heartiness of the Wild West and full of talk and knowledge of English literature', Coolidge was 'smart and slim, brushed up and very carefully dressed, and with his words so compressed, they were like meat lozenges, only more so'. But, despite this president's insularity and frosty and introspective character, Howard grew to like him: 'I knew I could trust him completely. He would never promise what he feared he could not perform.' On the other hand, Howard felt an immediate rapport with Charles Evan Hughes, the secretary of state. Howard believed that this man possessed in good measure a 'singularly balanced mind', 'equanimity and sound judgement', and 'perfectly level temperament'. Hughes, an eminent lawyer, had been the Republican presidential candidate who lost to Wilson in November 1916; and it was Howard's view that, had Hughes triumphed at that time, 'many of our troubles during the years that succeeded the War might have been avoided had he been the principal American delegate at the Paris Conference'. For the first year of his embassy in Washington – Hughes left the Administration early in 1925 – Howard had little difficulty in working with official Washington.

Howard also established political and social contacts. To tap into Congressional opinion, he sought out Senator Lodge, again the Chairman of the Senate Foreign Relations Committee. Although Lodge had difficulties with Coolidge because the senator supported American membership in the World Court, a League adjunct, and too willingly at times mouthed anti-British platitudes to placate his Irish constituents, Howard felt that Lodge had 'a sincere admiration and affection for Great Britain'.[25] Howard reaffirmed his friendships with prominent Washingtonians: James Garfield, now a respected elder of the Republican Party; Mabel Boardman, who had become one of the three commissioners of the city of Washington and the District of Columbia; Oliver Wendell Holmes, 'the Grand Old Man of the Supreme Court'; and Elihu Root, who, like Garfield, possessed elder statesman status within the Republican Party. To get a pulse on the Democratic Party's views on foreign policy, he cemented his ties with Colonel House. He also sought out members of the American diplomatic establishment like Edward Robinette, who had been American minister in Stockholm when Howard first arrived there in 1913 and, by 1924, occupied an executive position on the English-Speaking Union in Philadelphia.[26] In making the social rounds of the diplomatic corps, Howard realised the value of Jules Jusserand, the French ambassador and doyen of the Washington diplomatic corps, who was in the final period of a quarter century's service as France's chief representative in the United States. Howard found in Jusserand 'a perfect mine of information'. Within weeks of arriving in the American capital, Howard began to construct a network of political, social, and diplomatic contacts that could both give him valuable knowledge and allow him to get across the British view that much easier.

The 'old diplomacy' practised by Howard since 1903 had always involved using such contacts to help in the routine business of diplomacy. But, as he had confided to the London Pilgrims, given the size and heterogeneous nature of the United States, 'old diplomacy' had to be supplemented by Bryce's example of a visible and vocal ambassador. Therefore, during his first year in the United States, Howard made sixteen public speeches to a variety of organisations both within the Washington-New York-Philadelphia triangle, and outside on two excursions to Cleveland, Ohio and Louisville, Kentucky. The majority of these addresses, twelve of them, were little more than public relations exercises to outline British policy to Americans and anglophile groups: a few words to the St George Society of New York in April 1924; some remarks to the British Schools and Universities Club of New York in May; a eulogy to Bryce and his accomplishments to the St Andrews Society in Philadelphia in December; and so on.[27] Several constant themes emerged in these little speeches: emphasis on Britain's desire to have cordial relations with the United States; explaining some controversial British policies, like the Labour government's desire to normalise relations with Bolshevik Russia; and the need for Americans to appreciate the desire of Britain and the European Powers to effect a system of security on the continent. When the opportunity presented itself, especially when addressing American financial and commercial organisations, like the New York Board of Trade and Transportation, he stressed the importance of the close connexion 'between economics and foreign policies' in post-war reconstruction and as the underpin for sustained international peace.[28] A couple of times, he even appeared before non-political bodies and, as part of his strategy to be visible, talked engagingly about subjects near to his heart like 'The Art of Travel'.[29]

However, Howard delivered major speeches on four occasions to influential gatherings. Within a month of his arrival, the Pilgrim Society of New York honoured him with a dinner attended by more than a thousand people; the head table included key members of the Coolidge Administration, as well as diplomats like Jusserand. His message here, his first public address as ambassador, stressed the need for Anglo-American co-operation in international politics in order to preserve peace. This accorded with his 'Atlanticist' proclivities, but he went further by gently prodding his audience to consider the need for the United States to modify its political isolation from European affairs. After quoting the late President Harding, who had written about the impossibility of the United States maintaining 'an attitude of isolation and aloofness in the world', he commented:

This being so, I cannot believe that America will unquestionably feel the impulse to work in her own time and in her own way, for permanent peace in Europe on which, to put it on no higher grounds, so much of her own future prosperity depends.[30]

The lesson was one obviously delivered by a diplomat schooled in the tough world of European *realpolitik*: there would be nothing altruistic in American involvement in European affairs, as this course, not isolation, stood as the best safeguard of American external interests.

In Howard's other major speeches – to a gathering of American newspapermen the next month and, in December 1924, to the English Speaking Union in New York and a convention of American political scientists at Washington – he embroidered on this theme.[31] He also added new threads to give these influential Americans an appreciation of why Britain pursued the policies it did in Europe. The British government, whether Conservative or Labour, had little option but to involve itself in maintaining the balance of power. Though assuredly 'old diplomacy' of pre-war vintage, Americans had to realise that this diplomatic mechanism had worked successfully for several centuries in both Britain's interests and those of other European Powers. Even if it wanted, Britain could not ignore the continental ferment given Europe's geographic proximity to the British Isles. British diplomatists, it followed, were not tainted by seeking to have a say in creating a workable system of European security based on the balance of power. Besides, in the post-war era there existed instruments of the 'new diplomacy', like the League, which could be used to correct some of the weakness of the old. As he told the newspapermen, the 'new diplomacy' was 'less selfish, less violent, more considerate of the feelings and interests of others, more in accordance with Christian precept'. Howard confided that he shared the hope of many that the 'new diplomacy' would eventually become the norm, but until that time the British and the other Powers concerned about European security had to use the old.

Howard appreciated the power of the American press, both as an arbiter of American public opinion and as a compass showing in what direction that opinion lay. This had been driven home during his service at Washington twenty years before in matters like the Swettanham incident and the Lady Susan Townley affair. It was no coincidence that he chose to deliver one of his major speeches to the American Newspaper Publishers Association, accentuating the idea that the public in Britain and the United States would have an accurate image of either country only through the press. But it was not enough to reach audiences of up to a thousand people by delivering set speeches. This led Howard to consent to an interview with the *New York Sunday Times*, published on 1 June 1924 and then distributed to a wide audience by newspaper affiliates of the *New York Times* Syndicate.[32] The message in this interview conformed with what Howard had already spelled out in his other speeches, but its value came from its broad circulation. Moreover, when the opportunity arose, Howard used new communications technology to reach equally vast audiences. In speaking to the American Newspaper Publishers Association, he used a radio microphone – he had declined such a course for his New York Pilgrims speech out of deference to Jusserand, who would not consent to using such a device for his few words. According to the press report, Howard reached an estimated radio audience of two million people 'between the Atlantic Coast and the Middle West'.[33] Thus, in his first year in the United States, Howard attained his goal of being a visible and vocal ambassador along the lines established by Bryce.

For one who had made few public utterances in his career, and who expressed initial diffidence about taking the Washington Embassy because of the need to 'speechify', Howard quickly became accustomed to this part of his American duties. Naturally, no matter how anodyne, gentle, and moderate, speech-making on this scale was bound to raise some controversy. This happened when Howard spoke at Cleveland. In that speech, he discussed British policy towards Bolshevik Russia, which at that moment encompassed MacDonald's efforts to normalise Anglo-Soviet relations and conclude a commercial treaty. Some anti-communist Americans belonging to an organisation called the All-American Conference got his words garbled, so that they believed he had suggested that the United States follow Britain's lead.[34] Such was not the case, and the matter quickly died. This incident demonstrates the effectiveness with which Howard undertook this aspect of his diplomatic work in the United States. His speeches aroused almost no controversy, no critical editorials in newspapers or verbal attacks by politicians out to score easy political points by mouthing anglophobic sentiments. In fact, that he continued giving speeches throughout 1924 and into 1925, that his personal and diplomatic relations with American authorities remained unsullied, and that he never received Foreign Office censure shows he conducted himself with the utmost prudence in improving Britain's image within the United States.

For most of 1924, Howard concentrated on his public relations campaign, a function of the continuing smooth course of Anglo-American relations. This derived from the MacDonald government and the Coolidge Administration having different foreign-policy focusses and the need for each to concentrate on domestic affairs. For the MacDonald government, the chief diplomatic concerns centred on stabilising relations with Bolshevik Russia and finding some method to bring about a system of security on the continent. This led to the negotiation of Anglo-Russian trade and loans agreements by the late summer and the formulation of the Geneva Protocol.[35] For the Coolidge Administration, the passage of the Foreign Service Act in May saw substantial efforts directed towards the reorganisation and consolidation of the American diplomatic and consular services.[36] Moreover, on the one international issue in which the British and American governments participated together – the Dawes committee and report – there developed relative Anglo-American agreement on how to handle Germany's financial predicament.[37] In terms of domestic politics, MacDonald's minority government had to plan carefully every legislative move to avoid a non-confidence motion. As Anglo-Russian relations warmed, and as anti-communist sentiment in Parliament mounted, this became increasingly difficult. In the United States, combined presidential-congressional elections were scheduled for November. Burdened by corruption scandals he inherited along with Harding's Administration, Coolidge worked to present the Administration as efficient and the Republican Party as clean. The crunch in terms of domestic politics in both countries came in the autumn. In October, the MacDonald government fell over the issue of Anglo-Russian relations; a general election on 29 October saw a majority Conservative government elected under Baldwin. Baldwin's second ministry took power on 4 November, the same day that Coolidge and the Republicans won their elections to retain control of both the White House and Congress.

Although neither Howard nor his Foreign Office colleagues then realised it, the advent at the same moment of these two 'conservative' governments, both secure with the domestic political support accorded them, ushered in a new phase of Anglo-American relations. The quiescent period from the middle of 1923 to late 1924 had amounted to a respite in the troubled post-war Anglo-American relationship. Although financial differences had been resolved via the debt settlement, and initiatives like the Geneva Protocol demonstrated that Britain and the major European Powers were going to ignore the United States in achieving European security, the naval question in Anglo-American relations remained unsettled. The naval phase of Anglo-American relations occurred as the foreign-policy focus of the two governments began to converge in terms of national security and arms limitation. Difficulty arose because the goals behind those policies concerning naval construction differed fundamentally. During the Coolidge and early Hoover Administrations, the Americans undertook a concerted effort to achieve formal naval parity with Britain, something the British had to resist if their country had any chance of remaining the pre-eminent global Power.[38]

Howard became a central figure in meeting this American challenge. The diplomatic strategies devised by the Foreign Office and Cabinet to resist this challenge, one underpinned by American economic prosperity and industrial innovation, required advice from Howard on American motives, the vagaries of domestic American opinion, and other considerations which London had to weigh carefully in formulating policy. By the same token, as ambassador, Howard remained fundamental to the application of British policy towards the United States; it fell to him to utilise his diplomatic skills to 'obey his instructions' and, thereby, stymie the American threat to the security of Britain and the Empire. This American challenge to Britain continued until January 1930 – just two months before Howard completed his service as ambassador at Washington – when the Wall Street crash and the beginning of the London naval conference spelled the end of Anglo-American naval rivalry. But the five years between late 1924 and early 1930 taxed Howard, especially as Anglo-American relations were subjected to such strain that they almost ruptured in the winter of 1928–9. In this way, Howard found himself in Washington representing Britain in the United States, and explaining the United States to London, on an issue that increasingly became a matter of maintaining Britain as a Power of the first rank.

IV

For Howard, this new phase in responding to the American question began with the efforts of the new Baldwin Cabinet to help achieve European security. The first major foreign-policy issue considered by Baldwin and his colleagues involved whether to accede to the Geneva Protocol. The new foreign secretary, Austen Chamberlain, became a member of a CID sub-committee struck to examine the Protocol and recommend either its acceptance or rejection. In gathering information privately on the subject, Chamberlain instructed Howard to ascertain the American view of this proposed system.[39] Since the Protocol was essentially a League endeavour, and although Chamberlain admitted that 'I am under no delusion as to the prospect of the entry of the United States into the League in any time that I have to contemplate', the foreign secretary wanted to avoid any initiative that might push the Americans further away from the international organisation.

On receiving Chamberlain's instructions, Howard immediately saw Hughes. After indicating that the Baldwin government was considering the Protocol, Howard learnt of Hughes' unease towards this initiative.[40] Although designed mainly to ensure European security, the Protocol as a League contrivance had a theoretically universal application: in the Far East, Latin America, or anywhere a League member was threatened. '[Hughes] had hoped that the Protocol would die a natural death, because he saw in it numerous sources of trouble', Howard reported. 'In fact, if it went through as it was, America could hardly help regarding the League as a "potential enemy".' These were strong words. Suggesting with exaggeration that the Protocol could be considered a 'new Holy Alliance', Hughes showed that his chief concern lay with any League action that might occur under the provisions of the Protocol in Latin America. He postulated that American opinion would view such action as a violation of the Monroe Doctrine. Searching for a compromise, Howard suggested inserting a clause in the Protocol which would not bind the Imperial governments to support its application until there had been consultation and agreement with Washington. A similar clause had been in the old Anglo-Japanese alliance. Hughes thought this would suffice, though there could be no hint that the Coolidge Administration had agreed beforehand to such a course – anti-League feelings in the United States were too strong. Howard reported all of this, adding that Hughes had consulted Coolidge immediately afterwards, and that the president concurred with every word uttered by the secretary of state.

A month later, Howard received word from Chamberlain that Hughes' views would be included in the Foreign Office submission to the CID sub-committee.⁴¹ Chamberlain also squashed the compromise suggested by Howard. Although appreciating Howard's effort to breathe life into the Protocol, the foreign secretary believed it might undermine the League: 'It would turn the United States into a super-State with a vengeance, making them a court of appeal from all proceedings of the League and giving them a right of veto over its decisions...' Accordingly, although official American opposition to the Protocol was not the overriding factor in the Baldwin government's decision to reject – there existed reluctance to undertake its universal peace-keeping provisions, coupled with the fact it had been championed prior to November 1924 by Labour – Chamberlain added to the anti-Protocol sentiment by circulating a memorandum based on the Howard–Hughes conversation.⁴²

Whilst awaiting Chamberlain's reply, Howard assessed general American opinion about the Protocol.⁴³ He felt that the Foreign Office should be aware of this in order to understand the domestic constraints affecting the Administration's foreign policy. In the first place, Americans entertained legitimate concerns that 'the League of Nations may drive a wedge between them and South America'. If Britain or the other major League Powers wished American collaboration in applying sanctions against aggressive states, 'you must relieve the United States of their fear that the League of Nations will ultimately remove South America from their political sphere of influence'. Thus, in taking their hardline against the Protocol, Hughes and Coolidge were simply reflecting the concerns of their countrymen. In the second place, a political reality confronted the Administration. The Democratic Party had been weakened in the recent elections and could be discounted as an effective opposition for the foreseeable future. But, within the Republican Party, there existed a group of irreconcilables, strong isolationists who had led the successful fight against ratification of the Treaty of Versailles in 1919–20. By a quirk of fate, one of their most able members, Senator William Borah, now occupied the chair of the Senate Foreign Relations Committee. Lodge had died suddenly in November 1924, just days after the Republican victory. In assessing Borah's rise to this position of influence, Howard observed: 'I do not think we need expect Mr. Borah's Chairmanship to result in any particularly friendly attitude on the part of the Committee on questions which involve active American cooperation in international politics.'⁴⁴ It followed that if Coolidge wanted to ensure Republican unity to make governing the country easier, he would have to keep Borah's isolationist predilections in mind.

Howard's efforts in determining the American reaction to the Protocol, both generally and at the official level, were important in creating a good working relationship with the new foreign secretary. Chamberlain became foreign secretary, perhaps the most prestigious Cabinet post after the premiership, because Baldwin wanted to heal a rift within the Conservative Party between his followers and those of Chamberlain. This rift had developed at the time of Lloyd George's overthrow, so weakening the party that Labour formed its short-lived ministry in 1924. Because his career had suffered – Chamberlain had been the Conservative leader and had supported Lloyd George – he intended to use his position as foreign secretary to restore lustre to his reputation.[45] Baldwin gave Chamberlain complete control over British foreign policy, thereby reversing Lloyd George's experiment in prime ministerial control of diplomacy; this translated into the Foreign Office's re-emergence at the centre of the foreign-policy-making process in Britain. Howard impressed his new political chief in three ways. He showed that he could record and assess quickly a wide range of American opinion, thus assisting Chamberlain and the Cabinet in making difficult political decisions. Next, whilst he reinforced Chamberlain's opinions about the United States, he exposed the obstacles impeding a smooth League–United States relationship. Finally, Howard proved again that he could tread on dangerous political ground without alienating his hosts or compromising his government. For a foreign secretary intent on being successful, having an ambassador of Howard's mettle at Washington would make easier the pursuit of success. Getting Chamberlain's confidence assumed additional importance because, in April 1925, Crowe died unexpectedly. Although he used this untimely event as an excuse to move and retire some senior officials and diplomats, Chamberlain saw no reason to ease Howard out of the Washington Embassy.

Howard also aided Chamberlain in this early period of the second Baldwin government by shedding light on Hughes' retirement as secretary of state. On 9 January 1925, Howard learnt that Hughes would resign when the new Administration took office in March, and that Kellogg would be recalled from London to replace him.[46] Speculation arose within American press and political circles about Hughes' departure: that Hughes and Borah disagreed fundamentally on important issues like American membership of the World Court and the recognition of Soviet Russia; that Hughes and Coolidge were not getting along; and that the president sought a more 'pliable' secretary of state.[47] Supplementing a private conversation with Hughes with discreet enquiries around Washington, Howard found that Hughes' difficulties with Congress lay at the bottom of the change. Hughes wearied of his policies being deflected by senators and congressmen 'whose knowledge of foreign affairs was extremely limited' whilst, on the other side, Coolidge wanted an experienced man at the State Department who could work with Congress. Kellogg possessed such qualities. He had been a senator from 1917 to 1923 and, earlier, had risen to national prominence as the government's legal strategist who masterminded the dissolution of Standard Oil and the Union Pacific Railroad. By the time he replaced Hughes, however, Kellogg was 68. He had failed to impress the Foreign Office as an effective diplomat – he had been in London since 1923 – and, in the short time that Chamberlain dealt with him, he appeared 'a somewhat tired man, who had lost his power of grip and decision'.[48] Howard's enquiries suggested that Kellogg might hold office for only the first period of the new Administration because, at that moment, Coolidge required someone 'who was both personally conversant with European statesmen and had also a working knowledge of the Senate'.[49]

Howard knew of the president's strong desire for a new naval conference to extend the Washington treaty capital ship-building ratio to lesser craft. Coolidge had developed this theme in one of his first major speeches after his re-election, and similar views had been expressed to Howard in conversations with various members of the new Administration.[50] Although unstated in Howard's reports, this goal of the president would require a secretary of state who could not only get on with prickly politicians like Borah, but whose understanding of Congress's political caprices would help secure ratification of the resultant treaty. Hughes' dislike of Borah, coupled with enemies he had made within the American naval establishment during the Washington conference because of the concessions he had given the British and Japanese,[51] militated against his continuing in office. The advent of Kellogg augured well for a new naval conference. As new regimes took power in London and Washington, Howard and his Foreign Office colleagues recognised that key changes within the executive and legislative branches of the American government might have a significant impact on American policies towards Britain.

Howard's first exposure to the emotive issue of naval-arms limitation in the United States came with a series of events in late 1924 and early 1925. They fixed in him attitudes about the post-war United States, and its quest for global Power status, which lasted for the rest of his time in Washington and, thus, affected his diplomacy. The naval question had ceased to be a flashpoint in Anglo-American relations after late 1921, thanks to the Washington treaty, the troubles surrounding war debts and reparations, and the domestic political problems plaguing each country. But it still lurked in the shadows, threatening damage. The first event which drove this home to Howard came during the 1924 election campaign when John Davis, Coolidge's Democratic opponent, attacked the Washington treaty by charging that it gave certain strategic and technical advantages to Britain. Though Davis attempted to discredit a Republican diplomatic success, Howard's assessment implied that Davis' 'misrepresentations' had support in the United States.[52] Next, after the election, William Shearer, a naval expert and publicist, sued the American government to prevent it scrapping a battleship under provisions of the Washington treaty. Howard interpreted this as an effort by the United States 'Big Navy' party, a diverse group of politicians, journalists, retired naval officers, and steel, armament, and shipping interests, all navalist, jingo, and anglophobe, to arouse American opinion in favour of building the world's most powerful navy.[53] Finally, in late February 1925, Rear Admiral Phelps, a member of the United States Navy General Board, made a speech in which he argued that the 'possibility of serious differences with Great Britain regarding shipping policies could only be prevented by a strong United States navy'.[54] Howard reported that this assertion by a senior officer on the principal advisory committee of the United States Navy had forced the State Department to release a statement 'that no serious problem has arisen in Anglo-American relations and...that existing problems do not threaten serious complications'. Nothing came of these incidents in terms of disturbing Anglo-American relations, nor of some other minor ones that occurred at the same time.[55] However, that opposition politicians, 'Big Navyists', and even serving officers were willing to criticise Administration naval policies, and to do so by relying on anglophobic sentiments, raised concerns for Howard, Chamberlain, and the Foreign Office.

As Howard watched Davis, Shearer, and Phelps, he realised that the climate of American opinion had changed markedly since the days of Roosevelt. Although Britain had then presented some problems for American diplomatists – and the pathological anglophobia of Irish-Americans and others still existed – Bryce's achievement in helping to eliminate the earlier matters of contention had improved the tone of the Anglo-American relationship. But, by the middle of the 1920s, the pre-war rapprochement had begun to unravel. Whilst several American leaders recognised Japan's potential threat to American interests in the Far East,[56] the question for Howard was why had Britain been singled out by a range of influential Americans as their country's chief potential enemy? He knew from his Stockholm days that neutral rights at sea were fundamentally important to Americans. Given growing American isolationism, Americans were presupposing that the United States would not be drawn into another European war nor, as Hughes' words about the Protocol showed, any other conflict where the European Powers via the League were engaged. The United States seemed intent on being perpetually neutral. Hence, underneath the calls for 'a navy second to none' lay a determination to prevent Britain from again imposing a blockade against American seaborne commerce. Not only would an inability to break a British blockade be detrimental to American economic interests, it would indicate clearly the junior status of the United States in its global relationship with Britain. For both narrow national interests and reasons of prestige, influential Americans were advocating at least full naval equality with Britain. The anglophobia suffusing the comments of Davis and the others, especially Phelps' advocacy of a large navy to prevent future British interference with American shipping, showed that the possibility of an American naval challenge to Britain loomed large.

Howard realised that of all the problems in the Anglo-American relationship, the naval question held the potential of souring relations most and, given the economic strength and innovative capacity of American industry, of threatening the Royal Navy's ability to defend Britain's commercial and Imperial lines of communication. As an Atlanticist, he wanted to ensure the amity of the two principal English-speaking Powers. In the autumn of 1924, Howard had a conversation with House about the naval question. The nub of House's argument held that 'the American public was not really interested in armaments, that the best way to interest them and to make them willing to spend money on armaments was for a foreign government to oppose such arguments, and so give some colour to the accusations in the Hearst and other papers that the United States Government are bowing to the will of a foreign Power in not acceding to the demands of the Big Navy School'.[57] House stressed that if Anglo-American relations became embittered over naval construction, 'a spirit of national antagonism would at once be aroused which would carry Congress off its feet'. Thus, House suggested that Britain ignore the United States in determining Royal Navy strength; it could never out-build the United States given American economic resources and, besides, the idea of war between Britain and the United States was absurd.

Howard related this conversation to the Foreign Office, his despatch reaching London just as Chamberlain became foreign secretary. Howard believed that House's argument seemed 'very sound'. Public wrangling about technical issues like gun elevations would only serve to antagonise congressmen and senators, who would then push to have these things adopted. He surmised that if Britain made clear its desire not to enter into naval competition with the United States, 'Big Navy' propaganda would diminish. As a result, American public opinion and, therefore, Congress would not be inclined to spend money on 'a navy second to none'. Howard advised that it would serve British interests better if 'we act on the assumption that, war between Great Britain and the United States being impossible, we are indifferent as to what action the United States Government may take with reference to their navy'.

What Howard, with his Atlanticist leanings, proposed was a new approach to the most nettled problem not only in Britain's American policy, but also in its national security and Imperial defence. Such candour had rarely been part of British policy. Howard's words found guarded acceptance at the Foreign Office.[58] R. I. Campbell, the junior member of the American Department, concurred with Howard's support of House's views but stressed that the Foreign Office had to be wary of the 'Big Navy' propagandists who spoke and printed 'lies' in order 'to stir up that very racial tension antagonism which Col: House fears might carry Congress off its feet'. Endorsing Howard's arguments 'in view of our special relationship with the United States', Tyrrell cautioned that Britain's American policy had to be flexible. Vansittart also lined up with Howard though, typical of his suspicious nature, he warned of the folly in assuming that Britain and the United States might always be friends. When this despatch reached Chamberlain, he accepted Howard's assessment but ordered that nothing be done at that moment to tie his hands in his diplomacy towards the United States.[59] Howard's words had value. But the foreign secretary, in the midst of learning the intricacies of his office,[60] did not want to commit himself to anything that might mean a profound change in British diplomacy until he became familiar with both the policy and administrative sides of his new bailiwick.

As the New Year opened, Howard reported that both Coolidge and Borah seemed separately to be preparing the ground for a new naval limitation conference.[61] However, because of problems in Japanese–American relations caused by the passage of anti-oriental legislation in California, as well as Coolidge's reluctance to be seen to be prodded by Borah, an American call for such a conference would be delayed.[62] Coolidge's ostensible reason for retreating at this stage derived from League discussions about a world disarmament conference. In the light of these developments, Howard became acquainted with Chamberlain's general views on the American question in the context of the overall strategy the new foreign secretary would pursue.[63] By this time, March 1925, Baldwin's government had rejected the Protocol and Chamberlain had accepted the notion that a regional pact in Europe, giving security to both France and Germany, would offer the best defence of British interests. To prevent Britain from being sucked into another continental conflict, involvement in which would certainly weaken the country further, Chamberlain was prepared to have Britain guarantee the Franco-German border. 'With America withdrawn, or taking part only where her interests are directly concerned in the collection of money', the foreign secretary instructed Howard, 'Great Britain is the one possible influence for peace and stabilisation.' Howard learnt as well that whilst Chamberlain supported a new naval arms limitation conference, he would not push the president along. Chamberlain's problem stemmed from the French, chary of arms limitation until the security question was solved. For Howard, no doubt existed after reading Chamberlain's letters that the principal problem confronting the foreign secretary involved European security. He was going to do all possible to resolve this and then, if the situation merited, help tackle arms limitation; but first things first. The implication in this for Howard was that his Embassy had to do all in its power to ensure that Anglo-American discord on naval or other questions did not develop to threaten the delicate diplomatic manoeuvring then under way to bring about European security.

For two years, Howard worked to keep Anglo-American relations running smoothly whilst Chamberlain, the Cabinet, and the Foreign Office endeavoured to effect political and military stability in western Europe – and deal also with unexpected crises in Egypt and China.[64] By late 1925, Chamberlain succeeded in being 'the honest broker' in reconciling divergent Franco-German views on security: he played the pivotal role in the negotiation of the Locarno agreements, the series of treaties guaranteeing the Franco-German border whilst, simultaneously, stabilising Germany's eastern frontiers with several arbitration agreements.[65] But Chamberlain's efforts concerning European security did not end with Locarno, rather, he used this as a base on which to strengthen the co-operative spirit thus engendered. Part of the Locarno settlement involved Chamberlain's promise to Gustav Stresemann, the German foreign minister, to secure German membership in the League and acquire for Germany a permanent seat on the League Council, at once the formal acknowledgement of great Power status and a signal that Germany had returned to the comity of nations after its defeat in the war. Though Locarno was signed in October 1925, it took until September 1926 to get Germany into the League and on to the Council.[66] After this, Chamberlain used the League's apparatus – quarterly Council meetings and the annual Assembly – to keep the co-operative Locarno spirit alive. He, Stresemann, and Aristide Briand, the French foreign minister, used these League meetings to discuss face to face a variety of issues that had the potential of undermining European security.[67] In this process, Chamberlain tied British foreign policy firmly to the League, a strategy which, because of American isolationism and distrust of the international organisation, put greater distance between Britain and the United States.

Adding to Howard's need to keep the Anglo-American relationship running smoothly was the diplomatic corollary of Chamberlain's security diplomacy: arms limitation. In the summer of 1925, whilst the negotiations which culminated in Locarno were progressing, the League Council considered convening a League-sponsored disarmament conference to encompass air, land, and sea weapons.[68] In December, just as the exchange of the Locarno ratifications occurred, the Council established a Commission to prepare a draft treaty for an eventual World Disarmament Conference. Because naval limitation could not be handled adequately without United States involvement in the Preparatory Commission, the Baldwin government lobbied the League to issue an invitation to the Americans. This cut the political ground out from beneath Coolidge, who as recently as July 1925 repeated his desire for an American-sponsored naval conference in Washington.[69] However, as rejecting the League invitation would damage the United States reputation internationally and, as other important non-League members like Soviet Russia were also going to participate, the Coolidge Administration agreed to send a delegation to the Preparatory Commission in Geneva. In doing so, the American government added a caveat to its acceptance of the invitation: 'Participation in the work of the preparatory commission involves no commitment with respect to attendance upon any further conference or conferences on reduction and limitation of armaments.'[70] This statement genuflected to American isolationist sentiment whilst, cunningly, providing Coolidge with a way out should the Commission deliberations go against American interests. However, by the end of 1926, after holding two meetings, the commission had made little progress.

Throughout 1925 and 1926, Howard faced several incidents which, unless handled properly, had the potential of deflecting Foreign Office energies away from more pressing problems. They were of a minor nature but, because each possessed an emotive quality, threatened to inject poison into the Anglo-American relationship. Of these, two caused Howard real trouble. The first centred on the smuggling of bootleg liquor from Canada and the West Indies into the 'dry' United States. Little doubt existed that British subjects smuggled and that unscrupulous American politicians, like Borah, were willing to seize on this to attack Britain. Two days after Baldwin became prime minister, Howard wrote him a congratulatory letter and appended a lengthy discussion about the arrest of British schooners by American authorities creating 'serious tension' between Britain and the United States.[71] As he had done over tobacco smuggling into Spain, Howard recommended that the British government do what it could through the courts, for instance, declare British vessels engaged in this trade to be pirates, to aid his host government. This would reduce tension. But, as happened over tobacco, the Foreign Office, especially its legal adviser, Sir Cecil Hurst, argued that it was not up to Britain to enforce foreign legislation.[72] None the less, when it could, the Foreign Office did help Howard dampen the passions aroused by this contentious issue. For instance, in April 1925, when the vice-consul at San Salvador, William Gibson, was discovered to have been issuing false landing-certificates to British 'rum-running' vessels, the Foreign Office dismissed him.[73]

For Howard, these Foreign Office undertakings blunted but did not stop American pressures to have Britain cut off the illegal import of liquor at its source. In the latter half of 1925, the situation heated up when American patrol boats anchored less than three miles off Gun Cay in the Bahamas, a well-known smuggling base. This led to complaints by Bahamian authorities to Howard about American violation of British territorial waters and, thus, to representations by Howard to Treasury and State Department officials.[74] This put Howard in a delicate position between the Coolidge Administration and the Foreign Office, representing the United States to Britain as much as Britain to the United States. To the Americans, he protested that a British vessel laden with liquor and in United States territorial waters did not mean it was there for the purpose of smuggling; seizure could come only if there existed some evidence that such a vessel intended to violate American law.[75] To the Foreign Office, Howard suggested that American officials should be invited to London to discuss the problem, a suggestion that led Chamberlain to minute that 'Sir Esmé [sic] Howard is in great danger of becoming an exponent of the American case to the exclusion of the British case.'[76] Howard smoothed over the matter when he met with Kellogg and proposed minor administrative changes to reduce the amount of smuggled liquor.[77] This satisfied Washington and brought accolades from the Foreign Office, which reckoned that his 'language on this occasion and the terms of his note are excellent'.[78] The Gun Cay crisis blew over.

Howard continued throughout 1926 to press gently on the State Department the British dilemma over American prohibition laws: what was illegal in the United States was not necessarily so in other countries.[79] He and his staff also monitored a renewed debate in the United States between 'wets' and 'drys' – mid-term congressional elections were scheduled for November 1926 – which suggested weakening support for prohibition, a result of the cost of enforcement and the inability of American government at all levels to prevent the procurement, sale, and consumption of alcoholic drinks.[80] Whilst Chamberlain and his advisers occasionally guided Howard, ensuring that his efforts corresponded with the official British position concerning maritime rights and other issues,[81] the Washington Embassy handled the 'rum-running' problem on its own. By early 1927, this aspect of the American question had not become inflamed, a result of Howard balancing between London and Washington, hence, it did not divert Chamberlain's valuable time from far more important diplomacy in Europe, Egypt, and China.

The second troublesome issue with which Howard contended involved an American determination to collect 'blockade claims' from the British government.[82] During the war, until the United States joined the Allies in April 1917, American industrialists, shippers, and other traders who lost cargoes intercepted and seized by the British as war contraband filed private complaints against the British government at the State Department. Hurst discovered the American intention to collect these claims in a casual conversation with Kellogg on the liner carrying the secretary-designate back to the United States in February 1925. In Washington, Hurst informed Howard and then took the opportunity to learn as much as he could about the situation, finding that the push to present claims came from the State Department's legal division. Howard learned independently, from the lawyers who represented Britain in the United States, of the State Department's seriousness in pressing for a claims settlement.[83] Howard, Chamberlain, and the Foreign Office could never permit a settlement which questioned the legality of British blockade practices; a decision against Britain might imperil the Royal Navy's ability to defend the Empire by striking at the heart of British maritime belligerent rights. Thus, any American attempt to present claims in a way which threatened a future blockade had to be resisted. The matter simmered until late 1925 because of personnel changes in the State Department. Then, on 26 October, Howard reported that the blockade claims would soon be presented.

Howard's message inaugurated eighteen months of desultory diplomacy to achieve a suitable claims settlement. In this process, Howard and Vansittart served as the chief British negotiators – Howard, through his position in Washington, and Vansittart, to allow his superiors to direct their energies towards more important problems in British foreign policy. Between November 1925 and May 1927, when the settlement agreement was signed, Howard met with Kellogg several times to press British views and, on three crucial occasions, with Coolidge to ensure a fair hearing within the Administration for the British case. By May 1926 Howard reached an agreement with Kellogg whereby the American claims, numbering several thousand, were to be examined jointly by a State Department official, Spencer Phenix, and Howard's commercial counsellor, J. J. Broderick. A joint examination pre-empted any American call to arbitrate the claims. In September, Phenix travelled to London with a reduced list of about 1,100 claims, and deliberated there with Vansittart. This saw the number of legitimate claims shrink to below one hundred. Three months later Vansittart, using the pretext of a long-planned visit to his wife's family in Chicago, visited Washington secretly. The Vansittart mission settled the claims issue by reducing the American list further and, then, countering with British claims exactly equalling the remaining

American ones. Vansittart left and Howard was delegated to sign the final agreement once Coolidge had approved it.

Howard did not sign the agreement until five months after Vansittart left Washington. Delay occurred because Kellogg claimed that crises confronting him in China, Mexico, and Nicaragua diverted his attention. Instructed periodically to press for signature, Howard witnessed Kellogg's mounting irascibility deriving from the seriousness of these other problems. In fact, in March 1927, the exhausted Kellogg took two weeks' leave to regain spent energies. Whilst Kellogg was on vacation, Howard met Coolidge to impress on him Foreign Office desires for an early signature; he then realised that the president possessed only the sketchiest idea of what had been agreed. Foreign Office pressure to sign came from the need to keep this diplomacy completely secret. Blockade existed as a sensitive issue in both countries: in Britain, many authorities believed that blockade had been one of the chief reasons for Germany's defeat in the war; in the United States, the cry of 'the freedom of the seas', which had figured largely in Wilson's 'Fourteen Points', stood as a rallying point for navalists and isolationists. Thus the Foreign Office, and the State Department for that matter, wanted to avoid public discussion of blockade claims, since it might destroy the political basis for a settlement by opening an old wound in the Anglo-American relationship. It was thought better to present public opinion in each country with a *fait accompli*. Interestingly, formal signature occurred as a result of an unauthorised press leak. The *Baltimore Sun* had somehow received information that a claims settlement was near and published it on the morning of 19 May. Howard was summoned to sign and exchange the agreement that same day. Little public discussion ensued, so, for the British, another minor problem with the potential of damaging Anglo-American relations had been defused, this time by Howard working in partnership with Vansittart.

Howard's work in 1925 and 1926 involved a continuation of his efforts to be a visible ambassador. Between early 1925 and early 1927, he addressed more than thirty groups ranging from the English-Speaking Union to commercial organisations, at every instance emphasising the desire of the British government for co-operation with the United States.[84] He received two honorary doctorates – at McGill University in Montreal and George Washington University in Washington – and he even threw the first ball at the Columbia–Princeton game to inaugurate the Ivy League baseball season in April 1925. He granted more interviews to the press, laid a cornerstone at a small college, and became a member of the Phi Beta Kappa organisation. In all of these endeavours, when she could, and in the crucial social rounds in Washington and New York, Isa played an important part in helping raise the tone of the official British presence in the United States. Moreover, with her husband's encouragement, she attended some important functions on her own, for instance, the Italian-American Society at New York in May 1926. Thanks to Howard's judicious blend of the maxims of 'old diplomacy' with Bryce's ideas about the British ambassador being seen *and* heard, the British Embassy was being restored to the status not enjoyed since 1913.

But Howard did not leave the dissemination of information about his speeches and public appearances to chance. Because of his appreciation of the power of the press, and his belief in this institution as an arbiter of American public opinion, he did all possible to ensure that American newspapers received copies of his speeches and, when he travelled, prior notice of his itinerary. In this, Howard worked closely with the British Library of Information at New York – BLINY – the British government propaganda arm in the United States.[85] BLINY formed part of the British Diplomatic Service in the United States, though it answered to the Foreign Office News Department, not the American Department. In the early 1920s, the Foreign Office decided that BLINY would be more effective if its propaganda work was balanced by helping the Washington Embassy supply London with appraisals of American domestic opinion. Its dual mandate was stated explicitly: 'to serve as a clearing house, where information on British affairs is made available to the American public, while information is secured from American sources on various matters of interest to the Foreign Office and other departments'.[86] The Washington Embassy and BLINY worked closely together, especially after Howard became ambassador. Howard established a close relationship with Robert Wilberforce and Angus Fletcher, the two chief BLINY staff, soon after he arrived in the United States. By the end of 1924, Howard and Wilberforce had devised a procedure by which BLINY would send advance copies of important speeches Howard was to make to a large circle of regional newspapers.[87] This had never been done before, and it had the double advantage of ensuring the official British viewpoint on a range of issues affecting Anglo-American relations received wide publicity whilst providing 'a good opportunity for opening up relations' with newspaper editors whom the Embassy and BLINY might later be able to exploit to British advantage.

Howard's appreciation of the American press involved a recognition that as an institution it possessed a mind of its own, that it could not always be exploited. Like their British counterparts, American newspapers were strongly nationalist. Howard knew from his earlier service in the United States that, if American newspapers became enraged over an issue of national honour involving Britain, latent American anglophobia could easily be whipped up. The Swettanham incident showed this and, once Howard returned as ambassador, the same lesson was driven home again and again. In early 1925, the death of William Jennings Bryan, the populist politician, failed presidential candidate, and, at the moment of his passing, the prosecutor of a Tennessee teacher who dared instruct his students about the theory of evolution, led to uncomplimentary comments in some British newspapers about his political acumen. This unleashed a vitriolic attack on Britain as a whole by the newspaper chain owned by William Randolph Hearst, the most cynical and xenophobic of American journalists.[88] Although the issue quickly died, thanks to more newsworthy events in the United States, this demonstrated how easily a press war between American and British newspapers could erupt. As an Embassy official pointed out, although the importance of the Hearst attack could be discounted because of its source, 'nevertheless it serves to show how the slightest criticism of anything American is at once looked upon as a mortal insult'. Over the next two years, several incidents had the potential of embittering relations: hate-mongering speeches by Irish republican fund-raisers in various American cities; the desire of Hoover, Coolidge's secretary of commerce, to break British control of the international rubber market; the anger of British bond-holders over the default of several southern American states on bond payments; and ungrounded speculation that Britain might not honour its war debt.

Thanks to Howard, none of these questions led to a transatlantic shouting match between British and American newspapers. His handling of the speculation about Britain not paying its war debt is instructive. In August 1926, Howard met George Harvey, a strongly anglophile former American ambassador at London, who indicated that he was writing an article for an American journal. In this article, Harvey intended to argue that the United States should forgo the interest on the British debt to help Britain recover more quickly from its post-war economic problems. Howard said little but, worried about the impact of such a proposal on American opinion, suggested privately to Chamberlain that British newspapers follow the line which 'has met with a good press in this country – namely that we have signed an agreed settlement and that for our part we mean to stick to it'.[89] Chamberlain and his advisers approved of Howard's strategy, a strategy endorsed by the Treasury, which agreed 'to shepherd' British newspapers in the right direction once Harvey's article appeared.[90] As Howard predicted, Harvey's article created a debate in American newspapers about whether Britain could or should pay interest,[91] whilst British newspapers, like the *Manchester Guardian* which had been primed by the Treasury, criticised Harvey for raising an issue which could only hurt Anglo-American relations.[92] But the matter did not end there. Harvey's article misquoted a Howard speech made a few months earlier in which the ambassador allegedly said that Britain might not be able to meet its future financial obligations. Howard had not said this, but the story received wide circulation in the United States by newspapers serviced by the Associated Press. Howard and his staff realised that Harvey's misrepresentation had to be countered. Working with BLINY, the Embassy immediately issued a communiqué to the Washington papers giving Howard's precise words.[93] Howard went further by writing privately to Frank Noyes, the president of Associated Press, setting out the true situation and enclosing a copy of the communiqué for Noyes' organisation to distribute.[94] The correct story was then circulated and the matter died.

By the end of his third year in Washington, Howard re-established the dynamism and purpose of action at the British Embassy that had been eroded in the decade after Bryce's departure. He achieved this principally because of his understanding of the United States, both its domestic political ferment and the effect of this on American foreign policy. He not only impressed his Foreign Office colleagues with his handling of the American question, especially Chamberlain, who had more important problems to consider, but also many Americans. The greatest testament to Howard's success in the United States in this period occurred in March 1927 when he suffered a personal attack in the Senate by Senator Heflin of Alabama. Heflin, a rabid anti-Catholic, accused Howard of plotting with the papacy and American Catholic churchmen to embroil the United States in a war with Mexico. Heflin received almost universal censure from American newspapers and his senatorial colleagues. Howard, on the other hand, was accorded a spirited defence by several prominent Americans, including a few very isolationist senators like Senator King of Utah.[95] As Fletcher wrote to the Foreign Office: 'That a Senator from Utah should have defended the Br. Ambassador so vigorously in the Senate is indeed a solatium worth having.' Howard's work in Washington between early 1924 and early 1927, so important to re-establishing good Anglo-American relations in the long term, proved to be crucial in the last years of the 1920s. Because the Preparatory Commission proved to be barren throughout 1926 on the naval question, Coolidge delivered on his long-promised intention by issuing invitations in February 1927 to the major naval Powers to discuss separately naval arms limitation.[96] This initiated a renewed crisis in the Anglo-American relationship with which Howard wrestled for the rest of his tenure as ambassador at Washington. The effective ambassadorial presence he had built in the three years after February 1924 proved to be fundamental in meeting the American challenge to Britain's global Power status explicit in the naval limitation question and, more important, in ensuring that a firm Anglo-American relationship endured. Although Howard did not realise it in February 1927, he was entering the final and most important phase of his career in the Diplomatic Service.

10

Washington 'redux': meeting the American challenge, 1927–1930

> The Admirals here are in the saddle and intend to stay there, and Chilton who has just returned from the West tells me the impression he got there was the Big Navy programme was making headway all the time and that economy was no longer a word to conjure with. The fact is they feel themselves so rich that if they want a few extra toys they can [buy] them no matter how expensive they are.
>
> Howard, July 1927

I

Howard's accomplishments during his first three years in Washington occurred under a gathering cloud of personal crisis. In the summer of 1924, his eldest son, Esme, travelled to the United States after completing his term at Oxford. He had been ill for some time and, in Washington, the shattering discovery was made that he had leukaemia. Howard and his wife then began desperate efforts to seek a treatment for the disease in the hope of finding a cure, taking him first to London in the autumn of 1924 to consult specialists.[1] Although the universal opinion of prominent doctors in Britain, the United States, and the continent held the condition to be incurable, the parents continued searching for a miracle. Because Howard had to return to the United States before the end of the year – the presidential-congressional elections and the advent of a new administration necessitated his presence at the Embassy – Isa remained with her son in Britain and, later, Switzerland. By the next summer, young Esme's condition had worsened, but the entire family gathered at his clinic at Mürren to spend the holidays together. This contrasted sharply with that happiest of summers in 1919 when the end of the war and the seemingly endless round of visiting relatives, bicycling, and sharing the joys of family had appeared to begin a new, more optimistic period in Howard's life. Howard spent as much time as possible with his son that summer of 1925, recording later: 'Those were the last days he was able to walk a little, and he and I had occasional strolls to a seat from which he could drink in the great white purity of the Bernese Alps. We would sit in silence, which was better than words, for it brought us nearer together.'² When the summer ended, the family split up: Howard took the younger boys back to school in the United States; the two older ones returned to their studies in Britain; and Isa and young Esme stayed in Switzerland.

For the next year, whilst Howard wrestled with liquor smuggling, blockade, and the other problems confronting Britain's relations with the United States, the treatments continued at various Swiss clinics. Like any parent struck by such a calamity, Howard hoped against hope for a remission. It did not come. In September 1926, just as Phenix travelled to London, Howard received word from his wife's sister to go to Switzerland without delay. After a short stay at a clinic at Neufchâtel – 'we still had some happy hours...but he could walk no more with me' – Howard and Isa took their son to London in the vain hope that a new treatment there would succeed. On 15 November Howard wrote to his sister, Maud, to say Esme was 'really doing far better than we could have expected';³ but ten days later, because of his weakened condition, the boy succumbed to pneumonia and died on the 27th. Howard busied himself in comforting Isa and the three younger boys who were with them – Francis, now at Harvard, had to remain in the United States during the last crisis – and in making burial arrangements. But he sought to make sense of his loss by pouring out his grief to his sisters, Maud and Elizabeth.⁴ He confided to Maud:

I don't think I ever loved him more – much as I loved him before – but I am very glad now that he is no longer in that hell of suffering. These last $2\frac{1}{2}$ years have been agonising... I can't describe what he has meant to me ever since he was a little boy. I was relying on him to help me, as he could & would have done, with the younger ones in case I break down. One of his last words were [sic] that he offered up his sufferings as a sacrifice to help 'the little ones' as he always called them.

Howard's Catholicism proved vital in helping him come to terms with his son's death. His faith in the past had given him the inner strength at difficult times in his personal life to continue his work, notably in July 1918, when Isa and the three younger boys returned to Britain leaving him to complete his service in Stockholm. The chance still existed then of British steamers being torpedoed in the passage between Norway and Scotland; thus, it was possible that either his family or, later, he might not survive the journey. He and Isa decided to say their rosary together just before she departed.⁵ Sharing his faith in God with Isa offered the only way to assure that, should death suddenly separate them, life would continue for the other, a life marked by the joy and conviction that they would not be parted forever. These same sentiments permeated his handling of the loss of his son. 'God helped Esmetto to bear [his sufferings] without any revolt', he wrote to Maud. 'He will also help us to bear our sorrow at losing him without revolt.'[6] But Howard also asked what his son had accomplished in the world. Did he do something to make life better on earth? If one had faith in God, then God must have had some purpose in giving Esmetto life. The brevity of his son's life touched many people, a testament to which is seen in the more than 500 messages of condolence sent to Howard and Isa.[7] Howard therefore collected a number of his son's notes and other writings, published them privately, and sent copies to people who had known Esmetto.[8] This confirmed for Howard that his son had accomplished something in the world, despite being taken before he could serve his country, Church, or mankind in some more tangible way; it also perpetuated his memory amongst friends and others outside the family.[9] In this way, Howard's faith helped him weather this tragedy whilst, simultaneously, strengthening that faith. It also allowed him to get on with his own life and to continue his embassy as Anglo-American relations began to enter a more dangerous phase, thanks to Coolidge's desire for a separate naval conference.

On returning to Washington, Howard threw himself into his work, as much to keep his mind off his grief as to make certain that the improving relationship with the United States did not suffer. His immediate concern involved analysing the results of the mid-term elections held in November 1926 when the Republicans experienced setbacks in both houses of Congress: in the House of Representatives, the Republican majority fell from 60 to 39, a distressing but not disastrous result in a chamber of 435 seats; but in the 96-seat Senate, the Republican majority of 16 plummeted to just 2. The previous June, Howard had reported that the 'halcyon' days of Coolidge's Administration with the public were over, a result of three political issues: prohibition, farm relief, and isolationism.[10] BLINY's intelligence-gathering supported Howard's suspicions as the election campaign heated up,[11] so that, when the Republicans were worsted at the polls, the Embassy and the Foreign Office experienced little surprise.[12] By the time Howard returned to the United States in late December, the Foreign Office had begun to speculate about the presidential and party stakes in the 1928 elections.[13] The front-runners appeared to be Coolidge and Alfred Smith, the Democratic governor of New York. Howard's assessment suggested that the situation was not that cut and dried. Whilst Smith appeared to have the edge within the Democratic Party despite being a Roman Catholic and a 'wet', Coolidge did not occupy any clear advantage as an incumbent.[14] The staunchly Republican *Chicago Tribune* had begun to attack him over his reluctance to spend funds appropriated in 1924 for three cruisers, whilst some prominent Republican politicians like Hoover and Nicholas Longworth, the speaker of the house, were manoeuvring to secure the party nomination. Added to the president's problems was the idea that his seeking another term of office might violate the tradition of presidents serving only two terms, this despite Coolidge coming to the White House late in Harding's first term. Vansittart epitomised Foreign Office opinion about Howard's analysis by minuting that 'Mr. Coolidge is infinitely the best from our – and every – point of view. He is straight, and pro-British – and a great deal wiser than many of his countrymen profess to believe.'[15] About the other contenders, Vansittart found little to commend them. He especially deprecated Hoover, 'the most unpleasant personality I have ever met'. It was clear to Howard and his colleagues in London that, if Coolidge wished to serve a second full term, the president had to initiate some Republican-sponsored political success.

Whilst Howard and the Foreign Office pondered the changing political climate within the United States, Coolidge decided that a foreign-policy triumph would reflate his sagging reputation. Howard and BLINY grasped this immediately, but surmised that American diplomatic problems with Mexico, Nicaragua, and China, festering for some time, would be too difficult to settle quickly.[16] Naval-arms limitation, however, seemed a different proposition. A foreign-policy coup here offered several advantages for Coolidge: substantial economies in government spending could be realised and attributed to presidential initiative; his Republican Administration could complete the job begun by Harding's at the Washington conference, giving the party additional strength for the next campaign; and the sobriquet of 'peace-maker' would be tied to the president, reducing the appeal of both his Republican and Democratic adversaries. In the three months after the November 1926 elections, Howard was not surprised to see Coolidge begin clearing the way for a new naval conference: his support for extending the Washington treaty capital ship-building ratio to cruisers, destroyers, submarines, and auxiliary craft; a veiled reference to the lethargy of the Preparatory Commission; and the shelving of those appropriations for three cruisers despite 'Big Navy' opposition.[17] The American invitation of 10 February 1927 for separate naval talks stood as the logical consequence of these developments.

Howard had little to do with the formal preparations for what came to be known as the Coolidge naval conference.[18] First, because this meeting existed technically as an adjunct of the Preparatory Commission – the major naval Powers were to limit cruisers, destroyers, and so on and, because they had agreed amongst themselves, propose that the Commission endorse the resulting agreement – determining British policy fell to those who had been making British naval-limitation policy during the second Baldwin government: the Foreign Office Western Department, in charge of general disarmament questions; Cecil, the minister responsible for all disarmament matters; and William Bridgeman, the first lord of the Admiralty, and his ministry through their mandate to ensure the fighting capacity of the Royal Navy. This group had devised British naval policies for the Preparatory Commission and would do so for the Coolidge conference. Secondly, the governments involved decided to keep preliminary discussions to a minimum, something deriving from the fact that the naval experts who were to attend the Coolidge conference were those who had been meeting regularly in the important Sub-Committee A of the Preparatory Commission. These experts believed that they knew the naval requirements of the other delegations, and thus preliminary discussions were really unnecessary. In fact, the only preliminary discussions undertaken by the British occurred in March 1927 when the American delegation *en route* to a Preparatory Commission meeting in Geneva stopped in London to hold brief talks with Admiralty officials.

Howard realised that even a minor strain in Anglo-American relations during the run up to the conference, to begin in Geneva on 20 June, might imperil a naval agreement; it might compel the American delegation to adopt a hardline in order to show opinion at home that the United States could stand up to Britain. He, thus, took it upon himself to ensure that Britain's improving image in the United States remained unsullied, and these efforts consumed almost all of his time and energy as he sublimated his grief over the loss of his son. In essence, Howard sought to prevent the emotive issues like war debts, blockade claims, and liquor smuggling from inflaming the latent anglophobia prevalent in the United States. For instance, in October 1926, Chilton had submitted an *aide-mémoire* to the State Department outlining British views on a draft Senate bill providing American naval forces with the power to seize contraband liquor on foreign vessels outside of United States territorial waters.[19] Britain objected to the implication in this legislation that British vessels might be intercepted on the high seas if their customs declarations made no mention of liquor, as well as the chance that passengers and crews in international waters might be charged with breaking American law. Chilton had asked that these British views be circulated to American law-makers but, after the bill died in committee because Congress recessed in early March 1927, Howard discovered that the State Department had suppressed the *aide-mémoire*.[20] One of Kellogg's deputies told Howard that the British views might have galvanised support for the bill – which the State Department disliked because it meant the legislature was seeking to influence foreign policy, an executive responsibility – hence, nothing had been lost by not circulating them. Whilst Howard thought the State Department exaggerated the danger of Britain being painted as seeking to interfere in domestic American affairs, he acknowledged that some justification for this worry existed. Deciding not to protest the burking of the British observations, he urged instead that the State Department keep British concerns in mind should a new bill be drafted in another session of Congress. This constituted astute diplomacy: by not making an issue of State Department high-handedness, Howard prevented public ventilation of official British displeasure with American prohibition enforcement on the eve of the Coolidge conference.

Whilst expending energy on these sorts of political problems, Howard also continued making speeches and public appearances in the Washington-New York-Philadelphia triangle to polish further Britain's image in the United States. More important, he decided that his public relations campaign had to be extended into the far reaches of the continent where he had never travelled. He had mooted the idea of such a trip – to the South, the West Coast, and even western Canada – three weeks before the Coolidge Administration despatched invitations to a separate naval conference, this in response to numerous requests to visit these regions which he had received since being appointed ambassador.[21] Though he planned this journey to augment his successes on the East Coast and in the Middle West, he also saw it as a way both to occupy his time in planning the trip, and allow him and Isa an opportunity to get away together from Washington. However, the whole project assumed greater importance once the naval conference was in the offing. By having an ambassador make his presence known in areas outside of the northeast – important areas in terms of American domestic opinion to which few ambassadors of any Power, let alone Great Britain, had ever travelled – there were public relations gains to be made. Through Howard explaining aspects of British foreign policy to local notables and anglophile groups such as branches of the English-Speaking Union, the course of Anglo-American relations could be made that much smoother at a difficult moment.

Howard embarked on his 'journey to the Pacific Coast' on 25 April 1927 with the full support of the Foreign Office – recognising the value of this trek, Vansittart even secured funds for a secretary to go along to keep away 'importunates & undesirables who will be much in evidence'.[22] Over twenty-nine days, Howard visited New Orleans, Los Angeles, San Francisco, Portland, Seattle, Victoria, and Vancouver, with side trips to the Grand Canyon, Hollywood, the Yosemite Valley, and a couple of university campuses; he gave fifteen major speeches to civic chambers of commerce, branches of the English-Speaking Union and Concert of British Societies, and other bodies of local prominence. In assessing his efforts, Howard believed they had served 'a useful purpose' because of the positive publicity surrounding him at every function. His speeches were nearly always reported verbatim in newspapers whilst, more crucial, some of the ones at larger centres were broadcast on the radio. Personally, he confessed that he learnt much about political and economic conditions in the South and on the West Coast; in a wider sense the British consuls, who had made all the local arrangements, reckoned that his visit helped Britain's reputation. He had met privately with the 'principal industrial and commercial leaders' in each region, whilst his audiences, usually numbering several hundred, tended to be 'business men who on the whole appeared interested in what I had to say'. Although he came into contact chiefly with the financial community, the subjects of his addresses tended to be political, as he stressed the need for Anglo-American co-operation and explained British policy in troubled areas like China. In reporting to the Foreign Office, Howard judged that this tour had been a success, but it was not as fruitful as it might have been. In Vancouver, he collapsed from exhaustion, as much a result of the rigours of the trip as from the heavy workload he had undertaken on returning to Washington after his son's death. Thus, his scheduled appearances in Calgary, Regina, Winnipeg, and Detroit were cancelled as he sped back on a private rail car to rest in Washington. He had had no worry-free vacation since arriving in the United States in 1924; he needed time to refresh himself.

Howard's furlough proved to be short-lived because of the impact of the Coolidge naval conference on American public opinion. The three Powers established with little disagreement the classes and maximum displacement and armament for destroyers, submarines, and auxiliary craft like sloops.[23] Moreover, they did so within the Washington treaty building ratio. But, from the first plenary session, it emerged that the British and Americans were poles apart when it came to cruiser limitation – the Japanese goal at the conference had nothing to do with specific tonnage, instead, the Japanese sought to increase their cruiser construction above the 30 per cent of the combined British and American tonnage envisaged by adopting the Washington standard in Geneva. Cruisers, at once the weapons for defending and attacking seaborne lines of communication, constituted the backbone of any fleet for a Power with global pretensions. Because the United States had fewer overseas colonies than Britain, fewer international responsibilities, and decidedly less overseas trade as a percentage of national income to defend, the American delegation sought a fleet of 250,000 to 300,000 tons composed mainly of large cruisers – 10,000 tons with eight-inch guns. The British for the opposite reasons argued for a fleet of 500,000 tons comprised chiefly of smaller cruisers – 7,500 tons maximum with six-inch guns. (The difference in displacement between heavy and light cruisers came from the need to have more weight on the former to prevent them from flipping over because of the tremendous recoil created by firing a broadside.) The Americans indicated that they adhered to the doctrine of relative need, that American cruiser strength could be relative to that of other Powers. If the conference set a high tonnage, then the American allotment should be high; if set lower, then the United States could accept a lower tonnage. But, in the course of the negotiations, the Americans were adamant about not accepting a cruiser figure higher than 400,000 tons, a figure exceeding that set out by them at the first plenary session but one which Congress would accept. The British, on the other hand, argued for cruiser construction based on the doctrine of absolute need, that Britain required at least 500,000 tons to defend adequately its seaborne commerce and Imperial lines of communication, and that the total cruiser tonnage could not be set below this. Because the Americans desired naval equality with Britain, a function of the shibboleth of 'a navy second to none', a deadlock over cruiser limitation was soon reached. The line was drawn: should limitation be at figures convenient to Britain or the United States?

As these events unfolded in Geneva, Howard found that all of his work in repairing Britain's image in the United States began to unravel through what has been called 'the most bitter press war'.[24] Since the Foreign Office recognised the power of the American press in shaping American public opinion, a member of the Foreign Office News Department, George Steward, accompanied the British delegation and held daily press conferences to outline British policy to all the journalists covering the conference.[25] He also arranged for journalists to interview senior British delegates, distributed important British speeches, and ensured that 'general information' concerning British proposals was given quickly to eager newspapermen. Press liaison on this scale had rarely occurred at international conferences; thus, the British stole a march on both the Americans and Japanese, neither of whom had someone like Steward in their delegations. American officials in Washington and Geneva saw Steward's presence as an 'ungentlemanly act', which contributed to some anti-British feelings already existing in these circles because of intergovernmental problems involving commodity controls over cotton, rubber, and cinematographs and Britain's return to the gold standard in 1925.[26] Thus, the American position in Geneva became more intransigent as the conference progressed. On top of this, the 'Big Navy' propagandist, William Shearer, had been hired by several American steel and shipbuilding companies to write articles for domestic consumption which deliberately distorted British limitation policies.[27] Shearer was not alone in this, as several American journalists, especially the correspondent of the *Chicago Tribune*, engaged in 'cold-blooded and deliberate lying' about the British proposals.[28] The 'press war' in Geneva heated up as British journalists began to lambaste the American policies, with the result that the governments in London and Washington became more intransigent. In fact, anti-American hardliners in Baldwin's Cabinet, led by Winston Churchill, the chancellor of the exchequer, in an effort to disrupt the conference, succeeded in having the British delegation return to London for a week of consultations in late July. This antagonised the Americans and, after the return of the British, the conference ended in failure on 4 August.

Howard's worst fears about a tear in Anglo-American relations were realised as the conference broke down over the cruiser question. Throughout the entire six-week period, the American public became so agitated over the press reports they read regarding British limitation policies that Britain began again to be perceived as the arch-enemy of the United States. As early as 27 June, Howard warned Chamberlain that 'Jingo Congress men like Britten [chairman of the House Naval Affairs Committee] and Jingo papers such as 'Chicago Tribune' are doing all they can to break up [the] conference by persuading public opinion that it is really a snare set for Uncle Sam by Great Britain.'[29] He even sent advice directly to the British delegation in Geneva suggesting ways to present British proposals so as not to provide anglophobic American navalists with ammunition with which to attack those proposals.[30] Because of the gravity of the situation, he also left the British Embassy summer quarters in Manchester, Massachusetts to stay in hot, muggy Washington to explain British policy to Kellogg when the need arose. This had initial effect but, as the conference wore on, official Administration displeasure with British policy led to a State Department press release stating that American news despatches from the conference showed 'understanding of the naval situation'.[31] General American disfavour became clear when, on 21 July, Howard informed Chamberlain privately that Chilton had just returned from the areas in the West visited by Howard two months before with the disquieting news that 'the impression he got there was [that] the Big Navy programme was making headway all the time and that economy was no longer a word to conjure with'.[32] When it was obvious that the conference would fail because of Anglo-American wrangling over cruiser limitation after the British delegation's return to Geneva following consultations in London, the Americans made efforts publicly to suggest that the talks were to be adjourned rather than abandoned; the reasoning here stemmed from a desire to keep the ground clear for future discussions.[33] The British did the same through sweet words in their speeches at the final plenary session of the conference.[34] A delicate juncture in Anglo-American relations had been reached. Whilst the Baldwin government seemed prepared to build a cruiser fleet based on Britain's absolute need – and to be honest Britain worried as much about the French, Italians, and Japanese as they did about the Americans – American leaders were now confronted with a public willing to countenance increased government spending to build a fleet equal to that of Britain. Knowing that the Americans had the economic and industrial capacity to construct 'a navy second to none', Howard saw a deadly challenge to Britain's global Power status forming in the United States. His diplomatic skills would be put to the test to prevent this challenge from succeeding.

II

Howard had viewed British attempts to reach a naval accord with the United States as a dangerous move: failure could only create major diplomatic problems. As the decision to attend the conference was made by Baldwin's Cabinet, which agreed to the negotiations in order to achieve a naval settlement and the retrenchment that would entail, Howard did not record formally his concerns about the conference failing. But, within three days of the first plenary session, he wrote Chamberlain that there were 'times when I feel depressed and irritated almost beyond bearing by the tune and attitude of the Press here'.[35] As the conference ground to a halt because of the unscrupulous efforts of Shearer and the other American journalists of that ilk,[36] many Americans talked openly of war between Britain and the United States over the naval question.[37] In fact, within the British Embassy during the conference, some people, like Captain Arthur Stopford, the naval attaché, argued that Britain should re-align with Japan to oppose the United States in the world at large.[38] These sorts of sentiments on both the British and American sides prompted Howard to consider the possibility of mounting a public-education campaign on both sides of the Atlantic about 'the real absurdity' of an Anglo-American war. He broached the subject to Hoover at a dinner party in late July.[39] Sharing the ambassador's concern about the worsening state of Anglo-American relations, Hoover indicated that he would consider the matter.

A few days later, Howard met Hoover at a Washington club to discuss how a public-education campaign should be conducted. They agreed that two 'reports', one by a prominent American outlining the American case and a second by a prominent Briton doing the same for the British one, should be published jointly. Hoover then raised what he called 'certain political implications' likely to be drawn from public speculation about an armed struggle between the British Empire and the United States – that Canada would be forced into neutrality. This initiated discussion on the probable course such a conflict would take. Given that each side could not invade the other – the only exception being Canada suffering an invasion should it not be bullied into submission – the war would be fought at sea and entail mutual economic strangulation via a stringent application of belligerent rights: the United States would prevent western hemispheric countries, including Canada, from supplying Britain with foodstuffs and raw materials; Britain would blockade Europe and other markets from penetration by American merchantmen. Howard suggested to Chamberlain that it would be 'politic' to have such ideas included in the two reports, though this would have to be done 'unofficially' to obviate either government from being held accountable for raising this subject publicly. But, despite the political dangers of mounting this campaign, Howard argued strongly that something like this had to be done to prevent a naval arms race between Britain and the United States:

I cannot help feeling very strongly that the general public of both countries badly need education in this matter and that the only way of reducing the demands of the Big Navalists and Militarists for more and more armaments is by making the great mass of people understand clearly what the ultimate end of listening to their counsels is likely to be.

Howard's letter caused Chamberlain great consternation. He immediately ordered Howard to drop the public-education idea since 'the thought of war does not enter into anyone's calculations'.[40] Indeed, he opined that 'a peace propaganda conducted on such lines as Hoover suggests would have the very contrary effect to which is intended'. Chamberlain also instructed Howard on the reigning theory of Imperial unity in light of the suggestion that Canada might adopt a neutralist stance should an Anglo-American war break out. '[N]o one here will or can consent to admitting the hypothesis that, in a war in which the King is engaged', Chamberlain wrote, 'any part of his Empire can be neutral'. Howard relented over the idea of a public-education campaign. None the less, he put on record his disagreement with Chamberlain over both Canada and neutrality and 'the thought [that] war does not enter into the calculations of anyone in England'.[41] Concerning the former, Howard admitted that no responsible British leader could admit publicly that Canada would remain neutral in an Anglo-American armed struggle; however, British leaders who knew 'anything about the geographic, economic, financial and political position of Canada cannot *in petto* hold any other belief'. About the former, Howard recorded Stopford's ideas about a renewed Anglo-Japanese alliance to oppose American ambitions. With the cold-blooded realism that marked his professionalism in diplomacy, the more so when considering his Atlanticist proclivities, Howard instructed Chamberlain on the folly of assuming there could never be an Anglo-American war:

It might come – if we allow ourselves to be taken unawares – in more than one way – e.g. owing to a conflict over 'freedom of the seas' if again we are drawn into a European war, owing to League action in South America coming into conflict with the very strict interpretation the United States now places on the Monroe Doctrine against which South Americans are beginning to kick, owing to some act of 'hubris' by an American Government with regard to one of our many non-policed West India Islands, which can be used as bases not only for liquor-smuggling but become a nuisance in other ways. We must be prepared for such eventualities and be ready to deal with them, should they arise[,] by avoiding their natural consequences, viz. armed conflict.

Howard's argument was that whether a war with the United States was probable or not, the cruiser question had injected poison into Anglo-American relations. The 'Big Navy Party' seemed to be gaining strength in the domestic debate over naval spending so that, if Britain continued to be painted as a threat to United States trade and Imperial communications, something Shearer and his cohorts were doing,[42] American public opinion might just support massive naval appropriations to construct a huge cruiser fleet. With their tremendous economic resources and industrial capacity, the Americans could challenge the Royal Navy's pre-eminence, wreak havoc with Imperial unity by showing Canada, Australia, and New Zealand that Britain lacked the power to protect their interests, and push Britain on to the slope of second-class status. Removing American fears about British naval policy was an imperative. This would require concerted effort in both London and Washington.

Howard wrote to Chamberlain on 1 September when, at all levels, American opinion towards Britain seemed to be in a state of flux. As the conference ended, Howard surmised that the 'deliberate and anti-British campaign has met with so little success'.[43] The reasoned statements by the delegations at the final plenary session, coupled with general editorial opinion in both countries that the blame for failure had to be shared, had much to do with this.[44] In addition, Coolidge, realising the conference would fail, announced unexpectedly on 2 August that he would not seek a second full term. Howard's reports indicated that press speculation about why precisely Coolidge did this, and who possessed the best chance of succeeding him, diverted attention from the Geneva proceedings.[45] Admittedly, discussion in the United States was occurring over the need to have 'a conservative building up of the United States Navy to its proper position'. This statement came from Admiral Hilary Jones, the senior American naval expert on the American delegation, after his arrival home; it conformed to Coolidge's decision to endorse the construction of eight new cruisers asked for by the Navy General Board and supported by Congress.[46] These were essentially replacement vessels, and neither Howard nor his colleagues in London worried much about them.[47]

Howard's view since the conference began had been that 'as [the Americans] could of course outbuild us if they sought fit', 'I have always been of the opinion that it would be pure waste of time, money, and energy on our part to take U.S. armaments into consideration in deciding on our own requirements'.[48] Although British officials could never admit publicly that the United States could outbuild Britain – and, indeed, some would not – the point about Britain building a fleet large enough to protect its interests had been prominent in Geneva. After all, this stood at the heart of the doctrine of absolute need. Not wishing to force the Americans to have a smaller navy than the Royal Navy, British delegates suggested that the United States also build as large a fleet as it felt it needed. Britain's only concern here, especially after the delegation returned from consultations in London, involved not formalising cruiser parity with the United States. A time might come when Britain needed to expand its cruiser fleet, and to do this would entail breaking a treaty with the Americans. The assumption here was that the United States did not need and would not build as many cruisers as Britain – Howard, Chamberlain, and others saw the American call for parity as a policy of prestige more than necessity.[49] In the aftermath of the conference, several senior members of Baldwin's Cabinet made great play in their speeches about the necessity of each country building to the level it thought necessary to defend its maritime trade and communications.[50] If this meant that the Americans had to build cruisers to a number equalling Britain's, then Britain could live with this. But they also made the opposite argument: the United States had to respect British needs and the strength of the Royal Navy that the British government decided was necessary to look after those needs. This stance, in Howard's view, tended to ameliorate somewhat Anglo-American differences in the month or so after the conference ended.[51]

Howard's admonition of 1 September was designed to warn Chamberlain that American opinion, in the Administration, Congress, and amongst the press, should not find in British naval policy a scapegoat on whose horns the 'Big Navy Party' could hang the excuse to seek naval appropriations for more than a conservative build-up of American naval forces. By early September, Baldwin's government had weathered several minor problems which had the potential of whipping up anglophobia in the United States. The most important of these concerned Cecil, one of the two chief British delegates at the conference, who resigned from the Cabinet on his return to London. Although Cecil's resignation came as a result of a series of disagreements over domestic and foreign policy with his Cabinet colleagues, his letter of resignation had harsh words for the government's arms-limitation policies.[52] But thanks to concerted efforts by the Cabinet – those speeches, plus successful public relations by Baldwin and the Prince of Wales who, together on a state visit to Canada, attended the opening of the Peace Bridge at Buffalo, New York in early August and spoke soothingly – Cecil's resignation had little initial impact in the United States.[53]

As far as Howard was concerned, the failure of the Coolidge conference meant that the threat to good Anglo-American relations was more potential than actual. Whilst public opinion during the deliberations had been stirred up by American correspondents to question British intentions – Chilton's findings on his western tour showed this – the determination of Coolidge and his diplomatic and naval advisers in August and September to sanction only a conservative build-up of the United States Navy indicated that all had not been lost. As his 'war-talk' with Hoover showed, Howard believed that diplomatic confrontation with the Americans should be avoided, a stance supported by BLINY's information-gathering.[54] A British hardline would only antagonise the Americans, and little profit existed in this. It followed that Howard found himself representing the United States in London as much as Britain in Washington. Taking to heart the maxim of 'old diplomacy' that one should 'always give your opponents credit for being in good faith', he explained to the Foreign Office, and, through it, the Cabinet, why the Americans wanted a sizeable navy. Whilst he took the view that a large American navy would satisfy the general American desire for the prestige of having this powerful instrument of national policy, no doubt existed that American navalists wanted to prevent Britain from interfering with neutral trading rights should another European war break out. His time in Stockholm in this respect had made an indelible impression, and his American experiences since 1924 added to this, everything from American pique at rum-running from the West Indies and Canada through the blockade-claims controversy to his discussion with Hoover about mutual economic strangulation.

In the months after the Coolidge conference, Howard learnt from a variety of sources that many influential Americans saw a fundamental dichotomy between the British doctrine of maritime belligerent rights and the American theory of the freedom of the seas. By September, the anglophobe owner of the *Chicago Tribune*, Colonel Robert McCormick, had used his newspaper to argue that the West Indies existed as a potential base from which the Royal Navy could easily attack American shipping along the eastern coast of the United States and Panama.[55] At the same time, when lunching with House, Howard was told by the latter that 'there was only one possible source of war between our two countries and this was British interference with American neutral trade'.[56] Howard knew House's views, a result of earlier conversations and the recent publication of House's wartime and peace-conference memoirs. But, as

Howard confided in Tyrrell, now the permanent under-secretary, he was unprepared 'for his propounding [this argument] so vigorously'. Because House reckoned that both Republicans and Democrats were at one on this issue, he suggested to Howard that Britain should 'settle this question of the "freedom of the seas" now once and for all with the United States and thus eliminate a great danger of collision in the future'. Though Howard acknowledged that 'House of course does not any longer cut any ice politically', he confessed to Tyrrell that 'I am confident that he is quite justified in saying that Democrats and Republicans are agreed on this point and in the main I think his arguments are sound and logical'. A week later, Howard wrote Tyrrell about a private conversation the British military attaché, Colonel Ladislas Pope-Hennessy, had had with a senior American army officer, General Preston Brown. In discussing the impasse in Geneva, Brown remarked: 'The Conference failed because neither side would tell the truth; you (British) want numerous cruisers not only to protect your trade routes – which is obvious – but in order to apply in war your historic weapon of blockade...We (Americans) want a smaller number of big cruisers to ensure that your blockade does not interfere with our commerce as a neutral.'[57] By late September, therefore, Howard believed that 'the fear of future blockade is at the back of the minds not only of Senators but also of Generals and no doubt Admirals'. Because the United States might not always seek to restrict belligerent rights – what would happen, Howard asked, if the Americans in the future possessed a navy larger than the Royal Navy? – it might profit Britain to conclude some agreement with the United States on the future application of those rights.[58] In the short term, this might reduce the clamour in the United States for 'a navy second to none' whilst, in the longer view, it might protect British interests should the Americans ever steal a naval march on Britain.

Howard's reports, supplemented by BLINY assessments of American press opinion, greatly influenced the Foreign Office American Department. As early as 24 August, Robert Craigie, Vansittart's number two, addressed a memorandum to Chamberlain discussing the possibility of concluding an Anglo-American belligerent rights agreement as a means of weakening navalist arguments in the United States.[59] His basic premise held that such an agreement could reduce naval competition which, in turn, would improve the political relationship between the two countries so soured since the breakdown of the conference. Through Craigie, the American Department asked Chamberlain to consider an examination of the feasibility of approaching the Americans over reducing belligerent rights by agreement. Although the foreign secretary supported an examination, he shelved the proposal for a while to see if Anglo-American relations would improve. They did not. Howard's letters to Tyrrell showed the abiding concern of prominent Americans about the political and strategic aspects of the cruiser question. These rather than technical matters of displacement, gun calibres, and the like lay at the bottom of the problem. Just as telling, comment about the 'real reason' for the cruiser deadlock began to appear in the United States. Some influential American writers asserted that the cruiser impasse derived from British reluctance to surrender their ability to blockade.[60] Stoking the fires of discord were efforts by opposition politicians in Britain, mainly MacDonald and Lloyd George, to benefit politically by attacking Conservative arms-limitation policies.[61] By late October, thanks to all of these issues, Chamberlain approached the Cabinet about the need to examine whether it was in Britain's interest to seek a belligerent-rights agreement with the United States. His submission contained his own paper, in which he argued that the matter needed study, plus, to enhance his argument, a revised American Department submission and two of Howard's letters to Tyrrell.[62] Chamberlain's decision to go to the Cabinet – and he pointed out to his colleagues that Howard and the American Department had suggested an examination of belligerent rights independently of each other – led to a rear-guard action by British navalists and anti-Americans, centred by Hankey, to pre-empt this Foreign Office initiative.[63]

Howard continued assessing American events for the Foreign Office whilst it sparred with those in the British government who saw no reason to sacrifice British belligerent rights to appease the Americans. His reports helped swing Baldwin in favour of an examination. They began with the news that the parsimonious Coolidge had approved a $40 million appropriation for the construction of eight cruisers of the 1924 programme.[64] Two days later, Howard sent the disquieting news that Britten had announced his intention to put before Congress a five-year $400 million bill authorising the construction of thirty 10,000 ton cruisers and five aircraft carriers.[65] The 'Big Navy Party' had taken the high ground in the domestic American debate, though Howard suggested that this constituted a 'bargaining move'; the American navalists knew they could never get such a building programme through Congress and past the president, but they might achieve a level of construction above that which they might normally expect. Baldwin's Cabinet sought to reduce American fears and stymie attacks by the Labour and Liberal parties by having Bridgeman announce that Britain would build only one of three cruisers authorised in the 1927–8 building programme.[66] But Anglo-American relations continued to acidify, the catalyst being renewed American interest in why Cecil had resigned from the government, an interest fostered by Cecil who, with the petulance of a subaltern cashiered for improprieties everybody but he recognised, attacked the Cabinet's actions during the Coolidge conference.[67] Naturally, the American 'Big Navy' press paraded Cecil's remarks as proof that the British had been duplicitous at Geneva.[68] There existed nothing surprising in this. But, from private sources, Howard discovered the distressing news that the State Department saw Cecil's words as 'entirely justifying' the American position at Geneva.[69] The temper of domestic American opinion, from the Administration on down, seemed to be increasingly suspicious of British naval intentions.

Howard did his best in these difficult months to ensure that the British case had a fair hearing. He maintained his contacts with people like Kellogg, Hoover, and House to press the argument that Britain had no desire to dictate to the United States what American naval requirements should be whilst, at the same time, Americans should understand that British naval requirements differed from theirs, something that meant Britain required a substantial cruiser fleet.[70] Suspecting that a large number of speeches and addresses would have little impact at this difficult juncture, he spoke only once in the five months after 4 August, a major speech to the rigidly pro-American Society of Mayflower Descendants at Boston on 21 November.[71] Coming a week after an outburst by Cecil in the Lords, and in the midst of the swirl of anti-British propaganda surrounding Britten's $400 million naval construction programme, Howard's remarks went directly to the heart of the matter. Enmity between Britain and the United States threatened the post-war order and, although the two Powers might not agree on every issue, those in both countries who exaggerated those differences and distorted cynically the policies of the other were playing a dangerous game. 'It is difficult for me not to believe', he avowed, showing his Atlanticist leanings, 'that those who seek to undermine [good Anglo-American relations] are, consciously or unconsciously, actively promoting a state of things which will make permanent peace far more difficult to realize and the possibility of a new world war more threatening than at present.'

Howard's diplomacy in this period also entailed conducting normal business within the United States. Regular Embassy work had not ground to a halt because of the ill-feeling surrounding the cruiser question; indeed, although naval matters were clearly the chief preoccupation of the ambassador, concentration on lesser questions might suggest to members of the Administration, the State and Navy departments, and others outside of government that British diplomats had equally pressing tasks to undertake. For instance, Franco-American discussions had been progressing since April 1927, the tenth anniversary of American entry into the war, about an as yet amorphous international treaty to outlaw war and achieve peace and security. This concept had captured the imagination of many prominent Americans, including Borah. Howard and his staff set about gathering information on 'the desire of "responsible elements" in the USA to remove causes of international conflict by peaceful means'.[72] Additionally, arbitration treaties concluded by the United States in 1908, during Root's tenure as secretary of state, were coming up for renewal in 1928. Rumours circulated in Washington that Kellogg was not going to seek to exclude matters of honour and vital interests from the scope of the new treaties. Howard set about seeking information on the new Franco-American arbitration treaty, the first to be renegotiated.[73] None of this is to suggest that Howard ignored what had been his principal task for nearly four years: improving Britain's image. He continued to do this, for instance, in sending messages of congratulation to various regional organisations on their celebration days,[74] and in arranging with BLINY for national distribution of a press notice to announce Britain's semi-annual payment on its war debt, a practice which then became the norm.[75] Not only was the British government, through Howard, taking an interest in local American affairs, but Britain was seen to be honouring its debt to the country as a whole.

Howard did not hide his belief that the emotions stirred by the cruiser question and the freedom of the seas still had the potential of damaging, perhaps irreparably, the Anglo-American relationship. For that reason, he greeted with joy Tyrrell's news that Chamberlain would press the Cabinet for an examination of belligerent rights.[76] Although Howard realised that his government had to be cautious in handling this matter, he implored Tyrrell to push the examination along as quickly as possible. Despite the low point to which Anglo-American relations had dropped, Howard saw signs of improvement. Hoover, now the leading candidate to secure the Republican presidential nomination in 1928, had dropped the strident nationalism that had marked his campaign in 1926 against British control of the world rubber market. With the responsibility of power facing him, Hoover seemed anxious to avoid antagonising Britain.[77] There also existed the growing support of a range of Americans for a pact to outlaw war, an eventuality that would force the American government to involve itself in international politics in a major way. Tied to the support that many Americans gave to their country's membership in both the World Court and the League, there existed reason for optimism about improving Anglo-American relations should the belligerent-rights issue be resolved satisfactorily.

Howard's assessment held that all was not lost. The cruiser question had strained relations, but this did not mean that the situation could not be improved. Careful handling of the United States, as Howard had been doing since February 1924, could repair the tears in the fabric of Anglo-American cordiality. But, until the belligerent-rights issue was put to rest, any good Howard might do could just as easily be undone. He warned Tyrrell that time was a precious commodity. Preliminary Anglo-American discussions about future blockade, necessary before any conference to limit belligerent rights at sea could occur, should happen soon. Once the 1928 presidential election campaign began, probably in late August 1928, any conversations in progress might die. No certainty existed that a new Administration would accept what had been agreed by that date or, worse, continue discussions. Even if the preliminary meetings remained feasible, the elections and transition of power would create a hiatus of six to eight months; new Administrations took office in the March following the election. More worrying, the chance existed of any secret preliminary talks becoming known; if this happened during the election campaign, given the sanctity of 'the freedom of the seas' in the American national lexicon, the 'Big Navy Party' candidates who supported it and other anglophobes would exploit the situation thus poisoning any chance of agreement. Howard apprised Tyrrell that the time was ripe for beginning 'pourparlers' with the Americans:

The dead leaves of pure isolationism are, I think, beginning to be pushed off by the new spring buds of a will to cooperate... If, however, we leave the question too long in abeyance, we may find [American leaders] all so occupied with the emotion of the Presidential election that they may either have no time to think of anything else or no will to do so.

On 23 November, under pressure from Chamberlain and his American specialists, who had swung Baldwin to their side, the Cabinet agreed to establish a CID sub-committee to enquire into 'the subject of Belligerent Rights at Sea'.[78] Baldwin was to determine its members and terms of reference. Howard and the Foreign Office had won a major struggle within the Baldwin government about restructuring basic British policy towards the United States. Difficulty now centred on not having Foreign Office suggestions defused by those reluctant to countenance a modification of established blockade policy, a group composed of Hankey, the Admiralty, and other British navalists.

III

Howard learnt formally of the Cabinet's decision in early 1928 when Chilton, on leave in Britain, received briefings at the Foreign Office.[79] Whilst gratifying, as it demonstrated that Chamberlain and the Foreign Office shared the Embassy's assessment of the situation and were prepared to force the Admiralty and other interested parties in London to consider doing something to alleviate American concerns, this news reinforced

Howard's determination to follow a quiet diplomacy to repair the Anglo-American relationship. Efforts in London to come to grips with the American question could be jeopardised if relations were strained further, this by needlessly raising the hackles of anti-Americans in the Cabinet and Civil Service. Just as important, if American opinion became more negative towards Britain in the charged atmosphere created by the cruiser deadlock, the controversy surrounding Cecil's resignation, and the other emotive issues of late 1927, American anglophobes and navalists could exploit these feelings to Britain's detriment. Hence, by keeping public appearances to a minimum to deny American critics a target through which to attack Britain, Howard dedicated his efforts to ensuring a smooth working relationship with Kellogg and official Washington. Whilst public opinion on both sides of the Atlantic might be riled, and although some elements in each government might wish it otherwise, it remained essential that there be a clear and open line of communication between the British Embassy and those making American foreign policy in Washington. In this endeavour, Howard adhered to all of the diplomatic maxims he had outlined to the Pilgrims in February 1924. His original goal had not changed, just the tactics to achieve it. He began this quiet diplomacy as the Coolidge conference began to fizzle, and he continued on the same path for almost a year, until he began his leave in June 1928.

Howard's first foray in his quiet diplomacy concerned those ceremonies to open the new Peace Bridge connecting Canada and the United States near Buffalo, New York. Scheduled for 7 August 1927, planning for the event had been under way for months, though Coolidge and other prominent American leaders had indicated that they would not participate.[80] Because Baldwin and the Prince of Wales were to be on a state visit to Canada at that time, the possibility existed that they and the Canadian prime minister, William Lyon Mackenzie King, might attend the ceremonies. Speculation to that effect circulated in late June but, as no high-level Americans were travelling to Buffalo, the Canadian governor-general, Lord Willingdon, suggested in Ottawa that neither Baldwin, the prince, nor Mackenzie King attend. Howard agreed to this until he learnt in the middle of July that Charles Dawes, Coolidge's vice-president, would speak at the opening.[81] Howard reckoned that the Americans might see the absence of prominent Imperial leaders, despite their lack of attendance being based on the announced intention of American leaders to refrain from coming, as a deliberate slight on American honour. With the failure at Geneva more and more certain, such a course would damage Anglo-American relations further and, probably, impair Howard's relationship with official Washington. 'I am concerned', Howard admonished Willingdon, 'that to have cancelled this visit would have been the reverse of helpful in the future, simply because it would have annoyed a good many important people and given cause to the Hearst Press and others to say nasty things.' The ambassador lobbied to have Baldwin, the prince, and Mackenzie King attend and speak. Although these public utterances were to come just three days after the final plenary session in Geneva, which created a stir in the Foreign Office and saw the despatch of points which Baldwin might embrace in his speech – 'If we can't <u>agree</u> as friends let's differ as <u>friends</u>.'[82] – the result was successful.[83] Tempers on neither side were incensed, and a minor incident did not escalate into a major crisis at a tense moment in Anglo-American relations.

Howard's efforts over the Peace Bridge incident set the tone for the diplomacy he pursued for most of the next year. This amounted to meeting problems as they arose, working to ensure that any potential they might have to disrupt Anglo-American relations disappeared, and all the while trying to keep both his government and his American hosts from sensing that their honour was being besmirched by the other or that some diplomatic coup was about to be achieved by one at the other's expense. In the almost twelve months from August 1927 until June 1928, Howard represented Washington in London as much as he represented London in Washington. As he remarked to Chamberlain in March 1928, the purpose of seeking to understand the Americans and their policies – always giving one's opponents credit for being in good faith – was 'trying to change the trend of policy of this [American] Government by allaying the suspicion the people unfortunately entertain of Europe and everything European'.[84] This constituted realistic diplomacy. Britain would achieve nothing if disputes arose with the United States over matters of little consequence. Minor issues should remain minor issues, and if Britain had to make concessions to settle these, it would both build up credit in the bank of diplomacy and, when major problems came to the fore and British diplomatists stood firm, show the Americans that here lay an issue on which Britain would remain resolute. However, the fact that Britain would not, merely to appease America, abjectly give in on every minor point would put the Anglo-American relationship on a firmer footing. The deadlock in Geneva showed this. The issue had been met; no compromise existed; it was time to re-establish a working relationship so that diplomatic life could get on. Naturally, Howard had to respect Foreign Office direction in conducting policy.[85] But, at the same time, he wanted the Foreign Office, and the Cabinet and Whitehall behind it, to understand the American position and respond positively.

Howard confronted several issues in the year of his quiet diplomacy that tested his method of repairing the fabric of Anglo-American discussions: ensuring that an exchange of technical information concerning liquor smuggling went smoothly; warning Vansittart privately about a prominent Wall Street law firm trying to find a British buyer for $38 million worth of clandestinely purchased Mexican silver bullion which could not be sold on the American market; and monitoring the unsuccessful efforts of the Egyptian minister at Washington to secure State Department support 'to drive the British out of Egypt'.[86] Aware that each had the possibility of escalating into a crisis if tackled improperly, Howard worked behind the scenes to ensure that the Foreign Office remained completely informed of all developments and that American officials had no reason to doubt British goodwill. His efforts went beyond official Washington when, to achieve a better British hearing on these and other questions in the American press, he fostered a re-organisation of the Embassy to handle better United States journalists.[87] All of these matters except one were easy for Howard to defuse. The exception involved Kellogg's determination to conclude a multilateral treaty to renounce the use of war as an instrument of national policy.

Howard's problem in this matter centred on Kellogg's apparent conversion to the fantastic idea that all Powers should renounce war, whilst the Powers themselves, especially Britain, saw the impracticability of promising not to use force to protect themselves from unprovoked aggression. The genesis of the renunciatory pact lay with a proposal by Briand in April 1927 that France and the United States conclude a bilateral arrangement to renounce war in their relationship.[88] Kellogg did not reply until December 1927, when he informed Paul Claudel, the French ambassador in Washington, that the Coolidge Administration rejected a bilateral agreement but would pursue a multilateral one. With this, Kellogg seized the initiative from Briand and seemed prepared to push a multilateral renunciatory pact on the other major Powers.

Howard experienced little surprise at Kellogg's action. Over the autumn of 1927, as Congress reconvened and the usual jockeying for political kudos began in anticipation of the 1928 election campaign, the Republican Administration faced mounting domestic pressure to do something to build international peace and security amidst the shambles of the naval conference. In late 1927 several prominent politicians, private citizens, and peace groups had been vocally pressing for an international agreement 'to outlaw war'. Howard surmised that, for reasons of domestic politics, Coolidge and Kellogg had to address these concerns: public opinion demanded it and influential politicians, integral to getting Administration bills through Congress and who endorsed 'outlawry' wholeheartedly, needed to be courted.[89] The Foreign Office American specialists, including Chamberlain, tended initially to the opinion that the Americans would only talk about renouncing war but do nothing concrete to bring about such a treaty. This can be seen in Foreign Office reaction to Howard's report that Coolidge had confidentially informed a British journalist that 'the United States Government was anxious to do everything possible to promote peace, [but] they had also to safeguard their natural rights in time of war and the difficulty was now to draw the line between these two aims'.[90] But Howard's reports after Kellogg's reply to Briand forced the Baldwin government in early 1928 to confront the determination of the Coolidge Administration to have the world's great Powers sign a treaty renouncing war.

In private correspondence with Chamberlain, Howard deprecated the idea of renouncing war.[91] It lacked realism. If Britain suffered an attack, it would violate the treaty by defending itself. If a portion of the British Empire was threatened by or fell to invaders, Britain would be branded a treaty-breaker through mounting any sort of counter-attack, either by sending in forces to dislodge the invader or using the Royal Navy to blockade the offending Power. If the League moved under the Covenant's collective security provisions to defeat some League-defined transgressor of international peace, all League members would be in violation of Kellogg's pact. Most important for Britain, perhaps, if the Locarno treaty was broken, any British action taken as a guarantor would mean *ipso facto* a British violation of the renunciatory provisions. Hence, Kellogg's ideas struck at the heart of Britain's ability to defend itself, the Empire, and the system of international security that had evolved since the war. Chamberlain echoed all of Howard's misgivings though, worrying for Howard, the foreign secretary's comments were interlarded with disparaging remarks about Kellogg's lack of realism, his ignorance of the security problems faced by Britain and the European Powers, and his failure to consult before making such revolutionary proposals. Whilst Howard strove to make Chamberlain see the matter from Kellogg's perspective, the ambassador and foreign secretary agreed on the ludicrousness of Kellogg expecting Powers to abandon their ability to defend their national interests with armed force simply to assist the Republican election strategy for the 1928 elections.[92]

Howard realised that Britain could not reject outlawry out of hand. Some important sections of domestic British opinion supported the idea.[93] More important, a British rebuff would certainly antagonise Kellogg and embolden anglophobic elements in the United States which had been strengthened to a degree by the failure at Geneva. '[It] would be as well to consider', Howard candidly told Chamberlain, 'whether it is or is not worthwhile to try to make this geste on the part of the United States Government of some lasting account to us all and not to cast this country back into the arms of the jingoes, the big navyites and the isolationists who are already rejoicing over the prospective failure of the latest peace move.'[94] This constituted the British problem: finding a means of protecting Britain's ability to defend its interests with force whilst not tampering with Kellogg's dream to the extent that Anglo-American relations would suffer. Since the summer of 1927, Howard had expended much energy keeping his relationship with Kellogg running smoothly. Professionally, Howard had taken pains to listen attentively and make constructive observations when he and Kellogg met to discuss all manner of diplomatic business.[95] On the social side, Howard ensured that Kellogg had invitations to all important functions at the British Embassy, something complemented by Howard and Isa dining privately with Kellogg and his wife a few times during the winter.[96]

Howard found himself, as a consequence, balancing between mutually suspicious men in Washington and London. With gentleness and tact, he pressured Kellogg to clarify exactly what renouncing war meant;[97] in this, Howard was joined by other key members of the Washington diplomatic corps, notably Claudel. Thus, on 15 March, Kellogg addressed the American Council of Foreign Relations to put his proposals on the record.[98] In doing this, he created additional disquiet at the Foreign Office and other chancelleries in the world when he refused to make a distinction between aggressive and defensive war.[99] Howard then joined other diplomats in Washington to convince Kellogg that there had to be this distinction, something Kellogg had admitted to Howard earlier when questioned about possible American policy should force be necessary to uphold the Monroe doctrine.[100] Confronting pressures in Washington, behind which stood Howard and Claudel, and in Europe, where Chamberlain and Briand, each wanting to maintain the spirit of Locarno, stood united, Kellogg made another speech on 28 April which allowed that defensive wars would be excluded from his pact.[101] Along with reports from Howard showing that the Americans had no intention of abandoning their right to use force to defend the Panama Canal,[102] Chamberlain, his advisers, and the Cabinet were ready to agree to become a party to the proposed treaty, the formal British acceptance coming less than two weeks after Kellogg's second speech.[103] As wars of self-defence were to be exempted, and since the Americans were not surrendering their right to defend the isthmian canal, the British note made specific reference to Britain's right to treat any attack on the Suez Canal and adjacent territory as an attack on Britain; under the rubric of 'self-defence', Britain would commit armed force to defend this vital region. This became known as the 'British Monroe doctrine' and, when accepted by Kellogg, British concerns about renouncing war evaporated. With other notes of acceptance following similar lines – most Powers followed the American lead and reserved for themselves the right to use force to defend certain bits of vital territory[104] – the treaty was signed by nine major Powers in Paris in August 1928. Given its utopian goal and the fact that it was shot full of holes by reservations, the outlawry of war counted for nothing in international politics. But, in terms of Anglo-American relations, it gave the Republicans what they wanted whilst not endangering Britain's ability to protect its national and Imperial interests. Just as important, Anglo-American relations were not disrupted in the months prior to the despatch of the British note, when Howard helped iron out fundamental differences on the proposed pact's application.

Although Howard was just one of a number of British diplomatists who settled the problem, his role in Washington in explaining the Baldwin government's policy to Kellogg, in interpreting the American scene to Chamberlain, and in preventing a further tear in Anglo-American relations remained crucial. The Foreign Office had observed that during the diplomacy preceding the British note Howard had seen rather much of Kellogg.[105] Since the renunciatory proposals were ostensibly a Franco-American endeavour, the Foreign Office did not wish to slight the always hypersensitive French *amour propre*. But Kellogg obviously felt the British attitude to be crucial, and this necessitated several meetings with Howard. Chamberlain, his senior advisers, and Vansittart, who had been seconded to 10 Downing Street in February 1928 as Baldwin's private secretary responsible for foreign-policy matters, had no doubt that Howard's handling of this delicate matter had ensured that Anglo-American relations did not suffer during the difficult winter of 1927–8. The recognition of this came in the King's Birthday Honours List on 4 June 1928, the day Howard sailed from New York on his annual leave; he was made a GCB.

Howard's year of quiet diplomacy also touched an issue not purely Anglo-American. This involved the position of Canada in its relations with both Britain and the United States. From the beginning of his service as ambassador in Washington, Howard put a high priority on keeping Anglo-Canadian relations on a firm footing. This constituted a throwback to his time as Bryce's counsellor when Canadian affairs formed part of his responsibilities, and it also conformed to his notions about the Empire that had formed from his time with Carnarvon. For Howard, Anglo-Canadian relations were fundamental to maintaining Britain's position as a world Power, since at the base of this was the need for a united Empire. Howard made annual trips to Toronto, Ottawa, and Montreal in 1924, 1925, and 1926, and his transcontinental journey in 1927 had been designed in part to allow him to make the British presence felt in western Canada. In the course of events, Howard cemented a firm friendship with Mackenzie King, whom he had met at Washington in 1908 and of whom he formed a high opinion.[106] These feelings were reciprocated[107] and, just as crucial, Howard established firm contacts with other Canadian politicians, men of commerce, and leaders of the academic community.[108]

Howard viewed the Anglo-Canadian relationship as part and parcel of the Anglo-American one. In fact, American relations with all of the independent dominions, especially the Irish Free State, were perceived by Howard as components of the general Imperial relationship with Washington. He expanded on this theme in a speech to the British Empire Club in Providence, Rhode Island, in September 1924, characterising the attitude of 'certain Englishmen who take pride in the area and the population of the British Empire as a whole, who love to look at a map of the world and see the areas that are coloured red as forming parts of that Empire, who like to think of the sun never setting upon it and so on' as 'a mistaken and a foolish reason for glorification'.[109] Affirming what he had learnt since serving at Dublin in the 1880s, he emphasised that the Empire was not a static entity. The course of Imperial development since the war demonstrated clearly that the dominions had their own foreign-policy interests and were prepared to pursue them, even if they did not conform precisely with those of Britain. This did not mean that Britain and the dominions did not share certain interests; they did, chiefly international peace and security. They also shared the common interest of good relations with the United States; and this was not a one-way transaction, as it was just as much in American interests to be on good terms with the Empire. Howard made specific reference, as befitted his Atlanticism, to the 'Anglo-Saxon race'. Here lay the kernel of his comments:

I venture to think this problem of the British Empire or Confederation of free and equal nations cannot but be a matter of interest to Americans. If it is true, as many say, that a good understanding between America and the British Commonwealth of Nations is the best guarantee of the Peace of the World, it must be a matter of importance that the nations forming that Commonwealth should remain as united as possible in a foreign policy aiming at the maintenance of peace which is now generally recognised as the greatest of all our interests.

Howard's efforts concerning Anglo-Canadian relations were designed to keep Canada as close to Britain as possible in a period when that dominion was being drawn culturally, economically, and politically closer to the United States. For Howard, little benefit would come from bemoaning Canada's slipping into the American orbit.[110] Britain had to acknowledge this and fashion policy accordingly if it wanted a unified Empire to continue. Thus, in 1924 when the Canadian government wanted its unofficial representative at Washington to be accorded official recognition as a member of the British Embassy, Howard supported it unequivocally.[111] When he met with Mackenzie King and the Canadian Cabinet on his various trips north, he did all possible to assure them that the British government remained 'quite satisfied as to [Canada's] attitude on all questions' relating to the United States.[112] When Mackenzie King enquired about Howard's assessment of Canada's decision not to adhere to the Locarno treaty, for instance, the ambassador 'said he thought [Canada was] right not to become a party, when U.S. was not[;] he saw the position quite clearly'.[113] By the time the Coolidge conference broke down, Mackenzie King had become a staunch defender of Howard, seeing him and his endeavours on Canada's behalf as 'excellent'.[114]

By the winter of 1927–8, Howard confronted a concerted effort by Mackenzie King's government to put Anglo-Canadian relations on a new footing, an effort with the potential of weakening intra-Imperial bonds. By late 1927 Mackenzie King determined to have a permanent British diplomat posted to Ottawa. This had been an issue in Anglo-Canadian relations for more than a year, reflecting both the dislike Canadian nationalists like Mackenzie King felt towards the Dominions Office at London, the ministry through which the two governments officially conducted business, and the Canadian premier's suspicion of the office of the governor-general, deriving from a constitutional crisis in 1926.[115] Moreover, after the 1926 Imperial conference, which declared that the independent dominions were 'autonomous communities within the British Empire, equal in status, in no way subordinate to one another in any respect of their domestic or external affairs',[116] Canada and the United States exchanged permanent diplomatic missions.[117] In keeping with his views on the evolution of the Empire, Howard supported this exchange, doing all he could to help the new Canadian minister, Vincent Massey, establish the Canadian Legation in Washington.[118] But the closeness of Canadian–American relations that ensued precipitated a heated debate within Baldwin's government about whether a British permanent mission should be established in Ottawa.[119] Nothing was resolved because of a power struggle between the Foreign and Dominions offices over the nature of the appointment, over which ministry in London this British diplomat would be responsible to, and other matters of bureaucratic significance. Matters reached a head between December 1927 and February 1928. In December, Willingdon was to pay an official visit to Washington that had been arranged by Massey and bypassed Howard's Embassy. This caused consternation in London because British authorities were kept in the dark about what the Canadians and Americans were to discuss.[120] When Kellogg paid a return visit to Ottawa two months later and, again, the Washington Embassy was not consulted – and, in this instance, Willingdon had also been bypassed – the issue had to be met.

Howard's role in this affair is interesting. The dispute between the Foreign and Dominions offices over jurisdiction became one of interdepartmental in-fighting in which Chamberlain and Leo Amery, the dominions secretary, and their respective advisers fought each other with barbed memoranda and sharp words in committee.[121] The choice of Sir William Clark in March 1928 as the British high commissioner represented a compromise between the two competing ministries in London: Clark had been head of the Department of Overseas Trade, a Foreign Office adjunct, but would report to the Dominions Office. Clark's mission would have two junior members, one from the Foreign Office and one from the Dominions Office, a further indication of compromise. Thus, a permanent British representative in Ottawa was to become a fact in 1928 – Clark arrived in Ottawa in the autumn – and did so to serve the interests of both the Foreign Office and Dominions Office.[122] None the less, although the main fight occurred in London, Howard made very positive contributions to this revolutionary development in intra-Imperial affairs by his reportings from Washington in the eight months after the Coolidge conference.

In a series of letters to Foreign Office colleagues and other interested parties at London like the king, he emphasised time and again that British–American–Canadian relations had to be run efficiently.[123] The Canadian–American connexion was in place and, as the Willingdon and Kellogg visits showed, seemed to be functioning without a hitch in terms of those states' bilateral relations. Britain stood as the odd man out. If the British wanted to ensure a uniform Imperial viewpoint on what could be loosely called Imperial foreign policy, this rather than seeking to preserve Imperial unity – a mirage after the 1926 Imperial conference – any entrenched opposition to sending a permanent diplomatic mission had to be overcome. With the myriad of tasks confronting it in representing Britain in the United States, the Washington Embassy could no longer adequately handle Canadian affairs. Besides, the establishment of the Canadian Legation in the American capital militated against such a task, something seen starkly in Willingdon's December visit. Times had changed since Bryce served in Washington; London had to accept this. As Howard bluntly told Stamfordham, the king's private secretary:

Our policy if we want to hold the Empire together is, I think, to encourage the national feeling in the Dominions in every way we can. To do this we have ourselves to recast our old ideas about the Empire based on the fundamental conception of a Mother country, head of the house and still ruler in it, and a number of minors not yet completely of age. We must rather take as our pattern a firm in which the father has taken his sons into partnership and allows them an equal say in the household.

Tempered by his observations of Canadian–American relations over more than two decades, of the desire of Canadian leaders whether French or English to run their own affairs, and of United States power in the North American continent, Howard's realistic observations added to the readjustment of the North Atlantic community that an appointment of a British high commissioner to Ottawa implied. British leaders at every level had to respond wisely to the Canadian question if they wanted to preserve the Empire or, just as important, retain some influence in the North American balance of power now dominated by the United States.

IV

Howard's leave, which began in June 1928, lasted until late September. These three months proved to be a high point in Howard's service in the United States and, thanks to an indiscretion by Chamberlain, saw renewed crisis in Anglo-American relations. In the summer of 1928, Chamberlain completed a series of ambassadorial appointments in major capitals which capped efforts he had been making since becoming foreign secretary to ensure the professionalism of the British diplomatic representation abroad. With the exception of Cairo, where the British high commissioner, Lord Lloyd – a former MP and governor of Bombay – had been appointed in 1925, all of Chamberlain's appointments since 1924 had been members of the Diplomatic Service.[124] Now, all major embassies and legations were manned by professionals. The work begun by Crowe and Tyrrell in the early 1920s to reverse Lloyd George's revolution in conducting British diplomacy had finally been successful. It is obvious that Tyrrell, rewarded by Chamberlain with the Paris Embassy in July 1928 for his loyal work as permanent under-secretary, had much to do with this; appointments were the prerogative of the head of the Foreign Office in consultation with his political chief. Significantly, in Chamberlain's period as foreign secretary only two ambassadors, both Service men, were not transferred or retired. These were Howard and Sir Ronald Graham, the ambassador in Rome.

Howard's remaining at Washington is significant. Although transfers and retirements do not necessarily mean that the Foreign Office was concerned about the kind of representation the British government had in various capitals – shifts constituted the normal round of promotions and moves – Chamberlain had had plenty of opportunity to remove Howard from the United States if he had felt the ambassador lax or failing in his duty. That Howard remained in Washington throughout Chamberlain's tenure as foreign secretary shows the opposite to be true. The Foreign Office held him in high regard, personally and professionally,[125] and his success in representing British interests and interpreting the United States to his colleagues in London for more than four years can be seen in the award of his GCB. This accolade was as much a reflexion of the high regard the Foreign Office had of him – as had the prime minister's office after Vansittart's secondment there – as it was a signal to Howard's critics in Britain that Chamberlain and the professionals stood by the chief British diplomatic agent in the United States.

By the middle of 1928, Howard had come under criticism in a number of quarters in Britain. Most of this derived from personal pique and religious intolerance. The Prince of Wales had lobbied privately against Howard in August 1927 with Mackenzie King and Baldwin during the visit to Canada.[126] This stemmed from the prince's resentment at his father's refusal to allow him to travel to the eastern United States whilst in North America, something for which the prince blamed Howard. On a trip to New York in 1924, the heir to the throne had narrowly missed being arrested at a speak-easy and Howard had then advised that the prince's American friends were not terribly trustworthy.[127] Unfavourable press coverage of royal indiscretions could damage Britain's image in the United States. But in this course of events Howard found no fault with the prince; he simply recommended that the prince not return to New York after a scheduled visit to the West. In 1927, the orders that the prince stay out of the eastern United States came directly from Buckingham Palace and had no connexion with Howard.[128] More insidious, by early 1928 a campaign was being directed by British Christian Scientists, led by the American-born Lady Nancy Astor, against Howard and Tyrrell as popish agents. John Astor was the proprietor of *The Times*, thus having contacts with journalists in the United States. 'I am much amused by the legend started in the American papers with regard to my exile in Paris', Tyrrell confided to Howard. 'I trace it back to a story started by the Christian Scientists last year to the effect that the Vatican expected to capture England and the United States for the Church through your and my agency. Every effort was to be made to remove us both!'[129] That the Astors were behind this emerged in December 1928 when Thomas Jones, one of Baldwin's private secretaries, lunched with them and some other prominent people. When Howard's name was mentioned, Jones recorded: '"They are all Catholics", shouted Lady Astor. "All the servants are – the Military Attaché, Air Attaché – everybody is a Catholic."'[130] As Jones deduced correctly from this, the Astors would be only too willing to follow the Howards as the British ambassadors to the United States.

Attacks on Howard mounted by spoiled young men and the politically ambitious posed no problems. However, when Hankey decided to turn his guns on the British ambassador, that was another story. When Howard first began to press for an examination of belligerent rights in the autumn of 1927, Hankey suspected that a conspiracy existed amongst Howard,

Tyrrell, and Henry Wickham Steed, a British journalist who had been advocating the same course in speeches both in Britain and the United States.[131] No evidence for such a conspiracy exists, but this did not stop Hankey from privately deprecating Howard's diplomatic skills and analytical abilities to a range of men inside and outside the British government during late 1927.[132] The full force of Hankey's broadside came in January 1928 when the Cabinet secretary circulated a memorandum to the belligerent rights sub-committee explicitly arguing that Howard was failing to interpret the American situation accurately to the Foreign Office and the Cabinet.[133] Howard's views, Hankey observed, were that the United States had the power to resist a British blockade – this had not altered since 1914–17 – but now also had the will; their determination to achieve formal naval parity with Britain showed this. Hankey countered that that will had existed during the war but the Americans had chosen to do nothing. Hence, stressed Hankey, Howard's missives enshrined 'an old fallacy'. The Baldwin government should devise its future blockade policy on the basis that, just because the Americans could resist a British blockade, this did not mean they would decide to do so. When this issue came before the belligerent-rights sub-committee two weeks later, Chamberlain endorsed Howard's contention, forcefully putting this as the more realistic means of approaching the naval impasse, and emphasising 'that it was wiser to try to reach agreement now than to trust to circumstances and day to day diplomatic skill as we did in 1914–17'.[134] Honouring Howard in June and keeping him at the Washington Embassy showed all of his critics that the Foreign Office supported him and his views and would do all possible to ensure they had a fair hearing at London.

Whilst Howard and his colleagues wrestled with the various facets of the American question during the winter of 1927–8, the Preparatory Commission continued looking for a basis for arms limitation. The Coolidge conference had been called because in American eyes the Commission had failed to strike upon a draft treaty, a result of British and French differences and the divergence of requirements needed by maritime versus terrene Powers. In March 1928, with the Commission near to collapse, Chamberlain approached Briand at a League Council to suggest that an Anglo-French compromise on arms limitation might benefit both Britain and France and save the Commission.[135] Doing this at the request of the Cabinet committee responsible for British arms-limitation policy, Chamberlain's overtures initiated a complex diplomacy that led to such a compromise on 28 July 1928.[136] The British were willing to accept French demands that reserve soldiers not to be counted when determining terrene strength. For their part, the French agreed that only 10,000-ton cruisers be limited. At British insistence, the major naval Powers, Japan, Italy, and the United States, were to be told of the compromise privately, along with the caveat that this was not carved in stone but was only to serve as a basis for renewed discussion. A degree of guile existed in the compromise, however, as the terrene portion, certain to upset the Germans who, by the Treaty of Versailles, could have no trained reserves, was to remain secret until the naval question had been settled. But the point remains that the impasse in the Commission had been overcome and the Powers could now continue their discussions. The details of the naval portion of the compromise were telegraphed to Rome, Tokyo, and Washington on 30 July, the same day that Chamberlain's foreign policy suffered attack in the Commons because of the apparent failure of arms-limitation discussions. Chamberlain sought to defend himself by mentioning the compromise, a blunder as the three governments had yet to receive the details; time-zone differences, deciphering, and other problems creating delay. Although Chamberlain was fighting severe illness – the next day he collapsed and took more than three months' convalescence – he lacked Cabinet approval to make the announcement. Because of a muddle at the Foreign Office created by his sudden absence and the new permanent under-secretary, Sir Ronald Lindsay, not knowing the full details of the initiative when he was grilled by American diplomats seeking more information, reaction everywhere except Tokyo was unfavourable. Rome, Berlin, and Washington each suspected that the British and French were attempting a diplomatic coup in the Commission. Sensitive about the cruiser question, the Americans proved especially wary. Additionally, as the 1928 election campaign was heating up and American politicians, Big Navyites, and anglophobes were on the make, the compromise was deliberately distorted in the American press. By the time Howard returned to duty in Washington in October, he again confronted a major crisis created by the naval issue. It consumed him for the remainder of his time as ambassador.

Howard's arrival back in the United States coincided with the final phase of the election campaign. Whilst Howard had been in England, Hoover had secured the Republican presidential nomination; Alfred Smith, the governor of New York, had won that for the Democrats. Embassy assessments of the resultant fight gave Hoover a slight edge;[137] Howard did not quibble with this once he surveyed the situation from the American side of the Atlantic, but, when Hoover won a decisive victory on 6 November, the margin of his success exceeded that which the Embassy and most American pundits had expected. In summing up the situation for the Foreign Office, Howard argued that Smith's Catholicism, opposition to prohibition, and support for increased immigration had alienated a range of traditional Democratic voters.[138] This had provided Hoover with a firm political base on which to pursue his brand of political conservatism at home and economic diplomacy abroad.

Howard did not share the unfavourable view of Hoover then prevalent at London and encapsulated most pungently in a Foreign Office minute that stated: 'Mr. Hoover is nothing less than a cold, aggressive nationalist – an efficient calculating machine who will push commercial and maritime competition with this country to the utmost.'[139] Howard had watched Hoover function in political office for more than four years and this, coupled with conversations the two men had had over Anglo-American relations, prompted Howard to give London a dispassionate assessment of Hoover's attributes: on the positive side, a 'complete self-reliance and a belief in himself and his country, an immense power of work and talent for organisation, a hatred of what he terms the "European frozen strata of classes", and of tyranny in any form which prevents completely free development of an individual who has merit above his fellows'; and, on the negative, 'a contempt for what he does not understand and therefore has no sympathy with', a man 'very sure that he is in the right and...therefore inclined to give no consideration to, and to ride roughshod over, imponderabilia which, however, may be of immense importance to others'; a man 'almost painfully susceptible to personal criticism...[who] is entirely lacking in those lesser graces of life'.[140] Finally, Howard addressed the general supposition that Hoover embodied strong anti-British sentiments. 'I do not think this is the case', Howard observed. 'I think that he is without prejudice for or against any particular foreign country, though he has a general prejudice against all foreign countries which he shares with most of his countrymen.' In this way, Howard saw the change of administrations – which would occur in March 1929 – auguring well for the settlement of Anglo-American naval differences. The British could deal with Hoover, a man not motivated by anglophobia in fashioning policy concerning Britain but, rather, one who sought practical, workable solutions to problems. Of course, the British had to handle him carefully, avoiding anything that called into question his genuineness or sincerity, and making certain he understood completely the British position beforehand so as to prevent him from riding roughshod over issues judged crucial to Britain. For Howard, Hoover appeared to be a man who London could be assured would deliver on his promises if approached diplomatically.

The general situation in the United States on Howard's return convinced him that the British had to take an active role in settling their naval differences with the Americans. A fifteen-cruiser bill was before Congress and, thanks to the press distortions concerning the Anglo-French disarmament compromise, little doubt existed that it would pass in early 1929.[141] Just as important, Borah had indicated his desire earlier in the year to force the Administration to call an international conference to codify maritime law.[142] He reckoned that the cruiser impasse in Geneva derived from the divergence of British and American views on the freedom of the seas in wartime; the British surmise was that they would be forced by the pressures of domestic and international opinion to attend the conference should it be called. As several Powers would see this as a means of protecting their trading interests should war break out, and Howard had his Swedish experiences during the war to rely on, this would weaken British belligerent rights. By November 1928, Borah succeeded in tacking his resolution on to the fifteen-cruiser bill; as this legislative package would certainly pass, Britain now faced a legalistic threat to future blockade policy.[143] Finally, Coolidge seemed particularly incensed over the Anglo-French proposals to break the impasse in the Preparatory Commission. Frustrated at the failure of his Administration's arms-limitation efforts and almost free from the constraints of office, he uncharacteristically lashed out. In a speech on 11 November commemorating the tenth anniversary of the armistice, he castigated British naval-arms policy in truculent terms, questioned the sincerity of the European Powers generally in seeking international peace and security, and appeared to call for American naval supremacy as the best protection for United States' external interests.[144] Coming from one who had impressed the Foreign Office as holding pro-British views, and as the most parsimonious of presidents where government arms spending was involved,[145] a significant shift in official American opinion concerning Britain seemed to have occurred.

Howard saw a major threat to Britain's survival as a Power of the first rank: Congress willing to extend the American cruiser fleet significantly; an international conference to codify maritime law on the horizon; and the previously reticent Coolidge lending his voice to calls for American naval superiority. Not only did the United States have the economic and industrial capacity to build 'a navy second to none', it clearly had the will. Hence, the ambassador decided to return to the visible ambassadorial presence that had marked his first three years in Washington, this coupled with determined efforts behind the scenes to pre-empt American efforts to undermine belligerent rights in a future war.

Howard decided to approach Hoover privately to impress on him the dangers posed to both Britain and the United States by a conference on maritime law. He had clearance to do this. In March 1928, when Borah announced publicly that he would pursue the calling of such a conference, Howard urged that it would be profitable to hold secret preliminary talks with the Americans to achieve prior agreement on blockade – it would be just as much in American interest to support high belligerent rights.[146] But because of the uncertainty of who would win the 1928 elections, Howard and Chamberlain agreed that such preliminary discussions should wait until the new Administration took power a year hence – if a Democratic Administration took office, it might reject what its Republican predecessor had arranged.[147] Chamberlain wanted Howard fully apprised of what had been transpiring in the belligerent-rights sub-committee, thus, he arranged for Craigie to do this on the latter's visit to his wife's family in Georgia in April 1928. Craigie met with Howard, discussed the situation with him, and held some general conversations with State Department officials which, among other matters, touched belligerent rights.[148] Howard and Craigie confirmed the moment inopportune to hold preliminary discussions with American authorities; the renunciatory pact occupied all of their time. However, in his instructions to Howard, Chamberlain allowed that, should the ambassador judge that a maritime-law conference was imminent and that invitations might be suddenly despatched to Britain and other Powers, he had the freedom to discuss with Kellogg the need for preliminary Anglo-American conversations.[149]

Howard saw the wisdom of this, though he argued that a private approach to Borah might be all that was needed to pre-empt the call for such a conference.[150] The Foreign Office refused to sanction an approach to Borah because of the importance of questions like the renunciatory pact. When Howard was on leave in Britain, Chamberlain arranged for him to acquaint the belligerent-rights sub-committee with the situation as seen from the perspective of the Washington Embassy. Howard affirmed the need for prior consultations with the Americans should a conference be called, and in this he surprisingly had the support of Hankey.[151] But the committee avoided a decision on whether Borah should be headed off. Thus, whilst in Britain, Howard continued pressing for a private approach to Borah to abandon calling a conference on maritime law, an approach to be based on the argument that this conference might run counter to the renunciatory pact's intention to isolate a transgressor of international peace. Given Borah's suspicious nature concerning Europeans, Howard suggested that Vincent Massey, who the senator apparently trusted, could do this.[152] But the Foreign Office demurred.[153] So when Howard returned to Washington and within weeks the resolution tacked on to the fifteen-cruiser bill appeared on Congress's legislative agenda, he followed the belligerent-rights sub-committee decision to sound out the Americans about preliminary conversations.

When the Foreign Office reaffirmed its opposition to confronting Borah directly,[154] Howard canvassed his old friend, James Garfield, to see if he would warn Hoover about the danger to Anglo-American relations of a premature conference on maritime law. Garfield agreed to help but, as Hoover had gone on a short visit to South America after his victory, would be unable to talk to the president-elect for several weeks. Certain of Garfield's help, Howard sought Chamberlain's sanction for his strategy and, to underscore the seriousness of the situation, asked that Baldwin be apprised of what was intended.[155] To augment this pressure on the Foreign Office, Howard wrote privately to Vansittart to outline his views on the blockade question: he emphasised that the wartime blockade had worked because the United States had supported Britain, and that Britain could not rely on this happening in the future given apparent American support for the freedom of the seas and a determination to build a cruiser fleet equal to that of Britain. 'I don't see', he told Vansittart, 'any prospect of a successful war against any first class Power + America.'[156] He ended by stressing, yet again, that it would be 'wiser to agree with [the] U.S. on what we can do & how far we can go, before there is any danger of the excitement of war' and, before Borah's resolution was passed, that quiet and informal discussions with Hoover would allow for seeing 'if there is no way of reaching a terrain d'accommodement'.

Howard's letters found a receptive audience at both the Foreign Office and Downing Street. Chamberlain, Lindsay, Vansittart, and Baldwin all supported using Garfield as an intermediary, and Howard received instructions to use Garfield as he saw fit.[157] Borah's resolution, which came at the same time as a proposal from Fred Britten, the chairman of the House of Representatives Committee on Naval Affairs, to Baldwin to convene an inter-parliamentary conference on naval limitation – which Baldwin and Chamberlain carefully defused by conciliatory words about this being a matter for the executive branches of government[158] – galvanised the Baldwin government into finally determining its policies towards the United States. During Chamberlain's absence, the Foreign Office had been under increasing attack from anti-Americans in the Cabinet and the sub-committee on belligerent rights.[159] Because of the mishandling of the Anglo-French disarmament compromise and the resultant ill-will on both sides of the Atlantic, the Admiralty, the Dominions Office, and other critics of the Foreign Office ranging from Hankey to Churchill were seeking to prevent any new direction being made in Britain's American policy. If nothing was done, so the anti-Foreign Office argument went, Anglo-American relations would improve eventually. However, the Foreign Office took the view that all of the elements damaging good Anglo-American relations – naval arms limitation, belligerent rights, and even the proposed arbitration treaty – were not going to go away. In fact, the problem was that these elements constituted a 'vicious circle', each feeding off the others. Unless they were all settled at once, differences between the two countries would only intensify. The impending passage of the fifteen-cruiser bill, which had support from such usually pro-British press organs as the liberal *New York World*, offered clear testimony to this: a strengthened United States Navy was necessary to protect freedom of the seas in the event of a future great war. The Foreign Office sought a single overall policy to tackle all the problems in Anglo-American relations. There had to be balance between 'political' and 'technical' considerations, a reproach to the hypersensitive attitude of British navalists that had suffused official British discussion of the American question since the Coolidge conference. Once Chamberlain resumed his duties in late November, and assessed the situation, he moved quickly. He brought Baldwin around to the Foreign Office side, outflanked his ministry's critics in the Cabinet, and used his strong position in both the Conservative Party and the Cabinet to force constructive debate within the belligerent-rights sub-committee. By the middle of March 1929, thanks to Chamberlain, the belligerent-rights sub-committee had arrived at an overall American policy with which to resolve the American question.

Whilst his Foreign Office colleagues fought the bureaucratic battles in London, Howard pursued his active diplomacy within the United States. He again began to assume a visible presence, opening a home for aged British men and women in New York, speaking to groups like the Daughters of the American Revolution, and accepting an honorary degree at Trinity College in Hartford, Connecticut. If Britain's image within the United States had any chance of being revived to the level it enjoyed when he made his trans-continental trip in 1927, he could not wait until the Foreign Office overcame its enemies at home. Efforts he could make to affect a positive image of Britain in the United States, no matter how small the improvement, would only make easier the ultimate application of any new method of ameliorating Anglo-American relations. As he wrote to Bridgeman in early 1929 when the latter asked for Embassy assistance in correcting garbled American press reports about recently announced British cruiser construction: 'What we want for this, however, is the establishment of a spirit of friendly confidence between – not only the two peoples[;] that would not be so difficult – but also between the admiralties which is more difficult.'[160]

Howard even ventured into the nettled thicket of public comment on the naval question.[161] A week after the fifteen-cruiser bill passed the Senate in February 1929, a reporter from the Associated Press asked Howard what British naval policy would be now that the American cruiser fleet was to be strengthened. Without specific information but armed with statements made by Chamberlain, Bridgeman, and other British political leaders in the

Commons and on the public platform, Howard responded: 'Proposals for [a] new approach to [the] settlement [of the] disarmament problem may be made by [the] British government to [the] Uni[ted S]tates in [the] near future...'[162] As the next session of the Preparatory Commission was scheduled for April, American journalists immediately speculated that the British were about to make concessions of some kind to the United States. Hence, the idea that major proposals were in the offing gained currency. Howard, working closely with BLINY and the Foreign Office News Department, then issued statements that the British government was preparing for the next round of Preparatory Commission meetings, like every other Power, and hoped that there might be some progress then. The matter ended, but with the result that the Baldwin government was seen making efforts to come to grips in a positive way with the problem of naval arms limitation. The success of Howard's return to a visible presence in the United States began to be seen by the end of February 1929 when assessments of American opinion from places like California began to show a general improvement in feelings towards Britain.[163]

Howard's diplomacy in the months after the election also entailed the routine task of assessing the opinions held by American leaders. Given the state of the naval and blockade questions and the fact that the transition in administrations had begun, this assumed more importance than normal. Howard grasped that, whilst general American opinion seemed to be warming towards Britain by the New Year, a strong current of anglophobia amongst influential supporters of the 'Big Navy Party' could not be discounted. Frank Simonds, the foreign editor of the *American Review of Reviews* and a dedicated anglophobe who had distinguished himself in Geneva in 1927 with malicious distortions of British proposals, was especially prominent in this respect. He argued over and over again in print after the election that Anglo-American war would be the certain result of another European struggle in which Britain moved to blockade its enemies.[164] In addition, with the passage of the fifteen-cruiser bill and the resolution calling for a maritime law conference, plus the ratification of the renunciatory pact, powerful American newspapers in the 'Big Navy' camp – the *New York Herald Tribune* and the *Chicago Tribune* – were concerned that this might undermine sentiment in the United States against further naval expansion.[165] These press organs would be only too happy to use any British reluctance to conclude an agreement on future blockade as an excuse to press for increased naval construction. Thus, threats to improving Anglo-American relations lurked beneath the surface in the form of the dichotomy between the British doctrine of maritime belligerent rights and the American theory of the freedom of the seas. Seeing this, Howard kept up his pressure on the Foreign Office to do what it could in the belligerent rights sub-committee to strike upon a general policy towards the United States that would resolve the blockade matter and, thereby, remove the American threat of building a 'navy second to none'.[166]

On the positive side, Howard's discussions with congressional leaders and members of both the outgoing and incoming administrations convinced him of official Washington's desire to settle United States' differences with Britain. Publicly, this shift occurred when Coolidge seemed to recant his Armistice Day truculence in speeches in early December 1928 and late February 1929, a result of a reasoned British response and general foreign displeasure with the bombast of 11 November.[167] Privately, using opportunities presented by the normal social rounds, Howard had been able to draw out the views of Coolidge, Kellogg, Borah, Dwight Morrow, the American ambassador in Mexico City and one of Hoover's closest confidants, Reuban Clark, the under-secretary of state, and others.[168] Morrow's comment typified the softening of opinion towards Britain in the upper reaches of the American foreign-policy-making elite.[169] During desultory luncheon conversation with Hoover's friend in the middle of January, Howard discovered that feelings existed in influential quarters in Washington that an understanding with the British 'could be found and ought to be found without delay provided the matter was handled by real statesmen and not sailors'. The implication in these words was that the new leadership saw a settlement of Anglo-American differences residing with politicians and diplomats rather than naval experts. It harkened back to the Washington conference where, the general wisdom held, Balfour and Hughes had achieved a capital ship-building ratio only by shutting out their technical advisers from their deliberations. Morrow's observations were seconded by other men whom Howard consulted, like Clark who held that all that was required for a settlement of differences was 'two men of reasonable views and weight in their countries and the result is practically assured'.[170] The basis for some sort of Anglo-American settlement seemed possible as Hoover's inauguration neared.

Howard faced one major difficulty in this: determining Hoover's opinion. Despite his permission to use Garfield as an emissary, this initiative failed to bear fruit. Hoover's political commitments in the period after his return from South America prevented a meeting with Garfield. In early February, Garfield had to travel to Mexico on a long-planned business trip and, although he indicated that he would do what he could when he returned, Howard believed that Hoover had to be approached without delay: in the first week of February, the ambassador learnt that

Hoover had made promises to Borah to tackle the freedom of the seas at an early date.[171]

Howard felt that there had been enough procrastination in London. For nearly a year the threat of a maritime-law conference had hung over British heads, but nothing had been done to prepare for such an eventuality other than agreement within the belligerent-rights sub-committee to approach the White House directly should a conference seem imminent. The issue had now to be met, and Howard immediately sought Chamberlain's permission to approach Hoover about British concerns over a conference which might affect future blockade practices. Chamberlain wired back within a day that Howard should see the president-elect or, if that proved impossible given the new president's Cabinet-making and other tasks, put the matter privately to the State Department with the proviso that the British viewpoint be transmitted to Hoover.[172] The nub of Howard's instructions was that the British government 'earnestly deprecate[d]' an early conference and required that, whenever one was called, there be adequate time for full and confidential Anglo-American discussions beforehand. Howard worked quickly. Hoover was in Florida, so Howard approached William Castle, the assistant secretary of state and 'a personal friend' of the president-elect.[173] Howard outlined the British case and the desire of his government to have prior Anglo-American conversations. He also asked Castle to ensure a meeting with Hoover as soon as possible so that Howard could discuss the situation with him. Seeing the wisdom of pre-conference discussions, Castle promised to arrange a meeting between Hoover and Howard. He also added that it might be advantageous if, after the impending British elections, Baldwin might consider an autumn visit to the United States for private conversations with the president. That Congress would be in recess at the time would provide less domestic American pressures on both leaders. Howard supported this idea, adding only that if it was 'practicable' for Baldwin to visit Washington, the 'ground might be prepared and minor technical difficulties adjusted so that the discussions in September need not be needlessly prolonged'.

Howard's discussions with Castle received Foreign Office approval and, over several weeks, he received various instructions about specific matters he should bring up with Hoover.[174] Finally, on 16 March, after the inauguration, Howard met the president.[175] To ensure that he did not stray over the boundaries established by London, Howard read paraphrases of Foreign Office communications which the Embassy had received during the preceding month. Hoover took it all in and responded that nothing would be done for a while. The new secretary of state, Henry Stimson, the governor of the Philippines who had resigned this post to succeed Kellogg, had not yet arrived in Washington. Hoover indicated that, until Stimson had studied the problem, nothing would be done about calling a conference. The new president appeared completely non-committal, though he ended this conversation by remarking that 'No one desires cordial relations between our two countries more than I do.' Although Craigie did not see this meeting as promising much for Hoover's 'cordiality' towards Britain, at least there were to be preliminary Anglo-American conversations should a Borah-style conference be called.[176] But, as Craigie also saw, Hoover seemed unwilling to move until after the political air had cleared in Britain following the approaching General Election.

Howard's tasks were now simpler. The urgency of a maritime-law conference had receded, with every chance existing that some sort of settlement might come after the Baldwin Conservatives returned to office. Central to this settlement would be a visit by Baldwin to the United States. Castle's suggestion that the prime minister consider an autumn trip to the United States had been made because Baldwin, in a conversation with Castle when the latter visited London in late 1928, had broached the subject.[177] Although Howard remained unaware of Baldwin's overture to Castle, Baldwin had made the same suggestion to Howard during the summer of 1928. Whilst Howard mentioned nothing of this at the time to the Foreign Office, he began to suggest to both Vansittart and Chamberlain in late January 1929 that such a visit would do much to settle Anglo-American differences.[178] He told his two colleagues that Baldwin was held in high regard in Washington, a function of his work in 1923 when he was chancellor of the exchequer in settling the Anglo-American war debt.[179] Howard felt that even if the prime minister ultimately could not or would not make the journey, personal diplomacy held decided promise:

I cannot help feeling that if in the course of next Autumn, after the General Elections, H.M. Government would send over here some really important statesman, who would command respect and confidence both in England and America, to establish personal contacts and to talk the matter over with Mr. Hoover and his Secretary of State, whoever he may be, an arrangement re naval construction might be come to without great difficulty and in a comparatively short time.

This found a receptive audience at the Foreign Office, where even Chamberlain toyed with the idea of travelling to Washington.[180] But, as Vansittart told Howard, such plans had to be held in abeyance until after the General Election which, finally, was scheduled for 30 May.[181]

As Howard continued to assess the improving situation in Washington,[182] the Baldwin government prepared to go to the people. They also prepared to resolve the American question once they returned to power.

The belligerent-rights sub-committee had finished its work in the middle of March and, following the lead of Chamberlain and the Foreign Office, had produced a blueprint for settlement that had struck one overall policy to handle the various facets of British difficulties with the United States.[183] The Cabinet learnt of this policy in two reports. Circulated on 13 February 1929, the first held that if Britain had to sign an arbitration treaty with the United States along the lines of the Kellogg formula – Baldwin's government had delayed concluding such a treaty in order to work out these problems – Britain would not specifically reserve belligerent rights. The reason for this stemmed from the overwhelming majority of the committee supporting Chamberlain's view that should the United States become involved in war with another country, no American government and its diplomatic and naval advisers would want blockade practices of any sort subject to third-party restrictions. The second report, finished on 6 March, concluded that Britain should seek to maintain belligerent rights at the highest level possible – the Foreign Office had argued for this all along despite Hankey's shrieks to the contrary – and, should a conference on maritime law be called, defend these rights in preliminary conversations with the Americans to harmonise beforehand 'as far as possible the views of the two Governments'. Together, so the majority of the sub-committee argued, these initiatives would reduce Anglo-American friction and retard the growth of the United States Navy because Britain would not be seen as an adversary. Of course, ten days later, Howard broached the possibility of preliminary talks with Hoover. Although Baldwin delayed full Cabinet discussion of this proposed policy until after the election – he wanted his ministers to concentrate on the campaign – little doubt existed that Chamberlain and his supporters would get their way after 30 May.

From additional reports from Howard, it also appeared to the Foreign Office and the Cabinet that by early March Hoover was putting a conference on maritime law on a back-burner, despite his promise to Borah. Howard reported on 8 March that sources close to the president suggested that he had ordered American diplomats 'to sound out the Governments of the major Powers upon their willingness to hold another naval disarmament conference'.[184] This seemed a godsend; a naval settlement achieved before a maritime-law conference would render nugatory any effort to restrict belligerent rights legally. Anglo-American naval competition would end, and the arguments favouring a large American navy – protecting the freedom of the seas – would evaporate. Accordingly, in April 1929 at the next session of the Preparatory Commission, the American delegation made the novel suggestion that a 'naval yardstick' be found in order to determine how many light cruisers equalled a heavy one. With the Anglo-French compromise dead and the

Americans suddenly making a proposal which the Cabinet characterised as 'hopeful', an opportunity existed to resolve Anglo-American differences. Such hope received a boost when Hoover appointed Dawes to succeed Houghton in London. By having such a prominent man as ambassador, Hoover was sending a clear message that he placed a high priority on settling differences with Britain.[185] Even Craigie, so suspicious of Hoover, began to soften his assessment of the new president.[186] The resolution of the American question was there for Chamberlain and the Baldwin Cabinet; all the Conservatives had to do was win the election. However, in an unexpected turn of events, MacDonald and the Labour Party triumphed on 30 May and, though without a clear majority in the Commons, formed a minority government in the first week of June.

Howard did not see the advent of MacDonald as a blow to the process of settling Anglo-American differences. In a personal sense, Howard got on with the new prime minister. After all, he and MacDonald worked together well during Howard's first nine months in the American capital and, subsequently, the two had maintained a sporadic correspondence.[187] It had rankled with British diplomats when MacDonald used his position as leader of the opposition to muddy the waters of Anglo-American relations between late 1924 and the middle of 1929,[188] but this did nothing to lessen the ambassador's opinion of his new leader. Indeed, in the United States, MacDonald had a good reputation, a result of his generally pro-American comments during the years of crisis and his tendency to blame the Baldwin government and not the Coolidge Administration for the strain in the relationship[189] – not unnatural given the role of the opposition in Britain's parliamentary system. On the British side after 30 May 1929, MacDonald became central to the final settlement of Anglo-American differences. Although he appointed a Labour Party luminary, Arthur Henderson, as foreign secretary, the prime minister retained for himself control of British foreign policy towards the United States. He determined to engineer a settlement with the Americans both to accrue political credit for the Labour Party with British voters and to enhance his international image as peace-maker. This became evident within days of his replacing Baldwin and, amongst the foreign- and defence-policy specialists in the civil service, there ensued a struggle to win the heart and mind of the new premier. Almost immediately the Foreign Office, on the one hand, and the navalists led by Hankey, on the other, bombarded the new occupant of Downing Street with memoranda rehashing all of the arguments that had preoccupied the Baldwin government and the CID since the autumn of 1927.[190]

Howard joined in this lobbying. A week after Labour's victory, he wrote a lengthy letter to MacDonald, first, to ensure that his new political master could count on 'my acting in accordance with all instructions which I receive from your Government' and, secondly, 'that it seems to me *most important* for the settlement of the questions at issue between ourselves and this country that you should come here and get into personal contact with the President'.[191] Howard also outlined the situation in the United States as he saw it. Hoover, in his few months in office, had become 'much more interested' in achieving a naval agreement rather than one relating to belligerent rights. This stemmed from the former being 'immediately feasible', whilst the latter 'would take a very long time to settle internationally'. In fact, Howard had discovered that Dawes carried with him to London instructions 'not to go too far in the matter of the Freedom of the Seas'. Thus Hoover seemed bent on getting a naval-arms-limitation agreement with Britain and, perhaps, doing nothing about codifying maritime law. Even Borah, who had confided in Howard, acknowledged that practical difficulties existed in drawing up a contraband list. The frosty Anglo-American relations, which had begun to melt in the final months of the Baldwin government, seemed to be disappearing completely in a warming atmosphere of co-operation.

It is not surprising that Howard and the Foreign Office, the voices of moderation, succeeded in winning MacDonald to their side. Wanting to end Anglo-American discord, the prime minister was amenable to making some compromise. In addition, with a residual faith in the Foreign Office dating back to his brief tenure as foreign secretary in 1924,[192] and with Vansittart remaining as the principal foreign-policy adviser in the prime minister's office, MacDonald saw the wisdom of achieving a diplomatic settlement rather than letting matters slide, the policy of inactivity supported by Hankey and the anti-Americans. Full of confidence, MacDonald lunched with Dawes on 16 June; Howard's predictions encased in his 6 June letter came true. The thrust of Dawes' remarks was that an Anglo-American naval agreement was essential, that the other naval Powers had to be assured that they would not be presented with an Anglo-American *fait accompli*, that MacDonald visit Washington only when the chance for an agreement was possible so as to avoid raising hopes unnecessarily on both sides of the Atlantic, and that 'questions of belligerent rights, freedom of the seas, and so on, will not rise for the moment'.[193] Dawes also assured MacDonald that Hoover and his advisers were near to arriving at the formula that would constitute the 'yardstick' proposed in April. As soon as this was accomplished, the British would be given the figures, and these would serve as the basis for preliminary discussions. From other reports despatched by Howard, and from information Craigie brought back from the Preparatory Commission in April, the British understood that Hoover wanted a separate naval-arms conference to convene as soon as was practicable.[194] A diplomatic resolution of the American question now seemed at hand. All that had to be done was to smooth the rough spots so that MacDonald could travel to the United States to cement a settlement.

By September, MacDonald was ready to meet with Hoover. The story about how the final diplomatic ground was prepared for this crucial turn in the history of inter-war Anglo-American relations is well known.[195] The MacDonald government modified the belligerent-rights sub-committee proposals concerning Britain's American policy on only a single point: it decided not to conclude a new arbitration treaty with the United States. It was to rely on the League in matters of arbitration. In 1920 an amendment had been introduced to the Protocol of the International Court of Justice at the Hague, a League body, to aid in arbitration and conciliation procedures. It was not compulsory, hence it was called the 'Optional Clause', but once states signed it they were bound to accept the Court's jurisdiction without reservation in disputes involving any interpretation of treaties, all questions of international law, any 'breach of international obligation', and the level of award in the event any such breach occurred. This ended any chance for bilateral arbitration treaties with other Powers. Britain acceded to the 'Optional Clause' a week before MacDonald departed for the United States. With respect to belligerent rights, Dawes' talks with MacDonald indicated that this would not be a problem, but the Cabinet, although it argued about how 'high' belligerent rights were, conformed to what the Chamberlain Foreign Office had got the CID to accept. Concerning the naval limitation question, the 'yardstick' proved to be illusory given the task of actually sitting down and determining how many light cruisers equalled a large one. Regardless, both sides indicated their willingness to make compromises over the positions they had held in Geneva in 1927, the British reducing the number of light cruisers they sought and the Americans modifying their hardline over heavy ones. MacDonald embarked from Southampton on 28 September; that the diplomats rather than the sailors had the ear of the prime minister can be seen with the two chief advisers he took with him: Vansittart and Craigie.

Howard and his Embassy were to a large degree left out of the negotiating process that preoccupied the two governments during the summer. All the Embassy did in this respect was to act as a conduit for messages between the MacDonald Cabinet and the Hoover Administration.[196] This did not upset Howard. As he had known for almost thirty years, determining policy was the responsibility of those in London in charge of the big foreign-policy picture. Of course, normal diplomatic work continued. This meant ensuring that no problem, no matter how insignificant, escalated into a crisis that could damage the improving relationship. Howard understood the delicate state of Anglo-American relations at this juncture. As he told Craigie when the 'Big Navy' press circulated comments in July that the United States should demand a naval base in Ireland as compensation for any compromise with Britain: 'I thought I would call your attention to it as it may indicate a move on the part of the Big Navy Party here to make some sort of demand of this kind...in order to create difficulties and prevent any kind of understanding with Great Britain.'[197] As a result, Howard elected to stay in hot and humid Washington for the entire summer. If any problem developed, he was going to be there to deal with it personally.

Because of Howard's efforts, nothing occurred to disrupt the smooth course being charted by MacDonald and Hoover; and there were some potentially dangerous moments. For instance, just at the time of the change of government in Britain, charges were levelled by American prohibitionists that the British Embassy was engaged in selling bootleg liquor in the United States. In late May, as a result, Howard had private correspondence with an influential prohibitionist who was pressuring Hoover's Administration to end the consumption of liquor at embassies and legations by prohibiting the import of these beverages under bond.[198] The British diplomats were blameless, which Howard emphasised in his correspondence and in public statements. But, given the state of Anglo-American relations to that point, Howard made a move of public relations brilliance by announcing that the Embassy would 'abstain from any further application to the State Department for permission to bring wines and spirits into the country' for the time being.[199] More than this, amidst a flourish of publicity, he met with Stimson to clear the air, and the new secretary of state responded with the announcement that the importation of Embassy liquor remained 'a matter of diplomatic immunity and privilege'. Further discussions were to be held at some future date between Howard, now the doyen in Washington, and Stimson to clarify the matter concerning the entire diplomatic corps. Howard anticipated that the Administration would not restrict the privileges of diplomats working in the United States since this might create difficulties for those enjoyed by American ones in other countries. Stimson's support for immunity and privilege showed this.[200] But, for the meantime, the matter ceased to have any importance.

Despite his exclusion from the policy debates in London during the summer of 1929, Howard became pivotal in MacDonald's efforts to control British policy towards the United States. If MacDonald had any chance of dominating the discussions about policy towards the United States, that is in overcoming within the new Cabinet and the Civil Service the anti-

Americans, naval hardliners, and those reluctant to formalise some sort of naval-arms-limitation agreement with the United States, he had to have a grip on the situation in Washington. Rather than rely on Henderson to supply information from the Foreign Office confidential prints and via briefings, the prime minister decided to tap into Howard's well-established connections in Washington. Waiting until after his meetings with Dawes in the middle of June, in which everything the ambassador had said proved to be true, MacDonald replied to Howard in a private, hand-written letter – that it had not been dictated to a secretary for typing and later signature showed MacDonald's determination to impress on Howard the importance of a link between Downing Street and the Washington Embassy.[201] He supported the idea of meeting Hoover but for various reasons – he listed seven dealing with matters of internal and external policy – wished to delay going to the United States. 'The General [Dawes] said that America would welcome me', MacDonald confided to Howard, 'but I said I thought that it should be staged as the final & not as the opening act. I shall keep my hand upon the transactions here & then go over to cement the results if they are of any consequence.' He concluded by seeking Howard's comments on this, as well as any other points the ambassador might consider important. This exchange of letters in June set in train a highly secret correspondence between Howard and MacDonald which extended over the summer and cleared much of the way for MacDonald's successful visit to the United States in the autumn.

Howard's initial letters concerned the timing of the visit. Although unable to see Hoover because of the president's other commitments, Howard met with Stimson in late June and early July.[202] Whilst the Administration agreed that a hasty visit by MacDonald might be counter-productive before the general principles of a naval agreement were settled, once these were determined, he might with profit make the transatlantic crossing. Howard concurred, something he stressed in his report to MacDonald with the comment that a visit then 'would bring about the direct personal contact between yourself & the President which, unless I am mistaken, would do so much to help on an arrangement'. Naturally, a high-level meeting before determining the specific details of limitation was a gamble. Howard acknowledged this, but he counselled MacDonald that delaying a visit until it could serve as a 'final act' would rob any discussions with Hoover of 'a great deal of [their] utility'.

Howard's advice helped MacDonald make the decision to travel to the United States in the autumn. The prime minister's mind had been moving in this direction for most of July and, on the 24th, he announced in the Commons that he was intending to visit Washington in October.[203] To demonstrate his commitment to naval-arms limitation, MacDonald also announced the cancellation of two submarines and a submarine-depot ship, as well as the halting of construction on two new cruisers. Two days later MacDonald wrote to begin preparations for his meeting with Hoover – the president has responded to the British cuts by immediately suspending construction on three American cruisers. 'I think on this matter I might ask for your good services', Howard was told, 'as it would be far better to have it discussed personally than by slow correspondence.'[204] Howard also learnt that the prime minister would come only with his daughter, who served as his hostess, and a few secretaries, one of whom would be Vansittart. MacDonald did not desire 'to burden [himself] with papers or documents unless there were some topics upon which conversations of a detailed character were desired'.

Although Howard had no difficulty in working with Hoover, Stimson, and other members of the Administration in preparing for MacDonald's visit, problems arose in predictable quarters. The most serious concerned Borah. In late August, as the principles of Anglo-American naval agreement were being polished, Howard informed MacDonald that Borah might be moving to scuttle a settlement.[205] Howard surmised that this derived from the senator being excluded from helping to father this 'particular political egg'. Howard outlined the problem in precise terms:

[Borah] is therefore in a hypercritical mood, and, unless he can get all the reduction in the American cruiser programme which he wants and thinks G.B. should come down to, he is quite capable of joining forces with the Big Navyites in order to smash up the whole agreement in the Senate. To this alliance may also very likely be added many Democrats who will be inclined to 'play politics'.

Howard pointed out that Hoover 'doesn't trust Mr. Borah any more than Mr. Coolidge did', and the potential for trouble was enhanced through Borah's opposition to tariff proposals introduced by the Administration which, in the senator's view, did nothing for American farmers. Howard argued that Borah had to be persuaded 'not to start this Press and Senate campaign against the new naval agreement even if it doesn't give all he wants'. Howard suggested in the strongest possible terms that MacDonald have someone whom Borah respected – and Howard mentioned specifically Harold Laski, the radical economist – 'come out from England in order to show him that, if he persists in the course he seems now bent on following, he will wreck everything and probably end by bringing a real era of competitive building'. Sensing that his policy could be damaged irreparably by Borah, MacDonald took it upon himself to write directly to the senator. Howard learnt of this in a private telegram from the prime minister on 28 August;[206] as a result of the prime minister's personal intervention after Howard's warning, Borah ceased to be a problem in the final settlement of the naval question.

At the same time, Howard told MacDonald privately that Hoover and Stimson wanted a firm Anglo-American diplomatic front when the next naval-limitation conference met – such a conference had been mooted in the MacDonald–Dawes conversations held at London in July.[207] Howard put the American case to the prime minister:

> If other countries were able to divide us, which they might try to do, the results would be much more disastrous than in 1927. [Stimson] thought therefore that before the date of your visit was settled, there should be such measure of agreement between the two Governments that either before your arrival or while you are here a date for the calling of the Five-Power Conference could be made public, but that this should not be done until you and the President were assured that nothing could be brought up at that Conference that would be likely to cause any real difference of opinion between us.

On 11 September 1929, just as Howard's last letter about the need for a firm Anglo-American diplomatic front reached London, the principles to determine a naval settlement were finally agreed. The American secretary of the navy informed Hoover that his department could accept a British proposal that 339,000 British cruiser tons equalled 315,000 American cruiser tons, 'the difference being compensated for by a "yardstick" factor based on displacement and age'.[208] Two weeks later, MacDonald sailed for the United States.

The pinnacle of Howard's service as ambassador in Washington, perhaps, even of his diplomatic career, came with MacDonald's visit. Howard had surmised, when he broached the idea of a prime-ministerial journey to the United States in January 1929, that the despatch of 'some really important statesman, who would command respect and confidence both in England and America', would help immeasurably in resolving the Anglo-American naval impasse. He was correct. MacDonald's visit, the first by a British prime minister in office, healed the political rift in Anglo-American relations that had preoccupied both governments for two years. In reality, these high-level meetings failed to achieve much in the way of concrete gains.[209] The principles concerning naval limitation agreed with difficulty during the summer remained, but the specific details had to await the proposed five-Power conference. In this respect, though, the two leaders did agree that this conference should begin in London in late January 1930 and, on 7 October, whilst the British party was in Washington, invitations were sent to France, Italy, and Japan to attend. Despite the American promise made in June that belligerent rights be kept separate from naval limitation, Hoover raised the matter unexpectedly. After howls of protest from the Cabinet in London, directed by Hankey, and consultations with Howard, Vansittart, and Craigie, MacDonald gently deflected the president so that the matter died once and for all. This was the extent of the conversations. However, as Howard had predicted, the visit acted as a catalyst in replacing American suspicions about Britain with feelings of trust. The American people opened their hearts to the British prime minister. The Embassy in Washington was showered with messages for MacDonald expressing congratulations and good will. American churchmen, labour leaders, and large numbers of newspapermen gave him and his efforts glowing tributes. He even addressed the Senate in Washington and, thanks to Howard's efforts, in New York City spoke to the English-Speaking Union, a combined meeting of the St Andrew, St David, and St George societies, the Foreign Policy Association, and the Council on Foreign Relations. Because of Howard, who worked with BLINY to attain the widest possible press coverage for MacDonald's words, and who got the prime minister's Council on Foreign Relations address broadcast nationally on radio,[210] the British party's nine days in the United States constituted a propaganda achievement of the first magnitude for Britain amongst the American public. The tone of the Anglo-American relationship had changed dramatically from what it had been twelve months before. As MacDonald noted in his diary after returning to Britain: 'the unity & fairness of it all enabled me to do my very best'.[211] Although much credit has to be accorded to the prime minister for bringing a new atmosphere of understanding between Britain and the United States, a sizeable portion must also be accorded to Howard who, in a year of hard work after his return from leave in September 1928, paved the way for a prime-ministerial mission.

V

Howard's retirement had been a matter of press speculation in late 1928.[212] To settle the situation, Chamberlain announced that the ambassador would leave Washington in February 1930, after completing a term of exactly six years.[213] This arrangement had been confirmed privately by Henderson in June 1929 after Howard wrote to both him and MacDonald stressing that, though he would serve the Labour government as loyally as he had its Conservative predecessor, he would vacate the Embassy as soon as possible if the new regime in London should wish it.[214] Whilst at first glance it might seem that Howard's final months in Washington aided in part a return to the detestable practice of the prime minister's office controlling foreign policy, this was not the case. Foreign Office specialists were not squeezed out of the policy-making process, as the achievement of the diplomats in getting MacDonald to support a political settlement and the enhanced position of Vansittart and Craigie showed. Howard maintained contact with Henderson, Lindsay, and the other senior members of the Foreign Office, informing them of the thrust of American policy, shifts in attitude, and that sort of thing, as well as keeping the American Department abreast of regular diplomatic business.[215] But the division of responsibility over foreign policy in London – MacDonald controlling that relating to the United States; Henderson keeping the rest for himself – was a matter over which Howard had no control. As a Service man, he did as he was bid. Thus, the final period of his tenure in Washington witnessed an absence of rancour between the Embassy and the Foreign Office, a matter of decided import as the last bits of diplomatic debris were swept off the path of good Anglo-American relations.

With MacDonald's visit over, Howard and Isa began preparing to leave Washington in the New Year. As he would probably never return to the western hemisphere – Howard turned 66 that September – he decided to visit his plantation at Louis d'Or one last time. Although it had been reasonably successful under Thorlief Orde's stewardship for several years, it had never generated enough profit to allow Howard to retire without a government pension.[216] Accordingly, he travelled to Tobago, with side trips to Panama and Cuba, from late October to early December. Upon his return, he began a final round of official farewells in January and February 1930, which included dinners given in his honour by both Hoover and the new vice-president, Charles Curtis, and the diplomatic corps in Washington. He also received an honorary LLD from Georgetown University. In New York, during five days of social rounds before his departure, he spoke to both the British Empire Chamber of Commerce and the Pilgrims Society, and he made the effort to thank the BLINY staff for all they had done for him in making his embassy a success. He was also showered with praise for his six years in the United States by several prominent American newspapers, and this very public display of true appreciation was paralleled by private letters of thanks from Americans all over the country, some of whom he knew, most of whom he seems never to have met personally.[217] On 25 February 1930, he and Isa embarked for Britain and a much-needed holiday in Cumberland. In his speech to the Pilgrim Society a few days before he left, Howard had spoken eloquently about the importance of Anglo-American amity if there was to be true international peace and security. He told his audience:

The fact of the matter is that, unless our two countries should produce some remarkably stupid statesmen, the people inhabiting them are bound and obliged by the force of circumstances to learn that anything approaching serious conflict between them would be not only the most criminal and fratricidal proceeding, but also of such a nature that, whatever its outcome, it could only result in such economic and financial loss as could never be compensated by the fruits of victory.[218]

This statement is fundamentally important in assessing Howard's diplomacy during his six years in the American capital. He left Anglo-American relations better than he found them. That they had improved to the level they enjoyed when he retired – and good Anglo-American relations proved to be basic to the achievement of the London naval treaty of April 1930, the recognised end of Anglo-American naval rivalry in this period – owes much to his effective ambassadorial style. Chamberlain, MacDonald, and the Foreign Office, those who made British policy towards the United States, trusted him and his judgement. In almost all matters, they followed his advice and fixed policy accordingly. That 'serious conflict' had been prevented during his time at the Washington Embassy, especially in the two difficult years after the Coolidge conference, is eloquent testimony to Esme Howard's diplomatic gifts and talents. It was the cap to a distinguished career which had been directed to protecting Britain as a Power of the first rank.

Epilogue and conclusion
'A great ambassador'

At the beginning of 1924 Sir Auckland Geddes resigned the post of Ambassador at Washington, and Sir Esme Howard was appointed in his place. His mission was a great personal triumph. He remained six years in the United States, and takes rank with Stratford, Canning, Lord Lyons, and Bryce, among the greatest of his predecessors.

The Times, August 1939

I

Howard's work in the United States represented a monument, albeit one of spirit rather than substance, to good Anglo-American relations. More tangibly, he also left as a monument a new British Embassy. Whilst containing spacious reception rooms which made entertainment easy, the old Embassy's offices and chancery were built for another age. They were cramped for the number of diplomats needed to conduct British official business in the United States, and they were outmoded for modern typewriters, coding machines, and other technology fundamental to post-Great War diplomacy.[1] More important, Howard believed that the old Embassy, a forbidding Victorian structure with a dark interior, had for too long been a place of sorrow for the diplomats serving at Washington: Lord Pauncefote, Durand's predecessor, had died there in 1902; Durand had been the object of Roosevelt's private indignities; Spring Rice had been disgraced by his recall in 1917 and died before reaching Britain; and, most telling, Howard's first three years as ambassador had been marked by his eldest son's illness and death. A new Embassy building had been discussed by Foreign Office and Public Works officials shortly after Howard's arrival in 1924 so, with the course of his private life until December 1926, Howard began to press for the construction of a new edifice. He took a major role in planning the new Embassy, a bright, cheery, and airy place, on a new site with spacious gardens,[2] and, just as he and Isa left in February 1930, the new building was being prepared for the new ambassador, Ronald Lindsay. Howard never saw the new Embassy in its completed form. None the less, although several minor problems cropped up with this new structure, as they do with any new piece of construction,[3] the improved state of Anglo-American relations, at least from the point of view of British diplomats in Washington, began with improved working environs that lacked the funereal interior and unhappy history that had marked their workplace for thirty years.

Howard's major role in resolving British and American differences was recognised by King George V, by MacDonald and Vansittart at Downing Street, and by the Foreign Office. On 29 April 1930, just as the London naval conference ended successfully with Anglo-American agreement on cruiser limitation, MacDonald wrote to Howard offering him a hereditary peerage. 'I should like to do this,' the prime minister confided, 'not only as a mark of the obligations which your work – especially in the United States – have put the country under to you, but also because I should like to indulge in the luxury of giving you a proof of my own personal esteem.'[4] Howard accepted with his usual humility, expressing 'a real feeling of gratitude that I have been apparently able to render some service in [the] U.S. which was worthwhile',[5] and the announcement of his reward came in the King's Birthday Honours List in June. Although he toyed with the idea of being titled Baron Howard of Greystoke, his eldest brother's family were known generally as the Howards of Greystoke. Therefore, he asked the College of Heralds if he could have another name from his beloved Cumberland, suggesting either Penrith or Gowbarrow.[6] He could have either, so he chose the former, taking as his coat of arms that of the Duke of Norfolk. By doing this, Howard combined his Cumberland heritage with that of the Howard family that stretched back centuries into England's past.

The significance of Howard's reward cannot be overstressed. Few professional diplomats after Victoria's reign have been granted such a distinction. It is true that Bertie, Hardinge, and Nicolson received peerages, but they were men of another age. Drummond inherited his. Other than Tyrrell and Vansittart, none of Howard's contemporaries in the Foreign Office and Diplomatic Service was so honoured. However, Tyrrell and Vansittart both served as permanent under-secretary, which gave them constant and ready access to the centre of power in London. Tyrrell, for instance, counted Baldwin amongst his closest friends. Howard, on the other hand, had spent his career entirely in the Diplomatic Service abroad. Coupled with the fact that his was a hereditary peerage, one that would pass down through his family and not disappear when he died, this showed the debt paid him by the country and the Empire for his glittering record, especially that in Washington. The stream of congratulatory letters that reached Lord Howard of Penrith in the summer of 1930 all emphasised this point, especially from those who knew and appreciated the magnitude of Howard's accomplishments and the personal sacrifices he had made to achieve them.[7]

By the middle of 1930, Howard and Isa had settled down to enjoy their life of retirement. For the first time since returning from the Boer War, Howard had time to do the things he wanted – seeing family and friends, travelling for pleasure, spending time alone with his wife, and doing such mundane but blissful things like reading for enjoyment.[8] All of this occurred at a leisurely pace, an existence free from the pressures of diplomatic work and meeting one seeming crisis after another. Life soon took on a pattern; a visit to Italy each winter and spring, usually from February to May, and the rest of the year in London, with regular trips to Cumberland and to the country houses of family and friends. Occasionally, Howard and his wife would venture further abroad, notably in 1931, when they travelled extensively in the Holy Land. This particular expedition enhanced Howard's religious beliefs because, he believed, it brought him closer to Christ and the travails that his Lord-Saviour had undertaken for mankind.[9] In many respects, Howard's life in the years of his retirement mirrored that of his mother's family prior to her marriage: spending time with an established circle of relatives and acquaintances, travelling, seeing familiar places and experiencing new ones, reading about and discussing new ideas, and, if necessary through all of this, modifying established notions. Howard had done this between the time he left the Diplomatic Service in 1891 and rejoined it in 1903, but his almost three decades in the Diplomatic Service had demanded that his mental and physical energies be directed towards the conduct of British foreign policy. In his early years, before about 1900, Howard had been a man in a hurry, anxious to bring his great ideas to fruition. Now, in the twilight of his life, after a full career in the service of the country and the Empire, he simply enjoyed life to the fullest, building on what he had seen and heard since joining Carnarvon's staff in 1885.

None of this is to say that Howard's sense of public duty evaporated after his retirement. It remained as vital as ever, but found expression in different directions. He had never given up his concern for the less advantaged, something which saw him become a member of the committee that directed the Queen Mary Hospital in East London, the area where most of the capital's poorest classes lived. In addition, as the great depression of the 1930s created havoc with the nation's economy, Howard supported social activist organisations with programmes designed to find work for the unemployed. West Cumberland, especially, suffered extremely high rates of unemployment because its traditional industries of mining and iron and steel production had been savaged through the drop in international commodity prices abroad and reduced demand at home. Feeling that the old economic base of the region needed diversification, Howard lent his support to the British branch of a Roman Catholic society, The Grail, which sought to start new secondary industries. By the summer of 1936, The Grail had inaugurated a toy-making firm in West Cumberland which was beginning to have some success. As Howard told *The Times*, new methods like this had to be found 'to give men and boys who otherwise would stand idle the interest of manual work and so save them from the soul-destroying effects of years of idleness'.[10] He also pointed out other enterprises which could provide new opportunities, such as a soft fruit industry. Times were changing and British industry, so long tied to coal and steel, had to change with them. Howard's support of The Grail was directed in a small way to achieving this.

Because of his love of the unspoilt countryside, an echo of his happy boyhood exploring moorland, woods, and tarns of Greystoke, Howard took an active role in the work of the National Trust; he even became head of a Cumberland preservationist group called the Friends of the Lake District. In these endeavours, Howard managed to enlist Grey's help to have a rustic bridge built near Ullswater and dedicated to the memory of Cecil Spring Rice. Howard, through the Friends of the Lake District, led a subscription campaign to enable the bridge to be constructed. With a national publicity campaign and a dedication speech by Grey, a vice-president of the National Trust, an outdoor ceremony at Ullswater saw Howard's group turn the bridge over to the protection of the Trust.[11] As they had done so often in the past, Howard and Grey worked together well. Spring Rice's memorial served not only to remove some of the tarnish from the late ambassador's record; it aided in keeping a pristine area of Britain safe from development. Howard endorsed Grey's observation that 'this place becomes a sort of shrine, not because it is enclosed by walls or roof, but because it is encompassed by the sound of water, a sound which, if people do not interfere with the beck, will be more enduring than any walls or roof which human hands could make'. Along the same lines, Howard volunteered his energies canvassing for preservation projects in various parts of Britain, chiefly in the Lake District.[12] In 1932, he also immersed himself in a campaign to have Parliament pass legislation to protect endangered bird species from being hunted indiscriminately. Howard had seen an effective example of government providing sanctuary for birds in Italy,[13] and this resulted in him working with Lord Buckmaster, an equally dedicated preservationist, in heavy political lobbying in the House of Lords to achieve the same end in Britain by late 1933.[14] As much as he could, Howard dedicated his last years to protecting Britain's natural heritage from, as he once told a National Trust meeting, 'desecration'.[15]

Howard did not distance himself from political issues touching foreign and Imperial policies. In fact to a large degree these matters, given his career and interests, dominated most of his time during his retirement. On his last journey to the West Indies, in the autumn of 1929, he learnt from a variety of sources in the British colonial service, business, and other circles that this region of the Empire felt neglected by the home government. This dissatisfaction had a number of strands, which Howard outlined to Vansittart.[16] First, American airlines were dominating the aerial transport of freight and passengers in the region whilst no British group was yet organised to compete and so to maintain an Imperial presence in this new form of transportation. Secondly, the West Indian economy still relied heavily on sugar exports for survival and, although efforts were being made to diversify by producing cocoa, bananas, and citrus fruit, rumblings at London about eliminating a special tariff favouring Imperial sugar had an ominous sound in Jamaica, Tobago, and other sugar islands. Without Preference, large numbers of West Indian planters would be forced to close down, with the sure result of widespread unemployment for the lower classes and an increase in unrest. 'The question is, just as it is at home,' Howard instructed Vansittart, 'a social one & must be considered from that aspect quite as much as from the purely economic side.' Thirdly, West Indian political and commercial leaders recognised the problems that London faced, and thus seemed willing to increase commercial and other ties with Canada in order to preserve the essentially British nature of the Caribbean colonies. A Canadian steamship company, Canadian Pacific, realised the potential of the West Indian market, with the result that it maintained its routes there at a loss. Howard argued that this Canadian presence should be encouraged – his various trips to Canada had shown that Canadian political and business leaders looked on the Caribbean as a natural area of expansion for their interests – thus, London should do all possible to consult with Ottawa about any major policy changes for the region, as well as keep Canadian susceptibilities in mind in any Anglo-American agreements which might be concluded concerning the West Indies. Howard's point with this letter was to indicate that three things were essential 'for the development & maintenance of [West Indian] prosperity':

First, Good [sic] communications by sea with their markets.
Second, the establishment of secure & permanent markets for their produce.
Third. The introduction of new blood & new capital, which will bring them more economic & scientific methods of cultivation – let us call it the nationalism of cultivation.

As a source of 'new blood & new capital', Canada remained crucial in this equation: 'I am, after revisiting the West Indies[,] more than ever convinced the future of these islands, *within the British Empire*[,] depends on their being linked up as closely as possible with Canada...' (emphasis in original).

Recognising the force of Howard's argument and not wanting to allow the Americans any needless advantage in the West Indies, Vansittart used his influence within Whitehall to get a fair hearing for the ambassador.[17] Consequently, within three weeks of returning to London after his retirement, Howard received an invitation to attend a high-level policy meeting at the Air Ministry, also attended by experts from the Department of Overseas Trade and the Colonial, Dominions, and Foreign Offices, about an Anglo-American treaty covering air rights and landing privileges.[18] Howard's observations outlined at this meeting led Lord Thomson, the Air minister, to agree that Canada be consulted and encouraged to involve itself more heavily in West Indian air transportation. A beginning had been made. Over the next several years, Howard worked with West Indian officials, mainly S. V. Greig, the senior Colonial Office man at Tobago, to improve West Indian trade and get greater commitments from London to provide economic assistance for harbours improvement, the building of adequate airfields, and more.[19] Perhaps Howard's greatest success in this regard came in late 1931 when, through his lobbying, a West Indian trade commissioner was established in Montreal.[20] Howard's views about West Indian development – and they had little impact on his investments at Louis d'Or, which by as late as the 1930s were never going to make him rich – accorded with his conception about the evolution of the Empire and how the important dominions like Canada, growing in power and confidence, should be encouraged to assume greater Imperial responsibilities.

Howard's interest in foreign-policy matters found expression in a number of areas. One of the most sensitive of these concerned Anglo-Vatican relations, an issue of increasing importance in the 1930s owing to Britain's relationship with Italy and the problem of Britain's strategic position in the Mediterranean. Whilst he served as a diplomat, Howard distanced himself from seeking to influence Britain's policies towards the Holy See. During the Paris Peace Conference, when there had been some discussion of 'the Roman question', he outlined a method by which the pope, then still at odds with the Italian monarchy, could be recognised as a sovereign ruler in his own right: Italy could guarantee the Vatican's extra-territoriality, whilst the Powers could guarantee papal sovereignty over 'a small Mediterranean island'.[21] Such an arrangement, he surmised, would provide the pope with enough of a territorial base to support his claim as a temporal ruler and give Roman Catholics outside of Italy the security of knowing that their spiritual leader was not controlled by the Italian government. But, given the course of the peace negotiations, especially Italian distaste for their treatment by Lloyd George and Wilson, Howard's suggestion was not taken up. The only other proposal he made during his time in the Diplomatic Service came later that year when Lloyd George's government contemplated removing the British Legation at the Vatican. This Legation had been established in 1914 to counter 'the success of German and Austrian propaganda at the Holy See'.[22] With the war's end, some British leaders saw little need for a continued diplomatic presence there. Howard disagreed, asking Kerr and Curzon to put his case privately to both Downing Street and the Foreign Office.[23] He opined that maintaining the Legation would have benefits for Britain concerning Ireland (where the British faced a full-scale rebellion by predominantly Roman Catholic Irish nationalists), the Empire (which contained a sizeable Roman Catholic population), and the United States (with thirty million Roman Catholic citizens). In addition, as both the French and the Germans were about to appoint permanent diplomatic missions to the Vatican, the chance existed that British influence with the papacy would diminish whilst that of adversaries would increase. Howard's words added to a chorus of disapproval which persuaded the Lloyd George government to maintain a Legation to the Vatican.

In his retirement, freed from the constraints of public service, Howard became a vocal supporter of close Anglo-Vatican relations. His first effort came when, in 1930, a dispute broke out on the British island colony of Malta between the British governor, Lord Strickland, and Roman Catholic Maltese nationalists.[24] In this affair, the island's Roman Catholic bishops also opposed Strickland, who was notoriously heavy-handed in his administration; when elections were called in 1930, the bishops sent out a pastoral letter which informed all Roman Catholic voters, among other things, that: 'You may not, without committing a grave sin, vote for Lord Strickland and his candidates...'[25] London complained to the Vatican about Church interference in Malta's political affairs; the Vatican responded that Strickland was culpable. MacDonald's government suspended the island's constitution and recalled the British minister to the Vatican for an extended holiday.

Howard saw danger in these events because of the chance that Mussolini's government might become involved – the Lateran Treaty had been concluded in 1929 which finally reconciled the differences between the Vatican and the Italian government. He, therefore, penned a reasoned analysis of the problem – its history and immediate antecedents – and offered reasonable suggestions for settlement.[26] Employing a range of documents published by the British, Maltese, and Vatican governments, he pointed out that there was general agreement that the basis of the problem involved the Strickland government's determination to enforce the English language in Malta, where an Italian dialect was dominant. It was not just the Church which supported the Italian language in Malta, but also most of the professional, middle, and working classes. Moreover, Strickland and his supporters disagreed with certain Church powers, specifically that Franciscan authorities, who were not British, had ordered one of their number, a British monk on the island, to transfer to another monastery on the mainland. Here lay a question about who had jurisdiction over British subjects: Church or state. Howard pointed out that the pastoral letter had not been critical of the colonial government or its general policies, which were not anti-clerical; rather, it opposed those who sought to hurt the Church: Strickland and his agents.

Howard then outlined four possible solutions to the crisis: to impose the fiat of the governor despite the views held by the bishops and their Maltese supporters; to rule without the constitution; to hold the elections come what may, during which both sides might be persuaded to curtail their truculence towards one another; or, perhaps, to remove the Strickland administration, negotiate some agreement with the bishops to remove impediments to new elections, and hold the elections. Howard supported the third option but, regardless, something had to be done. His point was that the situation could not continue. Although he argued that the Italians had no intention of seizing the island – 'Italian public opinion has only regarded Malta as part of "Italia irredenta" in the most platonic sense' – this might not be the case if the crisis continued and the island split into two mutually hostile camps, one pro-British, the other pro-Italian:

> It would be difficult to imagine anything more disastrous for our interests in the Mediterranean. Such a consequence, leading to a struggle long-continued and bitter, would inevitably result in the Italian Government being compelled to take sides with the pro-Italians in Malta, especially if forcible measures had been taken to repress them. In that case Italy would become definitely antagonistic to Great Britain in the Mediterranean, with all that implies, instead of friendly as hitherto.

These wise words appeared just as a commission of enquiry under Lord Askwith was being created in Britain to travel to Malta to investigate. When it reported later in 1931, the Askwith Commission recommended that the constitution be reactivated and that several local reforms be implemented to reduce the tension between the two sides on the island and between London and the Vatican.[27] In March 1932, Strickland resigned, paving the way for elections in June which saw his opponents achieve a massive victory.[28] Although problems between London and Maltese nationalists continued sporadically afterwards, the crisis ended by late 1931.

Whilst Howard did not play a direct role in the settlement engineered by the Askwith Commission, he demonstrated publicly and to those who made foreign policy in London the strength of his religious beliefs and how these could be reconciled to national and Imperial interests. British foreign policy would not be helped by allowing disputes between the Vatican and London to escalate, especially if they had the potential of drawing in other Powers or weakening the Empire. Just as British relations with individual Powers should be maintained at the friendliest level possible, so long as Britain did not harm its interests in doing so, an amicable association with the Vatican should also be a goal of British foreign policy. His words to Kerr and Curzon in 1919 had not lost their force a decade later: the British relationship with the Holy See had implications for both the Empire and the wider world that went far beyond normal diplomatic intercourse with the papacy. This became more important for Howard throughout the 1930s, especially after the Ethiopian crisis of 1935-6, when many Cabinet members and Foreign Office officials reckoned that Pope Pius XI was a 'fascist Pope', a supporter of Mussolini and his foreign and imperial policies.[29]

Thus, as the 1930s unfolded, Howard nurtured good Anglo-Vatican relations when he could. As the Malta crisis subsided, he pressed Vansittart and Sir John Simon, the new foreign secretary, to get the British minister to the Vatican back to his post without delay; rabid Irish republican nationalists in the Irish Free State, led by a new prime minister, the treacherous and unscrupulous Eamon de Valera, would use continued British reluctance to revitalise relations as a weapon to help them distance Catholic southern Ireland from Britain and the Empire.[30] When some difficulty arose in 1933 over the selection of a new archbishop for New Zealand, Howard and his Catholic kinsman, Lord Fitzalan, helped behind the scenes to ensure that the appointment made would serve the best interests of the Empire and the Church.[31] Also in 1933, scurrilous reports appeared in the press organ of the Fianna Fail, de Valera's party in Ireland, indicating that Pope Benedict XV had blessed the Irish rebellion of 1916. On holiday in Rome, Howard used his connexions to get a *démenti* published in the *Osservatore Romano*, the official Vatican newspaper, which was then picked up and repeated in several British newspapers. Howard did this because he did not want this Irish falsehood to be accepted as a fact and used by anti-Catholic elements in Britain for their own ends.[32] Howard's position as a prominent English Catholic had other dimensions. In 1934, Queen Victoria Eugenia of Spain, in exile in London since 1931 following the end of the Spanish monarchy, asked Howard to help her get an annulment of her marriage. Alfonso had made public his adultery and now threatened to disinherit his children if they had anything to do with their mother. Howard wrote to his friend, Cardinal Pacelli, the Vatican secretary of state, to use his influence to help the poor woman.³³ In addition, in the late 1930s, the Foreign Office recognised Howard's importance as a Catholic. In 1938 he was canvassed about who might best serve as the Vatican's apostolic delegate to Britain – to facilitate Anglo-Vatican relations, there had been agreement that this man would be a British subject.³⁴ In 1939, during the selection of a successor to Pius XI, Vansittart and Lord Halifax, the foreign secretary, considered using Howard's connexions in Rome to lobby in favour of Pacelli. They contemplated this because it was thought that Pacelli would be less in the pocket of Mussolini; however, although Pacelli became Pius XII, the British government decided ultimately not to involve itself in the selection process.³⁵ In this way, throughout his retirement, Howard took an active role in promoting good Anglo-Vatican relations, something he deemed essential to national and Imperial interests.

As befitted a former ambassador who had retired after a successful career, Howard found his attention in his retirement focussing more and more on the international situation. His perception of the actions of Japan in the Far East after the Manchurian crisis began in 1931 and of Nazi Germany after Hitler took Germany out of the League and the World Disarmament Conference in October 1933 convinced him that Britain and the Empire faced circumstances abroad which paralleled closely those of the few years preceding the July Crisis. Given his long association with European affairs and his still pronounced anti-German sentiments, he saw the principal threat to British security residing in Europe. 'It is useless, I fear,' he told the Catholic Council of International Relations in late 1933, 'to disguise any longer the fact that the general condition of Europe to-day is, perhaps, even more unsettled than it was in 1913–14 just before the outbreak of the Great War.'³⁶ With his strong italophile feelings, Howard became a late convert to the idea that Mussolini's Italy posed a threat to international peace and security. His conversion came with the Italian invasion of Ethiopia in October 1935.³⁷ But the addition of fascist Italy to the group of Powers whose aggressive foreign policies threatened the existing international status quo and, thus, British interests did not alter Howard's views about how Britain should conduct its foreign and defence policies. These views had formed by early 1934, in the wake of Japan's success of arms in Manchuria and Hitler's nose-thumbing at the League, and they constituted a distillation of everything he had seen, learnt, and done since embarking on a diplomatic career almost fifty years earlier. They found expression in a series of speeches, pamphlets, and letters to *The Times* penned between late 1932 and early 1934.³⁸

Fundamental to Howard's arguments stood two firm beliefs: first, the absolute need for Britain and the United States to concert together to preserve international peace and security by presenting such a powerful economic and naval combination that no state or group of states would contemplate conducting aggressive war; and, second, the reliance on the rule of law in applying sanctions against transgressors of peace. From its creation in 1919, the League had Howard's support – his speech to the American political scientists in late 1924 showed this – though his enthusiasm had then been tempered by American reluctance to join the organisation and, until the League could show its utility in maintaining peace by enforcing the sanctions provisions of the Covenant, his belief in the balance of power offering security to Europe. But League inability to force Japan to disgorge the Chinese province of Manchuria, which it had seized in 1931 and transformed into a Japanese puppet state, disabused him of the idea that this body could enforce peace and security. That the Covenant's sanctions provisions were inadequate because of the American failure to join the League, and by 1931–2 there existed no chance of the United States joining, meant that a different approach to ensuring international security had to be found. But, as Howard told *The Times* in November 1932: 'I feel certain that the nations of the world, and especially the Great Powers, will ultimately be obliged to accept the logical conclusion that it is no use adding treaty to treaty and pact to pact without giving these instruments their value of law, having the penalties of the law behind them.'

Howard surmised that much time and effort would be wasted trying to negotiate a new security system, especially given isolationist sentiment in the United States. Why not, therefore, take an existing treaty to which the Americans were a party, even if it lacked 'the teeth' to enforce peace, make amendments to give it the ability to enforce peace, and end up with a renewed undertaking to maintain international security? Howard argued that the Kellogg–Briand pact renouncing the use of war as an instrument of national policy, signed with such fanfare in 1928, could serve as the basis for a renewed effort to ensure international peace and security. The Americans had pushed for its conclusion, hence the problem of getting the United States government to sign a multilateral peace-keeping initiative had already been solved. Moreover American leaders, notably Stimson, had continued to make reference to the pact as a cardinal element of American foreign policy. The difficulty to be overcome stemmed from this treaty lacking a mechanism to isolate a transgressor of peace; the breaking off of diplomatic relations with states that chose to use war as an instrument of national policy was not enough. Therefore, Howard suggested that the existing agreement be modified by the sixty-three nations which had signed it to compel them to undertake a complete economic boycott of any offenders. There had to be moderate rearmament to help achieve this. Amounting to a form of what Howard called 'collective security', his suggestions drew heavily on his Stockholm experiences when the efficacy of economic warfare had been proved in the defeat of Germany, especially after the United States entered the struggle in April 1917. Modern warfare required substantial economic and natural resources for its successful prosecution; if these could be denied transgressors of peace, especially if the two principal naval and economic Powers, Britain and the United States, could join in enforcing a total blockade, a major deterrent to war would be created. Howard reckoned that this sort of collective security, which would not require massive expenditures on new weapons, would allow governments to divert more revenues to combat domestic difficulties like unemployment. In these musings, Howard also drew on his war service in Sweden – clearly with Hammarskjöld's verbal juggling in mind – to castigate the theory of neutral rights in wartime. Neutral Powers profiting from war by loaning money or selling commodities to aggressive states were as guilty of making war as any belligerent because they supplied the wherewithal to conduct and sustain military operations. What Howard called for by early 1934 amounted to a judicious blend of arms and diplomacy to keep aggressive Powers in check.

Howard's proposals fell on barren ground. The British government confronted several problems deriving from the economic dislocation within Britain created by the Great Depression; this deflected the energies of Baldwin, MacDonald, and other leaders towards domestic policy.[39] As well, those who controlled British foreign policy seemed more willing to work within the existing network of international agreements and treaties to maintain British interests or, if this did not suffice, to pursue ad hoc bilateral arrangements with other Powers to meet the immediate problem.[40] Suffusing this second development was American reluctance to venture into the thicket of international security, something seen most tellingly in the passage of neutrality laws beginning in August 1935.[41] None the less, when the situation demanded, Howard continued lobbying for his vision of how the interests of Britain and the Empire could be better protected. He became a critic of what he called derisively 'the left' in Britain, with their unrealistic suggestions about achieving collective security at the same time as the government should reduce arms spending and pin all its hope on the League. In this, he was joined by others who argued for a sensible level of arms spending by Westminster coupled with consultations with the dominion governments so as to ensure that the Empire had a strong and united view for its defence. In late 1933 and early

1934, Howard, Sir Herbert Richmond, one of the country's foremost naval thinkers, Sir Edward Grigg, a former secretary at Downing Street, and Henry Wickham Steed, the journalist and advocate of close Anglo-American relations, put these views forcefully before the nation through the letters pages of *The Times*.[42] In this respect, Howard's ideas in the middle of the 1930s corresponded precisely with the critique he had levelled at the radical opponents of Grey's foreign policy before 1914, those who failed to understand 'the grammar' of diplomacy.

At the same time, Howard saw little merit in the rantings of old-style British militarists who saw the possession of unlimited arms as the only salvation for Britain and the Empire. For instance, when the Navy League began a propaganda campaign in late 1934 about Britain surrendering its naval superiority via agreements like the London naval treaty of 1930 – and in this lay a subtle attack on the United States – Howard penned a spirited defence of British naval-arms-limitation policy.[43] Navy League distortions were akin to the fulminations of the American 'Big Navy Party' in the 1920s, and they could not be allowed to be voiced without an exposition of the truth. What Howard proposed instead of unchecked idealism in the conduct of foreign and defence policy or a complete reliance on a heavily armed Britain unilaterally maintaining its interests – which was impossible given the economic difficulties of the time – was the need for collective security based on the combined armed and economic strength of those Powers willing to stand up to aggressors. His advocacy of a revised renunciatory pact and the efficacy of economic sanctions to ensure peace continued for the rest of his life.[44] When it became clear after the German occupation of the rump of Czechoslovakia in March 1939 that more extreme steps were needed to curtail Hitler's ambitions in Europe, Howard endorsed the British government's efforts to introduce peacetime conscription so as to better organise British manpower resources as a base for a firm foreign policy.[45] Howard did not want his country or the Empire involved in another great War – it would be a calamity of unknown proportions – thus, it had to do all possible to avoid it. But, if pushed, Britain had to be ready and able to defend itself and its interests. In December 1934 he wrote: 'The moral pointed by 1914 to the British Empire is becoming clearer every day, and it is this – "If you want peace, be ready to restrain any who threaten war, and show that readiness before events have rendered war inevitable."'[46] More than half a century in the service of his country, principally his efforts in the Diplomatic Service from 1903 to 1930, had taught him that this was the realistic thing to do. His efforts, and those of men who thought like him, ultimately came to nothing but, mercifully, Howard died before his worst fears were realised.

Howard's health had been uneven since his collapse on his tour of the western United States and Canada in the spring of 1927. His final three years in Washington had been difficult in a personal sense as the pressures of work had not allowed him to take extended periods of rest to regain spent energies which, as time passed, never seemed to recover to their old level. His retirement gave him the opportunity to rest but, at crucial times, he seemed to be as busy then as he had been whilst in the Diplomatic Service. In 1935 and 1936, he devoted himself to his myriad of endeavours – the National Trust and Friends of the Lake District, political work in the Lords, involvement in Catholic affairs, and speaking and writing on foreign policy – and to this he added work on his memoirs. By 1937, when he was seventy-three years old, he began to experience periods of ill health that required extended stays in the warmth of Italy and time in convalescent homes in England. After returning from Italy in the spring of 1939, he immediately went into a nursing home at Ridgecombe. He left there in late June and then spent the summer months at his home at Hindhead. His health worsened and on 1 August he died. He was buried at Arundel, next to his son, Esme, and, on 8 August 1939, a requiem mass was held in his honour in London attended by a large number of family, friends, and diplomatic colleagues. He had told his mother when he contemplated leaving the Diplomatic Service in 1890 that 'I shall never be satisfied all my life.' There was a grain of truth in this given his endeavours after 1932 concerning the foreign policy he thought that Britain ought to adopt. However, he had accomplished much in the fifty years after he had written those words, and for this there had to be contentment with what he achieved for himself, for his family, and for Britain and the Empire.

II

Howard's death brought an outpouring of appreciation for all that he had done for Britain as a member of the Diplomatic Service, especially his achievements in Washington between 1924 and 1930.[47] Perhaps the most eloquent testimony to his accomplishments came on 2 August 1939 with an obituary in *The Times* entitled 'A Great Ambassador'; along with a leading article the next day, this sought to put his record of achievement into perspective.[48] His service from the time he joined Carnarvon's staff in Ireland in 1885 until his retirement as the doyen of British ambassadors in 1930 was outlined, along with the high points of his career in Crete, Budapest, Berne, Stockholm, Paris, Madrid, and Washington. Just as important, the period of his temporary retirement between 1891 and 1903 received especial attention: his travels, work at the Foreign Office and with the Booth enquiry, war experience in South Africa, and his efforts to bring new kinds of agriculture to the West Indies. The essence of *The Times* tribute held that his character as much as his abilities as a diplomat might explain why he had done so well in a difficult and, as far as reputation was concerned, dangerous profession. The leading article put it best with the observation: 'Lord Howard of Penrith, whose death was recorded yesterday, was a great ambassador in spite of, or because of, the fact that his life had not been solely devoted to diplomacy.' But *The Times* equivocated on how important was the impact of Howard's character in assessing his contribution to the nation and the Empire; it was only natural given the lack of an adequate span of time between the end of his career and his death, along with the uncertainty and pace of events in the 1930s, to put what he had done in clearer focus. However, half a century after his death, sufficient time has passed. The observation about him being 'a great ambassador' because 'his life had not been solely devoted to diplomacy' is the only valid one on which to draw conclusions about Howard the man and Howard the diplomat; and how these two elements melded to produce one of the most important and gifted British diplomats in the first third of the twentieth century.

Howard was a man whose character had been shaped within the confines of a close and devoted family during a secure and prosperous period in Britain's history. His happy boyhood at Greystoke and Thornbury, along with those regular visits to his relatives' homes at Pixton Park and Charlton House, had steadily but imperceptibly driven home to him his heritage as an 'Englishman' and a Howard.[49] The 'old full-length portraits of Elizabethan Howards', 'the Whig and Stuart traditions' and 'the Protestant and Catholic atmosphere' of his house, as well as family stories about the old Norfolks, combined to create within Esme Howard a sense of his patrimony and the tradition of his family's place in the realm's past. More specifically, he was a member of the northern gentry, linked to the rugged Cumberland countryside in the games and explorations of his childhood and, in later life, hunting and shooting. This, too, enhanced his sense of being 'English'; and that he often returned there between postings or whilst on leave to revive his energies, and that he took a prominent part during his retirement in groups which sought to preserve its unspoilt state shows the almost spiritual importance of this part of England in his life.

At the same time, Howard never became so consumed by his nationality and all that it stood for that he would not or could not see that other places, with different pasts and ideas, had just as much to offer him. The smug and condescending snobbishness of his Farnborough headmaster seemed to permeate the British upper classes after the middle of the nineteenth century.[50] This attitude repelled Howard even at an early age, and for this he could thank his mother. Howard inherited the Long family's desire to experience different places and to learn about and discuss diverse ideas. A world existed outside of the narrow confines of that of the privileged classes in Britain, both within Britain itself and abroad. Working for Booth's enquiry amongst London's working classes provided as much insight into this foreign world as did prospecting in South Africa or sailing up the Amazon or exploring Morocco. Through his mother, Howard possessed in his character a desire to see and, more important, experience these different places. He rarely just observed; he tended to immerse himself fully in the life of the places he visited. Additionally, the world of ideas that the Longs had been part of in their peripatetic existence, which Howard tasted as a boy sitting with his mother at dinner with Tennyson and took to heart on his trips as a young man to France, Germany, and, especially, Italy, gave him an open and enquiring mind. By the time he embarked on a diplomatic career, Howard comprehended completely that because something was different – that is, not English – it was not necessarily bad. It remained crucial to understand different places, with their dissimilar histories and ideas, and judge them on their merit, not through the lens of preconceived notions about their worth in an English context.

Like any other man, Howard possessed seemingly paradoxical characteristics. In his case, these were a genuine and deep compassion for others and a hard-edged and, at times, cold-blooded realism in assessing people and situations. His compassion revealed itself in the deep love he had for his mother, his brothers and sisters, his children, and his wife. Part of the attraction that Greystoke held for him as an adult came from the memories of his boyhood, when family and friends played a central role in his life. This helps explain why during his career, all of which was spent abroad, he ensured that his own children experienced the same camaraderie and joy of being together, whether in an embassy abroad or, like that carefree summer of 1919, in the Lake District. This also underscores his initial reluctance to take the Washington Embassy in 1923, when to do so would mean long separations from the older boys. It almost goes without saying that the death of his eldest son in 1926 affected him deeply and created within him a sense of loss he carried till the end of his days. Finally, Isa stood at the centre of his emotional life after 1898. She existed as the rock on which Howard's whole existence was anchored, and theirs was as much a spiritual as a physical relationship. He remained unshakeably committed and faithful to her throughout their marriage. Whenever they parted, say during Isa's confinements at Rome in 1903 and 1905, or in July and August 1918 when she took the younger boys back to Britain, or between 1924 and 1926 when she spent time in European clinics with

Esmetto, they would say their rosaries together; this was as much a demonstration of their commitment to one another as to the teachings of the Church. To understand Howard the man is to appreciate his compassion for his family and its central place in his life.

Howard's compassion extended beyond his family. He had a concern for the less advantaged in life that was as deep and genuine as that he evinced for his family. His concern for the Irish and their aspirations, his efforts with the Booth enquiry, and, in his retirement, service on boards like that for Queen Mary Hospital show this side of his character. In his early life, his ideas about a non-Marxist 'State Socialism' were a manifestation of this, something which he sought to put into practice through his 'Economic Credo'. No doubt there existed a breath of paternalism in Howard's attitudes concerning the extension of a helping hand to the lower classes. But this was normal amongst those in Britain's upper classes who in the 1890s began to advocate 'social justice' in order to help the less advantaged. But pejorative connotations to the term 'paternalism' are of post-1945 vintage, the fruit of Marxist and feminist historiography, and have little bearing on the efforts of those who had benefited from the social and economic system in the generation or two before the great War to do something positive to improve society. It is also possible that Pope Leo XIII's encyclical, *De Rerum Novarum*, issued in 1891 as the Roman Catholic Church's answer to combating social and economic ills, helped turn Howard towards conversion seven years later.[51] However, compassion for others remained part of Howard's character throughout his life. His speeches and writings in the 1930s about the need to have a foreign policy strong enough to prevent another great War are, perhaps, the best example of this – though they did represent, as well, the assessment of a seasoned diplomatist. He had seen at first hand the terrible price of the war – the loss of sons and brothers of family and friends, the refugee camps outside Warsaw, and the devastation wrought on the battlefield. Concern for his fellow man motivated him to do what he could when he could to prevent or alleviate needless suffering.

Surfacing whilst he was a boy, Howard's realism encompassed two parts of his character: an innate ability to recognise his limitations; and the gift of being able to assess dispassionately people and situations. His Harrow Latin master's cruel remark that Howard was a 'respectable mediocrity' seems to have been the first sign that anyone had taken a dislike to him. Confronting this harsh reality for the first time makes an impact on everyone. But Howard accepted that there was some validity in these words – at least in the sense that he would never be a brilliant scholar – and got on with life. That, subsequently, they were never far from his consciousness can be seen in his search for a title to his memoirs; he suggested 'Respectable Mediocrity' but, because of his family and his publisher's opposition, he opted for 'Theatre of Life'.[52] This says much about how he approached his personal and professional life after leaving school. He did not lack ambition. Initially, he had wanted success in diplomacy but, when this vocation seemed barren, he left to pursue his great ideas. The various undertakings he involved himself with in the 1890s, culminating in the West Indian rubber syndicate, were all directed towards that end. However, falling in love, converting to Catholicism, and marrying Isa showed him that, realistically, he had to abandon his grandiose dreams. The plantation might work one day – that dream existed until after he retired in the 1930s – but unfulfilled dreams do not support a family or do much in the service of the nation and Empire.

Howard returned to diplomacy. Whilst appreciating that he lacked certain talents, he knew that he possessed others, languages and good analytical abilities, for instance. In his renewed career, he approached questions whether great or small with diffidence. After working to understand all facets of an issue, he would strive to come to grips with it. This is seen in his initial response to Curzon's offer of the Washington Embassy, knowing as Howard did Bryce's accomplishments and acknowledging the difficulty of equalling his friend's success. However, after accepting the challenge, he thought about how to make his embassy to the United States work, outlined how he would do so in his speech to the British Pilgrims, and then did the best job possible by overcoming personal and professional difficulties. Realistic self-assessment remained the key to his Washington achievements, just as it had contributed to those at every post from Crete to Madrid. This aspect of his character helps explain why he represented king and country in a way that made him a great diplomat.

Whilst his ability to assess himself developed rather quickly, a result of the ethos of the English public school, that relating to individuals and situations took longer. There is no mystery in that. Until one can gain experience outside of the cocoon of home and school, it is difficult to appreciate how the real world functions and how people in it conduct themselves. Howard's first period of government service, in Dublin, Rome, and Berlin, exposed him to the realities of the world and the need to judge men and policies as unemotionally as possible. The Embassy in Rome, controlled by the slothful ambassador, Lumley, and subject to the feuding of the three Chancery staff, revealed to him the internecine, back-biting struggles that often mar civil-service efficiency, but which Howard learnt were a fact of life. Malet's Embassy in Berlin existed as a place of quiet efficiency, the result of the ambassador's personality, but in the German capital Howard witnessed the Empress Frederick's mistreatment at the hands of her son and Bismarck; two years later he saw Bismarck's dismissal by the young emperor. Howard's subsequent fate at the hands of Conservative newspapers in the Worcester constituency and his efforts to create a business venture re-affirmed the need to recognise the world for the way it was rather than the way it should be. Howard grasped the problems posed by the multiplicity of human nature, which had to be assessed calmly and rationally if one was to make sense of the world and act accordingly. Emperor William and Bismarck might deal spitefully with an English princess, but relations between Germany and Britain had to continue. By 1903, he was a good judge of character. Prince George of Greece was not a cipher. Neither was Theodore Roosevelt, Hjalmar Hammarskjöld, or, for that matter, Lloyd George. Howard was rarely taken in by other men – an exception might have been Pilsudski, who set out successfully to charm Howard, though Howard's pro-Polish sympathies were by then established – because he had the ability to see them for what they were and to gauge accurately what they were doing and saying.

In the same way, Howard came also to appreciate the need to assess situations unemotionally. Working with Sir Percy Anderson on the division of East Africa showed him that the real world was unfair. Ideals were fine – in Howard's case, they were never abandoned; they were pursued when the time was right – but defending Britain's interests meant relying on calculated policies that would keep peace, deter aggression, or, if the need arose, ensure the military defeat of an adversary. Such attitudes characterised Howard's diplomatic career. Before 1914, for instance, when he saw a decided threat to British interests posed by Germany, he argued against idealists who wanted to stymie arms spending because they did not understand 'the grammar' of diplomacy. If Britain was to protect itself, its Empire, its strategic position, and its economic prosperity, this was not the time to weaken its foreign policy by limiting arms. Along the same lines, his emphasis in 1918–19 on building strong successor states in northern and northeastern Europe, or his defence of the balance of power before the American political scientists, shows how he appreciated the need for a realistic appraisal of the situation and the policies to respond to it. After 1903, he became a master of assessing difficult foreign policy problems for the Foreign Office, and the success of his missions for almost thirty years attests to this crucial element of his character.

This realism stood as the bridge between Howard the man and Howard the diplomat. Essential to his character lay an ability to separate his personal beliefs from what transpired in the world at large. This is most easily seen in his Catholicism. Following his conversion in 1898, Howard's commitment to the teachings of the Church of Rome was full and complete, so that Church orthodoxy pervaded every aspect of his existence.

But Howard held religious beliefs to be a strictly personal concern. It mattered not what others believed; it mattered what he believed. As he once wrote to his sister, Elizabeth, Catholicism was 'a great, and a glorious thing, and makes the struggle for a good life so much easier, in spite of raising the standard infinitely both as to thoughts, words, & acts'.[53] What remained essential for Howard was using his faith to ensure high personal standards for himself – and his immediate family. It would have been ideal if everyone shared his beliefs. But this was not how the real world operated, something made abundantly clear to him in his travels to Europe, Africa, and the Americas; other people were governed by different notions of how to conduct their lives. On Crete, he had befriended a man named Carlandi, who had separated from his wife and lived with another woman. When Carlandi tried once to explain the situation, Howard recorded: 'I told him I thought it was useless to tell me all about it as we should not agree. We are good friends as before, for I look upon him as a delightful person but as irresponsible as the god Pan.'[54]

This attitude explains much about Howard the diplomat. He experienced no inner conflict when separating personal beliefs from matters of state. As a diplomat, his task involved giving advice and carrying out policies designed to protect the interests of Britain and the Empire. On Crete, in one instance, this meant preserving the authority of the Moslem Ottoman sultan against the ambitions of Christian Greeks on the island and mainland. In Spain, in another, it involved doing all possible to aid the Spanish, corrupt and inefficient as they might seem, in maintaining their position in the western Mediterranean from French inroads. Throughout his career, Howard strove to protect British interests, and this constituted a matter of ends versus means. The end was to ensure that Britain's position did not suffer any sort of political, strategic, or economic erosion; the means involved supporting regimes which would help in this, though sometimes particular regimes might have little else in common with Britain. Even in foreign-policy matters where Howard's personal beliefs might be seen to have influenced his advice, say, in Poland in 1919 or Malta in 1931, no doubt exists that he put British interests above all else. His ideas about Catholic Poland were part of a larger issue which involved establishing equally strong regimes in Protestant Finland and the Baltic States to contain any revival of Germany and Russia. His argument concerning Malta held that the policies of Lord Strickland, who happened also to be Roman Catholic, might imperil the British position in the Mediterranean because Italy might be dragged into the dispute. Howard the diplomat stood as a realist above all else.

For Howard, realistic diplomacy meant conducting foreign policy from a position of strength. Before the great War, he had understood the intimate connexion between the possession of armed strength and the ability to project a nation's influence through the implied threat this meant. The inability of the Greeks to bring about the *enosis* of Crete with the mainland as a result of Venizelos' civil war occurred chiefly because of the overwhelming strength of the four occupying Powers and the support that they gave the gendarmerie. The same lesson was driven home to him during the final stages of the Bosnian crisis, when the Russians were forced to back down because of the German decision to support the Dual Monarchy in its annexation of the two Balkan provinces. Moreover, the ability of the Swiss to organise their manpower in the most expeditious way to keep their neighbours from seeking to violate Switzerland's neutrality or take territory made a decided impact on him. It was this Swiss example that formed the basis of his attack on the British radicals who criticised Grey's foreign policy and the efforts of the Liberal government to train effective armed reserves. But the course of the war and the imposition of the blockade convinced Howard about the importance of economic strength in underpinning foreign policy. Although strategic and political factors also contributed to the defeat of the Central Powers, the ability of the Allies, especially after the United States entered the war, to deprive Germany of basic raw materials played a major part in the final collapse of the Central Powers. Thus, Howard worked in Paris to make certain that Poland could sustain itself economically in the post-war period. This entailed not only ceding to the new Polish state coal- and iron-producing areas in Silesia and other areas, of course, based on principles of national self-determination, but, more importantly, assuring Poland unfettered access to the sea. Later, in Washington, Howard appreciated the tremendous economic strength of the United States as a potential threat which, if the Americans were handled improperly, could see the construction of 'a navy second to none' that might spell the end of the Royal Navy's paramountcy. Britain did not have the economic resources to outbuild the United States and other potential adversaries in naval craft, so there had to be an amelioration of Anglo-American differences to preclude a naval race. Howard's appreciation of the importance of economic power in conducting foreign policy was unusual for a British diplomat of this period.[55]

By the same token Howard looked on good Anglo-American relations as the basis of British external policy from at least his time as counsellor at Bryce's Embassy. There were several reasons for this. First, Howard reckoned that the two English-speaking Powers shared many common elements in their political, economic, and cultural life that made them natural allies. Whilst this might have been wide of the mark given the heterogeneous nature of American society and the anglophobia prevalent amongst Irish-Americans and others, the control by the 'eastern establishment' of the United States government and its dominance in the country's financial and industrial life during the period he served gave credence to his notions about Anglo-American similarities. Secondly, the United States possessed many qualities that Howard admired. American willingness to accept change, to innovate, and to put into practice new ideas appealed to Howard. He had been reared in an environment that put great store on appreciating the glories of the past, mainly in art, literature, and music, but also in valuing modern concepts – his reference to Spain's domestic turmoil in 1920 by an analogy to an impressionist painting shows this. Moreover, much of his father's wealth had come via the most notable innovation of nineteenth-century Britain: railway construction. American leads in matters of technology and industrial production only added to Howard's admiration of the United States. Finally, because of Canada's determination to assert itself in international affairs, the fate of the Empire was linked to the United States. The growing warmth in Canadian–American political and economic relations, which had entered a higher plane with the exchange of permanent diplomatic missions in 1927, suggested that Imperial unity had to be considered at all times when constructing policy touching the American question. His 'war talk' with Hoover at the moment the Coolidge conference sputtered to a halt showed Howard the imperative need to appreciate the Imperial dimension in any policy the British fashioned which touched the United States. If the Canadians were forced to choose between Britain and the United States in some crisis, no guarantee existed that Ottawa would align with London and the other Empire governments. More crucially, even if Canada wished to support Britain in such a crisis, the overwhelming strength of the United States would certainly force the Canadians into neutrality. Either way, the strength of the Empire would suffer, which would undermine Britain's position as a Power of the first rank. It followed that Howard's Atlanticism derived as much from a realistic assessment of the strength of the United States as from personal admiration of the inherent American disposition to change if change meant improvement.

The career of Howard the diplomat was also distinguished by a dedication to the Empire. From at least his time on Carnarvon's staff, he grasped that the Empire provided the *raison d'être* of Britain's position as the only truly global Power. He thereafter used every effort to make certain that this polity remained a vital, growing institution. But Howard's brand of Imperialism did not countenance efforts to retain as much of the Earth as possible, defend it against all comers, and exploit its riches to the detriment of colonial inhabitants. Such notions of Empire, tied to the pride of thinking 'of the sun never setting upon it', constituted 'a mistaken and a foolish reason for glorification'. The British Empire was not a static entity; it lived and breathed; it was constantly changing, evolving into an increasing number of independent governments tied to the mother country. Britain's leaders had to recognise this and, if they wished to preserve the Empire and thus Britain's position as a Power of the first rank, protect it, nurture it, and ensure that the interests of Britain and the constituent parts coincided as much as possible.

Importantly, Howard did not simply talk about these ideas; he also did what he could to foster Imperial unity, growth, and development. He sought to protect Imperial unity throughout his diplomatic career, mainly during his two Washington postings when Canadian efforts to attain increasing levels of independence in foreign policy had to be reconciled with Imperial interests. But he had also put his life on the line in South Africa in 1900 to prevent the Boers from splintering the Empire in a crucial region. In terms of nurturing the Empire, he did all he could in this regard from the time he left the Diplomatic Service in 1890 until his death. This entailed devoting most of his wealth to the fostering of the economic development of the West Indies; this investment, made with the intention of providing him and his family with financial security, also had as its goal improving the lot of native West Indians. As far as ensuring that the interests of Britain and the constituent parts of the Empire coincided, his efforts respecting British-Canadian relations, notably in the late 1920s when he supported a permanent Canadian mission in Washington, were directed towards this end. If London failed to appreciate the desire of the Canadians to go it alone in some areas of their foreign policy, Imperial unity would be eroded seriously. Along the same lines lay his continued support for some sort of Imperial Preference, as well as his lobbying in the early 1930s to have Canada shoulder more responsibility for Imperial interests in the Caribbean. Suffusing his entire diplomatic career, Howard's Imperialism reflected a belief that the British Empire, as much as possible, had to function as a single entity in international affairs if Britain's position as a global Power was to be maintained.

Finally, Howard the diplomat believed unbendingly in the need for professionalism in his field of endeavour. He was a 'Service' man, and he had identified himself as one to his friend, Spring Rice, several years before Hardinge plucked him out of private life and gave him an opportunity to re-establish his career. His appointments at the Rome and Berlin Embassies drove home to him the lesson about how competent ambassadors set the tone for British diplomatic representation in their host countries. Briefly serving in the Kimberley Foreign Office in the middle of the 1890s taught him how political squabbling can damage the administration of foreign policy by diverting the attention of those responsible for it. This is not to say that Howard deprecated the work of all political appointments in the Diplomatic Service. He did not, as his service under and subsequent friendship with Bryce showed. But, on the whole, Howard believed that the professionals should have predominance in the conduct of diplomacy. His work at the Paris Peace Conference, if he did not already know it, showed him clearly the problems that will ensue if politicians immerse themselves too deeply in the minutiae of diplomacy. The need to cut and trim policy for partisan political reasons led at times to uncertainty and contradictions which did nothing to strengthen the nation's foreign policy. Given the need for Lloyd George to consider a host of foreign and domestic issues, this also led to the rise in influence of unelected men like Kerr, so that uncertainty existed about whether the prime minister even saw important papers forwarded to him by the Foreign Office. None of this suggests that Howard did not want or desire political direction by the foreign secretary and the Cabinet. He did, supporting completely the political process in Britain. But directing policy along certain channels and actually creating and implementing it were different propositions. Policy had to be consistent, something rare when men like Lloyd George decided to run the country's external relations on the basis of their wits. That Howard appreciated the need for firm direction from London is seen in his acceptance of the idea that those responsible for the big diplomatic picture should have precedence over the man on the spot. Accepting this dictum served him well throughout his career. However, for Howard, the world seemed to be more complex as time passed, and the unravelling of these complexities, adjusting to new realities, and giving reasoned advice could come only from those who knew 'the grammar', understood the history of issues, and daily handled problems. His service was marked by a reliance on professionalism, something he admitted to the London Pilgrims in 1924 with the remark that he was guided by the maxims of 'old diplomacy'.

Esme Howard served Britain and its Empire in a period that coincided with the decline in Britain's position from the only truly global Power to just one of a number of great Powers. The great War had eliminated several British adversaries, either through disintegration or defeat. Simultaneously, it propelled others, chiefly, the United States, into the ranks of potential adversaries. But British decline was relative, so that by 1930 Britain still stood as the foremost Power in the world.[56] This derived from a small number of men responsible for British foreign policy. Howard was one of this group. The transition was smooth and benign, and in no small part due to the man who Austen Chamberlain once appreciatively called 'the gentle Sir Esme'.

Notes

I THE MAKING OF A DIPLOMAT, 1863-1903

1. Lord Howard of Penrith, *Theatre of Life*, vol. 1: *Life Seen from the Pit 1863-1905* (London, 1935), p. 13. Hereafter, Lord Howard's memoirs are abbreviated as *ToL*.
2. Lady Catherine Long, *The First Lieutenant's Story*, 3 vols. (London, 1853); and *Sir Roland Ashton. A Tale of the Times*, 2 vols. (London, 1854); *ToL*, vol. 1, p. 17.
3. Ibid., p. 16.
4. Ibid., p. 18. Also see Charlotte Howard's 'Register of Investments' for the period 1878-94, contained in DHW (Howard MSS, Cumbria County Record Office, Carlisle) 5/83; and the bank book of Charlotte Howard and her executors in DHW 5/84.
5. For Howard's recollections of his father, see *ToL*, vol. 1, pp. 18-20.
6. This is Howard's assessment. For this and his recollections about his mother, see ibid., pp. 25-7.
7. An indication of this can be seen in her 'Last Will and Testament', retained in DHW 5/91.
8. On the charms of Greystoke and Cumberland, see *ToL*, vol 1, pp. 22-4.
9. See his reaction on returning after four uninterrupted years of service in Scandinavia during the first World War; Howard diary, 2 Sept. 1918, DHW 1/4.
10. *ToL*, vol. 1, p. 26.
11. The following references to Pixton and Charlton are from ibid., pp. 26-7.
12. These reminiscences of Thornbury and Greystoke are from ibid., pp. 20-2, 28.
13. Ibid., p. 29.
14. Howard to his mother, n.d., DHW 3/9.
15. See his letters to his mother, all n.d., ibid.
16. *ToL*, vol. 1, p. 29. Also see Howard to Lady Wemyss, 15 Aug. 1933, Wemyss MSS (Churchill College, Cambridge) WYMS 6/2, in which the following passage occurs: '[Wemyss] and I were walking together when suddenly our Revered Head Master clasped his hand excitedly & exclaimed: "In what other school in England would you see the sons of three Cabinet Ministers walking together?" Another small boy might have been impressed, not so Rosy who at once whispered to me "Did you ever hear such an old snob?" It was the

first time I think that I ever came across snobbism in the flesh & it made a great impression on me.'
17 See *ToL*, vol. 1, pp. 30–1; and various letters to his mother for this period, all n.d., in DHW 3/9.
18 *ToL*, vol. 1, p. 31.
19 Ibid., p. 32.
20 The rest of this paragraph is based on ibid., pp. 33–48, as well as Howard to his mother, 13 June 1883 (Neuchâtel), 20 June (n.d., but 1883) (Geneva), 19 Nov. (n.d., but 1883) (Paris), all DHW 3/9.
21 Success in the examinations was only half the struggle to get into the Foreign Office and Diplomatic Service, the most prestigious branches of the civil service. Being the right sort of man had also to be weighed. See Zara Steiner, 'Elitism and Foreign Policy: The Foreign Office before the Great War', in B. J. C. McKercher and D. J. Moss, eds., *Shadow and Substance in British Foreign Policy, 1895–1939. Essays Honouring C. J. Lowe* (Edmonton, 1984). Also see Howard to his mother, 15 Feb. (n.d., but 1885), DHW 3/9.
22 *ToL*, vol. 1 p. 50. Cf. the first two chapters of M. Gilbert, *Sir Horace Rumbold. Portrait of a Diplomat 1869–1941* (London, 1973).
23 *ToL*, vol. 1, p. 49, and S. Gwyn, ed., *The Letters and Friendships of Sir Cecil Spring Rice. A Record* (London, 1930), pp. 29–50.
24 On Ireland and domestic politics at this juncture, see A. B. Cooke and J. R. Vincent, *The Governing Passion. Cabinet Government and Party Politics in Britain 1885–86* (London, 1974); L. P. Curtis, *Coercion and Conciliation in Ireland 1880–1892* (London, 1963); and R. Rhodes James, *The British Revolution. British Politics 1880–1939* (London, 1977), pp. 81–103.
25 Howard to his mother, 26 June (n.d., but 1885), DHW 3/9. Howard masked over this concern in his memoirs; cf. *ToL*, vol. 1, p. 53.
26 For an indication of Carnarvon's views on the Empire, see the Earl of Carnarvon, 'Imperial Administration', in the Earl of Carnarvon (ed. by R. Herbert), *Essays, Addresses and Translations*, vol. 3 (London, 1896), pp. 3–29. Cf. F. Harcourt, 'Disraeli's Imperialism, 1866–1868: A Question of Timing', *HJ*, 23 (1980), 88–109; and B. A. Knox, 'Reconsidering Mid-Victorian Imperialism', *JICH*, 1 (1973), pp. 155–72.
27 For opposition in Salisbury's Cabinet to Carnarvon, see Cooke and Vincent, *Governing Passion*, pp. 262, 264.
28 *ToL*, vol. 1, p. 61.
29 Ibid., p. 66.
30 For Blunt's iconoclastic views on Egypt, see W. S. Blunt, *Secret History of the British Occupation of Egypt* (New York, 1922). For criticism of Blunt, where he is described as 'that stormy petrel and wayward apostle of lost causes', see Marquess of Zetland, *Lord Cromer. Being the Authorised Life of Evelyn Baring, First Earl of Cromer* (London, 1932), pp. 163–7.
31 On the Crabbet Club, see *ToL*, vol. 1, pp. 72–3; and W. S. Blunt, *My Diaries. Being a Personal Narrative of Events 1888–1914* (London, 1932), pp. 41–2.
32 For Howard extolling Curzon's virtues, see Howard to Elizabeth, his sister, 18 Nov. 1902, DHW 3/10.
33 This and the following quotation are from *ToL*, vol. 1, pp. 84–5. Cf. G. A. Craig, *Germany 1865–1945* (Oxford, 1981), p. 170.
34 Malet to Salisbury, 6 July 1889, enclosing Howard to Malet, 5 July 1889, with Howard memorandum on the 'Summary of the Law for Insurance against Old Age and Infirmity', n.d., all DHW 1/10.

35 An indication is Bismarck's attack on a British diplomat, Sir Robert Morier. See F. B. M. Hollyday, '"Love Your Enemies! Otherwise Bite Them!" Bismarck, Herbert, and the Morier Affair, 1888–1889', *Central European History*, 1 (1968), 56–79; and A. Ramm, *Sir Robert Morier. Envoy and Ambassador in the Age of Imperialism 1876–1893* (London, 1973), pp. 270–304.
36 On this whole question, see D. R. Gillard, 'Salisbury's African Policy and the Heligoland Offer 1890', *EHR*, 75 (1960), 631–53; and G. N. Sanderson, 'The Anglo-German Agreement of 1890 and the Upper Nile', *EHR*, 78 (1963), 49–72.
37 Cf. *ToL*, vol. 1, pp. 95–6, and Howard to his mother, 20 June 1890, DHW 3/9. Subsequent quotations in this paragraph are from the former.
38 Howard to his mother, 20 July 1885, ibid.
39 Howard to his mother, 20 June 1890, ibid.; and Howard to Spring Rice, 1 Dec. 1888, CASR (Spring Rice Papers, Churchill College, Cambridge) 1/44.
40 Gunn (FO) to Howard, 4 Dec. 1890, DHW 1/35.
41 Howard to his mother, 1 June and 20 June 1890, both DHW 3/9. The rest of this paragraph, except where noted, is from these two letters.
42 Charlotte Howard's 'Investment Book', DHW 5/83.
43 *ToL*, vol. 1, p. 101.
44 Howard diary, 9 Mar. 1891, DHW 1/1.
45 On the nature of the agreement, see *ToL*, vol. 1, p. 112.
46 Howard diary, 22 and 25 Mar., and 8 and 13 Apr. 1891, all DHW 1/1.
47 His adventures can be followed in his South African diary, ibid.; and *ToL*, vol. 1, pp. 115–38.
48 Howard diary, 28 June 1891, DHW 1/1.
49 Howard diary, 25 June 1891, ibid.
50 Ibid.
51 Howard diary, 15 Dec. 1891, ibid. Quotations in the rest of this paragraph and the next are from this source.
52 On the division of the Liberal Party in 1886, see R. Rhodes James, *The British Revolution. British Politics 1880–1939* (London, 1977), pp. 81–134.
53 This interview is related in *ToL*, vol. 1, p. 142.
54 This is outlined in *The Birmingham Daily Gazette*, 27 May 1892.
55 *ToL*, vol. 1, p. 143; also see Howard's election manifesto, 'To the Electors of the City of Worcester', 20 June 1892, DHW 5/143.
56 The following quotations are from *The [Worcester] Daily Times*, 2, 21, and 22 June 1892.
57 These quotations are from *The Worcester Echo*, 12 June and 2 July 1892.
58 These statistics are in ibid., 4 July 1892.
59 *ToL*, vol. 1, pp. 158–9.
60 Howard's views are expressed in ibid., pp. 155–7.
61 On French ambitions in Morocco, see F. V. Parsons, *The Origins of the Moroccan Question, 1880–1900* (London, 1976), pp. 34–50. On Sanderson's later assessment, see *ToL*, vol. 1, p. 157.
62 C. Booth, *Life and Labour of the People of London*, 9 vols., 2nd edn. (London, 1892–7). On Booth and his work, cf. B. Norman-Butler, *Victorian Aspirations. The Life and Labour of Charles and Mary Booth* (London, 1972), pp. 116–38; and T. S. and M. B. Simey, *Charles Booth, Social Scientist* (Oxford, 1960).
63 The following is based on *ToL*, vol. 1, pp. 169–80; and Howard to his mother,

19 June, 9 and 25 July, 28 Aug., 27 Sept. 1893, all DHW 3/9. Howard erred in his memoirs about the period when he served on the Booth enquiry. He says he worked for Booth in the summer of 1895, but it is clear from his private MSS that he did the work two years earlier.
64 This 'credo' is outlined in *ToL*, vol. 1, pp. 176–7.
65 Howard's nephew, Aubrey, became enamoured with North Africa and the Middle East, subsequently carving an important place for himself both there and in the Balkans; see Mary Fitzherbert, *The Man Who Was Greenmantle: A Biography of Aubrey Herbert* (London, 1983).
66 *ToL*, vol. 1, p. 164.
67 Ibid., pp. 168. On the value of Grey as recognised by Rosebery, see K. Robbins, *Sir Edward Grey, A Biography of Lord Grey of Fallodon* (London, 1971), p. 44.
68 Rhodes James, *British Revolution*, pp. 141–55.
69 For instance, Howard to Spring Rice, 13 Nov. 1895, CASR 1/44.
70 Howard to his mother, 25 July 1893, DHW 3/9.
71 *ToL*, vol. 1, p. 183.
72 On Gray's views, see ibid., p. 180.
73 Ibid., p. 181.
74 The information which follows is based on ibid., pp. 184–208, as well as two of Howard's unpublished MSS: 'Wildfowl in Marajo – Amazon', and 'Visit to a Brazilian Country House', both in DHW 1/11.
75 *ToL*, vol. 1, p. 210.
76 Ibid.
77 Ibid., pp. 212–13.
78 Howard's inheritance from his mother's estate helped finance this investigatory process. See the bank book of Charlotte Howard and her executors, DHW 5/84; Charlotte Howard's 'Last Will and Testament', DHW 5/91; the record of Howard's investments for 1897–8 in DHW 1/56.
79 For Howard and Biffen's trip, see *ToL*, vol. 1, pp. 215–31; and Esme Howard, 'Impressions of an Englishman in the West Indies' (unpublished MSS), DHW 1/11.
80 The rest of this paragraph is based on *ToL*, vol. 1, pp. 232–3.
81 Howard to Elizabeth, his sister, 3 May 1897, DHW 3/10.
82 *ToL*, vol. 1, p. 233. Howard mentions here that his letter and Princess Bandini's reply were never kept. Indeed, they cannot be traced.
83 Howard to Elizabeth, his sister, 7 Apr. 1898, DHW 3/10.
84 See Isabella Bandini to Elizabeth Carnarvon, 13 Apr. 1898, and Howard to Elizabeth, his sister, 7 Apr. 1898, both ibid.; and Merry del Val to Howard, 16 Apr. 1898, DHW 3/29.
85 *ToL*, vol. 1, pp. 246–59.
86 Ibid., p. 260.
87 Howard to Elizabeth, his sister, 9 and 21 June 1898, both DHW 3/10.
88 For example, Elizabeth Carnarvon to Howard, 19 May 1898, enclosing Isabella Bandini to Howard, DHW 3/26.
89 Howard to Elizabeth, his sister, 15 Nov. 1898, DHW 3/10.
90 *ToL*, vol. 1, p. 266.
91 On British policy in South Africa in the period prior to the Boer War, that is the amalgam of policy emanating from London and Cape Town, see A. N. Porter, *The Origins of the South African War: Joseph Chamberlain and the*

Notes to pages 29–36

Diplomacy of Imperialism 1895–1899 (Manchester, 1980); and R. Robinson, J. Gallagher and A. Denny, *Africa and the Victorians. The Official Mind of Imperialism* (London, 1961), pp. 410–61.

92 On the German and French questions, see G. K. Burke, 'Anglo-French Relations in the African Crisis of 1898', Ph.D. dissertation (St John's University, 1973); and P. M. Kennedy, *The Rise of Anglo-German Antagonism 1860–1914* (London, 1982), pp. 157–250.

93 J. Butler, 'The German Factor in Anglo-Transvaal Relations', in P. Gifford and W. R. Louis, eds., *Britain and Germany in Africa* (New Haven, 1967).

94 For Howard's view, see *ToL*, vol. 1, pp. 269–72.

95 This can be traced in the letters to his wife published in ibid., pp. 274–85.

96 Howard to Stafford, his brother, 16 Aug. 1900, DHW 1/16.

97 On his time at Vrede, see ibid.; *ToL*, vol. 1, pp. 288–98; and Howard's untitled and unpublished MSS of his experiences in South Africa, DHW 1/15.

98 *ToL*, vol. 1, p. 292.

99 Ibid., pp. 297–308; Howard to Stafford, his brother, 16 Aug. 1900, DHW 1/16; and Howard's untitled and unpublished MSS of his experiences in South Africa, DHW 1/15.

100 On the Boer War, see B. Farwell, *The Great Anglo-Boer War* (Toronto, 1976); and T. Pakenham, *The Boer War* (London, 1979).

101 Howard to Elizabeth, his sister, 3 May 1897, DHW 3/10.

102 *ToL*, vol. 1, pp. 326.

103 Neither Howard nor Bertie have left any contemporary record of this meeting. The Howard and Bertie MSS do not contain any reference to it; thus I base this discussion on ibid. I would like to thank Dr Keith Hamilton of the University of Aberystwyth, who is writing Bertie's biography, for his advice with respect to searching Bertie's papers.

104 *ToL*, vol. 1, p. 326.

105 Ibid.

106 Ibid.

107 Cf. S. Lee, *King Edward VII. A Biography*, vol. 2: *The Reign* (New York, 1927), pp. 222–4; P. Magnus, *King Edward the Seventh* (New York, 1964), p. 307; and G. St Aubyn, *Edward VII. Prince and King* (London, 1979), pp. 320–3. Also see B. C. Busch, *Hardinge of Penshurst. A Study in the Old Diplomacy*, (Hamden, Conn., 1980), pp. 54–6; and C. J. Lowe and M. L. Dockrill, *The Mirage of Power*, vol. 1: *British Foreign Policy 1902–14* (London, 1972), pp. 4–11.

108 Balfour telegram to the king, 12 Apr. 1903, Hardinge MSS, Cambridge University Library (hereafter Har. MSS), vol. 4. Also see Barrington (private secretary to the foreign secretary) to Hardinge (FO official accompanying the king), 8 Apr. 1903; Balfour telegram to the king, 9 Apr. 1903; Hardinge telegram to Barrington, 9 Apr. 1903, all ibid.

109 See Barrington to Norfolk, 17 and 19 Apr. 1903, 15th Duke of Norfolk MSS. Also Norfolk to Hardinge, 7 Apr. 1903; Balfour telegram to the king, 9 Apr. 1903; Barrington to Hardinge, 10 Apr. 1903; Hardinge telegram to Lansdowne (foreign secretary), all Har. MSS, vol. 4.

110 Balfour telegram to the king, 12 Apr. 1903, ibid.

111 Bertie telegram to Hardinge, 18 Apr. 1903, enclosing Rampolla to Stonor, 15 Apr. 1903, ibid.

112 This is implied in Bertie telegram to Hardinge, 18 Apr. 1903; and Hardinge telegram to Bertie, 18 Apr. 1903, both ibid.

113 See Hardinge telegram to Barrington, 18 Apr. 1903, enclosing message for Norfolk, ibid. Cf. Rampolla to Norfolk, 23 Apr. 1903, 15th Duke of Norfolk MSS.
114 Howard memorandum, 21 Apr. 1903, DHW 1/9.
115 The following paragraph is based on ibid., as well as Howard memorandum, (n.d. but 21 Apr. 1903); Howard memorandum, 23 Apr. 1903; Bertie to Howard, 24 Apr. 1903; all ibid. Also Hardinge telegram to Balfour, 25 Apr. 1903; and Hardinge to Balfour, 29 Apr. 1903, both Har. MSS, vol. 4.
116 For instance, Bertie to Hardinge, 4 June 1902; and Hardinge to Bertie, 9 June 1902, both Har. MSS, vol. 3. Cf. R. A. Jones, *The British Diplomatic Service 1815–1914* (Waterloo, Ont., 1983), pp. 164–7; and Z. S. Steiner, *The Foreign Office and Foreign Policy, 1898–1914* (Cambridge, 1969), pp. 70–82.
117 Hardinge to Howard, 19 June 1903, DHW 2/8; also see Hardinge to Bertie, 25 May 1903, Bertie MSS, FO 800/163.
118 Hardinge to Howard, 21 July 1903, DHW 2/8. On the Levant Service, see D. C. M. Platt, *The Cinderella Service. British Consuls since 1825* (London, 1971), pp. 125–79. Criticism of Hardinge and his efforts to instil change came from a number of established diplomats who felt there was an element of self-aggrandisement in his efforts; for example, Goschen (ambassador at Copenhagen) diary, 6 Mar. 1904, C. D. H. Howard, ed., *The Diary of Edward Goschen 1900–1914* (London, 1980), p. 84.
119 See Jones, *Diplomatic Service*, p. 149. Cf. 22 May 1908, Hardinge to Bryce (ambassador at Washington), Har. MSS, vol. 13: '[Howard] has had the good fortune – having entirely retired from the Diplomatic Service – to be reinstated in a semi-diplomatic post at Crete...This was very exceptional treatment, and I only know of one other case where it has ever been done...'

2 CRETE: CONSULSHIP AND CIVIL WAR, 1903–1906

1 The following discussion of the Cretan question is based on Oakes (FO Library) memorandum, 31 Mar. 1904, FO 78/5349; M. S. Anderson, *The Eastern Question* (London, 1966), especially pp. 261–4; and D. Dakin, *The Unification of Greece, 1770–1923* (New York, 1972), pp. 107–14, 118–20, 149–58, 170–1.
2 *ToL*, vol. 2, p. 18. Cf. Howard to Hardinge, 17 and 23 July 1903, both DHW 1/17/1; and Hardinge to Howard, 21 July 1903, DHW 2/8.
3 For instance, Graves (consul-general, Crete) despatch (8) to Lansdowne, 2 Apr. 1903, with Sanderson minute, 11 Apr. 1903, and Lansdowne minute (n.d. but 11 Apr. 1903), all FO 78/5281.
4 *ToL*, vol. 2, p. 18.
5 Prince George of Greece, *The Cretan Drama, The Life and Memoirs of Prince George of Greece, High Commissioner in Crete (1898–1906)*, ed. by A. Pallis (New York, 1959), p. 186.
6 For example, Hardinge to Howard, 21 Oct. 1903, DHW 2/8.
7 Dakin, *Unification of Greece*, pp. 170–1.
8 The following paragraph is based on Howard to Hardinge, 17 July 1903, DHW 1/17/1.
9 Ibid.; also see Graves to Howard, 25 July 1903, DHW 2/8.

10 Hardinge to Barrington (Lansdowne's private secretary), initialled by Lansdowne, 29 Sept. 1904, Lansdowne MSS FO 800/141.
11 Howard despatch (36) to Lansdowne, 18 Sept. 1903, FO 78/5281.
12 Howard despatch (51) to Lansdowne, 26 Dec. 1903, ibid.
13 Hardinge to Howard, 13 Jan. 1904, DHW 2/8.
14 Howard despatch (10) to Lansdowne, 17 Mar. 1904, FO 78/5349.
15 The rest of this paragraph is based on Maxwell minute, n.d., and Lansdowne minute, n.d., both on ibid.; and Howard despatches (22 and 23) to Lansdowne, 12 May 1904, ibid.
16 The following paragraph is based on 'Quatrième Partie. Questions économiques et financières', in 'Report of International Commission on Cretan Affairs', 30 Mar. 1906, FO 371/48/12279/12279; Howard despatches (36 and 42) to Lansdowne, 22 Sept. and 2 Oct. 1903, both FO 78/5281; and Dakin, *Unification of Greece*, pp. 154–8.
17 Howard despatch (39) to Lansdowne, 22 Sept. 1903, FO 78/5281.
18 An indication of which can be seen in Lansdowne despatch (14) to Howard, 10 Sept. 1903, ibid.
19 Hardinge to Howard, 13 Jan. 1904, DHW 2/8.
20 Howard despatch (41) to Lansdowne, 1 Oct. 1903, FO 78/5281.
21 Howard to Prince George, 6 Aug. 1903, DHW 1/17/1; also Howard despatch (35) to Lansdowne, 11 Sept. 1903, with Maxwell minute, n.d., Sanderson minute, n.d., and Lansdowne initials, n.d., all FO 78/5281.
22 Wilkinson (acting British consul-general, Crete) despatch (45) to Lansdowne, 27 Oct. 1903, enclosing 'Collective Note to the High Commissioner', 26 Oct. 1903, ibid.
23 Howard despatch (42) to Lansdowne, 2 Oct. 1903, ibid.
24 The rest of this paragraph is based on Howard to Hardinge, 21 Oct. 1903, DHW 1/9; Sanderson to Howard, 13 Jan. 1904, DHW 2/8; and Sanderson to Howard, 10 Mar. 1904, with enclosure, DHW 1/17/1.
25 'I wish I could speak as nicely of Sir Thomas as he does of me, but I cannot. He gads about all summer & pays no attention to my despatches than if I were the man in the moon.': in Howard to Elizabeth, his sister, 7 Dec. 1903, DHW 3/10.
26 Villiers (assistant under-secretary, FO) telegram (unnumbered) to Howard, 17 Aug. 1903, FO 78/5281; and Villiers to Howard, 28 Aug. 1903, DHW 2/8.
27 Sanderson to Howard, 27 May 1904, DHW 2/9.
28 Cf. Howard to Hardinge, 23 July 1903, DHW 1/17/1; and Howard to Sanderson, 16 June 1904, DHW 2/9.
29 Cf. Prince George, *Cretan Drama*, pp. 23–9; and C. Kerofilas, *Eleftherios Venizelos. His Life and Work* (London, 1915), pp. 30–7.
30 The following paragraph is based on *ToL*, vol. 2, pp. 30–2; and Howard despatch (50) to Lansdowne, 19 Dec. 1903, with marginal comment, n.d., n.a., FO 78/5281.
31 Ibid.
32 For example, Howard despatch (35) to Lansdowne, 10 June 1904, with enclosures, FO 78/5349. This continued to underpin the prince's arguments long after he left Crete; see Prince George, *Cretan Drama*, pp. 189–90.
33 Howard despatch (19) to Lansdowne, 29 Apr. 1904, FO 78/5349.

34 Howard to Sanderson, 15 May 1904, enclosing Howard 'Memorandum of Conversation with High Commissioner of 14 May 1904', DHW 1/17/2; cf. the final drafts of these in FO 78/5349. Also see Cd 592.
35 For instance, Isabella Howard to Elizabeth Carnarvon, 16 June 1904, DHW 3/10.
36 Howard to Sanderson, 15 May 1904, DHW 1/17/2. For additional criticism of Papadiamondopoulos, see Howard to Elizabeth, his sister, DHW 3/10, in which he wrote: 'I cannot help thinking that our good friend Papa is trying to bring on a conflict with the Powers with a view of posing afterwards as hero champion of little Crete against the bullying nasty P[rotecting] P[ower]s.'
37 Howard despatches (16 and 19) to Lansdowne, 16 and 29 Apr. 1904, both FO 78/5349.
38 Howard telegrams (2 and 3) to FO, 8 and 12 July 1904, and Howard despatch (47) to Lansdowne, 13 July 1904, all FO 78/5349.
39 See *The Times*, 31 Aug. and 2 Sept. 1904.
40 Lansdowne minute to Villiers, 2 Sept. 1904, FO 78/5349.
41 Howard despatch (52) to Lansdowne, 29 July 1904, ibid.
42 For instance, Howard to Hardinge, 21 Oct. 1903, DHW 1/9; and Hardinge to Howard, 21 Oct. 1903, DHW 2/8.
43 Howard despatch (52) to Lansdowne, 29 July 1904, FO 78/5349.
44 Maxwell minute to Lansdowne, 13 Jan. 1904, and Lansdowne minutes, n.d., ibid.
45 Howard to Villiers, 13 Aug. 1904, and Howard despatch (64) to Lansdowne, 23 Aug. 1904, both ibid.; Howard to Villiers, 26 Aug. 1904, and Howard to Sanderson, 26 Aug. 1904, both DHW 1/17/2.
46 For example, Howard despatches (32 and 34), 3 and 4 June 1904, both FO 78/5349.
47 For instance, see the reports from St Petersburg: Hardinge (now ambassador at St Petersburg) despatches (467 and 485) to Lansdowne, 17 Sept. and 1 Oct. 1904, with Lansdowne minute, n.d., and initialled by the king, Prince of Wales, and Balfour, all FO 65/1681.
48 See C. M. Andrew, *Théophile Delcassé and the Making of the Entente Cordiale* (London, 1968); Lowe and Dockrill, *Mirage of Power*, vol. 1, pp. 1–28; G. M. Monger, *The End of Isolation* (London, 1963).
49 Lansdowne to Monson (British ambassador, Paris), 26 Dec. 1904, Lansdowne MSS, FO 800/126.
50 Cf. Hardinge to Lansdowne, 27 Oct. and 4 Nov. 1904, both Lansdowne MSS, FO 800/141.
51 *ToL*, vol. 2, pp. 36–7. Cf. Prince George, *Cretan Drama*, pp. 168–9.
52 Villiers to Howard, 26 Aug. 1904, DHW 1/17/2; Lansdowne minute to Villiers, 2 Sept. 1904, FO 78/5349.
53 *ToL*, vol. 2, p. 37.
54 Ibid.
55 Howard despatch (72) to Lansdowne, 11 Sept. 1904, FO 78/5349.
56 Lansdowne minute, n.d., on ibid.
57 Bertie telegram (unnumbered) to Howard, 1 Oct. 1904, ibid.
58 Howard telegram (unnumbered) to Bertie, 3 Oct. 1904, DHW 1/17/2; and Howard to Bertie, 14 Oct. 1904, DHW 1/17/1.

59 Howard despatch (80) to Lansdowne, 10 Dec. 1904, FO 78/5349.
60 'Proclamation of H.R.H. Prince George of Greece', 26 Nov./9 Dec. 1904, in the *Cretan Official Gazette*, enclosed in ibid.
61 Lansdowne to Prince George, 12 Nov. 1904, Lansdowne MSS, FO 800/131; and Elliott (British minister, Athens) to Howard, 23 Jan. 1905, DHW 2/8.
62 Howard despatch (4) to Lansdowne, 28 Jan. 1905, enclosing Howard memorandum on 'A summary of provisional financial statements for the years 1902 and 1903', n.d., and Howard despatch (9) to Lansdowne, 7 Feb. 1905, all ibid.
63 Howard despatch (7) to Lansdowne, 5 Feb. 1905; Sanderson despatch (7) to Howard, 23 Feb. 1905; and Howard despatch (23) to Lansdowne, 12 Mar. 1905, all ibid.
64 Howard to Sanderson, 21 Jan. 1905, DHW 1/17/3.
65 Howard despatch (17) to Lansdowne, 3 Mar. 1905, FO 78/5410.
66 Howard despatch (25) to Lansdowne, 16 Mar. 1905, ibid. Lansdowne also circulated this despatch to the king and the Prince of Wales.
67 The following is based on Howard telegram (10) to Lansdowne, 24 Mar. 1905, FO 78/5413; Howard despatch (28) to Lansdowne, 26 Mar. 1905, FO 78/5410. Also see *ToL*, vol. 2, pp. 38–42; and Prince George, *Cretan Drama*, pp. 205–12.
68 Monaco to Howard, 22 Mar. 1905, enclosed in Howard despatch (26) to Lansdowne, 23 Mar. 1905, FO 78/5410.
69 Balfour telegram (unnumbered) to Lansdowne, 25 Mar. 1905, and Lansdowne telegram (5) to Howard, 25 Mar. 1905, both FO 78/5413.
70 Howard despatch (34) to Lansdowne, 4 Apr. 1905, FO 78/5410.
71 Howard despatch (46) to Lansdowne, 20 Apr. 1905, ibid.
72 Howard despatch (41) to Lansdowne, 14 Apr. 1905, ibid.
73 Lansdowne minute, 25 Apr. 1905, on ibid.
74 Lansdowne minute (n.d. but 26 or 27 May 1905), ibid.
75 Howard despatch (Treaty 2) to Lansdowne, 22 Apr. 1905, with Davidson (FO legal adviser) and Lansdowne minutes, both 9 May 1905, all ibid.
76 FO telegram (37) to Howard, 27 Apr. 1905, FO 78/5413.
77 Howard despatch (102) to Lansdowne, 16 July 1905, FO 78/5411.
78 Sanderson minute to Lansdowne, 27 July 1905, on ibid.
79 See the correspondence in DHW 6/2 between Howard and the various British military and naval officers in Crete during the civil war. Cf. Sanderson to Howard, 7 Apr. 1905, enclosing Director of Military Operations (War Office) memorandum, 1 Apr. 1905, both DHW 1/17/3.
80 For example, Prince George to Lansdowne, 27 May 1905, enclosed in Howard despatch (76) to Lansdowne, 27 May 1905, both FO 78/5411. Also see FO Eastern Dept. memorandum on the 'High Commissioner's request for assistance in quelling insurrection' (unnumbered), FO 78/5413.
81 For instance, Hardinge to Howard, 27 Jan. 1906, DHW 2/9. Also see Maxwell to Howard, 17 May 1905, ibid; and Sanderson to Howard, 26 May 1905, DHW 1/17/3. Telling, too, is King Edward minute, n.d., on Howard to Sanderson, 18 May 1905, FO 78/5410.
82 The rest of this paragraph, and the next, based on Howard despatch (91) to Lansdowne, 1 July 1905, FO 78/5411.
83 See n. 10, above.

84 For instance, see King Edward minute, n.d., on Howard despatch (81) to Lansdowne, 12 June 1905, FO 78/5411. Also see Elliott to Howard, 14 June 1905, DHW 2/9.
85 Howard to Sanderson, 28 Apr. and 18 May 1905; and Howard despatches (65 and 66) to Lansdowne, 18 and 19 May 1905, all FO 78/5410. See Sanderson to Howard, 26 May 1905, DHW 1/17/3, which commends Howard's assessment and indicates that Lansdowne read the 18 May private letter to the Cabinet.
86 Lansdowne minute, n.d., on Howard despatch (66) to Lansdowne, 18 May 1905, FO 78/5410.
87 Howard despatch (73) to Lansdowne, 2 June 1905, FO 78/5411.
88 The rest of this paragraph, except where indicated, is based on *ToL*, vol. 2, pp. 48–50; Howard despatch (87) to Lansdowne, 22 June 1905, FO 78/5411; and Howard diary, 15 July 1905, DHW 1/2.
89 This proclamation, in French and Greek, is in DHW 4/Official/14.
90 'Discours du Doyen des Consuls à la délégation de Therisso', 15 July 1905, ibid.
91 *ToL*, vol. 2, p. 50.
92 The British and Russians had contingents of 900 men each in Crete, the French under 700, and the Italians under 300; see Lansdowne telegram (87) to Howard, 21 July 1905, FO 78/5413.
93 Howard to Panton, 21 July 1905, FO 78/5411.
94 Ibid.
95 Howard despatch (124) to Lansdowne, 17 Aug. 1905, enclosing Panton to Howard, 13 Aug. 1905, ibid.
96 Lansdowne minute, 31 Aug. 1905, on ibid.
97 Howard despatch (128) to Lansdowne, 21 Aug. 1905, ibid.
98 Ibid.; and Howard diary, 21 Aug. 1905, DHW 1/2.
99 The rest of this paragraph is based on Howard despatch (133) to Lansdowne, 1 Sept. 1905, with enclosures, FO 78/5411.
100 Lansdowne to Sanderson, 11 Sept. 1905, Lansdowne MSS, FO 800/116.
101 'Eothen', 'Crete under Prince George', *The Fortnightly Review*, new series, 78 (1905), 539–51.
102 Barrington minute to Lansdowne, 4 Sept. 1905, and Lansdowne minute, n.d., both FO 78/5413.
103 Barrington to Howard, 17 May 1905, DHW 1/17/3.
104 Howard diary, 22 Sept. to 21 Oct. 1905, DHW 1/2. Also see *ToL*, vol. 2, p. 53.
105 Howard despatch (174) to Lansdowne, 22 Oct. 1905, enclosing Venizelos and Manos to the four consuls-general, 18 Oct. 1905, and 'Procès-Verbal of Consular Meeting', 22 Oct. 1905, FO 78/5412.
106 Howard despatch (177) to Lansdowne, 3 Nov. 1905, ibid.
107 Howard despatch (187) to Lansdowne, 26 Nov. 1905, with enclosures, ibid.
108 The rest of this paragraph and the next are based on ibid. Cf. Prince George, *Cretan Drama*, pp. 328–9.
109 Robert Rhodes James, *The British Revolution. British Politics, 1880–1939*, vol. 1: *From Gladstone to Asquith 1880–1914* (London, 1976), pp. 225–30.
110 See the letters exchanged between the two on Grey's selection as foreign

secretary: Howard to Grey, 15 Dec. 1905, and Grey to Howard, 26 Dec. 1905, both DHW 1/17/3.
111 See Lansdowne telegram (129) to Howard, 15 Nov. 1905, FO 78/5413; and Egerton (British ambassador, Rome) despatch (216) to Grey, 27 Dec. 1905, FO 371/46/63/63.
112 For instance, Howard despatch (201) to Grey, 15 Dec. 1905, enclosing Howard 'Report on the Financial Situation in Crete and on the Budget Estimates for the Financial Years 1905–1906', 14 Dec. 1905, with Parker (FO Eastern Dept) minute, n.d., both FO 371/46/122/122.
113 For instance, Howard despatch (23) to Grey, 17 Feb. 1906, enclosing Panton 'Report on the British "Secteur" of Candia', 11 Feb. 1906, FO 371/46/6946/63.
114 King Edward minute, n.d., on Howard despatch (78) to Lansdowne, 4 June 1905, FO 78/5411.
115 Hardinge to Grey, 26 Apr. 1906, FO 371/50/15983/15983. Also see Law to Hardinge, 15 Apr. 1906, FO 371/50/16004/15983. Howard travelled to Athens for the Olympic Games in April and, with Elliott, visited with the king and Hardinge on the royal yacht; see Howard diary, 17 Apr. 1906, DHW 1/3.
116 Cf. Howard despatches (133 and 184) to Lansdowne, 1 Sept. and 12 Nov. 1905, both FO 78/5412.
117 Parker 'Memorandum on the situation in Crete', 26 Mar. 1906, FO 371/48/10900/10900.
118 Howard despatch (53) to Grey, 30 Mar. 1906, with enclosure, FO 371/48/12058/10476.
119 For instance, see Howard despatch (77) to Grey, 13 May 1906, enclosing Katzourakis (opposition leader) to Howard, 6 May 1906, Howard and de Bronewski to Katzourakis, 12 May 1906, 'Procès-verbal of the Consular Meeting' of 9 May 1906, and 'Notice issued by the Consuls of the Protecting Powers', 3 May 1906, FO 371/48/17456/10476.
120 Howard despatch (84) to Grey, 24 May 1906, FO 371/48/18638/10476; and Howard despatch (87) to Grey, 31 May 1906, FO 371/48/19963/10476.
121 Maxwell to Howard, 21 Dec. 1905, DHW 2/9.
122 *ToL*, vol. 2, pp. 66–7. The despatch to which he referred was Howard despatch (184) to Lansdowne, 12 Nov. 1905, FO 78/5412.
123 Howard despatch (57) to Grey, 6 Apr. 1906, with enclosure, FO 371/46/12770/320; and Howard despatch (74) to Grey, 4 May 1906, with enclosure, FO 371/46/17016/320.
124 Law to Grey, 28 Apr. 1906, FO 371/46/14660/320.
125 Cf. Howard despatch (81) to Grey, 20 May 1906, FO 371/46/18293/320; and Law to Howard, with Parker minute, 11 June 1906, and Maxwell minute, 13 June 1906, all FO 371/46/20012/320.
126 For example, Howard despatch (123) to Grey, 24 July 1906, FO 371/51/26475/15983.
127 Hardinge to Howard, 27 Jan. 1906, DHW 2/9.
128 Spring Rice (counsellor, British Embassy, St Petersburg) to Howard, 5 Mar. 1906, ibid.
129 Grey to Howard, 3 Apr. 1906, DHW 1/17/2.

3 WASHINGTON: IMPERIAL AFFAIRS AND ARBITRATION, 1906–1908

1. *ToL*, vol. 2, p. 98.
2. Howard diary, 18 Oct. 1906, DHW 1/3.
3. The rest of this paragraph is based on Howard diary, Oct.–Dec. 1906, ibid.; *ToL*, vol. 2, pp. 106–7; and Durand despatch (231) to Grey, 26 Dec. 1906, FO 371/357/618/618.
4. *ToL*, vol. 2, p. 107.
5. Except where noted, the following paragraph is based on B. Perkins, *The Great Rapprochement. England and the United States, 1895–1914* (New York, 1968), pp. 224–8; and P. Sykes, *The Right Honourable Sir Mortimer Durand. A Biography* (London, Toronto, Melbourne and Sydney, 1926), pp. 298–312.
6. On Roosevelt, see J. M. Cooper, *The Warrior and the Priest. Woodrow Wilson and Theodore Roosevelt* (Cambridge, Mass., 1983), pp. 5–14, 27–43; L. Einstein, *Roosevelt: His Mind in Action* (Boston, 1930); E. Morris, *The Rise of Theodore Roosevelt* (New York, 1978); and N. Roosevelt, *Theodore Roosevelt: The Man as I Knew Him* (New York, 1967).
7. On the ending of the Russo-Japanese war, see E. P. Trani, *The Treaty of Portsmouth. An Adventure in American Diplomacy* (Lexington, Ky, 1969); and J. A. White, *The Diplomacy of the Russo-Japanese War* (Princeton, 1964), *passim*. On Algeciras and the Moroccan question, see E. W. Anderson, *The First Moroccan Crisis, 1904–6* (Chicago, 1930); Lowe and Dockrill, *Mirage of Power*, vol. 1, pp. 11–29; and G. W. Monger, *The End of Isolation: British Foreign Policy, 1900–1907* (London, 1963), pp. 268–80.
8. Perkins, *Rapprochement*, pp. 227–8.
9. This is shown in Howard to Grey, 25 Dec. 1906, DHW 2/11.
10. *ToL*, vol. 2, p. 110.
11. Ibid., p. 111.
12. Howard to Grey, 25 Dec. 1906, DHW 2/11; and Howard despatch (239) to Grey, 31 Dec. 1906, FO 371/357/2300/622.
13. Hardinge to Howard, 11 Feb. 1907, DHW 2/11.
14. Hardinge to Howard, 8 Mar. 1907, ibid.
15. *ToL*, vol. 2, p. 108.
16. Hardinge to Bryce, 26 Dec. 1906, Bryce MSS, USA 27.
17. Except where noted, the rest of this paragraph is based on Howard diary, Dec. 1906, DHW 1/3; and *ToL*, vol. 2, pp. 109–17, 493–4.
18. On the 'Eastern Establishment', see, the following by E. D. Baltzell: *Philadelphia Gentlemen: The Making of a National Upper Class* (New York, 1958); *The Protestant Establishment: Aristocracy and Caste in America* (New York, 1965); *Puritan Boston and Quaker Philadelphia: Two Protestant Ethics and the Spirit of Class Authority and Leadership* (Boston, 1979); see also G. E. White, *The Eastern Establishment and the Western Experience: The West of Frederick Remington, Theodore Roosevelt, and Owen Wister* (New Haven, 1964). On the need to consider more carefully the question of the 'Eastern Establishment' and its influence on foreign policy prior to 1940, see P. M. Roberts, 'The American "Eastern Establishment" and Foreign Affairs: A Challenge for Historians' (unpublished paper delivered at the 8th Annual Meeting of the Society for Historians of American Foreign Relations, Boston University, Boston, Mass., August 1982).
19. *ToL*, vol. 2, p. 115.

20 A. E. Campbell, *Great Britain and the United States, 1895-1903* (Glasgow, 1960); C. S. Campbell, Jr, *Anglo-American Understanding, 1893-1903* (Baltimore, 1957); Lowe and Dockrill, *Mirage of Power*, vol. 1, pp. 96-106; and Perkins, *Rapprochement, passim*.
21 K. Bourne, *Britain and the Balance of Power in North America, 1815-1908* (London, 1967), pp. 313-401; and S. J. Wells, Jr, 'British Strategic Withdrawal from the Western Hemisphere, 1905-1906', *CHR*, 49 (1968).
22 For instance, R. G. Neale, *Britain and American Imperialism, 1898-1900* (St Lucia, Qld, 1965). Cf. War Office memorandum on 'The Conditions of a War between the British Empire and the United States', Dec. 1907, WO 106/40/B1/20.
23 K. Robbins, *Sir Edward Grey. A Biography of Lord Grey of Fallodon* (London, 1971), p. 170. Also see Hardinge of Penshurst, *Old Diplomacy. The Reminiscences of Lord Hardinge of Penshurst* (London, 1947), pp. 130-1. Cf. Roosevelt to Whitelaw Reid (US ambassador, London), 6 Nov. 1906, in E. E. Morison et al., *The Letters of Theodore Roosevelt*, vol. 5: *The Big Stick* (Cambridge, Mass., 1952), p. 488.
24 Hardinge, *Old Diplomacy*, pp. 131-2.
25 Bryce made six visits to the United States before becoming ambassador: 1870, 1881, 1883, 1890, 1901, 1904; see H. A. L. Fisher, *James Bryce*, vol. 1 (New York, 1927), pp. 222-3, 280, 329. See the description of a Roosevelt-Bryce conversation at the White House on the subject of business trusts; in *ibid.*, vol. 2, p. 6. Cf. Roosevelt to Bryce, 31 Mar. and 25 Nov. 1898, in Morison, *Roosevelt Letters*, vol. 2: *The Years of Preparation 1898-1900* (Cambridge, Mass., 1951), pp. 807, 889. J. Bryce, *The American Commonwealth* (London, 1888).
26 For instance, Irish Office memoranda on 'Irish constitutional reform', 12 June 1906, and on 'Irish administrative reform', 25 July 1906, CAB 37/83/54 and 70; and Bryce memoranda on 'Irish administrative council', 15 Dec. 1906, and on 'University Education in Ireland', 17 Dec. 1906, CAB 37/85/98 and 99.
27 E. Ions, *James Bryce and American Democracy 1870-1922* (London, 1960), pp. 199-200.
28 *Ibid.*, p. 202.
29 Howard despatch (238) to Grey, 31 Dec. 1906, FO 371/357/2300/622. After Bryce's arrival, criticism of him was voiced in German-American and Irish-American newspapers; for example, see Sanderson (consul-general, NY) to Howard, 8 Feb. 1907, FO 371/359/5523/4089; and Howard despatch (30) to Grey, 18 Feb. 1907, FO 371/359/7059/7059.
30 See King George V's remarks on Reid's death in 1912; in B. Willson, *America's Ambassadors to England 1785-1928* (London, 1928), p. 440. On Reid's life and accomplishments, see R. Cortissoz, *The Life of Whitelaw Reid*, 2 vols. (New York, 1921).
31 The rest of this paragraph is based on *ToL*, vol. 2, pp. 121-2.
32 See the Howard-Bryce correspondence in DHW 1/18 for proof of this.
33 *ToL*, vol. 2, p. 121.
34 The standard work on Canada for this period is G. P. de T. Glazebrook, *A History of Canadian External Relations*, rev. edn, vol. 1: *The Formative Years to 1914* (Toronto, 1966). Also see R. Bothwell, 'Canadian Representation at Washington: A Study in Colonial Responsibility', *CHR*, 53 (1972), 125-48;

Notes to pages 78–84

F. A. Coghlan, 'James Bryce and the Establishment of the Department of External Affairs', *Canadian Historical Association Historical Papers* (1968), 84–93; D. Farr, *The Colonial Office and Canada, 1867–1887* (Toronto, 1955); and C. P. Stacey, *Canada and the Age of Conflict*, vol. 1: *1867–1921* (Toronto 1977), pp. 85–121.
35 On the nature of Newfoundland's political structure, see F. W. Rowe, *A History of Newfoundland and Labrador* (Toronto, 1980), pp. 259–86. Also see P. Neary, 'The French and American Shore Questions as Factors in Newfoundland History', in J. Hiller and P. Neary, eds., *Newfoundland in the Nineteenth and Twentieth Centuries: Essays in Interpretation* (Toronto, Buffalo and London, 1980), pp. 95–122; and S. J. R. Noel, *Politics in Newfoundland* (Toronto, 1973), pp. 3–115.
36 See Bryce to Lord Grey, 11 Jan. 1907, Bryce MSS, FO 800/331.
37 For Bryce's itinerary during his service as ambassador, see Fisher, *Bryce*, vol. 2, pp. 317–23; his itinerary for 1907–8 is on pp. 317–18.
38 The following paragraph is based on *ToL*, vol. 2, pp. 118–19; Cd 3560, Cd 3796, Cd 4586, and Lindsay despatch (17) to Grey, 4 Feb. 1907, FO 371/358/5361/1806; and Colonial Office memorandum on the 'Jamaica Incident', 5 Feb. 1907, CAB 37/86/13.
39 This and the next paragraph are based on *ToL*, vol. 2, pp. 118–19.
40 On this question, see R. C. Brown and R. Cook, *Canada, 1896–1921. A Nation Transformed* (Toronto, 1974), pp. 33–48; J. Munro, *The Alaska Boundary Dispute* (Toronto, 1970); and N. Penlington, *The Alaska Boundary Dispute: A Critical Reappraisal* (Toronto, 1972).
41 Campbell, *Anglo-American Understanding*, pp. 88–119; and C. J. Chacko, *The International Joint Commission between the United States of America and the Dominion of Canada* (New York, 1932).
42 *Canadian Hansard, H of C*, 9th Parliament, 3rd Session, 23 Oct. 1903, p. 14812.
43 Ibid., 4th Session, 14 Mar. 1904, pp. 66–77.
44 For this and the next sentence, see Root to Durand, 3 May 1906; Bertram Cox (CO, under-secretary) to Gorst (FO, under-secretary), 22 Nov. 1906, enclosing Laurier to Lord Grey, 25 Sept. 1906; Gorst to Bertram Cox, 27 Nov. 1906, all FO 371/360/19366/19366. Cf. A. C. Gleuck, Jr, 'Pilgrimages to Ottawa: Canadian–American Diplomacy, 1903–1913', *Canadian Historical Association Historical Papers* (1968), 75; and P. Neary, 'Grey, Bryce, and the Settlement of Canadian–American Differences, 1905–1911', *CHR*, 49 (1968), 357–8.
45 Lord Grey to Howard, 12 Jan. 1907, enclosing Lord Grey to Sir Edward Grey, 25 Oct. 1906, DHW 2/11.
46 Howard to his wife, 17 Jan. 1907, DHW 3/4.
47 See the report of Root's speech to the Canadian Club of 22 Jan. 1907: 'Blood Thicker Than Water', 23 Jan. 1907, *Ottawa Evening Journal*.
48 Lord Grey to Howard, 24 Jan. 1907, DHW 2/11.
49 Ibid.
50 Bryce to Lord Grey, 11 Jan, 1907, Bryce MSS, FO 800/331. Also see Bryce to Lord Grey, 14 and 26 Feb. 1907, both ibid.
51 For Bryce's conversations with Laurier, see Bryce despatch (80) to Grey, 9 Apr. 1907, FO 371/360/19366/19366. For his initial discussions with Root, see Bryce despatch (70) to Grey, 19 Mar. 1907, ibid. Also see Bryce to Howard, 28 Mar. 1907, DHW 2/12.

52 Cf. Glueck, 'Pilgrimages', pp. 80–1; and Neary, 'Grey, Bryce', p. 364.
53 Brown and Cook, *Canada*, pp. 167–8; and J. E. Kendle, *The Colonial and Imperial Conferences, 1887–1911* (London, 1967).
54 J. W. Coogan, *The End of Neutrality. The United States, Britain, and Maritime Rights 1899–1915* (Ithaca and London, 1981), pp. 55–124. Also see C. D'A. Davis, *The United States and the Second Hague Peace Conference* (Durham, NC, 1975).
55 On Newfoundland's legal restrictions, see MacGregor (governor, Newfoundland) despatch (unnumbered) to Elgin (colonial secretary), 7 Sept. 1906, FO 371/185/32335/Case 607. Except where noted, the rest of this paragraph is based on H. A. Innis, *The Cod Fisheries. The History of and International Economy*, rev. edn (Toronto, Buffalo and London, 1978), pp. 454–6; and Noel, *Newfoundland*, pp. 39–40.
56 For insight into this, see F. W. Marks, III, 'Morality as a Drive Wheel in the Diplomacy of Theodore Roosevelt', *DH*, 2 (1978), 219–36.
57 Foreign Office, 'Memorandum communicated to Mr Whitelaw Reid', 25 Sept. 1906, FO 371/185/32335/Case 607; Reid to Grey, 6 Oct. 1906, and Grey to Reid, 8 Oct. 1906, both FO 371/185/34002/Case 607.
58 For example, R. Bond, *Speech on Modus Vivendi* (St John's, 1907); and editorial in *The [St John's] Evening Telegram*, 8 Oct. 1906.
59 On the American quest to dominate economically in Canada, cf. R. E. Hannigan, 'Reciprocity 1911: Continentalism and American *Weltpolitik*', *DH*, 4 (1980), 1–18; and G. T. Stewart, '"A Special Contiguous Country Economic Regime": An Overview of America's Canadian Policy', *DH*, 6 (1982), 339–57.
60 Howard to Grey, 25 Dec. 1906, DHW 2/11.
61 Hardinge minute, n.d. (probably 23 Jan. 1907); Grey minute, n.d.; and Grey despatch (33) to Howard, 11 Feb. 1907, all FO 371/387/2533/Case 607.
62 Bertram Cox to Under-Secretary, FO, with enclosures, 26 Feb. 1907, FO 371/388/6517/Case 607; and CO to FO, with enclosures, 24 May 1907, FO 371/388/16972/Case 607.
63 Bryce (but written by Howard) telegram (23) to Grey, 16 May 1907, FO 371/388/16076/Case 607.
64 Elgin to Grey, 17 May 1907, FO 371/388/16619/Case 607.
65 Grey telegram (25) to Bryce, 21 May 1907, ibid.; and Bryce (but written by Howard) telegram (25) to Grey, 21 May 1907, FO 371/388/16660/Case 607.
66 Mallet (Grey's private secretary) minute, n.d.; Grey minute, 22 May 1907; and Grey telegram (26) to Bryce, 23 May 1907, all ibid.
67 Grey telegram (unnumbered) to Bryce, 17 July 1907, FO 371/389/26447/Case 607; CO to FO, with enclosures, 10 Aug. 1907, FO 371/389/27081/Case 607; 'Memorandum Communicated by Mr Whitelaw Reid', 20 Aug. 1907, FO 371/389/28990/Case 607; CO to FO, 20 Sept. 1907, with enclosures, FO 371/389/31512/Case 607. Also Cd 3272; Cd 3754; and Cd 3765.
68 See Bryce (but drafted by Howard) despatch (131) to Grey, 3 June 1907, with enclosures, FO 371/388/19292/Case 607.
69 Reid to Grey, 12 July 1907, FO 371/389/23220/Case 607.
70 Mallet, Hardinge, and Grey minutes, all n.d., ibid.
71 Bertram Cox to Under-Secretary, FO, 7 Aug. 1907, FO 371/389/26512/Case 607.

72 The following paragraph is based on Howard to Hardinge, 16 Sept. 1907, DHW 2/11.
73 Howard memorandum, 26 Sept. 1907, FO 371/390/41663/Case 607; Bryce to Grey, 9 Dec. 1907, enclosing 'Memorandum by Mr Howard respecting proposed procedure as to terms of reference for Newfoundland arbitration', 9 Dec. 1907, FO 371/390/41593/Case 607.
74 Howard memorandum, 26 Sept. 1907, FO 371/390/41663/Case 607.
75 Howard to Stafford, his brother, 12 Sept. 1907, DHW 5/86.
76 Larcom (FO American Department) minute, n.d. (probably 21 Dec. 1907), with Mallet, Hardinge, and Grey initials, all FO 371/390/41593/Case 607.
77 See 'Special agreement between United States and Great Britain relating to North Atlantic coast fisheries', 11 Jan. 1909, in *British and Foreign State Papers*, vol. 102, p. 145.
78 Howard memorandum, 26 Sept. 1907, FO 371/390/41663/Case 607.
79 See J. M. Callahan, *American Foreign Policy in Canadian Relations* (New York, 1937), pp. 521–4.
80 For instance, see CO to FO, 8 Feb. 1908, FO 371/587/4707/Case 607; and Lucas (CO) to FO, 27 Mar. 1908, FO 371/587/10665/Case 607. At the 1907 Imperial Conference, Bond suggested arbitration as a means of settling the Newfoundland–United States fisheries dispute, but the British seem to have let it drop because it was seen to be another of his attempts to end the *modus vivendi*. See Elgin to Grey, 17 May 1907; Mallet to Grey, 18 May 1907; and Grey telegram (25) to Bryce, 21 May 1907, all FO 371/388/16660/Case 607.
81 Roosevelt to Reid, 29 July 1907, in Morison, *Roosevelt Letters*, vol. 5, 732–3.
82 Bryce (drafted by Howard) telegram (4) to Grey, 15 Jan. 1908, with Grey minute, n.d., both FO 371/587/1599/Case 607.
83 Grey despatch (123) to Bryce, 8 May 1908, enclosing Lucas (CO) to Under-Secretary, FO, 27 Mar. 1908, with enclosures, FO 371/587/7668/Case 607.
84 Howard's letter cannot be traced, but Mallet to Howard, 10 Mar. (1908), DHW 2/12 shows clearly what Howard had written.
85 Howard despatch (64) to Grey, 19 Feb. 1908, with enclosures, FO 371/565/7198/7198. There were also negotiations relating to the Canadian-American boundary which resulted in a treaty on 11 Apr. 1908; see *British and Foreign State Papers*, vol. 101, p. 210.
86 See Bryce (drafted by Howard) despatch (147) to Grey, 27 Apr. 1908, with enclosures, FO 371/565/16144/7198; and Bryce telegram (84) to Grey, 18 May 1908, FO 371/565/17163/7198.
87 For instance, see Bryce despatch (60) to Grey, 20 Feb. 1908, FO 371/562/6389/435.
88 Grey telegram (65) to Bryce, 9 May 1908, FO 371/587/15902/Case 607.
89 Bryce to Lord Grey, 20 Jan. 1908, Bryce MSS FO 800/331.
90 Bryce despatch (177) to Grey, 26 May 1908, FO 371/588/19117/Case 607.
91 For instance, the Americans wanted a five-man arbitration panel instead of the anticipated one of three; the Imperial governments agreed. See Mallet to CO, 12 Sept. 1908, FO 371/588/31541/Case 607.

92 Howard to Hardinge, 30 June 1908, and Howard to Bryce, 10 July 1908, both DHW 2/11.
93 For instance Howard to Laurier, 25 June 1908, enclosing Howard memorandum, 25 June 1908, ibid.; and Laurier to Howard, 26 June 1908, with Howard minute, n.d., DHW 2/12.
94 On the success of Bryce's ambassadorship, see Glueck, 'Pilgrimages to Ottawa'; Hardinge, *Old Diplomacy*, p. 132; and Neary, 'Grey, Bryce'.
95 See P. A. R. Calvert, 'Great Britain and the New World, 1905–1914' in F. H. Hinsley, ed., *British Foreign Policy under Sir Edward Grey* (Cambridge, 1977), pp. 382–94.
96 See K. E. Neilson, 'Wishful Thinking: The Foreign Office and Russia, 1907–1917', in McKercher and Moss, *Shadow and Substance*, pp. 151–80.
97 Bryce despatch (152) to Grey, 30 Apr. 1908, enclosing 'United States. Annual Report, 1907', Apr. 1908, FO 371/566/16149/16149.
98 For instance, see Howard despatch (31) to Grey, 18 Feb. 1907, FO 371/359/7059/7059.
99 Fisher, *Bryce*, vol. 2, pp. 96–8.
100 See Howard to Hardinge, 30 June 1908, DHW 2/11; and *ToL*, vol. 2, pp. 133–8.
101 Garfield to Howard, 9 July 1908, DHW 2/12; and Hardinge to Howard, 17 July 1908, DHW 4/Official/2.
102 Perkins, *Rapprochement*, p. 277.
103 Bryce despatch (120) to Grey, 3 Apr. 1908, enclosing Grant Watson, 'Report...on the Press of the United States and its Methods', Apr. 1908, FO 371/566/12701/12701.
104 The following paragraph is based on Howard to Grey, 25 Dec. 1906, DHW 2/11. Cf. Howard to Hardinge, 20 Mar. 1908, Har. MSS, vol. 11.
105 See D. Morton, *Ministers and Generals. Politics and the Canadian Militia* (Toronto, 1970).
106 Howard to Grey, 25 Dec. 1906, DHW 2/11, and Bryce to Lord Grey, 14 Dec. 1907, Bryce MSS, FO 800/331.
107 Elgin to Grey, 22 Feb. 1908, Grey MSS, FO 800/91.
108 Hardinge to Bryce, 22 May 1908, Bryce MSS, USA 28.
109 See Bryce despatch (84) to Grey, 6 Mar. 1908, FO 371/564/8763/1848. Cf. Coghlan, 'Bryce and the Establishment of the Department of External Affairs'.
110 D. Judd, *Radical Joe: A Life of Joseph Chamberlain* (London, 1977).
111 Howard to Stafford, his brother, 12 Sept. 1907, DHW 5/86.
112 Howard to Stafford, his brother, 9 Mar. 1908, ibid.
113 *ToL*, vol. 2, p. 106.
114 Howard to Esme, his son, 5 July 1926, DHW 3/11.
115 *ToL*, vol. 2, p. 131.
116 Howard to Hardinge, 30 June 1908, DHW 2/11.
117 Howard despatch (240) to Grey, 23 July 1908, FO 371/567/26944/26944.
118 For instance, Howard despatch (146) to Grey, 21 June 1907, FO 371/360/22521/22521.
119 See the appraisal of Howard at the time of his transfer in Bryce despatch (321) to Grey, 24 Nov. 1908, FO 371/567/42272/42272.

4 BUDAPEST AND BERNE: PRELUDE TO THE GREAT WAR, 1908–1913

1 *ToL*, vol. 2, pp. 129–30.
2 Hardinge to Howard, 18 Dec. 1907, DHW 5/2.
3 Hardinge to Howard, 18 June 1908, DHW 2/11.
4 Tyrrell telegram (unnumbered) to Howard, 30 Aug. 1908, ibid.; and Bryce to Howard, 28 Aug. 1908, DHW 2/12.
5 The rest of this paragraph is based on F. R. Bridge, *From Sadowa to Sarajevo. The Foreign Policy of Austria-Hungary, 1866–1914* (London and Boston, 1972), pp. 297–309; and B. E. Schmitt, *The Annexation of Bosnia* (London, 1937).
6 See Lowe and Dockrill, *Mirage of Power*, vol. 1, pp. 81–6. Cf. Grey of Fallodon, *Twenty-Five Years, 1892–1916*, vol. 1 (London, 1926), pp. 172–201.
7 In his memoirs, Howard glossed over this change in Foreign Office plans; see *ToL*, vol. 2, p. 143.
8 For example, Howard despatch (11) to Grey, 8 Feb. 1910, FO 371/826/6118/6118.
9 *ToL*, vol. 2, p. 149.
10 Ibid., p. 151.
11 Ibid., pp. 152–3.
12 This discussion of 'magyarisation' is from ibid., pp. 154–5. Cf. C. A. Macartney, *National States and National Minorities* (New York, 1934), pp. 113–22; and R. W. Seton-Watson, *The Southern Slav Question and the Habsburg Monarchy* (London, 1911).
13 *ToL*, vol. 2, p. 150.
14 Cartwright despatch (86) to Grey, 1 Aug. 1908, FO 371/399/27154/27154. Cf. K. Wilson, 'Isolating the Isolator. Cartwright, Grey, and the Seduction of Austria-Hungary 1908–12', *Mitteilungen des Osterreichischen Staatsarchiv*, 35 (1982), 169–98.
15 The Crowe biography has yet to appear. Until that time the best published discussion of him is in Steiner, *The Foreign Office*, pp. 109–18; also see E. T. Corp, 'Sir Eyre Crowe and the Administration of the Foreign Office, 1906–1914', *HJ*, 22 (1979), 443–59. Of interest is R. Cosgrove, 'Sir Eyre Crowe and the English Foreign Office, 1905–1914', unpublished Ph.D. dissertation (University of California, 1967).
16 Crowe Memorandum, 1 Jan. 1907, in *BD*, vol. 3, Appendix A.
17 This view is elaborated in Crowe to Howard, 10 Aug. 1913, DHW 4/Personal/19.
18 See F. R. Bridge, 'British Official Opinion and the Domestic Situation in the Hapsburg Monarchy, 1900–1914', in McKercher and Moss, *Shadow and Substance*, pp. 77–114.
19 For an indication, see F. R. Bridge, *Great Britain and Austria-Hungary* (London, 1972), pp. 179–80, 191–2.
20 *ToL*, vol. 2, p. 149.
21 Ibid., p. 143.
22 See Lowe and Dockrill, *Mirage of Power*, vol. 1, pp. 83–4.
23 The rest of this paragraph is based on Howard (1 and 2) to Cartwright, 19 and 24 Jan. 1909, both DHW 5/3.
24 Howard (4 and 5) to Cartwright, 16 and 21 Feb. 1909, both ibid.
25 On 24 February 1909 the Cabinet 'made it clear that war should be avoided

over these Balkan issues'; see Lowe and Dockrill, *Mirage of Power*, vol. 1, p. 84.
26 Foreign Office memorandum on the Russian attitude on the German ultimatum to Serbia, 29 Mar. 1909, CAB 37/98/56.
27 Howard to Hardinge, 31 Mar. 1909, DHW 5/3.
28 On Hungarian politics at this time, see R. Kann, *A History of the Habsburg Empire 1526–1918* (Berkeley, Los Angeles and London, 1974), pp. 456–7; and L. Valiani, *The End of Austria-Hungary* (London, 1973), pp. 25–40.
29 Howard despatch (1) to Cartwright, 18 Jan. 1909, FO 371/599/3263/3263.
30 Howard despatch (35) to Cartwright, 24 Apr. 1909, FO 371/599/16102/4018.
31 For instance, see Howard despatch (116) to Cartwright, 23 Dec. 1909, FO 371/600/46892/20432.
32 Howard despatch (22) to Grey, 22 Mar. 1910, FO 371/825/10329/532.
33 Howard despatch (45) to Grey, 6 June 1910, FO 371/827/20973/7859.
34 Crowe to Howard, 23 Nov. 1909; Law to Howard, 24 Nov. and 14 Dec. 1909; and Howard to Law, 18 Dec. 1909, all DHW 4/Official/16.
35 Howard despatch (5) to Grey, 19 Jan. 1910, with Crowe minute, 24 Jan. 1910, FO 371/825/2602/2602.
36 Tyrrell minute, 23 Sept. 1910, FO 371/825/34945/2602.
37 Crowe minute, 23 Sept. 1910, ibid.
38 The Russians had also been critical of the French for considering a loan to Hungary; see Nicolson (British ambassador, St Petersburg) despatch (681) to Grey, 28 Dec. 1909, with Crowe minute, 3 Jan. 1910, FO 371/825/157/157.
39 Hardinge minute, n.d., Grey initials, n.d., and Tyrrell minute, 26 Sept. 1910, all FO 371/825/34945/2602.
40 Howard despatch (67) to Grey, 17 Oct. 1910, FO 371/835/39578/2602.
41 This line was crossed out in the draft of Howard to Hardinge, 31 Mar. 1909, DHW 5/3.
42 The appraisals of these men can be seen in ibid.
43 Howard, 'Memorandum on the political situation in Hungary', 21 May 1909, enclosed in Howard despatch (48) to Cartwright, 23 May 1909, FO 371/600/20432/20432.
44 Cf. Howard's report on Hungary for 1909 in Cartwright despatch (8) to Grey, 21 Jan. 1910, FO 371/825/2580/904.
45 Crow minute, 7 Feb. 1910, and Grey minute, n.d., ibid; and Grey despatch (3) to Howard, 17 June 1909, FO 371/600/20432/20432.
46 Howard to Mallet, 8 Dec. 1909, DHW 1/9.
47 See Law to Howard, 14 Dec. 1909, DHW 4/Official/16.
48 *ToL*, vol. 2, pp. 165–6. For examples of subsequent Howard–Leipnik correspondence lasting until 1937, see DHW 4/27.
49 For instance, see Norman (FO) to Howard, 15 Sept. 1910, with enclosures, DHW 1/19.
50 The following paragraph is based on Howard to Hardinge, 19 May 1910, DHW 5/3.
51 Howard to Hardinge, 31 Mar. 1909, ibid.
52 Howard to Hardinge, 19 May 1910, ibid.
53 Howard to Hardinge, 31 Mar. 1909, ibid.

54 See *ToL*, vol. 2, p. 151; and Hardinge to Howard, 29 May 1909, DHW 4/Official/16.
55 There were seven of these letters between 19 Jan. and 1 Apr. 1909; for these and Cartwright's replies, see DHW 5/3.
56 See Bridge, 'Official Opinion', pp. 93–8.
57 H. and C. Seton-Watson, *The Making of New Europe. R. W. Seton-Watson and the Last Years of Austria-Hungary* (London, 1981), pp. 80–1.
58 See 'The Situation in Hungary. Troops at the General Election', 11 June 1910, *The Times*; and 'Hungarian Election Methods', 19 June 1910, *The Times*.
59 Howard despatch (51) to Grey, 20 June 1910, with Crowe minute, 28 June 1910, FO 371/827/22911/7859.
60 Langley minute, n.d., ibid.
61 Cartwright to Crowe, 25 June 1910, FO 371/827/22901/22477.
62 Bridge, *Great Britain and Austria-Hungary*, p. 19.
63 Crowe minute, 28 June 1910, plus Langley, Hardinge, and Grey minutes, all n.d., all FO 371/827/22911/7859.
64 See Tyrrell to Howard, 1 Nov. 1910, DHW 4/Official/16.
65 Howard 'Switzerland. Annual Report, 1912', enclosed in Howard despatch (8) to Grey, 28 Jan. 1913, FO 371/1756/6036/6036.
66 Rodd (British ambassador, Rome) despatch (34) to Grey, 24 Feb. 1911, FO 371/1227/8766/1464.
67 Crowe minute, 15 Mar. 1911, ibid. On Crowe as a student of military strategy, see Steiner, *Foreign Office*, p. 110.
68 See I. C. Barlow, *The Agadir Crisis* (Chapel Hill, NC, 1940); Lowe and Dockrill, *Mirage of Power*, vol. 1, pp. 37–48; and S. R. Williamson, *The Politics of Grand Strategy: Britain and France Prepare for War, 1904–1914* (Cambridge, Mass., 1969), pp. 143–66.
69 Howard despatch (26) to Grey, 13 Apr. 1911, FO 371/1227/16114/1464.
70 Parker minute, 2 May 1911, with Grey and Nicolson initials, both 3 May 1911, ibid. Hardinge had been appointed viceroy of India and left the Foreign Office in September 1910; see Busch, *Hardinge*, pp. 159–61.
71 Fairholme (military attaché, Paris) despatch (19) to Bertie, 15 Sept. 1911, FO 371/1227/36678/1464.
72 Parker marginal comment, 19 Sept. 1911, ibid.
73 Except where noted, the next three paragraphs are based on Howard despatch (18) to Grey, 22 Mar. 1911, FO 371/1227/10701/8160.
74 This is not at all true; see the views of Tancredi Saletta, the chief of the Italian General Staff, in R. J. B. Bosworth, *Italy, the Least of the Great Powers: Italian Foreign Policy before the First World War* (Cambridge, 1979), pp. 199–200.
75 Howard despatch (56) to Grey, 20 Sept. 1911, FO 371/1227/37242/8160.
76 Howard despatch (27) to Grey, 10 May 1912, FO 371/1480/20217/20217.
77 See Langley minute, n.d. (probably 10 Nov. 1911) FO 371/1227/44471/44471.
78 Howard 'Switzerland. Annual Report, 1912', enclosed in Howard despatch (8) to Grey, 28 Jan. 1913, FO 371/1756/6036/6036.

79 Howard despatch (67) to Grey, 7 Nov. 1911, FO 371/1227/44471/44471.
80 Drogheda and Langley minutes, both 10 Nov. 1911. ibid.
81 This and the next paragraph are based on Howard to Nicolson, 12 Jan. 1912, DHW 4/Official/4.
82 Nicolson to Stamfordham (private secretary to the king), 20 Jan. 1912, Nicolson MSS FO 800/353.
83 See Grey to Rodd, 14 Nov. 1911, Grey MSS FO 800/64. Also see Bosworth, *Italy*, pp. 290–8; and Lowe and Dockrill, *Mirage of Power*, vol. 1, pp. 92–5.
84 C. J. Lowe and F. Marzari, *Italian Foreign Policy 1870–1940* (London, 1975), pp. 116–17.
85 Howard despatch (1) to Grey, 3 Feb. 1912, FO 371/1479/5410/5410.
86 Ibid.
87 W. Martin and P. Beguin, *Switzerland from Roman Times to the Present*, 6th edn (New York and Washington, 1971), pp. 163–75.
88 Drummond (Foreign Office, Western Department) minute, 7 Feb. 1912, FO 371/1479/5410/5410.
89 Howard despatch (16) to Grey, 24 Feb. 1912, FO 371/1479/8693/5410.
90 Clerk (Foreign Office, Western Department) minute, 28 Feb. 1912, ibid.
91 The problems in Swiss–German relations are outlined in Howard 'Switzerland. Annual Report, 1911', Jan. 1912, enclosed in Howard despatch (80) to Grey, 26 Jan. 1912, FO 371/1479/4799/4799.
92 Howard despatch (65) to Grey, 27 Aug. 1912, FO 371/1480/36506/36246.
93 These are all outlined in the report cited in note 91, above.
94 For instance, see Howard despatch (68) to Grey, 9 Sept. 1912, FO 371/1480/38861/36246.
95 Orde (Foreign Office Western Department) minute, 16 Sept. 1912, with Villiers, Crowe, and Grey initials, all ibid.
96 Howard despatch (69) to Grey, 11 Sept. 1912, with Villiers, Crowe, and Grey initials, all FO 371/1480/38862/36246.
97 See Howard despatch (4) to Grey, 13 Jan. 1913, FO 371/1756/2266/2266; and Rodd despatch (33) to Grey, 13 Feb. 1913, FO 371/1756/7560/2260.
98 Howard despatch (26) to Grey, 23 Apr. 1913, FO 371/1756/19187/19187; and Howard despatch (28) to Grey, 24 Apr. 1913, FO 371/1756/19409/19187.
99 On the 1910 crisis, see N. Blewett, *The Peers, the Parties and the People: The General Elections of 1910* (Toronto, 1972). Also see Howard to Stafford, his brother, 26 Mar. 1911, DHW 4/Family/13.
100 Howard to Stafford, his brother, 13 Aug. 1911, ibid.
101 Howard to Stafford, his brother, 6 Oct. and 11 Nov. 1912, and 15 Feb. 1913, all ibid.
102 See K. Neilson, 'Wishful Thinking: The Foreign Office and Russia, 1907–1917', in McKercher and Moss, *Shadow and Substance*; and Robbins, *Grey*, pp. 252–4.
103 Howard to Stafford, his brother, 1 Feb. 1913, DHW 4/Family/13.
104 Howard to Stafford, his brother, 28 Mar. 1913, ibid.

5 STOCKHOLM: WAR AND DIPLOMACY IN NEUTRAL NORTHERN EUROPE, 1913–1916

1 *ToL*, vol. 2, p. 202.
2 Bryce to Howard, 4 Feb. 1911, DHW 4/Personal/12.
3 Rodd to Howard, 13 May 1913, DHW 4/Personal/16. On those who had served at Stockholm since 1851, see the *Foreign Office List* (London, 1914).
4 Tyrrell to Howard, 20 Feb. 1913, DHW 1/21.
5 Tyrrell telegram (3) to Erskine (chargé d'affaires, Stockholm), 8 Apr. 1913, FO 371/1755/16355/16355; and Erskine telegram (4) to Grey, 11 Apr. 1913, FO 371/1755/16694/16355.
6 Nicolson to Chalmers (Treasury), 29 May 1913, Nicolson MSS, FO 800/366.
7 *ToL*, vol. 2, p. 200.
8 For example, see Spring Rice to Nicolson, 'Jan,' and 13 Feb. 1910, 6 Jan. 1911, and 6 Aug. 1912, all Nicolson MSS, FO 800/343; Spring Rice to Nicolson, 8 Nov. 1910, Spring Rice MSS, FO 800/241; Spring Rice despatch (88) to Grey, 28 June 1910, FO 371/976/23712; and Spring Rice despatch (unnumbered) to Grey, 10 Feb. 1913, enclosing 'Sweden. Annual Report, 1912', Feb. 1913, FO 371/1755/7210/7210.
9 Spring Rice to Howard, 30 Nov. 1912, DHW 4/Personal/18. For an indication that Spring Rice suggested Howard as his replacement, see Tyrrell to Spring Rice, 13 Nov. 1912, Spring Rice MSS, FO 800/241.
10 Spring Rice to Howard, 13 Apr. 1913, DHW 4/Official/18. On the general accuracy of Spring Rice's views, cf. S. Koblik, *Sweden: The Neutral Victor. Sweden and the Western Powers 1917–1918* (Stockholm, 1972), p. 11; and F. D. Scott, 'Gustav V and Swedish Attitudes towards Germany, 1915', *JMH*, 39 (1967), 113–18.
11 Spring Rice to Howard, 13 Apr. 1913, DHW 4/Official/18.
12 *ToL*, vol. 2, pp. 251–2.
13 The rest of this paragraph is based on ibid., pp. 204–7.
14 See Howard despatch (28) to Grey, 2 Mar. 1914, enclosing 'Sweden. Annual Report, 1913', Feb. 1914, FO 371/2107/10077/10077.
15 For instance, see Howard despatch (57) to Grey, 21 July 1913, FO 371/1755/34420/3359.
16 On this issue, see F. D. Scott, *Sweden: The Nation's History* (Minneapolis, 1977), pp. 401–2.
17 *ToL*, vol. 2, pp. 208–9.
18 The next two paragraphs are based on Howard despatch (92) to Grey, 26 Oct. 1913, FO 371/1755/49603/49603; Howard despatch (100) to Grey, 7 Nov. 1913, FO 371/1755/51187/48759; Clive (second secretary, Stockholm) despatch (104) to Grey, 19 Nov. 1913, FO 371/1755/53203/48755; and Howard despatch (3) to Grey, 21 Jan. 1914, FO 371/2107/3644/3644.
19 Howard despatch (95) to Grey, 28 Oct. 1913, FO 371/1755/49606/49606.
20 Howard to Grey, 30 Oct. 1913, FO 371/1755/51472/49606.
21 Howard to Grey, 30 Oct. 1913, ibid. This is a different letter from that cited in note 20 immediately above.

22 Grey despatch (unnumbered) to Clive, 16 Dec. 1913, FO 371/1755/57190/57190.
23 Howard to Grey, 14 Feb. 1914, DHW 4/Official/6.
24 Crowe minute for Grey on 'Russia & Sweden', 23 Dec. 1913, enclosing Onslow (Foreign Office Western Department) minute for Crowe, Dec. 1913, FO 371/1755/57190/57190.
25 Howard despatch (5) to Grey, 21 Jan. 1914, FO 371/2107/3644/3644.
26 Craigie (Foreign Office Western Department) minute, 26 Jan. 1914, with Crowe and Nicolson initials, all ibid.
27 This paragraph is based on Howard to Grey, 14 Feb. 1914, and Howard to Nicolson, 16 Mar. 1914, both DHW 4/Official/6.
28 Howard despatch (19) to Grey, 16 Feb. 1914, FO 371/2107/8087/3645.
29 See ibid.
30 Howard telegram (6) to Grey, 17 Feb. 1914, FO 371/2107/7257/3645.
31 Ibid.; and Vansittart (Foreign Office Western Department) minute, 23 Feb. 1914, FO 371/2107/8088/3645.
32 Howard to Grey, 14 Feb. 1914, DHW 4/Official/6.
33 Howard despatch (62) to Grey, 25 Apr. 1914, FO 371/2108/19334/19334.
34 Lowe and Dockrill, *Mirage of Power*, vol. 2, pp. 135–8.
35 Howard memorandum, 29 May 1914, DHW 1/21.
36 A holograph note by Howard on ibid. indicates that Crowe approved of the memorandum's contents.
37 Howard to Grey, 22 June 1914, ibid.
38 Crowe to Howard, 27 June 1914, DHW 4/Official/18.
39 On this anti-Germanism, see Steiner, *Foreign Office*, pp. 103–4.
40 See Rodd to Howard, 10 Dec. 1912, DHW 4/Personal/16; and Howard to Nicolson, 8 July 1913, DHW 4/Official/5.
41 The rest of this paragraph is based on *ToL*, vol. 2, pp. 211–16.
42 These obligations were tenuous at best; see T. Wilson, 'Britain's "Moral Commitment" to France in August 1914', *History*, 64 (1979), 380–90.
43 Ibid., pp. 217–18. Also see D. French, *British Strategy and War Aims 1914–1916* (London, 1986), pp. 20–41.
44 On the blockade, see A. C. Bell, *A History of the Blockade of Germany and the Countries Associated with her in the Great War...1914–1918* (London, 1937); and M. Siney, *The Allied Blockade of Germany, 1914–1916* (Ann Arbor, 1957).
45 A. Nekludoff, *Diplomatic Reminiscences before and during the World War, 1911–1917* (London, 1920), pp. 337–40. Cf. Howard despatch (67) to Grey, 6 May 1914, FO 371/2108/21812/19334, which shows this consultation had its roots before the war began.
46 *ToL*, vol. 2, p. 219.
47 On the pre-war plans of the Russian navy, see N. E. Saul, *Sailors in Revolt. The Russian Baltic Fleet in 1917* (Lawrence, Kan., 1978), pp. 1–12, 37–44.
48 As cited in Bell, *Blockade*, p. 89. Also see the Foreign Office memorandum on Sweden's protest against the treatment of iron ore as contraband, 4 Oct. 1914, CAB 37/121/116.
49 Howard to Grey, 7 Aug. 1914, Grey MSS, FO 800/78.
50 For an example of Howard's views, see Howard to Grey, 28 Oct. 1914, DHW 4/Official/6. See the opposition cited in Bell, *Blockade*, p. 89.

51 A. Marsden, 'The Blockade', in Hinsley, *Grey*, p. 495.
52 Howard to Grey, 22 Nov. 1914, DHW 4/Official/6.
53 K. E. Neilson, *Strategy and Supply. The Anglo-Russian Alliance, 1914–17* (London, 1984); and N. Stone, *The Eastern Front, 1914–1917* (London, 1975).
54 Grigorovich to Sazanov, 1 Jan. 1915, as cited in J. Barros, *The Aland Islands Question: Its Settlement by the League of Nations* (New Haven and London, 1968), p. 21.
55 Marsden, 'Blockade', p. 498.
56 For example, see Findlay to Howard, 29 Aug. 1914, DHW 4/Official/6; and Findlay to Howard, 28 Nov. 1914, DHW 4/Official/18.
57 Findlay to Howard, 14 Nov. 1914, DHW 4/Official/6.
58 Findlay to Grey, 21 Nov. 1914, DHW 5/6.
59 Howard's proposal cannot be found, but it is easily seen in Findlay to Howard, 15 Dec. 1914, DHW 4/Official/18. On Grey's August 1914 communication to the neutrals, see O. Riste, *The Neutral Ally. Norway's Relations with Belligerent Powers in the First World War* (Oslo and London, 1965), pp. 36–7.
60 Howard telegram (69) to Grey, with Clerk minute, 19 Dec. 1914, Grey minute, n.d., and FO to Treasury, 20 Dec. 1914, all FO 371/2108/84385/84385; and FO telegram (1) to Howard, 1 Jan. 1915, FO 371/2108/88695/84385.
61 Marsden, 'Blockade', p. 502; and Siney, *Allied Blockade*, pp. 109–10.
62 Howard to Bryce, 3 Mar. 1915, DHW 4/Official/7.
63 Crowe to Howard, 22 Mar. 1915, DHW 4/Official/6. On the wartime restructuring and functioning of the Foreign Office, see Z. Steiner, 'The Foreign Office and the War', in Hinsley, *Grey*, pp. 516–31.
64 *ToL*, vol. 2, p. 225.
65 Ibid.
66 Howard despatch (180) to Grey, 13 Apr. 1915, FO 368/1402/47312.
67 Buchanan to Howard, 28 June 1915, DHW 5/5.
68 See Neilson, *Strategy and Supply*, pp. 86–7, 97–107; and Stone, *Eastern Front*, pp. 144–93.
69 The rest of this paragraph is based on Barros, *Aland Islands*, pp. 23–4.
70 See Marsden, 'Blockade', p. 498.
71 Howard telegram (64) to FO, 29 Mar. 1915, with Vansittart minutes, 30 Mar. and 1 Apr. 1915, and Crowe minutes, 1 and 3 Apr. 1915, all FO 382/155/36726/1249.
72 Grey minute, n.d., on Findlay to Grey, 21 Nov. 1914, Grey MSS, FO 800/69.
73 See the correspondence cited in Siney, *Allied Blockade*, pp. 113–14.
74 Buchanan to FO, 24 June 1915, FO 371/2452/84106.
75 Siney, *Allied Blockade*, pp. 111–13.
76 N. Rose, *Vansittart, Study of a Diplomat*, (London, 1978), p. 41.
77 The best discussion of the Vansittart mission and the attitudes of the various Powers is in Bell, *Blockade*, pp. 331–43; and Siney, *Allied Blockade*, pp. 116–17.
78 Grey to Buchanan, 12 Aug. 1915, CAB 37/132/31.
79 Cf. *ToL*, vol. 2, pp. 241–7; and Lord Vansittart, *The Mist Procession. The Autobiography of Lord Vansittart* (London, 1958), pp. 145–9. For a specific

example of Howard removing a diplomatic impediment thrown up by the Swedes to embarrass the British during the negotiations, see Howard despatch (114) to Grey, 24 July 1915, with Crowe minute, 31 July 1915, Nicolson minute, 2 Aug. 1915, and Crowe to Howard, 7 Aug. 1915, all FO 371/2473/103717/103717; and Howard despatch (135) to Grey, 19 Aug. 1915, FO 371/2473/121347/103717.
80 For instance, see Vansittart to Howard, 15 Dec. 1926, DHW 5/33; and Vansittart to Howard, 12 Sept. [1930], DHW 1/35.
81 For example, see the correspondence appended to FO to Board of Trade, 25 Mar. 1915, FO 382/265/49585/113. Cf. Findlay to Howard, 14 June 1915, DHW 5/5; and Findlay to Howard, 31 July 1915, DHW 4/Official/7.
82 Howard to Crowe, 10 June 1915, DHW 5/6; and Crowe to Howard, 7 July 1915, DHW 4/Official/7. On the dispute between Howard and Consett, see B. J. C. McKercher and K. E. Neilson, '"The Triumph of Unarmed Forces": Sweden and the Allied Blockade of Germany, 1914–1917', *Journal of Strategic Studies*, 7 (1984), 178–99.
83 Cleminson to Parker, 16 Oct. 1915, FO 382/330/161822.
84 See Howard despatch (805) to Grey, 1 Nov. 1915, with Crowe minute, 11 Nov. 1915, FO 382/330/166083.
85 Grey to Howard, 23 Nov. 1915, ibid. Also see Drummond (Grey's private secretary) to Howard, 10 Dec. 1915, DHW 5/5.
86 But informal contacts were different. When Emperor Francis Joseph died in November 1916, Howard sent personal condolences to the Austro-Hungarian minister in Stockholm; see Howard to Hadik, 23 Nov. 1916, DHW 6/3.
87 On this issue, see M. Pitt, 'Great Britain and Belligerent Maritime Rights from the Declaration of Paris, 1856, to the Declaration of London', unpublished Ph.D dissertation (London, 1964).
88 The following information is from *ToL*, vol. 2, pp. 239–41.
89 Howard despatch (85) to Grey, 8 June 1915, FO 371/2473/79883/79883.
90 For instance, Howard despatch (135) to Grey, 19 Aug. 1915, FO 371/2473/121347/103717.
91 On Queen Victoria, see Howard to Grey, 19 May 1915, Grey MSS, FO 800/78. On von Lucius, see Howard to Nicolson, 18 Oct. 1915, ibid.
92 Howard to Nicolson, 23 July 1915, DHW 4/Official/7.
93 Howard to Nicolson, 18 Oct. 1915, Grey MSS FO 800/78.
94 Howard to Crowe, 10 June 1915, DHW 5/6.
95 Crowe to Howard, 7 July 1915, DHW 4/Official/7.
96 Marsden, 'Blockade' makes this clear.
97 On intelligence-gathering see Lowther (British minister, Copenhagen) to Howard, 31 Oct. 1914, DHW 4/Official/18; and Howard (Admiralty) to Howard, n.d. (but late May 1915), with enclosures, and British Consulate, Stockholm memorandum, 29 June 1915, both DHW 4/Official/7. On getting additional manpower, see Leverton Harris (Contraband Department) minute to Crowe, 17 Apr. 1915, with minutes, FO 382/315/46263/46263; Howard telegram (64) to FO, 29 Mar. 1915, FO 382/155/36726/46263; British Consul, Stockholm telegram (17) to FO, 10 Apr. 1915, FO 382/154/42143/307; Howard to Crowe, 4 Dec. 1915, DHW 5/6; Malcolm (Foreign Office) to Howard, 7 Jan. 1916, DHW 4/Official/18.
98 Howard despatch (130) to Grey, 18 Mar. 1915, FO 382/265/34722/113;

and Howard despatch (144) to Grey, 29 Mar. 1915, FO 382/265/39589/113. Also see Howard telegram (236) to FO, 5 May 1915, FO 382/155/55105/1249; and Howard despatch (264) to Grey, 12 May 1915, FO 382/155/64122/1249.
99 On the Netherlands Overseas Trust, see Bell, *Blockade*, pp. 68–72; and Siney, *Allied Blockade*, pp. 37–42.
100 Howard despatch (130) to Grey, 18 Mar. 1915, FO 382/265/34722/113. Cf. Sargent (Contraband Department) 'Memorandum respecting Russian transit trade through Sweden', 27 Apr. 1915, FO 382/265/32907/113.
101 Buchanan telegram (572) to FO, 25 Apr. 1915, FO 382/265/49585/113.
102 Stone & Company (metal merchants) to FO, 23 July 1915, FO telegram (875) to Howard, 27 July 1915, and FO telegram (1590) to Buchanan, 27 July 1915, all FO 382/155/100631/1249; and Buchanan telegram (1110) to FO, 5 Aug. 1915, FO 382/155/107493/1249.
103 *ToL*, vol. 2, pp. 249–51.
104 Howard telegram (unnumbered) to FO, 14 Dec. 1915, DHW 4/Official/7.
105 See *ToL*, vol. 2, pp. 249–52; B. E. Nolde, *Russia in the Economic War* (New Haven, 1928), pp. 35–7; and E. Turlington, *Neutrality, its History, Economics and Law*, vol. 2: *The World War Period* (New York, 1936), pp. 35–7.
106 *ToL*, vol. 2, p. 249.
107 'It was a great pleasure to me on grounds of personal friendship to recommend you for a K.C.M.G. and there is no one in the Diplomatic Service who has deserved recognition better for the post he fills during this war than you have done.': in Grey to Howard, 24 Mar. 1916, DHW 4/Official/8.
108 Howard to Grey, 16 Jan. 1916, initialled by Asquith, Balfour, Grey, Kitchener, Nicolson, Grey MSS FO 800/78.
109 Hambro to Howard, 13 Jan., 7 Feb., and 3 Mar. 1916; and Cecil (minister of Blockade) to Howard, 12 Mar. 1916, all DHW 4/Official/8.
110 Robertson memorandum on 'The strategical consequences of Swedish intervention in the war on the side of the Central Powers', 31 Jan. 1916, CAB 42/7/24/2/G.54.
111 Robertson to Hanbury-Williams (British Military Mission, Russia) 16 Feb. 1916, Robertson MSS I/35/20.
112 Caldwell (British fact-finding mission, Russia) to Robertson, 22 Mar. 1916, Robertson MSS I/35/20.
113 Buchanan to FO, 5 May 1916, FO 371/2748/85629.
114 Cecil to Howard, 12 Mar. 1916, DHW 4/Official/8. For a less optimistic report, see Phillimore (Admiralty Representative, Russia) Report No. 23, 13 Apr. 1916, ADM 137/1389.
115 Hurst memorandum, 21 Mar. 1916, CAB 37/144/57.
116 See C. M. Mason, 'Anglo-American Relations: Mediation and Permanent Peace', in Hinsley, *Grey*, pp. 466–87; and D. C. Watt, *Succeeding John Bull. America in Britain's Place 1900–75* (Cambridge, 1984), pp. 30–2.
117 Grey to Asquith, 15 Feb. 1916, Grey MSS, FO 800/100. Also see two memoranda by Asquith (16 Feb. 1916) and Cecil (probably 1936) reprinted in G. M. Trevelyan, *Grey of Fallodon, Being the Life of Sir Edward Grey afterwards of Fallodon* (London, 1937), pp. 308–11.
118 Howard to Cecil, 14 Apr. 1916, DHW 4/Official/8.
119 Cecil to Howard, 6 Apr. 1916, ibid.

120 Cecil to Howard, 6 June 1916, ibid.
121 T. Kaarstad, *Great Britain and Denmark, 1914–1920* (Odense, 1979).
122 This antagonism increased over time; see M. W. W. P. Consett, *The Triumph of Unarmed Forces (1914–1918)* (London, 1923).
123 Howard's letter cannot be traced as Consett left no papers and Howard kept no copy; but what it said can be gleaned from Consett to Howard, 2 May 1916, DHW 4/Official/18.

6 STOCKHOLM: DIPLOMACY AND WAR IN NEUTRAL NORTHERN EUROPE, 1916–1918

1 On the Somme, see B. H. Liddell Hart, *History of the First World War* (London and Sydney, 1976 [first published in 1934]), pp. 231–53.
2 French, *British Strategy and War Aims*, pp. 220–43 is the best recent evaluation of the strategic and political reasons for Asquith's ouster – and it introduces all the literature in the footnotes.
3 Viscount Grey of Fallodon, *Twenty-Five Years 1892–1916* (London, 1926), vol. 2, p. 70; and K. Robbins, *Sir Edward Grey* (London, 1973), pp. 301–4.
4 J. C. Stokesbury, *A Short History of World War One* (New York, 1981), pp. 216–26.
5 For instance, see Howard to Hardinge, 28 Jan. 1917, DHW 4/Official/9. Stone, *Eastern Front*, pp. 264–81; and A. K. Wildman, *The End of the Russian Imperial Army* (Princeton, 1980), pp. 105–20.
6 For example, Hardinge to Howard, 11 Mar. 1915, DHW 4/Personal/15.
7 Kaarstad, *Great Britain and Denmark*, pp. 28–9.
8 Howard to Hardinge, 23 Aug. 1916, Har. MSS, vol. 24.
9 On these reforms, see Bell, *Blockade*, p. 452 and *passim*; and Siney, *Allied Blockade*, pp. 136–55.
10 Hardinge to Howard, 2 Sept. 1916, Har. MSS, vol. 25.
11 Cecil to Howard, 6 July 1916, DHW 4/Official/18.
12 Howard to Hardinge, 17 Sept. 1916, DHW 4/Official/8.
13 W. M. Carlgren, *Neutralität oder Allianz, Deutschlands Beziehungen zu Schweden in den Anfangsjahren des ersten Weltkrieges* (Stockholm, Gothenburg and Uppsala, 1962) gives an indication.
14 Hardinge to Howard, 4 Oct. 1916, Har. MSS, vol. 26.
15 Consett's views are reported in Paget to Hardinge, 25 Nov. 1916, Har. MSS, vol. 27.
16 Findlay to Hardinge, 9 Oct. 1916, Har. MSS, vol. 26.
17 Carlgren, *Neutralität* shows this.
18 For example: 'I really do not think that for the moment there is anything to fear. The main point, however, is that the Russians are genuinely nervous as to what would happen if Sweden on some point of honour suddenly took it into her head to join Germany.'; in Howard to Hardinge, 17 Sept. 1916, DHW 4/Official/8.
19 Howard memorandum, 26 Feb. 1917, DHW 5/6.
20 Howard to Cecil, 12 Dec. 1916, DHW 4/Official/8. Howard's letter to Findlay cannot be traced, but what it said is seen easily in Findlay to Howard, n.d. (but 1 or 2 Dec. 1916), DHW 4/Official/18.
21 Ibid.

22 On Paget's initial favour towards Consett, see Paget to Cecil, 18 Oct. 1916, Paget Papers, BL Add. MSS 51254. For an example of subsequent friction, see Consett to Paget, 21 Nov. 1916, and the reply, 23 Nov. 1916, both Paget Papers, BL Add. MSS 51256.
23 Paget to Hardinge, 25 Nov. 1916, Har. MSS, vol. 27.
24 See Cecil and Grey minutes, both n.d., both on ibid.
25 K. M. Burk, *Britain, America and the Sinews of War, 1914–1918* (London, 1985) shows this.
26 Findlay to Hardinge, 28 Nov. 1916, Har. MSS, vol. 27; and Findlay to Howard, 14 Dec. 1916, DHW 4/Official/18.
27 Paget to Cecil, 8 Dec. 1916, Paget Papers, BL Add. MSS 51254.
28 Howard to Cecil, 12 Dec. 1916, DHW 4/Official/8.
29 This interdepartmental struggle is related in Hardinge to Paget, 16 Jan. 1917, Har. MSS, vol. 29.
30 For example, Howard to Cecil, 12 Dec. 1916, DHW 4/Official/8; and Paget to Hardinge, 25 Jan. 1917, Har. MSS, vol. 29.
31 Cecil to Paget, 9 Jan. 1917, Paget Papers, BL Add. MSS 51254.
32 For example, Paget to Hardinge, 25 Jan. 1917, Har. MSS, vol. 29; and two Howard memoranda, both 26 Feb. 1917, DHW 5/6.
33 See Hardinge, Steel (Carson's private secretary), and Shane (Jellicoe's private secretary) minutes, all n.d., all on Paget to Hardinge, 25 Jan. 1917, Har. MSS, vol. 29.
34 Paget to Hardinge, 8 Apr. 1917, Paget Papers, BL Add. MSS 51253.
35 Kaarstad, *Great Britain and Denmark*, pp. 31–3; Paget to Hardinge, 7 Apr. 1917, Paget Papers, BL Add. MSS 51253; Hardinge to Findlay, 30 Apr. 1917, Har. MSS, vol. 31; and Hardinge to Findlay, 4 May 1917, Har. MSS, vol. 32.
36 M. W. W. P. Consett, *The Triumph of Unarmed Forces (1914–1918)* (London, 1923). For Howard's rebuttal, cf. Howard to Belloc (English writer), 15 Sept. 1923, DHW 9/6; and *ToL*, vol. 2, pp. 218–19.
37 Buchanan to Balfour, 10 Jan. 1917, FO 371/3021/3184; Buchanan to Hardinge, 28 Oct. 1916, Har. MSS, vol. 26; and Buchanan to FO, 17 Nov. 1916, FO 371/2752/232510.
38 Knox to Military Intelligence 3, 'Northern Front', V2, 16 Oct. 1916, WO 106/1086.
39 Howard to Hardinge, 16 Oct. 1916, DHW 5/6; and Howard to Buchanan, 11 Oct. 1916, DHW 4/Official/8.
40 Buchanan to Howard, 20 Oct. 1916, and Hardinge to Howard, 27 Oct. 1916, both DHW 5/5.
41 Except where noted, the next two paragraphs are based on Howard to Cecil, 12 Dec. 1916, DHW 4/Official/8; and Howard to Hardinge, 18 Jan. 1917, DHW 4/Official/9.
42 Howard telegram (unnumbered) to Hardinge, 13 Dec. 1916, DHW 4/Official/8.
43 On these negotiations, see Koblik, *Neutral Victor*, pp. 15–40.
44 Cecil to Howard, 16 Nov. 1916, DHW 4/Official/8.
45 For example, Harcourt Rose (Ministry of Blockade) to Howard, 18 Nov. 1916, DHW 4/Official/8; Harcourt Rose to Howard, 30 Nov. 1916, DHW 4/Official/18; and Cecil to Howard, 18 Jan. 1917, DHW 4/Official/9.
46 Koblik, *Neutral Victor*, pp. 24–33. Cf. I. Schuberth, *Schweden und das Deutsches*

Reich im Ersten Weltkrieg. Die Aktivistenbewegung 1914–1918 (Bonn, 1981), pp. 107–18.
47 'Wallenberg, Hellner and Frisell are very friendly, and sincerely anxious to make an agreement. But I suspect that they are a good deal hampered by their instructions, and still more by the presence of Westman.': in Cecil to Howard, 16 Nov. 1916, DHW 4/Official/8.
48 Howard to Hardinge, 19 Dec. 1916, ibid.
49 Koblik, *Neutral Victor*, p. 36.
50 War Cabinet Minute 40(17), 22 Jan. 1917; and War Cabinet Minute 52(6), plus Appendix II, 2 Feb. 1917: both CAB 23/1.
51 Lowe and Dockrill, *Mirage of Power*, vol. 2, pp. 247–56. Also see War Cabinet Minute 9(2), 16 Dec. 1916; and War Cabinet Minutes, 10(1–4), plus Appendices I–IV: both CAB 23/1.
52 Bell, *Blockade*, pp. 534–6; and Siney, *Allied Blockade*, pp. 220–4.
53 Howard to Findlay, 20 Mar. 1917, DHW 5/6.
54 Howard telegram (858) to FO, with Cecil, Hardinge, and Balfour initials, FO 371/3037/50095/49286.
55 On the domestic crisis in Sweden, see Koblik, *Neutral Victor*, pp. 41–63.
56 For instance, Howard to Findlay, 20 Mar. 1917, DHW 5/6.
57 Howard to Hardinge, 19 Mar. 1917, Har. MSS, vol. 30.
58 Howard telegram (962) to Balfour, 18 Mar. 1917, Balfour MSS, FO 800/206.
59 Yarde Buller (military attaché, Christiania) to Howard, 2 Apr. 1917, DHW 4/Official/18.
60 This and the next sentence are based on Howard telegram (unnumbered) to Balfour, 2 Apr. 1917, Balfour MSS, FO 800/206; and Howard to Hardinge, 17 Apr. 1917, Har. MSS, vol. 31.
61 See Howard telegram (1272) to FO, 21 Apr. 1917, FO 371/3037/82571/49286; Howard telegram (1303) to FO, 25 Apr. 1917, FO 371/3037/84013/49286; Howard telegram (1332) to FO, 2 May 1917, FO 371/3037/89548/49286; and Howard telegram (1425) to FO, 6 May 1917, FO 371/3037/92057/49286.
62 Koblik, *Neutral Victor*, pp. 65–6.
63 Howard despatch (53) to Balfour, 6 Apr. 1917, FO 382/1467.
64 War Cabinet Minute 110(1), plus Appendix I, 2 Apr. 1917; CAB 23/2.
65 Crowe to Howard, 3 Apr. 1917, FO 382/1467.
66 Buchanan to Howard, 1 and 16 Apr. 1917; and Lindley (counsellor, British Embassy, Petrograd) to Howard, 16 Apr., 27 July, and 5 Sept. 1917, all DHW 4/Official/19.
67 Koblik, *Neutral Victor*, p. 73.
68 Margaret to Howard, 5 July [1917], DHW 4/Official/18; Howard to Hardinge, 27 Dec. 1917, DHW 5/6; and *ToL*, vol. 2, pp. 251–2.
69 Howard to Hardinge, 30 June 1917, DHW 4/Official/9.
70 For example, Howard to Hardinge, 29 June 1917, DHW 5/6.
71 The rest of this paragraph is based on Howard to Hardinge, 22 Aug. 1917, ibid.
72 Howard to Hardinge, 18 Sept. 1917, DHW 4/Official/9.
73 C. M. Andrew, *Secret Service. The Making of the British Intelligence Community* (London, 1985), p. 107; Koblik, *Neutral Victor*, pp. 95–152; and Schuberth, *Schweden und das Deutsches Reich*, pp. 135–43.

74 Howard to Hardinge, 18 Sept. 1917, DHW 4/Official/9.
75 See K. E. Neilson, 'The Breakup of the Anglo-Russian Alliance: The Question of Supply in 1917', *IHR*, 3 (1981), 62–75. Cf. L. P. Morris, 'The Russians, the Allies and the War, February–July 1917', *Slavonic and East European Review*, 50 (1972), 29–48.
76 G. F. Kennan, *Soviet–American Relations, 1917–1920*, vol. 1: *Russia Leaves the War* (Princeton, 1956); A. B. Ulam, *The Bolsheviks. The Intellectual, Personal and Political History of the Triumph of Communism in Russia* (New York, 1965), pp. 314–81; R. H. Ullman, *Anglo-Soviet Relations, 1917–1921*, vol. 1: *Intervention and the War* (Princeton, 1961), pp. 58–127; and J. W. Wheeler-Bennett, *Brest-Litovsk. The Forgotten Peace, March 1918* (London, Melbourne and Toronto, 1966).
77 The next two paragraphs are based on Bell, *Blockade*, pp. 651–64; and Koblik, *Neutral Victor*, pp. 169–211.
78 Howard diary, 14 Mar., 2, 20 and 27 Apr. 1918, DHW 1/4.
79 Howard diary, 15 Mar. and 15 Apr. 1918, ibid.
80 Bell, *Blockade*, pp. 664–6.
81 *ToL*, vol. 2, p. 257. Cf. Howard diary, 27 Mar., 3 and 7 Apr. 1918, DHW 1/4.
82 This and the next quote are from Howard diary, 22 May 1918, ibid.
83 For example, Howard despatch (95) to Balfour, 15 Mar, 1918, FO 371/3352/54026/3351; and Howard despatch (7) to Balfour, 27 Apr. 1918, FO 371/3358/80597/75297.
84 Lowe and Dockrill, *Mirage of Power*, vol. 2, p. 273.
85 The following two paragraphs are based on I. Morris, *From an American Legation* (New York, 1923), pp. 129–32; Howard diary, 11, 13 and 24 Mar., 20, 29 and 30 Apr., and 4, 6, 11, and 27 May 1918, DHW 1/4; and Hardinge to Howard, 11 July 1918, and Howard to Hardinge, 31 July 1918, with enclosure, both DHW 4/Official/10.
86 Barros, *Aland Islands*, pp. 28–31; and C. J. Smith, Jr, *Finland and the Russian Revolution, 1917–1922* (Athens, Ga., 1958), pp. 11–12.
87 See A. F. Upton, *The Finnish Revolution, 1917–1918* (Minneapolis, 1980), pp. 26–101.
88 Howard despatch (39) to Balfour, 26 Jan. 1918, FO 371/3205/27732/144.
89 For instance, see Howard telegram (386) to FO, 9 Feb. 1918, FO 371/3209/27069/25367; and Howard diary, 29 May, 12 and 14 June 1918, DHW 1/4.
90 Howard to Hardinge, 3 Mar. 1918, Har. MSS, vol. 36.
91 E. Lyytinen, *Finland in British Politics in the First World War* (Helsinki, 1980), pp. 136–7.
92 Ibid., p. 137.
93 Ibid., p. 169.
94 Howard diary, 27 June 1918, DHW 1/4; Howard telegram (1758) to FO, 27 June 1918, FO 371/3211/115570/95029; and Howard telegram (1759) to FO, 27 June 1918, FO 371/3211/115575/95029.
95 Gregory and Clerk minutes, both 29 June 1918, both ibid.
96 See Balfour to Cambon (French ambassador, London), 15 July 1918, FO 371/3206/126337/144.
97 Howard despatch (245) to Balfour, 8 July 1918, ibid.

98 Thwaites (War Office) to FO, 6 Aug. 1918, FO 371/3206/135959/144.
99 Geddes to Cecil, 6 July 1918, FO 371/3206/125951/144.
100 Lyytinen, *Finland in British Politics*, pp. 180–1.
101 Barros, *Aland Islands*, p. 69.
102 Ibid., pp. 602–3. Howard did learn about the German offer by the spring of 1918; see Howard telegram (1141) to FO, 24 Apr. 1918, FO 371/3352/73129/2371.
103 See Howard telegram (50) to FO, 7 Jan. 1918, with Hardinge and Balfour minutes, both n.d., all FO 371/3352/4219/2371; Howard telegram (195) to FO, 24 Jan. 1918, with Hardinge and Balfour minutes, both n.d., and FO telegram (153) to Howard, 26 Jan. 1918, all FO 371/3352/15556/2371; and Howard telegram (355) to FO, 7 Feb. 1918, FO 371/3352/24794/2371.
104 Howard despatch (21) to Balfour, 11 Jan. 1918, FO 371/3352/11626/3271.
105 Hardinge and Cecil minutes, both n.d., both ibid.
106 Howard telegram (195) to FO, 24 Jan. 1918, FO 371/3352/15536/2371.
107 Political Intelligence Department [Foreign Office] 'Memorandum on Sweden and the Aland Islands', 10 Apr. 1918, FO 371/3351/57934/2159.
108 Barros, *Aland Islands*, p. 80.
109 Howard telegram (576) to FO, 2 Mar. 1918, FO 371/3352/39636/2371.
110 Howard despatch (49) to Balfour, 5 Feb. 1918, FO 371/3352/27742/2371.
111 Howard telegram (637) to FO, 7 Mar. 1918, FO 371/3352/42735/2371.
112 For instance, Howard telegram (1708) to FO, 23 June 1918, FO 371/3358/111423/80588; and Howard telegram (1680) to FO, 18 June 1918, FO 371/3359/108975/106561. Also see Howard diary, 21 June 1918, DHW 1/4.
113 '*Note Verbale*', 14 Mar. 1918, enclosed in Howard despatch (98) to Balfour, 16 Mar. 1918, FO 371/3352/54030/2371.
114 On the Treaty of Paris, see Barros, *Aland Islands*, pp. 3–12.
115 For instance, Howard diary, 19 July 1918, DHW 1/4.
116 Howard diary, 17–18 July 1918, ibid.
117 Howard diary, 29 June 1918, ibid.
118 Howard despatch (248) to Balfour, 13 July 1918, with Cecil and Balfour initials, all FO 371/3357/126340/42190.
119 For example, Howard to Hardinge, 3 Mar. 1918, Har. MSS, vol. 36.
120 Howard diary, 26 July 1918, DHW 1/4.
121 Russell to Howard, 15 Mar. 1915, DHW 4/Personal/19.
122 For example, Dering (British minister, Bangkok) to Russell, 29 July 1916, Grey MSS, FO 800/76.
123 Hardinge minute, n.d., to Balfour, with Balfour minutes, both n.d., Davidson (Foreign Office legal adviser) minute, 28 Sept. 1917, and FO to Director of Public Prosecution, 28 Sept. 1917, all FO 371/3037/187449/187449; and Director of Public Prosecution to FO, 25 Oct. 1917, with enclosure and minutes, all FO 371/3037/205180/187449.
124 Cf. Drummond to Howard, 31 Aug. 1917 and 12 Feb. 1918, both DHW 5/5.

125 Drummond to Howard, 31 Aug. 1917, ibid; and Hardinge to Howard, 23 Oct. 1917, DHW 4/Official/9.
126 'Asked Mme. Corinne Wikstrom to try to sell for us my Napoleon Miniature, one of Isa's diamond ornaments and a ring...Hope we may get £1,000 for the lot.': in Howard diary, 1 June 1918, DHW 1/4.
127 See Howard diary, 23 Mar., 20 Apr., and 16 May 1918, ibid.
128 This and the next sentence are based on Hardinge to Howard, 8 May 1918, DHW 5/5.
129 Howard despatch (256) to Balfour, 13 July 1918, with Drummond minute, 22 July 1918, Hardinge minute, n.d., and FO telegram (1467) to Howard, 29 July 1918, all FO 371/3360/126348/126348.
130 Howard diary, 1 Sept. 1918, DHW 1/4.
131 Howard diary, 2 Sept. 1918, ibid.

7 PARIS: POLAND, THE BALTIC STATES, AND THE TREATY OF VERSAILLES, 1918–1919

1 Howard diary, 13 Oct. 1918, DHW 1/4.
2 Howard diary, 2 Oct. 1918, ibid.
3 This and the next sentence are based on Howard diary, 22 and 23 Oct. 1918, ibid.
4 Howard diary, 26 Oct. 1918, ibid.
5 Howard diary, 28 Oct. 1918, ibid.
6 Howard diary, 8 Nov. 1918, ibid.
7 Howard diary, 13 Nov. 1918, ibid.; and Hardinge to Howard, 8 Nov. 1918, enclosing Hardinge 'Preparations for the Peace Conference', 8 Nov. 1918, DHW 9/29.
8 Howard diary, 13 Nov. 1918, DHW 1/4.
9 Also see M. L. Dockrill and Z. S. Steiner, 'The Foreign Office at the Paris Peace Conference in 1919', *IHR*, 2 (1980), 55–86; and M. L. Dockrill and J. D. Goold, *Peace without Promise. Britain and the Peace Conferences 1919–1923* (London, 1981), pp. 24–6.
10 For instance, see Union of Democratic Control, Pamphlet No. 1, *The Morrow of the War* (London, n.d. [but September 1914]); Pamphlet No. 4, *The Origins of the Great War* (London, n.d.); and Pamphlet No. 14, *The Balance of Power* (London, n.d.). Cf. C. A. Cline, *E. D. Morel, 1873–1924. The Strategies of Protest* (Belfast, 1980); H. Swanwick, *Builders of Peace* (London, 1924); and M. Swartz, *The Union of Democratic Control in British Politics during the First World War* (Oxford, 1971).
11 The best study in this respect is K. E. Neilson, *Strategy and Supply. The Anglo-Russian Alliance, 1914–1917* (London, 1984). But also see K. M. Burk, 'The Diplomacy of Finance: British Financial Missions to the United States 1914–1918', *HJ*, 22 (1979), 351–72; K. M. Burk, 'The Treasury: From Impotence to Power', in K. M. Burk, *War and the State: The Transformation of British Government, 1914–1919* (London, 1982), pp. 84–107; and J. Gooch, 'Soldiers, Strategy and War Aims in Britain 1914–18', in B. D. Hunt and A. Preston, eds., *War and Strategic Policy in the Great War* (London, 1977), pp. 21–40.
12 K. O. Morgan, 'Lloyd George's Premiership: A Study in "Prime Ministerial

Government"', *HJ*, 13 (1970), 130–57; J. Turner, 'Cabinets, Committees and Secretariats: The Higher Direction of the War', in Burk, *War and the State*, pp. 57–83; and R. M. Warman, 'The Erosion of Foreign Office Influence in the Making of Foreign Policy, 1916–1918', *HJ*, 15 (1972), 133–59.
13 Howard diary, 13 Nov. 1918, DHW 1/4.
14 He wrote that Carr was 'a most intelligent able fellow'; in ibid.
15 See S. Roskill, *Hankey. Man of Secrets*, vol. 2: *1919–1931* (London, 1972), pp. 19–42; and Dockrill and Steiner, 'The Foreign Office at the Peace Conference'. Also see Foreign Office, *The Foreign Office List 1919* (London, 1919), 9E–9K.
16 Dockrill and Goold, *Peace Without Promise*, p. 114; T. Komarnicki, *Rebirth of the Polish Republic. A Study in the Diplomatic History of Europe, 1914–1920* (Melbourne, London and Toronto, 1957), p. 298 and *passim*; and H. I. Nelson, *Land and Power. British and Allied Policy on Germany's Frontiers 1916–19* (London and Toronto, 1963), *passim*. It is necessary to set off by itself the work of Professor K. Lundgreen-Nielsen, whose studies of the re-establishment of Poland in 1918–20 are probably the last word on this important diplomatic question. Howard's pro-Polish views are highlighted in K. Lundgreen-Nielsen, *The Polish Problem at the Paris Peace Conference. A Study of the Policies of the Great Powers and the Poles, 1918–1920* (Odense, 1979), *passim*; and 'The Mayer Thesis Reconsidered: The Poles and the Paris Peace Conference, 1919', *IHR*, 7 (1985), 68–102. Cf. K. Lundgreen-Nielsen, 'Woodrow Wilson and the Rebirth of Poland', in Link, *Revolutionary World*, pp. 105–26.
17 *ToL*, vol. 2, p. 298.
18 Headlam-Morley (FO Political Intelligence Department) diary, n.d., but probably 18 May 1919, in A. Headlam-Morley, R. Bryant, and A. Cienciala, eds., *Sir James Headlam-Morley. A Memoir of the Paris Peace Conference 1919* (London, 1972), p. 117.
19 This is implied throughout Lundgreen-Nielsen, *Polish Problem*.
20 Headlam-Morley, *et al.*, *A Memoir*, p. 193.
21 The problem in all of this, a problem which is admitted in Lundgreen-Nielsen, *Polish Problem*, p. 22, is that Howard's papers have till now not been available for use by historians studying this or any other period of his diplomatic career.
22 The historiography on Poland from the 1790s to 1918 is large, the interpretations diverse, and the scholarly debate vituperative. The following three paragraphs are based on A. Dallin *et al.*, *Russian Diplomacy and Eastern Europe, 1914–1917* (New York, 1963); N. Davies, *God's Playground. A History of Poland in Two Volumes*, vol. 2: *1795 to the Present* (New York, 1982), pp. 3–392; M. K. Dziewanowski, *Poland in the Twentieth Century* (New York, 1977), pp. 1–84; L. L. Gerson, *Woodrow Wilson and the Rebirth of Poland, 1914–1920. A Study in the Influence on American Foreign Policy of Minority Groups of Foreign Origin* (New Haven, 1953); S. Kieniewicz and H. Wereszycki, 'Poland under Foreign Rule, 1795–1918', in Gieysztor, *Poland*, pp. 399–633; R. F. Leslie, *et al.*, *The History of Poland since 1863* (Cambridge, 1980), pp. 1–138; W. F. Reddaway, *et al.*, eds., *The Cambridge History of Poland from Augustus II to Pilsudski* (Cambridge, 1941); and P. Wandycz, *The Lands of Partitioned Poland, 1795–1918* (Seattle and London, 1974).
23 This and the next sentence are based on Drummond to Howard, 26 May

Notes to pages 206–209

1916, and Howard to Grey, 1 June 1916, with enclosures, both DHW 4/Official/8.
24 See D. Read, *England 1868–1914. The Age of Urban Democracy* (London, 1979), pp. 505–8. For Howard's sympathy for Irish Home Rule, see Howard to Grey, 16 Sept. 1913, DHW 4/Official/6.
25 A. E. Senn, 'The Entente and the Polish Question, 1914–1916', *Jahrbücher für Geschichte Osteuropas*, 25 (1977), 21–33.
26 Howard to Hardinge, 2 Nov. 1916, DHW 5/6; Howard to Hardinge, 19 Dec. 1916, DHW 4/Official/8; and Howard to Hardinge, 10 May 1917, DHW 4/Official/9.
27 Howard to Hardinge, 17 Nov. 1917, enclosing Howard to Lubecki, 14 Nov. 1917, DHW 4/Official/9.
28 Cf. K. J. Calder, *Britain and the Origins of the New Europe, 1914–1918* (Cambridge, 1976), pp. 145–74; W. Fest, *Peace or Partition, The Habsburg Monarchy and British Policy, 1914–1918* (New York, 1978), pp. 156–60; and V. H. Rothwell, *British War Aims and Peace Diplomacy, 1914–1918* (Oxford, 1971), pp. 155–8. In fn. 47, p. 158 of Rothwell's book, he refers to a letter from the director of special intelligence to Hardinge of 6 Nov. 1917. This alleges that an intercepted letter from *The Times*' correspondent at Stockholm to his editor revealed that Howard wanted *The Times* to propagandise in favour of an independent Poland. Although it might be true, Howard's MSS contain no corroborating evidence.
29 Calder, *New Europe*, p. 185. Also see P. Latawski, 'Count Horodyski's Plan "To Set Europe Ablaze"', June 1918', *Slavonic and East European Review*, 65 (1987), 391–8.
30 Howard to Hardinge, 27 Dec. 1917, Har. MSS, vol. 35.
31 Hardinge to Howard, 7 Dec. 1917, enclosing Hardinge memorandum on 'Poland', 5 Dec. 1917, DHW 5/5.
32 See his diaries for November–December 1918, DHW 1/4; and January 1919, DHW 1/5. Key documents in circulation within the Foreign Office included Political Intelligence Memorandum on 'The Settlement', November 1918, FO 608/435; and Foreign Office Historical Section, *Peace Handbooks*, vol. 1: *Austria-Hungary*, vol. 7: *Germany*, vol. 8: *Poland and Finland*, vol. 9: *The Russian Empire*, vol. 23: *International Affairs*, and vol. 25: *Indemnities, Plebiscites etc*. Hardinge to Howard, 8 Nov. 1918, DHW 9/29 gave Howard permission to read 'a series of short papers' which Balfour had prepared for circulation to the War Cabinet; for instance, see Balfour memorandum on 'The Baltic Provinces', 18 Oct. 1918, GT6356, CAB 24/70.
33 For example, on assessing incoming information, see Howard diary, 14 Nov. 1918 ('Very conflicting news from Germany but it seems that moderate Socialists have things in hand.'); 25 Nov. 1918 ('Bolshevik revolution seems to have got upper hand in Berlin.'); and 6 Dec. 1918 ('No officers visible in Berlin but no disorder as yet.'), all DHW 1/4. On his meetings, see Howard diary, 15 Nov. 1918 (Sobanski); 17 and 20 Nov. 1918 (Mannerheim); 14 Dec. 1918 (Kokotseff, a former Russian premier); and 17 Dec. 1918 (Belaieff, 'White' Russian envoy), all ibid.
34 Howard diary, 18 Nov. 1918, ibid.
35 Except where noted, the rest of this paragraph is based on Lyytinen, *Finland in British Politics*, 191–6.
36 E. Anderson, 'British Policy towards the Baltic States, 1918–1920', *Journal*

of *Central European Affairs*, 19 (1955), 276–89; and W. A. Fletcher, 'The British Navy in the Baltic, 1918–1920: Its Contribution to the Independence of the Baltic Nations', *Journal of Baltic Studies*, 7 (1976), 134–44.
37 Howard diary, 13 Dec. 1918, DHW 1/4.
38 Ibid.
39 This and the rest of this paragraph are based on O. Hovi, *The Baltic Area in British Policy, 1918–1921* (Helsinki, 1980), pp. 55–7.
40 Howard diary, 13 Dec. 1918, DHW 1/4.
41 Lord Howard of Penrith, 'Paderewski, Musician–Patriot–Statesman', unpublished MSS (*c.* 1935), DHW 1/51.
42 Howard diary, 15 Jan. 1919, DHW 1/5.
43 This paragraph is based on Lundgreen-Nielsen, *Polish Problem*, pp. 63–4; and Nelson, *Land and Power*, pp. 93, 98–100. For this and the next two paragraphs, also see Komarnicki, *Rebirth of Polish Republic*, pp. 298–460 *passim*.
44 This paragraph is based on Lundgreen-Nielsen, *Polish Problem*, p. 67.
45 This paragraph is based on ibid., p. 109. Cf. Wade memorandum on 'War Aims and Publicity', 1 Jan. 1918, DHW 4/Official/10; Kenney to Howard, 24 Dec. 1918, DHW 1/24; and R. Kenney, *Westering. An Autobiography* (London, 1939), pp. 239–67. For political reporting, see Howard diary, 2 Feb. 1919, DHW 1/5.
46 See Wade to Howard, 21 Dec. 1918, DHW 1/21.
47 Lundgreen-Nielsen, *Polish Problem*, pp. 147–8.
48 Ibid., p. 20.
49 Howard memorandum, June 1919, DHW 4/Official/11; and Howard to Curzon, 3 Dec. 1919, DHW 9/33/5.
50 For instance, Lindley to Howard, 16 Dec. 1917 and 2 Feb. 1918, both DHW 4/Official/19; and Howard diary, 12 Mar. 1918, DHW 1/4.
51 Clive (British Legation, Stockholm) to Howard, 13 Feb. 1918, enclosing Pares to Appleton (British trade-union official) Feb. 1918, on 'Russian Affairs. Rights of the People', and 18 Feb. 1918, on 'Russian Affairs. The Dictatorship of the Proletariate [*sic*]', both DHW 4/Official/10; and Pares memoranda on the 'Situation in Russia', 2 Mar. 1918, and 'Questions which representatives of the Bolcheviks [*sic*] should be required to answer when they speak or write in the Press in England', Mar. 1918, both DHW 5/3. Cf. B. Pares, *My Russian Memoirs* (London, 1931), p. 486.
52 Lockhart to Howard, 18 Nov. 1918, DHW 1/35.
53 For example, Howard diary, 30 Nov., 2 Dec., and 14 Dec. 1918, all DHW 1/4.
54 For example, Bryce to Howard, 8 Dec. 1918, DHW 1/24.
55 Howard to Curzon, 3 Dec. 1919, DHW 9/33/5.
56 'The Bolsheviks have taken Narva and committed hideous atrocities... I saw a good definition of the aims of Bolshevism the other day. All capital owning classes to be destroyed by murder or starvation. No one but women without capital to have any civil rights. No representative Gov.t because that represents all classes but direct Gov.t or dictatorship guided by Soviets of workmen and soldiers.'; in Howard diary, 3 Dec. 1918, DHW 1/4.
57 Howard diary, 10 Jan. 1919, DHW 1/5; and Howard to his wife, 10 Jan. 1919, DHW 3/32.
58 Howard diary, 13 Jan. 1919, DHW 1/5.

59 Howard diary, 16 Jan. 1919, ibid.
60 Howard diary, 17 Jan. 1919, ibid.
61 This and the next quotation are from Howard diary, 11 Jan. 1919, ibid.
62 Howard diary, 14 Jan. 1919, ibid.
63 For instance, Wade telegram to Balfour, 16 Jan. 1919, FO 608/61.
64 Howard minute, 18 Jan. 1919, ibid.
65 On Namier having access to Lloyd George through Kerr, see Lundgreen-Nielsen, *Polish Problem*, p. 24. For Namier's anti-Dmowski stance, which entailed more than just opposition to Dmowski's antisemitism, see T. Hunczak, 'Sir Lewis Namier and the Struggle for Eastern Galicia, 1918–1920', *Harvard Ukrainian Studies*, 1 (1977), 198–210.
66 Lundgreen-Nielsen, *Polish Problem*, pp. 65–7.
67 Howard diary, 21 and 22 Jan. 1919, DHW 1/5.
68 Howard diary, 23 Jan. 1919, ibid.
69 Ibid.
70 Howard diary, 24 Jan. 1919, ibid.
71 Ibid.
72 Howard to his wife, 27 Jan. 1919, DHW 3/32.
73 Howard diary, 25 Jan. 1919, DHW 1/5.
74 See R. H. Lord, *The Second Partition of Poland* (Cambridge, Mass., 1915).
75 Howard diary, 27 Jan. 1919, DHW 1/5.
76 Howard diary, 29–31 Jan. 1919, ibid.
77 Balfour to Howard, 7 Feb. 1919, enclosing 'Final Instructions for the Delegates of the Allied Governments in Poland' (extract), 1 Feb. 1919, DHW 4/Official/11.
78 Howard diary, 3 to 8 Feb. 1919, DHW 1/5; also Howard memorandum for Hardinge, 2 Feb. 1919, FO 608/58.
79 Lundgreen-Nielsen, *Polish Problem*, pp. 174–5; and Nelson, *Land and Power*, pp. 147–50.
80 Nelson, *Land and Power*, p. 149.
81 Howard diary, 11 and 12 Jan. 1919, DHW 1/5; and P. A. Gajda, *Postscript to Victory. British Policy and the German–Polish Borderlands, 1919–1925* (Washington, DC, 1982), p. 7.
82 Balfour to Lloyd George, 30 Jan. 1919, LG MSS F/3/4/9.
83 Nelson, *Land and Power*, p. 147.
84 Headlam-Morley memorandum, 6 Feb. 1919, in Headlam-Morley, *et al.*, *A Memoir*, pp. 21–3; and Carr minute, 12 Feb. 1919, FO 608/57.
85 Howard diary, 9 Feb. 1919, DHW 1/5.
86 On Lloyd George getting rid of opponents by sending them on missions, see J. M. McEwen, 'Northcliffe and Lloyd George at War, 1914–1918', *HJ*, 24 (1981), 651–72; and Neilson, *Strategy and Supply*, p. 227.
87 On the work of the Inter-Allied Commission, see A. Carton de Wiart, *Happy Odyssey. The Memoirs of Lieutenant-General Sir Adrian Carton de Wiart* (London, 1950), pp. 92–102; Lundgreen-Nielsen, *Polish Problem*, pp. 180–93; and *ToL*, vol. 2, pp. 322–3.
88 For Howard's record of these negotiations, see Howard diary, 7–19 Mar. 1919, DHW 1/5.
89 Komarnicki, *Rebirth of Polish Republic*, pp. 395–748; and J. Korbel, *Poland between East and West. Soviet and German Diplomacy toward Poland, 1919–1933* (Princeton, 1963), pp. 9–67.

90 Howard diary, 12 Feb. 1919, DHW 1/5; and Howard to his wife, 12 Feb. 1919, DHW 3/32.
91 On Pilsudski charming Howard, see Lundgreen-Nielsen, *Polish Problem*, pp. 222, 255–8. Cf. Howard diary, 14 and 15 Feb. 1919, DHW 1/5; and Howard, 'Paderewski'. Howard wrote a poem whilst in Warsaw in which Poland is personified as 'a horseman on a wintry plain', whose horse is weary and whose weapons are old and blunted. Then there is the refrain: 'Yet from his lance there floats the eagle white / On blood red ground, arisen from the dead, / And tho' all terrors on his path are spread / His heart is true and ready to fight'. This seems to be an allegorical reference to Pilsudski; see Howard, 'Warsaw February 1919', Feb. 1919, DHW 1/23.
92 For instance, Howard diary, 8 and 23 Mar. 1919, DHW 1/5.
93 See Howard diary, 13, 17, 20, and 22 Feb., 8 Mar. 1919, all ibid; and Howard despatch to British Delegation (Paris), 20 Feb. 1919, FO 608/65.
94 Howard diary, 17 Feb. 1919, DHW 1/5.
95 Howard diary, 27 Feb. 1919, ibid. Howard's friend, Bryce, had headed an investigation into German atrocities during the war; see T. Wilson, 'Lord Bryce's Investigation into Alleged German Atrocities in Belgium, 1914–1915', *JCH*, 14 (1979), 369–83. Cf. Bryce to Howard, 23 Sept. 1915 and 14 Mar. 1917, both DHW 4/Personal/12.
96 This paragraph is based on Howard diary, 7 to 19 Mar. 1919, DHW 1/5. It would seem that Howard was more hardline in these negotiations than is suggested in Lundgreen-Nielsen, *Polish Problem*, p. 225.
97 See Gajda, *Postscript*, pp. 6–27 *passim*; Lundgreen-Nielsen, *Polish Problem*, pp. 215–63 *passim*; and Nelson, *Land and Power*, pp. 176–97 *passim*.
98 For instance, see '... v. particularly Mr. Namier's minute. He apparently did all he could to saboter Poland.': on record of Balfour despatch to Howard, 6 Mar. 1919, in Howard memorandum on 'Poland. Inter-Allied Commission. Tels & despatches to FO' (n.d., but recorded as received), DHW 1/51.
99 Headlam-Morley to Howard, 4 Mar. 1919, DHW 1/24; Cf. Howard diary, 11 Mar. 1919, DHW 1/5.
100 Quoted in Gajda, *Postscript*, p. 19. Cf. 'L.G.'s remarks are interesting & characteristic[,] amounting to "Put off anything immediately required for Poland by any argument you can[.]"': on record of War Cabinet minute, 5 Mar. 1919, in Howard memorandum on 'Poland. Inter-Allied Commission. Tels. & despatches to FO', (n.d., but recorded as received), DHW 1/51.
101 For an indication of how Lloyd George's mind was working, see R. K. Debo, 'Lloyd George and the Copenhagen Conference of 1919–1920: The Initiation of Anglo-Soviet Negotiations', *HJ*, 24 (1981), 429–41; and M. L. Dockrill, 'Britain, the United States, and France and the German Settlement, 1918–1920', in McKercher and Moss, *Shadow and Substance*, pp. 203–20.
102 Howard diary, 10 Apr. 1919, DHW 1/5. The next four paragraphs except where indicated, are based on Howard to Lloyd George, 10 Apr. 1919, LG MSS F/57/6/1.
103 Howard had suggested this earlier in private discussions at the Foreign Office; see Howard diary, 16 Nov. 1918, DHW 1/4.
104 Headlam-Morley to Namier, 24 Mar. 1919, in Headlam-Morley, *et al.*, *A Memoir*, pp. 54–5. See references to Namier minutes in Lundgreen-Nielsen, *Polish Problem*, fns. 217 and 222, p. 542.

105 Howard diary, 26 and 27 Mar. 1919, DHW 1/5; and Howard despatch to Balfour, 2 Apr. 1919, FO 608/66.
106 Cf. Howard diary, 6 Mar. 1919, DHW 1/5.
107 Howard memorandum on 'Russia and the Baltic States', 21 Apr. 1919, LG MSS F/199/1/1.
108 Howard diary, 22 Apr. 1919, DHW 1/5.
109 This and the rest of this paragraph are based on Dockrill and Steiner, 'Foreign Office at the Paris Peace Conference'.
110 See Hovi, *Baltic Area*, pp. 143–206, especially: 'In its initial stages, the significance of the commission, led by the British political representative Esmé [sic] Howard was not very great, because it could only make recommendations.', p. 143. See 'Proceedings of 1st Meeting of the Baltic Commission', 14 May 1919, FO 608/186.
111 Howard diary, 19 June 1919, DHW 1/5.
112 Howard diary, 1 July 1919, ibid.
113 For instance, Howard diary, 4 Jan. 1919, ibid.
114 C. J. Lowe and F. Marzari, *Italian Foreign Policy, 1870–1940* (London, 1975), pp. 172–80.
115 Howard diary, 23 Apr. 1919, DHW 1/5.
116 Howard diary, 6 May 1919, ibid.
117 Also see Z. Steiner and M. L. Dockrill, 'The Foreign Office Reforms', *HJ*, 17 (1974), 131–56.

8 MADRID: ANGLO-SPANISH RELATIONS, 1919–1924

1 Howard diary, 26 June 1919, DHW 1/5.
2 Drummond to Russell, 9 Apr. 1919, Balfour MSS, FO 800/216. Cf. A Sharp, 'The Foreign Office in Eclipse, 1919–22', *History*, 61 (1976), 198–218.
3 See Drummond to Balfour, 22 Jan. 1919, Balfour MSS, FO 800/215; and Curzon to Balfour, 12 May 1919, Balfour MSS, FO 800/216. For an indication that Howard was canvassed about going to Washington and declined the offer, see Bryce to Howard, 20 Mar. 1920, DHW 1/25.
4 Curzon to Balfour, 20 July 1919, Balfour MSS, FO 800/217; Curzon to Howard, 4 Aug. 1919, DHW 8/14; and Howard diary, 24 July and 7 Aug. 1919, DHW 1/5.
5 Howard diary, 12 Sept. to 2 Oct. 1919, ibid.
6 This and the next paragraph are based on Sperling (Foreign Office American and African Department) 'Memorandum...respecting Morocco', 3 Sept. 1919; 'Memorandum respecting the Status of Tangier', 28 July 1919; and FO to French government, 19 Oct. 1919, all enclosed in Sperling to Howard, 19 Oct. 1919, DHW 4/Official/22.
7 Cecil memorandum for Hardinge and Steel-Maitland (secretary, Department of Overseas Trade), 20 Nov. 1918, Cecil Papers, BL Add. MSS 51094.
8 Howard diary, 10 July 1919, DHW 1/5; and Howard memorandum, 2 Aug. 1919, DHW 4/Official/11.
9 On Howard's views of the 1919 miners' strike and the kind of problems it posed for Britain both internally and externally, see Howard diary, July–September 1919 *passim*, DHW 1/5.
10 *ToL*, vol. 2, pp. 418–19.

11 On the problems in Spain in this period, see S. Ben-Ami, *Fascism from above. The Dictatorship of Primo de Rivera in Spain 1923–1930* (Oxford, 1983); C. P. Boyd, *Praetorian Politics in Liberal Spain* (Chapel Hill, 1979); R. Carr, *Spain, 1808–1939* (Oxford, 1966), pp. 430–563; J. Harrison, 'Big Business and the Failure of Right-Wing Catalan Nationalism, 1901–1923', *HJ*, 19 (1976), 901–18; and C. Petrie, *King Alfonso XIII and his Age* (London, 1963), pp. 136–78.
12 Ben-Ami, *Fascism from above*, p. 37.
13 Ibid., fn. 85. Ben-Ami asserts that Howard wrote the Introduction to Petrie, *Alfonso XIII*, which was published first in 1963. If true, this would be the greatest coup in two millennia; this book has no 'Introduction' and, more important, Howard died in 1939.
14 *ToL*, vol. 1, p. 101.
15 Howard, 'Spain. Report for 1919–1920', Feb. 1921, enclosed in Howard despatch (112) to Curzon, 19 Feb. 1921, FO 371/7130/1975/1975.
16 Carr, *Spain*, pp. 497–523, 558–63.
17 Ben-Ami, *Fascism from above*, p. 8, fn. 37.
18 Howard despatch (765) to Curzon, 27 Nov. 1920, with Butler (Foreign Office Western Department) minute, 2 Dec. 1920, FO 371/5493/2635/19.
19 Howard despatch (663) to Curzon, 25 Oct. 1920, enclosing Deakin 'Weekly Report on the Industrial Situation in Spain', 25 Oct. 1920, FO 371/5493/1616/19.
20 Wingfield despatch (561) to Curzon, 8 Sept. 1920, with Butler minute, 22 Sept. 1920, and Tufton (head, Foreign Office Western Department) minute, 23 Sept. 1920, all FO 371/5494/859/170.
21 For instance, Howard despatch (620) to Curzon, 9 Oct. 1920, enclosing Deakin 'Industrial Situation in Spain', n.d., FO 371/5493/1098/19.
22 Howard 'Spain. Report for 1919–1920', Feb. 1921, enclosed in Howard despatch (112) to Curzon, 19 Feb. 1921, FO 371/7130/1975/1975.
23 See Deakin 'Weekly Report on the General Industrial Situation in Spain', 25 Oct. 1920, enclosed in Howard despatch (663) to Curzon, 25 Oct. 1920, FO 371/5493/1616/19.
24 Wingfield despatch (834) to Curzon, 23 Dec. 1920, enclosing Deakin 'Weekly Report', n.d., FO 371/5493/3659/19.
25 Howard despatch (780) to Curzon, 23 Dec. 1920, enclosing Deakin 'Weekly Report on the General Industrial Situation in Spain', 29 Nov. 1920, FO 371/5493/2810/19.
26 See Howard despatch (762) to Curzon, 26 Nov. 1920, FO 371/5498/2632/2632; and Howard 'Note' (listing the people he met at Bilbao), n.d., DHW 6/4.
27 Howard to Tufton, 26 Oct. 1920, FO 371/5495/1478/170; and Howard to Tufton, 30 Oct. 1920, FO 371/5495/1670/170.
28 Butler minute, 12 Oct. 1920, FO 371/5494/859/170; and Howard despatch (674) to Curzon, 28 Oct. 1920, FO 371/5495/1622/170.
29 Howard to Denbigh, 8 Oct. 1920, enclosed in Howard to Tufton, 8 Oct. 1920, with Tufton minutes (2), both 12 Oct. 1920, and Butler minute, 12 Oct. 1920, all FO 371/5494/859/170.
30 Howard despatch (756) to Curzon, 24 Nov. 1920, FO 371/5495/2046/170.

Notes to pages 242–247

31 Wingfield despatch (844) to Curzon, 24 Dec. 1920, FO 371/5496/3666/551.
32 Howard, 'Spain. Report for 1919–1920', Feb. 1921, enclosed in Howard despatch (112) to Curzon, 19 Feb. 1921, FO 371/7130/1975/1975.
33 Except where noted, this paragraph is based on Howard despatch (765) to Curzon, 27 Nov. 1920, FO 371/5493/2635/19.
34 Howard telegram (409) to FO, 14 Dec. 1920, FO 371/5493/3237/19; and Wingfield despatch (844) to Curzon, 24 Dec. 1920, FO 371/5496/3666/551.
35 Howard despatch (600) to Curzon, 4 Oct. 1920, FO 371/5496/714/551.
36 Wingfield despatch (844) to Curzon, 24 Dec. 1920, FO 371/5496/3666/551.
37 *ToL.* vol. 2, p. 425.
38 See Carr, *Spain*, pp. 509–16; Howard telegram (409) to FO, 14 Dec. 1920, FO 371/5493/3237/19; and Howard despatch to Curzon, 3 Feb. 1921, FO 371/7119/1436/355.
39 Howard despatch (796) to Curzon, 7 Dec. 1920, enclosing Deakin 'Weekly Report', n.d., FO 371/5493/3070/19.
40 Wingfield despatch (844) to Curzon, 24 Dec. 1920, FO 371/5496/3666/551.
41 The rest of this paragraph is based on Carr, *Spain*, pp. 500–3.
42 This and the next paragraph are based on Boyd, *Praetorian Politics*, pp. 142–7; *ToL,* vol. 2, p. 419; and Howard 'Spain. Report for 1919–1920', Feb. 1921, enclosed in Howard despatch (112) to Curzon, 19 Feb. 1921, FO 371/7130/1975/1975.
43 Ibid.
44 Ibid.
45 Howard despatch (650) to Curzon, 21 Oct. 1920, FO 371/5497/1482/1482. Also see Secret Intelligence Service memorandum on 'Germany. The Ambassador to Madrid', 19 Oct. 1920, enclosed in Tufton despatch (675) to Howard, 8 Nov. 1920, FO 371/5497/1726/1482.
46 See the report on the heads of foreign missions in Spain contained in Howard despatch (836) to Curzon, 23 Dec. 1920, FO 371/5498/3661/3661.
47 Howard despatch (764) to Curzon, 27 Nov. 1920, FO 371/5497/2634/1507.
48 Duff (Foreign Office News Department) minute, 6 Dec. 1920, and Duff to Deakin, 19 Dec. 1920, both ibid.
49 For instance, Howard despatch (376) to Curzon, 13 June 1921, with enclosures, FO 371/7120/6838/357.
50 Campbell (Foreign Office Western Department) minute, 25 June 1921, with Crowe and Curzon initials, ibid.
51 Sperling 'Memorandum...respecting Morocco', 3 Sept. 1919, DHW 4/Official/22.
52 Merry del Val (Spanish ambassador, London) to Curzon, 5 Mar. 1919, enclosing Merry del Val memorandum on 'Interview with Lord Curzon of Kedleston', 5 Mar. 1919, with Curzon minute, n.d., and Merry del Val to Curzon, 30 Apr. 1919, all Curzon MSS, FO 800/157.
53 For example, Merry del Val to Lloyd George, 23 Apr. 1921, ibid.
54 Crowe minute, 23 July 1920, FO 371/4512/4743/639.
55 See the list of claimants in FO 371/4512/4573/639.

56 For example, Howard to Hardinge, 21 Apr. 1920, and Hardinge to Howard, 6 and 25 May 1920, all FO 371/4511/2559/6393; and Howard despatch (461) to Curzon, 8 July 1920, enclosing de Lema to Howard, 2 July 1920, FO 371/4512/4742/639.
57 Lidderdale (Foreign Office Western Department) minute, 2 Mar. 1921, FO 371/7077/1968/1968; and Villiers (Foreign Office Western Department) memorandum, 6 May 1921, FO 371/7077/4972/1968.
58 Howard despatch (335) to Curzon, 28 May 1921, with Crowe and Curzon minutes, both 2 June 1921, and Campbell to Howard, 6 June 1921, all FO 371/7077/5877/1968.
59 Howard to Curzon, 1 June 1920, with Curzon minute, n.d., Curzon MSS, FO 800/157. On the Spa conference, see W. N. Medlicott, *British Foreign Policy since Versailles 1919–1963* (London, 1968), pp. 6–8.
60 Wingfield despatch (859) to Curzon, 31 Dec. 1920, FO 371/7114/361/3; and Rowley (British consul-general, Barcelona) to Curzon, 10 Jan. 1921, FO 371/7114/502/3.
61 Butler minute, 4 Feb. 1921, FO 371/7114/1197/70.
62 Howard despatch (794) to Curzon, 4 Dec. 1920, FO 371/5497/3068/781.
63 Howard despatch (795) to Curzon, 11 Dec. 1920, with enclosures, plus Butler and Villiers minutes, 15 Dec. 1920, FO 371/5497/3067/781.
64 Howard despatch (276) to Curzon, 30 Apr. 1921, FO 371/7116/4758/76; and Butler minute, 30 June 1921, FO 371/7117/6867/76.
65 Howard to Villiers, 19 Mar. 1921, FO 371/7116/3348/76; and Howard telegram (76) to FO, 30 Mar. 1921, FO 371/7116/3374/76.
66 On Annual, see Boyd, *Praetorian Politics*, pp. 168–82; S. G. Payne, *Politics and the Military in Modern Spain* (Stanford, 1967), pp. 159–72; and D. Woolman, *Rebels in the Riff* (Stanford, 1968), pp. 80–102.
67 Howard telegram (143) to FO, 23 July 1921, FO 371/7067/7921/184; Wingfield telegram (144) to FO, 24 July 1921, FO 371/7067/7947/184; and Howard telegram (147) to FO, 29 July 1921, FO 371/7067/8149/184.
68 Howard despatch (462) to Curzon, 3 Aug. 1921, enclosing Wingfield 'Report on Operations in Morocco and State of Public Opinion in Spain', 1 Aug. 1921, FO 371/7067/8512/184.
69 Villiers minute, 9 Aug. 1921, FO 371/7067/8528/184.
70 Crowe minute, 15 Aug. 1921, FO 371/7122/8660/367.
71 Boyd, *Praetorian Politics*, pp. 184–98 gives an indication. Cf. S. G. Payne, 'Fascism and Right Authoritarianism in the Iberian World – The Last Twenty Years', *JCH*, 21 (1986), 163–5.
72 For example, see Howard despatch (768) to Curzon, 21 Nov. 1921, FO 371/7118/12461/76; and Crowe minute, 13 Dec. 1921, with Crowe to Merry del Val, 16 Dec. 1921, both FO 371/7119/12996/76.
73 FO Western Department Memorandum on 'The Spanish Tariff', 20 Dec. 1921, with Curzon minute, 22 Dec. 1921, FO 371/7119/13122/76. This memorandum was circulated to the Cabinet as CP3588. Also see Cabinet Minute, 92(21)6.
74 On Howard's 'volte-face', see Campbell minute, 20 Nov. 1921, FO 371/7118/12461/76.
75 See Howard telegram (259) to FO, 31 Dec. 1921, FO 371/8381/2/1.

76 Howard to Crowe, 30 Dec. 1921, FO 371/8381/360/1.
77 Cmd 1592: *Correspondence Respecting Egyptian Affairs*; and Cmd 1617: *Despatch to His Majesty's Representatives Abroad Respecting the Status of Egypt*.
78 Howard to Crowe, 24 Aug. 1921, with enclosure and minutes, and Crowe to Howard, 7 Sept. 1921, all FO 371/7127/9314/937; Spanish Embassy, London, '*Note Verbale*', 23 Sept. 1921, FO 371/7127/10281/937; and Howard to Crowe, 15 Sept. 1921, with Crowe minute, 28 Sept. 1921, FO 371/7127/10312/937.
79 The next two paragraphs are based on Villiers and Crowe minutes, both 13 Jan. 1922, and Curzon minute, 15 Jan. 1922, all FO 371/8381/360/1.
80 Crowe to Howard, 23 Jan. 1922, ibid.; and Howard to Crowe, 5 Feb. 1922, FO 371/8394/1666/1666.
81 Crowe minute, 23 Feb. 1922, ibid.
82 Eugenia Victoria to Howard, 29 Aug. 1921, with Howard minute, 4 Sept. 1921, both DHW 1/25; and Howard despatch (804) to Curzon, 8 Dec. 1921, FO 371/7134/12885/12885. Also see Howard telegram (238) to Curzon, 29 Nov. 1921, with Vansittart minute, 30 Nov. 1921, Curzon initials, and Vansittart telegram (unnumbered) to Howard, 1 Dec. 1921, all ibid.
83 Howard despatch (336) to Curzon, 27 Apr. 1922, with Howard to Gaselee, 29 Apr. 1922, and Gaselee minute, 5 May 1922, all FO 371/8396/3714/3714.
84 Gaselee to Belloc, 8 May 1922, ibid.; and Belloc to Gaselee, 10 May 1922, FO 371/8396/4282/3714.
85 Howard despatch (493) to Balfour (acting foreign secretary), 3 July 1922, FO 371/8396/5717/3714. Also see Jimenez (English Society in Spain) to Howard, 10 Jan. 1923, DHW 1/25.
86 Alba to Howard, 23 June 1924, DHW 5/8.
87 Except where noted, this paragraph is based on Butler's 'Memorandum showing the present position in regard to negotiations for a commercial treaty with Spain', 6 Feb. 1922, and Curzon minute, 10 Feb. 1922, FO 371/8381/1426/1.
88 Howard to Crowe, 30 Dec. 1921, FO 371/8381/921/1.
89 See *Gaceta de Madrid*, 13 Feb. 1922, in FO 371/8381/1549/1.
90 Howard despatch (180) to Curzon, 4 Mar. 1922, enclosing Howard to Hontoria, 2 Mar. 1922, FO 371/8381/2069/1. Also see Howard's outline of his negotiating strategy in Howard despatch (155) to Curzon, 24 Feb. 1922, FO 371/8381/1867/2029/1.
91 Howard despatch (190) to Curzon, 9 Mar. 1922, FO 371/8388/2469/268; and Howard despatch (306) to Curzon, 15 Apr. 1922, FO 371/8388/3347/268.
92 Cabinet Conclusion 15(22)5: CAB 23/40, and FO telegram (24) to Howard, 9 Mar. 1922, FO 371/8381/2044/1.
93 For instance, Howard telegram (49) to FO, 5 Apr. 1922, FO 371/8382/3167/1.
94 'Memorandum of Press Comments on Spanish Tariff', Feb. 1922, in Howard despatch (151) to Curzon, 24 Feb. 1922, FO 371/8381/2053/1.
95 Howard to Villiers, 18 Mar. 1922, FO 371/8382/2516/1.
96 FO telegram (30) to Howard, 22 Mar. 1922, ibid.
97 Howard despatch (340) to Curzon, 28 Apr. 1922, FO 371/8382/3727/1.

98 Howard memorandum, 24 May 1922, enclosed in Howard despatch (390) to Curzon, 24 May 1922, FO 371/8382/4513/1.
99 Howard to Fountain, 27 May 1922, FO 371/8382/4876/1.
100 See Campbell and Villiers minutes, both 31 May 1922, FO 371/8382/4513/1.
101 Butler minute, 31 May 1922, FO 371/8382/4522/1.
102 Fountain to Under-Secretary, FO, 12 June 1922, FO 371/8382/4846/1.
103 Crowe memorandum, 16 May 1922, FO 371/8382/4176/1.
104 Ibid.
105 See note 100, above.
106 The rest of this and the next paragraph are based on Howard telegram (93) to FO, 20 June 1922, FO 371/8383/5154/1; and Howard telegram (92) to FO, 20 June 1922, FO 371/8383/5158/1.
107 Howard despatch (474) to Curzon, 24 June 1922, FO 371/8383/5340/1.
108 Wills to Villiers, 6 July 1922, with enclosures, Villiers minute, 7 July 1922, Mounsey (Treaty Department) minutes, 8 and 10 July 1922, and FO telegram (1) to Howard, 11 July 1922, all FO 371/8383/5649/1.
109 An example of this hard bargaining can be seen in Howard telegram (9) to FO, 19 July 1922, FO 371/8383/6069/1; and Fountain to Under-Secretary, FO, 19 July 1922, with FO telegram (6) to Howard, 20 July 1922, FO 371/8383/6091/1. Also see Charles to Howard, 31 July 1922, FO 371/8384/6570/1; and Wills to Howard, 27 July 1922, DHW 5/8.
110 Howard telegram (1) to FO, 11 July 1922, with Campbell minute, 13 July 1922, both FO 371/8383/5810/1.
111 Howard telegram (13) to FO, 23 July 1922, with Butler minute, 25 July 1922, both FO 371/8383/6197/1; and FO telegram (10) to Howard, 24 July 1922, FO 371/8383/6183/1.
112 Balfour (acting foreign secretary) despatch (400) to Howard, 2 Aug. 1922, FO 371/8383/6444/1.
113 Nugent (Federation of British Industries) to Howard, 9 Nov. 1922, FO 371/8385/9282/1; and Vansittart to Howard, 9 Jan. 1923, DHW 5/8.
114 Wills minute, 23 Nov. 1922, FO 371/8386/9722/1; and Wills to Howard, 2 Aug. 1922, DHW 4/Official/22.
115 Howard telegram (198) to FO, 31 Dec. 1922, FO 371/9458/1/1.
116 For a general discussion of the Turkish imbroglio, see Dockrill and Goold, *Peace Without Promise*, pp. 131–252; and P. C. Helmreich, *From Paris to Sevres: The Partition of the Ottoman Empire at the Peace Conference of 1919–1920* (Columbus, Ohio, 1974).
117 Howard despatch (8) to Curzon, 4 Jan. 1923, FO 371/9458/247/1; and Howard telegram (22) to FO, 22 Mar. 1923, and FO telegram (19) to Howard, 23 Mar. 1923, both FO 371/9458/2154/1.
118 Howard despatch (62) to Curzon, 30 Jan. 1923, with Crowe and Curzon minutes, both 8 Feb. 1923, FO 371/9458/1008/1.
119 Villiers to Howard, 24 Apr. 1923, DHW 9/37/5; Curzon despatch (1547) to Crewe (British ambassador, Paris), 2 May 1923, with Crowe and Curzon minutes, both 5 May 1923, all FO 371/9458/3476/1; and Curzon to St Aulaire (French ambassador, London), 24 May 1923, FO 371/9458/4029/1.
120 For example, Howard despatch (317) to Curzon, 25 May 1923, with enclosures, FO 371/9458/4122/1.

121 Howard to Curzon, 28 Oct. 1921, DHW 9/37/3.
122 Howard to Crowe, 5 Feb. 1922, FO 371/8394/1666/1666.
123 Crowe minute, 13 Jan. 1922, FO 371/8381/360/1.
124 Howard despatch (365) to Curzon, 12 May 1922, FO 371/8388/4110/268.
125 Wingfield despatch (819) to Curzon, 21 Dec. 1922, FO 371/8389/10435/268.
126 The rest of this paragraph is based on Wingfield despatch (768) to Curzon, 20 Nov. 1922, FO 371/8389/9737/268.
127 Ben-Ami, *Fascism from above*, fn. 37, p. 8.
128 Howard despatch (479) to Balfour (acting foreign secretary), 24 June 1922, FO 371/8390/5342/279.
129 Ben-Ami, *Fascism from above*, pp. 1–52.
130 Howard despatch (193) to Curzon, 31 Mar. 1923, FO 371/9489/2501/623.
131 Wingfield despatch (819) to Curzon, 21 Dec. 1922, FO 371/8389/10435/268.
132 Howard despatch (193) to Curzon, 31 Mar. 1923, FO 371/9489/2501/623.
133 Howard despatch (835) to Curzon, 30 Dec. 1922, FO 371/9469/242/44.
134 Howard despatch (263) to Curzon, 2 May 1923, FO 371/9489/3521/623.
135 Howard despatch (277) to Curzon, 9 May 1923, FO 371/9489/3780/623.
136 Ibid.
137 Howard despatch (531) to Curzon, 21 Sept. 1923, enclosing Lloyd Thomas memorandum, n.d., FO 371/9490/7602/623. Cf. Boyd, *Praetorian Politics*, pp. 243–57.
138 Howard telegram (unnumbered) to FO, 13 Sept. 1923, FO 371/9490/7238/623; and Howard telegram (84) to FO, 14 Sept. 1923, FO 371/9490/7265/623.
139 Howard despatch (704) to Curzon, 8 Dec. 1923, FO 371/9490/9602/623.
140 Howard despatch (531) to Curzon, 21 Sept. 1923, FO 371/9490/7602/623.
141 Howard despatch (795) to Curzon, 3 Dec. 1921, FO 371/7134/12877/12877.
142 Howard to King George V, 21 Sept. 1923, DHW 9/37/5; and Howard despatch (517) to Curzon, 15 Sept. 1923, FO 371/9490/7311/623.
143 Villiers minute, 18 Sept. 1923, ibid.
144 Villiers minute, 28 Sept. 1923, FO 371/9490/7656/623.
145 Cf. Howard despatch (531) to Curzon, 21 Sept. 1923, FO 371/9490/7602/623; and Howard despatch (699) to Curzon, 7 Dec. 1923, FO 371/9493/9599/6376.
146 Howard telegram (111) to FO, 11 Dec. 1923, FO 371/9466/9643/1; and Howard telegram (118) to FO, 18 Dec. 1923, FO 371/9467/9827/1.
147 Carr, *Spain*, p. 573.
148 Graham (British ambassador, Rome) despatch (1032) to Curzon, 23 Nov. 1923, FO 371/9493/9345/6376.
149 Howard telegram (107) to FO, 15 Nov. 1923, FO 371/9493/8967/6376.

150 Campbell minute, 16 Nov. 1923, ibid.
151 Howard, *ToL*, vol. 2, p. 476.

9 WASHINGTON *REDUX*: REBUILDING GOOD RELATIONS, 1924–1927

1 *ToL*, vol. 2, p. 476.
2 Curzon telegram (unnumbered) to Howard, 14 Dec. 1923, DHW 9/39.
3 Tyrrell telegram (unnumbered) to Howard, 14 Dec. 1923, ibid.
4 *ToL*, vol. 2, p. 476.
5 Howard to Curzon, 15 Dec. 1923, DHW 9/39.
6 Howard telegrams (both unnumbered) to Curzon and Tyrrell, both 17 Dec. 1923, both ibid.
7 *ToL*, vol. 2, p. 479.
8 Curzon to Howard, 23 Dec. 1923, DHW 9/39.
9 See Crowe telegram (unnumbered) to Howard, 17 Dec. 1923, ibid.
10 Crowe to Howard, 9 Jan. 1924, ibid.
11 Spring Rice to Howard, 26 Mar. 1913, DHW 4/Personal/18.
12 Spring Rice to Howard, 10 June 1913, ibid.
13 This paragraph is based on L. E. Boothe, 'A Fettered Envoy: Lord Grey's Mission to the United States, 1919–1920', *RP*, 33 (1971), 78–94; G. W. Egerton, 'Diplomacy, Scandal, and Military Intelligence: The Craufurd-Stuart Affair and Anglo-American Relations, 1918–1920', *INS*, 2 (1987), 110–34; D. Judd, *Lord Reading: A Life of Rufus Isaacs, First Marquess of Reading, 1860–1935* (London, 1982), pp. 141–84; B. D. Rhodes, 'The Image of Britain in the United States, 1919–1929: A Contentious Relative and Rival', in McKercher, *Struggle for Supremacy*; and D. C. Watt, *Succeeding John Bull, America in Britain's Place, 1900–75* (Cambridge, 1984), pp. 27–48 *passim*.
14 See Curzon to Balfour, 12 and 27 May 1919, both Balfour MSS, FO 800/216.
15 See the seminal discussion of 'Atlanticism' in D. C. Watt, 'United States Documentary Sources for the Study of British Foreign Policy, 1919–39', in Watt, *Personalities and Policies*, pp. 1–15. Also see M. G. Fry, *Illusions of Security, North Atlantic Diplomacy 1918–22* (Toronto, 1972), pp. 3–67.
16 On these people, see B. J. C. McKercher, *The Second Baldwin Government and the United States, 1924–1929: Attitudes and Diplomacy* (Cambridge, 1984), pp. 1–33 *passim*.
17 The Pilgrim Society, *Speeches at a Dinner in Honour of His Excellency Frank B. Kellogg...and His Excellency The Rt. Hon. Esmé [sic] Howard* (London, 1924): in DHW 9/8.
18 *ToL*, vol. 2, p. 489.
19 Ibid., pp. 565–8.
20 Ibid., p. 488.
21 Ibid.
22 This and the next paragraph are based on K. M. Burk, *Britain, America and the Sinews of War, 1914–1918* (London, 1985); G. W. Egerton, 'Britain and the "Great Betrayal": Anglo-American Relations and the Struggle for United States Ratification of the Treaty of Versailles, 1919–1920', *HJ*, 21 (1978), 885–911; K. Middlemas and J. Barnes, *Baldwin. A Biography* (London, 1969), pp. 136–48; K. Nelson, *Victors Divided: America and the Allies in Germany, 1918–1923* (Berkeley, 1975); S. W. Roskill, *Naval Policy between*

the Wars, 2 vols. (London, 1968, 1976), vol. 1, pp. 71–130, 204–32, 300–55; D. P. Silverman, Reconstructing Europe after the Great War (Cambridge, Mass., and London, 1982); D. G. Williamson, 'Great Britain and the Ruhr Crisis, 1923–1924', BJIS, 3 (1977), 70–91. Howard was informed periodically of Anglo-American problems during his time at Madrid; for instance, see Tyrrell to Howard, 16 Nov. 1920, DHW 9/37/2.

23 The Foreign Office archives rarely have any information on promotions, transfers, and retirements; usually, such information is in private papers. But Tyrrell left no papers, and Crowe's, which do exist, are closed.

24 The next two paragraphs, except where noted, are from ToL, vol. 2, pp. 491–6. In this portion of his memoirs, Howard indicated in passing that he also met the vice-president. This is a slip of memory, since Coolidge had no vice-president from the time he succeeded Harding in August 1923 until he formed his own Administration in March 1925.

25 Howard despatch to Chamberlain (British foreign secretary), 10 Nov. 1924, FO 371/9636/6546/6359.

26 See Robinette to Howard, 16 Jan. 1924, DHW 9/10.

27 'Praises St. George as British Saint. Sir Esme Howard Says Slaying Dragon is Typical of Nation's Help to Weak' – 24 Apr. 1924, NY Times; 'Dr Butler Cheered at Dinner…Sir Esme Howard Also a Guest' – 25 May 1924, NY Times; and 'Howard Proposes a Memorial to Bryce' – 2 Dec. 1924, NY Times.

28 'British Diplomat Invites Merchants. Ambassador Urges Them to Visit Him at Washington to Talk Business'; and 'Howard Sees More Good Will Abroad' – both 22 Oct. 1924, NY Times.

29 'Sir Esme Howard Lotos Club Guest. British Ambassador Avoids Politics and Talks on "The Art of Travel"' – 10 Apr. 1924, NY Times.

30 'London Hears Us Greet Her Envoy' – 19 Mar. 1924, NY Times.

31 'British Premier Sees Press as Peace Aid. Tells Publishers Here World's Hopes Lie in Anglo-American Friendship' – 25 Apr. 1924, NY Times; 'Sir Esme Howard Praises Protocol. British Ambassador Calls It an Honest Effort by Honest Men to End War' – 10 Dec. 1924, NY Times; and E. W. Howard, 'British Policy and the Balance of Power', APSR, 19 (1925), 261–7.

32 P. W. Wilson, 'British Ambassador Foresees a New Era', 1 June 1924, NY Sunday Times Magazine, 8 (1924), 4.

33 'British Premier Sees Press as Peace Aid' – 25 Apr. 1924, NY Times.

34 'Howard is Criticized for Remark on Soviet. All-American Conference Assails Ambassador as Urging Policy on America', 17 May 1924, NY Times.

35 Cf. C. F. Brand, The British Labour Party, A Short History, rev. edn (Stanford, 1974), pp. 106–15; and P. J. Noel-Baker, The Geneva Protocol for the Pacific Settlement of International Disputes (London, 1925).

36 F. M. Bemis, ed., The American Secretaries of State and their Diplomacy, vol. 10 (NY, 1929), pp. 395–6; and M. J. Pusey, Charles Evans Hughes, vol. 2 (NY, 1951), pp. 419–20.

37 S. A. Schuker, The End of French Predominance in Europe. The Financial Crisis of 1924 and the Acceptance of the Dawes Plan (Chapel Hill, 1976), pp. 171–382. Cf. M. Trachtenberg, Reparation in World Politics: France and European Economic Diplomacy, 1916–1923 (NY, 1980).

38 McKercher, Baldwin Government; and Roskill, Naval Policy, vol. 1.

39 Chamberlain to Howard, 22 Dec. 1924, Chamberlain MSS, FO 800/256.

40 Howard to Chamberlain, 9 Jan. 1925, ibid. FO 800/257. Cf. D. D. Burks, 'The United States and the Geneva Protocol of 1924: "A New Holy Alliance"?', *AHR*, 64 (1959), 891–905.
41 Chamberlain to Howard, 28 Jan. 1925, Chamberlain MSS, FO 800/257.
42 On the anti-Protocol sentiment, see Cecil to Baldwin, 23 Jan. 1925, Cecil Papers, Add. MSS 51080. Cf. CID Report (559B), 23 Jan. 1925, CAB 4/12; and Chamberlain memorandum (CP 48(25)), 27 Jan, 1925, CAB 24/171.
43 Howard to Chamberlain, 13 Feb. 1925, Chamberlain MSS, FO 800/257.
44 Howard despatch to Chamberlain, 13 Nov. 1924, FO 371/9636/6553/6359.
45 B. J. C. McKercher, 'Austen Chamberlain's Control of British Foreign Policy, 1924–1929', *IHR*, 6 (1984), 570–91.
46 Howard telegram (9) to FO, 10 Jan. 1925, FO 371/10639/171/171.
47 This and the next two sentences are based on Howard despatch (82) to Chamberlain, 16 Jan. 1925, FO 371/10639/450/171; and Howard despatch (90) to Chamberlain, 16 Jan. 1925, FO 371/10639/457/171.
48 Vansittart minute, 12 Jan. 1925, FO 371/10639/450/171; and Howard despatch (90) to Chamberlain, 16 Jan. 1925, FO 371/10639/457/171.
49 Howard to Chamberlain, 13 Feb. 1925, ibid.
50 Howard telegram (374) to FO, 14 Dec. 1924, FO 371/9619/6948/435; also see Howard despatch (13) to Chamberlain, 2 Jan. 1925, FO 371/10633/191/6.
51 Roskill, *Naval Policy*, vol. 1, pp. 307–9, 501.
52 Howard despatch to MacDonald, 30 Oct. 1924, with enclosures, FO 371/9618/6340/635.
53 Howard despatch to Chamberlain, 21 Nov. 1924, FO 371/9619/6701/435.
54 Howard telegram (71) to FO, 25 Feb. 1925, FO 371/10633/1049/6.
55 See Howard despatch (1885) to Chamberlain, 18 Dec. 1924, FO 371/10633/10/6.
56 See the views of Curtis Wilbur, secretary of the Navy, reported in Howard despatch to MacDonald, 25 Sept. 1924, FO 371/9612/5763/218.
57 Howard despatch to MacDonald, 30 Oct. 1924, FO 371/9618/6340/435. On American navalism, see G. T. A. Davis, *A Navy Second to None* (New York, 1940); and H. and M. Sprout, *Toward a New Order of Sea Power* (Princeton, 1946). For a different perspective, see R. W. Turk, 'Edward Walter Eberle', in Love, *The Chiefs*, pp. 37–46.
58 Except where noted, the rest of this paragraph is based on R. I. Campbell minute, 11 Nov. 1924, Vansittart and Tyrrell minutes, both 12 Nov. 1924, all FO 371/9618/6340/435.
59 Chamberlain minute, 12 Nov. 1924, ibid.
60 D. Johnson, 'Austen Chamberlain and the Locarno Agreements', *University of Birmingham Historical Journal*, 8 (1961), 62–81.
61 Howard telegram (374) to FO, 14 Dec. 1924, FO 371/9619/6948/435; and Howard telegram (26) to FO, 22 Jan. 1925, FO 371/10636/381/49.
62 On anti-oriental legislation, see Howard despatch to Chamberlain, 8 Dec. 1924, FO 371/9587/7005/2; on Coolidge and Borah, see Howard despatch (20) to Chamberlain, 6 Jan. 1925, FO 371/10636/373/49; and on the American delay, see Howard telegram (69) to FO, 24 Feb. 1925, FO 371/10636/1031/49.

Notes to pages 291–296

63 Chamberlain to Howard, 18 and 31 Mar. 1925, both Chamberlain MSS, FO 800/257.
64 For instance, see B. J. C. McKercher, 'A Sane and Sensible Diplomacy: Austen Chamberlain, Japan, and the Naval Balance of Power in the Pacific Ocean, 1924–29', *CJH*, 21 (1986), 187–93.
65 J. Jacobson, *Locarno Diplomacy. Germany and the West, 1925–1929* (Princeton, 1972), pp. 3–67; and D. Johnson, 'The Locarno Treaties', in Waites, *Troubled Neighbours*, pp. 100–24.
66 Cf. D. Carlton, 'Great Britain and the League Council Crisis of 1926', *HJ*, 11 (1968), 354–64; and McKercher, 'Chamberlain's Control', pp. 581–5.
67 J. Jacobson, 'The Conduct of Locarno Diplomacy', *RP*, 34 (1972), 67–81.
68 Viscount Cecil of Chelwood, *A Great Experiment* (London, 1941), p. 171; F. P. Walters, *A History of the League of Nations* (London, 1960), pp. 363–76; and J. W. Wheeler-Bennett, *Disarmament and Security since Locarno, 1925–1931* (London, 1932), pp. 43–102.
69 Chilton despatch (1925) to Chamberlain, 29 July 1925, FO 371/10637/4067/49.
70 Coolidge, 'Message to Congress', 4 Jan. 1926, *FRUS 1926*, vol. 1, pp. 42–4. Cf. Chamberlain to Howard, 24 Nov. 1925, Chamberlain MSS, FO 800/259.
71 Howard to Baldwin, 6 Nov. 1924, FO 371/9590/6461/8.
72 Hurst minute, 24 Nov. 1924, Vansittart and Chamberlain minutes, both 25 Nov. 1924, and Chamberlain to Howard, 3 Dec. 1924, all ibid.
73 The documentation on this case is in FO 371/10634/1390/31.
74 Cordeaux (governor, Bahamas) to Howard, 7 May 1925, FO 371/10649/2784/2497; and Chilton to Kellogg, 25 June 1925, FO 371/10649/3454/2497.
75 Howard to Kellogg, 16 Nov. 1925, FO 371/10649/6008/2497.
76 Howard telegram (321) to FO, 25 Nov. 1925, Chamberlain minute, 30 Nov. 1925, and Chamberlain telegram (unnumbered) to Howard, 1 Dec. 1925, all FO 371/10649/5913/2497.
77 Howard despatch to Chamberlain, 16 Nov. 1925, FO 371/10649/6008/2497.
78 R. I. Campbell minute, 8 Dec. 1925, ibid.
79 For instance, Howard despatch to Chamberlain, 13 Apr. 1926, with enclosures, and Chamberlain to Howard, 12 May 1926, all FO 371/11176/2243/88.
80 For example, Howard despatch to Chamberlain, 23 Mar. 1926, with Craigie (FO American Department) minute, 9 Apr. 1926, both FO 371/11173/1870/44; and Howard despatch to Chamberlain, 28 May 1926, with Vansittart minute, 9 June 1926, both FO 371/11173/3029/44.
81 See Chamberlain to Howard, 12 May 1926, FO 371/11176/2243/88.
82 Except where noted, the following three paragraphs are based on B. J. C. McKercher, 'A British View of American Foreign Policy: The Settlement of Blockade Claims, 1924–1927', *IHR*, 3 (1981), 358–84.
83 Howard despatch to Chamberlain, 20 Mar. 1925, with enclosures, FO 371/10646/1697/1490.
84 See Howard's entries in Anonymous, *The New York Times Index. A Book of Record. 1925*, 2 vols. (New York, 1926); *1926*, 2 vols (1927); and *1927*, vol. 1 (1928).

85 B. J. C. McKercher, 'The British Diplomatic Service in the United States and the Chamberlain Foreign Office's Perception of Domestic America, 1924–1927: Images, Reality, and Diplomacy', in McKercher and Moss, *Shadow and Substance*, pp. 221–48.
86 'British Library of Information. Annual Report. 1926', FO 395/420/284/58.
87 Wilberforce to J. Balfour (2nd secretary, British Embassy, Washington), 1 Dec. 1924; Wilberforce to Howard, 3 Dec. 1924, and Howard to Wilberforce, 8 Dec. 1924, all DHW 5/12.
88 This and the following quotation are from Chilton despatch to Chamberlain, 6 Aug. 1925, FO 371/10651/4134/4057.
89 Howard to Chamberlain, 26 Aug. 1926, FO 371/11198/4989/3895.
90 R. I. Campbell minute, 6 Sept. 1926, Vansittart and Wellesley minutes, both 7 Sept. 1926, and Chamberlain minute, 9 Sept. 1926, all ibid; and Niemayer (Treasury) to Vansittart, 22 Sept. 1926, FO 371/11198/5046/3895.
91 See BLINY despatch to FO, 29 Oct. 1926, FO 371/11198/5924/3895.
92 'The American Debt Settlement', 6 Oct. 1926, *Manchester Guardian*.
93 'Trade Outlook Good Here. Embassy Issues Statement in Direct Contradiction of Harvey Article', 9 Dec. 1925, *Washington Post*.
94 Howard to Noyes, 10 Dec. 1926, with enclosure, DHW 5/14.
95 This and the next sentence are based on Howard despatch to Chamberlain, 4 Mar. 1927, FO 371/12038/1569/128; and Willert to FO American Department, 4 Apr. 1927, enclosing Fletcher to Willert, 24 Mar. 1927, FO 371/12038/2098/128.
96 Kellogg to Herrick (US ambassador, Paris), 3 Feb. 1927 (*mutatis mutandis* to London, Rome, and Tokyo), *FRUS 1927*, vol. 1, pp. 1–5.

10 WASHINGTON *REDUX*: MEETING THE AMERICAN CHALLENGE, 1927–1930

1 See Thayer to Howard, 14 Sept. 1924, Earle to Howard, 16 Nov. 1924, and Washburn to Howard, 8 Dec. 1924, all DHW 9/11.
2 *ToL*, vol. 2, p. 526.
3 Howard to Maud, his sister, 15 Nov. 1926, DHW 9/26.
4 Howard to Maud and Elizabeth, his sisters, both 28 Nov. 1926, both ibid.
5 Howard diary, 22 July 1918, DHW 1/4.
6 Howard to Maud, his sister, 28 Nov. 1926, DHW 9/26.
7 Howard to Maud, his sister, 25 Dec. 1926, ibid.
8 *In Memoriam E.J.H.S.H.* (privately, 1927).
9 See Spooner (New College, Oxford) to Howard, 2 Nov. 1927; and Ramsay (Downside) to Howard, 11 Dec. 1927, both DHW 9/13.
10 Howard despatch to Chamberlain, 11 June 1926, with Vansittart minute, 23 June 1926, and Chamberlain minute, 24 June 1926, all FO 371/11185/3319/179.
11 Wilberforce to Willert, 9 Sept. 1926, FO 371/11185/5050/179.
12 Chilton despatch to Chamberlain, 5 Nov. 1926, FO 371/11185/6070/179.
13 Montgomery (assistant under-secretary) to Craigie, 8 Dec. 1926, with

enclosures, plus R. I. Campbell and Craigie minutes, both 15 Dec. 1926, and Vansittart minute, 24 Dec. 1926, all FO 371/11185/6500/179.
14 Howard despatch to Chamberlain, 27 Jan. 1927, FO 371/12038/795/128.
15 Vansittart minute and Tyrrell initials, both 11 Feb. 1927, ibid.
16 See BLINY despatch to FO, 28 Jan. 1927, FO 371/12038/897/128.
17 Chilton despatch to Chamberlain, 10 Dec. 1926, FO 371/11185/6729/179; and Howard despatch to Chamberlain, 27 Dec. 1926, FO 371/12034/93/93.
18 This paragraph is based on McKercher, *Baldwin Government*, pp. 62–5.
19 Chilton despatch to Chamberlain, 29 Oct. 1926, enclosing Chilton *aide-mémoire*, 26 Oct. 1926, FO 371/11173/5838/44.
20 Howard despatch to Chamberlain, 10 Mar. 1927, with Chamberlain initials, 28 Mar. 1927, both FO 371/12015/1712/27.
21 Howard despatch to Chamberlain, 21 Jan. 1927, FO 371/12052/673/673.
22 On Foreign Office support, see Vansittart minute, 4 Feb. 1927, Chamberlain initials, 5 Feb. 1927, and Vansittart to Howard, 17 Feb. 1927, all ibid. On his trip, see Howard despatch to Chamberlain, 3 June 1927, enclosing Howard 'Journey to the Pacific Coast', n.d., FO 371/12052/3485/673. Cf. *ToL*, vol. 2, pp. 547–58.
23 On the Coolidge conference, see D. Carlton, 'Great Britain and the Coolidge Naval Conference of 1927', *PSQ*, 83 (1968), 573–98; L. E. Ellis, *Frank B. Kellogg and American Foreign Relations, 1925–1929* (New Brunswick, NJ, 1961), pp. 164–84; McKercher, *Baldwin Government*, pp. 55–74; and Roskill, *Naval Policy*, vol. 1, pp. 498–516.
24 Watt. *Succeeding John Bull*, p. 58.
25 McKercher, 'Images, Reality, and Diplomacy', p. 234.
26 F. C. Costigliola, 'The Other Side of Isolationism: The Establishment of the First World Bank', *JAH*, 59 (1972), 602–20; and 'Anglo-American Financial Rivalry in the 1920s', *JEH*, 37 (1977), 911–34; and M. Leffler, *The Elusive Quest: America's Pursuit of European Stability and French Security* (Chapel Hill, 1979).
27 Steward memorandum, 15 Aug. 1927, FO 395/422/862/256.
28 Yencken (FO News Department) minute, 12 July 1927, FO 395/421/699/256.
29 Howard telegram (293) to Chamberlain, 27 June 1927, *DBFP*, *1A*, vol. 3, pp. 619–20.
30 Howard telegram (283) to Chamberlain, 23 June 1927, ibid., p. 613.
31 For Howard's success in explaining policy to Kellogg, see Howard telegram (322) to Chamberlain, 6 July 1927, ibid., pp. 641–2. For the State Department press release, see 'Lauds Geneva News in American Press', 27 July 1927, *NY Times*.
32 Howard to Chamberlain, 21 July 1927, Chamberlain MSS, FO 800/261.
33 Chilton telegram (unnumbered) to Chamberlain, 29 July 1927, *DBFP*, *1A*, vol. 3, p. 706.
34 See Bridgeman telegrams (228 and 232), both 4 Aug. 1927, both ibid., pp. 725–6. Cf. Cmd 2964.
35 Howard to Chamberlain, 23 June 1927, Chamberlain MSS, FO 800/261.

36 This was not lost on some Americans. The editor of the *NY Times* reminded his Geneva correspondent that 'he was reporting a disarmament conference not a battlefield'; see Watt, *Succeeding John Bull*, pp. 58–9.
37 This is seen in Howard to Chamberlain, 23 June 1927, Chamberlain MSS, FO 800/261. This is a different letter from that cited in note 35, above.
38 Howard to Chamberlain, 1 Sept. 1927, ibid.
39 The rest of this paragraph and the next are based on Howard to Chamberlain, 29 July 1927, ibid.
40 Chamberlain to Howard, 10 Aug. 1927, ibid.
41 Howard to Chamberlain, 1 Sept. 1927, ibid.
42 Cf. 'After the Disarmament Failure', *Literary Digest*, 99 (Sept. 1927), 18–19; E. F. Baldwin and K. K. Kawakami, 'What Happened at Geneva', *Outlook*, 146 (Aug. 1927), 535–7; J. Carter, 'American Correspondents and British Delegates: Some Reasons for the Failure at Geneva', *Independent*, 119 (Aug. 1927), 150–2; and J. T. Gerould, 'Failure of the 3 Power Naval Conference', *Current History*, 26 (Sept. 1927).
43 Howard despatch (1549) to Chamberlain, 12 Aug. 1927, FO 371/12040/4935/133.
44 See McKercher, *Baldwin Government*, p. 76, fn. 80.
45 Howard despatch to Chamberlain, 5 Aug. 1927, FO 371/12039/4793/128. Cf. J. L. Blair, 'I Do Not Choose to Run for President in Nineteen Twenty-Eight', *VH*, 30 (1962); and B. D. Rhodes, 'British Diplomacy and the Silent Oracle of Vermont, 1923–1929', *VH*, 50 (1982).
46 Howard telegram (382) to FO, 11 Aug. 1927, FO 371/12035/4731/93; and Howard despatch to Chamberlain, 18 Aug. 1927, FO 371/12035/5073/93.
47 See Howard despatch cited in note immediately above; plus Craigie minute, 1 Sept. 1927, ibid.; and Thompson (FO American Department) minute, 10 Sept. 1927, and Craigie minute, 12 Sept. 1927, both FO 371/12035/5309/93.
48 Howard (2) to Chamberlain, both 23 June 1927, Chamberlain MSS, FO 800/261.
49 Howard to Chamberlain, 13 July 1927, and Chamberlain to Howard, 10 Aug. 1927, both ibid.
50 See McKercher, *Baldwin Government*, p. 87, fn. 50.
51 For instance, Howard despatch to Chamberlain, 13 Oct. 1927, FO 371/12035/6205/93.
52 See Cecil to Chamberlain, 10 Aug. 1927, Cecil Papers, BL Add. MSS 51079; Hankey memorandum, 30 Aug. 1927, CAB 21/297; and Cecil to Baldwin, and Baldwin to Cecil, both in *The Times*, 30 Aug. 1927.
53 Baldwin's speech at 'The International Peace Bridge', 7 Aug. 1927, in S. Baldwin, *Our Inheritance. Speeches and Addresses* (London, 1928), pp. 153–4; and Vansittart minute, 12 Sept. 1927, FO 371/12035/5309/93.
54 For instance, BLINY memorandum on 'Anti-British Propaganda in the United States', 7 Oct. 1927, FO 395/420/1054/75.
55 Howard despatch to Chamberlain, 30 Sept. 1927, FO 371/12035/5931/93; and BLINY despatch to FO, 23 Sept. 1927, FO 371/12035/5846/93.
56 Howard to Tyrrell, 15 Sept. 1927, FO 371/12040/5846/93.
57 Howard to Tyrrell, 22 Sept. 1927, ibid.
58 The rest of this paragraph is based on ibid. and Howard to Tyrrell, 12 Oct. 1927, FO 371/12040/6213/133.

59 Craigie memorandum, 24 Aug. 1927, FO 371/12040/5042/133; and Chamberlain minute, 25 Aug. 1927, FO 371/12040/4935/133.
60 For example, J. T. Gerould, 'Britain's Opposition to the Freedom of the Seas', *Current History*, 27 (Oct. 1927), 112–15.
61 McKercher, *Baldwin Government*, pp. 88–91.
62 Chamberlain memorandum on 'Belligerent Rights at Sea and the Relations between the United States and Great Britain', 26 Oct. 1927, with enclosures, CP 258(27), CAB 24/189.
63 McKercher, *Baldwin Government*, pp. 98–100.
64 Howard telegram (472) to FO, 5 Nov. 1927, FO 371/12035/6445/93.
65 Howard telegram (477) to FO, 7 Nov. 1927, FO 371/12035/6504/93.
66 Bridgeman speech, 16 Nov. 1927, H of C Debs., vol. 210, col. 1013.
67 Cecil speech, 16 Nov. 1927, H of L Debs., vol. 69, cols. 84–94.
68 Howard telegram (488) to FO, 21 Nov. 1927, FO 371/12035/6776/93.
69 Howard despatch to Chamberlain, 18 Nov. 1927, FO 371/12036/6894/93.
70 For example, see Howard to Tyrrell, 26 Oct. 1927, *DBFP*, 1A, vol. 4, pp. 412–14.
71 'Sir Esme Howard Sees Peace Threat. Anti-British Agitation Bears Elements of New War Ambassador Says', 22 Nov. 1927, *NY Times*.
72 Howard despatch to Chamberlain, 18 Nov. 1927, FO 371/12041/6974/133; and Howard despatch to Chamberlain, 23 Nov. 1927, FO 371/12041/7070/133.
73 Howard despatch to Chamberlain, 16 Dec. 1927, FO 371/12058/7559/3827.
74 For instance, 'Battle Pageantry Inaugurates Saratoga State Park...British Ambassador's Message', 9 Oct. 1927, *NY Times*.
75 Howard telegram (506) to FO, 2 Dec. 1927, FO 371/12025/7000/25; FO telegram (514) to Howard, 8 Dec. 1927, FO 371/12025/7104/25; and FO telegram (519) to Howard, 14 Dec. 1927, FO 371/12025/7155/25.
76 Except where noted, the following two paragraphs are based on Howard to Tyrrell, 10 Nov. 1927, FO 371/12041/6746/133.
77 See Howard to Craigie, 14 Sept. 1927, FO 371/12039/5583/128.
78 Cabinet Conclusion 57(27)7, CAB 23/55.
79 Chilton to Howard, 27 Jan. 1928, DHW 4/Official/23. Until this time, Howard had been pressing for an examination; see Howard to Tyrrell, 10 Nov. 1927, FO 371/12041/6746/133; Howard to Tyrrell, 16 Dec. 1927, FO 371/12822/133/133; Howard to Tyrrell, 29 Dec. 1927, with various minutes, FO 371/12822/228/133; and Howard to Vansittart, 20 Jan. 1928, FO 371/12822/782/133.
80 For instance, Kellogg to Howard, 13 June 1927, Kellogg MSS, Reel 26.
81 Willingdon to Howard, 25 July 1927; and Howard to Willingdon, 30 July 1927, both DHW 9/57.
82 Chamberlain telegram (unnumbered) to Baldwin, 30 July 1927, with various minutes, FO 371/12059/4502/4021.
83 Howard despatch to Chamberlain, 11 Aug. 1927, with Craigie minute, 24 Aug. 1927, and Chamberlain initials, all FO 371/12059/4928/4021. Cf. Mackenzie King diary, 7 Aug. 1927, PAC MG 26 J13 1927; and Chamberlain to Howard, 22 Aug. 1927, DHW 9/51.
84 Howard to Chamberlain, 9 Mar. 1928, DHW 9/59.
85 For instance, in 1927, Howard wanted to make a speech on the naval

question but the Foreign Office refused permission; see Howard telegram (527) to FO, 16 Dec. 1927, with Vansittart and Chamberlain minutes, both 20 Dec. 1927, and Chamberlain telegram (529) to Howard, 21 Dec. 1927, all FO 371/12036/7267/93. Cf. Howard to Lindley (British Legation, Oslo), 12 Feb. 1928, DHW 9/59.
86 On Canadian–American exchanges, Howard despatch to Chamberlain, 13 Sept. 1927, with enclosures, FO 371/12061/5628/5628; on the bullion matter, Howard to Vansittart, 10 Dec. 1927, DHW 9/58; and on the Egyptian minister, Howard to Tyrrell, 17 May 1928, DHW 9/59.
87 Howard despatch to Chamberlain, 30 Sept. 1927, FO 371/12035/5931/93. Also see BLINY memorandum (on anti-British propaganda in the USA), 7 Oct. 1927, FO 395/420/1054/75.
88 The rest of this paragraph is based on McKercher, *Baldwin Government*, pp. 104–5.
89 Howard despatch to Chamberlain, 23 Nov. 1927, FO 371/12041/7070/133; Howard despatch to Chamberlain, 25 Nov. 1927, FO 371/12041/7083/133; and Howard despatch to Chamberlain, 2 Dec. 1927, FO 371/12041/7216/133.
90 Howard despatch to Chamberlain, 9 Nov. 1927, with Craigie and Vansittart minutes, both 25 Nov. 1927, and Chamberlain minute, 28 Nov. 1927, all FO 371/12058/6759/3827.
91 Howard to Chamberlain, 2 Feb. 1928, DHW 9/58; and Chamberlain to Howard, 13/14 Feb. 1928, and Howard to Chamberlain, 9 Mar. 1928, both DHW 9/59.
92 By May 1928, Kellogg had been designated to draft the foreign-policy plank for the Republican Party's 1928 campaign; see White (Republican National Committee) to Kellogg, 9 May 1928, Kellogg MSS, Reel 32. The renunciatory pact became integral to the Republican campaign; see Chilton despatch to Cushendun (acting foreign secretary), 13 Sept. 1928, FO 371/12800/6697/1.
93 Cecil was prominent; see Howard telegram to FO, 16 Mar. 1928, with Craigie minute and press cuttings, and Chamberlain initials, 20 Mar. 1928, all FO 371/12790/1879/1.
94 Howard to Chamberlain, 2 Feb. 1928, DHW 9/58; and Howard to Chamberlain, 9 Mar. 1928, DHW 9/59.
95 For instance, on Peruvian problems, Howard telegram to FO 15 Nov. 1927, FO 371/12061/6675/6597; on naval matters, Howard telegram (535) to FO, 29 Dec. 1927, FO 371/12036/7523/93; on the proposed Anglo-American arbitration treaty, Howard telegram (89) to FO, 7 Mar. 1928, FO 371/12824/1681/154.
96 Kellogg to Howard, 5 Oct. 1927, and Kellogg to his wife, 5 Oct. 1927, both Kellogg MSS, Reel 28. On the private dinners: interview with Lord Howard of Penrith and his brother, the Hon. Edmund Howard, 13 July 1984.
97 For example, Howard telegram (17) to Chamberlain, 12 Jan. 1928, FO 371/12789/290/1; and Howard despatch to Chamberlain, 2 Mar. 1928, FO 371/12790/1774/1.
98 F. B. Kellogg, 'The War Prevention Policy of the United States', *FA Special Supplement*, 6 (1928), i–xi.
99 Tyrrell minute (on a conversation with US ambassador, London), 13 Apr. 1928, with minutes, FO 371/12790/2542/1.

100 Howard telegram (115) to FO, 3 Apr. 1928, with Craigie minute, 4 Apr. 1928, FO 371/12790/2355/1; and Howard telegram (127) to FO, 22 Apr. 1928, with Hurst (FO legal adviser) minute, 24 Apr. 1928, FO 371/12790/2730/1.
101 See Ellis, *Kellogg and American Foreign Relations*, pp. 205–6; and R. H. Ferrell, *Peace in their Time. The Origins of the Kellogg–Briand Pact* (New Haven, 1952), pp. 173–6. Cf. BLINY despatch to FO, 20 Apr. 1928, FO 371/12791/2903/1.
102 Howard to Chamberlain, 2 Feb. 1928, DHW 9/58.
103 McKercher, *Baldwin Government*, pp. 113–27.
104 The Japanese were going to reserve their right to intervene in Manchuria; see Dormer (chargé, Tokyo) telegram (106) to FO, 23 May 1928, with minutes, FO 371/12792/3516/1.
105 McKercher, *Baldwin Government*, p. 112.
106 Howard to Hardinge, 30 June 1908, DHW 2/11; and Mackenzie King to Howard, 3 Dec. 1908, DHW 4/Official/15.
107 Howard to Mackenzie King, 7 May 1926, King MSS, PAC MG 26 J1/132; and Mackenzie King diary, 1 May 1926, ibid., J13 1926.
108 Howard despatch to MacDonald, 4 July 1924, FO 371/9633/4531/3673; Wrong (University of Toronto) to Howard, 14 June and 25 July 1924, and Howard to Crowe, 31 July 1924, all DHW 9/42; and Howard to Chamberlain, 11 May 1926, Chamberlain MSS, FO 800/258. Also Cockburn (Bank of Montreal) to Howard, 28 June and 26 Aug. 1926, both DHW 9/56.
109 Howard 'Address to the British Club at Providence', 17 Sept. 1924, DHW 5/20.
110 'What you say about the position of the so-called Canadian companies established in Canada though really financed by United States capitalists and operated by parent companies in the United States is interesting. It would be well worth looking into but I doubt whether the present Government or any Canadian Government would care to touch this rather prickly subject.'; in Howard to Armstrong (British consul-general, NY), 25 Jan. 1925, DHW 5/13.
111 Howard to Crowe, 4 June 1924, with enclosures, Crowe to Howard, 26 June 1924, and Howard to Mackenzie King, 13 July 1924, all DHW 5/15.
112 Mackenzie King diary, 30 Apr. 1926, King MSS, PAC MG 26 J13 1926.
113 Ibid., 1 May 1926.
114 Mackenzie King diary, 4 Aug. 1927, King MSS, PAC MG 26 J13 1927.
115 On anti-Dominions Office feelings, see ibid., 5 July 1927: 'We will yet get the Dominions Office out of the Br. cabinet circle – It is a fifth wheel to the coach and save as a post office is wholly unnecessary.' On the 1926 constitutional crisis, see W. L. Morton, *The Kingdom of Canada. A General History from Earliest Times* (Toronto, 1963), pp. 450–3.
116 H. D. Hall, 'The Genesis of the Balfour Declaration of 1926', *JCPS*, 1 (1963), 169–93; A. Toynbee (for the Royal Institute of International Affairs), *The Conduct of British Empire Foreign Relations since the Peace Settlement* (London, 1928), pp. 72–110; and P. G. Wrigley, *Canada and the Transition to Commonwealth. British–Canadian Relations 1917–1926* (Cambridge, 1977), pp. 248–77.

117 McKercher, *Baldwin Government*, p. 168; and Toynbee, *Empire Foreign Relations*, pp. 64–7.
118 Howard to Chamberlain, 18 Nov. 1926, FO 371/11193/6099/977; Howard telegram (56) to FO, 25 Jan. 1927, FO 371/12020/560/14; Howard despatch to Chamberlain, 18 Feb. 1927, FO 371/12020/1305/14; and Massey to Tyrrell, 24 Mar. 1927, FO 371/12020/2704/14.
119 N. Hillmer, 'A British High Commissioner for Canada, 1927–28', *JICH*, 1 (1979), 339–56.
120 Chamberlain telegram (unnumbered) to Howard, 13 Oct. 1927, and Howard telegram (unnumbered) to Chamberlain, 14 Oct. 1927, both FO 371/12021/6056/14; and Chamberlain to Stamfordham (the king's private secretary), 17 Oct. 1927, Chamberlain MSS, FO 800/261.
121 For instance, Amery to Chamberlain, 15 Aug. 1927, and Chamberlain to Baldwin, 2 Nov. 1927, both PREM 1/65.
122 Hillmer, 'British High Commissioner' is, thus, wide of the mark by stating that Clark's appointment 'represented almost total victory for Amery'. He is also factually in error by saying that Clark was appointed in April 1928; see Clark to Baldwin, 26 Mar. 1928, PREM 1/65.
123 For instance, Howard to Vansittart, 6 Dec. 1927, DHW 9/58; Howard to Tyrrell, 4 Apr. 1928, DHW 9/59; and Howard to Stamfordham, 11 July and 10 Aug. 1928, both DHW 9/60.
124 See Foreign Office, *Foreign Office List, 1930*, pp. 477–87.
125 For example, Vansittart to Howard, 15 Dec. 1926 and 27 June 1927, both DHW 5/33; Tyrrell to Howard, 21 June 1927, DHW 5/9; and Tyrrell to Howard, 5 May 1928, DHW 4/Personal/13.
126 Mackenzie King diary, 4 Aug. 1927, King MSS, PAC MG 26 J13 1927.
127 Lascelles (the prince's private secretary) to Howard, 23 Sept. 1924; Howard telegrams (both unnumbered) to Prince of Wales, both 29 Sept. 1924; Howard to the King, 30 Oct. 1924, all DHW 9/55; and Stamfordham to Howard, 15 Oct., 17 Nov., and 18 Nov. 1924, and Howard to Stamfordham, 28 Oct. 1924, all DHW 9/44.
128 Mackenzie King diary, 5 Aug. 1927, King MSS, PAC MG 26 J13 1927.
129 Tyrrell to Howard, 5 Mar. 1928, DHW 4/Personal/13.
130 Jones diary, 5 Dec. 1928, in K. Middlemas, ed., *Thomas Jones: Whitehall Diary*, vol. 2: *1926–1930* (London, New York and Toronto, 1969), pp. 159–60.
131 Howard had met Steed in his Budapest days. Hankey diary, 12 and 13 Dec. 1927, HNKY 1/8; and Hankey to Esher (Conservative peer), 17 Dec. 1927, HNKY 4/19.
132 On the absence of a conspiracy, see the record of a conversation with Chamberlain in Casey (Australian liaison officer, London) to Bruce (Australian prime minister), 22 Dec. 1927, in W. J. Hudson and J. North, eds., *My Dear P.M. R. G. Casey's Letters to S. M. Bruce, 1924–1929* (Canberra, 1980), pp. 227–31. This shows that the Foreign Office had formed its view of the American problem independently of Wickham Steed and that Chamberlain, unwilling to be rushed by the Foreign Office, saw Wickham Steed's efforts in the United States as planting seeds in ground already ploughed by Howard. On Hankey complaining privately, see Hankey to Richmond (principal, Imperial Defence College), 5 Nov. 1927, CAB 21/307; and Hankey to Richmond, 25 Jan. 1928, returning papers sent by Richmond.

Notes to pages 330–334

especially 'Comments on Sir E. Howard's letter of 29.12.27', Richmond MSS, RIC 7/3d.
133 Hankey 'A Rejoinder to Sir Esme Howard', 26 Jan. 1928 (BR 15), CAB 16/79.
134 BR 2nd Meeting, 6 Feb. 1928, CAB 16/79.
135 Chamberlain telegram (64) to Cushendun (minister responsible for disarmament) and the Cabinet, 7 June 1928, *DBFP 1A*, vol. 5, pp. 683–4; Chamberlain memorandum, 10 Mar. 1928 (CP 81(28)), CAB 24/193; and PRA Meeting 27(6), Appendices I and II, CAB 27/361.
136 The rest of this paragraph is based on Cmd 3211; D. Carlton, 'The Anglo-French Compromise on Arms Limitation, 1928', *JBS*, 8 (1969), 141–62; McKercher, *Baldwin Government*, pp. 140–9; and A. Toynbee et al., *Survey of International Affairs 1928* (London, 1929), pp. 61–81.
137 For instance, Chilton despatch to Cushendun (acting foreign secretary) 30 Aug. 1928, FO 371/12811/6395/39.
138 Howard despatch to Cushendun, 9 Nov. 1928, FO 371/12812/7952/39.
139 Thompson minute, 29 Oct. 1928, FO 371/12812/7450/12.
140 Howard despatch to Cushendun, 16 Nov. 1928, FO 371/12812/8126/39.
141 Howard telegram (366) to FO, 1 Dec. 1928, FO 371/12823/8232/133. Cf. Wilberforce to Willert, 30 Nov. 1928, FO 371/12810/8464/36; and Craigie memorandum on 'Limitation of Naval Armament. Timetable of impending political events in the United States', 27 Nov. 1928, FO 371/12913/8248/39.
142 Howard telegram (74) to FO, 23 Feb. 1928, FO 371/12822/1302/133; and Howard despatch (726) to Chamberlain, 4 Apr. 1928 (BR 32), CAB 16/79.
143 Howard telegram (329) to FO, 15 Nov. 1928, FO 371/12823/7862/133.
144 Office of the President, *Address of President Coolidge at the Observance of the 10th Anniversary of the Armistice, under the Auspices of the American Legion* (Washington, 1928). Cf. Howard despatch to Cushendun, 16 Nov. 1928, FO 371/12812/8128/39.
145 On the earlier favourable assessment of Coolidge, see Howard telegram (81) to FO, 29 Mar. 1926, and R. I. Campbell minute, 30 Mar. 1926, both FO 371/11162/1757/6.
146 Howard to Chamberlain, 23 Mar. 1928, Chamberlain MSS, FO 800/262.
147 Chamberlain despatch to Howard, 5 Apr. 1928, FO 371/12823/2280/133.
148 Howard telegram (121) to FO, 19 Apr. 1928, Howard telegram (122) to FO, 19 Apr. 1928, and Howard telegram to FO, 20 Apr. 1928, all (BR 32), CAB 16/79; plus Craigie memorandum on 'Conversations at Washington Respecting Belligerent Rights', 8 June 1928 (BR 37), and Craigie memorandum on 'Conversations at Washington during April between Sir Esme Howard, Sir John Broderick, and Mr Craigie', 1 June 1928 (BR 38), both ibid.
149 See note 146, above.
150 Howard despatch to Chamberlain, 25 Apr. 1928 (BR 34), CAB 16/79.
151 BR 4th Meeting, 27 July 1928, ibid. Also see Craigie minute, 25 July 1928, FO 371/12823/5183/133.

152 Howard to Chamberlain, 28 July 1928, and Howard to Craigie, 2 Aug. 1928, both FO 371/12823/5809/133.
153 Craigie to Howard, 2 Sept. 1928, DHW 5/9; and Howard to Craigie, 19 Sept. 1928, FO 371/12823/6652/133.
154 FO telegram (389) to Howard, 21 Nov. 1928, FO 371/12823/7862/133.
155 Howard to Chamberlain, 30 Nov. 1928, FO 371/12823/8765/133.
156 Howard to Vansittart, 29 Nov. 1928, ibid.
157 Lindsay to Vansittart, 10 Dec. 1928, Chamberlain to Lindsay, 11 Dec. 1928, Chamberlain minute, 17 Dec. 1928, all ibid.; and Chamberlain to Howard, 18 Dec. 1928, Chamberlain MSS, FO 800/263.
158 McKercher, *Baldwin Government*, pp. 178–9.
159 The rest of this paragraph is based on ibid., pp. 171–99; and B. J. C. McKercher, 'Belligerent Rights in 1927–1929: Foreign Policy Versus Naval Policy in the Second Baldwin Government', *HJ*, 24 (1986), 963–74.
160 Howard to Bridgeman, 8 Mar. 1929, DHW 9/61.
161 Except where noted, the rest of this paragraph is based on Steward (FO News Department) minute to Craigie, 15 Feb. 1929, with minutes and FO telegram (118) to Howard, 15 Feb. 1929, all FO 371/13518/1170/30; Howard telegram (94) to FO, 15 Feb. 1929, and FO telegram (120) to Howard, FO 371/13518/1171/30; and Willert and Chamberlain minutes, both 19 Feb. 1929, FO 371/13518/1187/30.
162 This is from the Associated Press telegram quoting Howard's words; see King (Associated Press) to Willert, 18 Feb. 1929, with enclosures, ibid.
163 Howard despatch to Chamberlain, 28 Feb. 1929, FO 371/13510/1799/12.
164 Howard despatch to Chamberlain, 11 Jan. 1929, enclosing F. Simonds, 'Anglo-American Clash is Considered Possible. Trouble over embargo is foreseen should Britain go to war with European nation', 23 Dec. 1928, FO 371/13510/474/12; and Fletcher to Willert, with enclosures, 18 Jan. 1929, FO 371/13510/736/12.
165 Howard despatch to Chamberlain, 8 Feb. 1929, with Thompson and Craigie minutes, both 22 Feb. 1929, all FO 371/13519/1249/30. Cf. Howard despatch to Chamberlain, 24 Jan. 1929, with Craigie minute, 8 Feb. 1929, and Chamberlain minute, 9 Feb. 1929, all FO 371/13518/846/30.
166 See the various despatches, private letters, and telegrams from Howard to Chamberlain and the Foreign Office circulated to the belligerent-rights sub-committee: documents BR 67 (30 Jan. 1929), BR 75 (25 Jan. 1929), BR 79 (1 Feb. 1929), BR 80 (9 Feb. 1929), BR 83 (31 Jan. 1929), and BR 94 (8 Feb. 1929), all CAB 16/79.
167 On the December speech, see Coolidge speech, 3 Dec. 1928, *FRUS 1929*, vol. 1, pp. v–xxx; Howard telegrams (359 and 360), 28 Nov. 1928, FO 371/12813/8182/39; and Dodds (British Legation Stockholm) to Cushendun, 23 Nov. 1928, FO 371/12812/8146/39. On the February speech, see Office of the President, *Address of President Coolidge...22 February 1929* (Washington, 1929); and Howard despatch to Chamberlain, 1 Mar. 1929, FO 371/13510/1802/12.
168 Howard to Chamberlain, 25 Jan. 1929, Chamberlain MSS, FO 800/263.
169 Howard to Vansittart, 24 Jan. 1929, DHW 9/61.
170 Ibid.
171 Howard to Vansittart, 8 Feb. 1929, ibid.

Notes to pages 339–343   433

172 Howard's request is missing from the Foreign Office Archives, but it can be seen in Chamberlain telegram (103) to Howard, 7 Feb. 1929, with the footnote, in *DBFP 1A*, vol. 6, pp. 642–3.
173 Howard telegram (91) to FO, 11 Feb. 1929, with Lindsay minute, 12 Feb. 1929, and Chamberlain minute, 13 Feb. 1929, all FO 371/13541/1040/279.
174 For instance, Chamberlain telegram (103) to Howard, 7 Feb. 1929, FO 371/13541/1142/279; FO telegram (121) to Howard, 16 Feb. 1929, FO 371/13541/1208/279; and FO telegram (132) to Howard, 22 Feb. 1929, FO 371/13541/1227/279.
175 Howard telegram (143) to FO, 17 Mar. 1929, FO 371/13541/1932/279.
176 Craigie minute, 19 Mar. 1929, and Lindsay minute, 20 Mar. 1929, both ibid.
177 Cf. Jones diary, 1 Nov. 1928, Middlemas, *Whitehall Diary*, vol. 2, p. 155.
178 Howard to Vansittart, 24 Jan. 1929, and Howard to Chamberlain, 25 Jan. 1929, both DHW 9/61.
179 K. Middlemas and J. Barnes, *Baldwin. A Biography* (London, 1969), pp. 136–48.
180 Chamberlain minute, 13 Feb. 1929, FO 371/13541/1040/1864.
181 Vansittart to Howard, 9 Apr. 1929, DHW 9/61.
182 For instance, Howard to Chamberlain, 3 Apr. 1929, FO 371/13541/2634/279.
183 The rest of this paragraph is based on McKercher, *Baldwin Government*, pp. 186–94; and McKercher, 'Belligerent Rights'.
184 Howard telegram (128) to Chamberlain, 8 Mar. 1929, DHW 9/61.
185 Howard telegram (140) to FO, 13 Mar. 1929, FO 371/13548/1864/1864.
186 See Craigie minute, 19 Mar. 1929, ibid.; and Craigie minute, 5 Apr. 1929, FO 371/13548/2429/1864.
187 See the correspondence in DHW 4/Personal/10.
188 For instance, see Fletcher to Willert, 4 May 1928, with enclosures and Chamberlain minute, 21 May 1928, both FO 371/12792/3266/1.
189 D. Marquand, *Ramsay MacDonald* (London, 1977), pp. 467–9; MacDonald to Henderson (Labour Party National Executive), 20 Sept. 1927, MacDonald MSS, PRO 30/69/5/38; and *H of C Debates*, vol. 210, cols. 2089–98. On congratulations from a prominent American, see Borah to MacDonald, 5 June 1928, and MacDonald to Borah, 15 June 1928, both MacDonald MSS, PRO 30/69/5/39.
190 See Craigie memorandum on the 'Question of an Agreement with the United States in Regard to Maritime Belligerent Rights', the 'Question of the Conclusion of an Anglo-American Arbitration Treaty', and '...the Naval Disarmament Question', all 10 June 1929, all MacDonald MSS, PRO 30/69/1/267. Cf. Hankey diary, 18 Oct. 1929, in S. Roskill, *Man of Secrets*, vol. 2: *1919–1931* (London, 1972) p. 458, which summarises Hankey's efforts.
191 Howard to MacDonald, 6 June 1929, DHW 9/62.
192 For instance, see MacDonald's defence of the Foreign Office against Labour Party critics: MacDonald to Woolf, 9 Mar. 1926, MacDonald MSS, PRO 30/69/5/37; and MacDonald to Greenwood, 4 Mar. 1928, ibid., PRO 30/69/5/132.
193 Henderson despatch to Howard, 24 June 1929, *DBFP 2*, vol. 1, pp. 8–10.

194 Howard telegram (128) to Chamberlain, 8 Mar. 1929, DHW 9/61; and Craigie memorandum, 27 June 1929, *DBFP 2*, vol. 1, pp. 15–16.
195 The rest of this paragraph is based on D. Carlton, *MacDonald versus Henderson. The Foreign Policy of the Second Labour Government* (London, 1970), pp. 100–13; McKercher, *Baldwin Government*, pp. 195–9; R. G. O'Connor, *Perilous Equilibrium: The United States and the London Naval Conference 1930* (Kansas, 1962); and Roskill, *Naval Policy*, vol. 2, pp. 21–44.
196 For instance, Howard telegram (328) to FO, 25 July 1929, *DBFP 2*, vol. 1, pp. 30–1.
197 Howard to Craigie, 5 July 1929, DHW 9/63.
198 'Diplomatic Liquor. Sir E. Howard's Statement', 27 May 1929, *The Times*.
199 'Diplomatic Liquor. Mr Stimson's Statement', 7 June 1929, ibid.
200 Howard to Henderson, 13 June 1929, DHW 9/63. Actually, the Embassy was to blame in a way. The family cook Isa Howard brought to Washington was Italian and had family in New York involved in bootlegging. This cook sold empty wine and liquor bottles of no use to the Embassy to his family and they, in turn, filled them up with their own concoctions and sold them on the black market. Of course, the bond seal indicating these bottles were the property of the British government added to their appeal and the profits of the bootleggers. Howard and his staff knew nothing of this at the time. Years later the cook, on his death bed, confessed his part in this imbroglio to Howard's son, Hubert. From an interview with Lord Howard of Penrith and his brother, the Hon. Edmund Howard, 13 July 1984.
201 MacDonald to Howard, 17 June 1929, DHW 9/63. This proves barren the claim in Carlton, *MacDonald versus Henderson*, p. 22 that Howard appeared to have no value in Washington and London at this time and 'played no decisive part in the naval disarmament discussion which dominated Anglo-American relations during the first year of the Labour Government's tenure in office'.
202 Howard to MacDonald, 12 July 1929, DHW 9/63.
203 *H of C Debs.*, vol. 130, cols. 1304–7. Cf. Marquand, *MacDonald*, pp. 503–4.
204 MacDonald to Howard, 26 July 1929, DHW 9/63.
205 Howard to MacDonald, 22 and 23 Aug. 1929, ibid.
206 This can be followed in Howard to MacDonald, 30 Aug. 1929, ibid.
207 Ibid.
208 Roskill, *Naval Policy*, vol. 2, pp. 43–4.
209 Except where noted, the rest of this paragraph is based on Carlton, *MacDonald versus Henderson*, pp. 114–18; Marquand, *MacDonald*, pp. 506–9; and Roskill, *Naval Policy*, vol. 2, pp. 45–8.
210 Howard to Vansittart, 24 Sept. 1929, in Middlemas, *Whitehall Diary*, vol. 2, p. 211.
211 Quoted in Marquand, *MacDonald*, p. 508.
212 See *NY Times*, 14 Oct. 1928.
213 Chamberlain to Howard, 3 Jan. 1929, DHW 9/61. Cf. *NY Times*, 10 Jan. 1929.
214 Howard to MacDonald, 6 June 1929, Howard to Henderson, 13 June 1929, and Henderson to Howard, 24 June 1929, all DHW 9/62.
215 For instance, Howard to Henderson, 2 July and 27 July 1929, and Howard

to Lindsay, 16 Aug. 1929, all DHW 9/62; and Howard to Lindsay, 7 Dec. 1929, DHW 9/63.
216 For the financial and other records of Louis d'Or, see DHW 1/13, DHW 2/5, and DHW 9/22.
217 For instance, the correspondence in DHW 9/17. For an example of a laudatory editorial, see the *NY Times*, 2 Feb. 1930.
218 'Sir Esme Howard's Retirement. Review of Anglo-American Relations', 21 Feb. 1930, *The Times*.

EPILOGUE AND CONCLUSION 'A GREAT AMBASSADOR'

1 *ToL*, vol. 2, pp. 559–61.
2 For instance, see the correspondence between Howard and the Foreign Office between 16 July and 13 Aug. 1926 in Chamberlain MSS, FO 800/259.
3 See Lindsay to Howard, 19 Aug. 1930, DHW 4/Personal/17.
4 MacDonald to Howard, 29 Apr. 1930, DHW 4/Personal/10.
5 Howard to MacDonald, 11 May 1930, ibid.
6 Howard to Burke, 25 June 1930, DHW 4/Personal/31.
7 For instance, Tyrrell to Howard, 29 June 1930, DHW 4/Personal/13; R. I. Campbell (counsellor, British Embassy, Washington), to Howard, 7 July 1930, DHW 4/Personal/14; and Vansittart to Howard, 12 Sept. (1930), DHW 1/35. Cf. Henderson to Howard, 10 Mar. 1930, DHW 9/65.
8 Interview with Lord Howard of Penrith and his brother, the Hon. Edmund Howard, 13 July 1984.
9 *ToL*, vol. 2, pp. 582–608. Also see his diary for this trip in DHW 1/6.
10 Howard to the Editor, 12 Aug. 1936, in *The Times*, 19 Aug. 1936.
11 'Lord Grey's Tribute. Memorial Accepted by the National Trust', 10 Aug. 1932, *The Times*. Cf. the correspondence in DHW 1/47.
12 For example, 'Tree Planting in the Lake District', 20 Aug. 1935, *The Times*.
13 Howard to the Editor ('Capri as a Bird Sanctuary'), 12 Dec. 1932, ibid.
14 Buckmaster to Howard, 23 Sept. 1933, with Howard minute, 27 Sept. 1933, and Buckmaster to Howard, 14 Nov. 1933, all DHW 1/37.
15 'Preservation in the Lake District. Work of the National Trust', 25 Jan. 1936, *The Times*. Cf. the correspondence in DHW 1/53 and 1/54.
16 Howard to Vansittart, 6–9 Nov. 1929, DHW 9/70.
17 This can be seen in Howard to Vansittart, 3 Feb. 1930, DHW 9/64. For an example of Vansittart's consistent desire to deny the United States a free hand in the Caribbean, see Vansittart minute, 23 Mar. 1927, FO 371/12038/2249/128.
18 'Notes of Interdepartmental Meeting on Air Developments in the West Indies and South America held at Air Ministry...20th March, 1930', and a draft of the 'Air Navigation Agreement', plus Thompson (FO American Department) to Howard, 31 Mar. 1930, all DHW 9/70.
19 For instance, see St Johnston (governor, Leeward Islands) to Howard, 1 Mar. 1930, ibid.; and Greig to Howard, 28 Oct. 1930 and 28 May 1933, with Howard minute, 13 June 1933, both DHW 4/Personal/20.
20 Greig to Howard, 24 Feb. 1930, DHW 4/Personal/20; and Greig to Howard, 24 June 1930 and 4 Apr. 1931, both DHW 1/38.

21 Howard diary, 12 Jan. 1919, DHW 1/5; and Howard to Drummond, 13 Jan. 1919, Balfour MSS, FO 800/215.
22 T. E. Hachey, ed., *Anglo-Vatican Relations, 1914–1939: Confidential Annual Reports of the British Ministers to the Holy See* (London, 1972), p. xvi.
23 Howard to Kerr, 9 Nov. 1919, and Howard to Curzon, 5 Dec. 1919, both DHW 9/35/1.
24 Except where noted, this paragraph is based on D. Austin, *Malta and the End of Empire* (London, 1971), pp. 9–13; O. Chadwick, *Britain and the Vatican during the Second World War* (Cambridge, 1986), p. 5; and Hachey, *Anglo-Vatican Relations*, pp. xxxi–xxxii, 182–6, 206–7.
25 'Holy See. Annual Report, 1930', in ibid., p. 184.
26 Lord Howard of Penrith, *Memorandum Regarding the Malta Crisis* (January 1931) (London, 1931).
27 Cmd 3993.
28 Austin, *Malta*, p. 13.
29 Chadwick, *Britain and the Vatican*, pp. 7–13.
30 Howard to Vansittart, 23 June and 10 July 1932, and Vansittart to Howard, 24 June and 4 July 1932, all DHW 9/23/1.
31 Fitzalan to Howard, 28 Apr. and 12 May 1933, with Howard minute, 23 May 1933, and Howard to Fitzalan, 4 May 1933, all DHW 9/23/2.
32 Howard to Fitzalan, 3 and 10 June 1933, both with enclosures, and Fitzalan to Howard, 19 June 1933, with enclosures, all ibid.
33 Howard to Victoria Eugenia, 3 Dec. 1934, enclosing draft of Howard to Pacelli, n.d., and Victoria Eugenia to Howard, 3 Dec. 1934, DHW 9/23/3.
34 Ingram (FO) to Howard, 4 Aug. 1938, with Howard minute, 6 Aug. 1938, DHW 9/23/4.
35 Vansittart to Halifax, 14 Feb. 1939, in Chadwick, *Britain and the Vatican*, p. 36.
36 Howard of Penrith, *The Prevention of War by Collective Action* (issued by the Friends of Europe) (London, 1933), p. 1. A copy is retained in DHW 5/123.
37 On Howard's belief that Mussolini wanted 'first a long spell of peace & secondly a real measure of disarmament to enable him to spend all the money required for his social legislation', see Howard to Fitzalan, 10 June 1933, DHW 9/23/2. Cf. his comments in the Lords about sanctions against Italy, reported in 'Plea for Prearranged Action', 24 Oct. 1935, *The Times*.
38 The following two paragraphs are based on Lord Howard of Penrith, *Sanctions: Confidence: Disarmament: Recovery* (London, 1932); Howard, *Prevention of War*, which are publications of two speeches, copies of which are in DHW 5/123; and Howard to the Editor, 19 Nov. 1932 and 14 Nov. 1933, *The Times*. Cf. Howard, 'Law or Chaos?', unpublished MSS, Nov. 1934, DHW 7/5.
39 D. H. Aldcroft, *The Inter-War Economy: Britain, 1919–1939* (London, 1970); N. Branson and M. Heinemann, *Britain in the Nineteen Thirties* (London, 1971); S. Glynn and J. Oxborrow, *Interwar Britain: A Social and Economic History* (London, 1976); and Rhodes James, *British Revolution*, pp. 239–331. Cf. M. Cowling, *The Impact of Hitler: British Politics and British Policy, 1933–1940* (London, 1975).
40 For instance, see A. Goldman, 'Sir Robert Vansittart's Search for Italian Co-operation against Hitler, 1933–1936', *JCH*, 9 (1974), 93–130; E. Haraszti,

Treaty Breakers or 'Realpolitikers'? The Anglo-German Naval Agreement of June 1935 (Boppard/R, 1974); J. C. Robertson, 'The Hoare-Laval Plan', *JCH*, 10 (1975), 433–64; and L. G. Schwoerer, 'Lord Halifax's Visit to Germany, November 1937', *Historian*, 32 (1970), 353–75.

41 R. A. Divine, *The Illusion of Neutrality* (Chicago, 1962), pp. 57–228; D. F. Drummond, *The Passing of American Neutrality, 1937–1941* (Ann Arbor, 1955), pp. 21–82. Cf. W. S. Cole, 'Senator Key Pittman and the American Neutrality Policies, 1933–1940', *Mississippi Valley Historical Review*, 46 (1960), 644–62.
42 Howard, Richmond, Grigg, and Wickham Steed to the Editor, 19 Dec. 1933 and 28 Mar. 1934, *The Times*.
43 Howard to the Editor, 29 Oct. and 8 Nov. 1934, ibid.
44 'Further Protocol Suggested' (speech in the Lords), 21 Feb. 1935; and Howard to the Editor, 3 Jan. and 3 July 1936, all ibid.
45 Howard to the Editor, 21 Apr. 1939, ibid.
46 Howard, *Prevention of War*, p. 1.
47 See the file of letters of condolence to Lady Howard, DHW 3/34.
48 'Lord Howard of Penrith. A Great Ambassador', 2 Aug. 1939; and 'Lord Howard of Penrith', 3 Aug. 1939, both *The Times*.
49 The terms 'Englishman' and 'England', on the one hand, and 'British' and 'Britain', on the other, are not used interchangeably.
50 Cf. C. Aslet, *The Last Country Houses* (New Haven and London, 1982), *passim*; and M. Wiener, *English Culture and the Decline of the Industrial Spirit, 1850–1980* (Cambridge, 1981), *passim*.
51 On British 'social justice', see J. Rose, *The Edwardian Temperament, 1895–1919* (Athens, Ohio, 1986), pp. 16–27. I would like to thank Professor Alan Cassels for his comment about *De Rerum Novarum*; see A. Cassels, 'Afterword: Diplomats in an Age of Alien Ideologies and Bureaucratization', *IHR*, 9 (1987), 612–20, which discusses in part B. J. C. McKercher, '"A Dose of fascismo": Esme Howard in Spain, 1919–1924', in ibid., 555–85.
52 Howard to Hodder Williams (his publisher), 22 Feb. 1935, DHW 1/45.
53 Howard to Elizabeth, his sister, 21 June 1898, DHW 3/10.
54 Howard to Elizabeth, his sister, 21 Dec. 1903, ibid.
55 See D. G. Boadle, 'The Formation of the Foreign Office Economic Relations Section, 1930–1937', *HJ*, 20 (1977), 919–36; and V. Cromwell and Z. S. Steiner, 'Reform and Retrenchment: The Foreign Office between the Wars', in Bullen, *Foreign Office*, pp. 85–107. Cf. C. Barnett, *The Audit of War. The Illusion and Reality of Britain as a Great Nation* (London, 1986), pp. 1–37.
56 For an indication, see B. J. C. McKercher, 'Wealth, Power, and the New International Order: Britain and the American Challenge in the 1920s', *DH*, 12 (1988), 411–41.

Bibliography

I PRIVATE PAPERS

Arthur Balfour	Public Record Office, Kew (FO 800 Series)
Francis Bertie	Public Record Office, Kew (FO 800 Series)
James Bryce	Bodleian Library, Oxford (Bryce Series)
	Public Record Office, Kew (FO 800 Series)
Robert Cecil	British Library, London (BL Add. MSS Series)
	Public Record Office, Kew (FO 800 Series)
Austen Chamberlain	Public Record Office, Kew (FO 800 Series)
Marquess Curzon	Public Record Office, Kew (FO 800 Series)
Foreign Office General	Public Record Office, Kew (FO 800 Series)
Edward Grey	Public Record Office, Kew (FO 800 Series)
Maurice Hankey	Churchill College, Cambridge (HNKY Series)
Charles Hardinge	University Library, Cambridge (Har. MSS)
Esme Howard	Cumbria County Record Office, Carlisle (DHW Series)
Frank Kellogg	Minnesota Historical Society, Minneapolis (Microfilm Series)
Marquess of Lansdowne	Public Record Office, Kew (FO 800 Series)
David Lloyd George	House of Lords Record Office, London (LG Series)
J. Ramsay MacDonald	Public Record Office, Kew (PRO 30 Series)
W. L. Mackenzie King	Public Archives of Canada, Ottawa (MG 26 Series)
Arthur Nicolson	Public Record Office, Kew (FO 800 Series)
15th Duke of Norfolk	Arundel Castle
Ralph Paget	British Library, London (BL Add. MSS Series)
Herbert Richmond	National Maritime Museum, Greenwich (RIC Series)
William Robertson	Kings College, London (Robertson MSS)
Cecil Spring Rice	Churchill College, Cambridge (CASR Series)
	Public Record Office, London (FO 800 Series)
Rosslyn Wemyss	Churchill College, Cambridge (WYMS Series)

II GOVERNMENT ARCHIVES (GREAT BRITAIN ONLY)

ADMIRALTY
ADM 116   Political Correspondence
ADM 137   Historical Section

CABINET
CAB 4   Committee of Imperial Defence Memoranda
CAB 16   Committee of Imperial Defence. *Ad hoc* Sub-committees
CAB 21   Cabinet Registered Files
CAB 23   Cabinet Minutes after December 1916
CAB 24   Cabinet Memoranda after December 1916
CAB 27   Cabinet Committees. General Series
CAB 37   Cabinet Papers, 1880–1916
CAB 42   Copies of the Papers of the War Council, Dardanelles Committee, and War Committee

FOREIGN OFFICE
FO 65   Political Correspondence. Russia
FO 78   Political Correspondence. Turkey (Crete)
FO 368   General Correspondence. Commercial
FO 371   General Correspondence. Political
FO 382   General Correspondence. Contraband
FO 395   General Correspondence. News Department
FO 608   The Paris Peace Conference of 1919

PRIME MINISTERS OFFICE
PREM 1   Premier Files

WAR OFFICE
WO 106   Directorate of Military Operations and Intelligence

III GOVERNMENT PUBLICATIONS

BRITAIN
Foreign Office
  British and Foreign State Papers, vols. 101–2
  British Documents on the Origins of the War, vol. 3
  Documents on British Foreign Policy, Series 1A
  Documents on British Foreign Policy, Series II
  Foreign Office List 1914 (London, 1914)
  Foreign Office List 1919 (London, 1919)
  Foreign Office List 1930 (London, 1930)
  Peace Handbook
    No. 1: *Austria-Hungary* (London, 1918)
    No. 7: *Germany* (London, 1918)
    No. 8: *Poland and Finland* (London, 1918)
    No. 9: *The Russian Empire* (London, 1918)
    No. 23: *International Affairs* (London, 1918)
    No. 25: *Indemnities, Plebiscites, etc.* (London, 1918)
Parliament
  Command Papers. Cd Series
  Command Papers. Cmd Series
  Hansard (House of Commons)
  Hansard (House of Lords)

CANADA
Parliament
  Hansard (House of Commons)

NEWFOUNDLAND
Office of the Prime Minister
  R. Bond, *Speech on Modus Vivendi* (St John's, 1907)

UNITED STATES
Department of State
  Papers Relating to the Foreign Relations of the United States. 1926, 2 vols. (Washington, 1941); *1927*, 3 vols. (Washington, 1942); *1929*, 2 vols. (Washington, 1943)
Office of the President
  Address of President Coolidge at the Observance of the 10th Anniversary of the Armistice, under the Auspices of the American Legion (Washington, 1928)
  Address of President Coolidge...22 February 1929 (Washington, 1929)

IV NEWSPAPERS

The Birmingham Daily Gazette
The [Worcester] Daily Times
The [St John's] Evening Telegram
Manchester Guardian
New York Times
Ottawa Evening Journal
The Times
Washington Post
The Worcester Echo

V BIOGRAPHIES, DIARIES, MEMOIRS, SPEECHES

Andrew, C. M. *Théophile Delcassé and the Making of the Entente Cordiale* (London, 1968)
Baldwin, S. *Our Inheritance. Speeches and Addresses* (London, 1928)
Blunt, W. S. *My Diaries. Being a Personal Narrative of Events, 1888–1914* (London, 1932)
Booth, C. *Life and Labour of the People of London*, 9 vols., 2nd edn (London, 1892–7)
Busch, B. C. *Hardinge of Penshurst. A Study in the Old Diplomacy* (Hamden, Conn., 1980).
Carton de Wiart, A. *Happy Odyssey. The Memoirs of Lieutenant-General Sir Adrian Carton de Wiart* (London, 1950)
Cecil of Chelwood, Viscount. *A Great Experiment* (London, 1941)
Chamberlain, A. *Down the Years* (London, 1935)
Cline, C. A. *E. D. Morel, 1873–1924. The Strategies of Protest* (Belfast, 1980)
Consett, M. W. W. P. *The Triumph of Unarmed Forces (1914–1918)* (London, 1923)
Cooper, J. M. *The Warrior and the Priest. Woodrow Wilson and Theodore Roosevelt* (Cambridge, Mass., 1983)
Cortissoz, R. *The Life of Whitelaw Reid*. 2 vols. (New York, 1921)

Dutton, D. *Austen Chamberlain: Gentleman in Politics* (Bolton, 1985)
Einstein, L. *Roosevelt: His Mind in Action* (Boston, 1930)
Fisher, H. A. L. *James Bryce*. 2 vols. (New York, 1927)
Fitzherbert, M. *The Man Who Was Greenmantle: A Biography of Aubrey Herbert* (London, 1983)
Gilbert, M. *Sir Horace Rumbold. Portrait of a Diplomat, 1869–1941* (London, 1973)
   Winston S. Churchill, vol. 5: *1922–1939* (London, 1976)
Grey of Fallodon, Viscount. *Twenty-Five Years, 1892–1916*. 2 vols. (London, 1926)
Gwyn, S., ed. *The Letters and Friendships of Sir Cecil Spring Rice. A Record* (London, 1930)
Hardinge of Penshurst, Baron. *Old Diplomacy. The Reminiscences of Lord Hardinge of Penshurst* (London, 1947)
Headlam-Morley, A., Bryant, R., and Cienciala, A., eds. *Sir James Headlam-Morley. A Memoir of the Paris Peace Conference 1919* (London, 1972)
Herbert, R., ed. *Earl of Carnarvon, Essays, Addresses and Translations*, vol. 3 (London, 1896)
Howard, C. H. D., ed. *The Diary of Edward Goschen 1900–1914* (London, 1980)
Howard of Penrith, Baron. *Theatre of Life*. 2 vols. (London, 1935–6)
Hudson, W. J., and North, J., eds. *My Dear P.M. R. G. Casey's Letters to S. M. Bruce, 1924–1929* (Canberra, 1980)
Ions, E. *James Bryce and American Democracy, 1870–1922* (London, 1960)
Judd, D. *Radical Joe: A Life of Joseph Chamberlain* (London, 1977)
   Lord Reading: A Life of Rufus Isaacs, First Marquess of Reading, 1860–1935 (London, 1982)
Kenney, R. *Westering. An Autobiography* (London, 1939)
Kerofilas, C. *Eleftherios Venizelos. His Life and Work* (London, 1915)
Lee, S. *King Edward VII. A Biography*, vol. 2: *The Reign* (New York, 1927)
Magnus, P. *King Edward the Seventh* (New York, 1964)
Marquand, D. *Ramsay MacDonald* (London, 1977)
Middlemas, K., ed. *Thomas Jones: Whitehall Diary*. 2 vols. (London, New York and Toronto, 1969)
Middlemas, K., and Barnes, J. *Baldwin. A Biography* (London, 1969)
Morison, E. E., et al. *The Letters of Theodore Roosevelt*, vol. 2: *The Years of Preparation, 1898–1900* (Cambridge, Mass., 1951); and Vol. 5: *The Big Stick* (1952)
Morris, E. *The Rise of Theodore Roosevelt* (New York, 1978)
Morris, I. *From an American Legation* (New York, 1923)
Nekludoff, A. *Diplomatic Reminiscences before and during the World War, 1911–1917* (London, 1920)
Nicolson, H. G. *Sir Arthur Nicolson, Bart., First Lord Carnock: A Study in the Old Diplomacy* (London, 1930)
Norman-Butler, B. *Victorian Aspirations. The Life and Labour of Charles and Mary Booth* (London, 1972)
Pallis, A., ed. *The Cretan Drama. The Life and Memoirs of Prince George of Greece, High Commissioner in Crete (1898–1906)* (New York, 1959)
Pares, B. *My Russian Memoirs* (London, 1931)
Petrie, C. *The Life and Letters of the Rt Hon. Sir Austen Chamberlain*, vol. 2 (London, 1940)
   King Alfonso XIII and his Age (London, 1963)

Pusey, M. J. *Charles Evans Hughes*, vol. 2 (New York, 1951)
Ramm, A. *Sir Robert Morier. Envoy and Ambassador in the Age of Imperialism, 1876–1893* (London, 1973)
Robbins, K. *Sir Edward Grey. A Biography of Lord Grey of Fallodon* (London, 1971)
Ronaldshay, the Earl of. *The Life of Lord Curzon*, vol. 3 (London, 1928)
Roosevelt, N. *Theodore Roosevelt: The Man as I Knew him* (New York, 1967)
Rose, N. *Vansittart. Study of a Diplomat* (London, 1978)
Roskill, S. *Hankey, Man of Secrets*, vol. 2: *1919–1931* (London, 1972)
Rowland, P. *Lloyd George* (London, 1975)
St Aubyn, G. *Edward VII. Prince and King* (London, 1979)
Seton-Watson, H., and Seton-Watson, C. *The Making of New Europe. R. W. Seton Watson and the Last Years of Austria-Hungary* (London, 1981)
Simey, T. S., and Simey, M. B. *Charles Booth, Social Scientist* (Oxford, 1960)
Swanick, H. *Builders of Peace* (London, 1924)
Sykes, P. *The Right Honourable Sir Mortimer Durand. A Biography* (London, Toronto, Melbourne and Sydney, 1926)
Trevelyan, G. M. *Grey of Fallodon, Being the Life of Sir Edward Grey afterwards of Fallodon* (London, 1937)
Vansittart, Lord. *The Mist Procession. The Autobiography of Lord Vansittart* (London, 1958)
Zetland, Marquess of. *Lord Cromer. Being the Authorised Life of Evelyn Baring, First Earl of Cromer* (London, 1932)

VI MONOGRAPHS AND BOOKS

Aldcroft, D. H. *The Inter-War Economy: Britain, 1919–1939* (London, 1970)
Anderson, E. W. *The First Moroccan Crisis, 1904–6* (Chicago, 1930)
Anderson, M. S. *The Eastern Question* (London, 1966)
Andrew, C. M. *Secret Service. The Making of the British Intelligence Community* (London, 1985)
Anonymous. *The New York Times Index. A Book of Record. 1925*, 2 vols. (New York, 1926); *1926*, 2 vols. (1927); *1927*, 2 vols. (1928); *1928*, 2 vols. (1929); *1929*, 2 vols. (1930)
Aslet, C. *The Last Country Houses* (New Haven and London, 1982)
Austin, D. *Malta and the End of Empire* (London, 1971)
Baltzell, E. D. *The Protestant Establishment: Aristocracy and Caste in America* (New York, 1958)
  Philadelphia Gentlemen: The Making of a National Upper Class (New York, 1965)
  Puritan Boston and Quaker Philadelphia: Two Protestant Ethics and the Spirit of Class Authority and Leadership (Boston, 1979)
Barlow, I. C. *The Agadir Crisis* (Chapel Hill, NC, 1940)
Barnett, C. *The Audit of War. The Illusion and Reality of Britain as a Great Nation* (London, 1986)
Barros, J. *The Aland Islands Question: Its Settlement by the League of Nations* (New Haven and London, 1968)
Bell, A. C. *A History of the Blockade of Germany and the Countries Associated with her in the Great War…1914–1918* (London, 1937)

Bemis, F. M., ed. *The American Secretaries of State and their Diplomacy*, vol. 10 (New York, 1929)
Ben-Ami, S. *Fascism from above. The Dictatorship of Primo de Rivera in Spain, 1923–1930* (Oxford, 1983)
Blewett, N. *The Peers, the Parties and the People: The General Elections of 1910* (Toronto, 1972)
Blunt, W. S. *Secret History of the British Occupation of Egypt* (New York, 1922)
Bond, R. *Speech on Modus Vivendi* (St John's, 1907)
Bosworth, R. J. B. *Italy, the Least of the Great Powers: Italian Foreign Policy before the First World War* (Cambridge, 1979)
Bourne, K. *Britain and the Balance of Power in North America, 1815–1908* (London, 1967)
Boyd, C. P. *Praetorian Politics in Liberal Spain* (Chapel Hill, 1979)
Brand, C. F. *The British Labour Party. A Short History*, revised edn (Stanford, 1974)
Branson, N., and Heinemann, M. *Britain in the Nineteen Thirties* (London, 1971)
Bridge, F. R. *From Sadowa to Sarajevo. The Foreign Policy of Austria-Hungary, 1866–1914* (London and Boston, 1972)
Great Britain and Austria-Hungary (London, 1972)
Brown, R. C., and Cook, R. *Canada, 1896–1921. A Nation Transformed* (Toronto, 1974)
Bryce, J. *The American Commonwealth* (London, 1888)
Bullen, R., ed. *The Foreign Office, 1782–1982* (Fredericksburg, Md, 1984)
Burk, K. M. *Britain, America and the Sinews of War, 1914–1918* (London, 1985)
Burk, K. M.\ed. *War \and \the \State :\ The Transformation\ of the British Government, 1914–1919* (London, 1982)
Calder, K. J. *Britain and the Origins of the New Europe, 1914–1918* (Cambridge, 1976)
Callahan, J. M. *American Foreign Policy in Canadian Relations* (New York, 1937)
Campbell, A. E. *Great Britain and the United States, 1895–1903* (Glasgow, 1960)
Campbell, C. S. Jr. *Anglo-American Understanding, 1893–1903* (Baltimore, 1957)
Carlgren, W. M. *Neutralität oder Allianz. Deutschlands Beziehungen zu Schweden in den Anfangsjahren des ersten Weltkrieges* (Stockholm, Gothenburg and Uppsala, 1962)
Carlton, D. *MacDonald versus Henderson. The Foreign Policy of the Second Labour Government* (London, 1970)
Carr, R. *Spain, 1808–1939* (Oxford, 1966)
Chacko, C. J. *The International Joint Commission between the United States of America and the Dominion of Canada* (New York, 1932)
Chadwick, O. *Britain and the Vatican during the Second World War* (Cambridge, 1986)
Coogan, J. W. *The End of Neutrality. The United States, Britain, and Maritime Rights 1899–1915* (Ithaca and London, 1981)
Cooke, A. B., and Vincent, J. R. *The Governing Passion. Cabinet Government and Party Politics in Britain, 1885–86* (London, 1974)
Cowling, M. *The Impact of Hitler: British Politics and British Policy, 1933–1940* (London, 1975)
Craig, G. *Germany, 1865–1945* (Oxford, 1981)
Curtis, L. P. *Coercion and Conciliation in Ireland, 1880–1892* (London, 1977)
Dakin, D. *The Unification of Greece, 1770–1923* (New York, 1972)

Dallin, A., et al. *Russian Diplomacy and Eastern Europe, 1914–1917* (New York, 1963)
Davies, N. *God's Playground. A History of Poland in Two Volumes*, vol. 2: *1795 to the Present* (New York, 1982)
Davis, C. D'A. *The United States and the Second Hague Peace Conference* (Durham, NC, 1975)
Davis, G. T. A. *A Navy Second to None* (New York, 1940)
Divine, R. A. *The Illusion of Neutrality* (Chicago, 1962)
Dockrill, M. L., and Goold, J. D. *Peace without Promise. Britain and the Peace Conferences, 1919–1923* (London, 1981)
Drummond, D. F. *The Passing of American Neutrality, 1937–1941* (Ann Arbor, 1955)
Dziewanowski, M. K. *Poland in the Twentieth Century* (New York, 1977)
Ellis, L. E. *Frank B. Kellogg and American Foreign Relations, 1925–1929* (New Brunswick, NJ, 1961)
Farr, D. *The Colonial Office and Canada, 1867–1887* (Toronto, 1955)
Farwell, B. *The Great Anglo-Boer War* (Toronto, 1976)
Ferrell, R. H. *Peace in their Time. The Origins of the Kellogg–Briand Pact* (New Haven, 1952)
Fest, W. *Peace or Partition. The Habsburg Monarchy and British Policy, 1914–1918* (New York, 1978)
French, D. *British Strategy and War Aims 1914–1916* (London, 1986)
Fry, M. G. *Illusions of Security. North Atlantic Diplomacy, 1918–1922* (Toronto, 1972)
Gajda, P. A. *Postscript to Victory. British Policy and the German–Polish Borderlands, 1919–1925* (Washington, DC, 1982)
Gerson, L. L. *Woodrow Wilson and the Rebirth of Poland, 1914–1920. A Study in the Influence on American Foreign Policy of Minority Groups of Foreign Origin* (New Haven, 1953)
Gieysztor, A., et al. *The History of Poland* (Warsaw, 1968)
Gifford, P., and Louis, W. R., eds. *Britain and Germany in Africa* (New Haven, 1967)
Glazebrook, G. P. de T. *A History of Canadian External Relations*, revised edn, vol. 1: *The Formative Years to 1914* (Toronto, 1966)
Glynn, S., and Oxborrow, J. *Interwar Britain: A Social and Economic History* (London, 1976)
Hachey, T. E., ed. *Anglo-Vatican Relations, 1914–1939: Confidential Annual Reports of the British Ministers to the Holy See* (London, 1972)
Haraszti, E. *Treaty Breakers or 'Realpolitikers'? The Anglo-German Naval Agreement of June 1935* (Boppard/R, 1974)
Helmreich, P. C. *From Paris to Sèvres: The Partition of the Ottoman Empire at the Peace Conference of 1919–1920* (Columbus, Ohio, 1974)
Hiller, J., and Neary, P., eds. *Newfoundland in the Nineteenth and Twentieth Centuries: Essays in Interpretation* (Toronto, Buffalo and London, 1980)
Hinsley, F. H., ed. *British Foreign Policy under Sir Edward Grey* (Cambridge, 1977)
Hogan, M. *Informal Entente: The Private Structure of Cooperation in Anglo-American Economic Diplomacy, 1918–1928* (Columbia, Mo., 1977)
Hovi, O. *The Baltic Area in British Policy, 1918–1921*
Howard, E. W. *In Memoriam E. J. H. S. H.* (privately, 1927)

Howard of Penrith, Lord. *Memorandum Regarding the Malta Crisis* (London, 1931)
  Sanctions: Confidence: Disarmament: Recovery (London, 1932)
  The Prevention of War by Collective Action (London, 1933)
Hunt, B. D., and Preston, A., eds. *War and Strategic Policy in the Great War* (London, 1977)
Innis, H. A. *The Cod Fisheries. The History of and International Economy*, revised edn (Toronto, Buffalo and London, 1978)
Jacobson, J. *Locarno Diplomacy. Germany and the West, 1925–1929* (Princeton, 1972)
Jones, R. A. *The British Diplomatic Service, 1815–1914* (Waterloo, Ont., 1983)
Kaarstad, T. *Great Britain and Denmark, 1914–1920* (Odense, 1979)
Kann, R. *A History of the Habsburg Empire, 1526–1918* (Berkeley, Los Angeles and London, 1974)
Kendle, J. E. *The Colonial and Imperial Conferences, 1887–1911* (London, 1967)
Kennan, G. F. *Soviet–American Relations, 1917–1920*, vol. 1: *Russia Leaves the War* (Princeton, 1956)
Kennedy, P. M. *The Rise of Anglo-German Antagonism, 1860–1914* (London, 1982)
Koblik, S. *Sweden: The Neutral Victor. Sweden and the Western Powers. 1917–1918* (Stockholm, 1972)
Komarnicki, T. *Rebirth of the Polish Republic. A Study in the Diplomatic History of Europe, 1914–1920* (Melbourne, London and Toronto, 1957)
Korbel, J. *Poland between East and West. Soviet and German Diplomacy toward Poland, 1919–1933* (Princeton, 1963)
Leffler, M. *The Elusive Quest: America's Pursuit of European Stability and French Security* (Chapel Hill, 1979)
Leslie, R. F., et al. *The History of Poland since 1863* (Cambridge, 1980)
Liddell Hart, B. H. *History of the First World War* (London and Sydney, 1976 [first published in 1934])
Link, A. S., ed. *Woodrow Wilson and a Revolutionary World, 1913–1921* (Princeton, 1982)
Long, Lady C. *The First Lieutenant's Story*, 3 vols. (London, 1853)
  Sir Roland Ashton. A Tale of the Times, 2 vols. (London, 1854)
Lord, R. H. *The Second Partition of Poland* (Cambridge, Mass., 1915)
Love, R. W., Jr. *The Chiefs of Naval Operations* (Annapolis, 1980)
Lowe, C. J., and Dockrill, M. L. *The Mirage of Power*, 3 vols. (London, 1972)
Lowe, C. J. and Marzari, F. *Italian Foreign Policy, 1870–1940* (London, 1975)
Lundgreen-Nielsen, K. *The Polish Problem at the Paris Peace Conference. A Study of the Policies of the Great Powers and the Poles, 1918–1920* (Odense, 1979)
Lyytinen, E. *Finland in British Politics in the First World War* (Helsinki, 1980)
Macartney, C. A. *National States and National Minorities* (New York, 1934)
McKercher, B. J. C. *The Second Baldwin Government and the United States, 1924–1929: Attitudes and Diplomacy* (Cambridge, 1984)
McKercher, B. J. C. ed. *The Struggle for Supremacy. Aspects of Anglo-American Relations in the 1920s* (Edmonton and London, forthcoming)
McKercher, B. J. C., and Moss, D. J., eds. *Shadow and Substance in British Foreign Policy, 1895–1939. Essays Honouring C. J. Lowe* (Edmonton, 1984)
Martin, W., and Beguin, P. *Switzerland from Roman Times to the Present*, 6th edn (New York and Washington, 1971)

Medlicott, W. N. *British Foreign Policy since Versailles, 1919–1963* (London, 1968)
Monger, G. M. *The End of Isolation: British Foreign Policy, 1900–1907* (London, 1963)
Morton, D. *Ministers and Generals. Politics and the Canadian Militia* (Toronto, 1970)
Morton, W. L. *The Kingdom of Canada. A General History from Earliest Times* (Toronto, 1963)
Munro, J. *The Alaska Boundary Dispute* (Toronto, 1970)
Neale, R. G. *Britain and American Imperialism, 1898–1900* (St Lucia, Qld, 1965)
Neilson, K. E. *Strategy and Supply. The Anglo-Russian Alliance, 1914–1917* (London, 1984)
Nelson, H. I. *Land and Power. British and Allied Policy on Germany's Frontiers, 1916–19* (London and Toronto, 1963)
Nelson, K. *Victors Divided: America and the Allies in Germany, 1918–1923* (Berkeley, 1975)
Noel, S. J. R. *Politics in Newfoundland* (Toronto, 1973)
Noel-Baker, P. J. *The Geneva Protocol for the Pacific Settlement of International Disputes* (London, 1925).
Nolde, B. E. *Russia in the Economic War* (New Haven, 1928)
O'Connor, R. G. *Perilous Equilibrium: The United States and the London Naval Conference 1930* (Lawrence, Kan., 1962)
Page, S. W. *The Formation of the Baltic States. A Study of the Effects of Great Power Politics upon the Emergence of Lithuania, Latvia, and Estonia* (New York, 1970)
Pakenham, T. *The Boer War* (London, 1979)
Parrini, C. *Heir to Empire: United States Economic Diplomacy, 1916–1923* (Pittsburgh, 1969)
Parsons, F. V. *The Origins of the Moroccan Question, 1880–1900* (London, 1976)
Payne, S. G. *Politics and the Military in Modern Spain* (Stanford, 1967)
Penlington, N. *The Alaska Boundary Dispute: A Critical Reappraisal* (Toronto, 1972)
Perkins, B. *The Great Rapprochement. England and the United States, 1895–1914* (New York, 1968)
Platt, D. C. M. *The Cinderella Service. British Consuls since 1825* (London, 1971)
Porter, A. N. *The Origins of the South African War: Joseph Chamberlain and the Diplomacy of Imperialism, 1895–1899* (Manchester, 1980)
Read, D. *England 1868–1914. The Age of Urban Democracy* (London, 1979)
Reddaway, W. F., et al. *The Cambridge History of Poland from Augustus II to Pilsudski* (Cambridge, 1941)
Rhodes James, R. *The British Revolution. British Politics 1880–1939* (London, 1976)
Riste, O. *The Neutral Ally. Norway's Relations with Belligerent Powers in the First World War* (Oslo and London, 1965)
Robinson, R., Gallagher, J., and Denny, A. *Africa and the Victorians. The Official Mind of Imperialism* (London, 1961)
Rose, J. *The Edwardian Temperament, 1895–1919* (Athens, Ohio, 1986)
Roskill, S. W. *Naval Policy between the Wars*, 2 vols. (London, 1968, 1976)
Rothwell, V. H. *British War Aims and Peace Diplomacy, 1914–1918* (Oxford, 1971)

Rowe, F. W. *A History of Newfoundland and Labrador* (Toronto, 1980)
Saul, N. E. *Sailors in Revolt. The Russian Baltic Fleet in 1917* (Lawrence, Kan., 1978)
Scally, R. J. *The Origins of the Lloyd George Coalition. The Politics of Social-Imperialism, 1900–1918* (Princeton, 1975)
Schmitt, B. E. *The Annexation of Bosnia* (London, 1937)
Schuberth, I. *Schweden und das Deutsches Reich im Ersten Weltkrieg. Die Aktivistenbewegung 1914–1918* (Bonn, 1981)
Schuker, S. A. *The End of French Predominance in Europe. The Financial Crisis of 1924 and the Acceptance of the Dawes Plan* (Chapel Hill, 1976)
Scott, F. D. *Sweden: The Nation's History* (Minneapolis, 1977)
Seton-Watson, R. W. *The Southern Slav Question and the Habsburg Monarchy* (London, 1911)
Silverman, D. P. *Reconstructing Europe after the Great War* (Cambridge, Mass., and London, 1982)
Siney, M. *The Allied Blockade of Germany, 1914–1916* (Ann Arbor, 1957)
Smith, C. J., Jr. *Finland and the Russian Revolution, 1917–1922* (Athens, Ga., 1958)
Sprout, H., and Sprout, M. *Toward a New Order of Sea Power* (Princeton, 1946)
Stacey, C. P. *Canada and the Age of Conflict*, vol. 1: *1867–1921* (Toronto, 1977)
Steiner, Z. S. *The Foreign Office and Foreign Policy, 1898–1914* (Cambridge, 1969)
  Britain and the Origins of the First World War (London, 1977)
Stokesbury, J. C. *A Short History of World War One* (New York, 1981)
Stone, N. *The Eastern Front, 1914–1917* (London, 1975)
Swartz, M. *The Union of Democratic Control in British Politics during the First World War* (Oxford, 1971)
Temperley, H. W. V. *A History of the Peace Conference of Paris*, 6 vols. (London, 1920–4)
Toynbee, A. *The Conduct of British Empire Foreign Relations since the Peace Settlement* (London, 1928)
Toynbee, A., et al. *Survey of International Affairs 1928* (London, 1929)
Trachtenberg, M. *Reparation in World Politics: France and European Economic Diplomacy, 1916–1923* (New York, 1980)
Trani, E. P. *The Treaty of Portsmouth. An Adventure in American Diplomacy* (Lexington, Ky, 1969)
Turlington, E. *Neutrality, its History, Economics, and Law*, vol. 2: *The World War Period* (New York, 1936)
Ulam, A. B. *The Bolsheviks. The Intellectual, Personal and Political History of the Triumph of Communism in Russia* (New York, 1965)
Ullman, R. H. *Anglo-Soviet Relations, 1917–1921*, vol. 1: *Intervention and the War* (Princeton, 1961)
Union for Democratic Control. *The Balance of Power* (London, n.d.)
  The Origins of the Great War (London, n.d.)
  The Morrow of the War (London, n.d.)
Upton, A. F. *The Finnish Revolution, 1917–1918* (Minneapolis, 1980)
Valiani, L. *The End of Austria-Hungary* (London, 1973)
Waites, N., ed. *Troubled Neighbours. Franco-British Relations in the Twentieth Century* (London, 1971)
Walters, F. P. *A History of the League of Nations* (London, 1960)

Wandycz, P. *The Lands of Partitioned Poland, 1795–1918* (Seattle and London, 1974)
Watt, D. C. *Personalities and Policies. Studies in the Formulation of British Foreign Policy in the Twentieth Century* (London, 1965)
Succeeding John Bull. America in Britain's Place, 1900–75 (Cambridge, 1984)
Wheeler-Bennett, J. W. *Disarmament and Security since Locarno, 1925–1931* (London, 1932)
Brest-Litovsk. The Forgotten Peace, March 1918 (London, Melbourne and Toronto, 1966)
White, G. E. *The Eastern Establishment and the Western Experience: The West of Frederick Remington, Theodore Roosevelt, and Owen Wister* (New Haven, 1964)
White, J. A. *The Diplomacy of the Russo-Japanese War* (Princeton, 1964)
Wiener, M. *English Culture and the Decline of the Industrial Spirit, 1850–1980* (Cambridge, 1981)
Wildman, A. K. *The End of the Russian Imperial Army* (Princeton, 1980)
Williamson, S. R. *The Politics of Grand Strategy: Britain and France Prepare for War, 1904–1914* (Cambridge, Mass., 1969)
Willson, B. *America's Ambassadors to England 1785–1928* (London, 1928)
Woolman, D. *Rebels in the Riff* (Stanford, 1968)
Wrigley, P. G. *Canada and the Transition to Commonwealth. British–Canadian Relations 1917–1926* (Cambridge, 1977)

VII ARTICLES

Anderson, E. 'British Policy toward the Baltic States, 1918–1920', *Journal of Central European Affairs*, 19 (1955)
Anonymous. 'After the Disarmament Failure', *Literary Digest*, 99 (Sept. 1927)
Baldwin, E. F., and Kawakami, K. K. 'What Happened at Geneva', *Outlook*, 146 (Aug. 1927)
Blair, J. L. 'I Do Not Choose to Run for President in Nineteen Twenty-Eight', *VH*, 30 (1962)
Boadle, D. G. 'The Formation of the Foreign Office Economic Relations Section, 1930–1937', *HJ*, 20 (1977)
Booth, L. E. 'A Fettered Envoy: Lord Grey's Mission to the United States, 1919–1920', *RP*, 33 (1971)
Bothwell, R. 'Canadian Representation at Washington: A Study in Colonial Responsibility', *CHR*, 53 (1972)
Bridge, F. R. 'British Official Opinion and the Domestic Situation in the Hapsburg Monarchy, 1900–1914', in McKercher and Moss, *Shadow and Substance*
Burk, K. M. 'The Diplomacy of Finance: British Financial Missions to the United States, 1914–1918', *HJ*, 22 (1979)
'The Treasury: From Impotence to Power', in Burk, *War and the State*
Burks, D. D. 'The United States and the Geneva Protocol of 1924: "A New Holy Alliance"?', *AHR*, 64 (1959)
Butler, J. 'The German Factor in Anglo-Transvaal Relations', in Gifford and Louis, *Britain and Germany*
Calvert, P. A. R. 'Great Britain and the New World, 1905–1914', in Hinsley, *Grey*
Carlton, D. 'Great Britain and the Coolidge Naval Conference of 1927', *PSQ*, 83 (1968)

'Great Britain and the League Council Crisis of 1926', *HJ*, 11 (1968)
'The Anglo-French Compromise on Arms Limitation, 1928', *JBS*, 8 (1969)
Carnarvon, Earl of. 'Imperial Administration', in Herbert, *Essays*
Carter, J. 'American Correspondents and British Delegates: Some Reasons for the Failure at Geneva', *Independent*, 119 (Aug. 1927)
Cassels, A. 'Afterword: Diplomats in an Age of Alien Ideologies and Bureaucratization', *IHR*, 9 (1987)
Coghlan, F. A. 'James Bryce and the Establishment of the Department of External Affairs', *Canadian Historical Association Historical Papers* (1968)
Cole, W. S. 'Senator Key Pittman and the American Neutrality Policies, 1933–1940', *Mississippi Valley Historical Review*, 46 (1974)
Corp, E. T. 'Sir Eyre Crowe and the Administration of the Foreign Office, 1906–1914', *HJ*, 22 (1979)
Costigliola, F. C. 'The Other Side of Isolationism: The Establishment of the First World Bank', *JAH*, 59 (1972)
'Anglo-American Financial Rivalry in the 1920s', *JEH*, 37 (1977)
Cromwell, V., and Steiner, Z. S. 'Reform and Retrenchment: The Foreign Office between the Wars', in Bullen, *Foreign Office*
Debo, R. K. 'Lloyd George and the Copenhagen Conference of 1919–1920: The Initiation of Anglo-Soviet Negotiations', *HJ*, 24 (1981)
Dockrill, M. L. 'Britain, the United States, and France and the German Settlement, 1918–1920', in McKercher and Moss, *Shadow and Substance*
Dockrill, M. L., and Steiner, Z. S. 'The Foreign Office at the Paris Peace Conference in 1919', *IHR*, 2 (1980)
Egerton, G. W. 'Britain and the "Great Betrayal": Anglo-American Relations and the Struggle for United States Ratification of the Treaty of Versailles, 1919–1920', *HJ*, 21 (1978)
'Diplomacy, Scandal, and Military Intelligence: The Craufurd-Stuart Affair and Anglo-American Relations, 1918–1920', *INS*, 2 (1987)
'Eothen'. 'Crete under Prince George', *The Fortnightly Review*, 78, new series (1905)
Fletcher, W. A. 'The British Navy in the Baltic, 1918–1920: Its Contribution to the Independence of the Baltic Nations', *Journal of Baltic Studies*, 7 (1976)
Gerould, J. T. 'Failure of the 3 Power Naval Conference', *Current History*, 26 (Sept. 1927)
'Britain's Opposition to the Freedom of the Seas', *Current History*, 27 (Oct. 1927)
Gillard, D. R. 'Salisbury's African Policy and the Heligoland Offer 1890', *EHR*, 75 (1960)
Gleuck, A. C., Jr. 'Pilgrimages to Ottawa: Canadian–American Diplomacy 1903–1913', *Canadian Historical Association Historical Papers* (1968)
Goldman, A. 'Sir Robert Vansittart's Search for Italian Co-operation against Hitler, 1933–1936', *JCH*, 9 (1974)
Hall, H. D. 'The Genesis of the Balfour Declaration of 1926', *JCPS*, 1 (1963)
Hannigan, R. E. 'Reciprocity 1911: Continentalism and American *Weltpolitik*', *DH*, 4 (1980)
Harcourt, F. 'Disraeli's Imperialism, 1866–1868: A Question of Timing', *HJ*, 23 (1980)
Harrison, J. 'Big Business and the Failure of Right-Wing Catalan Nationalism, 1901–1923', *HJ*, 19 (1976)

Hillmer, N. 'A British High Commissioner for Canada, 1927–28', *JICH*, 1 (1979)
Hollyday, F. B. M. '"Love Your Enemies! Otherwise Bite Them!" Bismarck, Herbert, and the Morier Affair, 1888–1889', *Central European History*, 1 (1968)
Howard, E. W. 'British Policy and the Balance of Power', *APSR*, 19 (1925)
Hunczak, T. 'Sir Lewis Namier and the Struggle for Eastern Galicia, 1918–1920', *Harvard Ukrainian Studies*, 1 (1977)
Jacobson, J. 'The Conduct of Locarno Diplomacy', *RP*, 34 (1972)
Johnson, D. 'Austen Chamberlain and the Locarno Agreements', *University of Birmingham Historical Journal*, 8 (1961)
  'The Locarno Treaties', in Waites, *Troubled Neighbours*
Kellogg, F. B. 'The War Prevention Policy of the United States', *FA Special Supplement*, 6 (1928)
Kieniewicz, S., and Wereszycki, H. 'Poland under Foreign Rule, 1795–1918', in Gieysztor, *Poland*
Knox, B. A. 'Reconsidering Mid-Victorian Imperialism', *JICH*, 1 (1973)
Latawski, P. 'Count Horodyski's Plan "To Set Europe Ablaze", June 1918', *Slavonic and East European Review*, 65 (1987)
Lundgreen-Nielsen, K. 'Woodrow Wilson and the Rebirth of Poland', in Link, *Revolutionary World*
  'The Mayer Thesis Reconsidered: The Poles and the Paris Peace Conference, 1919', *IHR*, 7 (1985)
McEwen, J. M. 'Northcliffe and Lloyd George at War, 1914–1918', *HJ*, 24 (1981)
McKercher, B. J. C. 'A British View of American Foreign Policy: The Settlement of Blockade Claims, 1924–1927', *IHR*, 3 (1981)
  'Austen Chamberlain's Control of British Foreign Policy, 1924–1929', *IHR*, 6 (1984)
  'The British Diplomatic Service in the United States and the Chamberlain Foreign Office's Perception of Domestic America, 1924–1927: Images, Reality, and Diplomacy', in McKercher and Moss, *Shadow and Substance* (1984)
  'A Sane and Sensible Diplomacy: Austen Chamberlain, Japan, and the Naval Balance of Power in the Pacific Ocean, 1924–29', *CJH*, 21 (1986)
  'Belligerent Rights in 1927–1929: Foreign Policy Versus Naval Policy in the Second Baldwin Government', *HJ*, 24 (1986)
  '"A Dose of Fascismo": Esme Howard and Spain, 1919–1924', *IHR*, 9 (1987)
  'Wealth, Power, and the New International Order: Britain and the American Challenge in the 1920s', *DH*, 12 (1988)
McKercher, B. J. C., and Neilson, K. E. '"The Triumph of Unarmed Forces": Sweden and the Allied Blockade of Germany, 1914–1917', *Journal of Strategic Studies*, 7 (1984)
Marks, III, F. W. 'Morality as a Drive Wheel in the Diplomacy of Theodore Roosevelt', *DH*, 2 (1978)
Marsden, A. 'The Blockade', in Hinsley, *Grey*
Mason, C. M. 'Anglo-American Relations: Mediation and Permanent Peace', in Hinsley, *Grey*

Morgan, K. O. 'Lloyd George's Premiership: A Study in "Prime Ministerial Government"', *HJ*, 13 (1970)
Morris, L. P. 'The Russians, the Allies, and the War, February–July 1917', *Slavonic and East European Review*, 50 (1972)
Neary, P. 'Grey, Bryce, and the Settlement of Canadian–American Differences, 1905–1911', *CHR*, 49 (1968)
 'The French and American Shore Questions as Factors in Newfoundland History', in Hiller and Neary, *Newfoundland*
Neilson, K. E. 'The Breakup of the Anglo-Russian Alliance: The Question of Supply in 1917', *IHR*, 3 (1981)
 'Wishful Thinking: The Foreign Office and Russia, 1907–1917', in McKercher and Moss, *Shadow and Substance*
Payne, S. G. 'Fascism and Right Authoritarianism in the Iberian World – The Last Twenty Years', *JCH*, 21 (1986)
Rhodes, B. D. 'British Diplomacy and the Silent Oracle of Vermont, 1923–1929', *VH*, 50 (1982)
 'The Image of Britain in the United States, 1919–1929: A Contentious Relative and Rival', in McKercher, *Struggle for Supremacy*
Robertson, J. C. 'The Hoare-Laval Plan', *JCH*, 10 (1975)
Sanderson, G. N. 'The Anglo-German Agreement of 1890 and the Upper Nile', *EHR*, 78 (1963)
Schwoerer, L. G. 'Lord Halifax's Visit to Germany, November 1937', *Historian*, 32 (1970)
Scott, F. D. 'Gustav V and Swedish Attitudes towards Germany, 1915', *JMH*, 39 (1967)
Senn, A. E. 'The Entente and the Polish Question, 1914–1916', *Jahrbücher für Geschichte Osteuropas*, 25 (1977)
Sharp, A. 'The Foreign Office in Eclipse, 1919–22', *History*, 61 (1976)
Steiner, Z. S. 'The Foreign Office and the War', in Hinsley, *Grey*
 'Elitism and Foreign Policy: The Foreign Office before the Great War', in McKercher and Moss, *Shadow and Substance*
Steiner, Z. S., and Dockrill, M. L. 'The Foreign Office Reforms', *HJ*, 17 (1974)
Stewart, G. T. '"A Special Contiguous Country Economic Regime": An Overview of America's Canadian Policy', *DH*, 6 (1982)
Turk, R. W. 'Edward Walter Eberle', in Love, *The Chiefs*
Turner, J. 'Cabinets, Committees, and Secretariats: The Higher Direction of the War', in Burk, *War and the State*
Warman, R. M. 'The Erosion of Foreign Office Influence in the Making of Foreign Policy', *HJ*, 15 (1972)
Watt, D. C. 'United States Documentary Sources for the Study of British Foreign Policy, 1919–39', in Watt, *Personalities and Policies*
Wells, S. J., Jr. 'British Strategic Withdrawal from the Western Hemisphere, 1905–1906', *CHR*, 49 (1968)
Williamson, D. G. 'Great Britain and the Ruhr Crisis, 1923–1924', *BJIS*, 3 (1977)
Wilson, K. 'Isolating the Isolator. Cartwright, Grey, and the Seduction of Austria-Hungary 1908–12', *Mitteilungen des Österreichischen Staatsarchiv*, 35 (1982)
Wilson, P. W. 'British Ambassador Foresees a New Era', *New York Sunday Times Magazine*, 8 (June 1924)

Wilson, T. 'Britain's "Moral Commitment" to France in August 1914', *History*, 64 (1979)
'Lord Bryce's Investigation into Alleged German Atrocities in Belgium, 1914–1915', *JCH*, 14 (1979)

VIII UNPUBLISHED DISSERTATIONS AND PAPERS

Burke, G. K. 'Anglo-French Relations in the African Crisis of 1898', Ph.D. (St John's University, 1973)

Cosgrove, R. 'Sir Eyre Crowe and the English Foreign Office, 1905–1914', Ph.D. (University of California, 1967)

Pitt, M. 'Great Britain and Belligerent Maritime Rights from the Declaration of Paris, 1856, to the Declaration of London', Ph.D. (University of London, 1964)

Roberts, P. M. 'The American "Eastern Establishment" and Foreign Affairs: A Challenge for Historians', unpublished paper (delivered at the 8th Annual Meeting of the Society for Historians of American Foreign Relations, Boston University, August 1982)

Index

Adams, Henry (American writer), 75
Admiralty and belligerent rights, 304, 318, 335; and blockade (1914–18), 156–7, 161, 167–71; and Finland, 190–1; and Foreign Office, 167–71, 318, 335; and naval limitation, 304, 306–9
Aehrenthal, Baron Alois von (Austro-Hungarian foreign minister), 102, 108, 115, 117
Africa, 33
  Boer War (1899–1902), 29–32; Howard's service in (1900), 30–2, 374
  East Africa (1890); Howard and Anderson mission, 12–13, 370
  South Africa; Howard's expedition to (1891), 14–17
Aguilera Egea, General Francisco (Spanish military commander), 266
Air Ministry, 357
Aland Islands, 147–8, 151, 171, 187; and Finnish civil war, 187, 190
Alaska boundary question (1903), 75, 81, 83, 89, 93
Alba, Duke of (Spanish anglophile), 255
Alexandra (Queen of Great Britain, 1901–10), 40
Alexandra (Tsarina of Russia, 1894–1917), 172
Alfonso XIII (King of Spain, 1885–1931), 237, 239, 245, 255, 264, 267, 360–1
Allied Powers, *see* 'Triple Entente'
Amery, Leo (British colonial secretary, 1924–9, and dominions secretary, 1925–9), 327
Anderson, H. N. (Danish premier), 170
Anderson, Sir Percy (Foreign Office African Department), 19, 370; mission to Berlin on East Africa, 12–13, 14, 130

Andrassy, Count Julius (Hungarian politician), 112
Anglo-French disarmament compromise (1928), 330–1, 341
Annual crisis (1921–3), 249–50, 250–1, 256–7, 263–7
Apponyi, Count Albert (Hungarian politician), 112
Ariluce, Marquess de (Spanish financier), 241
Asquith, Herbert (after 1925, first Earl of Oxford and Asquith) (British prime minister, 1908–15), 93, 127–8, 161, 164; and his governments, 127, 128, 129–30, 140, 143, 170
Assanovitch, Colonel (Russian military attaché, Stockholm), 137–8, 140, 141
Astor, John (proprietor of *The Times*), 329
Astor, Lady Nancy (American-born, self-important British politician), 329
Aunay, Count d' (French Minister, Berne), 120, 121
Austria-Hungary: and Bosnia and Herzegovina, 102–3; and 'Bosnian solution', 47, 102, 143; and Crete, 39, 40, 53, 54, 68–9; defeat of (1918), 198, 207, 208–9; and France, 111–12, 113, 114, 125; and Germany, 39, 40, 53, 54, 68–9, 103–4, 105, 108, 110, 111, 112, 113, 114–15, 120–1, 122–5, 134; and Great Britain, 39, 40, 53, 54, 68–9, 102–3, 107, 108–9, 111–12, 113; and Italy, 103, 122–4; and Poland, 204, 205; and Russia, 102–3, 108, 118, 134, 137; and Serbia, 103, 107–8, 143; and Switzerland, 118, 120–1, 124–6
Austria
  and 'German' Austrians, 103, 106, 110–11, 114–15, 116–17; and

453

Germany, 108, 110, 111, 112, 113, 114–15, 122–5; and Magyars, 103, 106, 108–9, 110–11, 116–17

Hungary
and anglophobic press attacks, 107, 115, 116; and Bosnian crisis (1908–9), 103, 107, 108; domestic politics, 108–10, 112–13, 116–17; impact on Austro-Hungarian foreign policy, 108–9, 110–11; and 'German' Austrians, 103, 106, 110–11, 113–14, 115, 117; Hungarian anti-Germanism, 105, 114–15; and Germany, 108, 110, 111, 112, 113, 114–15, 120–1; and Great Britain, 105, 107, 108–9, 111–12, 113, 116–17, 125; and Magyars, 103, 106, 110–11, 116; and subject peoples, 103, 105, 106, 108, 110, 116; and Russia, 108
Also see 'Triple Alliance'

Bacon, Robert (American State Department official, 1906–8), 75
balance of power: Europe, 106, 118, 122, 124, 126, 127, 128–30, 133, 137, 186–95, 203, 212–15, 215–17, 227–30, 236, 237, 245, 251–5, 267–8, 281–2, 362–3, 370, 371; North America, 324–8
Baldwin, Sir Stanley (after 1937, first Earl Baldwin of Bewdley)
(British president of the Board of Trade, 1921–2), 259
(chancellor of the exchequer, 1922–3), 340
(prime minister, 1923–4, 1924–9, 1935–7), 270, 283–4, 312–13, 319–20, 329, 335, 336, 341; and his proposed trip to the USA (1929), 340; and his second government, 286–7, 292–3, 303–4, 306–9, 312, 313, 320, 321–4, 327, 336, 342
Balfour, Sir Arthur (after 1922, first Earl of Balfour), 261
(British prime minister, 1902–5): and Crete, 55; and Edward VII – Leo XIII meeting, 35–6; resigns, 66
(foreign secretary, 1916–19), 200–1; appointment, 164–5; and Czechoslovakia, 221; and Finland, 189, 190, 194, 209, 210; and Germany, 223; and Howard, 165, 178, 189, 193, 194, 208, 209, 210, 212–15, 218, 221, 223, 235, 261; and League of Nations, 210; and Paris Peace Conference (1918–19), 200–1, 208, 212–15, 218, 221, 223; and Poland, 208, 210, 212–15, 221, 223; resigns, 233; and Russia, 188, 189, 190, 210, 212–15; and Sweden, 178, 193, 194, 210; and the United States, 188, 210, 235, 273, 274, 338
Balkans: and the Cretan question, 38–40; and Russian influence in, 40, 51, 372; *also see* 'Bosnian crisis'
Baltic
and balance of power, 186–95, 203, 207, 216–17, 222, 227, 370
and Baltic States, 199–200, 203, 205, 216–17, 218, 222, 370, 371; Estonia, 210, 218, 222; Latvia, 210, 218, 222; Lithuania, 208–9, 210, 222
and Finland, 186–95, 203, 207, 216–17, 222, 227, 370
and Howard: Baltic Commission, 202, 231, 234; Baltic League, 190, 191, 192, 194–5, 203, 210
Bandini, *see* 'Giustiniani-Bandini'
belligerent rights, British doctrine of, 169, 313–14, 314–15, 318, 329–30, 337–8, 341, 342–3, 348; and maritime law conference (1928–9), 333, 333–6, 338–40, 341; *also see* 'blockade' and 'freedom of the seas'
Belloc, Hillaire (British man of letters), 255
Benedict XV (Pope, 1914–22), 360
Bertie, Sir Francis (later Viscount Bertie of Thame)
(British ambassador, Rome, 1903–5): and Crete, 53, 55; and Edward VII – Leo XIII meeting, 35–6; and Foreign Office reform, 36–7; and Hardinge, 36–7; and Howard's reappointment to the Diplomatic Service (1903), 34   1903), 34
Biffen, Rowland (Tobago rubber syndicate), 25–6
'Big Navy Party', 289–90, 303, 312, 315–16, 331, 345, 347
Bildt, Axel de (Swedish anglophile businessman), 135, 157–9, 185–6, 235
Bismarck, Prince Otto von (German chancellor, 1871–90), 11–12, 370
blockade (1914–18)
Anglo-Swedish negotiations (1914), 147, 149, (1915), 147, 148, 149,

Index

152–3, 157, (1916), 162, (1917),
173–4, 175, 178, 181, (1918),
182–5
and British Legation, Stockholm, impact
on, 195–6
and British policy, 144–6, 147, 148,
149, 151–3, 156–7, 160–1, 166–7,
171, 181–2, 182–5, 363, 372; and
blockade claims (1925–7), 295–6,
304, 313
and Consett, 148, 155, 156–7, 160–3,
165, 167–71
and Findlay, 148, 153, 155, 160,
167–8, 169
and Germany, 144, 149, 151, 155–6
and Hammarskjöld, 148, 151, 154–5,
158–9, 173–5, 176, 177, 363
and Howard, 144–6, 148, 151–2,
155–6, 159–60, 363, 372; criticism
of, 148, 149, 150, 167–71, 179;
instructions to, 144, 146–7, 150,
156; and Inter-Allied Trade
Committee, 183; and neutral Powers
(*tertii gaudentes*), 150, 154–5, 363
and Russia, 144–6, 150–1, 160–1,
171–3, 181–2; and trans-shipment
to, 148, 149, 150–1, 157–9, 161,
171, 178, 181–2, 182–5
and Sweden, 144–6, 146–7, 148, 149,
151–3, 166–7, 171, 173–5, 181–2,
182–5, 363, 372
and *Transito Aktiebilag*, 157–9, 161, 175
and the United States, 161, 165, 169,
179, 372; and blockade claims
(1925–7), 295–6, 304, 313
Also see 'belligerent rights' and 'freedom
of the seas'
Blunt, Wilfred Scawen (English eccentric),
11
Board of Trade, 113, 200, 222, 248,
255–61
Boardman family (Washington, DC,
society), 74, 280
Boer War, *see* 'Africa'
Bond, Sir Robert (Newfoundland premier,
1900–9), 82–3, 85–8, 90, 91, 92,
391n80
Bond–Blaine treaty (1891), 82–3, 90
Bond–Hay treaty (1902), 82–3, 87, 90
Booth, Charles (British businessman and
reformer): his enquiry, 20–1, 33, 367,
378n63; and rubber syndicate,
23–4, 26
Borah, William (chairman, Senate Foreign
Relations Committee, 1924–33), 286,
287, 288, 291, 317, 338, 342; and

maritime law conference, 333, 333–6,
341, 347
Bosnian crisis (1908–9), 102–3, 118, 372
'Bosnian solution', 102; and Crete
(1901–6), 47–8, 49; rejected by
Lansdowne, 52–3
Branting, Hjalmar (Swedish politician),
180, 181
Brazil, 33; Howard's trips to, (1895),
23–4, (1897), 26
Brest Litovsk (negotiations and treaty),
187, 188, 189, 192, 193
Briand, Aristide (French foreign minister in
the late 1920s), 292, 330–1; and
renunciatory pact (1928), 316–17,
321, 362
Bridgeman, Sir William (first lord of the
Admiralty, 1924–9), 315, 336,
336–7; and Coolidge naval conference
(1927), 304, 306–9
British Chamber of Commerce in Spain,
236–7, 248, 249
British Delegation, Paris Peace Conference,
see 'Paris Peace Conference'
British Library of Information, New York,
297, 299, 302, 303, 313, 314, 317,
337, 350
British South Africa Company, 15, 17; and
Boer war, 29, 30; and Howard's
criticism of, 16
Britten, Fred (chairman, US House Naval
Affairs Committee, 1924–33), 308,
335
Broderick, J. J. (commercial counsellor,
British Embassy, Washington,
1920–30), 295
Bronewski, Baron de (Russian consul-
general, Crete), 58, 62, 64
Brown, General Preston (US military
commander), 314
Browning, Walter (Rio Tinto Mining
Company manager, Spain), 241–2
Brusilov, General Alexis (Russian military
commander), 161, 165, 166, 171
Bryan, William Jennings (American
politician), 297–8
Bryce, Sir James (after 1914, Viscount
Bryce) (British ambassador,
Washington, DC, 1907–13), 74, 102,
132, 197, 215, 270, 271, 280
and Anglo-American relations, 77–8,
85, 87, 95–6, 271
appointment, 76–7
and Canada, 78–9, 84–5, 87, 90, 93–4,
98
and Lord Grey, 79, 84, 94

and Howard, 76–7, 84, 90, 93–4, 197;
and influence on Howard, 96, 215,
270, 272–3, 275–6, 280, 297, 369
and Newfoundland, 78–9, 90
and Roosevelt, 76, 93–4
and Root, 87, 93–4
and United States press, 97; and public
opinion, 79, 297
Buchanan, Sir George (British ambassador
at St Petersburg [Petrograd],
1910–17), 151, 160–1, 172, 215
Buckmaster, Lord (British preservationist),
355
Butler, Neville (Foreign Office Western
Department), 258–60

Cameron, Mrs (Washington, DC, socialite),
74, 75
Campbell, R. I. (Foreign Office American
Department), 291
Campbell-Bannerman, Sir Henry (British
prime minister, 1905–8), 77, 86;
appointed, 66; resigns, 93
Canada
autonomy in foreign policy, 98–7,
324–8
and Bryce, 78–9, 84–5, 87, 93–4, 96,
98
and fishing rights (1906–7), 81, 82–3,
84, 85, 88; arbitration of, 88–90,
91–4
and Howard
(1906–8), 78–9, 81, 82–3, 84, 85, 86,
88–91, 93–4, 98–9, 101–2; visits
(1907), 84, (1908), 94
(1924–1930), 273, 277, 293, 310–13,
324–8, 356–7, 429n110; visits
(1924–30), 324–8
and Canadian–American relations,
78–9, 88, 89–90, 91–4, 96, 98–9,
273, 324–8
and Canadian sovereignty, 91, 98–9,
324–8
and Newfoundland, 90–1
and pelagic sealing, 81, 94
and reciprocity, 81, 84, 90–1
and Root, 82, 83–4, 87, 273
and the United States
(1906–8), 80–2, 83–4, 88, 93; and
Joint High Commission, 81, 82
(1924–30), 273, 324–8
and West Indian development, 356–7
Caprini, Count (gendarmerie commander,
Crete), 42, 43
Carlisle, Lord (Howard cousin), 26

Carnarvon family, 3, 5
Carnarvon, the third Earl of (Howard's
uncle), 5
Carnarvon, the fourth Earl of (Howard's
cousin and brother-in-law) (viceroy of
Ireland, 1885)
Imperial ideas of, 9–10; impact on
Howard, 9–10, 17–18, 128, 325
death, 14
Carr, Edward Hallett (Howard's secretary,
Paris Peace Conference), 201, 218
Carson, Sir Edward (first Lord of the
Admiralty, 1916–17), 170
Carton de Wiart, General Sir Adrian
(British military adviser, Paris Peace
Conference), 223, 224
Cartwright, Sir Fairfax (British ambassador,
Vienna, 1908–13), 106, 272
and Austria-Hungary, 105, 107–8, 110,
115, 116–17
and Bosnian crisis (1908–9), 107
and Foreign Office, 106, 117
and Germany, 105, 110, 116–17
and Howard, 104, 105, 106–8, 110,
111, 115, 272; Cartwright's
opposition to, 115–17, 118
Castle, William (American State
Department official), 339, 340
Caulfield, Algernon (Howard's
companion, South Africa, 1891),
15–16
Cecil, Lord Robert (after 1923, first
Viscount Cecil of Chelwood), 304,
306–9
(Foreign Office blockade official,
1915–18, and minister of blockade,
1916–18), 161, 161–2, 167; and
Consett, 169, 170; and Howard, 166,
167, 169–70, 178, 184–5, 192, 197;
and Sweden, 173–5, 178, 181, 182,
184–5, 192, 197
(member, British Delegation, Paris Peace
Conference, 1919): and Poland, 207
(chancellor of the Duchy of Lancaster,
1924–7): and Anglo-American
relations, 274, 306–9, 312–13,
315–16, 319
Central Powers, see 'Triple Alliance'
Chamberlain, Sir Austen (British foreign
secretary, 1924–9), 285–7, 291–2,
294, 342
and belligerent rights, 314–15, 318,
330, 335–6, 342
and the Empire, 310
and European security, 285–7, 291–3,
323

Index 457

and Howard, 285-7, 291, 308-9, 309-10, 311-13, 324, 328-9, 330, 351, 375
and League of Nations, 285-7, 292
and renunciatory pact, 316-17, 321-4
and the United States, 285-7, 291-3, 294, 298-9, 308-9, 309-10, 330-1, 336-7, 340, 342; and belligerent rights, 314-15, 317, 318, 329-30, 333-6, 341

Chamberlain, Sir Joseph (British Colonial secretary, 1895-1903), 31, 98

Chambers, F. (Howard's secretary, Budapest, 1909-10), 115

Charles, Captain Ulick (commercial attaché, British Embassy, Madrid, 1919-28), 257, 260-1

Chilton, Henry (counsellor, British Embassy, Washington, 1921-8), 279, 305, 308, 313, 318

Churchill, Sir Winston (chancellor of the exchequer, 1924-9), 308, 335

Clark, Reuban (American State Department official), 338

Clark, Sir William (British high commissioner, Ottawa, after 1928), 327

Clarke, Captain (medical adviser to Prince George of Greece), 41

Claudel, Paul (French ambassador at Washington after 1925), 323

Clemenceau, George (French premier, 1917-20), 202, 217

Cleminson, H. H. (Foreign Office blockade official), 153

Clerk, Sir George (head, Foreign Office War Department), 189-90

Colleoni, Count (Howard's brother-in-law), 123

Colleoni, Countess (Howard's sister-in-law), 123, 198, 301

Colonial Office, 78-9, 87, 92-3, 324-8, 357

Commission on Polish Affairs (1919), 226, 230
  suggested by Howard, 219; created, 222-3

Committee of Imperial Defence, 342; and belligerent rights sub-committee (1927-29), 314-15, 318, 329-30, 333-6, 341; and European security (post-1919), 285-7

Consett, Captain Montagu (British naval attaché, Scandinavia, 1914-18): and blockade, 148, 155, 156-7, 160, 162-3, 167-71; and Denmark, 162, 168-9, 170; and Howard, 148, 159, 162-3, 165, 167-71; and Norway, 148; and Sweden, 155, 162, 167; and Russia, 162, 167

Coolidge, Calvin (American president, 1923-9), 273, 277, 283-4, 287-8, 291-2, 293, 302-3, 321-2, 338, 347
  and his Administration, 281, 283, 284, 287-8, 294, 299, 303-4
  and Howard, 279, 294, 303
  and naval limitation, 288-91, 299, 303-4, 333, 338; and Coolidge naval conference (1927), 303-4, 306-9, 426n36

Coolidge naval conference, *see* 'naval limitation'

Cowles, Anna (Theodore Roosevelt's sister), 73, 75

Crabbet Club, 11, 93

Craigie, Sir Robert (Foreign Office American Department, 1925-8; head, 1928-35), 314, 334, 340, 343-4, 345, 348, 349

Crawley, George (rubber syndicate), 23-4

Cretan Commission of Enquiry (1906), 63, 64, 66; work of, 67-9

Crete, 73, 229
  and 'Bosnian solution', 47, 53
  civil war (1905): course, 56-64; end, 64-5; origins, 54-6
  and the consuls, 41, 44, 45, 48, 49, 55, 57-9, 60, 63-4
  and Cretan Commission of Enquiry (1906), 63, 64, 66, 67-9
  and Eastern question, 38, 40-1
  and *enosis*, 39, 42, 47, 50-1, 54, 103, 372
  and finance, 44-6, 49, 52, 56, 58; and four-Power loan, 44-6
  and gendarmerie, 42, 49, 52, 56, 57-8, 60, 62, 372
  and Greece, 39, 40, 45, 50, 53, 56, 68, 372; and 'Bosnian solution', 47
  and Greek-Cretans, 39, 40, 44, 47-8, 50, 371
  and international troops, 42-3, 54, 55, 56, 57-8, 61-2, 63-4, 372; and Moslem-Cretans, 39, 46, 68-9
  and Prince George's administration, 39, 42-3, 54-6, 59-60; and finance, 44-6, 52, 56; and opposition to, 46-7, 48-9, 50-1, 54, 60-2, 66-7, (and civil war), 55-65, (and Howard's analysis), 48-9

and Protecting Powers, 39–40, 43, 45, 46, 49, 51–3, 54, 55, 56, 60–1, 63–4, 67–9, 372
and Turkey, 38–9, 46–7, 371
Crewe, first Marquess of (Moncton Milne), 11; (colonial secretary, 1908–10), 93
Crowe, Sir Eyre
(head, Foreign Office Western Department), 104; and Austria-Hungary, 106, 111–12, 115, 116, 117, 118; and Bosnian crisis (1908–9), 106; and Germany, 106, 111–12, 115, 116, 117, 118; and Switzerland, 119
(head, Foreign Office Contraband Department), 149–50, 156–7, 161, 181; and Russia, 140–3; and Sweden, 133–4, 138, 140–3, 149–50, 181
(diplomatic adviser, British Delegation, Paris Peace Conference), 200, 202, 208, 223, 230
(permanent under-secretary, Foreign Office, 1920–25), 233; and Spain, 250, 251–5, 256, 259; and United States, 270–1, 272, 278–9; death of, 287
and Howard, 106, 111, 113, 116, 117, 133–4, 138, 140–3, 149–50, 156–7, 165, 181, 200, 202, 208, 223, 230, 251–5, 256, 270–1, 272
and Lloyd George, 230, 270–1; and Lloyd George revolution in foreign policy, 270–1, 328
Cumberland, 3, 5, 25, 29, 71, 73, 196, 197, 234, 350, 353, 366, 367
Curtis, Charles (American vice-president, 1929–33), 350
Curzon of Kedleston, first Marquess of (George Nathaniel Curzon), 11, 74, 75, 197, 261, 272, 276, 369
(foreign secretary, 1919–24); and France, 261–2, 267–8; and Morocco, 247, 251–5, 267–8; and Poland, 212–15; and Spain, 242, 245, 247, 251–5, 261–2, 267–8; and Tangier, 261–3, 267–8; and the United States, 235, 269–71, 272, 273; and Vatican, 358
Cuso, Viscount de (Spanish tariff expert), 257, 259–60
Czechoslovakia, 205, 208–9, 224; and Silesia, 208–9, 221; and Teschen, 208–9, 211, 221, 223–4

Danzig, 211, 221–2, 226–7, 228
Davis, Admiral (American naval commander), 79–80
Davis John (American Democratic Party presidential nominee, 1924), 288
Dawes, General Charles (American vice-president, 1925–9), 319 (American ambassador, London, 1929–31), 342, 343, 346, 348
Deakin, Frederick (press attaché, British Embassy, Madrid, 1919–24), 237, 247
Degrand, Baron (French Polish expert, French Foreign Ministry), 217, 220, 221
Delmé-Radcliffe, Colonel Charles (British military attaché, Paris, 1911–13), 119–20, 122, 123
Denbigh, Lord (senior director, Rio Tinto Mining Company), 241
Deniken, General Anton ('White' Russian leader), 214, 216
Denmark, 150, 162, 168–9, 190
Department of Overseas Trade, see 'Foreign Office'
Destelle, Captain (French commander, Crete), 43
Diplomatic Service
Hardinge, Bertie, and, 36–7, 381n118
Howard on, 22–3, 69, 77, 129–30, 131, 136, 202, 207, 231–3, 270–1; Howard as 'Service man', 22–3, 374–5
Levant Service critical of Howard (1903), 37
Lloyd George revolution and, 200–2, 223, 230, 231–3, 235, 272; Crowe seeks to reverse, 270–1; reversed, 328
Di San Giuliano, Antonio (Italian foreign minister), 23–4, 127
Disraeli, Sir Benjamin (British prime minister, 1868), 9
Dmowski, Roman (Polish nationalist leader), 205, 210–11, 217–18, 219; his critics, 207, 219
Dominions Office, 326–8, 335, 357, 429n110
Douglas, Count (Swedish earl marshall), 139
Draft Treaty of Mutual Assistance, 278
Drogheda, Lord (Foreign Office Western Department), 123
Drouin, Monsieur (French consul-general, Crete), 44
Drummond, Sir Eric (Balfour's private secretary, 1916–19), 195, 197–8, 218, 220, 235, 353

Duckworth, George (secretary, Booth enquiry), 20
Duke of Cambridge's Own, 30, 32
Durand, Sir Mortimer (British ambassador, Washington, DC, 1903-7), 75, 76, 352; and Howard, 71, 72-3, 73-4, 94; his recall, 71, 80, 82, 94, 95, 97
Dyer, Sir Thisselton (curator, Kew Gardens), 25

Eastern Establishment, 74-5, 79
Eastern Galicia, 208, 209, 221, 223, 224
Eastern Question (1903-6), 38, 40-1, 44, 45, 48, 51, 70; (1908-9), 102-3, 118; (1912-14), 127, 128-30
Eden, Nils (Swedish prime minister after 1917), 181, 184
  his government, 182-5, 194; and Brest-Litovsk, 192, 193
Edward VII (King-Emperor of Great Britain, 1901-10), 33, 76, 97; meeting with Leo XIII (1903), 34-6; and Prince George of Greece, 40, 55, 67-8
Edward, Prince of Wales (1910-36), 313, 319-20
Egypt, 19, 247, 252, 321
Ehrensvärd, Count (Swedish foreign minister), 135, 137
Elgin, Lord (British colonial secretary, 1905-8), 87, 93, 98
English Committee in Spain, 255
English-Speaking Union (United States), 280, 281, 296, 305
Entente, see 'Triple Entente'
Estonia, see 'Baltic'
Etter, Baron de (Russian consul-general, Crete), 48

Fașciotti, Signor (Italian consul-general, Crete), 58, 61, 64
Federation of British Industries, 248, 257, 261
Fernandez-Silvestre, General Manuel (Spanish commander, Annual), 251
Fielding, Sir Charles (chairman, Rio Tinto Mining Company), 241-2
Findlay, Sir Mansfeldt (British minister, Christiania, 1911-23); and blockade, 148, 155, 160, 167-8, 169; critical of Howard, 148, 159, 167-8; criticism of Findlay, 153, 200; and Hardinge, 167-8; and Norway, 148, 153; and Sweden, 155
Finland
  and Aland Islands, 147-8, 151, 187, 190, 191-4
  and Britain, 187, 188, 189, 190-1, 191-4, 207, 209
  and civil war, 187-9, 190-1, 209
  and Bolshevik Russians, 187, 189, 209
  and Germany, 189, 190, 191-4
  and 'White' victory, 188-9; and 'White' policy, 189, 191, 207, 209
  and Germany, 151, 186-7, 187, 188, 189, 191-4
  and independence, (1915), 151, 187, (1917-18), 186-7, 187-8, 189-90, 191, 209
  and Russia, 151, 187, 186-7, 187-8, 189-90, 209
  and Sweden, 151, 187, 186-7, 191-4
Fitzalan, Lord (Howard's cousin), 360
Fitzpatrick, Sir Charles (Canadian chief justice), 89, 94
Fletcher, Angus (British Library of Information, New York), 297, 299
Fontenay, Baron de (French minister, Berne), 114
Foreign Office
  and Admiralty, 167-71, 180-1, 318, 335
  and Austria-Hungary, 102-3, 106, 108-9, 111, 112, 113, 116, 117
  and 'big picture', 69, 112, 144, 252
  and Canada, (1906-8), 81, 82-3, 84, 85, 88-90, 91-4, 101-2, (1924-30), 276, 324-8
  and Crete, 40, 43, 44, 45-6, 50, 52-3, 55-6, 57, 59
  Department of Overseas Trade, 236-7, 327, 357
  and Dominions Office, 326-8, 335
  and France, 111-12, 118, 178, 204-6, 212, 220-1, 246, 247-8, 249-50, 251, 252, 253, 255-6, 261-3, 264, 267-8, 330-1
  and Germany, 106, 119, 120, 124, 129, 133-4, 137, 139, 143, 147, 155-6, 212-15, 215-17
  and Italy, 120-1, 267-8, 331
  and Lloyd George, 200-2, 217, 223, 271, 272, 375
  and MacDonald, 342, 343, 349
  and Morocco, 247, 249-50, 251-5, 263-7; and Annual, 249-50, 251-5, 263-7; and France, 246-8, 249-50, 251, 252, 253, 255, 261-3, 267-8; and Tangier, 236, 246, 247-8, 261-3, 267
  and Paris Peace Conference (1919): and British Delegation, 199-202, 208-9, 217, 218-19, 220-1, 223, 226-7;

460   *Index*

and domestic criticism, 200; and
  Hardinge, 199–202, 233; and Lloyd
  George, 164–6, 202–2, 217, 223,
  230, 231–3, 270–1, 273, 328–9; and
  Polish borders, 211–12, 217, 226–7
and Poland, 199–200, 203–4, 208–9,
  212–17, 217–19, 220, 222–3,
  226–7; Foreign Office critics of, 219,
  223, 227; Foreign Office opposition to
  Howard, 223, 226–7
and Russia, 95, 128, 129–30, 133–4,
  137, 144, 155, 160–1, 161–2,
  172–3, 188, 189–90, 204–7,
  212–15, 215–17
and Spain: and commercial treaty,
  236–7, 246, 248–9, 251, 252, 254,
  255–61; and domestic politics,
  238–40, 241–2, 243, 245, 246,
  246–7, 249–51, 252, 254, 255–61,
  263–7, 267–8; and foreign policy,
  246, 246–7, 247–8, 249–50, 250–1,
  251–5, 261–3, 263–7, 267–8; and
  Gibraltar, 246, 252–3; and Howard,
  247, 251–5, 258–9, 261, 261–3,
  263–7, 267–8
and Sweden, 132–4, 137, 139, 140,
  144, 146–7, 149–50, 152–3, 155,
  156–7, 159–61, 174, 182–5, 193,
  194, 197;
and blockade, 144–5, 146–7, 149–50,
  151–3, 156–7, 165–6, 167–71, 178,
  182–5; and blockade claims
  (1925–27), 295–6; and trans-shipment,
  148, 149, 150–1, 157–9, 161, 171,
  178, 182, 185; and the United States,
  161, 169, 183
and Consett, 156–7, 167–71
and Finland, 187, 188, 189–90,
  191–4, 207
and Howard: criticism of, 148, 149,
  150, 151–2, 179; and Ministry of
  Blockade, 161, 161–2, 167, 169–71,
  182–5; opposition to, 151–2, 153,
  159, 162–3, 165–6, 195
and Switzerland, 119, 120–1, 122–3,
  124, 125–6
and United States: (1906–8), 71, 73,
  75–6, 77–8, 87, 91, 92, 93, 94;
  (1912), 272; (1914–18), 165, 175,
  178, 179, 183, 185–6, 187, 188;
  (1919), 235; (1924–30), 269–71,
  278–9, 283, 284, 285–7, 287–8,
  293–4, 297–9, 309–13, 317–18,
  319–20, 330–1, 331–2, 333–6,
  338–40, 344–8, 348–9, 349

and arbitration treaty, 317, 333–6,
  338–40, 341
and belligerent rights, 309–13,
  313–15, 317–18, 330–1, 333–6; and
  maritime law conference, 333, 333–6,
  338–40, 343
and Dominions Office, 324–8, 335
and European security, 285–7,
  291–3
and Foreign Office support for Howard,
  324, 330, 344–8, 348–9, 351
and Hoover, 332, 333–6, 338–40,
  341, 341–2
and League of Nations, 285–7, 292
and naval arms limitation, 277–8, 284,
  288–91, 299, 313, 330–1, 333–6,
  336–7, 338–40, 341–2; and Coolidge
  naval conference (1927), 303–4,
  306–9; and Preparatory Commission,
  292–3, 299, 303, 304, 330, 333,
  337, 341–2
and renunciatory pact, 317, 333–6,
  338–40, 341
Fort, Seymour (secretary to the governor,
  Cape Colony), 15
Foumis, Constantine (Venizelos supporter),
  49, 56, 59, 63–4
Fountain, Henry (Board of Trade official),
  258–9
France, 1, 8, 13, 367
  and Austria-Hungary, 111–12, 113,
    125, 394n38
  and Boer War, 29
  and Crete, 39, 58, 61, 64, 66, 67–9,
    371
  and Finland, 187
  and Germany, 51, 107, 108, 111–12,
    119–20, 120–1, 125, 143, 165, 212,
    221, 224–6
  and Great Britain, 5, 51, 111–12, 118,
    124, 130, 165, 204–6, 212, 216,
    220–1, 224–6, 236, 246, 247–8,
    249–50, 251, 252, 253, 255, 256,
    261–3, 263–4, 267–8, 291–2, 309,
    324, 330–1, 348, 371
  and Italy, 124
  and Morocco: (1893); 19–20; (1904),
    235; (1911), 119, 124; (1914),
    235–6; (1919–24), 236, 246, 247–8,
    249–50
  and Poland, (1914–18), 204–6,
    (1918–19), 212, 216, 221, 228; and
    Inter-Allied Commission to Poland,
    220–1, 224–6
  and Russia, 106, 107, 108, 187,
    204–6, 212, 216, 221

and Spain, 236, 246, 247–8, 249–50, 251, 252, 253, 255, 255–61, 261–3, 267–8
and Switzerland, 118–19, 120
and Tangier, 236, 247–8, 261–3
and the United States, 316–17, 321–4, 330–1, 348
Francis Joseph I (Emperor of Austria, 1848–1916), 109, 110, 115, 400n86
Frederick I (Emperor of Germany, 1888), 11–12
freedom of the seas, American theory of, 165, 313–14, 333, 337–8, 343, 348; and maritime law conference, 333, 333–6, 338–40, 341; *also see* 'belligerent rights' and 'blockade'
Frisell, Erik (Swedish businessman), 17, 404n47

Garfield, James (Republican statesman), 77, 96, 273, 280, 334–5, 338
Gaselee, Sir Stephen (Foreign Office librarian), 253
Geddes, Sir Auckland (British ambassador, Washington, 1920–4), 269–70, 272, 273
Geddes, Sir Eric (first lord of the Admiralty, 1917–19), 191
Geffecken, Professor Heinrich (German liberal), 12
Geneva Protocol, 283, 284, 285–7
George I (King of the Hellenes, 1863–1913), 39, 40, 66
George V (King-Emperor of Great Britain, 1910–36), 124, 134, 140, 170, 197, 327, 329, 353
George of Greece, Prince (high commissioner, Crete, 1898–1907), 102, 170
and his administration, 39, 46–7, 48–9, 54–6, 58–60
appointment, (1898), 39; reappointment (1901), 39, (1904), 53–4
and 'Bosnian solution', (1901–4), 47–8, 49, 102; Lansdowne rejects, 52–3
and civil war (1905): course, 56–64; end, 64–5; origins, 54–6
and consuls, 39, 45, 49, 55, 57–9, 60, 63–5
and Cretan opposition, 46–7, 50–1, 52, 54, 56–7, 60, 66–7; and Venizelos, 46–7, 49, 50–1, 52, 54–5, 59–60, 62, 64–5, 66–7
and *enosis*, 39, 41, 42, 47–8, 50–1, 54
and gendarmerie, 42–3, 55, 56, 57, 60
and Howard, 39, 41–2, 43, 44–5, 48–9, 52–3, 54–6, 57–8, 60, 64–5, 67, 68, 370; retrospective criticism of Howard, 40, 69
and international troops, 42–3, 54, 57, 63–5
and Isabella Howard, 41
and Italy, 41, 42–3, 50, 66
and Lansdowne, 49, 52–3, 54, 63; and *Fortnightly Review* article, 63
and Protecting Powers, 39, 41, 42–3, 45, 49–52, 54, 57, 59–60, 63–5; tour of capitals (1904), 49–52
Germany, 1, 11–13, 367
and Austria-Hungary, 39, 40, 53, 54, 68–9, 103–4, 105, 108, 110, 111, 112, 113, 114–15, 120–1, 122–5, 134
and Boer War, 29
and Crete, 39, 40, 51, 53, 54, 68–9
and Danzig, 211, 221–2, 226–7, 228
and East Prussia, 211, 221–2, 228
and Finland, 151, 186–7, 188, 189, 191–4
Foreign Ministry, 114, 118, 121, 138–9
and France, 51, 107, 108, 111–12, 119–20, 120–1, 125, 143, 165, 212, 224–6, 291–2
and Great Britain, 51, 75, 86, 103–4, 112, 113, 114–15, 118, 133–4, 143, 155, 165, 185–6, 187, 208–9, 211–12, 212–15, 215–17, 224–6, 227–31, 246, 277, 283, 291–2, 331; and Anderson mission (1890), 12–13
and great War: defeat, 198–9, 207; domestic conditions, 155–6; unrestricted submarine warfare, 165, 169, 175
and Howard, 1, 8, 11–13, 103–4, 107, 114–15, 118, 122–5, 143–4, 186, 198–9, 206–7, 211–12, 212–15, 215–17, 224–6, 227–31, 246, 255, 361–5, 367
and international peace and security (1933–9), 361–5
and Italy, 120–1, 122–4, 124–6
and July crisis, 143–4
and Morocco, 246
and Norway, 148
and Poland, 204–5, 206–7, 208–9, 210–11, 212–15, 215–17, 221–2, 224, 225–6, 227–30; and Polish corridor, 209, 210, 221–2, 227–30; and Poznan negotiations, 224, 225–6
and Russia, 106, 108, 114, 133–4; and Brest-Litovsk treaty, 187, 188, 189, 192, 193; and separate peace (1915), 155

462 Index

and Spain, 246, 255
and Sweden, 133–4, 138–9, 143, 144, 153–4, 155, 167, 168, 177, 180–1, 183–5, 185–6, 193, 194
and Switzerland, 118–19, 120, 125–6, 127
and Turkey, 39, 40, 51, 68–9, 155, 213
and the United States, 165, 175, 179
and Versailles Treaty, 231
Also see 'Triple Alliance'
Gibraltar, 20, 246, 252–3, 267
Gibson, William (British vice-consul, San Salvador), 294
Giustiniani-Bandini, Isabella, *see* 'Howard, Isabella'
Giustiniani-Bandini, Prince (Howard's father-in-law), 24, 33
Giustiniani-Bandini, Princess (Howard's mother-in-law), 27, 29
Gladstone, William (British Liberal Party leader, 1868–94), 17–18, 21
Gleichen, Lord Edward (British military attaché, Washington, DC), 73
Goluchowski, Count (Austro-Hungarian foreign minister, 1895–1906), 54
Grant Watson, Herbert (third secretary, British Embassy, Washington, DC, 1908), 97
Graves, Robert (British consul-general, Crete, 1899–1903), 41, 42
Gray, Christian (Tobago rubber syndicate), 23, 25
Great Britain
  and anti-Americanism, 274, 308, 315, 319, 329–30, 335, 343, 345–6
  and Atlanticism, 274
  and Austria-Hungary, 102–3, 107, 108–9, 114–15, 116, 129–30; and Bosnian crisis (1908–9), 104, 107, 115; and Hungary, 105, 107, 108–9, 111–12, 113, 116
  and Baltic, 189, 190, 203, 208–9, 211–12, 212–17, 218
  and belligerent rights, 289–91, 309–13, 313–15, 318, 329–30, 333–6, 337–8, 341, 342, 343, 348; and blockade claims (1925–7), 295–6, 304, 313; and maritime law conference, 333, 333–6, 338–40, 341, 343
  and Canada, 78–9, 81, 82–3, 84, 85–8, 89–90, 91, 276, 319–30, 324–8, 356–7
  and Crete, 38–40, 50, 51, 52–3, 59, 64, 66, 67–9
  and Czechoslovakia, 208–9, 221; and Inter-Allied Commission to Teschen, 223–4
  and Denmark, 150
  and Eastern Question, 38–40, 70, 103, 127, 128–30
  and European security arrangements (1924–30), 278, 280–1, 284, 285–7, 291–3, 323
  and Finland, 187, 188, 189–90, 191, 203, 208–9, 212–17
  and France, 5, 111–12, 118, 178, 204–6, 212, 220–1, 246, 247–8, 249–50, 251, 252, 253, 256, 261–3, 263–4, 267–8, 291–2, 309, 324, 330–1
  and Germany, 5, 12, 12–13, 75, 86, 120–1, 124, 128–30, 133–4, 136, 139–40, 143–4, 147, 155, 165, 169, 175, 185–6, 187, 208–9, 211–12, 212–15, 215–17, 224–6, 227–31, 246, 277, 283, 291–2, 361–4
  and Gibraltar, 246, 252–3, 267
  and Greece, 40
  and Imperial isolationism, 274–5
  and Italy, 10–11, 39, 42, 43, 58, 61, 64, 66, 67–8, 122–4, 150, 267–8, 309, 331, 358–60
  and Japan, 288, 306–9, 330–1
  and Malta crisis (1930–1), 358–60
  and Morocco, 235–6, 246, 247–8, 249–50, 250–1, 251–5, 261–3, 263–7; and Annual, 249–50, 250–1, 251–5, 256–7, 263–7
  and naval limitation, 277–8, 284, 288–91, 299, 315–16, 333–6, 338, 338–40, 343–4, 344–8, 348–9
  and Coolidge naval conference (1927), 303–4, 306–9, 426n36
  and London naval conference (1930), 348, 353
  and Preparatory Commission, 292–3, 299, 303, 304, 330, 333, 337, 341–2, 343–4; and Anglo-French disarmament compromise (1928), 330–1, 341
  and Newfoundland, 78–9, 82–3, 84, 85–8, 89–90, 91–4, 391n91; and fishing *modus vivendi*, 86, 87, 88, 391n91
  and Poland, (1914–18), 204–5, 409n28, (1918–19), 208–9, 211–12, 212–15, 215–17, 218, 219, 220–1, 222–3, 227–30
  and Dmowski, 205, 207, 210–11, 217–18, 219

and Inter-Allied Mission to Poland, 202, 220-1, 222-3
and National Committee, 204-6, 207, 210, 212, 217-18, 219
and Pilsudski, 205, 210-11, 218
and Russia (tsarist regime), 38-9, 40, 48, 51, 58, 59, 64, 66, 67-8, 70, 107, 114, 129-30, 133-4, 136, 144, 144-6, 146-7, 150-1, 155, 160-1, 168, 187; and Eastern Question, 38, 70; Provisional and Bolshevik regime, 171-3, 174, 175, 181-2, 187, 188, 189-90, 204-6, 211-12, 212-15, 215-17, 218, 219-20, 282-3, 283-4,
and Spain
  and Alfonso XIII, 237, 239, 241, 245, 255, 264, 267
  and domestic politics, 237-8, 239-40, 241-2, 242-5, 250-1, 255, 255-61, 263-7; fascism, rise of, 263-7, 267-8; and juntas, 238-9, 243, 244-5, 263-7; and working-class radicalism, 238, 238-40, 241-2, 242-3, 245, 264-5
  and foreign policy, 235-7, 239, 241, 245, 246, 247-8, 249-50, 250-1, 251-5, 255-61, 261-3, 363-7, 367-8; and commercial treaty, 236-7, 246, 248-9, 251, 252, 254, 255-61; and Gibraltar, 246, 252-3
  and Primo de Rivera, 251, 263, 266-8
and Sweden, 133-4, 136, 138, 139-40, 140-3, 144, 144-6, 146-7, 148, 149-50, 150-1, 152-3, 160-1, 166-7, 173-4, 175, 176, 177-9, 180-1, 182-5, 185-6, 191-4, 197
  and blockade, 144-6, 149-50, 150-1, 152-3, 154-5, 160-1, 165, 166-7, 173-4, 175, 176, 177-9, 181, 182-5; and *Transito Aktiebilag*, 157-9, 161, 175
and Switzerland, 118-19, 120-1, 126
and Tangier, 236, 246, 247-8, 261-3, 267
and Turkey, 38-40, 70, 103, 127, 128-30, 213, 254, 263
and the Ukraine, 199-200, 208-9, 219, 221, 223, 225
and the United States, 72, 75-6, 81, 86, 91-4, 98-9, 101-2, 161, 165, 175, 178, 179, 183, 185-6, 187, 217-18, 218-19, 271-2, 279-83; 285-7, 288-91, 296-9, 302-3, 306-9, 315-316, 319-20, 330-1, 333-6, 338, 338-40, 340-1, 341-2, 342-3, 344-8, 348-9, 391n80
  and anglophobia, 274-5, 288-91, 296-9, 302, 315-16, 319, 331, 337-8, 345
  and arbitration, 317, 333-6, 341, 344
  and Canada, 80-2, 83-4, 88, 93, 273, 324-8
  and Dawes Plan, 277, 283
  and isolationism, 274, 281, 289-90
  and liquor smuggling, 292-3, 304, 313, 321
  and naval limitation, 277-8, 284, 288-91, 299, 315-16, 333-6, 338, 338-40, 343-4, 344-8, 348-9
  and Coolidge naval conference (1927), 303-4, 306-9, 426n36
  and London naval conference (1930), 348, 353
  and Preparatory Commission, 292-3, 299, 303, 304, 330, 333, 337, 341-2, 343-4; and Anglo-French disarmament compromise (1928), 330-1, 341
  and Prohibition, 292-3, 304, 313, 321, 331, 345, 434n200
  and war debt, 275, 277-8, 298-9
  and Vatican, 360-1; (1903), 34-6; (1919), 357-8; (1931-9), 358-60
Greece
  and Crete, 39, 40, 45, 50, 53, 56, 68, 372; and 'Bosnian solution', 47
  and *enosis* with Crete, 39, 42, 46-7, 49-50, 68, 103, 372
  and Great Britain, 40
Gregory, John (Russian Section, Foreign Office War Department), 189-90
Greig, S. V. (Colonial Office official), 357
Grey, Albert, Earl of Howick (Imperialist and governor-general of Canada, 1904-11), 14, 82, 83, 84, 86; and Canadian-American relations, 79, 82, 94
Grey, Sir Edward (after 1916, first Viscount Grey of Fallodon),
  (parliamentary under-secretary, Foreign Office, 1892-5), 22
  (foreign secretary, 1905-1916), 116, 127, 128, 143
  appointment, 66
  and Austria-Hungary, 102, 103, 105, 107, 108, 111-12, 113, 116, 117, 124, 129
  and Consett, 169
  and Crete, 66, 70
  and Findlay, 148, 151-2, 153

and Germany, 124, 129, 143, 147,
   155
and Howard, 22, 70, 113, 122,
   128–30, 139–40, 149, 151–2, 153,
   159, 169, 197, 199, 205–6, 372,
   401n107
and Italy, 122, 124
and Norway, 148, 153
and Poland, 205–6
radical criticism of, 95, 128, 129–30,
   199, 372
resignation, 164–5
and Russia, 155; and Anglo-Russian
   entente (1907), 95, 128, 129–30,
   137–8
and Sweden, 137–8, 139–40, 147,
   149, 153, 161, 169
and Switzerland, 120, 121
and the United States, 71, 73, 75–6,
   80, 83, 86, 87, 88, 92, 94, 161, 169,
   197, 272
Greystoke, 5–6, 71, 99, 196, 353, 355,
   365, 366, 367
Grigg, Sir Edward (British political writer),
   364
Grigorovich, Vice-Admiral Ivan (Russian
   minister of marine), 147
Gustav V (King of Sweden, 1907–50),
   135, 138, 139–40, 176, 235; pro-
   Germanism of, 133–4, 147, 177

Habsburg Empire, see 'Austria-Hungary'
Halifax, Lord (British foreign secretary,
   1938–40), 361
Haller, General Joseph (Polish military
   commander), 212
Hambro, Eric (Anglo-Swedish banker),
   160
Hammann, Otto (German diplomatist),
   114, 118
Hammarskjöld, Hjalmar (Swedish premier,
   1914–17), 135–6, 140, 141, 142,
   151, 158, 159, 162, 170, 171,
   173–5, 180, 181, 182, 363, 370;
   argument with Howard, 154–5; his
   government, 148, 154, 158–9, 171,
   173–5, 176–7; resigns, 176
Hankey, Sir Maurice (secretary to the CID,
   1912–37, and the Cabinet, 1916–37),
   274, 342; and belligerent rights, 315,
   329–30, 334, 335, 341, 342, 343,
   348; criticises Howard, 329–30; and
   Paris Peace Conference, 201–2, 230
Harding, Warren (American president,
   1921–3), 277, 281, 283

Hardinge, Sir Arthur (British ambassador,
   Madrid, 1913–19), 234, 237, 238
Hardinge, Sir Charles (after 1910, first
   Baron Hardinge of Penshurst), 120,
   143, 353, 381n118
   (assistant under-secretary, Foreign Office,
   1903–4)
   and Crete, 50, 55; instructions to
      Howard, 40, 43; and Prince George of
      Greece, 41
   and Howard; impressed with Howard,
      36, 70; gets Howard Crete consul-
      generalship, 36–7, 381n118
   (permanent under-secretary, 1906–10)
   appointed, 66, 96
   and Austria-Hungary, 102, 103,
      110–11, 115, 117, 118
   and Bryce, 74, 76
   and Canada, 98, 102
   and Crete, 70
   and Howard, 70, 71, 74, 101–2
   and the United States, 71, 73, 77, 87,
      89, 102; and Durand's recall, 71,
      73–4
   (permanent under-secretary, 1916–20):
   and blockade, 166
   and Consettt, 166
   and Finland, 188, 207, 210
   and Germany, 207, 210
   and Howard, 166, 167, 179, 185,
      188, 192, 195, 197, 199–201, 208,
      230
   and Paris Peace Conference (1919):
      and Howard, 199, 203–4; and ideas
      concerning, 199 201; and Lloyd
      George, 201–2, 230; and loss of
      power, 201–2, 230
   reappointed, 166
   resigns, 233
   and Russia, 167, 172–3, 210
   and Sweden, 174, 179, 185, 192, 207,
      210
Harris, Walter (*Times* correspondent), 19,
   21
Harvey, George (American anglophile
   diplomatist), 298–9
Headlam-Morley, Sir James (Political
   Intelligence Department, Foreign
   Office, 1919), 223, 227
Hearst, William Randolph (American
   anglophobic newspaper publisher),
   298, 320
Hedin, Sven (Swedish anglophobe
   academic), 139, 141, 194
Heflin, Senator (American politician),
   299

Index

Heidenstam, Werner von (Swedish poet), 139
Hellner, Johannes (Swedish businessman), 174, 404n47; (Swedish foreign minister after 1917), 181, 182, 184, 186, 193, 194
Henderson, Sir Arthur (British foreign secretary, 1929–31), 342, 346; and Howard, 342, 349, 350
Herbert, Arthur (Carnarvon cousin), 19
Herbert, Aubrey (Howard nephew), 21
Herbert, Mervyn (Howard nephew), 21, 237
Hindenburg, Field Marshal Paul von (German military commander), 194, 198–9
Hitler, Adolph (German dictator, 1933–45), 361, 364
Hofmeyr, Jan (Cape Colony politician), 15
Holmes, Oliver Wendell (American Supreme Court justice), 75, 280
Hontoria, Manuel Gonzalez (Spanish foreign minister), 256, 258
Hoover, Herbert
  (American secretary for commerce, 1921–8), 298, 309–10, 317, 373
  (American president, 1929–33), 331–2, 338–40, 341
  his Administration, 284, 338
  and Borah, 333–6, 347
  and Great Britain, 317, 333–6, 341, 342–3, 348–9
  and Howard, 309–10, 317, 331–2, 333–6, 338–40, 341, 342–3, 344–8, 348–9, 350, 373; and MacDonald visit, 344–8, 348–9; and MacDonald–Hoover conversations, 348
  and maritime law conference, 333–6, 338–40, 341, 343
  and naval limitation, 341–2, 344–8, 348–9
Houghton, Alanson (American ambassador, London, 1925–29), 342
House, Colonel Edward (American foreign-policy expert): and Anglo-American relations (1924–30), 273, 280, 290–1, 313–14, 316; and Paris Peace Conference (1919), 210, 217, 220
Howard, Charlotte (Howard's mother): background, 3; and Howard, 4, 8, 14, 24; illness and death of, 24–5; religion, 4, 25
Howard, Edmund (Howard's son), 117, 135, 197, 225, 230, 234, 301, 367

Howard, Cardinal Edward (Howard's cousin), 11
Howard, Elizabeth (Howard's sister; after 1878, the Countess of Carnarvon), 9, 21, 26, 29, 32, 209, 301, 371; widowed, 14
Howard, Esme William (after 1930, first Baron Howard of Penrith)
attitudes
  anti-bolshevism, 21, 215–17, 218, 220, 227–30, 237, 410n56
  'Atlanticism', 99, 274, 281, 290–1, 325, 361–5, 372–3
  and Austria-Hungary, 104–5, 109–12, 114–15, 117–18, 124–5, 372
  and balance of power, 118, 124, 126, 127, 128–30, 137, 186–95, 203, 212–15, 215–17, 227–30, 236, 237, 245, 251–5, 267–8, 281–2, 324–8, 362–3, 370, 371
  and Baltic Powers, 186–95, 202, 203, 207, 210, 216–17, 222, 227, 370
  and Boers, 16, 31
  and Cumberland, 3, 5, 25, 29, 71, 73, 196, 197, 234, 350, 353, 366, 367
  and diplomacy
    armed strength, need for, 128–9, 199, 212–15, 252, 333, 371–2
    and balance of power, 106, 118, 122, 124, 126, 127, 128–30, 133, 137, 186–95, 202–3, 212–17, 227–30, 236, 237, 245, 251–5, 267–8, 281–2, 324–8, 362–3, 370, 371
    'big picture', 69, 112, 144, 156, 252, 374–5
    dispassionate, need to be, 13, 70, 130, 136, 144, 203, 212, 215–17, 224, 254–5, 368–9, 371
    economics and foreign policy, connexion between, 15, 17, 20–1, 98–9, 145–6, 157–9, 161, 174, 175, 181–2, 195–6, 211–12, 222, 227, 228–9, 237,276–7, 362–3, 372
    non-partisan, need to be, 95, 128, 129–30
    'old diplomacy' maxims, 275–6, 280, 281–2, 296–7, 313, 319, 375
    patience, need for, 65–6
    professionalism, need for, 22–3, 77, 118, 129–30, 131, 136, 202, 207, 231–3, 270–1, 328–9, 369–70, 370–3, 374–5; and unschooled critics of British foreign policy, 128, 129–30, 199, 263–4, 370, 372

466 Index

Howard (cont.)
  realism, need for, 91, 112, 129–30, 136, 144, 203, 207, 212–15, 215–17, 224, 251–5, 270–1, 281–2, 369–70, 371–2, 375
  'Service man', 69, 96, 130, 269–71, 350, 374–5
  and visible ambassador, 275–6, 280–3, 290, 296–9, 305–6, 336–7, 348–9
  dislikes: city life, 5; 'Society', 8
  likes: countryside, 5, 71, 243, 355, 365; and Greystoke, 3, 5–6, 99, 196, 197, 355, 366, 367
  'Economic Credo', 21, 23, 25, 33, 99, 237, 355, 365, 368
  and Empire, 3, 9–10, 90, 91, 98, 105, 118, 143, 277, 309–13, 322, 356–7, 361–5
    and Canada, 78–9, 81, 82–3, 84, 85, 86, 88–91, 93–4, 98–9, 101–2, 273, 277, 293, 310–13, 324–8, 356–7, 429n110
    and dominion sovereignty, 91, 98–9, 324–8
    and Imperial federation, 14, 17, 23; and Boer War, 30
    and Imperial preference, 15, 17, 20–1, 98–9
  and Ireland, 9–10, 17–18, 128, 206, 325, 360
  and France, 1, 8, 19–20, 118–19, 120, 125, 126, 212, 216, 220–1, 228, 235–6, 246, 247–8, 249–50, 251, 252, 253, 256, 261–3, 264, 267–8, 316–17, 321–4, 330–1, 367
  and Germany, 1, 11–13, 20–1, 103–4, 105, 108, 111–13, 114–15, 118, 127, 133, 138–40, 143–4, 186, 211–12, 212–15, 215–17, 224–6, 227–31, 246, 255, 361–5, 367, 371, 372;
    and Howard's anti-Germanism, 8, 11–13, 103–4, 105, 107, 114–15, 118, 122–5, 143, 198–9, 206–7, 224–6, 227–31, 361, 370
  and Ireland, 9–10, 128, 345, 368; and anti-British propaganda, 246, 360; and Home Rule, 9–10, 15, 206
  and Italy, 3, 10–11, 24–5, 122, 267–8, 361–5, 367, 371; and Howard's italophilia, 8, 10–11, 124, 132, 232–3, 354, 358–60, 361, 367; and Mussolini, 361, 436n37
  'July crisis', 143–4, 198–9, 370
  and League of Nations, 281–2, 361–5
  and Lloyd George, 203, 217, 218–19, 219–20, 223, 227–30, 274
  and Poland, 199–200, 202, 203–4, 207, 211–12, 212–17, 217–18, 219, 224–5, 226–7, 227–30, 273, 370, 371, 409n28, 412n91
  press, power of the, 97, 185–6, 246, 275–6, 282–3, 297–9, 305–6, 307–8, 331, 336–7, 337–8; and radio (1924–30), 282, 306, 349
  and Roman Catholicism, 26–7, 28–9, 33, 301–2, 367–8, 369
  and the Empire, 358, 361
  and foreign policy, 370–1; and Anglo-Italian relations, 34–6, 358–60, 361; and Britain's apostolic delegate, selection of (1938), 361; and Ireland, 246–7, 360; and Malta crisis (1930–1), 358–60; and Poland, 203, 216–17; and Pope Pius XII, selection of (1939), 361; and Roman question (1919), 357–8; and Spain, 246–7
  and Russia
    (tsarist regime), 38–9, 40, 48, 51, 58, 59, 64, 66, 67–8, 70, 107, 114, 128, 129–30, 133–4, 137–8, 143, 145–6, 148, 149, 150–1, 155, 159, 162–3, 167, 168, 212–15, 372
    (Provisional and Bolshevik regimes), 171–3, 203, 210, 211–12, 212–15, 218, 227–30, 240, 371, 410n56; and 'White Russians' (1918–19), 213–14, 215–16
  and social reform, 12, 20–1, 237, 354–5, 365, 368
  and Spain, 238–40, 242–5, 246, 247–8, 248–9, 249–50, 251, 252–3, 256–7, 257–61, 263–7, 267–8
  and 'State Socialism', 14, 20, 368
  and Sweden, 132–3, 136, 138, 139–40, 140–3, 144–6, 148, 149, 153–4, 159–60, 161–2, 167, 171, 183–5, 194–5, 210, 273
  and Turkey, 128, 213, 254, 371
  and the United States, 26, 372–3; (1906–8), 76, 79, 83, 96, 99, 99–100, 101–2; (1908–24), 161, 165, 175, 178, 179, 180, 181–6, 187, 205, 212, 218–19, 220, 271–2; (1924–30), 272–6, 276–7, 279–83, 285–7, 288–91, 291–3, 295–6, 302–3, 304–5, 307–8, 309–13, 314–15, 316–17, 317–18, 319–21, 321–4, 330–1, 331–2, 333–6, 337–8

Index

awards (in chronological order), 165
  Royal Victorian Order (1904), and Commander of the Royal Victorian Order (1906), 70
  Knight Commander of the Order of St Michael and St George (1916), 159, 162, 185, 401n107, and Grand Cross of the Order of St Michael and St George (1922), 261
  honorary doctorates (1924–30): McGill University, 296; George Washington University, 296; Trinity College (Hartford, Connecticut), 336; Georgetown University, 350
  Grand Cross of the Order of the Bath (1928), 324, 329
  peerage (1930), first Baron Howard of Penrith, 353
character, 69–70, 365–75
  ambition to succeed, 13–14, 23, 32–3, 365, 369
  analytical abilities, 7, 14, 32–4, 69–70, 100, 107–8, 109–11, 113, 124, 125–6, 183–5, 212–15, 227–30, 251–5, 276–7, 285–91, 302–3, 309–13, 313–15, 315–17, 317–18, 321–4, 324–8, 329–30, 331–2, 333–7, 358–9, 361–5, 369–70, 370–3
  compassion for others, 20–1, 225, 367, 368
  dispassionate in assessment, 13, 70, 130, 136, 144, 203, 212, 215–17, 224, 254–5, 268–9, 368–9, 369–70, 370–1
  history, sense of, 5–6, 99, 353, 366
  recognition of limitation, 7, 14, 32–4, 368–9
  shaped: as a boy, 3–6, 99, 367, 376n16; as a young man, 13–33, 369
  tolerance towards other people, 9–10, 33, 99–100, 206, 366–7, 371, 376n16
and Cumberland, 3, 5, 25, 29, 71, 73, 196, 197, 234, 350, 353, 366, 367
and family, 2–3, 366–7
  ancestors: Howards, 3, 366; Longs, 3, 367; Walpoles, 3
  connexion with England's history, 3–6, 366–7
  relationships with: his children, 99, 196, 197, 234, 270, 300–2, 367, his parents, 4, 5, 8, 14, 24–5, 367, his siblings, 5, 367, his wife, 24–5, 26–7, 33, 38, 42, 48, 63, 71, 123, 132, 134, 135, 136, 179, 196, 197–8, 234, 300–2, 367–8, 369
finances, 72, 101, 117, 374
  Louis d'Or cocoa plantation, 25–6, 30, 72, 101, 379n78
  mother's endowment, 14
  need to sell valuables (1917), 195–6, 407n126
  and rubber syndicate, 25–6, 30, 72, 101, 379n78
'great ideas', 14, 23, 368
and languages, facility for, 7, 8, 13
and religion
  family's Protestantism, 4, 28
  Howard's early agnosticism, 26
  Roman Catholicism, 354, 367–8, 369, 370–1
  converts, 28–9
  initial uncertainty about, 26–7
  and Isabella Bandini (Howard), 27, 367–8, 369
  and Howard: his character, 33, 301–2, 367–8, 369; criticised because of, 203, 299, 329; Foreign Office approaches because of, 361
life and career
  (boyhood and youth, 1863–85) (chronological)
  boyhood (1863–73), 2–6, 366–7; and Greystoke, 3, 5–6; relationship with: his father, 4, his mother, 4–5, his siblings, 3; sense of history, 5–9, 99, 366–7; Thornbury, 5
  school life (1873–81): Farnborough, 6–7, 367, 376n16; Harrow, 7, 368
  abroad (1881–4), 8, 367
  Scoones (1884–5), 8
  passes Civil Service examinations and enters Diplomatic Service (1885), 8
  (Foreign Office Western Department, 1885), 9
  (assistant private secretary to the Viceroy of Ireland, Dublin, 1885), 9–10
  (3rd secretary, British Embassy, Rome, 1886–8), 10–11
  (private secretary to the ambassador, Berlin, 1888–90): assesses German social legislation, 12; assists Anderson mission, 12–13; decides to take leave and retire, 13–14; growing anti-Germanism, 11–12
  (gold prospecting in South Africa, 1891), 14–17; and British South Africa Company, 16–17; and Cecil Rhodes, 15–17

Howard (cont.)
  (Liberal candidate, Worcester, 1892 general election), 17–19
  (explores Morocco; 1893, 1894): (1893), 19–20; (1894), 21
  (research assistant, Booth enquiry, 1893), 20–1, 378n63; impact on Howard, 21, 33, 367, 368
  (assistant private secretary to the foreign secretary, 1894–95), 21–3, 66; impact on Howard, 22–3, 374–5
  (establishes rubber syndicate, 1895–1903): conceives, 23; expeditions: to Brazil (1895), 23–4, and (1897), 26, to Mexico (1897), 26, to Tobago (1898), 27–8; establishes, 25–6; progress of, 30, 72; fails, 101
  (yeoman trooper, Duke of Cambridge's Own, Boer War, 1900): captured, 30–1; enlists, 30; escapes, 31; final months, 32; opinion of Boers, 31
  (return to Diplomatic Service, honorary second secretary, British Embassy, Rome, 1903): offered consul-generalship, Crete, 36–7, 381n119; offered honorary position, 34; reasons, 32; and visit of Edward VII, 34–6
  (consul-general, Crete, 1903–6), 133, 254, 371
  and Bertie, 53, 55
  and British troops, 42–3, 54, 55, 56, 57–8, 61–2, 63–4
  and civil war (1905), origins and course of, 54–5, 56–64; end, 64–5
  and consuls, 41, 44, 45, 48, 49, 55, 57–9, 60, 63–4, 65, 67–8; Howard becomes doyen, 58–9
  and Cretan Commission of Enquiry, (1906), 64, 66, 67–9; and Howard, 66–7
  and Eastern Question, 40–1, 48
  and *enosis*, 39, 42, 47, 50, 52–3, 59, 60, 68, 372
  and financial question, 44–5, 68–9
  and gendarmerie, 42–3, 55, 56, 60, 64, 372
  and Hardinge, 36–7, 40, 41, 43, 55, 68, 381n119
  instructions to, 38–9
  and international troops, 39, 42–3, 55, 56, 57–8, 61–2, 63–5, 372
  and Lansdowne, 43, 50, 52–3, 55–6, 60, 61, 62–3
  and Maxwell, 43, 50
  and Papadiamondopoulos, 41, 42, 44, 46, 47, 48–9, 50–1, 54, 59, 383n36; Howard and his removal, 59
  and Prince George, 41–2, 43, 44–5, 48–9, 52–3, 54–6, 57–8, 58–9, 60, 64–5, 67, 68, 74; 'Bosnian solution', 47–8; and retrospective criticism of Howard, 40, 69
  and Sanderson, 37, 40, 46, 48, 53, 54; Howard criticises, 45, 382n25
  and Venizelos, 46–7, 49, 50–1, 52, 55, 57, 58, 59, 63–5
  (counsellor, British Embassy, Washington, DC, 1906–8)
  and Bryce, 76–7, 84–5, 90, 93–4, 95–9, 369
  and Canada, 78–9, 86, 88–91, 93–4, 98–9; fishing rights, 81, 82–3, 84, 85, 101–2, and arbitration of, 88–90, 91–4, 101–2; visits to (1907), 89, (1908), 94
  contacts, 73, 74–5
  and Durand's recall, 71, 72–4, 352
  Howard seeks early transfer, 101; Hardinge denies, 101–2
  instructions, 71–2
  and Newfoundland–American relations, 78–9, 85–8; and Newfoundland–American fishing rights, 82–3, 84, 85–8, and arbitration of, 88–90, 91–4
  and Roosevelt, 73, 80, 93–4, 99, 352
  and Root, 87, 93–4
  selection, 71–2
  and Swettenham incident, 79–80, 99
  and the United States: domestic politics, 76, 95–6; press, 76, 80, 97; Senate, 83, 90, 92
  (consul-general, Budapest, 1909–11)
  and Bosnian crisis (1908–9), 102–3, 107, 115, 372
  and Cartwright, 104, 105, 106–8, 110, 111, 115; opposition to Howard, 115–17, 118
  contacts, 104, 112, 113–14, 115, 117
  and Crowe, 104, 106, 111–12, 117
  Hungarians, attitude to, 104–5, 112; and domestic politics, 108–9, 112–13, 394n38, and impact on Austro-Hungarian foreign policy, 108–9, 114–15; and Hungarian anglophobic press, 107, 115, 116
  instructions, 104
  transfer to Vienna, 102; changed to Budapest, 103

(consul-general, Berne, 1911–13): and Anglo-Swiss relations, 118–19, 120–1, 126; appointment, 117; and Austria-Hungary, 118, 120–1, 124–6; and Delmé-Radcliffe, 120, 122, 123; and France, 118–19; and Germany, 118–19, 120–1, 124–6, 127, 372; and Italy, 120–3, 124, 127; and Swiss neutrality, 119, 120–3, 128, 129–30, 272
(minister, British Legation, Stockholm, 1913–18)
and Balfour, 165, 178, 188, 189, 190
and blockade, 144–6, 147, 148, 149, 161–2, 167–71, 173–5, 199, 402n18; and Anglo-Swedish negotiations, 183, (1914), 147, 149, (1915), 147, 148, 149, 152–3, (1916), 162, (1917), 173–4, 175, 178, 181, 404n47, (1918), 182–5; and Howard: criticism of, 148, 149, 150, 151–2, support for, 151–2, 153, 159, 162–3, 165–6; and Ministry of Blockade, 161, 161–2, 166, 167, 182–5, 404n47; and neutral Powers (*tertii gaundentes*), 150, 161, 184, 363; and Nordiska Presscentralen, 185–6; and Transito Aktiebilag, 157–9, 161; and the United States, 161, 165, 289
and British Legation staff, 195–6
and Cecil, 161–2, 166, 167, 169–70, 178, 182–5, 192, 404n47
and Consett, 148, 150, 155, 162–3, 164, 165, 167–71
and contacts, 134–5, 135–6
and Crowe, 149–50, 156–7, 165, 181
and Ehrensvärd, 135, 137
and Findlay, 148, 150, 151–2, 153, 155, 160, 167–8, 169
and Finland, 187–8, 189–90, 191–4, 203, 207, 209, 370, 371; advocates pro-'White' policy, 188, 189, 190, opposed by Foreign Office; advocates Baltic bloc, 190, 191–4; and Mannerheim, 188, 195, 207, 209
and Germany, 133–4, 138, 143, 143–4, 155–6, 168, 177, 180–1, 187, 191–4; and Howard's anti-Germanism, 181–2, 193; and separate Russo-German peace (1915), 155; and Swedish pro-Germanism, 133–4, 143, 154, 168, 177, 179, 180–1, 185–6, 193, 194, 402n18
and Grey, 137–8, 139–40, 147, 149, 151–2, 153, 159, 164–5, 199, 205–6, 400n107
and Gustav V, 139, 147, 177
and Hammarskjöld, 135–6, 140, 141, 142, 148, 151, 153–4, 173–4, 183, 363, 370; argument with Howard, 154–5
and Hardinge, 166, 167, 179, 185, 188, 192, 402n18
and Hellner, 182, 186, 193, 194–5
instructions, 144, 146–7, 150, 156
and Kogrund Passage deal, 175, 178–80, 183; threatens resignation over, 179–80
and Lindman, 178, 179, 183
and Norway, 148
and Paget, 166, 168–9
and Poland, 205–7, 409n28
and Russia, 133–4, 137–8, 143, 145–6, 148, 149, 150–1, 155, 159, 162–3, 167, 168, 171–3, 187; and separate Russo-German peace (1915), 155; and trans-shipment to, 148, 149, 150–1, 157–9, 161, 171, 173–4
and Staaff, 135, 137, 138, 139
and Swedish domestic politics, 135–6, 138, 139–40, 173, 175–6, 177–9, 180–1, 185–6
and Swedish foreign policy, 134, 137–8, 139–40, 140–3, 144–6, 148, 149, 153–4, 159–60, 161–2, 167, 173–4, 175–6, 177–9, 180–1, 182–5, 185–6, 191–4, 404n47; and Inter-Allied Trade Committee, 183; and neutrality, 133, 144–6, 152–3, 154–5, 160–1, 166, 180–1, 182, 363, 402n47
and *Tatler* libel, 195
transfer, 132–4
and Transito Aktiebilag, 157–9, 161, 175
and Vansittart, 152–3, 166, 192
and Wallenberg, 135–6, 140–1, 142, 151, 155, 186
(diplomatic adviser, British Delegation, Paris Peace Conference, 1918–19)
appointed, 199–200, 202
and Baltic States, 199–200, 208–10, 212–15, 215–17, 222, 231, 370, 371; Baltic Commission, 202, 231, 234; Baltic League, 210; Estonia, 210, 216–17, 218, 222; Finland,

Howard (cont.)
  203, 207, 209, 215–17, 371;
  Latvia, 210, 216–17, 219, 222;
  Lithuania, 210, 216–17, 219,
  222
and Bolshevik Russia, 199–200, 203,
  209, 211–12, 212–15, 218, 219,
  226, 410n56; and Prinkipo
  conference, 219–20, 223; and
  'White' Russians, 213–14, 215,
  216, 220
and Caucasus, 199–200, 208
and Czechoslovakia, 221, 223–4, 225
and Germany, 198–9, 206–7,
  211–12, 212–15, 215–17, 224–5;
  and Poznan negotiations, 224,
  225–6, 229
and Hardinge, 199, 199–202
Howard–Lord agreement, 221–2, 226,
  227, 372
and League of Nations, 197
and Lloyd George, 203, 218–19,
  219–20, 223, 226, 227, 227–30;
  Howard's dislike for, 203, 218,
  227, 375, 412n100
and Namier, 219, 223, 227, 229,
  412n98
and Neufahrwasser, 211, 222, 372
opposition to Howard, 203, 217, 223,
  226, 227, 229
and Poland: and borders of, 211–12,
  212–15, 215–17, 221–2, 224–5,
  226–7, 227–30; and Commission
  on Polish Affairs (1919), 219,
  222–3; contacts: Paris, 208,
  Stockholm, 203–4, 206–7, Warsaw,
  224, 225–6; and Dmowski, 205–6,
  207, 210–11, 217–18, 219; and
  Howard's pro-Polish views, 203,
  207, 212–15, 215–17, 218, 219,
  224–5, 226–7, 227–30, 370, 371,
  opposition to Howard's views, 203,
  217, 223, 226, 227; Inter-Allied
  Mission to Poland, 202, 220–1,
  222–3, 223–5, 372; and
  Paderewski, 210–11, 212, 218,
  223, 228; and Pilsudski, 210–11,
  212, 218, 223, 224, 225, 228,
  370, 412n91; and Polish Corridor,
  211–12, 221–2, 226–7, 228–9,
  372, and Danzig, 211, 221–2,
  226–7, 228–9; and Polish National
  Committee, 205–6, 207, 210, 212,
  219; and Polish Regency Council,
  206–7; and Silesia, 211, 221, 226,
  372; and Teschen, 208–9, 221,
  223–4, 226, and Inter-Allied
  Mission to Teschen, 222,
  223–4
preparations for conference, 201,
  203–4, 212–17; and Roman
  question, 357–8; and Sobanski,
  206, 207, 208, 210, 212, 217,
  218; and Sweden, 210; and the
  Ukraine, 199–200, 208, 219, 221,
  222, 223–4, 225, 228–9; and
  Wade mission, 212, 223
(ambassador, Madrid, 1919–24)
  and Alfonso XIII, 237, 239, 241, 245,
    255, 264, 267
  appointed, 197–8, 234–5
  and British policy, 251–5
  and British propaganda in Spain,
    246–7, 255
  criticism of Howard, 238, 258–9,
    414n13
  and de Cuso, 257, 259–60
  and domestic politics, 237–8, 239–40,
    241–2, 242–5, 248–9, 251–5;
    263–7; and Annual, 249–51,
    251–5, 263–7; and business
    interests, 239–40, 241, 245,
    248–9, 256–61; and Cortes,
    242–5; fascism, rise of, 263–7; and
    juntas, 238–9, 243, 244–5, 263–7;
    and de Lema, 242; and Rio Tinto,
    241–2, 249; and working-class
    radicalism, 238, 238–40, 241–2,
    242–3, 245, 264–5; and
    Bolshevism, 240, 241, 243, 265;
  and foreign policy, 237–8, 239, 241,
    245, 246, 247–8, 249–50, 251–5,
    261–3, 263–7; and commercial
    treaty, 236–7, 246, 248–9, 251,
    252, 254, 255–61; and Gibraltar,
    246, 252–3, 267
  and Hontoria, 256, 258
  instructions, 235–7, 238
  and Morocco, 235–6, 246, 247–8,
    251–5, 256–7, 261–3; and
    Annual, 249–50, 251–5, 263–7;
    and France, 235–6, 246, 247–8,
    252, 253, 261–3, 267–8; and
    Tangier, 236, 246, 247–8, 261–3,
    267
  and Primo de Rivera, 263, 266–8
  support for Howard, 255, 261
(ambassador, Washington, DC,
  1924–30)
  and anglophobia, 274–5, 288–91,
    296–9, 302, 308, 315–16, 319,
    331, 337–8, 345, 347

Index

appointed, 269–71, 369; almost appointed (1919), 235
approach to the United States, 271–6, 372; 'old diplomacy' maxims, 275–6, 280, 281–2, 296–7, 313, 319; visible ambassador, 275–6, 280–3, 296–9, 305–6, 316, 336–7
and arbitration, 317, 333–6, 344
and belligerent rights, 289–91, 309–13, 313–15, 317, 330–1, 343, 348
and blockade claims (1927–8), 295–6, 304, 313
and Borah, 286, 287, 288, 291, 317, 333–6, 338, 341, 342, 347
British Embassy, new, 352–3
British prime ministerial trip, 339, 340, 342–3, 344–8, 348–9
and Canada, 276, 324–8, 429n110
and Chamberlain, 285–7, 291, 294, 299, 308–9, 309–10, 311–13, 314–15, 317, 321–4, 330, 333–6, 340, 350
contacts, 279–80, 421n24
and Coolidge, 279, 287–8, 291, 292–3, 296, 302–3, 303–4, 338
criticism of Howard, 329, 329–30
and domestic politics, 280–3, 286–8, 288–91, 296–9, 302–3, 304–5, 315–16, 331, 331–2, 337–8, 345, 347, 372; impact on foreign policy, 273, 286–8, 290–1, 296, 304–5, 307–8, 315–16, 317–18, 321–4, 331, 332–3, 333–6, 337–8, 342–3, 347, 372
and foreign policy, 273, 280, 285–7, 288–91, 291–3, 295–6, 302–3, 303–4, 309–13, 313–14, 314–15, 316–17, 317–18, 319–20, 321–4, 330–1, 333–6, 337–8, 338–40, 342–3, 344–8, 348–9; and Canada, 273, 277, 293, 310–13, 319–20, 324–8; and European security, 277–8, 281–2, 284, 285–7; and liquor smuggling, 293–4, 304, 313, 321; and Prohibition, 293–4, 304, 313, 321, 331, 345, 434n200; and war debts, 275, 277–8, 298–9, 304, 317
and Hankey, 330–1, 334, 335, 342, 343
and Henderson, 342, 349, 350
and Hoover, 309–10, 313, 317, 331–2, 333–6, 338–40, 341, 343, 346, 347, 348
and House, 273, 280, 290–1, 313–14, 316
and Hughes, 279, 285–7, 338
and Kellogg, 287–8, 295–6, 306–9, 316, 321–4, 338
and King, 319–20, 324–8
and MacDonald, 275, 342, 345–7, 350, 352; visit to United States, 342–3, 344–8, 348–9
and maritime law conference, 333, 333–6, 338–40, 341, 343
and naval limitation, 277–8, 288–91, 292–3, 299, 303–4, 309–13, 315–16, 317–18, 330–1, 332–3, 337, 338, 338–40, 343–4, 344–8, 348–9; and Coolidge naval conference (1927), 303–4, 306–9; and London naval conference, (1930), 348
and renunciatory pact, 316–17, 321–24; retirement from Washington, 349–50; and Stimson, 345, 346, 347, 348; support for Howard, 275, 330, 350, 352

(retirement, 1930–9)
Anglo-Vatican relations, 357–8; Irish Catholic anglophobia (1932), 360; Malta crisis (1930–1); 358–60; selection of: Britain's apostolic delegate (1938), 361, New Zealand archbishop (1933), 360, Pope Pius XII (1939), 361;
and British 'Left', 363, 364;
death, 365, eulogies, 365–6;
and Empire, 363–4;
Holy Land, visit to (1931), 354;
and international peace and security (1931–9): and Germany, 361, 364, and Great Britain, 361, 363–4 – and need for rearmament, 364, and the United States, 362–3; and Italy, 361; and Japan, 361, 362; and League of Nations, 362; and lessons of his life, 362–5; and the United States, |362–3 – and Britain, ' 362–3; and renunciatory pact, 362–3;
and neutralism, 363–4;
memoirs, Howard's 365, 368–9;
peerage, rewarded with, 353–4;
preservationist work, 355, 365;
Roman Catholic affairs, 357–61, 365
– and Victoria Eugenia, divorce for, 360–1;
social agencies work, 354–5, 365;
West Indian development, 356–7;

Howard (cont.)
  Also see 'Balfour', 'Bryce', 'Cartwright', 'Cecil', 'Austen Chamberlain', 'Consett', 'Crowe', 'Curzon', 'Findlay', 'Edward Grey', 'Charles Hardinge', 'W. L. M. King', 'Lansdowne', 'MacDonald', 'Malet', 'Nicolson', 'Sanderson', 'Spring Rice', 'Tyrrell', and 'Vansittart'
Howard, Esme (Howard's son), 63, 71, 99, 104, 135, 196, 197, 230, 234, 376, 368; illness and death of (1924–6), 300–2, 304
Howard, Francis (Howard's son), 63, 71, 104, 135, 196, 197, 230, 234, 301, 367
Howard, Lord Henry Thomas Molyneaux-(Howard's grandfather), 3
Howard of Greystoke, Henry (Howard's father), 3–4
Howard of Greystoke, Henry (Howard's brother), 25
Howard, Henry (Howard's son), 133, 135, 230, 234, 301, 367
Howard, Hubert (Howard's son), 101, 135, 197, 230, 234, 301, 367
Howard, Isabella (Howard's wife), 32, 38, 42, 48, 63, 71, 123, 132, 197, 198, 225, 230, 234, 237, 269, 270
  and Crete: Prince George's suspicion of, 41
  and Howard: her love for, 26–7, 33, 301–2, 369; Howard's love for her, 24–5, 26–7, 33, 301–2, 369
  and Hungary, 104, 109
  and Roman Catholicism, 25, 26–7, 301–2, 369
  Scottish ancestry, 25, 41
  and Sweden, 277, 297, 323, 350
  and the United States, 73, 277, 297, 323, 350
Howard, Maud (Howard's sister) (later Mrs Popham), 8, 301–2
Howard, Mowbray (Howard's brother), 7
Howard, Stafford (Howard's brother), 13, 14, 91, 98, 127, 128–30, 135, 199
Howard–Lord agreement (1919), 221–2, 226, 227
Hughes, Charles Evans (American secretary of state, 1921–5), 279, 285–7, 288, 289, 338
Hungary, see 'Austria-Hungary'
Hurst, Sir Cecil (Foreign Office legal adviser), 161, 293, 295

Inter-Allied Mission to Poland (1919), 202; composition, 220; Howard–Lord agreement (1919), 221–2, 226, 227; instructions, 220–1, 221–2; work of, 223–5
Ireland, 76
  and Carnarvon, 9–10, 325
  and Home Rule, 9–10, 128; Howard's support for, 17–18
  Irish Roman Catholic anglophobia, 246–7, 360; and Roman Catholicism, 35
  and United States navalists, 345
Isvolsky, Alexander (Russian foreign minister, 1906–10), 102, 107, 108
Italy
  and Austria-Hungary, 103, 122–4
  and Crete, 39, 42, 43, 58, 61, 64, 66, 67–8
  and France, 124
  and Germany, 120–1, 122–4
  and Great Britain, 10–11, 39, 42, 43, 58, 61, 64, 66, 67–8, 122–4, 150, 267–8, 330–1, 348, 357–8, 358–60
  and Howard, 3, 10–11, 24–5, 122–4, 361, 367; and his italophilia, 8, 10–11, 124, 132, 232–3, 354, 358–60, 361, 367
  and Malta crisis (1930–1), 358–60, 371
  and Poland, 205
  and Roman question, 357–8
  and Spain, 267–8
  and Switzerland, 118–19, 120–3, 127
  and Triple Alliance, 120, 122–4, 127, 136, 150
  and Turkey, 122–4
  and the United States, 330–1, 348
  and the Vatican, 34–6, 357–8

Jameson, Leander (British South Africa Company official), 15; Howard's assessment of, 16
Japan: and Anglo-American relations (1924–30), 288, 289, 306–9, 330–1, 348; and international peace and security (1931–9), 361, 362; and Russia (1904–5), 43, 46, 51, 58
Jellicoe, Admiral Sir John (first sea lord, 1916–17), 170
Jenkinson, Edward (Tobago rubber syndicate), 26
Jerningham, Sir Hubert (governor of Trinidad-Tobago), 28
Jones, Thomas (private secretary to the prime minister in the 1920s), 329
Juntas de Defensa, see 'Spain'
Jusserand, Jules (French ambassador, Washington, DC), 280, 281, 282

Justh, Julius de (Hungarian politician), 109

Kellogg, Frank B.
  (American ambassador, London, 1923–5), 275
  (American secretary of state, 1925–9), 287–8, 294, 316, 326, 327, 338; and arbitration, 317, 341; and blockade claims, 295–6; and Coolidge naval conference (1927), 306–9; and Howard, 287–8, 295–6, 306–9, 316, 321–4, 338; and renunciatory pact, 316–17, 362, 428n92
Kenney, Rowland (Foreign Office Political Intelligence Department), 212
Keppel, Alice (Edward VII's mistress), 97
Kerr, Philip (Lloyd George's private secretary), 201, 209, 218, 219, 223, 230, 274, 358, 375
Khuen-Hedevary, Count (Hungarian premier), 110
Kimberley, first Earl of (foreign secretary, 1894–5), 21, 21–3
Kimens, Richard (assistant commissioner, British Mission, Warsaw, after December 1918), 212
King, Senator (American politician), 299
King, William Lyon Mackenzie (Canadian prime minister, 1921–6, 1926–30), 319–20, 329; and Great Britain, 326–7, 429n110; and Howard, 324–5, 326; and the United States, 326–8
Kitchener, first Viscount (viceroy of Egypt, 1911–14), 123
Kogrund Passage, 175; and Howard's deal regarding, 178–9, 183, Howard's threatened resignation over, 179–80
Kolchak, Admiral Alexander ('White' Russian leader), 214, 216
Kossuth, Francis (Hungarian politician), 109, 110, 112
Kruger, Paulus (Transvaal president, 1882–1900), 29, 32

Lamsdorff, Count (Russian foreign minister, 1900–6), 51
Lanczy, Leo (Hungarian financier), 113
Langley, Walter (assistant under-secretary, Foreign Office), 116, 117, 123
Lansdowne, fifth Marquess of (British foreign secretary, 1900–5), 130
  and Crete, 43, 45, 50, 55–6, 57, 60, 61, 62–3, 68;
  and note of 1904, 52–3; and Prince George, 54
  and Howard, 37
  and Prince George, 49
Laski, Harold (British radical economist), 347
Latvia, see 'Baltic'
Laurier, Sir Wilfrid (Canadian prime minister, 1896–1911), 82, 83, 84, 85, 87, 91, 92, 93, 94
Law, Algernon (Foreign Office Commercial Department), 111
Law, Sir Edward (British member, Cretan Commission of Enqury, 1906), 66–7, 68
League of Nations, 194, 197, 210, 247, 284, 285, 292–3, 362–3
  and Howard, 281–2, 361–5
  and Preparatory Commission, 292–3, 299, 303, 304, 330, 333, 337, 341–2; and Anglo-French disarmament compromise (1928), 330–1, 341
  and the United States, 197, 210, 281–2, 285–7, 292–3, 317, 322, 362–3
Leipnik, Dr Ferdinand (Hungarian academic and journalist), 113–14, 117, 118
Leiter, Mrs (Washington, DC, grande dame), 74, 75
Lema, Marquess de (Spanish foreign minister), 242
Lenin, Vladimir (Bolshevik Russian leader), 181, 208, 216
Leo XIII (Pope, 1878–1903), 27, 29; and De Rerum Novarum (1891), 368; and Edward VII meeting, 34–6
Liberal Party of Great Britain, 127–8; and Asquith governments (1908–15), 127, 128, 129–30, 140, 143; and Campbell-Bannerman government (1905–8), 66, 77, 86, 93; and Howard as Liberal candidate (1892), 17–19; and Irish Home Rule, 17–19; and radicals and foreign policy, 95, 129–30, 143; and Rosebery government (1894–5), 21–3
Lindley, Francis (counsellor, British Embassy, Petrograd, 1915–17), 215
Lindman, Admiral Arvid (Swedish foreign minister, 1917), 176, 177, 178, 180, 184
Lindsay, Sir Ronald, 352
  (second secretary, British Embassy, Washington, DC, 1905–7), 74, 75
  (permanent under-secretary, Foreign Office, 1928–30), 331, 335, 350
Lithuania, see 'Baltic'

Lloyd George, David, 274, 315
(British chancellor of the exchequer, 1908–15), 127–8
(prime minister, 1916–22), 171, 178
and Diplomatic Service, 200–2, 223, 230, 231–3, 235, 271, 329, 375
and Foreign Office, 164–6, 200–1, 217, 223, 230, 231–3, 235, 271, 375
and foreign policy, 200–2, 217, 223, 271, 272, 375
and his government; and Morocco, 251; and Spain, 251, 257
and Howard, 203, 217, 218–19, 219–20, 223, 227–30, 274, 370, 375; Howard's dislike for, 202, 203, 227, 230, 231–3, 375, 412n100
and Paris Peace Conference (1918–19), 217, 218–19, 223, 226–7, 227–30, 231–3, 357–8, 375; and British Delegation, 201–2, 217, 223, 230, 231–3
and Poland, 219, 226, 227, 230, 231, 412n100
rise to power, 164–5
and War Cabinet, 165, 178, 181–2
Loch, Sir Henry (governor, Cape Colony, 1891), 15
Lockhart, Robert (British agent, Moscow, 1917–18), 215, 219
Lodge, Henry Cabot (chairman, Senate Foreign Relations Committee): (1906–8), 74, 75, 83, 97; (1924), 279–80
Lodge, Mrs. Henry Cabot, 74, 75
London naval conference (1930), see 'naval limitation'
Long family, 3, 23
Long, Henry Lawes (Howard's grandfather), 3
Long, Samuel (ancestor), 3
Longworth, Nicholas (American politician), 302–3
Lord, Professor Robert (American Polish expert), 220, 223, 224; and Howard–Lord agreement (1919), 221–2, 226, 227
Louis d'Or, 30, 32, 72, 101, 350, 357, 374
Low, Maurice (*Times* correspondent, 1906–8), 74
Lowther, Edward (British minister, Copenhagen, 1913–16), 162, 166
Lubecki, Prince (representative, Polish Regency Council), 206
Lucius, Baron von (German minister, Stockholm), 155
Ludendorff, General Erich (German military commander-politician), 194, 198–9
Lumley, John Savile (British ambassador, Rome, 1883–8), 10, 369
Luxburg affair, 180–1, 182
Lvov, see 'the Ukraine'

McCormick, Colonel Robert (anglophobe American journalist), 313
MacDonald, James Ramsay, 270, 275, 283–4, 315, 363
(prime minister, January–October 1924), 270, 275, 283–4
(prime minister, 1929–31)
and Borah, 347
and Dawes, 343, 346, 348
and Foreign Office, 342, 343, 346
and his government, 342, 358–60
and Hankey, 342, 343, 348
and Henderson, 342, 350
and Hoover, 344–8, 349; and MacDonald–Hoover conversations, 348
and Howard, 275, 342, 345–7, 348–9, 349, 351; offers Howard peerage, 353
and Malta crisis (1930–1), 358–60
and the United States, 342, 343–4, 350; visit to the United States 342–3, 344–8, 348–9
Macedonia: and Crete, 38–9, 40, 46, 51, 68
Madeley, Charles (honorary attaché, British Legation, Stockholm), 135
Malet, Sir Edward (British ambassador, Berlin, 1884–95), 11, 12, 14, 103; influence on Howard, 272, 275, 369
Mallet, Louis (Grey's private secretary), 92, 93
Malta crisis (1930–1), 358–60, 371
Mannerheim, General Carl (Finnish patriot and leader), 188, 208; and Howard, 188, 195, 207, 209
Mappin, Herbert (yeoman trooper, Duke of Cambridge's Own), 31
Margaret (Crown Princess of Sweden), 134, 179
Marie (Dowager Tsarina of Russia), 40
Manos, Constantine (Venizelos supporter), 63–4
Massey, Vincent (Canadian high commissioner, Washington, DC, 1927–30), 326–7, 334
Maude, Alwyne (Englishman resident in Sweden), 135
Maura, Antonio (Spanish premier), 250
Maurouard, Monsieur (French consul-general, Crete), 58, 61

Maxwell, Richard (head, Foreign Office Eastern Department), 43, 50
Merry del Val, Marquess (Spanish ambassador, London, in the 1920s), 259
Merry del Val, Monsignor Raphael (Roman Catholic churchman; later a cardinal): and Edward VII–Leo XIII meeting (1903), 36; and Howard's conversion, 27, 28; marries Howard and Isabella, 29
Mihalis, Hadji (Cretan opposition leader), 48–9
Milner, first Viscount (colonial secretary, 1919–21), 223
Ministry of Blockade, 161, 162, 166, 167, 170–1, 173–5
Ministry of Shipping, 201
Monaco, Captain (commander, Cretan gendarmerie), 43, 54, 55, 56, 57
Monroe doctrine (American), 285, 323
Monroe doctrine (British), 323–4
Morgan, J. P., Sr, (anglophile American financier), 74
Morocco, 51, 124, 235–6, 246, 247–8, 249–50, 251–5, 263–7
 and Annual, 249–50, 256–7, 263–7
 and France, 235–6, 246, 247–8, 249–50, 252, 261–3, 264, 267–8
 and Germany, 246
 and Great Britain, 235–6, 246, 247–8, 249–50, 250–1, 251–5, 256–7, 261–3, 263–7, 267–8
 and Howard, 235–6, 246, 247–8, 249–50, 251–5, 261–3, 263–7, 267–8; his visits to (1893), 19–20, (1894), 21; his views on (1893), 19–20
 and Tangier, 236, 246, 247–8, 261–3, 267
Morris, Ira (American minister, Stockholm, 1917–18), 183, 185–6
Morrow, Dwight (American ambassador, Mexico City), 338
Munthe, Axel (Swedish Court physician), 135
Murmansk, see 'Nikolaev'
Mussolini, Benito (Italian dictator, 1922–43), 264, 267–8, 358–60, 436n37; Howard's opposition to, 361

Namier, Lewis (Foreign Office Political Intelligence Department), 219, 223, 227, 229, 412n98
naval limitation, 277–8, 288–91, 291–2, 299

Coolidge naval conference (1927), 303–4, 306–9, 426n36
London naval conference (1930), 348, 353, 364
 and MacDonald–Hoover conversations, 344–8, 348–9
 and Preparatory Commission, 292–3, 299, 303, 304, 330, 333, 337, 341–2; and Anglo-French disarmament compromise (1928), 330–1, 341
Negri, Count (Italian consul-general, Crete), 41, 50, 58–9, 60
Nekludoff, Anatole (Russian minister, Stockholm), 145–6, 147, 150, 155, 158, 159, 173
Neufahrwasser, 211, 222
Newfoundland:
 and Bryce, 78–9
 and fishing righs, 82–3, 84, 85–8; and arbitration of, 88–90, 91–4, 391n80
 and Howard, 78–9, 85–8
 and the United States, 82–3, 85–8
newspapers: *Aftontidningen*, 186; *American Review of Reviews*, 337; *Baltimore Sun*, 296; *Chicago Tribune*, 302, 307, 308, 313; *Daily Times*, 18; *Fortnightly Review*, 63; *Manchester Guardian*, 207, 298; *Militär Wochenblatt*, 139; *New York Herald Tribune*, 337; *New York Times*, 282, 426n36; *Tatler*, (libels Howard), 195; *Times*, 107, 116, 239, 362, 364, 365–6, 409n28; *Svenskhandelstidning*, 186; *Svenska Dagblad*, 139, 185; *Worcester Echo*, 18–19
Nicholas II (Tsar of Russia, 1894–1917), 160–1, 168, 172; overthrow, 165, 181
Nicolson, Sir Arthur (permanent undersecretary, Foreign Office, 1910–16), 353; and Germany, 120, 143; and Howard, 120, 123, 133; and Italy, 123–4; retires, 166; and Switzerland, 120
Niessel, General (French military adviser, Paris Peace conference), 223
Nikolaev, 146, 161, 171, 189
Nordiska Presscentralen, 185–6
Norfolk, Dukes of, 353, 366
Norfolk, eleventh Duke of, 6
Norfolk, twelfth Duke of, 3, 99
Norfolk, fifteenth Duke of: and Edward VII–Leo XIII meeting (1903), 35–6
Norway, 136, 145, 190

Noulens, Joseph (chairman, Inter-Allied Mission to Poland), 220–1, 224, 225–6
Noyes, Frank, (president, Associated Press), 299

O'Conor, Sir Nicholas, (British ambassador, Constantinople, 1898–1908), 45
Orde, Thorlief, (manager, Louis d'Or plantation): and cocoa plantation, 101, 350; and rubber plantation, 26, 27–8, 32

Pacelli, Cardinal, *see* 'Pius XII'
Paderewska, Madame, 225
Paderewski, Jan Ignace (Polish patriot, pianist, and politician), 210–11, 212, 218, 228; and Inter-Allied Mission to Poland (1919), 223
Paget, Sir Ralph
  (British minister, Copenhagen, 1916–18), 166; and Howard, 166, 168–9
  (diplomatic adviser, British Delegation, Paris Peace Conference), 200, 202
Panama Canal, 94, 313
Panton, Lieutenant-Colonel (British commanding officer, Crete), 61, 66
Papadiamondopoulos, Andrew (private secretary to Prince George of Greece), 42, 44, 46, 47, 48–9, 50–1, 54–5, 59, 65; and Cretan civil war (1905), 54–5, 55, 59; and Howard, 383n36; his removal, 59; 'sinister influence' of, 41
Pares, Bernard (British russophile academic), 215, 219
Paris Peace Conference, 201–2, 217, 218–19, 221
  and Baltic Commission, 202
  and Bolshevik Russia, 211–12, 212–15, 215–17, 219–20, 221, 227–31; and Prinkipo conference, 219–20, 223
  and British Delegation, 199–202, 208, 209, 211–12, 217, 218–19, 223, 226–7, 227–31, 231–33
  and Council of Ten, 221
  and Czechoslovakia, 205, 208–9, 211, 221, 223–4
  and Germany, 198, 210, 211–12, 212–15, 215–17, 224–6, 227–31
  and Poland, 208–9, 211–12, 212–15, 215–17, 218–19, 220–2, 223, 226–7, 227–31
  and Commission on Polish Affairs (1919), 219, 222–3, 230
  and Howard–Lord agreement, 221–2, 223
  and Inter-Allied Mission to Poland, 202, 220–1, 222–3; composition, 220; instructions, 220–1, 221–2; and Poznan negotiations, 224, 225–6; and work, 223–5
  and Polish Corridor, 211–12, 221–2, 226–7, 228; and Danzig, 211, 221–2, 226–7, 228; and East Prussia, 221–2, 226–7
  and Roman question, 357–8
  and the Ukraine, 199–200, 208, 219, 221, 223, 225
Parker, Alwyn
  (Foreign Office Library), 201, 230
  120
  (Foreign Office Library), 201
Pauncefote, Sir Julian, 9, 352
Peruchetti, General (Italian military commander), 121
Phelps, Admiral (United States Navy General Board), 289, 290
Phenix, Spencer (American State Department legal adviser), 295, 301
Pilgrims Society, 275–6, 280, 281, 350–1
Pilsudski, General Joseph (Polish soldier, patriot, and statesman), 205, 210–11, 218, 228; and Howard, 223, 224, 225, 370, 412n91; and Inter-Allied Mission to Poland, 223
Pius XI (Pope, 1922–39), 360, 361
Pius XII (Pope, 1939–58), 361
Poland
  and Austria-Hungary, 204
  and Czechoslovakia: and Silesia, 208–9, 211, 221, 226, 227, 372; and Teschen, 208–9, 211, 221, 223–4, 226, 228
  domestic politics
  (1914–18), 204–5
  (1918–19), 206–7, 211, 212, 218, 223–5, 227–30; and coalition government (1919), 211, 218; and Pilsudski, 205, 211, 212, 218, 223, 224, 225; and Polish National Committee, 204–5, 205–6, 207, 212, 218
  and Dmowski, 204–5, 205–6, 207, 210–11, 217–18
  and France, 204–6, 212, 216, 220–1, 228
  and Germany, 204–5, 208–9, 211–12, 224–6, 227–30; and Danzig, 211, 221–2, 226–7, 228; and East Prussia, 221–2, 226–7; and Polish Corridor, 211–12, 221–2, 226–7, 228

and Great Britain, 204–5, 208–9,
211–12, 212–15, 216–17, 218, 219,
220–1, 222–3, 227–30, 409n28
and Haller's Army, 212
and Howard, 199–200, 202, 203–4,
207, 211–12, 212–17, 217–18, 219,
221, 222, 224–5, 226–7, 227–30,
368, 372, 409n28
and Paderewski, 210–11, 212, 218,
223
and Paris Peace Conference, 208–9,
211–12, 212–215, 215–17, 218–19,
221–2, 224–6
and Commission on Polish Affairs
(1919), 226; ceated, 210–11;
Howard's suggestion, 219
and Howard–Lord agreement, 221–2,
226, 227, 372
and Inter-Allied Mission to Poland, 202
composition, 220
instructions, 220–1, 221–2, 223
work, 223–5; and Poznan
negotiations, 224, 225–6
and Russia
(Bolshevik regime), 204–5, 208–9,
211–12, 221–2, 227–30
(tsarist regime), 204
and the Ukraine, 205, 208–9, 219, 223,
225, 228–9
Polish Corridor, 205, 211–12, 221–2,
226–7, 228
Pope-Hennessy, Colonel Ladislas (British
military attaché, Washington, DC),
314
Preparatory Commission for the World
Disarmament Conference, 292–3,
299, 303, 304, 333, 337, 341–2;
and Anglo-French disarmament
compromise (1928), 330–1, 341
Primo de Rivera, General Manuel (Spanish
military commander and leader), 251,
263, 266–8
Prothero, G. W. (Foreign Office Historical
Section, 1918–19), 201

Rampolla, Cardinal (Vatican secretary of
state), 35–6
Rathenau, Walter (German industrialist),
114, 118
Reading, first Marquess of (British
ambassador, Washington, DC,
1918–20), 272
Redl, Colonel Alfred (Austro-Hungarian
staff officer), 137
Reid, Whitelaw (American ambassador,
London, 1905–12), 77, 88, 92, 94

Rennell Rodd, Sir James (British
ambassador, Rome, 1908–19), 123,
133, 198
renunciatory pact (1928), 316–17, 321–4,
362–3, 428n92
Rhodes, Cecil (Imperialist and head, British
South Africa Company), 14, 15, 16,
82; and Boer War, 29, 30; and
Imperial 'Customs Federation', 17,
98
Richmond, Admiral Sir Herbert (British
naval intellectual), 364
Rimmern, Baron Langwerth von (German
ambassador, Madrid), 246
Rio Tinto Mining Company, 239, 241–2,
249
Robertson, Arnold (British consul,
Tangier), 262
Robertson, General Sir William (chief of
the Imperial General Staff, 1915–18),
160–1, 167
Robinette, Edward (executive, American
English-Speaking Union), 280
Romei, General (Italian military adviser,
Paris Peace Conference), 223
Roosevelt, Theodore (American president,
1901–9), 71, 72, 73, 224, 272, 279,
352; his Administration and Britain,
72, 75–6, 81, 83–4, 86, 91–4, 95;
and Bryce, 76; and Canada, 75, 81,
83–4, 85–6, 87, 92, 277; and
Durand, 71, 72–3, 80, 352; and
Howard, 73, 80, 99, 370; and Russo-
Japanese war (1904–5), 72; and
Swettenham incident, 80
Root, Elihu (American secretary of state,
1905–9), 73, 86, 273; and
arbitration, 88–90, 91–4, 317; and
Canada, 82, 83–4, 87, 88–9, 92, 93,
95; and Durand, 73–4; and Howard,
87, 92, 95, 281; and Newfoundland,
82–3, 83–4, 87, 88–9, 92, 93, 95
Rosebery, fifth Earl of (British prime
minister, 1894–5), 21–3, 76
Ruchet, Monsieur (president of the Swiss
Confederation), 120, 121, 124
Russell, Theo
(counsellor, British Embassy, Vienna,
1908–14), 106, 116
(secretary to the foreign secretary,
1915–19), 165–6
Russia
(tsarist regime)
and Aland Islands, 147–8, 151
and Austria-Hungary, 102–3, 107,
108, 137, 394n38

Russia (cont.)
  and Blockade, 144–6, 160–1; and trans-shipment, 148, 149, 150–1, 157–9, 161, 178
  and Bosnian crisis (1908–9), 102–3, 107
  and Crete, 38–9, 40, 48, 51, 58, 59, 64, 66, 67–8
  and Eastern Question, 38, 40, 51, 102–3, 127, 128–30, 134
  and Finland (1915), 151, 187
  and France, 106, 107, 108, 204
  and Germany, 106, 108, 114, 133–4, 136, 151; and separate peace (1915), 155
  and Great Britain, 38–9, 40, 48, 51, 58, 59, 64, 66, 67–8, 70, 107, 114, 128, 129–30, 133–4, 136, 137–8, 144, 144–6, 150–1, 160–1, 168
  and great War, 144–6, 150–1, 160–1
  and Japan, 43, 46, 51, 58
  and Poland, 204–5
  and Serbia, 103, 143
  and Sweden, 133–4, 136, 136–7, 138, 139–40, 140–3, 144–6, 147–8, 150–1, 160–1; and Assanovitch spy affair, 137–8, 140, 141
  (Bolshevik regime), 165, 171, 181
  and Aland Islands, 171, 187
  and Brest-Litovsk negotiations, 187, 188, 189
  and Finland, 187, 189–90, 191–4, 208–9, 212–17
  and France, 187, 206, 212, 216
  and Germany, 187, 188, 189
  and Great Britain, 171–3, 174, 175, 181–2, 187, 188, 189–90, 208–9, 211–12, 212–15, 215–17, 218, 227–30, 283–4
  and Paris Peace Conference (1918–19), 208, 209, 210–11, 212–17, 218–19, 227–30; and Prinkipo conference, 219–20, 223
  and Poland, 208–9, 210–11, 212–17, 218–19, 227–30
  and revolutions of 1917, 165, 171, 181
  and Sweden, 173–4, 175, 176, 177–9, 181–2, 187
  and 'White' Russians, 213–14, 215, 220

Salazar, Manuel Allende (Spanish premier), 250
Salisbury, third Marquess of (British prime minister, June 1885–February 1886), 9, 10 (British prime minister, 1886–92), 11–12
Sanderson, Sir Thomas (permanent under-secretary, Foreign Office, 1894–1906)
  and Crete, 45, 48, 53, 54, 59, 62–3; instructions to Howard, 40, 46
  and Howard: opposes Howard's Cretan appointment, 34, 37; Howard criticises, 45, 382n25; influence on Howard, 275
  and Morocco, 19–20
  retires, 66
Sanlucas, Duke of (Spanish nobleman), 269–70
Sazanov, Sergei (Russian foreign minister, 1910–16), 147, 155, 171
  ('White' Russian spokesman), 215, 216, 220
Scollenberger, Professor (Swiss germanophile academic), 120–1
Serbia, 103, 107–8, 143
Seton-Watson, Robert (British austrophobe writer), 116
Shearer, William (American anglophobe naval writer), 289, 307, 309
Silesia, 208–9, 211, 221, 226, 227, 372
Simon, Sir John (British foreign secretary, 1931–5), 360
Simonds, Frank (American anglophobe editor), 337
Smith, Alfred (American Democratic Party presidential nominee), 302, 331–2
Sobanski, Count Wladyslaw (Polish National Committee agent), 206, 207, 208, 210, 212, 217, 218
Sophie (Dowager Queen of Sweden), 135
Sota, de, family (anglophile Spaniards), 241
Spain
  and Alfonso XIII, 237, 239, 245, 255, 264, 267
  and business interests, 239–40, 241, 245, 248–9, 257–1
  and Cortes, 242–5, 263–7
  domestic politics, 238, 238–40, 242–5, 246, 263–7; and Annual, 249–51, 263–7; and Catalonia, 238, 240, 242, 248; fascism, rise of, 263–7, 267–8 – and Directorate, 251, 267–8; and juntas, 238–9, 243, 244–5, 263–7; and working-class radicalism, 238, 238–40, 241–2, 242–3, 245, 264–5
  and foreign policy, 238, 246, 247–8, 248–9, 249–50, 256–7, 261–3,

267–8; and commercial treaty,
236–7, 246, 248–9, 251, 252, 253,
255–61
and France, 235–6, 246, 247–8,
249–50, 251, 252, 253, 256, 261–3,
264, 267–8
and Germany, 246
and Gibraltar, 246, 252–3, 267
and Italy, 264, 267–8
and Morocco, 235–6, 238, 246–7,
250–1, 261–3, 263–7; and Annual,
249–50, 256–7, 263–7
and Primo de Rivera, 251, 263, 266–8
and Tangier, 236, 246, 247–8, 261–3,
267
Spanish Tariff Commission, 257–61
Sperling, Rowland (head, Foreign Office
American and African Department),
236
Springardi, Paolo (Italian war minister),
124
Spring Rice, Cecil (British diplomat), 9,
132, 143, 352; on Howard and Crete,
70; Howard honours, 355; and
Sweden, 134, 136, 149, 181; and the
United States, 76, 181, 270–1, 272,
275
Staaff, Karl (Swedish premier), 135, 137,
138, 139
Stamfordham, Lord (private secretary to
George V), 327
Steward, George (Foreign Office News
Department), 307
Stimson, Henry (American secretary of
state, 1929–33), 339–40, 345, 346,
347, 348, 362
Stonor, Monsignor Edmund (Vatican
official): and Edward VII–Leo XIII
meeting (1903), 35–6
Stopford, Captain Arthur (naval attaché,
British Embassy, Washington, DC),
309
Stresemann, Gustav (German foreign
minister), 292
Strickland, Lord (governor of Malta),
358–60, 371
Suez Canal, 323–4
Suffolk, Earl of (Howard's uncle), 5
Swartz, Carl (Swedish premier, 1917),
176, 177, 180–1
Sweden
and Aland Islands, 147–8, 151, 171,
187, 191–4
and blockade, 144–6, 146–7, 148, 149,
151–3, 166–7, 171, 173–5, 181–2,
182–5, 363, 372; and Anglo-Swedish

negotiations (1914), 147, 149,
(1915), 147, 148, 149, 152–3, 157,
(1916), 162, (1917), 173–4, 175,
178, 181, (1918), 182–5
domestic politics, 135–6, 137, 138–40,
173, 175–6, 177–9, 180–1; and
Luxburg affair, 180–1, 182
and Eden government, 176, 177,
180–1
and Ehrensvärd, 135, 137
and Finland, 151, 186–7, 190, 191–4
foreign policy, 133, 136, 137, 138–9,
140–3, 147–8, 159, 162, 173–4,
175, 178, 181, 182–5, 191–4; and
neutrality, 133, 144–6, 152–3,
154–5, 159, 160–1, 165, 180–1, 182
and Germany, 133, 136, 138–9, 144–6,
153–4, 155, 159, 167, 183–5,
185–6, 193, 194; and Brest-Litovsk
conference, 187, 188, 189, 192, 193;
and germanophilia of Swedes, 133–4,
136, 140, 144, 153, 159, 168, 177,
179, 180–1, 185–6, 193, 194; and
growing anti-Germanism of Sweden,
181–2, 193, 194
and Great Britain, 133–4, 136, 138,
139–40, 140–3, 144–6, 147, 152–3,
157–9, 160–1, 161–3, 165, 173–4,
175, 176, 176–9, 180–1, 181–2,
182–5, 185–6, 191–4, 197; and
anglophobia of Swedes, 134, 136,
154–5, 185–6; British propaganda in,
185–6
and Gustav V, 133–4, 135, 138,
139–40, 147, 177; and court of, 134,
135, 155, 159, 168, 179
and Hammarskjöld, 135–6, 140, 141,
142, 148, 151, 154–5, 158–9, 162,
170, 171, 173–5, 180, 181, 182
and Norway, 148, 153
and Russia, 133, 136, 136–7, 139–40,
140–3, 144, 144–6, 160–1, 181–2;
and Assanovitch spy affair, 137–8,
140, 141; and russophobia of Swedes,
133, 136, 136–7, 138, 140, 153,
168; and trans-shipment, 148, 149,
150–1, 157–9, 161, 171, 178,
181–2, 182–5
and Staaff, 135, 137
and Swartz government, 176, 177,
180–1
and Transito Aktiebilag, 157–9, 161,
175
and the United States, 165, 185–6
and Wallenberg (Knut), 135–6, 140,
147–8, 151, 158, 162, 184, 185

Swedish Telegram Bureau, 185–6
Swettenham, Sir Alexander (governor of Jamaica), 79–80, 297
Switzerland, 132, 133
and Austria-Hungary, 118, 120–1, 124–6
domestic politics, 119, 120–1, 122–3
foreign policy, 119, 122–3, 127; and neutrality, 120–1, 122–3, 124–5, 127, 133
and France, 118–19, 120, 125, 126
and Germany, 118–19, 120–1, 124–6, 127
and Great Britain, 118–19, 120–1, 126
and Italy, 118–19, 120–3, 127

Tangier, 236, 246, 247–8, 261–3, 267
Tennant, Hugh (Howard's private secretary, Washington, DC, 1924–30), 279
Tennyson, Alfred Lord (poet-laureate), 4, 367
Teschen, 208–9, 221; and Inter-Allied Mission to Teschen, 222, 223–4, 226
Thiébaut, Monsieur (French minister, Stockholm), 145, 183, 192
Thomson, first Lord (secretary for air, 1929–30), 357
Thornbury, 5, 135, 365
Tobago, 33, 356–7; Howard's cocoa plantation, 30, 32, 72, 101, 350, 357; Howard's rubber plantation, 27–8, 30, 32, 72
Townley, Lady Susan, 97
Transito Aktiebilag, 157–9, 161, 174
Treasury, 133, 149, 200, 201, 248, 298–9
Triple Alliance, 103, 105, 110, 111, 113, 115, 118, 119, 120, 121, 122–3, 124–5, 127, 129, 131, 136, 141, 150; and Central Powers, 144–6, 147, 150, 159, 171–2; and great War, 136, 144–6, 159, 165, 169, 171–2; and Italy, 120, 122–4, 127, 136, 150
Triple Entente, 104, 106, 108, 111–12, 113, 114, 118, 119, 124, 131, 134, 135, 136, 139, 141, 143, 190; and Anglo-Russian entente (1907), 95, 128, 129–30, 137–8, 140–3; and great War, 136, 144, 190
Turkey, 102–3, 145, 147, 150, 198, 213, 254, 263
and Balkan wars (1912–13), 122–4, 127–8, 129–30
and Bosnian crisis (1908–9), 102–3, 107
and Crete, 39–40, 47, 51, 56, 371; and 1898 settlement, 39, 47
and Germany, 39, 40, 41, 68–9, 155, 213
and Howard, 128, 213, 254, 371
and Italy, 122
Tyrrell, Sir William, 272, 353
(private secretary to the foreign secretary, 1905–15), 102, 117, 132–3, 195, 197, 198
(Political Intelligence Department, Foreign Office): and Paris Peace Conference, 201, 222
(assistant undersecretary, Foreign Office, 1918–25, and permanent undersecretary, 1925–8): and the United States, 269–71, 278–9, 291, 313–14, 315, 317, 318, 329–30
(ambassador, Paris, 1928–34), 328
friendship with Howard, 166, 269–271, 329
and Lloyd George revolution in foreign policy, 270–1, 328

Ukraine, the, 199–200, 205, 208–9, 219, 221, 223, 225, 228–9
Union of Democratic Control, 200
United States of America, 1, 26, 33
anglophobia in, 274–5, 288–91, 302, 315–16, 319, 330–1, 337, 345, 347, 372–3; and Irish-Americans, 76, 96, 274, 279, 289, 296, 372–3
anti-Catholicism, 299, 331
and arbitration, 88–90, 91–4, 317, 333–6, 341, 344
and Baltic States, 222
and belligerent rights (1924–30), 289–91, 309–13, 313–15, 333–6, 343, 348; and maritime law conference, 333, 333–6, 338–40, 341, 343
and 'Big Navy party', 289–90, 303, 315–16, 345, 347
and blockade (1914–18), 161, 165, 169, 179, 183; and blockade claims (1925–7), 295–6, 304, 313
and Bolshevik Russia, 187, 218–19, 222, 280, 296–9, 302, 308, 315–16
and Canada, 75, 78–9, 81, 83–4, 85–8, 88–91, 91–4, 98–99, 101–2, 276, 324–8, 391n91, 429n110; and fishing rights, 81, 82–3, 85–8, 88–90, 91–4, 101–2; and Joint High Commission, 81, 82
and Coolidge naval conference (1927), 303–4, 306–9, 426n36

and Dawes Plan, 277, 283
and Democratic Party, 273, 286, 288–9, 302–3, 331–2, 347
and domestic politics, 83, 95–6, 280–3, 286–8, 288–91, 296–9, 302–3, 304–5, 331, 331–2, 372–3; and connexion with foreign policy, 80, 83, 95–6, 233, 273, 304–5, 306–8, 321–4, 333–6
and Eastern Establishment, 74–5, 279–80, 372–3
and European security, 277–8, 280–1, 284, 285–7, 292–3
and Finland, 187
and France, 316–17, 321–4, 330–1
and Germany, 165, 175, 179, 185–6, 278
and Great Britain, 72, 75–6, 81, 86, 91–4, 95, 161, 165, 175, 178, 179, 183, 185–6, 217–18, 271–2, 280–3, 284, 288–91, 291–3, 299, 303–4, 305–9, 315–16, 319–20, 330–1, 333–6, 336–7, 338, 338–40, 341–2, 342–3, 344–8, 348–9, 372–3
and great War, 165, 175, 178, 179
and Howard, 26, 76, 79, 83, 96, 99, 99–100, 101–2, 161, 165, 175, 178, 179, 180, 181–6, 187, 205, 212, 218–19, 220, 271–2, 272–6, 276–7, 279–83, 285–7, 288–91, 291–3, 295–6, 302–3, 304–5, 307–8, 309–13, 314–15, 316–17, 317–18, 319–21, 321–4, 330–1, 331–2, 333–6, 337–8, 372–3
and isolationism, 274, 281, 289–90
and Japan, 288, 289
and League of Nations, 197, 281–2, 285–7, 317
and liquor smuggling, 293–4, 304, 313, 321
and naval limitation, 277–8, 288–91, 291–2, 299, 315–16, 338, 338–40, 341, 341–2, 342–3, 344–8, 348–9, 372
and Preparatory Commission, 292–3, 299, 303, 304, 333, 337, 341–2; and Anglo-French disarmament compromise (1928), 330–1, 341; and Coolidge naval conference (1927), 303–4, 306–9, 426n36; and London naval conference (1930), 348
and Newfoundland, 78–9, 82–3, 84, 85–8, 89–90, 91–4, 391n91; and fishing *modus vivendi*, 86, 87, 88, 391n91
and Paris Peace Conference (1918–19), 232–3

and fourteen points, 198, 296
and Poland, 205, 212, 218–19, 220
and Inter-Allied Mission to Poland (1919); composition, 220; Howard–Lord agreement, 221–2, 226, 227; instructions, 220–1, 221–2; work, 223–5
and Versailles treaty, 273, 286
and Poland, 205, 212, 218–9, 220, 221–2, 223–5, 226, 227
and Prohibition, 293–4, 304, 313, 321, 331, 345, 434n200
and Protectionism, 17, 81, 84
and renunciatory pact (1928), 316–17, 321–4, 428n92
and Republican Party, 75, 271–2, 273, 280, 283–4, 286, 302–3, 331–2, 428n92
and Spring Rice, 76, 271–2
United States press, 76, 80, 275–6, 280–3, 296–9, 329, 331, 337
and war debts, 275, 277–8, 298–9

Valera, Eamon de (Irish terrorist and politician), 360
Vansittart, Sir Robert, 353
(assistant clerk, Foreign Office, 1914–20), mission to Sweden (1915), 152–3, 157, 158, 159, 183, 321
(head, Foreign Office American Department, 1924–8), 278–9, 291, 295–6, 305, 314
(private secretary, prime minister's office, 1928–30), 324, 335, 340, 344, 347, 348, 349
(permanent under-secretary, Foreign Office, 1930–8), 356, 360, 361
and friendship with Howard, 153, 166, 198, 278–9, 324
Vatican
Anglo-Vatican relations
Edward VII–Leo XIII meeting (1903), 34–6
and Irish Roman Catholic Anglophobia (1932), 360
Malta crisis (1930–1), 358–60
Roman question (1919), 357–8
and selection of Britain's apostolic delegate (1938), 361
and selection of New Zealand archbishop (1933), 360
and selection of Pius XII (1939), 361
and Howard
his conversion, 27
divorce of Victoria Eugenia (1934), 360–1

early contacts, 11
meeting of Edward VII–Leo XIII (1903), 34–6
Venezuela border dispute (1895–6), 75
Venizelos, Eleutherios (Cretan opposition leader), 46–7, 49, 50–1, 52, 69
and Cretan civil war (1905), 372; and course of, 55, 57, 58, 59, 63–4; and end, 64–5; and origins, 54–5
and Prince George of Greece, 46–7, 49, 50–1, 52, 54–5, 57–60, 62
Victoria I (Queen, 1838–1901, Empress, 1878–1901), 12
Victoria (Queen of Sweden), 139, 155
Victoria (Empress Frederick of Germany), 11–12, 370
Victoria Eugenia (Queen of Spain), 255, 360–1
Villiers, Gerald (Foreign Office Western Department), 250, 253
Vladivostock, 145, 146

Wade, Colonel Harry (British liaison officer, Poland), 212, 223
Wallenberg, Knut (Swedish foreign minister), 135–6, 140–1, 142, 147–8, 151, 155, 158, 162, 180, 182, 184, 185
Wallenberg, Marcus (Swedish financier), 149, 162, 174, 182, 184, 185, 404n47
Walpole, Catherine (Howard's grandmother), 3
War Office, 120, 190–1
Washington naval conference (1921–2), 252, 278, 303
Wemyss, Admiral Sir Rosslyn (first sea lord, 1917–19), 7, 377n16
Wekerle, Alexander (Hungarian premier), 108, 109, 112

West Indies
and Anglo-American relations, 313
and Howard: family connexion, 3; Tobago plantation, 23–4, 25, 26, 27–8, 30, 32, 72, 101, 350, 357, 374
and Imperial economic development (1930s), 356–7
and Imperial Preference, 17, 374
and Jamaica (1907), 79–80
and liquor smuggling (1920s), 294, 313
Westman, Cläes (Swedish Foreign Ministry official), 174, 182, 404n47
Wickham Steed, Henry (British journalist), 116–17, 329–30, 364, 430n132
Wilberforce, Robert (British Library of Information, New York), 297
William II (Emperor of Germany, 1888–1918), 11–12, 34, 114, 126, 198–9, 370
Williams, Sir Rhys (Rio Tinto Mining Company executive), 241
Willingdon, Viscount (governor-general of Canada, 1926–31), 319, 326–7
Wills, J. J. (Board of Trade official), 260–1
Wilson, Woodrow (American president, 1913–21)
and fourteen points, 198, 210; and Poland, 205, 210
and Howard, 232, 218–19, 232–3, 279
and Paris Peace Conference, 202, 217, 218–19, 233, 273, 357–8
and Russia, 187, 218–19, 219–20, 221
Wingfield, Charles (counsellor, British Embassy, Madrid, 1919–26), 238
Wodehouse, Armine (private secretary to Lord Kimberley), 21–2
Wrangel, Count (Swedish minister, London), 137, 138